SELECTED LETTERS
OF WILFRED OWEN

Selected Letters of

Wilfred Owen

Edited by

JANE POTTER

OXFORD
UNIVERSITY PRESS

OXFORD
UNIVERSITY PRESS

Great Clarendon Street, Oxford, OX2 6DP,
United Kingdom

Oxford University Press is a department of the University of Oxford.
It furthers the University's objective of excellence in research, scholarship,
and education by publishing worldwide. Oxford is a registered trade mark of
Oxford University Press in the UK and in certain other countries

Published in the United States of America by Oxford University Press
198 Madison Avenue, New York, NY 10016, United States of America

British Library Cataloguing in Publication Data
Data available

Library of Congress Control Number: 2022950497

ISBN 978–0–19–968950–7

DOI: 10.1093/oso/9780199689507.001.0001

Printed and bound in the UK by
Clays Ltd, Elcograf S.p.A.

For
Jon Stallworthy (1935–2014)
&
Peter Owen (1940–2018)

ACKNOWLEDGEMENTS

This book owes its genesis to Elizabeth Owen. She is the first among many whom I want to thank for the help, support, and love that made it possible for me to complete what at times seemed a daunting task.

I carried out research at the key institutions that look after Owen's archives, and am enormously grateful to: the Harry Ransom Humanities Research Centre at the University of Texas at Austin, in particular to Dr Jean M Cannon, Elizabeth L. Garver, and all the staff in the Reading Room; Sue Usher at the English Faculty Library at Oxford; Judith Priestman and Oliver House in the Weston Library Special Collections at the Bodleian Library, Oxford; the staff at the Rare Book and Manuscript Library at Columbia University, New York. I am grateful to the John Rylands Library, University of Manchester, for its permission to reproduce John Gunston's photograph of a smiling Wilfred Owen.

I am indebted to Oxford Brookes University, where my Faculty of Technology, Design and Environment and the School of Arts, especially Professor Paul Whitty and Professor Daniela Treveri-Genari, provided generous financial support, which allowed me to travel to Texas to work on Owen's manuscripts and to be released from teaching to focus on research and writing. On a day-to-day basis, my colleagues at the Oxford International Centre for Publishing have been consistently enthusiastic in their support of me and this project. I am sure they often wondered if W. E. S. Owen had actually become a member of the department. I could not hope to work with a better team of people and they have my heartfelt appreciation. I am especially grateful to Dr Leander Reeves, Dr Caroline Davis, and Sarah Franklin, who read drafts, gave wise criticism, and provided personal encouragement along with a healthy dose of humour when it was most needed.

I thank my sister Vickie Noll, who has been a continual source of love and encouragement; she has been on this Owen journey with me ever since I first encountered his work as a teenager. It was wonderful to have her as my co-researcher in Texas, where she painstakingly checked the manuscripts against copy and provided welcome company at the end of long days in the Reading Room. Owen's letters often brought us to tears, but, not infrequently, they would collapse us into fits of giggles when we came across passages where he gave free rein to his wicked sense of humour.

Other colleagues and friends who have read drafts, offered research advice, and generally supported and cajoled me to keep going are: Dr Carol Acton, Professor John Barnard, Dr Sandie Byrne, Professor Elaine Chalus, Dr Margaret

Connolly, Meg Crane, the late Jan Crosser-Cooke, Dr Julie Curtis, Vanessa Davis, Dr Ann-Marie Einhaus, Professor Alison Fell, Grace Freeman, Professor Toby Garfitt, Professor Susan Grayzel, Philip Guest, Dr Philip Hoare, Martin Impey, Dr Alice Kelly, Professor Tim Kendall, Dr Edmund King, Dr Philip Lancaster, Professor Dame Hermione Lee, Dr Sarah Lubelski, Dr Neil McLennan, Dr Kate McLoughlin, Helen McPhail, Yvonne Morris, Dr Niall Munro, Dr Paul Norgate, Dr Ray Ockenden, Professor Angela K. Smith, Dr Trudi Tate, Julia Ribeiro S C Thomaz, Dr Shaf Towheed, Dr Vincent Trott, Dr Anja Tschörtner, Susan Werbe, and Janet Woods. All have my most sincere thanks.

I am so grateful to the late Dr Dominic Hibberd, whose devotion to Owen and detailed scholarship inform many aspects of the references in this edition.

Although I was not lucky enough to meet the original editor of Owen's letters, the late John Bell, his exemplary work is the foundation of this volume and I am grateful to his estate for allowing me to reproduce and augment his notes. I stand in his shadow.

I am honoured to be published once again by Oxford University Press. My editors Jacqueline Norton and Eleanor Collins and my Production Manager Emma Varley deserve every note of thanks I can give for their professionalism—and kindness—in bringing this book to fruition.

Spouses and partners of biographers and literary scholars have to be remarkably patient as they accommodate the ghostly presences of any number of poets, novelists, playwrights, and other strange figures from the past in their lives. My husband, Dr Andrew Woods, is no exception. He has with love, good grace, and humour accepted Wilfred Owen as the third person in our marriage for a very long time.

The mentorship of Jon Stallworthy and the friendship of Peter Owen have been amongst the greatest privileges of my life. Their deaths marked the opening and closing years of the Centenary, and it is my deep regret that neither is here to see the completion of this book. I hope they would think it is at least a worthy tribute to them.

CONTENTS

CONTENTS

LIST OF PLATES

LIST OF ABBREVIATIONS

The following abbreviations are used after the first reference, which is given in full.

DH   Dominic Hibberd

GC   Guy Cuthbertson

HO   Harold Owen

JB   John Bell

JS   Jon Stallworthy

LG   Leslie Gunston

PN   Paul Norgate

SS   Siegfried Sassoon

CL   Harold Owen and John Bell, eds., *Wilfred Owen: Collected Letters* (Oxford University Press, 1967)

CPF   Jon Stallworthy, ed., *Wilfred Owen: The Complete Poems and Fragments* (Chatto & Windus, 2013)

JFO   Harold Owen, *Journey from Obscurity: Memoirs of the Owen Family,* 3 vols, (Oxford University Press, 1963–5)

SL   John Bell, ed., *Selected Letters of Wilfred Owen* (Oxford University Press, 1993)

WO   Jon Stallworthy, *Wilfred Owen* (Oxford University Press, 1974, new ed., Pimlico, 2013)

WOANB   Dominic Hibberd, *Wilfred Owen: A New Biography* (Phoenix, 2003)

PREFACE

The Life

Wilfred Edward Salter Owen was born to Tom and Susan Owen (née Shaw) on 18 March 1893 at the home of his maternal grandfather, Edward Shaw—Plas Wilmot, Oswestry, Shropshire. He was their first child. His sister Mary was born in 1896, his brothers Harold and Colin in 1897 and 1900 respectively. After four seemingly blissful years, the Owen family fortunes changed dramatically due to debt in the wake of Edward Shaw's death. Plas Wilmot and all but a few of its contents were sold. The Owen family moved first to Shrewsbury to live with Tom's parents, then to Birkenhead, where Tom Owen was stationmaster at Woodside and Wilfred attended the Birkenhead Institute. In 1907, Tom was promoted to Superintendent of the Great Western Railway and the family returned to Shrewsbury, where Wilfred continued his education at Shrewsbury Technical School and, as a temporary pupil-teacher, at Wyle Cop School.

In 1911 Wilfred Owen sat the matriculation exam at the University of London; he passed, but not with the honours marks required for a scholarship. Without a scholarship his way to a university education was closed, so—in the hope of an opportunity for additional tuition and further study—he accepted the position of lay assistant to the vicar of Dunsden church, near Reading, Berkshire. During this time he also took classes at University College, Reading (now the University of Reading), and received tuition from Edith Morley, Professor of English Language, who encouraged his writing and his university ambitions: 'The kindly Minerva was favourably impressed by my genuine, (and well-founded, goodness knows) self-depreciations, said they were a good sign, and pressed me to go on with attempts' (Letter 167). But he found that 'real study' was incompatible with parish duties, 'the meetings, classes, spiritual excitements, and such like that prevail, and will prevail in this place', he wrote in December 1912 (Letter 167).

Moreover, his pastoral duties brought home the disparity between the poor of the village and the cosseted, genteel life of the vicarage. Religious doubts and his break with the evangelical church in which he had been brought up—'I have murdered my false creed' (Letter 172)—precipitated what some have suggested was a nervous breakdown, but was more likely depression compounded by lung problems. Having failed in his attempt to obtain the scholarship to University College, Reading, he made the decision to leave Dunsden: 'It amounts to finding out whether my sanest moments are really my maddest. If they are I am still— mad' (Letter 178).

In search of a new profession, Owen became an English tutor in France, a country he grew to love, and where he 'reached perhaps the highest point of happiness that life would offer him'.[1] Owen began teaching English at the Berlitz School in Bordeaux in the autumn of 1913, and his letters are filled with the frustrations of hours of lessons ('I am getting positively stultified by the nature of my employment...we have anything between 7 and 10 hours per day', Letter 230), but also the joys of French life and friendships. There was even discussion of running his own Berlitz School in Angers in the north of France (Letters 235 and 238). In July 1914, he took up the post of tutor to Madame Léger and her daughter Nénette at the Villa Lorenzo, near Bagnères-de-Bigorre in the La Gailleste valley at the foot of the Pyrenees. It was an idyllic location with enchanting hosts (Letter 278). Monsieur Léger was a former engineer who had given up the profession for a career in the arts. Nénette was 'perfectly a child' with 'more than her fair share of intellect', while her mother, Madame Léger, was 'elegant rather than *belle*' with 'shapely features luxuriant coiffure' (Letter 278). She 'has a considerable liking for me, both in a physical and intellectual sense' (Letter 284), and not for the first time Owen reassures his mother that he is not being seduced by the charms of women: 'She is now equally conscious that the former liking is not reciprocated—not one little bit—and continues to like me for my mind's nature. If it were not so,—I should hop it, immejit.'

Just as Owen was fully ensconced at the Villa Lorenzo, Bagnères was overcome by news of war: 'Women were weeping all about; work was suspended. Nearly all the men have already departed', and he had 'to declare' himself to the authorities and 'get a permit to remain' (Letter 278). Yet he continued 'to be immensely happy and famously well', becoming fluent in French, immersing himself in French literature, and making the acquaintance of the poet Laurent Tailhade, who guided him to the work of Paul Verlaine, Gustave Flaubert, and others. This elderly, formerly radical French poet took a great liking to the young Englishman, which Owen describes with characteristic wryness: 'he quite slobbered over me' (Letter 285). As the war carried on around him, Owen felt his 'own life all the more precious and more dear in the presence of this deflowering of Europe' that might 'effect a little useful weeding' (Letter 285). Yet he was not entirely oblivious to press rhetoric about shirking young Englishmen, and he told his mother that the real reason he would go to fight—'what would hold me together on the battlefield'—was 'the sense that I was perpetuating the language in which Keats and the rest of them wrote!' (Letter 302). It was only after his harrowing experiences on the Western Front that the 'the poet of Pity' would emerge.

---

[1] Jon Stallworthy, 'Owen, Wilfred Edward Salter (1893–1918)', *Oxford Dictionary of National Biography*, Oxford University Press, 2004 (http://www.oxforddnb.com/view/article/37828, accessed 22 June 2022).

Thus Owen's letters of this early period of the war and through most of 1915 reveal him weighing many options (including joining the French or the Italian army; see Letters 365 and 376), as he continued to tutor in Bordeaux and attend courses at the University there. Madame Léger suggested he accompany her on a business trip to Canada (Letter 284), but instead, in December, Owen took up the post of tutor to two English boys, Johnny and Bobbie de la Touche, at Mérignac (Letters 304–81).

By June 1915 Owen had made his decision to enlist: 'I don't want the bore of training, I don't want to wear khaki; nor yet save my honour before inquisitive grand-children fifty years hence. But I <u>now</u> <u>do</u> most <u>intensely</u> <u>want</u> <u>to fight</u>' (Letter 357). The boys were meant to return to their public school, Downside in Bath, but the threat of submarines in the Channel continually delayed their leaving until September 1915. After accompanying Johnny and Bobbie back to England, Owen, in mid-October, enlisted in the Artists' Rifles at its headquarters in London (Letter 383).

Having completed training at various posts in the south and north-west of England, including Romford, Southport, and Fleetwood, Owen arrived at the Western Front in January 1917. In his five months in and out of the front line, he 'suffered seventh hell'. At Beaumont Hamel, though physically unscathed, he came face to face with the shocking realities of war: trenches that 'had been blown flat out', machine guns that 'spluttered every few minutes', and mud—'not sloppy mud, but an octopus of sucking clay' (Letter 480). The blinding of a sentry in the same action provided the source of the eponymous poem that has since become one of Owen's most iconic creations.

At Le Quesnoy-en-Santerre, in March, Owen fell into 'a kind of well', hit his head on the way down, and was concussed (Letter 494). In April, during an attack on Savy Wood, he was blasted into a railway cutting by a shell and lay next to a dead fellow officer for a number of days (Letters 505 and 508). Diagnosed with neurasthenia (shell shock) and invalided back to England in June, Owen was sent first to the Royal Victoria Hospital, Netley, on Southampton Water, then to Craiglockhart Military Hospital in Edinburgh. Here he was treated by Dr Arthur Brock, RAMC, and met Siegfried Sassoon. Sassoon had been sent to 'Dotty-ville', as he called it, in lieu of a court martial for his outspoken 'Soldier's Declaration' against the war, which was published in *The Times* and addressed in Parliament.

Owen was a nervous acolyte when he introduced himself to Sassoon at Craiglockhart that summer of 1917 (Letter 541). After reading some of Owen's poems, Sassoon became his mentor. Urging the younger officer to 'Sweat your guts out writing poetry', Sassoon helped Owen to channel his memories of the Western Front, which had been haunting his dreams, into poems such as 'Dulce et Decorum Est'. Their friendship was a deep one. There is no evidence that their relationship was physical, but it was profound. As Owen wrote to Sassoon in

November of 1917, 'You have <u>fixed</u> my Life—however short. You did not light me: I was always a mad comet; but you have fixed me' (Letter 557).

Owen spent the final year of his life composing his most famous poems as he recovered his physical and emotional fitness at postings in Scarborough and Ripon. He arrived on the London literary scene, thanks to Sassoon, and letters from late 1917 throughout 1918 relate his meeting such figures as Osbert Sitwell, H. G. Wells, Arnold Bennett, Charles Scott Moncrieff, and the publisher William Heinemann. He lunched at the Reform Club with Robert Ross (Letters 559, 565, 585) and attended the wedding of Robert Graves and Nancy Nicholson (Letter 584) while on leave. The 'schemes' of his friends, especially Scott Moncrieff, to get him a posting at the War Office or as an Instructing Staff Officer to a cadet battalion (Letter 621) came to nothing, and in August 1918 Owen was declared fit for draft (Letter 643) back to the Western Front.

Fierce fighting in the final months of the war tested Owen 'to the limits of my Abhorrence', and for leading a resistance against a heavy counter-attack by the Germans in October on the Fonsomme Line, which included personally capturing a machine gun and taking prisoners, he was awarded the Military Cross. As he wrote to Susan, 'I can find no word to qualify my experiences except the word SHEER...I lost all my earthly faculties, and fought like an angel' (Letter 662). By this time, it was known that the Germans were falling back and there were rumours that the war might soon end. On 31 October, he wrote to his mother from 'The Smoky Cellar of the Forester's House' (Letter 673). In this letter, which was to be his last, Owen's powers of vivid—and affectionate—description are on full display as he describes 'the inmates' crammed with him in that small space. A 'Coy. Commander snores on a bench'; 'Kellett, a delightful servant of A Coy. in The Old Days radiates joy & contentment from pink cheeks and baby eyes'; an 'old soldier with a walrus moustache peels & drops potatoes into the pot'. The letter ends with some of the most poignant words he ever wrote: 'Of this I am certain you could not be visited by a band of friends half so fine as surround me here.' Early on the morning of 4 November, as the 2nd Manchesters attempted to cross the Sambre–Oise Canal near the tiny village of Ors under heavy shelling and machine-gun fire, Owen was hit and killed. His death one week before the Armistice was just one more tragic irony of the Great War.

The Letters

> I like to think you'll keep this letter; as indeed all, not, of course, [for a] megalomaniac's reason; but just because I keep no Diary; and the landmarks of one's Thoughts fade away still quicker than Events.
>
> Wilfred Owen to Susan Owen, 5 March 1915, Letter 330

The chronology of Owen's life is not extraordinary. Indeed, it could have been the trajectory of any young man of his class and generation. Save for his having met Sassoon, who would (along with others such as Edith Sitwell and Edmund Blunden) go on to promote his posthumous poetic reputation, the bare facts of Owen's war service, highlighted by his Military Cross, are not unlike those of many other soldiers and officers during the Great War. What is remarkable is the writing he left behind. His poetry has come to define 1914–18 in the cultural imagination, the words of the draft preface to the volume of poems he had been planning coining the now iconic phrase 'the Pity of war'. Yet equally remarkable is his correspondence. As Dominic Hibberd argued, '[E]ven if he had written no poems he would deserve to be remembered as one of the finest letter writers of his century.'[2]

Owen's letter writing began early—his first letter to his mother was written in 1898 when he was 5 (Plate 1)—and continued regularly until that final October of the war. Read cover to cover, Owen's letters constitute his autobiography, a *Bildungsroman*. Cut off as he was at the height of his powers, they are also his extended epitaph.

Owen's letters are crucial if we are to understand the man, the soldier, and the war poet, for they reveal his developing literary powers and provide the raw material for his famous poetry. His correspondence chronicles his 'journey from obscurity' to 'poet's poet'. The early letters are peppered with drawings and sketches to animate his accounts of holidays in Wales and Cornwall, of his schoolwork, essays, exam results, various ailments, and concerns for his mother's health. They show his close, affectionate relationship with his siblings; the fractious squabbles and frustrations that sometimes came to the surface between him and his brother Harold are testament to the fact that, as in any family, brotherly and sisterly relationships are not always easy.

Owen's letters reveal his life as emblematic of many young men of his generation and lower-middle-class background, of those struggling to shrug off the perceived constructions of the Victorian age and to find a role in life that promised more than just drudgery. The longings of a Leonard Bast or Jude Fawley for an education were also those of the young pupil-teacher in Shrewsbury and the vicar's assistant in Dunsden. The confusions and deep emotions of adolescence and young adulthood were for him complicated by the pious religiosity and strict moral codes learned at his mother's knee. Undoubtedly, as the eldest son/brother, he could at times be overbearing, pompous, and self-important. His younger siblings could often only stand in his shadow, but they were his compass home and he loved them dearly.

Owen's sense of humour is perhaps the most surprising aspect of the letters. He could be wickedly funny, something that belies the more sombre image of the 'poet of Pity' we have come to know, just as the photograph of the cheerily smiling, newly enlisted recruit contrasts sharply with that of the enigmatic officer (Plates 2 and 3). The image of a 20-year-old Owen in Bordeaux, 'Revelling! in the Carnival!', is thus likely unexpected:

---

[2] Dominic Hibberd, *Wilfred Owen: A New Biography* (Phoenix, 2003), p. xxii.

> I had huge success with my Costume: Nothing more elaborate than my Gown on my back
> a laurel wreath on my head, & a palm branch in the hand. These 3, (with of course a
> Mask—my own home-made domino) made an imposing combination! I was with a stu-
> dent (whom I like very much), & his friends. The crowds were enormous, & I was twice
> choked with confetti. Weather magnificent.   (Letter 239)

Owen's letters transport us to the Edwardian world he inhabited and which
shaped him before he encountered 'the abode of madness' (Letter 481) on the
Western Front.

From an early age he could evoke a sense of place and write a good character,
attuned as he was to the idiosyncrasies and pretensions of people. In London on
his way to Craiglockhart to be treated for his shell shock, Owen lost none of his
capacity to see and communicate the absurd:

> I had tea at the Shamrock Tea Rooms, perhaps the most eminently respectable exclusive
> and secluded in Town. There was the usual deaf old lady and her Companion holding
> forth upon the new curate. I happen to know that a few stories higher in the same build-
> ing is an Opium Den. I have not investigated. But I *know*. That's London.   (Letter 528)

Owen's time at Craiglockhart may have been plagued by 'disastrous dreams'
(Letter 545), but these subsided under Brock's ergotherapy or work cure, which
encouraged activity and engagement with the world. The letters from this time
are filled with the delights of Edinburgh: visits to friends, walks on the Pentland
Hills, teaching at Tynecastle School, editing the hospital magazine *The Hydra*, and
poetry discussions with Sassoon. Owen even played 'Mr. Wallcomb, in Lucky
Durham: a fashionable young fellow, whose chief business in the play is introducing people' (Letter 538). He packed much living into what was little more than
four months. When he returned to light duties in October 1917, he continued his
mental and physical recovery, writing and revising his poems, and making plans
for publication. We can hear the voice of a mature, more self-assured young
officer emerging.

Owen's correspondence reveals his 'speech communities'—the Bible and
Shakespeare, the poetry of the English Romantics, Georgians, and Modernists,
the writings of French Symbolists and Decadents, and the lingo of the British
Army.[3] And, as he negotiated his experiences of the Western Front, these speech
communities gave him the power of vivid description, of cadence, sound, and
detail that are also the hallmarks of his best poems. His letters are lyrical, imagina-
tive, and arresting, even when written in his most distressed states of mental
anguish.[4] The rather isolated and lonely young man, who before the Great War

[3] Douglas Kerr, *Wilfred Owen's Voices: Language and Community* (Clarendon Press, 1993).
[4] See Jane Potter, '"I can find no word to qualify my experiences except the word SHEER":
Wilfred Owen's Letters and his Baptisms of Fire', in *Writing the Great War / Comment écrire la
Grande Guerre? Poétiques francophones et anglophones / Francophone and Anglophone Poetics*, ed. Nicolas
Bianchi and Toby Garfitt (Peter Lang, 2017).

seemed at times to prefer the company of the dead poets he admired (in particular Keats and Shelley) to that of the living, shared the suffering of his men and became their witness—in prose as well as poetry.

The Truth Untold

In Owen we have a paradox: a large number of detailed letters for such a short life are extant, letters that are, in essence, his autobiography; and, at the same time, these represent a very small portion of the nuances of that life—we have only what Owen wanted his recipient to know. As the list on page 421 shows, the majority of extant letters are addressed to Susan Owen, his mother. He wrote with her in mind, though in the knowledge/expectation that she would share his writing within the family: 'You will impart my messages to Father. I never begin "Dear Mother and Father" because I have the feeling of addressing an audience' (Letter 330). Only on rare occasions does he tell Susan to keep a letter strictly to herself. However candid Owen might have been in correspondence throughout his life, what might he *not* have said? While the letters give us a remarkably vivid picture of the life of an aspirational young poet thrown into the maelstrom of the First World War, they cannot tell us everything. For instance, where are all the letters Owen wrote to other correspondents, for surely there *were* others? And of those correspondents, how many may have simply discarded the letters of a then-obscure young man, later wartime army officer? Or, as Dominic Hibberd wistfully mused in the epilogue to his biography of Owen, 'maybe in some attic in Edinburgh perhaps or Bordeaux, a bundle of Wilfred's letters, tied in faded purple ribbon, still waits to be discovered'.[5] It is tempting to want to speculate—to fill in a more complete picture, a fuller life, to know, in short, everything about Owen—but as historians and literary scholars we have to be guided by evidence.

Over the years, certain key personal aspects have been foregrounded by close readings of Owen's letters and poems. The first has been Owen's sexuality. Denial of his likely homosexuality was vigorous by some of a generation for whom homosexuality was not only illegal (it was not decriminalized in England and Wales until 1967, the year the *Collected Letters* were published) but immoral and distasteful. Jon Stallworthy, Owen's first biographer (1974/2013) and editor of *The Complete Poems and Fragments* (1984/2013), was circumspect; Dominic Hibberd, Owen's second biographer (2003) and poetry scholar, concluded categorically that Owen *was* gay (although that term is an anachronism); Guy Cuthbertson, author of the third Owen biography (2014), highlighted more bisexual leanings. Most recently, Paul Norgate has investigated Owen's brief, but important, acquaintanceship with Mamie Knox Fullerton (Mrs Fullerton), an intriguing

---

[5] *WOANB*, p. 466.

episode in Owen's time in Edinburgh.[6] But Owen's letters themselves reveal
nothing definite and, unsurprisingly given that they were written mainly to his
mother and siblings, they do not mention whether he had any sexual encounters.
He certainly tries hard to reassure his mother that he is not cavorting with loose,
predatory women—it seems women found him very attractive—and he speaks
candidly of male friendships. His relationship with Sassoon was undoubtedly
profound: 'I love you, dispassionately, so much, so very much, dear Fellow, that
the blasting little smile you wear on reading this can't hurt me in the least. [....]
you have fixed my Life—however short' [Letter 557]. Thankfully, in the twenty-
first century the issue of Owen's sexuality, whatever it was and however it might
have been expressed had he lived, is no longer something 'that dare not speak its
name'. We can acknowledge, without the unease that earlier generations might
have felt, the power of Owen's intimate rendering of the male body in agony or in
repose as well as the vigour and intensity with which he brings that body into full
view in his poems.[7]

It is undoubtedly the case that Owen has at times suffered from being
presented in an over-sentimentalized or idealized way, and that this in turn has
provoked a natural reaction in some readers, a wish to bring out his possibly less
admirable, or simply more human, qualities. This is understandable, and to a
degree legitimate, but as biographers and readers we must be careful not to con-
fuse the desire to see a complete life with the temptation to 'reveal' some hitherto
'hidden', unsubstantiated details. As early as the 1920s, Robert Graves in *Goodbye
to All That* (1929) effectively accused Owen of cowardice, causing untold distress
to his family and friends. Graves's slur was based on hearsay, of a comment sup-
posedly made by one of Owen's senior officers, but military records contain no
supporting evidence. His shell-shock diagnosis obviously indicates that he had
been rendered incapable of effectively fulfilling his duties, but the care taken by
the authorities to ensure that capability was properly restored, and the way in
which Owen subsequently conducted himself after his return to the front line in
1918, are reminders of the importance of substantial evidence.

More recently, the joy with which Owen wrote about children has been
adduced as an occasion for suspicion. The 'furore' which precipitated his leaving
Dunsden, as described in Letter 172, has been interpreted (partly due to Harold's
redactions) as having something to do with an inappropriate, intimate relationship with a child of the parish. This in turn, however, is again not based on

[6] Paul Norgate, 'Reading "Hiawatha", Writing Friendships: Wilfred Owen & Mrs Fullerton',
The Annual Wilfred Owen Birthday Lecture, recorded on 18 March 2021, https://www.you-
tube.com/watch?v=60LdOcOFHH0&t=198s.
[7] See Santanu Das, *Touch and Intimacy in First World War Literature* (Cambridge University Press,
2005).

evidence, and Owen returned to visit Dunsden during the war without any hint of embarrassment or censure. As Owen's letters reveal, Owen was not averse to being a disciplinarian, either as elder brother or employed tutor. But he loved children and children flocked to him. The gentle, easy manner he had with his own siblings was extended to those he interacted with in Dunsden and in France. To suggest that his relationships with children were in any way inappropriate, or that his dealings with young people were somehow predatory, is both cruel and insupportable.

Manuscripts and Publication History

Compiled, edited, and interpreted by various hands after Owen's death, the letters, in their very materiality and conservation, expose the competing public and private interests in Owen's reputation over the course of 100 years. They have been instrumental in shaping Owen's afterlife. They form the basis of, and are quoted at length in, the three major biographies of Owen, literary-critical and historical studies, journalism, and various media.

The manuscript letters were kept in haphazard fashion. Both Susan and Mary were 'perfect squirrels' when it came to storage, as Harold Owen and John Bell noted in their introduction to the *Collected Letters* (1967):

> In every room and outbuilding of the little house in Emmer Green, near Reading, bundles of Wilfred's letters and postcards were found. There was no chronological order, no yearly sequence. Tied up with string, wool, odd bits of ribbon or tape, some of these bundles also contained letters from other people with receipted bills...Some letters were found in the garden shed in nailed-down boxes and tea-chests, unopened for many years; others had been hidden amidst remnants of materials, oddments of wool, and silk-embroidery work. In one box a few letters had been packed with a tea-set. And in another nailed-down box, incidentally opened by the Emmer Green Boy Scouts on Mary's instructions, was Wilfred's heavy army revolver, loaded, with a pouch of live ammunition.
>
> From time to time an odd bundle or single letter had been handed by Mary to her brother for safe-keeping; but she, like her mother, had forgotten or did not realize how many letters had been stored in this haphazard way. Only one letter had been carefully preserved, the first; and this was discovered in Susan Owen's jewel-box after Mary's death. Carefully sealed in an envelope, it was inscribed in pencil 'Wilfie's first letter, 1898'.

Yet, despite the family having moved house eight times, 'Wilfred's letters survived, somehow'.[8]

On Mary's death, the contents of Wilmot House in Emmer Green were transferred to Harold's home, Rodgarden Shaw, Ipsden, Oxfordshire. Here, Harold Owen wrote *Journey from Obscurity*, using Wilfred's letters from time to time but refusing all requests from scholars and critics—especially Dennis Welland,

---

[8] *Wilfred Owen: Collected Letters*, ed. Harold Owen and John Bell (Oxford University Press, 1967), p. 1.

author of the first serious critical study of Owen's poetry (1963)—to see or publish his brother's correspondence. As he explained in *My Dear Old Wolf* (appendix A), he would release them only once he had finished his own family biography. Harold Owen's refusals, his intractableness, were seen as censorship; ignorant and naïve at best, paranoid and malicious at worst—charges confirmed when the extent of his redactions became publicly known. Some passages of the originals had been pencilled over (mostly likely by Susan Owen) and were easily retrievable, but others were blacked out in Indian ink or completely scissored out and destroyed. The Introduction to the *Collected Letters* asserted that 'this was done…in good faith, and without a realization of the difficulties that might arise later'. Arguably, such 'difficulties' included not just transcription (in order to reinstate what was deleted) but speculation by future readers about how salacious the excised material might actually be. The original intention was merely

> to remove names of people whose families might have been upset by some particularly scathing reference, or simply by the unexpected appearance of their names in print; and to remove words or expressions that seemed displeasing or unworthy.…It all appears harmless, almost comically so. Auntie for Aunt, dinner for lunch, unattractive slang expressions, words with mildly disagreeable associations such as pimples, boils, and so on, disparaging comments on casual acquaintances who cannot now be identified; and some sentences so respectable that the original impulse to obscure cannot now be recalled.[9]

Harold Owen and John Bell attempted 'to decipher and restore all the obliterations' and even used 'infra-red treatment in one or two particularly obstinate cases' involving the Indian ink redactions. (These were found to involve disparaging comments about the Royal Navy, for instance in Letter 488.) They largely succeeded, and it was not unreasonable for them to argue that, taken in context, 'the content is the surest indication of triviality'.[10]

Since then, further efforts have been made to get below the redactions, most recently by Dr Jean M. Cannon, during her tenure as Archivist of the Owen Collection in Texas.[11] But the process is costly and has not yet been realized by modern technology. Would the revealed passages make a difference to our understanding of Owen? Perhaps. But it is likely that what Harold Owen excised was more about *himself* than his brother. Even with these (in)famous redactions, Owen's letters are documents of remarkable candour. Notwithstanding interventions that seem to us now as misplaced, Susan, Mary, and Harold Owen's collective devotion to a son and brother, and John Bell's consummate editorial skills, have preserved for us a remarkable collection of the words of one of the great poets of the English language.

---

[9] CL, p. 5.
[10] CL, p. 6.
[11] Jean M. Cannon, 'Censorship in Surprising Places: Uncovering the Letters of Wilfred Owen' (2014), https://notevenpast.org/censorship/.

The *Collected Letters* contained 673 letters, picture postcards, and incomplete letters. Owen's field service (twelve in total) postcards were not included as, by design, they did not include any additional information beyond what was printed on the card. The overwhelming majority of the letters are to Susan Owen.

Within the Family	Susan Owen	554
	Mary Owen	41
	Colin Owen	22
	Harold Owen	9
	Tom Owen	5
Outside the Family	Leslie Gunston	30
	Siegfried Sassoon	7
	Alec Paton	3
	Osbert Sitwell	1
	Nelly Bulman	1
	Charles Scott-Moncrieff	1

The sheer volume of Owen's letters to his mother has been seen as overly needy, as the missives of a 'mama's boy'. But for his generation it was not unusual to address most of one's correspondence to one's mother. As Mary Ragge, a contemporary of Colin Owen and neighbour of the family, pointed out, 'that was the order; that is what you must do for the women. My father said to [my brother] John, "write to your Mother". And it was the same with Tom Owen—write to your Mother.' With absence or loss of a child, 'it's the Mother who is to suffer a bit more'.[12] In the years after his death, Susan found comfort in returning to the letters which contained the ghostly spirit of her son: 'Oh! How I miss his beautiful letters but I read all the old ones. I am sure no mother ever had such loving letters—and always so interesting.'[13]

The publication of the *Collected Letters* was received with great interest and favourable reviews. Letters of appreciation poured in to Harold Owen. One admirer wrote that the *Collected Letters* helped readers 'to understand much more' of his brother, 'his thoughts, his dreams, his hopes, his life'. Another called them 'inexpressibly moving'. In many ways, it is impossible to overstate the significance of the *Collected Letters*. Prior to their publication, extracts reproduced by Edmund Blunden (1931) and C. Day Lewis (1967) gave only a hint of what was, in fact, a treasure trove.

[12] Mary Ragge, Personal Interview with Peter and Elizabeth Owen, February 1998.
[13] Susan Owen to Alec Paton, 1919, Oxford, Bodleian Libraries, MS. 12282/33.

After the publication of the *Collected Letters*, Harold Owen offered the manuscripts to the Bodleian Library in Oxford for £3,000. The response was slow and not particularly enthusiastic, perhaps because in the late 1960s, despite the fact that his poems provided the basis for Benjamin Britten's *War Requiem* and featured in the BBC's *The Great War* series, Owen was still seen by some as rather a minor poet.[14] Thus the manuscripts were auctioned at Sotheby's and bought for £6,500 in 1970 (over £90,000 today) by the University of Texas at Austin, where they form the cornerstone of the Wilfred Owen Collection at the Harry Ransom Humanities Research Center. Owen's personal library, schoolbooks, and family photographs were bequeathed to the English Faculty Library at Oxford by Harold's widow, Phyllis, in 1975, and are now housed in the Bodleian's Weston Library. In this latter sense, Harold's words ring poignantly true: 'So you see, Old Wolf, although you could not get to your coveted Oxford, your work has done this for you'.[15] The current locations of the originals of all of Owen's letters may be found in Appendix B.

Selected Letters of Wilfred Owen: New Edition

John Bell included 329 letters in his editions of Owen's *Selected Letters* (1985, 1998) and made a number of corrections based on scholarship that appeared in the wake of the *Collected Letters*. I adhered to the same sensible editorial principles established by Bell for these selected editions, namely that early years are 'cut severely', the Dunsden and Bordeaux years truncated, and the war years left 'more or less intact'. I have not deleted any of the letters that appeared in Bell's *Selected* edition, but I have added twenty-three more letters/postcards which I found especially interesting and worthy of inclusion, bringing the total up to 352. Among these are letters to Mary Owen and to Leslie Gunston which were not included in Bell's shorter edition. What is especially new and distinctive about this revised edition is the reinstatement of deciphered redactions as well as previously omitted names and sentences; further details of each are included in the footnotes.

John Bell's footnotes provide the foundation for those in this edition, but I have amended and added to them to provide fresh information and context, and to assist a twenty-first-century audience in their reading. Aspects which Owen and Bell took for granted as understood in 1967, or even in 1985 or 1998, may not now be familiar. Updated to reflect the most recent scholarship from inside and

---

[14] Owen did not appear in the *Dictionary of National Biography* until 1993, when the supplementary volume *Missing Persons* (Oxford University Press), edited by Christine Nicholls, was published.

[15] Harold Owen, *My Dear Old Wolf: An Undelivered Letter to Wilfred Owen from His Brother Harold* (Backwater Press, 1996); see Appendix A.

outside the academy, this new edition provides today's reader with the resources to see Owen in the context of his time and to appreciate the nuances of his writing. Much work has been done by independent scholars, unattached to any university or academic organization, and references in the footnotes to meticulously researched articles in such publications as *The Wilfred Owen Association Journal* demonstrate just how vibrant this work is.

Throughout, references to the poems come from the authoritative *Complete Poems and Fragments*, edited by Jon Stallworthy.

Owen's dating of his letters could be idiosyncratic—often simply a day (e.g. 'Monday') with no date—and his brother Harold had separated many from their postmarked envelopes: thus, in many cases years later, it was left to Harold and John Bell to assign reasonable dates of composition. Subsequent scholarship by Dominic Hibberd (1982)[16] and Paul Norgate (1986)[17] established more accurate dates for a significant number of letters, some of which have implications for the narrative of Owen's life (as well as for the dating of some of the poems).The revised dates (which mostly affect letters from the war years) have been incorporated into this edition in two ways:

1. Where the date of composition is incorrect by only a day or two, it does not generally affect the chronology of the selection, the dates have been amended accordingly and referenced with a footnote.
2. In the few instances where the corrected date significantly impacts on the sense of the narrative, whether by a week, month, or year, the letters in question have been moved to their correct or approximate chronological place with an amended date. But in order not to cause confusion for those who wish to consult the manuscripts, the *Collected Letters*, or the *Selected Letters*, I have retained the original manuscript number and placed it in square brackets, [ ].

Owen in the Twenty-First Century

Academic and general interest in Owen's life and work shows no signs of abating and indeed was amplified during the Centenary. His role as a cultural icon of the Great War became more firmly entrenched than ever. In *Wilfred Owen: An Illustrated Life*, I outlined what in 2014 was an already impressive range of monuments, spaces, and awards dedicated to Owen over the preceding

---

[16] Dominic Hibberd, 'Wilfred Owen's Letters: Some Additions, Amendments and Notes, *The Library* (Sept 1982), sixth series, Vol. 4, no. 3, pp. 273–87.

[17] Paul Norgate, '"Dulce et Decorum Est" and Some Amendments to the Dating of Wilfred Owen's Letters', *Notes and Queries* (June 1986), Vol. 33, no. 2, pp. 186–90.

decades.[18] During the Centenary, that list expanded exponentially. Owen was a touchstone of commemorations in Britain. His words appeared on a special £2 coin from the Royal Mint and on a Royal Mail stamp in a series marking the Armistice. New statues, memorials, and sculptures were dedicated in Oswestry, Birkenhead, Shrewsbury, and Edinburgh, and the Wilfred Owen Violin was created using wood from a sycamore tree at Craiglockhart. The anniversary of his death was marked in the misty early morning hours of 4 November 2018 on the banks of the Sambre–Oise Canal and later at his graveside in the Communal Cemetery at Ors. With the Centenary behind us, the opportunity to encounter and appreciate the man behind the myth, in his own words, now seems particularly apt.

Owen's importance, as this edition intends to show, extends far beyond the Centenary. Sadly, while the dates may have changed, human beings' capacity for hurting each other has not. War continues around the globe and today's veterans, now women as well as men, continue to work through their experiences via literary forms.[19] Owen's message—conveyed in his letters as well as his poetry—that urges us to recognize the horror and pity of war resonates still. As Jon Stallworthy asserted, 'Owen's readiness to express his feelings—of grief, tenderness, delight, as well as indignation' is what draws readers to him.[20]

After three major biographies and countless scholarly works that have interpreted Owen's life and writing, his work still invites study and literary criticism. Thus I also hope that this edition will provide material to researchers, the general reader, and, especially, a new generation of students who might carry out future scholarship. The new *Selected Letters* allows Owen to speak for himself once again, revealing not so much the cultural icon he has become but a man, human with all his foibles, whose twenty-five years were marked by great highs and lows, by emerging modernity and the violence of war.

---

[18] See Jane Potter, *Wilfred Owen: An Illustrated Life*, ch. 6, 'Owen's Afterlife' (Bodleian Library Publishing, 2014).

[19] See, for example, *'My teeth don't chew on shrapnel': an Anthology of Poems by Military Veterans* (Oxford Brookes Poetry Centre, 2020), https://doi.org/10.24384/dnqr-wm30.

[20] Jon Stallworthy, *Wilfred Owen* (Pimlico, 2013), p. 295.

1

Shrewsbury and Dunsden
1902–1913

1. To Susan Owen

Addressed *Mary and Mother* with a pattern of kisses

[1898]   [Birkenhead]

my dear mother

i no that you have got there safely. We are making huts. I have got a lantern, and we are lighting them up to-night.

With love from Wilfred I remain your loving son Wilfred

2. To Susan Owen

Saturday 19th [April 1902]   [Underdale Road, Shrewsbury]

Dear Mother,

Grandpa[1] has given me as much garden as what you see from the dining room window only where the bricks are and I have got about six potatos planted, I have made another path and on the right side of it is the Vegeatble Garden and on the left is the fruit and the one you saw is the flower. It has just been raining a little for the first time but now it has stopt. We are going to Market this afternoon and I might buy some seeds. I know the children next door they have got a horse and carriage which will fit me comfortably and the path slopes like Grandpa's and I can go down without anybody touching me, I can sit or stand which ever, I like.

I look something like this standing.

I'm glad Mary is better I expect Harold is. Now I must stop, my hands are begining to shake.

Kisses for all.

From your loving Wilfred

¹ Grandfather William Owen (1837–1914). The 9-year-old Wilfred is staying with his Owen grandparents at 2 Hawthorn Villas, Underdale Road, Shrewsbury. Early in 1907 the Owen family leaves Birkenhead for 1 Cleveland Place, Underdale Road, Shrewsbury, a few houses away from the grandparents. See Harold Owen, *Journey from Obscurity: Memoirs of the Owen Family*, Vol. 1 (Oxford University Press, 1963), pp. 122–4.

3. To Mary Owen

[1903]   [Wales]²

Dear Mary,

I have really not much to tell you. I went up the hill the day before yesterday. I am afraid you or Colin could not have climbed up it, dear, it was so hard. I hope the young ladies in your school are very good & all your large family is well. I am trying to learn Welsh. I should like to have been with you on Sunday & at our service. Mind you have it next Sunday & I shall think about you. I shall expect you to read more of that story book by the time I am home.

With best love & kisses from your brother Wilfred

² Owen was staying with his school friend Alec Paton, whose uncle farmed in North Wales at Rhewl, near Ruthin, Denbighshire.

35. To Vera and Leslie Gunston

15 November 1907   Shrewsbury

TO OBSERVE THE WORLD.

(To be read together if possible)

Dear Vera & Leslie,

At last, (by the way how often I begin my letters thus, I notice, too, that you have commenced so, no less than 4 times!) But I have no time for trifles now for

I have much to say yet little time. I'm afraid that this scribble will have to be the last 'Soc. Letter'³ before I make my proposed visit, (to which I look forward with the keenest delight). For in less than 4 wks the exams will be upon us, & between that time who knows what I've got to do! Well I must get to the point. On thinking over the Rules, (for which I believe I have never yet thanked you) a new subject came into my head, that of Mountain Climbing. It is, as you will see, an almost essential branch of each of our studies, and mountaineering is also to the ambitious & strenuous outdoor naturalist, not only the noblest but the most insatiable of all noble sports. I propose that the aims of the movement shall be:

(1) The promotion of scientific study & exploration of certain glacial regions.
(2) *The cultivation of Art in relation to mt. scenery.
(3) The Christian education of the inhabitants to an appreciation of their mt. heritage.
(4) The encouragement of the mt. craft, & the opening of new regions as a national playground.
(5) The preservation of the natural beauties of the mt. places, & of the fauna & flora in their habitat (with special reference to V.)

 * It is hoped that you, V. will become the Photographic Representative, for what is Astronomy without its sister-art Photography? & some pictures showing strata, etc. would be invaluable to me. Hence I earnestly hope you will accept this office, for none is better fitted for it than you, surrounded as you are by some of the foremost works in Alpine Photography.

As for You, Les: I don't know what you will think of me for not writing to tell you of the lecture on Nov. 7. (I certainly did get 'flurried' when I received a second letter from you!) The lecture was by A.R. HINKS. M.A.⁴ chief asstnt. to Sir Robt. Ball,⁵ Cambridge. It was entitled—'Our Place in the Universe' & the slides were as excellent as the Lecture was instructive. It really was, however, too boring to sit there in pleasure, knowing you were missing it all. I am glad you like long letters, (I do of course) but I really can't stay at it much longer, I will answer your last letter as soon as possible. And V. dear I will write too you but if my epistles are long you must expect them to be 'far between'. How are you progressing in your Bot: studies at the Tech: ?

Amor ad omnes omnibus mittitur est! (as this flowery ending is wrong don't try it)

I remain, not doubting that you are equally faithful, A most zealous member of the A.G.B.S.

W.E.O.

P.S. I hope you will get this before Sunday, so I am going to the post myself tho' it's 10 P.M. It is a lovely night—a brilliant moon, & Orion looks superb in the Eastern sky. Have you seen it? It is nice, tho' we are separated by hundreds of miles to be able to gaze on the same objects! If possible would you tell me how to find Mars. I am rather vague as to its position at present, so I would be grateful for some directions.

W

[3] The AGBS, or Astronomical, Geological, and Botanical Society; the members were Vera and Leslie Gunston and Wilfred Owen. See Letter 535. Leslie (1895–1988) was the youngest of the four Gunston cousins, the others being Gordon (b.1887), Dorothy (b.1888), and Vera (b.1891). Their father, John Gunston, married Emma (1861–1934), second eldest of the three Shaw sisters, the others being Mary 'May' (Mrs Loughrey) (1860–96) and (Harriet) Susan (1867–1942), Wilfred's mother.

[4] Arthur Robert Hinks, FRS (1873–1945), Secretary of the Royal Geographical Society 1915–45.

[5] Robert Stawell Ball, FRS (1840–1913), Professor of Astronomy at Dublin University and Royal Astronomer of Ireland 1874–92. He was Lowndean Professor of Astronomy at Cambridge from 1892 until his death.

39. To Harold Owen

[10 April 1908]   [Wimbledon]

My dear Harold,

I was so pleased with your letter this morning I did not expect one from you so soon.

Jimmy is grown into quite a cat now but he is so lazy. The dove has gone; a cat got it Leslie says, so there is only one left of the family. I went for a short walk on the common yesterday morning after going to school with Leslie, but it was very misty, so I soon came in. Leslie came home in a frightful bluster from the class. He was given homework! 'Why couldn't I have homework when Wilfred is gone. Why couldn't Wilfred come when I have no homework? Eh? Mother! Mother! What on earth's the good of me having homework when Wilfred's here?' When he began to do it, I heard nothing but 'Wilfred, Wilfred, do look here!' I tried to explain, but that was the way Mr. Latham[6] did it, which was wrong, quite wrong! I then did one of the sums for him, but he said 'Do you think I am going to copy that?' at which I left him to his own methods.

I should like to see the peculiar skeletons of flies you have found you must keep them till I come home. I will write to Colin and Mary next time.

With best love from   Wilfred

I WILL WRITE TO COLIN SOON.

[6] Leslie Gunston was having special holiday tuition under Mr Latham, a master of King's College School, Wimbledon.

42. To Susan Owen

18 April 1908   *Alpina*[7]

My own dear Mother,

   I must send you another little note while I have got the chance, as Leslie is now doing his homework. (that is I am doing one half of it, & Auntie the other.) Gordon did <u>not</u> get up at 6 to go bug-hunting, but he is going this morning. I think it is going to be fine although it began to rain this morning. Yesterday we had beautiful weather, the sun was out nearly all day. We went to the lantern service. I did enjoy it; the pictures were very beautiful, thirty-nine in all & all selected by Mr. Moore.[8]

   He explained all the slides, so that each was quite a little sermon. The Church Room was crowded, so that about 20 people were standing at the doors! After some of Mr. Moore's graphic descriptions there was a great deal of suspicious blowing of noses & one person fainted at the door.

   I don't think I told you Mr. Moore's text yesterday morning. It was Pilate's <u>sermon</u>, as he called it: 'Behold the man' He told us a lot about Pontius Pilatus, & then about 'The Man'. In this he referred to Mr. Macdonald's sermon on 'man' (*Gen.* 2. 7.) on Thurs. afternoon.—did I tell you we went to church on Thurs. with Dorothy? It was a very good address. He took the meaning of the word 'man' in <u>Hebrew</u> where it means 'a weak, feeble one'.

   In <u>Greek</u> mng: 'one who prays'
   In <u>Latin</u> mng: 'a <u>strong</u> one'
   & in Eng. mng: 'one who has the power of thought.'

   Well I must stop this letter now, as I suppose Harold will like a note. Love to Father, hope your poor cold is gone.

                                                            Your loving boy Wilfred

   [7] The Gunston house at 3 Clement Road, Wimbledon.
   [8] Rev. E. W. Moore, evangelical preacher, Emmanuel Church, Wimbledon. He was one of the founder clergy of the Keswick Convention. See Letters 132(n. 144) and 148.

51. To Susan Owen

31 December 1908   *Alpenrose, Kidmore End, Reading*[9]

Dearest Mother,

   So sorry to keep you waiting for a letter till next year but when you read the programme I have been filling up these days you will see I had not much time for writing.

The journey was <u>most</u> uncomfortable. In half an hour's time my feet were frozen & went on getting worse and worse, & my sufferings were increased by the prospect of three hours more with no means of relief. However a lady ordered a 'portah to bwing a foot warmah' which comforting article she invited us to share.

Vera met us at Reading; we drove up in a kind of trap, I in Leslie's Inverness & Mary in sundry cloaks of Auntie's.

Before tea the fowls etc. were inspected & Leslie took me (on bicycles) to the Smithie & Mrs. Baker's cottage.[10]

The snow was very thin down here then, but on Tuesday it snowed all day, and froze hard, with the result of a fine dry covering so deep that the snow-plough was used yesterday. We went to Kidmore Pond to see if there was skating but found ice broken & covered with snow.

On Wednesday morning Uncle had made a toboggan, the height of whose runners was 2 ins., so that it was useless in thick snow. Howbeit Dorothy, Vera, Leslie, Mary & I were going to try it on Peppard Common when we met the Cates with the news that Kidmore Pool would bear. Thither therefore proceeded Leslie, George, Geoff, & I, to find we could skate around the sides, But the ice was fright-fully hard being composed of wet snow frozen, & so presenting a surface like a species of nutmeg-grater. Dorothy was meanwhile tobogganing down Peppard Common, Mary & Vera not indulging in the dangerous pastime. I stayed in in the afternoon & imbibed *Cassell's Popular Science*.[11]

In the evening Dorothy Leslie the Cates's[12] & I took the toboggan to Peppard Common, & had a simply splendidrippinggrandmajesticgloriousdelightful-scrumtiousexquisitelyexcruciating time. The moon was overclouded but there was light enough to see the dark forms against the snow.

When I went to bed last night I found blocks of ice floating about in my water-jug and this morning it was thicker still so you can imagine what a time we are having.

After breakfast Uncle spied tracks of a hare all about the garden. Uncle loaded his gun & we stealthily made our way to the Pit where it was supposed to be hiding. Approaching the stable the sound of many waters broke upon our wondering ears—thrusting the loaded gun into Leslie's hand he broke in to find a deluge of water spurting about over the bags of meal, etc, the tools, & the cows. The first thing to be done was to turn off the water at the main.

Now the main tap was in the road covered with quickly melting snow, & to find it was no easy thing. We frantically scraped, & kicked & shovelled & dug like searchers for hidden treasure until at last it was unearthed & the supply stopped. The tools & nails were conveyed to the house to dry, but the bags of meal were ruined. One sack worth £1. is utterly soaked, & unless used up at once will rot or turn sour, so I think Uncle will sell it for the pheasants.

It is fast thawing now but still horribly cold & a thick mist envelopes the land.

I am glad the boys had some tobogganning.

I had myself looked out that iron for sledge-runners!

Tea will soon be ready—the last day of the year is now closing.—so must this letter.

With best love from Wilfred

---

[9] John Gunston's newly built house at Kidmore End, 5 miles north of Reading, had been completed earlier in the year.

[10] Two adjoining cottages at Peppard, near Reading. Mrs Baker's cottage was possibly Fern Brae. The Gunstons occasionally stayed there while Alpenrose was being built.

[11] *Cassell's Popular Science*, ed. Alexander S. Galt. The announcement of its publication in the journal *Nature* (26 November 1903) noted that it 'is profusely illustrated and contains a well-selected series of brightly written essays on various subjects of pure and applied science. The volume may be recommended as a suitable present to boys and girls, who will probably by its means be led to study more deeply one of the many branches of science of which some of the methods and results are described' (p. 78).

[12] Wimbledon friends. The three Cates boys were George, Henry, and Geoffrey.

54. To Susan Owen

Postcard

[*Postmark 18 July 1909*]   [*Postmark Brest*][13]

Dearest Mother,

This is a summary of events:

Friday Night. Did not once lose consciousness in train.

Sat. Mng. Almost got carried on to Penzance, there being 'change' at North Road, Plym. Embarked *IBEX*.[14] Slept in clothes in common saloon. Awoke (tired) at 8. Passed thro' various fogs, till about 5 o'clock engines suddenly stopped, & ship lay tossing frightfully (deck angle 35°.) Fog increased—so did anxiety. We were lost! Soundings were made but to no purpose, & we lay helplessly drifting. The log showed we were only a few miles off the most dangerous coast of the channel, & we could only see a few furlongs! However, the melancholy siren attracted a pilot. Such was the state of the sea, that the great bowsprit of his boat was smashed like a match! Pilot finally lost himself, until certain lighthouse loomed ahead. Again we proceeded but finally were forced to anchor. We slept on deck, & only reached B. at 7 this mng. Breakfasted at H. Continental. Then discovered Mme. Berthou's to be a dirty little house over a wine-shop! Wandered about—were told of an English 'Mees' who has directed us to an apartment. Are now at Hotel de France, comfortable but cheaper than Continental. Had an excellent lunch, and am now about to rest being exceedingly tired. (Went to Church this morning) No more news now.

---

[13] Tom Owen had taken Wilfred for a holiday in Brittany in June 1908. This was a repeat visit.

[14] TSS *Ibex*, a passenger vessel owned by the Great Western Railway.

56. To Colin Owen

July 1909   *Torquay*[15]

My dear Colin,

It <u>was</u> stupid of me to forget your birthday. I'm sure I was more sorry when I found out, than you were on receiving not even a post card! However I hope you will like the paint box. We have got a <u>real</u> lizard, too, — dead of course and in a bottle of spirits.

There is something else in that bottle, something long, green, and thin, ... ugh!

One day as Father and I were going up over a cliff not far from the hotel, I suddenly saw what I thought was a great worm wriggling across the path. In an instant it flashed upon me that it was a snake!

'Look, look,' I cried, 'A snake'.

'What !! Where!' says Father.

'Ah, quick, quick!' and he rushed upon it, just as it was escaping down the cliff, and nearly overbalanced himself over the precipice.

The first blow did not kill it, and it coiled up with his head in the air just like the pictures you have seen.

However, the second hit finished it, and we cautiously took it up and carried it on the end of the stick. Since we are going right over the cliff & back we hid the serpent under some stones. We found it again coming back, and Father was putting it in his pocket when it moved, and wriggled its tail feebly! It was a pity to spoil it, by smashing its head, so I carried it home holding it securely round the neck, with its wicked little eyes open.

However, I think it was quite dead when we reached the hotel. They said it was a Viper! which very much surprised me, for I had thought it quite harmless & was not even disgusted by its wriggling. It is only a <u>small</u> one, you know, but still, if it <u>is</u> a viper it is very dangerous indeed, and I am glad we saw it in time. I hope Mother will not let this incident stand in the way of her visiting Brittany, for Morgat has one of the very finest shores I have seen and Mother never need venture on to the moors.

I have found no stones worth a place in your museum, but some very good shells, (if they are not broken)

It has rained all day. I am sorry for Father, but I am quite all right in the house with hundreds of books to choose from.

I hope someone will be able to read this letter, my good writing is taking a holiday.

Give my birthday wishes the cane for being so late. Their late arrival is too due to a <u>fog</u> in the memory <u>channel</u>.

Your loving brother Wilfred

[15] No. 264 Union Street, Torquay, home of Uncle John Taylor and his wife Ann, Tom Owen's sister. John Taylor was a newsagent, stationer, and bookseller in Stockport before retiring to Torquay around 1906.

62. To Susan Owen

24 December 1909   *Alpenrose*

Dear Mother,

A happy Christmas to you all!

I am writing on the veranda, with no coat on—in warm sunshine. There is not a cloud in the sky. Can't imagine I was skating the day before yesterday.

They have had hardly any snow here.

I did spend a delightful afternoon yesterday!

I am not sure of the exact time I arrived. The box being carried by an 'outside' porter, I reached the station yard & looked about for old Mildenhall.[16]

I was not disconcerted to find him not there, since you had warned me. I waited five minutes, ten minutes, quarter of an hour—then enquired of the person in charge of the 'Inquiry Office' whether he had gone. Official didn't know.—Thought he had.

Three quarters of an hour gone! How I anathemised that unlucky carrier!

Imagine me with nothing whatever to do, couldn't even think—for fear of losing sight of the box, or missing the cart—watching every wretched carriage, trap, bus, van, cart, motor, etc. etc. that passed, without a moment's rest. And one eye on the box at the same time.

Then darkness drew on with vast and rapid strides, and when neither Perrin nor any other carrier appeared after two hours waiting, there remained nothing but to leave the box at Station & walk. I was not at all sure of the way and in the dark too! However, people had begun to look at me askance. Was I a detective? A Spy? And perhaps they would order me off the place for loafing. So I boldly set out, resolving to pass the night in some one-roomed cottage if I got lost. By force of much enquiry I reached the hill after Caversham[17] and there I overtook Perrin, & got in.

I arrived safely without box & passed a good night after the nervous prostration of the afternoon; the only discomforts being a dirty collar, & muddy trousers after this morning's walk.

The poultry etc. are much the same. The calf is very pretty really.

As you prognosticated—fattened fowls for Christmas!

However I descried a hare, 2 pheasants, & a tongue in the larder as well. Oh! I had a cup of tea on arriving, & a chop for supper at 8.

We are going out again this afternoon to gather decorating materials from the woods.

Best love & Christmas Wishes to all especially dear Mary,

from Wilfred.

[16] The Kidmore End carrier.
[17] Caversham Hill, the area of Reading north of the Thames.

69. To Susan Owen

Aug. 1910   *Torquay*

Dearest Mother,

I daresay you will be as astonished as I was to find a Postal Order in my letter!
The accompanying note will doubtless explain.

Leslie says he is delighted to hear of some fixed arrangements. What are they
please? And is it fixed that we leave Torquay on Tuesday? Really, I am by no means
'fed up' with it!

The whole day to Harold & me centres round the bathing. The most enjoyable
we have ever had, I think.

It is one of those rare cases where the actuality exceeds, does not fall short of,
the expectation.

Since yesterday afternoon my senses have been considerably fluttered. For
I then discovered that a few furlongs away there lives a descendant of Coleridge—
Miss Christabel Coleridge.[18] I promptly discovered the house by means of a
directory, and a few minutes later my heart (liver and cerebellum included)

Would it savour too much of the tradesman's invitation to Lord Roberts if
I were to interview her?

But what relics must she possess, and what information with regard to the
truth of the anecdotes about Coleridge!

Archaeological interest next consumes me. My American friend[20] tells me of
a prehistoric Cavern near Meadfoot (Kent's Cavern).[21] I, however, have found out
(from a Guide Book) about another and Prehistoricer cavern (as well as a Roman
Camp)[22] near Brixham.

So we are together going to Brixham on Monday afternoon (if fine.)... [*one
line missing*] nearly gone.

I hear scanty news of your throat!

Is it therefore quite better?

---

[18] The novelist Christabel Rose Coleridge (1843–1921), daughter of the Rev. Derwent
Coleridge, was Samuel Taylor Coleridge's granddaughter. She lived at Cheyne, Torquay, and
her brother, Ernest Hartley Coleridge, must have been visiting her at this time, for they both inscribed their names with the date 10 August 1910 in Owen's copy of *The Golden Book of Coleridge*.

[19] From 'An Evening Song' by Frances Anne 'Fanny' Kemble (1809–93), actress and author.

[20] Russell Tarr. For a detailed account of this boy, and the Torquay holiday, see *JFO* I, pp. 186–99 (and see also Letter 79). His father, Ralph Stockman Tarr (1864–1912), was Professor of Geology at Cornell University, and organized the Cornell Greenland Expedition which was part of the Peary Arctic expedition of 1896. Robert Edwin Peary (1856–1920) was an American admiral and Arctic explorer credited with leading the first expedition to the North Pole in 1909.

[21] One of the oldest identifiable human habitations in the British Isles, dating from *c.*2,000,000 BC.

[22] Berry Head, near Brixham, was probably a Roman encampment, and many Roman remains have been found there. Tradition has it that Vespasian and Titus landed at this spot.

73. To Susan Owen

18 August 1910   *Alpenrose*

My dearest Mother,

Sorry I have not written before; I have been so actively occupied these last days.

So far I have thoroughly enjoyed myself. After all, open air coursing about is the only thing I can comfortably do here. For when I try to read, I can not lose sight of a figure sprawled across the table, kicking his slippers about the floor, tossing up a coin, a pencil, (or a pair of scissors if nothing else comes to hand), and whistling between his teeth some annoying tune.

Consequently I welcome the excursions he has planned out. I don't think I am getting overdone,—if I ever do I can counter-balance the effect by eating meat which is indisputably underdone!

To get to the point, on Tuesday we went to Silchester since Mr. Colyer was going away the next day.[23] Rather disappointed since the mounds have been levelled down and the pits filled up, so that the city presents the same appearance as the ordinary country, except for the walls. We found nothing particular.

Yesterday Leslie's friend Mr. Wilsher,[24] (who is a young married gentleman just beginning to collect fossils, etc.) took us (cycling) to see a great geologist and collector of prehistoric implements, who lives at Twyford, about 8 miles away. I never have seen in museum or house such a magnificent collection. Hardly less interesting was the mighty range of books on Geology, History, etc. And Mr. Treacher[25] himself, with his long grey hair, philosophical manner, and dirty old coat, was character I would go a long way to see. Hearing I was interested in Roman remains, he took me round to a shed and fished out a small sack. 'You can have all this pottery from Silchester,' he said, 'No, don't open it, because if I should keep half, I should always be regretting that I gave the other half away.' If you, dear Mother, cannot picture to yourself my feelings, and the semi-reluctance with which I took that sack,—then you don't know your own son.

For I knew that it contained treasures—whether I smelt or heard, or felt or tasted them I cannot say, but I <u>knew</u>!

Well, it turned out after Leslie carried them home on his carrier, that there were almost a hundred large pieces of various wares, (crowds so-called Samian) including 2 with actual potter's names on (rare treasures)—and, above all, just half of a superb bowl.

We have divided the fragments between us, and tossed up for the bowl. Leslie won but I secured an equal amount of other stuff, and a bone pin. We both have several genuine Roman nails.

Today we cycled out about the same distance to another place, a chalk pit in search of fossils. Found several.

Mr. W. and Leslie helped me along at times, so I am not unduly tired.

Tomorrow we hope to see the last achievements of civilization instead of its earliest records, namely the aeroplanes (real, large ones) of a friend of Mr. Wilsher's.

And next day—the Exhibition ![26]

We are debating whether I should go on early with one of the family to see the Brit. Museum in the morning, because the party do not get the Exhibition till half past 3 ! !

If I pack my pottery, etc. in a suitable box, can I send it free and in safety—in advance?

Shall never get it into the porkmantle.

Excuse such quantity of matter, and such a quality of writing.

I do hope you see something of the sea, and not

> 'the creeping tide come up along the sand
> And o'er and o'er the sand
> And round and round the sand
> As far as eye could see!'[27]

Fondest love Wilfred

[23] T. W. Colyer was Assistant Curator at Reading Public Museum and Art Gallery, where the Silchester Collection is housed. The Roman town of Calleva Atrebatum, near Silchester, 10 miles south-west of Reading, was first excavated in 1864.

[24] Managing Director of the Abstainers and General Insurance Company, Reading.

[25] Llewellyn Treacher (1859–1943), Fellow of the Geological Society, author of a paper on 'The Occurrence of Stone Implements in the Thames Valley between Reading and Maidenhead', *Man*, Vol. 4 (1904), pp. 17–19. His collection was presented to the Oxford University Museum of Natural History in 1946 by his widow, Mrs M. S. Treacher.

[26] Probably the annual exhibition of the Royal Photographic Society. To Uncle John Gunston, a passionate amateur photographer, it would have been the exhibition of the year.

[27] 'The western tide crept up along the sand / And o'er and o'er the sand...'; Charles Kingsley (1819–75), 'The Sands of Dee'.

74. To Susan Owen

23 August 1910[28]   *Alpenrose, Kidmore End, Reading*

My dearest Mother,

Many, many thanks for your long letter.

Do please call upon the Canon and ask him about the fees, etc. Certainly, if it is possible, it is my wish to get into such a College. As to whether I mean [to] be a clergyman is a different matter. You well know that I don't ask myself 'Is the life congenial to me' but 'am I fitted for, am I called to, the Ministry?' And it is my sure conviction that it is possible to serve Him, as you say, in any station just as well. Still, I say, as things stand, I see nothing I should rather do than enter—if possible—St. Aidan's.[29] For even if I have the brains I don't think I have the strength to read up for a degree in a situation in a school.

And really I have no desire to be chained to an <u>elementary</u> school for the best years of life by the King's scholarship. Of a secondary school is very different.

As for taking up French. I never thought of it seriously, but if the opportunity should occur, I confess I do not look upon it as the last thing in the world I should take up. Very disagreeably as experience is forcing upon me the fact that <u>money</u> must purchase even such pleasures as good books, still do I place first things first, and regard the life whose sole aim is money-making to be the most pitiable.

Perhaps you think me still hopelessly undecided, but I hope that the Canon's advice may clear things up a bit.

Auntie is going to Brixton on Friday, and returning on Tuesday. Hence we may stay till Wednesday (for Auntie must needs see Leslie off), <u>or</u>, if my inclinations so direct me, I may fly back on Friday or Saturday. I am hoping to see you much less tired-looking. Tho' I sometimes have sight of you in the night-season, the visits are short and unsatisfying and leave me full of anxiety about Mary (see Mary's letter)! Your verse was really clever, and in correct metre too!

Your loving son W.

[28] During the next five weeks he wrote 'Written in a Wood, September 1910' (*CPF*, p. 7).
[29] St Aidan's Theological College, Birkenhead, founded in 1846, was located in Shrewsbury Road. It closed in 1969 and the building was demolished in 1970. The College archives are housed at the University of Liverpool.

77. To Colin Owen

1 January 1911   *Alpenrose*

My dearest Colin,

How glad I was to have your little letter,
To know your throat is really, truly better.

(My words, you see, are falling into verse-gear,
I hope it will not make you any worse, dear!
A bout your new Bird's Egg Book worth six shillings
What <u>can</u> I say until myself I see it?
But now it's bought so dearly, so dearly
                              so dearly

O carefully use it!
Oh brown-paper-bind it!
Or you'll certainly lose it,
Yes, and <u>I</u>'ll find it!
                    (Oh really!
                    Oh really!)
<u>Then</u> you'll see it never more
So don't you leave it on the floor!
                    (D'you hear me,
                    D'you hear me?)
Now let me tell you something of my doings—
We all went out to tea last night to Painter's
And played a game I know you'd like to play at:
We shot an air-gun at a target on their door
And even Vera did her level best to score.
Hence excepting Auntie (for such sports too aged)
We might have been all <u>Bis(i)ley</u> engaged.
That afternoon we also saw the 'Pictures'
The French boys always charm me, but the mixtures
Of Blood and Thunder Stories sometimes shock me.
How does Mary like her Book of Botany?
I wish I could find some Pheasant's Eggs or Partridges
To bring you; but I got you lots of empty cartridges.

———————————————

<u>P.S.</u>   'There was a boy so wondrous wise   ⎫
                He tried to see his nose   ⎪
                And turning inwards both his eyes   ⎬
                He now in glasses goes :—'   ⎪
                    must now be changed to   ⎭
                'There is a boy of Shrewsbury   ⎫
                On whom all doctors dote,   ⎪
                He lets them take hot iodine   ⎬
                And burn out half his throat.'[30]   ⎭

[30] The references are to Colin's new spectacles and Harold's tonsillitis.

78. To Susan Owen

2 April 1911   [Shrewsbury]

Dear Mother,

Thank you so much for your letter, and for interviewing Mr. Robson.[31] I am very anxious to know 'what else' he has found or will find out.

I am not able to get much study done in school yet, but Mr. Edwards[32] is going to approach Mr. Lightbown[33] on the subject (of allowing me to study when not actually teaching) as soon as I find out exactly what is done in other schools in the town where P.T.'s[34] are.

Leslie tells me you are often hearing the Nightingale. Is it indeed so enchanting? I crave to hear it, and yet I should almost be afraid lest it should not be as fine as I imagine it. At present my soul is in a ferment, and the 'leafy month of June' promises as many terrors as leaves.

> 'It is a flaw
> In happiness to see beyond our bourne,
> It forces us in summer skies to mourn,
> And spoils the singing of the nightingale.'
>   (Keats)[35]

You ought, if you feel so moved, dear Mother, to read the 'Ode to the Nightingale' by the same Poet, which you will find in his Poems, in the bookcase. Furthermore, if you [are] at a loss at any time for good literature, why not study the Introduction to this volume?

But let me warn you about believing what it says of Keats' 'attitude to knowledge, which cannot be justified, must not be copied, etc.' I know of something which proves the contrary to this view.

If you could find room for it in your trunk, I should be obliged by a present of some lumps of soft chalk. And might I ask for some complete specimens of Woodruff from the wood, of Mary (who seems to have dwindled into oblivion for ought I hear, of or from her, or her doings.)

                                                              W.

---

[31] The Rev. Herbert Eric Robson (1877–1917), Vicar of Kidmore End 1909–16.
[32] A master at Shrewsbury Technical School.
[33] S. J. Lightbown, Headmaster of Wyle Cop School, Shrewsbury, where Owen was a pupil-teacher in the summer of 1911. WO refers to him as 'Lightbourn' in Letter 295.
[34] Pupil-teachers.
[35] 'Epistle to J. H. Reynolds', ll. 82–5.

79. To Susan Owen

Apr. 1911   *Torquay*

My dearest Mother,

I was very glad to hear of your early exodus to Alpenrose, and I hope it means a longer holiday there for you. But since I shall not see you on Saturday to give a verbal account of myself here, I must write a longer letter now, which shall suffice for some days to come. I am really disappointed not to see you for those few days; our absence will now amount practically to a month. However I shall not 'rush home' on Friday as I have all too short a time to make my pilgrimage to Teignmouth,[36] the passport[37] for which I expected in your letter. Will it arrive on time?

I have bought at last a Life of Keats[38] (in the same edition as that of Dickens) and began this morning 'with fear and trembling' to learn the details of his life. I sometimes feel in reading such books that I would give ten years of life to have been born a hundred years earlier (always providing that I have the same dear mother.)

Up to to-day I have been reading on the beach of course the French-books, bought as bargains from I.P. Williams, Esq. It was strange that after gazing for a long while upon the waves (which are now quite rough), I should come upon this passage which I will translate to you giving a very true picture of how I am spending some of my time:

'…I used to go and put myself between two rocks almost on a level with water, in the midst of the sea-gulls, blackbirds, and swallows, and I stayed there almost the whole day in that kind of stupor and delicious "overwhelmedness" which the contemplation of the sea gives. You know, don't you, this lovely intoxication of the soul? You are not thinking, you are not dreaming either. All your being escapes you, flies off, is scattered. You are the plunging wave, the dust of foam which floats in the sun between two waves, the white of that receding steamer,… this bead of water, this flake of mist, everything except yourself.'

(Daudet: *Lettres de mon Moulin*)[39]

Well, I was reading the book at Meadfoot the other afternoon when who should I see but the boy—youth whom we met with Russell Tarr, and played croquet with us on the hotel lawn, as Harold will [*remainder missing*]

---

[36] Keats lodged from March to May 1818 at 20 The Strand (now Northumberland Place), Teignmouth. See Letter 80.

[37] The railway ticket. Tom Owen always provided, or was called on to provide, tickets for railway journeys, free or at much reduced rates.

[38] *Keats* by Sidney Colvin. An autographed copy, inscribed 'Torquay, Spring 1911', survives among Owen's books. A few days later he wrote a sonnet, 'Written at Teignmouth, on Pilgrimage to Keats's House' (CPF, p. 10).

[39] *Lettres de mon moulin* (*Letters from My Windmill*) (1869), a collection of short stories by the French novelist Alphonse Daudet (1840–97). This excerpt is from Chapter VI, *Le Phare des Sanguinaires* ('The Lighthouse on the Sanguinaires').

80. To Susan Owen

25 April 1911   *Shrewsbury*

Dearest Mother,

Father has arrived safely but has not written before being busy. Let me tell you of my holiday, now a thing very much of the past, for I have plunged deep into work again—(did not get out till 5.25 yesterday, an object lesson requiring preparation today, and so on).

I went to Teignmouth on Friday. Perhaps it was a good thing that the soft buffeting sheets and misty drifts of Devonshire rain renewed themselves almost the whole day, since Keats's letters from here are full of objurgations against the climate.

'You may say what you will of Devonshire' he writes, 'The truth is it is a splashy, rainy, misty, snowy, foggy, haily, floody, muddy, slip-shod county'[40] and so on.

I long to tell you of my good fortune in discovering the house (of Keats)—I will only say now that I saw it, and gaped at it (regardless of people in the window who finally became quite alarmed, I fancy)—to my heart's content. If I had only had a little more time, and a photograph or two, perhaps I might have made up a magazine article upon it—the district certainly lends itself to picturesque description.

Would you please ask Dorothy whether (1) she knows of Leigh Hunt's cottage in the Vale of Health Hampstead? (2) Whether the house she has described to me (in what is known as Keats' Road) is, or was, in Well Walk? (3) Or is it a house (once semi-detached) now known as Lawn Bank, originally Wentworth Place,[41] near the bottom of John St. In this garden the 'Ode to a Nightingale' was written so that it is one of London's most holy spots.

I shall never be able to approach the metropolis without being drawn there. If therefore Dorothy would ascertain something about its position and accessibility, I should be deeply obliged to that dear cousin.

Mrs. Timpany[42] called yesterday evening, her mission being to warn me against the Teaching Profession (Elementary). Her husband could not candidly do this, she said, but she thinks it 'wicked' that young people should enter it without a fair premonition of the hopelessness of their fate, and without knowing of the profound dissatisfaction among all who are now teachers.

Civil Service is her cry, and I am to see Mr. Timpany about it one of these evenings. I wish you were here to approve or condemn this good lady's counsel.

Have you ever asked Uncle John's opinion on these matters?

Really, indecision is rapidly turning into distraction. When I begin to eliminate from my list all those professions which are impossible (seemingly) from a financial point of view, and then those which I feel disinclined for—it leaves nothing. But is my inclination to matter after all? Yet what I do find so hard to distinguish between is aimlessly drifting, and waiting upon God.

If it must be done, I suppose I am not too young to destroy all my love of literature and such study, and turn to Office Routine, Customs, Revenues, Taxation, etc.— (I suppose this is what is meant by Civil Service, but as a matter of fact my ideas of this life are of the vaguest.)

Dreams of the power of money, and the necessity of obtaining it in the easiest way, have run before me with special brightness at such times as a stay at Meols;[43] yes and Alpenrose, too.

But of all those visions none is so powerful as one which I almost think has been cherished from my earliest remembrance, that of my sweet Mother, in a delightful garden, passing a bland old age among her greenhouses, and in a small carriage drawn by an ambling pad-pony...But till this comes, don't, oh don't, sign yourself, 'your old mother.'

There was no class on Sunday—we went to the Mission instead. I would not like to write down an opinion of Mr. Alexander: nor yet of Dr Chapman; More than once my sense of reverence and 'decently—and—in orderness' was outraged by an attempt at wit on the part of a certain 'Sergeant' who spoke, and by the perfectly deafening shout which his voice passed into towards the end of his address. Nor did the words he spoke tend to disprove the words of Ruskin, which then came to my mind: 'Your converted children who teach their parents...your converted dunces, who, having lived in cretinous stupefaction half their lives suddenly awaking to the fact of there being a God, fancy themselves therefore His peculiar people and messengers:—these are the true fog-children—clouds these without water; bodies these of putrescent vapour and skin, "swollen with wind and the rank mist they draw." '[44]

(Not that I quite hold with Ruskin either.)

However, I shall try and go again.

Please give my love to Mary, Auntie, Dorothy, etc. etc. etc. Small need for me to send it to One to whom it has been given for these last sixteen years.

[40] 13 March 1818, to Benjamin Bailey, from Teignmouth (Letters of John Keats, ed. Hyder Edward Rollins [Cambridge, 1958], Vol. I, p. 241).

[41] Keats lodged with his brothers in Well Walk before moving to share with Charles Armitage Brown in one of the attached houses then known as Wentworth Place, later converted into one house and renamed Lawn Bank. Keats House, 10 Keats Grove, London NW3, is now a museum

[42] Wife of the headmaster of Shrewsbury Technical School, Harold Timpany.

[43] Home in Cheshire of Uncle Edward Quayle, prosperous tinplate broker of Liverpool, whose first wife was Tom Owen's eldest sister, Edith (1864–92).

[44] John Ruskin (1819–1900), Sesame and Lilies I: 'Of Kings' Treasures' (1865).

83. To Susan Owen

18 June 1911   *Alpenrose*

My dearest Mother,

I have been to see Mr. Robson this afternoon. He had prepared some notes to aid him in his discourse, which he gave me in his study, smoking mean-while....My pre-eminent plan is to borrow or become possessed of just £150, with which sum I can get a degree at College. If I have a rich relation, I ought to try and get them to lend, repaying in the process of time at, say, 4%. Failing this, teaching in a secondary school might be tried, studying with a Corresp. College at the same time, but this is 'killing' work, he says.

Finally, he revealed what he had in his mind as being 'easier' than teaching.

It is:—to become the 'assistant' of some hardworked or studiously inclined parson, helping in parish work, correspondence etc. and being generally com-panionable to a lonely country-sequestered bachelor, such as himself. Not to himself actually, however, one reason being—that it would never do to have one with relations in the parish! He had heard, however, that 'Wiggan[45] of Dunsden' wanted help in the parish this winter, and suggested applying to him, especially as his views coincide with ours.

For we must be most careful as to the kind of parson I go to. Some would keep me trotting round the parish all day: some, (who have no servant perhaps) would require me to scrub floors. He knows of one priest, moreover, who celebrates Mass daily, and requires someone to say 'amen' in the consecration prayer since it is uncanonical to have no congregation.

On the other hand, however, it is a post not easily procured, and they are eas-ily 'snapped up'. About £20. a year might be given, or less than that if coaching is required.

Mr. Robson would be pleased to frame an advertisement for me in the *Churchman*[46] or some such paper, if we like the proposal.

What do you think?

Parish work would not be by any means uncongenial to me, and as I suppose, far less worrying than teaching. And I could render myself 'companionable' to anyone if at all literary-inclined. But everything depends upon the kind of person the parson is.

Which risk shall I take then—(1) borrowing money (supposing such available from E.Q.[47] Esq.—and why not?) and thus sail with a fair wind to B.A. or (2) put myself at the mercy of a reverend man, who may be exacting, eccentric, intoler-ant and all that?

I mentioned my scheme of getting a thorough knowledge of French *in* France, and he considered it a very good thing, but far better if a degree be obtained first. A year or two in France after that, and I should be worth something.

I am to go to see him again on Wednesday afternoon; and to play tennis with another priest who is staying at the Vicarage—a Mr.Thackrah,[48] who, in his purple socks, looks about as <u>secular</u> as the 'secularist' of laymen. I was asked to be prepared for tennis today, but it rained. One Allwright, however, was there, helping Rev. Mr. Thackrah to pass the afternoon at tennis. So we four bachelors had afternoon tea in the drawing room. The comfort afforded by the luxurious armchairs however, was somewhat impaired by the fact that we held our cups in our hands and had no plates. Nevertheless Mr. Robson, by his humorous stories, made us so much at home that I remained perfectly placid and imperturbable when I dropped a large portion of cake into my unfortunate tea-cup. No liquid escaped the cup, and I am firmly convinced that I succeeded in conveying (by degrees) the soppy blobs of dough into my mouth without my host suspecting it; and thinking me a bounder. That most or all elem- teachers <u>are</u> bounders is his unshaken faith. During our conversation in the study I had asked, 'Am I then to avoid <u>elem</u>^{ty}. teaching?' He screwed up his visage, raised his hands, turned aside his head, and murmured 'AS PITCH !!' Now I have often touched pitch and not been defiled, but too much handling has always resulted in defilement. Hence in answer to the question 'Can a man touch <u>pitch</u> and not be defiled ?' I reply— 'Certainly, for a certain length of time.'

    <u>Moral</u>: If I don't want to be defiled I must <u>drop</u> the <u>pitch</u> with all speed.

Another power has sprung up to hold me in Shrewsbury.—'<u>Uriconium is to be excavated in the near future.</u>' according to Mr. Colyer.[49]

Awaiting your reply to this budget before Wednesday (if you get it in time), including Father's opinion of course,

I am, Your own Wilfred

[45] The Rev. Herbert Wigan (1862–1947), Chaplain of Bloxham School 1891–9, Curate of Sonning 1903–4, Vicar of Dunsden, near Reading, 1904–47. Owen would spend sixteen months in his charge. The Rev. Bernard Wigan, his nephew, wrote: 'He was brought up in a tractarian rectory in Kent, and until middle age was an "advanced" exponent of that school of thought. As a young man, he had a bout of "Roman fever", of which he was cured by a trip round the world. And, when he died, a biretta and signed portrait of Leo XIII were found buried beneath a mountain of evangelical divinity. He must have been a particular protégé of Edward King, for he went and stayed with him at Lincoln for his enthronement. One interest of the first half of my uncle's life was genealogy; and he printed a pedigree of the family in Crispe's *Visitations* series. But after he had been some years at Dunsden, he changed into a strong evangelical, and gave a family living to a protestant trust, although his sisters were still living in the parish. But in later life he mellowed considerably, and was always pleased to see me, although I was Curate at St. Barnabas, Oxford; and we discussed ecclesiastical affairs (and even his "unregenerate" past) amiably enough.'(CL, pp. 75–76)

[46] An evangelical Anglican monthly periodical founded in 1879. Published by the Church Society, it moved to quarterly publication in 1920 and continues today.

[47] Edward Quayle.

[48] The Rev M.W. Thackrah.

[49] Uriconium, the Roman city at Wroxeter on the Severn east of Shrewsbury. The city and its inhabitants were destroyed by fire and sword *c.* AD 400. First excavated in 1859–61, the more important finds went to the Shrewsbury Museum. The site had great fascination for Owen. See 'Uriconium: An Ode' (*CPF*, p. 65), written in July 1913. Jon Stallworthy has argued that 'Uriconium' 'anticipates…the tender physicality of Owen's mature work' (Jon Stallworthy, 'Owen's Afterlife', in *Survivors' Songs* [Cambridge University Press, 2008], p. 68). It could be considered Owen's first 'war poem'.

84. To Susan Owen

Postcard

23 June 1911   *Alpenrose*

I have chosen the 3 o'clock train on Sat. to carry me back to Scrobbesbyrig,[50] where I expect to set foot on the nineteenth minute after seven. The lights from 10 Bonfires could be seen from here last night.[51] I have written to Miss W. and Miss J.[52]

Glad you are satisfied with the Result. Went to see Mr. Wigan this morning with Leslie as an introducer. I can only say here that he is a most delightful parson, and what he has said may or may not come to anything.

We stayed 'lunch', at which was another cleric (who knows Mr Brownlow), and Mr. Kemp,[53] who is the assistant of Mr. Wigan, and whom I choose to consider as my mortal enemy and rival, for reasons which you may guess.

W

[50] The original Saxon settlement derived from two Old English words, 'scrubb' (meaning scrubland) and 'burh' (meaning fortified place). The name was corrupted over the years to Shrewsbury, and pronounced either 'Shrows-bury' or 'Shroos-bury'.

[51] They celebrated the coronation of George V, 22 June 1911.

[52] Miss Elizabeth Wright and Miss Mary Jones, two of Owen's teachers at Shrewsbury Technical School. Wright gained a science degree from Durham; Jones a geography degree from Liverpool. See also Letter 88. Dominic Hibberd asserted, 'These two young women seem to have done more than anyone else to develop his interest in literature and nature, and it may well be that it was in 1907–08 that he felt the stirrings of an ambition to become a poet in the Wordsworthian tradition' (Dominic Hibberd, *Wilfred Owen: A New Biography* [Phoenix, 2003], p. 50).

[53] The Rev. Alfred George Saxelby-Kemp was ordained in 1914 and went to Holy Trinity, Kilburn. See Letter 98.

88. To Susan Owen

[*12 or 13 September 1911*]   *The Doldrums, Seven-times-heated—*
                                                          —Furnace Road, Dumpshire[54]

Ah me! What a time! The heat has been simply appalling during every exam so far! And what with the excitement and the four hundred roasting bodies jammed around me my brains have been spluttering in my head. As a proof that it was not all <u>mental</u> heat, I may say that the Vigilators kept on flapping their foreheads, and taking great breaths and snatching whiffs of air at the open door as often as they could.

Not only did a morning like this melt the crystal sharpness of my wits, but it gave me a strong revulsion to any [food], but I conquered this rebellion of the lower man and went to the Imperial Restaurant.

Perhaps it is a good thing the weather has been so oppressive, it will be a really good excuse in case of 'Found Wanting.'

Have I passed? I <u>do</u> think so! even in Arith. & Geometry. At least I have done enough right to score pass marks. I might have left hours of work untouched for the last few weeks for all the good it's done me in <u>this paper</u>. But of course all that will come in for the <u>next attempt</u> (?)...

As I was asking for the Institute at Kensington, a young gent. from Cheltenham overheard me, and immediately asked me if our destinations were the same. I saw him again & he says he has certainly failed, having been sent to sleep (mentally) by the oppressive atmosphere; and so did about 2 questions only.

Was asked by a gent. in Restaurant if I was a Matric. Candidate. He said he had been in a few years ago & failed hopelessly first time, but passed at the next. Showed him the papers & he pronounced them harder than in his day. Did not see my Chelsea friend this morning but instead—for I conceal nothing from you—I was spotted as a Candidate by a young lady who was in mortal terror of being transported to the other side of London by those wretched District trains, and accordingly I acted the part of Sydney Carton to the poor Seamstress.[55]

The entrance hall or clock room is nothing but a horrid stuffy vault, where for half an hour the boys stand waiting packed like sardines. I could have thought myself in the Black Hole of Calcutta, especially as there was a fair sprinkling of black faces among us, and a pompous old Rajah of an Examiner—gorgeous in his silken hoods—came glaring at us from over a barred gate on the staircase. This gate was at last opened, and then followed a maddening rush up the stairs, which changed in a moment to a death-like stillness when we entered the vast Hall of Torture. For all its solemnity, I could not help being tickled by the sight of a learned-looking parson, past the middle age, sitting in his little desk and scratching away at his paper under the stern gaze of a fair young graduate very much like Miss Wright!

All of the men seem much older than I expected, many of them remind me of say Dr. Simpson.[56]

Many thanks for your letter.

I am, as you may guess, very lighthearted, and really am enjoying the <u>high</u> spirits which always connote <u>low</u> marks.

Slept very soundly, too, last night.

Love in abundance—like the rain which has just begun.

W

[54] Owen was in London taking the London University Matriculation exam, for which he had been working while a pupil-teacher at the Wyle Cop School, Shrewsbury. The exam was held in the Imperial Institute, Kensington. He stayed at Glenmore, 38 Worple Road, Wimbledon, a private school a short walk from the Gunstons' house in Clement Road.

[55] Characters in Charles Dickens, *A Tale of Two Cities* (1859).

[56] The family doctor in Shrewsbury.

90. To Susan Owen

17 September 1911   *Wimbledon*

My dearest Mother,

As Gordon is going to Kidmore on Sat., and as that day will just complete my fortnight here, I think I shall even stay on till then. For I have not half accomplished my sight-seeing and holy-ground-treading, as you will see from the following summary:

Friday—British Museum: spent some hours there in subdued ecstasy— reading two letters of J.K's and two books of manuscript poems (open at 'Eve of St. Mark' & 'Hyperion') which, of course, show all his corrections and crossings out.

These and the letters must form the subject of many a discourse to my dear willing Hearer, but I will note a few things—'before I forget'— I was going to say, but I can never do that.—At the side of the title to 'St. Mark's Eve' (unfinished) he has drawn an ivy leaf (not very like one, and it would shock Prof. Cavers)[57]—this of course while going round and round his subject and not knowing where or how to begin. Even then he made a false start, and struck out several lines. His writing is rather large and slopes like mine—not at all old fashioned and sloping as Shelley's is. He also has my trick of not joining letters in a word. Otherwise it is unlike anybodies' I know, and yet I seem to be strangely familiar with it. It is none too precisely formed—a proof that he is thinking of nothing but the matter and not of himself and his pen. The letters are to Fanny (i.e. the sister) but, poor fellow, he can't keep the name of Brawne out of it! I was highly jealous of other people seeing this at first, but was nevertheless gratified when various French visitors seemed familiar with his name!

Other manuscripts there are in abundance—Scott is absolutely illegible. George Eliot, Shelley, Milton, Byron, Tennyson, Browning, etc. are all represented. In the afternoon I drifted into the audience of the newly-appointed free lecturer, who conducted a party all round the Mummy- and Egyptian-Rooms.

On Sat. morning I went to Hampton Court by tram: more of this later. Got home in time to join Gordon [*several words illegible*]

Hence we made our way to L'pool St. and so to Cheshunt at about 4 p.m.[58] Spent the time very pleasantly in recalling our reminiscences of the common fountain-head of our existences, known by all as the 'old Home'. Nelly has also an album of very old photographs of the family in which Gordon was very interested.

Today, mng. and evening, have listened with delight to Mr. Moore.[59] For tomorrow, I have luckily one more S. Kensington Ticket. I shall then be blocked, unless more arrive in time. I want Orders on District Rly: to the following stations:

(1) Wim[ldn] to Westminster
(1) „   „ Mark Lane.
(3) „   „ Charing Cross.
on to <u>Hampstead Rly:</u>
(1) Charing Cross to Hampstead

(*Monday*) Am off to S. Kensington this morning. In the matter of *Macbeth*,[60] I am again between two fires. On the very same afternoon, Benson Co.[61] are giving in Wimbledon *Henry V*, which I have read, and learnt, and spouted these last two years. Depend upon it, whichever Fire draws me, I shall but extract the brilliance and fervour of the flames, and shall come out unscathed. I think *Macbeth* will shall be the one, specially as I have seen *Punch*'s Criticism on the same,[62] this week. Am keeping well, except for the gum, and my nose, which is, like Bardolph's, 'all barbukles and whelks, and knobs and flames of fire!'[63]

Your own Wilfred

Love to Mary and me brethren twain. Had a card from Stanley.[64] No time for more now. I must apply to myself the nerve-lacerating speech of the pompous vigilator, when every exam was almost over—

Laydeezanjenulmun, You have abow-oot Five Minutes Maw!

[57] Unidentified.
[58] To visit Nelly, formerly a maid at Plas Wilmot, Oswestry, the 'old Home'.
[59] Rev. E. W. Moore, Emmanuel Church.
[60] A production opened at His Majesty's Theatre on 5 September 1911 with Herbert Beerbohm Tree (1852–1917) and Violet Vanbrugh (1867–1942).
[61] The company founded by Sir Frank Benson (1858–1939), actor-manager. See also Letters 536 and 598 from Craiglockhart.
[62] A mixed review. The production seemed notable only for 'the extraordinary reality of the scenery' (*Punch*, 13 September 1911, p. 194).
[63] *Henry V*, III, vi., l. 110.
[64] [Henry] Stanley Webb. The Webbs were a Shrewsbury family who lived at Elmhurst, Abbey Foregate, and whose children were friendly with the Owens. See Letters 503, 613.

91. To Susan Owen

September 1911   *Wimbledon*

Dearest Mother,

    I have just returned from *Macbeth*. My pleasure has been completely marred by a most trying circumstance:—I had to stand the whole time. Thought I was in the queue 1¼ hrs. before the time, every seat was taken when I got in, i.e. every seat under 5s. or 10/6 and these had to be booked. Hearing <u>and</u> seeing were therefore quite difficult at times; having promenaded the National Gallery all morning, I had much same feeling as used to overtake me at the '<u>Cop</u>'[65] of amiable memory, towards the end of the day. Hence I never 'lost consciousness' in the sense that I should have liked to have done; though two ladies close to me, also standing, lost consciousness in a very disagreeable way, and both dropped like logs simultaneously to earth.

    The scenes in the witches' cave were simply marvellous, and quite took the breath out of the audience. At no time, however, was I so moved by the acting, as I was moved earlier in the day by a <u>lifeless face-mask</u> and a <u>painted canvas</u>. This was none other than a mould of Keats's face taken during life, so that of <u>him</u> as of no other writer, I and the world may gain a true idea of the countenance! Two paintings of his 'extraordinary beauty' are also there.—One of the whole figure, <u>painted by Severn in Rome, after his Friend's death</u>! Of this, <u>of course</u>, I have bought a copy, which you, as I hope, will be most anxious to see. It represents him in the Hampstead House. I have not yet been there, but have fixed Friday for this, the last of my 'sermons in stone'. On this day Miss Jones[66] has asked me to Finchley, which I can easily reach from the Heath. For tomorrow, therefore, there is the Tower, or Westminster & St. Paul's, and maybe another peep into the National Gallery at some other Faces there, which have woven a spell over me. I must not begin to describe or to name even the pictures hanging there, and must stop not for 'lack of argument', but for sheer excess of matter.

Your own loving Wilfred

    Thank you for this morning's parcel and letter: its newsiness and its assurance of Mary's good-health. Have you written to Mrs. Timpany?

---

[65] Wyle Cop School.
[66] Mary Jones, favourite teacher at Shrewsbury Technical School, who was then teaching at Finchley.

92. To Harold Owen

20 September 1911   [*Wimbledon*]

Dear Harold,

Such was the effect of receiving so unexpected a card from you, and such the imperative force of the underlining, that I <u>immediately</u> sent off your compasses. I hope that you got them in time. I have thought much of you today, and during the week. I mean when I have been gladdening my eyes by the sights of works of Art,—of sculptures, and buildings, and portraits. So that now more than ever seems Art a noble profession, and to have a brother now fairly launched out upon its wide stream is enough to make me proud indeed. In my present state, I could wish for no better choice of profession for you than this; and then my only wishes for you will be Skill, Sense, and Success. Study the Fine, Strive for Finesse, and Strike the First, and you <u>will do</u>—you must...

So far I have seen no Galleries of Design (they are at S. Kensington, I think), but I wish you [could] have seen with me the loveliest of Designs,—the human face,[67] as drawn by the greatest artists. I was so rapt in gazing at one of these today, that I kenned not of a human Toe belonging to a lady behind me, and made a sudden retrograde motion which brought my heel upon it—much to the confusion of both parties.

To return to the serious, I wished you could have seen the marvellous <u>sketches</u> both in oil and pencils of people's heads. I wondered if <u>you</u> would ever, ever rise to the supreme height of—<u>mastery in Portraiture.</u>

Has Mr. Dane[68] supped with you yet? Thank you for your last letter and its very pointed birthday message. It has at least pricked my memory as to your <u>advancing age</u>, to which I begin to think I have been for some years forgetful. Soothly, I must now treat you—as I have begun to in this letter—as a responsible individual arrived at years of discretion, and as a schoolboy no longer. Indeed I must endeavour to cultivate your acquaintance [*one or two words missing, the corner of the sheet has been torn away*]

Best wishes for a prosperous & happy Term,

Your loving brother, Wilfred

---

[67] Owen had visited the National Portrait Gallery earlier in the day.

[68] The assistant master at the Shrewsbury School of Art, where HO was a pupil. See *JFO, I,* pp. 204–5.

94. To Colin Owen

26 September 1911   *Alpenrose*

My dear Colin,

I was very pleased to have your letter, and have real pleasure in answering it. As for my head, you may be sure it is not busting with knowledge, for that was squeezed out of it upon certain sheets of paper, now enshrined in one of the grandest buildings of the greatest city on the earth. Consequently, when a vacuum began to be formed, a 'cold' flooded in, for I never could be <u>empty</u>-headed. This, indeed, makes my brain-bag feel as if it would go bang if you hit it. But the fair breezes which are blowing up here should soon make me better—as I am glad to hear <u>you</u> are.

I have spent a good part of this morning picking mushrooms which abound in these fields. I said Father would like some, and a tin box has been filled with the best ones, and will soon find its way to Mahim. There are four fine turkeys now. They walk just about as awkwardly as I do on the polished floors here. This reminds me that at the Tate Gallery where the floors are just the same, a middle-aged lady came a cropper close to me. To add to her discomfort, an official came up with a note-book and pencil asking her name and address! 'Yes'm' I heard him say, 'We tikes the nimes of all lidies as slips dahn in the gelries.' Poor thing! You know I like London, but it worries me when I get into a 'bus or train where women are talking, because I could believe that it was full of thing but Mrs. Raggs![69] I did not go to the wax-works. Nor did I find time for the Tower. But I spent a whole day at Kew, where every tree is ticketed; and all the plants have names attached. In the green-houses, I saw pitcher-plants with wasps caught in them—some alive and buzzing, but trapped, and never to escape!

This morning I was awakened at quarter past seven by Uncle calling me to see the huntsmen, who were in the wood just opposite. Leslie and I stood on the window-sill of our bedroom in our pyjamas and wrapped the rosy curtains round our selves like woodland nymphs. But we saw no fox. This evening, we had a supper supposed to be of mushrooms, but the whole quantity was contained in a gravy tureen, and they were done in the daftest way imaginable, and tasted like boot-polish mixed with warm water.

Since supper, and while I have been writing this, Leslie has had me out eight times in succession to see a new comet.

This is the second visible now.[70] The first may be seen with the naked eye; it has a faint tail. You will find it if you can understand this 'heavenly' map (!)

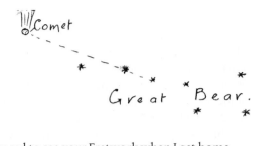

Shall be pleased to see your Fretwork when I get home.

Your affectionate brother, Wilfred

[69] The correct spelling is Ragge. The Ragges and their two children, John (b.1899) and Mary (b.1902), lived next door but one to the Owens in Monkmoor Road, Shrewsbury. HO and JB in CL noted that the family was 'much liked', but omitted the Ragge name in a later letter (298), perhaps not to cause offence. John was later killed in France. See JFO, III, pp. 106–7, and Letter 518.

[70] The two new comets were seen in 1911. Quenisset's Comet, first sighted 23 September, and Brooks's Comet, discovered 31 July and easily visible to the naked eye on 26 September.

95. To Susan Owen

28 September 1911 *Alpenrose*

My dearest Mother,

I had your very welcome letter this morning. Leslie and I walked to Dunsden yesterday, only to find the Vicar in London for the day. He had gone by Auntie's train, and they saw him at Padd. and he appointed us to go to tea today. We played croquet most of the time, and once again put off finalities till 'another day'. This is to be as soon as I hear the Result. But I told him that my wants would be the same, whether I pass or fail. And he reminded <u>me</u>, that his offer still holds. Really, I am even more charmed with the Vicarage than ever, and nothing but the uncertainty as to the amount of Work—scholastic or parish that I should accomplish there, would prevent me from going—since it seems the time is ripe for me to wrench myself from Home.

Miss Jones urged me, <u>if I pass</u>, to state my case to the Registrar of L' pool or London University, and try for a three years' course, which under 'the Scholarship', will cost only £40 for the whole time. <u>Living</u> would be in a Hostel. Our old enemy, 'the Obligations', would certainly include such a school as Miss Jones is now at; i.e. Secondary. Further information would of course be supplied, if I wrote to the 'Varsity'. I shall at least do this, <u>if</u>...(?)

I think to stay on till the <u>Intimation</u> comes, then. 'Tis awfully near at hand—I feel its shadow upon me. But I am not a prey to doubts and fears on this matter: my mind is filled with cogitation and perplexities and despondencies which spring from deeper depths than that.

May I quote you a sentence of a Poet— (need I name which?) that is marvellously expressive of what I want to say:

'The imagination of a boy is healthy, and the mature imagination of a man is healthy; but there is a space of life between in which the soul is in a ferment, the character undecided, the way of life uncertain, (yes!), and the ambition thick-sighted (yes indeed!)'[71]

Well, I am prosing instead of giving News—which seems to be the main intendment of the Letter in these days. Herbert Billing[72] is coming on Tues, to rest after <u>his</u> exam; but I need not turn out on that account.

Mrs. Lea[73] charged the same as for Gordon: my accompt was therefore 30s. Thank you for the Convention Notice; Auntie knows Mr. Buchanan; he is a great friend of the Sharwoods.[74]

I am already feeling a touch of <u>Nostalgia</u> (consult dictionary). What if it becomes chronic in the Future?

Your own Wilfred

[71] From the Preface to Keats' *Endymion* (1818).
[72] A Wimbledon solicitor, friend of the Gunston family.
[73] Headmistress of Glenmore.
[74] Mr Sharwood was Managing Director of J. A. Sharwood and Co. (founded 1889), makers of Green Label Chutney. They were Wimbledon acquaintances of the Gunstons, and a Christmas hamper of Sharwood products arrived each year at Kidmore End. Sharwood's continues as a brand.

98. To Susan Owen

23 October 1911   *Dunsden Vicarage*

My dearest Mother,

It is about time that I began to give you some account of my mode of life here. First as to the premises. The house is even larger than I ever thought—two staircases—and quite a labyrinth of passages upstairs. My bedroom is quite large, and handsomely furnished—containing a bureau and a wardrobe (which one might make a home of) as well as the usual appointments. The chamber is softly carpeted. Mysterious ministering spirits keep the room in order, for surprising things happen, though I have never seen a living wight therein. Thus—every night I find my pyjamas scrupulously laid out upon the coverlet in exactly that position in which it is easiest to put them on!

At seven every morning a meek voice announces to the noble sir that his shaving water waits outside. Presently the noble sir deigns to rise—but 'uneasy is the head that lies on Down', for it has to wash in a silly pot of a basin, the bathroom being somehow connected with Mr. Wigan's room, and therefore unused. Having then moistened as it were his boiley neck in soap-solution, his lordship applies to it a towel like a white Turkish carpet, and then selects his suit. At the stroke of the awe-inspiring gong, he takes a large chair on one side of the fire, in the dining room, with Mr. Kemp[75] on the other, the Vicar at the table, and the domestics sitting in respectful admiration in a row at the end of the room. After prayers the said admiring domestics withdraw, and breakfast is taken, when (as in all meals) his noble highness brandishes the bread-knife, and dispenses his cuttings as required.

Left alone, and with something of my gravity thrown off, I then set to work at a bureau-bookcase in the dining room till lunch. This afternoon the Vicar took me with him visiting, till afternoon tea. Then dinner at 7.30. of such things as jugged hare!

On Sat. we went to the Prayer Meeting in the Hall, where I read the Portion—to less than a dozen people only! On that afternoon I went to Alpenrose, but Auntie was out and I had tea alone with Leslie. There is a pony, but his only work is to pump the water from a deep well to the housetop, by a circular movement, just like the elephantine pigo-ox in the Chinese Scroll.[76] The garden is still very beautiful.

In fact every [thing] is on the scale of a fine country <u>manor</u>, and my

or

only sorrow is that you are not in a like man(ner) established!

Mr. Kemp is very pleasant indeed; thoroughly enjoying his parochial work, if not so much his studies; and, I believe, he is well liked about the parish. His exam.[77] is in December. He has already failed (twice I think), tho' he has no very advanced work, so far as <u>I</u> can see.

I will say nothing about dear Mr. Wigan. I never do sketch the characters of those on a higher plane than myself. But I was much enlightened concerning certain doubts in my mind when he talked of literary people at dinner today. He is a sixth cousin of the great William Morris! has heard Ruskin lecture !! was introduced to Holman Hunt !!! Furthermore, is thoroughly at home in Dickens' country in Kent !! read Romola <u>in Florence</u> overlooking Ponte Vecchia! ! was acquainted with the original of Sam Weller! and other Characters!

Other revelations may come out later! (Oh, also, he has dined with Marconi.) Do not think, however, that my admiration of him is vastly eased by all this, though it is somewhat, you may guess! I know, indeed, certain unlovely minds who would be shocked to hear him take any interest in these matters.

I have written to Torquay. I am anxiously looking forward to the time when I can present these new surroundings to you, and you to them, and when I can present to you my cheeks for the good-night kiss which I so much miss. Love to Father & all the stay-at-homes, with 'heaps and loads' for You.

W

[75] The Rev. Alfred Saxelby-Kemp remembered Owen: 'I liked him, and thought him pleasant and clever, a natural student (unlike me). Mr. Wigan had a soft spot for him. I had no idea that he was writing poetry, though I do remember that he wrote home a good deal. He had a room on the first floor; I had an attic room, but a study downstairs to myself as well. The house and garden were run smoothly and expensively; the servants were very good. Wigan was rather lordly, and I remember the village women curtseying to him; but he took little interest in the parish, and rarely seemed to go out. He was a silent, reserved, rather prosy man, always bringing out the same three standard jokes at dinner when anyone came to stay. I remember most the awful evening silences. I was homesick, watching the smoke of the London trains in the valley. It was all very quiet, and very dull.'

[76] The Chinese scroll on which this splendid creature appeared had been presented to the Owens by a missionary returned from China.

[77] The entrance examination for St John's Hall, the London College of Divinity, then at Highbury. It relocated to Northwood, Middlesex, in 1946 and then to Nottingham in 1970, where it is now run as St John's College.

99. To Susan Owen

31 October 1911   *Dunsden Vicarage*

My dearest Mother,

I find my weekly epistle is overdue, so I will forthwith set upon this pleasant task.

I took the address to Children on Thurs. in the Hall, did minor parts at the Prayer Meeting on Saturdays, and have been visiting several times. Other duties than these, I cannot find, except the very important one of talking at meals and in the evening. Dead silence sometimes prevails, which Mr. Kemp (Brother Kemp) is sometimes powerless to break; Brother Lewty[78] used even to talk nonsense for the sake of saying something, Kemp tells me! However, I don't think this is the case now. After dinner we sit round the study fire till bed-time, (about 11 to 11.30); during which time poor Kemp is on pins and needles, I imagine, feeling he ought to be at his Greek. Generally the Vicar reads to us about the Irish Revival of 1859. Then, instead of family prayers as was formerly the custom, we have a private prayer meeting every evening. The Vicar has the hope of a Revival in the place much on his mind, during these times.

On Wednesday, the Vicar took me to a Bible Society Meeting at Henley. (For this, I gave up going to a lecture <u>in French</u> for which Leslie offered me a Ticket). Never was at a B.S. Meeting before. Most entertaining concerns I find. Vicar says

<u>he</u> never was at a Bible Soc. meeting where there was <u>so much humour!</u> Dr. Dunn[79] gave a really fine address on its work. You must get him at Shrewsbury. My tyre went flat on the way, and we were somewhat late. But the Vicar was quite glad, for he didn't want to be elevated to the platform. Henley Town Hall is new, and (therefore) beautiful. The staircase is of pure marble every whit, and what with a statue of Hermes at the top, and strains of delicious music floating about, I could have imagined it a Greek Temple.[80] This was while we were waiting alone to enter the meeting hall. There was, as I have said, some musical concert at the same time, and, when Vicar asked the attendant the way to the meeting, the man looked first at him in his frowsy old habiliments, and then at me in my most unbiblical garb, and was fain to enquire—'Which meetin' may it be, sir?'

Last evening I went to a lecture on Charles Lamb, by Prof. Sir Walter Raleigh (!);[81] in Univ. College Hall—with Leslie. Paid only 6d. for a splendid seat. The lecture was good, but the lecturer but so so. Next fortnight there's one on Radium. These will beat your Abbey Forgates[82] for abstruseness and refinement, if not for humour, too, for F. C. Gould[83] gives one on Caricature next week.

I have got U.C.C.[84] some books <u>almost new</u>, at second hand price (half price) in Reading! Will you please cause enquiries to be made for *Modern Eng. Lit.* at Wilding's,[85] before you come? I am hardly expecting a Latin Bible from the Gleaning's People. Am not very inclined with the hymn, which I sent just in time, yesterday. I prefer indeed original compositions to linguistical competitions.[86]

I spent yesterday evening at Alpenrose with Dorothy, etc. Saw Gordon in Church on Sunday, with Auntie [*two-three words illegible*] Leslie I have not yet got my parcel; but expect to today.

So glad you are coming so soon. The Vicar asked when next you were owing, before I had said anything, and of course said that you must come over. I will try and meet you, you may be sure. I must get my features into training for a Photograph![87] Love to Father, Mary, etc.

Your loving, Wilfred

Thank Harold for his honest attempts to get my hair off. Luckily, some miles intervene between us, or I should have tweaked his nose for it, i.e. if I could get a grip of the thing.

[78] The Rev. Walter Lewty (ordained 1903). He started the children's Scripture Union, a Bible study group, at Dunsden that Owen led. Lewty went to South Africa in December 1911, presumably to become a missionary.

[79] The Rev. J. W. Bradney Dunne, Deputation-Assistant of the Bible Society 1898–1913.

[80] The Town Hall was built 1900–1. The only statue is that of a woman known locally as the Black Widow; the Town Clerk of Henley on Thames told HO and JB that there never had been a statue of Hermes at the head of the main staircase (see *CL*, p. 93, n. 2).

[81] Sir Walter Raleigh (1861–1922) was Professor of English Literature at Oxford from 1904 and a Delegate of Oxford University Press.

[82] A fashionable road within the precincts of the Abbey Church, Shrewsbury.

[83] Sir Francis Carruthers Gould (1844–1925), cartoonist and stockbroker, contributed to the *Pall Mall Gazette* and the *Westminster Review*, and edited his own (staunchly Liberal) paper *Picture Politics* from 1894 to 1914; he was knighted in 1906.

[84] The University Correspondence College, founded at Cambridge in 1887.

[85] A Shrewsbury bookshop and printing business.

[86] *Bible Society Gleanings* in 1911 offered a prize Bible for the best verse translation of a French hymn by any reader not over 19. The prize-winning poems were not printed. Owen's entry won and the prize, a leather-bound Latin New Testament, *Novum Testamentum*, ex Interpretatione Theordori Bazæ (Berlolini, 1909), survives in Owen's Library in the Bodleian.

[87] A photograph was taken at the Arcade Studio, Reading, at about this time, and is reproduced as Plate 8b in *JFO*, I.

100. To Mary Owen

7 November 1911   *Dunsden Vicarage*

My dear Sister,

Mother told me you would like me to write to <u>you</u> while she is here; and I am indeed pleased to cover a few sheets of this my Tablet for your benefit.

Mother has not been over here yet. Perhaps she is coming on Friday. But she came to church on Sunday Morning.

I addressed the Children's Service in the Parish Hall on Sunday Afternoon. I am also booked for the Scripture Union on Thurs. I enjoy speaking very much. I use no notes, and spend no great time in preparation; but I use no high falutin' words, but try to express myself in simple, straightforward English. I believe the children are impressed for the time being. I hope they will really benefit, for, of course, I give them the Messages, with one Purpose, and not with any idea of displaying my own bumptiousness.

Yesterday, the Vicar took me & Mr. Kemp to hear an address by Bishop Ingham[88] at Earley Court,[89] the fine residence of some of the Sutton Seeds people. I was introduced to the Bishop, and spoke a few words with him. I need hardly say that the Address more than justified the great praise which I heard of him from you at Shrewsbury. He told the story of the Tiles of Budda's Shrine! In addition to his Lordship, I met about half a dozen clergy at the Meeting. This was at the afternoon tea which followed, (in the immense billiard room.)

From such mansions as these, I pass, next afternoon, to the wretched hovels of this Parish, and carry myself with equal ease in the crazy, evil-smelling huts of the poor, as in the wide, luxurious chambers of the rich.

Numbers of the old people cannot read; those who can seldom do so. Scores of them have passed their whole lives in the same stone box with a straw lid, which they call their cottage; and are numbed to all interests beyond it. Those who have within them the Hope of a Future World are content, and their old faces are bright with the white radiance of eternity. Those who, like the beasts, have no such Hope, pass their old age shrouded with an inward gloom, which the reverses of their history have stamped upon their worn-out memories, deadening them to all thoughts of delight.

There is one poor creature who cannot be said to live—she exists and no more: She can neither speak, hear, nor see; I suppose she can taste, smell, and feel. But alas, all her feeling must be that of pain, for she has a disease of the bone; all her smell must be the smell of a foul cottage; all her taste, the taste of bread and of tea. What a life! Why am I telling you these dreadful things? Simply to let them educate you, as they are educating me, in the Book of Life, and to make us rejoice in our own happy state.

I spend my afternoons in going round to these cottages. I am at my books in the morning; while there is nearly always some meeting to keep me busy in the evening. I have been so busy, indeed, that I have not been able to finish this letter till this morning (Friday). Let me hear from you when you have something to say—(I will not say when you have time—I <u>know</u> you have time to write me a note). Give my benedictions to the boys, and my love to Father, and take as much as you like for yourself.

Your loving brother, Wilfred

<hr>

[88] The Rt Rev. Ernest Graham Ingham (1851–1926), Bishop of Sierra Leone 1883–97, Home Secretary of the Church Missions Society 1904–12.
[89] Near Reading.

101. To Susan Owen

21 November 1911   *Dunsden Vicarage*

My dearest Mother,

I had half expected a line from you on Sat. and I was delighted to have the sweet little note:—to have an account of the barometric changes of your dear, warm temperament, instead of details concerning the temperature of the weather; the falling of a tear is more precious to me than the holding-up of any volume of atmospheric rain... I was not alone as you were, or I might have sought relief in a verse or two. As it was, I was mightily cheered, by finding several large volumes of the *Quarterly Review*,[90] c. 1830-5, exposed for sale at Poynder's,[91] 1d the volume! I was astonied, for some of these must be quite valuable. Only a ten years earlier one would be priceless to me. (as, of course, you know, it was an article in this that helped to kill J.K.)[92] Strangely enough, a critic, in one of the vols. that I possess, apologises (half-mockingly, I believe) for the dastardly attack, and condescends, as it were, to pat Johnny Keats on the back, now he has been ten years dead. And warned by their mistake in his case, they hope to show more justice to <u>young Mr. Tennyson</u>, now making his second appearance in poetry! So far from this, they have not a good word to say for him, and make merciless fun of some of his best-beloved pieces ! ! Even I was, for the time, disenchanted, and roared with laughter with the *Quarterly* at his nonsense, and silly conceits.

The best pennyworth of humour I ever bought, albeit I would not let every-body enjoy it, lest Tennyson should come to shame. Thus, with all the guilty consciousness of infidelity to a professed hero, I spent a morning in naughty levity. But I am improved thereby, and look upon things now with a saner eye than formerly. Lamb, who died only a few years before, receives much attention in another vol. Byron, etc., etc. figure in others. So please don't tell [me] not to grind too much at regular study. I am rather in danger of falling into this desultory style of reading. I also at another shop picked up for 3d, a five shilling book of poetry by a modern aspirant, (unknown to me).[93] The book is quite new (1911) and is also in a new condition (many leaves uncut) so I am idly-busy in trying to discover the talent of our own days, and the requirements of the public (if such requirements exist).

Thank you for the Book forwarded. I hope to glean much from this, too.

Brer Kemp and your servant are to take the choir boys to the C.M.S.[94] Sale in Reading Town Hall this afternoon. We shall have to walk there and back, but as I am 'ever so' happy in the society of boys and youths of intelligence (even if unlettered) I trust I shall not find the way long. However, armed with your last injunctions, I flatly refused to go into Reading this morning for Tickets! Brer Kemp, therefore, had to bundle his lusty limbs there; he will be lucky indeed, if I don't make him carry me up the hills coming home, for we are not supposed to have tea there, and you know how restful a C.M.S. Sale of Work is.—I ought to say, that we are not going in order to patronise the stalls, but to witness the side-shows, and to enjoy the thrilling effects of puerile cantatas. 'Tis called a 'Trip to the East'. I ween the hungry choristers would trip more gaily if there were an 'F' somewhere in the title!

One of our cherubs (nomine Laurence Ambrose,[95] if you please!) cannot come, because engaged in the pressing duties of 'bird-starving', so he told me. This, of course, means scaring birds from newly-sown fields; but you notice how humanitarian these country folk are, (or birdy-manitarian, I should say) for they quite look at things from the bird's point of view.

The blue envelope, which I also thought to be the Matric. Tystisgriffe,[96] proved to be a 'tystisgriffe' to the excellence of the borrowed-brain-stuff which I imbibed to help me through the Exam.—Sanatogen.[97]

Therewith was appended a Chapter on Formamints. [98] This reminds me of Miss Goshkins herms—I mean Miss Hoskins[99] germs—and the thought thereof fills me with distress. If the fair Gipsy Smith[100] so much as thinks she's going to succumb, deny her entrance to the academical portals. Yea, an 'twere well to s'Macbeth, saying: 'Is this a Cadger that I see before me ?—a cadger of microbes, With the (h)air all full of the signs of Scarlet death!'

But I am trifling with a serious matter, and I would pass on to you the excellence, hetsetterer, hetsetterer, of Formamint. For though it be expensive, it may be worth a guinea a suck, and may, indeed, form a mint of blessing in dis to you all. Tis time this foolish monologue was rung off,

So adieu, until your next 'call':

Your own Wilfred

[90] Founded in 1809 as a Tory rival to the *Edinburgh Review*.

[91] G. A. Poynder was a bookshop at 96 Broad Street, Reading. Poynder's also had a printing business, based at Minster Street. DH noted how many of Owen's textbooks (now in the Bodleian) have labels for Poynder's, Golder's, and Smith's in Reading (*WOANB*, p. 489, n. 6).

[92] This was the notorious article on *Endymion* in 1818, thought to have hastened Keats's death in 1821. The reviewer was John Wilson Croker (1780–1857), secretary to the Admiralty and a regular contributor to the *Quarterly Review*.

[93] DH identified this as Harold Monro, *Before Dawn: Poems and Impressions* (Constable, 1911), among Owen's books in the Bodleian.

[94] The Church Missionary Society, founded in 1799 by members of the Clapham Sect, including William Wilberforce, who campaigned for the abolition of the slave trade, social reform, and world evangelism. In 1995 its name changed to the Church Mission Society and its headquarters are now based in east Oxford.

[95] He became a gamekeeper and HO met him, years later.

[96] A Welsh word meaning certificate.

[97] Sanatogen was marketed as a 'brain tonic' and was invented by the German Bauer Chemical Company in 1898.

[98] Formamint was comprised of formaldehyde and milk sugar, marketed as 'the germ-killing throat tablet', and was believed to alleviate any number of ailments from sore throat to tonsillitis, bad breath, and influenza.

[99] Mistress, with Miss Goodwin, of the infant school, which was then being run at Mahim in the mornings. Susan would read the daily prayers with the children.

[100] Beth Smith, nicknamed Gipsy, a friend of Mary. Her father farmed near Shrewsbury.

104. To Harold Owen

2 December 1911   *Dunsden Vicarage*

My dear Harold,

You will find enclosed an original design which shaped itself one evening when I was in idle mood. I want a Cover for an Everyman[101] and in case your design might not please me, I venture to ask you to adopt this, altering the size, etc. as you see fit.

I have no idea how you are going to execute it, for of course it is not for a Stencil, but I trust to your ingenuity to produce some sort of cover. I want the whole surface light green; the 'branches' dark green; the 'roses' (they are not cabbages) red; and the 'nameplate' yellow or yellowish-green. I imagine that my Monogram and the other ovals would look well in Blue.

For I want a 'rich' effect; and not a rigidly pure scheme of colour. If the whole thing is not worth copying, don't be afraid to say so: and please make another and better design. (Leaving the Printing to me, please, unless you have mightily improved in that way of late.)

Supposing you have time for such a useful exercise, I am in need of a <u>cover for</u> <u>a large 'Atlas Antiquus'</u> (9½ ins. × 14½ins. and ⅓ in. thick.) So should you like to design and make such an article, I should be much obliged. It might do for my Christmas Present?

The aspect of the Chiltern Downs is perfectly wintry now, but the land is by no means devoid of beauty or interest. The village of Sonning is one of the prettiest in the Thames Valley, and no wonder Holman Hunt chose to live there.[102] I have not yet seen his house.

I do not often venture out of the Parish; but yesterday I spent a morning in Reading. The shops are already beginning to wear their Christmas glories. When I view the triumphs of Fine Art to be seen in some of the most expensive Christmas Cards and books, I am overcome by an access of thriftlessness, and positively have to look the other way. Anyhow I shall be forced to spend a considerable amount on <u>something</u> because <u>all</u> the household staff expect something for Christmas. For that reason alone I should be glad to be at home for that season. But I hardly expect to, seeing no word has been said on that subject yet.

Brother Lewty is coming today, to spend Sunday. Brother Kemp departs in perfect peace to the City of Distraction on Monday.

If he stays over the next Sunday, I shall act Superintendent of the Sunday School, as well as Presiding on Thursday.

Fare thee well! I rejoice that you <u>work hard</u>, even as much as to hear that you are happy therein.

(I remember that I did not remember to remember Mary and <u>her</u> last letter, in <u>my</u> last letter. But I will respond anon.) Likewise to Mother's and Colin's last notes: to whom and to Father, Greeting!

From the faithful Wilfred

[101] This cover, and that for the *Atlas Antiquus* mentioned later, were duly executed by HO.

[102] William Holman Hunt, OM (1827–1910), the painter, and one of the three founders of the Pre-Raphaelite Brotherhood, lived at 'The Acre', Sonning-on-Thames, where he painted the second version of *The Light of the World*, which was presented to St Paul's Cathedral in 1908. The Acre was designed by Holman Hunt's daughter Gladys in 1901.

105. To Mary Owen

7 December 1911   *Dunsden Vicarage*

My dearest Sister,

It is more than a fortnight since I had your last letter, so you well deserve a 'full' one from <u>me</u>. I am pleased that you can exhibit some amount of spirit in your replies, and particularly because they are <u>well expressed</u> (!). I have no book called 'Notes' on L.L.[103] but a copy <u>with Notes</u>, which, of course, you will abstract from my shelves when required.

I was altogether shocked by the News of Kathleen's[104] death, and, possibly because of the similarity of our ages, took it much more to heart than I imagine the 'other branch' of Cousins did. I even thought I had rheumatic fever one night—because I found my socks had been wet for hours.

Strangely enough, on that day, I went to the first funeral I have ever been to in my life; and I wore black and mourned there—for other cause than people thought.[105] Ah, at such times, like Lamb, 'I begin to count the probabilities of my duration, and grudge at the expenditure of moments like miser's farthings. In proportion as the years both lessen and shorten, I set more count upon their periods, and would fain lay my finger upon the spoke of the great wheel.'[106] For every circumstance of my present life reminds me that I am no more a Boy. Can a Boy speak at Meetings, as I speak; can a Boy superintend a Sunday School and six teachers as I shall do; Can a Boy carve a Pheasant at late dinner as I did?...

Well, even now, you see my moralising does not last long; and at the present moment my heart is filled with music. 'Tis thus: After the Scrip. Union Meeting which I took alone, and thoroughly enjoyed, I took upon myself (at Mrs. Lott's[107] desire,) to teach a Carol to the 'Sowers' and others; which they are to sing at the Sunday School Treat to my accompaniment. There were about a dozen, from ten to fourteen years old, and some have really exceptional voices, and all seem most intelligent; so it [is] with real pleasure that I 'doh-ray-me' before them; harp on first piano, then organ; insist on pauses, slurs and crescendo's, and beg the rosy mouths to ope a trifle widah!

Two choir boys came Carol singing here on Tues. and I enjoyed that, also. The skies have been warm and sunny here, and I enjoy that also. The moon rose in full splendour last night, and I enjoyed that also. But alas! I do not enjoy the long hours spent doing absolutely nothing in the study nearly every night. Imagine me slobbering over my can of shaving-water and blinking over my candle these dark mornings—when I only get to sleep as near twelve as eleven! I tell you the honey-dew of warm sleep is not to be compensated by the honey (literal) on the breakfast-table...But I want something to complain of, don't I, when I hear of carters getting up at 4, and having no holiday from year to year—no not Sunday!

Mr. Lewty spent Sunday here—for the last time. He is a splendid speaker, and an M.A. and is or was a reader of Modern Poetry; so it was a pleasure to be able to speak with him, and an honour to be called 'brother' by him. Harold is not to show my cabbage-patch[108] to Mr. Dane—where's his self-respect!

I have had no information about Christmas. The Vicarage is not decorated, I believe; but after all it accords better with my tastes to have a house well swept than garnished—and that it verily is. Mr. Kemp's exam is over, and he writes about it with confidence.

I think very often about you, on Sunday Evenings especially. You will, of course, thank dear Mother for her letter; (for whom this is half intended) Thanks be to Miss Rose[109] for her very kind and valued message—but 'tis not a fresh message to me, if <u>Mother</u> ever gave me a piece of advice.

Your affectionate brother, Wilfred

[103] Sir Walter Scott, *The Lady of the Lake*. Owen had three copies, all of which survive in his Library at the Bodleian.

[104] Kathleen Loughrey, a cousin, fourth child of Susan Owen's sister May.

[105] On 15 October 1912 Owen assisted at the double funeral of Alice Mary Allen and her 4-year-old daughter, Hilda Agnes. The resulting poem, 'Deep under turfy grass' (*CPF*, p. 59), is a compassionate yet unflinching response whose features 'would characterize his writings from the western front' (Jon Stallworthy, *Wilfred Owen* [Oxford University Press, new ed. 2013], p. 80.)

[106] Charles Lamb, *The Essays of Elia*, 'New Year's Eve'.

[107] The vicarage housekeeper.

[108] The rose design for the *Everyman* cover.

[109] A missionary friend of Susan Owen.

109. To Susan Owen

Postcard

29 December 1911   [*Postmark Reading*]

It seems very strange to be writing to you now, when only this morning I was talking—aye and <u>grumbling</u>, over my specimens but prithee put this down to an excess of zeal in the cause of Science.

I landed in full time for the Treat which began at 4. The Conjurer was just as might be expected—but sometimes above the comprehension of the infant multitude. His dummy in Ventriloquism, Mr. Marmalade, struck terror to the heart of one of these, while it gave the keenest pleasure to the rest. It was lucky I snatched my bowler hat this morning—for it was the only one in the hall, & was therefore used, and abused till we all had clear proof as to the truth of miracles. I wish your little party had been transferred here, tonight, and could stay here till I get used to the Silence, the State, and the Stiffness.

W

111. To Mary Owen

January 1912   *Dunsden Vicarage*

My dearest Mary,

I wonder how you are today. I am hoping to hear soon that you feel stronger, dear. The 'change' to this part of the country would not benefit you much at present, for today is the very worst day of the season. Rain is incessant; Temperature as near freezing as it can manage, Wind—East; Clouds—yellow and black, about

5 miles thick ! ! Anyhow it was so dark this morning as to send me to sleep at ten o'clock—over my book. Perhaps this was also due to the late hour of retiring— nearly twelve! We had been to Fritz and Arthur Wood's meetings.[110] Kemp & I went in to the 3 o'clock, with Mrs. & Miss Fordham, had tea at Mrs. F's expense, & then went to the 8 o'clock meeting. The 'Singer' Wood is simulating the Great Alexander in his spiral-staircase-windmill-arm-feats; he also has Alexander's trick of stamping, clapping, and grinning by turns, and what is more, complimenting individuals on their singing—(one of which individuals was the Vicar.)

Apart from all this preamble which led to nothing, I enjoyed the services. Brother Kemp has gone in this afternoon to hear their dicta on 'Questionable Amusements'. I had not the strength to wallow through and underneath the mud, and to treadmill back again, with twenty gallons of rain-water in one's clothing. Moreover I don't need to hear what I could say myself, and I don't want to hear what I don't think myself.

The social evening, considering the short notice given to performers, was distinctly successful. I simply couldn't sing my song with less than three mistakes in practice. I didn't the least know the tune, but read it. However, the actual thing went off splendidly and compliments upon the song, and the voice (when it matures (!)) were numerous. So I have made my debut in one of the Fine Arts! Mr K's voice is very good indeed, I think; much better than the Woods' for instance.

I am thankful to say I was able to 'throw myself into' my recitations, and out of that stupefying nervousness which might have frozen me at your age. But I doubt whether the audience enjoyed the pieces as well as I did myself. I am sending you the programme that you may see what all the others did. The people numbered nearly 80 I should think.

My little patient, (not sufferer you will be glad to know) is on a fair way to recovery. I infuse life and mirth into him drop by drop, day by day; chiefly through the nasal channels of Mr. Punch's Voice. He has a Punch & Judy Book, and his little brother of about 3 will bring it open to a certain picture, gravely saying 'Laugh at this' whereat I laugh. 'Now laugh at this,' whereat we all laugh. He was asleep when I took Colin's crackers, and his pleasure on finding them by his bed on waking was, says his Mother, very, very real.

I find that Shelley lived at a cottage within easy cycling distance from here.[111] And I was very surprised (tho' really I don't know why) to find that he used to 'visit the sick in their beds; kept a regular list of the industrious poor whom he assisted to make up their accounts;' and for a time walked the hospitals in order to be more useful to the poor he visited! [112] I knew the lives of men who produced such marvellous verse could not be otherwise than lovely, and I am being confirmed in this continually. I find my very slight medical knowledge of some use— not perhaps to the patients but rather to myself, in giving topics of confabulation, and in commanding respect to my advice, and, it may be, in winning a way into the homes.

Would I could give <u>you</u> some advice which would lead to better health. But myself am feeling at low vitality. No doubt this time of year is like the third hour of morning. For you know that at 3 a.m. our life ebbs at its lowest; that is 'the hour when sick men die.'[113]

I hope to take a trip to Town next week (or this), when I want to buy my Bible. Would one of you send my Royal Autographs,[114] which you will find in my cash box ? I may take it to the Brit: Museum.

Fondest love to all, Yrs. Wilfred

Canon B. Laurence[115] from London speaks tonight : I must get ready.

[110] Travelling brother evangelists. See Letter 512.

[111] Albion House, Marlow, Buckinghamshire.

[112] Owen had been reading *Shelley*, by John Addington Symonds (Macmillan, 1809); his marked copy survives. 'His charity, though liberal, was not weak. He…visited the sick in their beds…and kept a regular list of industrious poor, whom he assisted with small sums to make up their accounts.'

[113] Sir Lewis Morris (1833–1907), *The Epic of Hades*, 1879, 'Andromeda', ll. 137–8: '…the dead dark hour before the dawn / When sick men die….'. Owen later returned to the theme in 'The Unreturning' (*CPF*, p. 107): 'Then peered the indefinite unshapen dawn / With vacant gloaming, sad as half-lit minds, / The weak-limned hour when sick men's sighs are drained.'

[114] HO and JB, in *CL* (p. 107, n. 1), remarked: 'We can throw no light on these.'

[115] Arthur Evelyn Barnes-Lawrence (1852–1931), Hon. Canon of Southwark 1905–15, later Vicar of St John the Evangelist, Boscombe, Bournemouth.

112. To Susan Owen

5 January 1912   *Dunsden Vicarage*

My dearest Mother,

Our Sunday School Treat went off with great success. I must not spend words describing it, but will just mention that the Carol was tolerably well sung, & that the games were most enjoyable. The boys were rough, but so were we, and no one was hurt. They derived great fun from my innovation of Earth, Air, etc., and also from Oranges and Lemons, when they passed under Miss Reading's and my hands joined. Had that young lady of (doubtful age) been anything but a farmer's daughter she must surely have gone home minus both arms and numerous locks of hair.

At this treat the Vicar announced a Bible Class in the Vicarage, starting next Sunday, held by Mr. Owen. (Mr. O. had only had definite knowledge that such a Class had been decided upon half an hour previously.) However, I have about 20 names eligible, and expect quite ten or a dozen. I shall enjoy it, and everything is as one could desire except the capacity of the Leader for such an undertaking.

I am very much interested in a sweet little boy of 5 who a day or two ago was at the point of death (from Peritonitis.) His whiteness was as the whiteness of snow. Now he seems past the crisis. I do want to give him some of my faithful veterans of <u>Soldiers</u>. Could you make a packet bulky enough to travel free per G.W.R.? I particularly want them soon, but rather than spend their worth on postage, would wait till you come.

—Not a moment to spare for more—Choir Supper tonight!

Your loving Wilfred

114. To Susan Owen

11 January 1912   Dunsden Vicarage

My dearest Mother,

Your news was a great disappointment. I had reserved all latest news of mine to <u>tell</u> you, and quite thought of meeting you at the station today. How long will you have to wait now?

There is one thing I am glad of—That I need have no fear of your appearing at the 'Concert'.

I am taking the Bass in three part songs, and may sing the *Arrow and the Song*[116] (to another tune). But unless I improve wonderfully by Monday, I shall substitute for it a pianoforte solo or more recitations.

Last Monday we went to Mrs Reading's of Caversham to tea. The house is new and large—you pass it on Caversham Hill. We actually stayed till after nine—playing bagatelle and another competitive game, 'Carnations', which I will explain for our diversion someday. The Children made no appearance; but we had the pleasure of the company [of a] step-daughter of Mrs Reading's, who is a fashionable young lady from Town, and who, having travelled over Europe, and having, as I soon discovered, a tolerable leaning towards literature, made the evening most agreeable. Particularly as Mrs. R. is very nervous and jerky about the face. (But she was once a house-keeper to Mr R. and no doubt finds Self-possession and Placidity the most difficult of all lady-like qualities to assume.)

On Tuesday, the Sunday School Teachers assembled here for tea, and an hour's sitting on the Drawing Room sofas. A duller time I have seldom spent. We looked at albums of photographs and things—very nice in themselves, but when they run into thousands one begins to nauseate of 'A Street in Japan', Street in Winnipeg, Street in Norway, Street in Normandy, and a painful spirit of unrest begins to assert itself somewhere behind the eyes.

Miss Cheshire, missionary from India, is here now. She took Wednesday night, and will address Mothers, and Children today. We amassed some seventy people in the Hall for the occasion.—Alas! I am beginning to tire of all these meetings, and the goings and comings connected with them—not that they themselves are in any way disagreeable, but that I want to be <u>reading</u>. The time

I am at Book and Pen seems to be growing smaller and smaller, and the worst of it all is that in the mornings, I am as dull as I used to be, say at eleven o'clock at night in the term-times. Given ten minutes quiet at any time of day, and a fire to sit before, I could go into a sound sleep for hours. I am just now reading a Life of Shelley, and I find that he exhibited these characteristics too. So I am comforted. But even this does not relieve the tense nervous strain of two to three hours solid idleness per night.

You will think I am all complaints—but believe me none hears them but you—unless a mutual sigh with the 'other Brother' as we light our candles—partakes of the nature of a complaint.

During the afternoons, I am mostly very happy, and the consciousness of bringing a stray gleam of pleasure into a sick room is in itself ineffably pleasurable. It will be hard to part with the boys and others if I stay much longer. Surprising how my opinions of ploughmen's sons have changed now I know some. Thought they had round vacant eyes and mouths and intellects to correspond—Find them possessed of (sometimes) fine features, and (somehow) nice manners...I wish I could enlarge upon my experiences and the thoughts they engender. That must be put off till anon, while I now distribute some invitations for the Social.

Good-bye.

Thank dear Colin for his presents to my little patient. It seems that nothing short of prayer answered has brought round this little fellow. But even yet he must be in terrible danger—for years—I suppose. It was contracted after measles. Consumption may take hold on him—and then?

Consumption is all round us here. Scarlet Fever and Diphtheria are at work near by. God grant that His mercies in keeping our dear family together may be continued long, long years to come! And do you mind and not get influenza. Some one has got Quinsy[117] here—O what tremors I have lest you should get it again.

Your devoted son, Wilfred

[116] A poem by Henry Wadsworth Longfellow, set to music by M. W. Balfe *c.*1850.
[117] A bacterial infection and complication of tonsillitis, quinsy is an abscess between the tonsils and the wall of the throat.

125. To Susan Owen

March 1912   *Dunsden Parish Hall*

Dearest Mother,

This letter is a few days late, in consideration of my rather frequent epistles lately. Once again, you see, I am writing at the Club while timing Red Lanterns (otherwise Boxers.) This is because after tea today the Vicar wanted us to go a ride with him; The evening was indeed very lovely; and I enjoyed seeing new country. You remember I half promised to give some music lessons to one of my favourite Boys (Vivian); well, he is very keen (at present speaking) and I have given him two on the Hall Piano after 'Thurs. Afternoon's'. I promised indeed to give him four lessons gratis, and after that to exact a slight fee.

This has set his Mother all agog to get a piano. She saw an advertisement for one; and begged the favour of my going to examine and pronounce upon it. This I did; and again rode in today (to Reading) to meet the lady and help her to decide. All these negotiations are done unbeknown to the rest of the Parish (I hope): & the Vicarage in particular.

I could get no farther with my writing at the club, and so, having had my 9.15 o'clock repast in solitude and happiness, I now sit down before your distant presence and finish this communication.

Mr. Moore came in time for tea yesterday and stayed the night. We had a full enough Hall, made fuller by the Gunston Family complete, Mrs. Cates, & Mrs. Francis.[118]

The Text was: 'And the yoke .. (pause) .. shall be BROKEN...(pause & gasp)...because of the anNOINTing!' (This extraordinary ciphering is meant to represent the manner of delivery.)

What the dear old man said, it is not the time to repeat here, but I must remark upon How he spoke.

Just precisely as if he had never slept, eaten, or stopped delivering since we saw him in Wimbledon—so unchanged is he. How I revel in his dramatism. With what absolute command he modulates his voice-tones. The shrill declamatory top-note (almost passing into a shriek) in an instant changed for a hollow, deep, sepulchral groan, that seems to feel its way beneath the very tables of the heart!

The subdued persuasive undersong quietly leads us through labyrinths of agreeable meditation...Then like a thunderbolt, flashes and roars a sentence, making one jump in his seat.

Gradually the storm subsides, until once more we are brought up with a jerk...and so on; until we fairly hang upon his words and it is impossible not to attend.

Then there is the hand-play—how he finishes off a thought with a trail of the fingers instead of words; clinches a statement with a clap, instead of an epigram; points to a long-dead figure, and we see it; sparing epithets.

Then there is the body-play: advancing, he forces an argument upon our brains; retreating he is horrified as if at the audience, bending forward he drives home his points as with a mallet; leaning backwards he pleads, as before a court.

Then there is the Foot-play, for he even drags heavily his boot upon the floor under the weight of some distressing thought.

Then there is the Face-play: the sharp grey eyes, shooting right and left at the close of every period; and never letting a single person out of sight for two minutes together. And how extraordinary sometimes is his resemblance to 'the Canon'. When he compresses his lips; droops the eyebrows, takes in a deep breath, and pats nervously with his hand upon the table—then the scene changes; I am in Christchurch!

What I like so is the sighs; and the 'tut-tut-tut's'; the apostrophes; the hand-on-chin asides; the confidential, confirmatory repetition of 'you do (click of tongue, shake of head) .. you do (click of tongue, shake of head) .. you do' in a whisper, after some telling affirmation…

Well, well; all this is beside the mark, perhaps you think, and to notice such is to defeat the purpose for which they were intended. And alas, the boys present could scarce keep from laughing. Ah! how could I have laughed ever!

For now he is among the chiefest prophets in my—what shall I call it ?—Theogony. Yes—Theogony; for such aged benignity and saintliness on the one hand; and the youthful genius of poets on the other, press home to me the secret of much in Religion—at least false religions. I could (if I did not hear the 'See thou do it not!' within), fall down and worship either. And had I lived in the days of Buddha, Confucian, Zoroaster, or Mahomet, I should have been the first to start preaching their deification.

The dear man was seriously shocked to hear of Dorothy's apostasy;[119] quite unnecessary to tell him; for his quarter-hour expostulation with her before us all after the meeting was of none effect. I plied him with a few questions after supper; but gained nothing conclusive; where shall I?

The Vicar presides over the Plumber![120] Kemp is pretty sure of Highbury now.

I really mean you to send by rly. the 'Andersen'; and if needs, to eke it out with any 'school' Shakespere's[121] you find; and my Arabian Nights; also the MS. book, I mentioned.

Do you know I have an idea of versifying such Fairy Tales as are suitable; and of trying to publish them. They always had an immense attraction for me; and if I don't spoil them in trying 'to paint their roses, and throw perfume on their violets',[122] they ought to do.

At any rate, some settled task, may kill my present lassitude. The very thought has made me sleepy, and so—a fair Good-night!

From your affectionate son, Wilfred

P.S. I hope you will be agreeably disappointed to hear that what you thought a 'Quotation' is perfectly original; 'a poor thing, but mine own'; & so far as I know not expressed before : it was 'printed' simply for the sake of emphasis. As you dwelt on 'When I survey', I might say what Canon Barnes Lawrence told me—Matthew Arnold was once in a Church in Liverpool, in 1888, when that was sung; and he was very moved, saying it was the finest piece of religious poetry in our tongue—or something like that. That day he fell down dead—from heart failure.[123]

Do you remember a girl at the Mothers' Meeting who looked ill, having had appendicitis. On Monday she thought herself dying; and was in a state of fearful terror. Mrs. Fordham dealt with her; and she has found peace now. She is better, too. You do not say how you are feeling; or whether a new maid has been found.

I am, of course, all right again; (and much enjoyed the Gingerbreads).

How did Father enjoy Torquay?

---

[118] Her husband managed a game-rearing farm in the neighbourhood owned by a cousin of John Gunston.

[119] Later, however, Dorothy Gunston became a missionary. DH notes that 'she had probably just announced that she had made Wigan's spiritual journey from Evangelicalism to the High Church beliefs she was to hold for the rest of her life' (WOANB, p. 97).

[120] A reformed character, much in demand at public evangelical meetings.

[121] This was Owen's own idiosyncratic spelling of 'Shakespeare', and it has been retained throughout.

[122] King John, IV, ii.

[123] Matthew Arnold (1822–88), poet and cultural critic, died suddenly of heart failure in Liverpool on 15 April 1888, running to catch a train to the Liverpool Landing Station to meet his daughter on her return from America.

126. To Susan Owen

11 March 1912   *Dunsden Parish Hall*

My dearest Mother,

I am taking out a few minutes from the Club Time to answer your letter. There are ten stalwart youths now under my eye, so pardon if I wander. The vicar & Mr. Fordham left early today, & a telegram tells us they are safe at a hotel.

Mrs. Fordham invited Kemp & me to tea, together with Miss Hendy; our music was cut short (as far as I am concerned) at seven. My photographs are not yet finished; but I am afraid they are all 'mucked up',—Kemp did not even expose one of the 3 plates, tho' he thinks he has! But I mean to try again.

You were right in guessing my occupation last Saturday at 6.45; I fancy I was thinking of you then—at least in my extensive mind-travels at that hour I touch usually upon Mahim, England. I indeed wished for your presence on Sunday. Most enjoyable service. I really shall never tolerate St. Julian's crashing organ-blasts and choking boys after our clear, stirring melodies and dim religious light. The sermons I could only bear interchanged once a month (say). The Concertina improves minute by minute. I was required to accompany the wheezy concert-screamer on the organ, and 'soothly one might imagine it a violin, so pleasant were some tones.

I had an Ambrose to tea on Sunday. With an easy glide, I entered upon Deep Waters, when we were alone, and the poor lad is in a fearful Fog. It thickens every day. I can get him to say little, but by <u>talking</u> what I <u>knew</u> was in his mind (for an hour) I have nearly apprehended his state. Marvellous how a farmhand should be inflicted with earnest self-questioning every time he is alone. Like many a famous philosopher, he leans to the opinion that the personality of man becomes utterly extinct upon Death, and he cannot profess a Christian's hope. How shall I answer?

If others knew the fog, fog fog which rolled in <u>my</u> mind, they would wonder that I should try to lighten another being. But I spend most of my time now in reading, analysing, collecting, sifting, and classifying Evidence, whereas <u>he</u> has neither time nor powers to probe the mysteries of Reason and Revelation. Of course I do not talk to him quite in this strain, but I try to uncover the grappling-hooks which are holding down his soul (supposing he has one.) His chief difficulty is <u>Language</u>. So is mine. In <u>his</u> case, <u>Bad</u> Language though one would never have thought it. He hates it, and he cannot escape it.

In <u>my</u> case, <u>Fine</u> Language, to yield wholly to the glamours of which would be accounted 'of this world' by those who aver they are not of this world.

I love it, and I cannot escape it.

More, I dare not say now. You will think I have been 'in the clouds'. Nay, I have been in my Cor Cordium, my heart of hearts.

I must return to externals again to say that I shall probably <u>not</u> go to a Doctor. This bright weather puts my mopes to shame. My body needs no physician. Then my eye got better without any pharmaceutical fumbling; for, feeling it slightly less painful, I went into the Library, and there, with a parting stab, the grit seemed suddenly to leave me [*final sheet missing*]

127. To Susan Owen

16 March 1912   *Dunsden Vicarage*

My own dear Mother,

I hope you will get this by your Birthday; though I know you must have given up hope of getting the Pen Case by the 17th. Anyhow I say Many and Happy be the Returns of the Day to thee! What would you like me to give you at the next 'return'?—so I may set about to think about beginning to start to choose something?

The Lantern worked splendidly under my manipulation on Wednesday; tho' I only brought up the Slides from the Station at the last moment. There was no solo-singing. Brother Kemp was rather amusing over his part of the duties; for not wanting to <u>stand</u> up to read; he had the Study Reading Lamp taken to the Hall, and <u>seated</u> himself at the table at my side, with the result that all behind were 'blinded with excess of light.' Of course this conduct was soon nipped in the bud.

I got (or rather allowed) a favourite boy (Vivian) to help me with the slides; and on Thurs. managed to smuggle the same urchin to tea with me, having conveniently drafted the 'Kemptitude' upon the Fordhams. Such a tête-à-tête tea, by the open window of the Den, with the odours of the Currant-Shrubs balmily wandering in and commingling with the essences in the solid-silver tea-pot—is a thing to enjoy.

On Friday afternoon, I was also in a pleasure-vein; spending an hour and a half in the School. I made a careful inspection of the drawings, dealt out the usual supplies of encouraging praise, and found the usual merriment in the dunces' work; tigers, for instance, which looked like your slavey's old boots thus:

Nevertheless, there were some very fine Drawings from some; and Lorrie Ambrose, now a 'bird-starver', showed unmistakable <u>talent</u>! His paintings should startle Harold, if he saw them. Then, I went out to see Mrs. Hulcoop[124] drill the smaller boys and girls; begged permission to give them a few commands; was accorded the same with great pleasure; and so put them thro' the old familiar Hips—FIRM! Neck—RESST! Darlings some of them are! I could have hugged them, rather than put any in the corner. Such is the force of the reaction—from now living where the voice of children is not heard, because they are not! After this I went thro' a collection of fossils and flints brought by scholars, and found one <u>genuine</u> chipped implement.

From school, I rendered myself to Fordhams' for tea with Kemp, and thence went a walk under lovely clear sky to Caversham Heights to visit an invalid lady; friend of Mrs. F.'s and also visited at her word, by the Vicar. This invalid lives with her old mistress, a lady, old-maid, accomplished, and having a rather nice house. Next door lives a boy (of 15) who has composed music to a Hymn, and the old lady would have hustled this prodigy in for us to behold, if he had not been out. Now this school-boy has an older brother who aspires to be a journalist; and when I heard this I pricked up my ears the more: apparently <u>visibly</u>, for I received an invitation to meet one or other next Friday. I wonder what I shall make of them! It was strange enough to find oneself 'at home' in a totally new household <u>last</u> Friday: It will be stranger still next week.

Is the Burden of your household shifted for a lighter one yet?

The Vicar has just returned: <u>plus</u> antiques as we had prophesied! Mrs. Lott wants me to teach her Niece Pianoforte Music, with some slight remuneration, of course! Her late teacher & Kemp will come no more. I shall not refuse, tho'

I feel something of a Charlatan over it. What I receive <u>may</u> pay for one or two lessons <u>for me</u>.

Kisses & Love from

Your own Wilfred

[124] Correct spelling: Hullcoop. Wife of the village schoolmaster.

[124.][125] To Susan Owen

5 March [*April*] *1912. Good Friday*   *Dunsden Vicarage*

Dearest Mother,

The slippers are in every way to my fancy, and I thank you for your promptitude in making them. The 'bars sinister', furrows, chasms and ridges, or whatever they may be, are indeed suggestive of Mme. <u>Defarge</u>,[126] or as you evasively write it *"the frauumm"*, and I fear you must have been as constant a Knitter as she: (well since writing this I have been idly employed on the accompanying sketch, and as it somewhat realizes my 'Madame' I cannot resist sending it.) I'm bothered if I know how you adjust your digits when knitting, tho'.

My carbuncle is almost well now, thank you.

When you send a letter late on Monday Night, say, I do not get it till Wednes. mng! (*Interval: Friday to Tues. Night !*)

I quite forgot whether I acknowledged 'the Parcel' or not. Anyhow the surprising amount of 'goodies' is worth a second time of thanking. I hardly can take a taste of the things, when I picture the delight of the Child when she hears the rustling of the paper-bags in my pocket! To quote Scott (for a marvel)

'All sunk and dim her eyes so bright
Her form decayed by pining,
Till through her wasted hand at night
You saw the taper shining.'[127]

How am I occupying myself? Well, 'but so so' on Monday; seeing the Spider invited me into his parlour, and there I was caught nicely, and had my patience sucked out of me, while bad blood took its place. During the whole afternoon we accomplished <u>Nothing</u>, save deciding that a whole batch of pictures, costing about 15s. each, were <u>No good</u> (i.e. for this house).

'Ha! Hum! Well! I'm puzzled. Very puzzled. Try <u>this</u> frame! Now that. Now this. Hum! well, I'm puzzled! Perfectly G H A S T L Y, isn't it? Rather smitten with <u>that</u>, I must confess.' And so on, till it was time to go to the Fordhams to tea. My boredom was completed there! Talked of nothing worth rememb'ring; except I recollect, when the Vicar repeated a snatch of 'To the Cuckoo', and finished up with, 'Well, Wordsworth <u>may</u> have been a nice old man, and a lover of "Nācher", but he was <u>not</u> a poet.' The Vicar's eyes caught mine, and the conversation speedily resumed a non-literary line. I shall remember <u>that</u>. And oh! I remember how they all committed young Selwood to his grave; shoved him in, one might say; locked the vault; trampled the earth down tight.

Vicar : ...thinks if he can only get away, he'll get better.
    Well, poor thing, <u>we</u> know better.
Mr. F.: I should just think so.
Vicar: Yes, humanly speaking, there is not a particle of hope.
Mr. F.: Absolutely; <u>absolutely</u>.
Mrs. F.: Well, vicar, as I was thinkin' jest now, when I 'eard you say 'e thought 'e
    was getting' better, well, I says, orfentimes, one 'as such delusions, an perchance
    its the doin' of Satan, and its jest a sign for us.
Miss F.: Yus. I only ope e may reelise it soon.'

What will you think of me, for this naughtiness! Perhaps you had better burn my letter at once. Yet no! I would suggest what Junkets (so he sometimes styled himself) said to his Sister,
    <u>'You will preserve all my Letters and I will secure yours—and thus in the course of time we shall each of us have a good Bundle—which, hereafter, when things may have strangely altered and God knows what happened, we may read over together, and look with pleasure on times past that now are to come.'</u>[128]
Ah! in my hours of 'ennui' as hinted above, what balm I find in saying over and over to myself such lines as these;
        ... 'The solitary breeze
        Blustered and slept, and its wild self did teaze
        With wayward melancholy, and I thought,
        Mark me, Peona!, that sometimes it brought
        Faint fare-thee-wells', and sigh-shrilled adieus.'
                                    (Endymion)[129]

I left Fordham's early to be at the Club, for the boys could not spend Bank Holiday Evening better than at the Hall and would not be put off.
    On Sat. I secretly met with Vivian*[130] at a stile and went a delicious ramble; lay in hawthorn glades, where antlered stags[131] would come within a few yards of us.

He read to me, and I told him tales. I took some figs of Mary's for him, (for I … [*two words illegible*] and arriving home at 6, <u>I</u> went without tea, willingly. The weather last week was glorious; and one afternoon I half spent in a daisy-meadow, with the 'Fairy Bray', with another and (to me) more enchanting elf, being older and well-spoken, and with various insignificant brothers and sisters. We sought the Biggest Daisy, and the <u>Reddest</u>† Daisy. My elf found them (oh yes, honestly!) <u>and I</u> found the Golden Age. Talk of Miss Moses!

What a <u>black-slander</u> about the brute black-hand, son of Bruce Blaxland![132] All the blacker‡ being true; but you don't circulate it do you?

I sang a solo on Good Friday—'O come and mourn'. I enjoyed it thoroughly and now quite wish you could hear me in the Hall. 'Such a lot of people turned up'; (not to hear me, for I was only asked at lunch-time.)

Gordon stayed all day Sunday here; but I had to entertain Willie, who left our establishment today. A Dissenter is now installed here!

I don't expect to get any sort of Easter holiday. Vicar is going away next week for Spring Cleaning.

Really, I could go on all night with letter-writing <u>To You</u>: but now I drop pen, for I want to read over your last dear kind letter and wonder how you enjoyed today, before I tap-tap at the Study-door, and banish <u>candid expression</u>.

À *Dieu*, Wilfred

Make up what loving messages you like to M, H, & C, <u>and</u> Father; you know my heart.

* —an' mind you, not the feminine termination '-en'.

† Little did I reck that the adjectives of colour have no comparative or superlative degree!

‡ There I am again!

---

[125] Moved here in chronological order. DH identified that certain letters from this March–April period were labelled and thus printed 'slightly out of sequence' in *CL* and *SL*. In the case of Letter 124, Easter Sunday, 1912, was 5 April not 5 March (*WOANB*, p. 489, n. 17; Paul Norgate, '"Dulce et Decorum Est" and Some Amendments to the Dating of Wilfred Owen's Letters', *Notes and Queries* (June 1986), Vol. 33, no. 2, pp. 186–90 [hereafter PN], p. 188)

[126] The formidable leader of the knitting women of St Antoine in *A Tale of Two Cities* (1859) by Charles Dickens.

[127] 'Till through her wasted hands at night, / You saw the taper burning.' Sir Walter Scott, 'The Maid of Neidpath'.

[128] Keats to his sister Fanny, 10 September 1817 (*Letters* I, p. 156).

[129] Book I, ll. 686–90.

[130] Vivian Rampton. See Letter 126.

[131] There was a herd of deer at Crowsley Park, near Dunsden.

[132] The full name was originally omitted in *CL* and *SL*. The source of this 'slander' could not be explained.

132. To Susan Owen

16 April 1912   *Dunsden Vicarage*

My dearest Mother,

What do you think of the latest work of Kemp's Camera?[133] I took Kemp, and I think it is splendid of him. I am not very struck with the 'Hatted' one of me, but the other appears to me very <u>natural</u>, almost animated. Would you like one to keep? Because you must please send all these three back, together with the 'unearthly' one.

This morning I went into Reading with the iron-clenched purpose of beard- ing the College Tutorial Secretary in his Den. After a long wait, I saw him, and settled to take only Botany Classes, this term:

> 2 hrs. on Tues!
> 3 hrs. on Wed ! !
> 1 hour on Thurs. (afternoon).

This is grand. Now can you let me have £3? I may be able to return it in a <u>few months'</u> time. Classes start tomorrow. So please send off my <u>Gown</u>[134] at once per G.W.R.; and with it, if you find any, <u>my</u> Shakesperes (*Julius Caesar; As You Like It; Mid Night's Dream.*) (<u>No</u> Chamber's.) I don't think I need a <u>Cap</u>. I spoke to one of the Lecturers, Miss Rayner,[135] and she seems very nice indeed. Premises and all appurtenances are <u>admirable</u>. The lady, with her satellites was photographing the eclipse[136] when I interviewed her. I was riding home at <u>12.10</u>; the sky was clear; and very weird the universe seemed; the atmosphere dulled as if charged with volcanic dust, especially on the horizon.

I am so glad you had a good time on your picnic. We go to tea at Fordhams' on Friday next.

Yes, the Vicar did speak thus contumeliously of Wordsworth; he sinned in ignorance. Did my tongue well in cleaving to the roof of my mouth?

Ah, <u>Junkets</u>, who ? Why, Jun-kēts, John Keats; (so <u>he</u> signed a letter,[137] or I should not have dared . . .) Marvel ye, that I handle thus lightly his Name? Well, thro' reading his Letters, as I have just begun to do, I see him in a truer light; not one whit less to be reverenced, and fifty whits more lovable; having so many 'wits' unrevealed to me before. He didn't lack <u>humour</u>, narrabitavit, and his <u>laugh</u> lived in many ears, long after death 'had fed on his mute voice'.[138]

Small time I now shall get for <u>private</u> reading; I am '<u>Correspondent of Dunsden School</u>'; Yes, ma'am; hi! you there, on your knees, man; don't-cher-know who I am? Fancy Colin tweaking the conk of the Correspondent of Dunsden School! All manner of red-lined accounts, greasy vouchers, and type-written letters come under my lock and key. I pull the strings, and set five teachers and a hundred scholars chattering. You know how I detest 'ledgery'. Still, I suppose, it can do no harm to gain a working knowledge of moneys and usurances.

The Vicar is hiding his nose from the Spring Dust Storms among the rocks of Clevedon. Despite household-conditions which make Study or Composition impossible, Kemp & I are having a delightsome se'nnite; 'ho, ho, ho; we make good sport, —with—ho! ho! ho!'[139]

Kemp carols, from a full heart, indeed; his Course at Highbury is a fixed thing; £200 have been raised!

I am looking forward immensely to showing Father round about, and in and out; but they said something about being unable to have him sometime at the end of the month. I don't know!

A holiday in Scotland,[140] magnificent! I suppose I shall be taken to Keswick[141] in July.

Leslie looked a very ducal personage on Monday, spoke very distinctly too. Shylock gesticulated rather well; but spoke far too choppily; every other word seemed to have a full-stop after it.

Portia & Nerissa beautifully feminine; but P. must have had a cold; positively saying—'It droppeth as a ged-tle raid from heaved upud the place bedeath.' Oh, it must have been the outcome, the issue of a bunged up nose; like something else of which the quotation is somewhat descriptive. Bassanio's (Hulcoop's) tights were all baggy!—No more of this Critique; my charge is ninepence, please.

Your own, Wilfred

[133] Probably the photograph reproduced as Plate IVb in CL and as frontispiece in JFO II.

[134] HO recalled a cap and gown at Mahim, presumably those worn by Wilfred when he took the matriculation examination in London.

[135] M[abel] M[ary] C[heveley] Rayner (d.1948) was Lecturer in Botany at University College, Reading, 1908–13. She was awarded her DSc from University College London in 1915 and published a number of textbooks on plant biology. She was one of those to whom Owen later planned to give a copy of his collected poems after the war.

[136] 16 April 1912. It began at 10.51 a.m. and reached its maximum at 12.11 (as Owen was riding home). It was the largest solar eclipse seen in the British Isles for fifty-four years.

[137] To Leigh Hunt from Margate, 10 May: 'Your sincere friend John Keats alias Junkets—' (Letters I, p. 140.).

[138] 'Death feeds on his mute voice, and laughs at our despair.' Shelley, Adonais, 1.27.

[139] Traditional ballad, 'The Mad Merry Pranks of Robin Goodfellow', the lyrics of which were influenced by A Midsummer Night's Dream.

[140] With Mrs Bulman and her family at Kelso.

[141] The Keswick Convention, an evangelical summer convention, in the Lake District run by Anglicans and Free Churchmen. It was established by Canon Thomas Hartford-Battersby, Vicar of St John's Church, Keswick, and Robert Wilson, a Quaker, and has been held every summer since 1875. It continues today.

133. To Susan Owen

23 April 1912   *Dunsden Vicarage*

Dearest Mother,

I had your Letter this morning, and your Parcel tonight! It got out of the Station before I could catch it on Sat; and Carriers have been bandying it about ever since. You must please, in future, label conspicuously—'To be left till called for—<u>not</u> per Carrier.' if it is small enough for my bicycle. Many are the thanks I owe you for so carefully detecting anything Shakesperean in my shelves. I suppose I must thank you for the cates[142] too. But you must positively send no more. I am most distressed to hear about the Bills; and I <u>do</u> wish, for your sake, a scramble might be made to get, and keep 'Cr.' The College Sec. does not seem to want my fees yet; so I shall do nothing until father brings me some 'spondoolick'[143] (as Kemp calls it). Then, in a month or two, I shall be able to repay;—if I 'take Mr. Kemp's place' on the <u>accounts</u>, as I hope I shall do <u>in space</u>; having already more than done so in the spear of dooty.

One thing in your letter made me exceedingly ratty! <u>the tent</u>;[144] scandalous; I could not make out what you meant at first; and still can't make out <u>why</u>! Cussed be Canaan a servant of servants shall he be; for dwelling in the tents of ours. Had a letter from Stanley this morning too; I'll ha' none on't. They have enough 'putheriveleges', (as Canon Barnes-Laurence would say.) Here am I, my fee for <u>one</u> course of lectures, unpaid, with no-wherewithal to buy a College Cap, or a pair of Flannels. 'The Revolutionary Ideals, crossing the Channel into England, inspired the British School of revolt and reconstruction in Burns, Shelley, Byron, Wordsworth, Coleridge and Tennyson, <u>till its fires have died down today</u>.'[145] Have they! They may have in the bosoms of the muses, but not in my breast. I am increasingly liberalising and liberating my thought, spite of the Vicar's strong Conservatism. And when he paws his beard, and wonders whether £10 is too high a price for new curtains for the dining room, (in place of the faded ones you saw); then the fires smoulder; I could shake hands with Mrs. Dilber who stole Scrooge's Bed-Curtains; and was affronted that old Joe[146] was surprised, or questioned her right! From what I hear straight from the tight-pursed lips of wolfish ploughmen in their cottages, I might say there is material ready for another revolution. Perhaps men will <u>strike</u>, not with absence from work; but with arms at work. Am I for or against upheaval? I know not; I am not happy in these thoughts; yet they press upon me. I am happier when I go to '<u>distribute dole</u>

> <u>To poor sick people, richer in His eyes,</u>
> <u>Who ransomed us, and haler too than I</u>'.[147]

These lines I quote, have haunted me incessantly. Perhaps because they are true. Anyhow, in obedience to you, <u>and certain inward monitions</u>, I have been to Dr. Gandy:[148] nominally to ask whether I can play tennis. No! No! No! and on no account to ride up hills! He sounded me most thoroughly, travelling round my trunk two or three times; and this was his conclusion <u>at once</u>. So I am eased; yes, I am glad I went.

This morning I had my first 'lecture' and also an hour's practical work with the microscope. I am sure I shall enjoy the Course.

If any more of my old set call, do tell them to <u>write</u>.

Here are some more photographs. The Best 'Smiler' is yours. The other (taken in eclipse, doncherknow) for Mary.

The one I like, and the boys, is Harold's—proviso—he takes care of it; for they are costly affairs. And we spent hours 'doing them' today; and Kemp's turned out no good; <u>though he taught me</u> with them. I mean to have one taken in gown. One of <u>these</u> for Colin. Now—no more.

Your own, Wilfred

I am really anxious to see Father again; despite the Tent affair.

<u>Can't you get your camera to take you</u>? At least you might do this; if you don't come with Father, to see your Mother-languishing <u>son</u>.

W

[142] Cates: choice foods or delicacies. HO corrected this in the MS to 'eats', which subsequently became the word printed in *CL* and *SL*.

[143] Slang for money or cash, especially a reasonable amount of spending money. Also spelled 'spondulicks' or 'spondulix'.

[144] A small tent, used in the garden at Mahim, had been lent to Stanley Webb. DH notes how 'Stanley Webb had borrowed a tent with Tom's permission. The Webbs were better off than the Owens, and Wilfred thought they could perfectly well afford to buy their own tent' (*WOANB*, p. 99).

[145] Laurie Magnus, *Introduction to Poetry* (1902), p. 146, among Owen's books. DH identified this quotation.

[146] All from *A Christmas Carol*.

[147] Tennyson, *Idylls of the King: Guinevere*.

[148] The doctor at Peppard (whose wife wrote plays and poetry and published several books for children).

139. To Susan Owen

20 May 1912   *Dunsden Vicarage*

O most sweet among Mothers,

Blessed is thy hand which writes to me so often! Blessed is thy heart which perceives the Sorrows of mine! O Blessed art thou among women!

Cheering was the testimony of a Bygone friend to thy youth and gladsomeness of countenance! And cheering thy words of counsel to me. I did not know before that weak hearts went with craven spirits. I had hoped it were otherwise.

How can I tell what a Book is going to say next! 'Lavengro'[149] is one of the most agreeable autobiographies; but suddenly Borrow must needs describe one of his fits of the horrors. These are preceded by unmistakable physical sensations. He feels the sensations coming on again and—Oh Horrors!...

Well, to return (if ever I started on them) to things more definite, you will be sorry to hear that Selwood is breathing, or trying to breathe, his last breath. He is nothing to me; but I cannot be indifferent, or dismiss him from my thoughts even in a letter. Perhaps because it puts me in mind (if ever I needed it) of another Consumptive—long ago—ah too long ago...

There I am on the old Junkets track once again, you say! And now I'm on, I'll not omit to tell you I lit on a picture of Isabella, in the Gunstons' Academy Pictures, the other day. There flourishes the Basil, tho' not so balmy as it should be, and fair Isabella kneels at a marble console-table (I leave the pun on this to you). Her features are almost those of Keats himself (feminised)—I suppose intentionally.

Now I do think you should have had yourself 'snapped' before you sent the camera. Oh how do I stand (yes and sit, lie, kneel & walk, too,) in need of some tangible caress from you.

Ink-slung ones are all very well in their way, and no one appreciates them more than I do; but my affections are physical as well as abstract—intensely so— and confound 'em for that, it shouldn't be so.

What if I feel 'strange' in your company after all this time apart; as I have done before after but a fortnight—surely that was the same I and the same you.

Then, when I recall the past, I often feel pretty sick at all the abominable rude-nesses, ingratitudes, huffs, grumps, snaps, and sulks levelled at you. Oh my works do follow me

---

How marvellously you have wrought upon my garments. And how well-packed was the parcel! What cannot you darn between Sun & Moon? I found something in a pocket! That was tangible, and mange-able too. I must not write more—my head troubles me, which it has not done for months. And a weird kind of spiral

has been rolling round and round in front of my vision—what ever I look at; so to bed—and sleep it off.

Goodbye, which being interpreted, is God be with you.

Wilfred.

[149] *Lavengro: The Scholar, the Gypsy, the Priest* by George Barrow (John Murray, 1851).

142. To Susan Owen

12 June 1912   *Dunsden Vicarage*

Dearest Mother,

It was very good of you to be writing for my Tuesday pleasure at 10 p.m. on Sunday. As it happens it is just that time now, on Tuesday.

Public & Business Matters are very pressing just now, & I must deal with them first. I answered that U.C.C. Letter indecisively & <u>not</u> in the negative. I daren't do anything till the Vicar comes home. But as 3 months of the Course-Time have lapsed, and as you are or were wanting me to 'put off till yet another year'; and as opportunities for reading are not abundant here; and as my Latin is so tarnished; and as my machinery has a wonderful exhaust-system; perhaps I will wait till <u>1914</u>! What a time, alas! Seemingly, <u>too long</u>! But a brilliant idea seizes me! I will take one or more <u>Honours</u> if I take that unconscionable time over the Business!

What this means you will please learn from p. 30 and pp. 3–7 (Intro.) of the Guide, I am sending for your & Father's reference.

What you think after reading this (& as much other pertinent matter as you can e.g. Syllabuses) I shall be interested to know.

Just now I am in a fearful stew about it all. I know I could <u>pass</u> in 1913 with <u>all day free</u>,—other factors of course being propitious. But the last U.C.C. letter warns me I want 400 hours study in each subject. i.e. 400 hrs. x 5 = 2,000 hrs. Taking 1 day = 5 hours, nearly I require 400 days, or 18 mths. allowing for Sundays, Holidays, Illness (?) etc.

The Vicar 'said something' about teaching me Greek. I dread it; and Hebrew & all Theological dustiness. But would substitute it for Latin willingly; and am going to attack the Vicar about it. I should love to read Greek; whose spirit giveth life to so much poetry: <u>only the letter killeth</u>.

One thing I may state, and that is—I definitely abandon the <u>thought</u> of Divinity Training <u>till</u> at least an Arts Degree is won. Such at present is my resolve. All Theological lore is growing distasteful to me. All my recent excursions into such fields proves it to be a shifting, hypothetical, doubt-fostering, dusty and unprofitable study. Such a conclusion at my time of life is not to be wondered at. It may change hereafter. All I can now is to groan with Meredith:

> 'Ah what a <u>dusty answer</u> gets the soul
> When hot for certainties in this our life.'[150]

I need not this as a Wall-Text, though they are the verses of Meredith which have more than <u>any</u> others, appealed to me. <u>I</u> see them after 'Finis' in every book which takes upon itself to answer the soul with 'certainties.'

———————————————

I am sorry this important letter is so badly written. It is not Private to the Addressed unless you choose to consider it so.

Do not haste to answer it; and be not at pains to concoct a sedative reply. I can come to no Fixation of Plans till I get closeted with the Vicar.

Meantime I <u>may</u> dissipate these clouds by a day at Shakespere's England. The Vicar wrote to ask me and the Fordhams to join him tomorrow in Town. I have not heard more. But I know the F.s' have backed out. I have every respect for Mr. F. as 'a fellow that hath had losses; and one that hath two gowns, and everything handsome about him',*[151] but I should choose him last of all people as a companion round Shakesperean realms.

Methinks, 'that unlettered, small-knowing soul'†[152] would worry me beyond bearing if he began to pat Wild Will on the back: an actor too! and dead against his principles!

'He hath never fed of the dainties that are bred in a book‡;'[153] however admirable his appearance, diction and cosmogony may be.

Have you seen anything about a Keats-Shelley Matinée[154] in London? I am nearly beside myself to know more; and I <u>told the Vicar</u> I was fluttered! Leading exponents are going to recite <u>and sing!</u>

Here is a letter from Kemp. Really interesting, isn't it?

Adieu, sweet Mother. Give me particulars of your pulse, when next you write. I think about it, oftener than mine own.

Your loving, Wilfred

*Shakespere.   †Shakespere.   ‡Shakespere.
Can I get Cheap Tickets again?

[150] George Meredith, *Modern Love: L*, ll. 11–12.
[151] *Much Ado about Nothing*, IV, ii, l. 92.
[152] *Love's Labour's Lost*, I, I, l. 251.
[153] *Love's Labour's Lost*, IV, ii, l. 25.
[154] Two special matinees took place on 25 and 28 June at the Haymarket Theatre to raise funds for the Keats–Shelley Memorial House in Rome. Marie Löhr, Ellen Terry, and others recited poems by Keats and Shelley, and there were also songs and tableaux.

143. To Mary Owen

23 June 1912   *Dunsden Vicarage*

My dear Mary,

I wonder how you are feeling today. I hope you are now in such a <u>taedium vitae</u> as I am; I, having already given two discourses to boys of 14 and 4 respectively; as well as attending two Church Services myself. Evening Service is coming on apace; so I seize this hour for a Letter to you; which I must write <u>currente calamo. O sancta simplicitas!</u> I perceive I am in a Latin strain just now. Pray have your English Dictionary to hand; open to 'Words & Phrases from Latin'; or else this example of my cacoēthis scribendi will be a caput mortuum to you.

On the night preceding the morning when Mother told me you were fallen in recrudescence, I dreamed of you. You were decked in fine raiment, and methought I was treating you to a Show at a Picture Palace! Absit omen! When inside, we found ourselves surrounded by religio loci, in the form of the Sowers' Band. And so we made merry.

'Twas but one of my frequent aegri somnia—brought on my a magnificent romp with the Sowers, and the inevitable amabilis insania—must I call it—that you may some day be imbued with like spirits and like lissome limbs.

The firm Superintendent of their Sunday School, the silence-loving, and the melancholy-voiced, on that day capered about the lawn among them, a very Pan amid the nymphs. To Charades, 'Old Man from Botany Bay',[155] and so on, I initiated them; and great was the delight. Oh! dulce est desipere in loco! Amantes: Amantes!

Mrs. Lott's River Trip is to be next Tuesday. Most of the anile population of this aldea compose the Party. Our destination is Dorchester.[156]

On Monday Week the Choir draws me with it to Bournemouth. I may possibly be taken to Shakespeare's England. I am not very keen. Unless we see a representation in The Model of the Globe,[157] I doubt if there is much of interest. Not to see a play, and yet to go to the Place seems to be saying to Shakespeare, (whatever that name may represent): 'Yes, have done wondrous works, and we quite appreciate you'—but crying, as soon as he would open his mouth as it were, 'Hold your tongue—we wouldn't listen to you for worlds.'

. . . . .

O tempora, O mores! The meanest seat at the Keats-Shelley Matinée is 7/6!

In one way this is very flattering. In what more forcible way can the man of the world be made to set value on a Poet, than by seeing the Price at his Matinée is 30s!

But that those two names should ever help to breed in me amor sceleratus habiendi! How long shall 'virtus post nummos' be detestable to me, when such spirits are under the foot of Mammon. I feel inclined to hang on my wall that striking picture in Bibby's Annual[158] (of Mammon) and buffet it daily.

When Mother asks whether I state my sum of ducats available for holiday-expenses, you must say 'zonam perdidit', for I shall only have about two gold pounds.

I thought at first, when Mother's letter came—'adieu paniers, vendanges sont faites!'[159] but tomorrow I got to make enquiries as Mother directs; and my reluctantly-closed volumes [one sheet missing]

My own countree likewise begins to feel romantic—if these lines
    are true—
'Where Severn flows she stands, —the encircled town.
Two spires uplift the jewels of her crown,
Two bridges are the portals to her feet.
Through Wyle Cop to Dogpole climbs the street,
And westward to the hills down Mardol goes,
            Where Severn flows.'

These verses are not mine; I <u>don't</u> wish they were. I came across them in my
deporably desulatory reading.

<u>Basta!</u> I must keep my [*one line missing, one line illegible*] loosen my tongue.

Do not get impatient with the formidable <u>loci classici</u> here given; and tear up
the whole <u>amphigouri</u>.

<u>Aequam memento rebus in arduis servare mentem.</u>

Forgive and forget!

Your most loving, Wilfred

Mrs. Ambrose's address
1. Bishop's Lands,
        nr. Kidmore End,
            Reading
or 2. Royal Berkshire Hospital,
    Reading

[155] A game invented by Tom Owen.
[156] Dorchester-on-Thames, 16 miles upriver from Reading. But the excursion got no farther
than Wallingford. See Letter 144.
[157] A model of the Globe Theatre was a feature of this Earls Court exhibition. See Letter 156.
[158] See Letter 545, n. 211
[159] From 'À son ami, Chapelain', by Honorat de Bueil, seigneur de Racan (1589–1670).

144. To Mary Owen

27 June 1912   *Dunsden Vicarage*

Dear Mary,

What an idiot I was to send you such a letter! And what a marvel you are in
spite of it! I think Mother's Card must have carried something of the Malady to
me; for as I was reading Scott this morning an obstinate Black Spot foisted itself
upon the Print; and danced in front of me, like a malicious goblin. Finally it took
this shape

and appeared to be going round in opposite directions at the same time. This phenomenon so flabbergasted me that I lay down and dozed; but at lunch time woke up with a violent headache. After lunch I felt sick; but went out to do some business at the school, and tried to get into Reading. Finally I became so afraid of losing some of that refractory lunch upon the road that I made all speed home and slept again—until even now, when I am better already. There is going to be a meeting in the Hall to explain the Insurance Act,[160] tonight. I hope to be able to go.

Now, in order to prevent any germs of my latest complaint communicating themselves to you through this letter I will sprinkle it with that excellent disinfectant <u>mirth</u>—and tell you something of our river trip last Tuesday.

The clouds hung very heavily when we embarked; and at odd moments swelled so tremendously about the waist and cheeks that they had perforce to drop some of their fatness to earth—as the Psalmist hath it—as a balloonist might drop sand.

We started more than half an hour late—the last arrivals being the Fordhams. Annette by some extraordinary manoeuvring soon anchored herself by me; and as I looked so extremely happy, as the Vicar said, his riverence rallied me on the subject afterwards. Bless his soul—I <u>was</u> happy. For one thing the old <u>ladies</u> (as Mother would say) puffed and blinked so complacently in their snug quarters astern and in the bows, that it was a sight to be thankful for. Then, then... (see how candid I am—don't betray me) the cargo was not all anile, and behold, in blissful proximity, mine own favourite Milly![161] My favourite boys were not aboard; instead a regular rascal (as I had thought him) was there. Oft had I been down on him like a load of bricks at the Scrip. Union; and indeed he needed it. At school he goes by the universal name of 'Knowledge'—of course because that commodity has no part in his being. Well, on the boat, I 'noticed' him, so to speak; chatted with him, and joked; and was astonished to find what good points, what tender ones, are hidden under the somewhat spiky ones that fringe his shaggy head. The <u>comble</u> (there I am again—I mean the crowning-point) came when for about quarter of an hour, he fought Milly for the place next to me. Sometimes the struggle was subdued, and carried on by craft; sometimes it was a matter of elbow-point and finger-nail. No interesting sights on the banks could make Knowledge

forget to squeeze up to my side; no bribery could tempt him to go below for
lemonade. Until at last he was caught napping and Beauty won. The adjacent
good folk were immensely amused at all this; but they saw not the magnificent Allegory therein: <u>Knowledge</u> and <u>Beauty</u> wrestling for me! Heaven for-
fend that they should be antagonistic forces in my life; and that Beauty should
win!...

Why! I had almost forgotten the most important thing of the day—
incessant rain all morning. I preferred the dry but 'thick' air of the tiny cabin to
the sodden deck, & the views of the sodden fields seen from underneath a sodden overcoat; so I stayed below all the way there. Coming back, however, it
cleared; and everything was delightful.

We had about two hours at Wallingford; where the Vicar took me (only) to a
Hôtel. We had an excellent lunch of *'Poulet Fricassé'*, green peas, etc. —and—veil
not thy face, O Goddess Temperentia—a whopping beaker of Cider each!

Then the Vicar explored the Antique Shops. For tea, we moored up against a
beech-wooded escarpment, miles long, on the left bank.

I and three élite, adventuresome children climbed to the top; and came down
at a breathless rate; nursing the delicious fear that the boat had gone. Sailing
home, Hymns were sung; but as different ones were crooning astern and 'fore,
and I was just between, it was anything but pleasant.

We reached Caversham about 7.30; and I of course rode home; but I thought
of two little feet that had to <u>walk</u>, even to beyond the Vicarage, and was troubled.

So ended that happy day; and I kept an aromatic weed, the Sweet Flag,
(*Acorus*, N. Order *Orontiaceae*, don't you know) as a '<u>memory</u>', as the children
called it. I didn't correct them. Memento is an infinitely less pretty word for
such a thing than 'memory'.

Childe Mary, I hope <u>we</u> are to have many such happy days, before long! Keep
battling Unhealth; and I will do the same. And having won, watch dear, dear
Mother that she overstrain not herself at this time.

I am expecting to hear very soon what Father has ascertained about my journey. The Vicar must be told. I am not particularly anxious to go to Meols; but
'shouldn't mind if I did.'

'God bless you, my dear Sister.'

Your loving Brother, Wilfred

[160] Lloyd George's 'Medical Panel', the first form of National Insurance and the introduction
of the panel doctor system.
[161] Milly Montague. Her brother Willie was a stable boy and the Montagues lived next to the
Ramptons at Binfield Heath at Dunsden. She was the same age as Vivian Rampton.

146. To Susan Owen

2 July 1912   *Dunsden Vicarage*

Dearest Mother,

Your proposal to hustle me up in 1 day I readily accept, seeing it concerns pretty well all at Pringle Bank. Of course Mrs. Lott will find, (I sh'd say <u>has found</u>) no objection whatever to the time. What's 6 o'clock to me! who got up the other day at 3! Your dictum about my not wanting books from Shrewsbury, must be either ironical or abjectly unreasonable. Of course I want my Scotts'; and I wonder whether Mrs. Davies has the key of the house, & could open my Bookcase & send them; as well as Wordsworth. Fancy being among the Lakes without e'er a Wordsworth!—But perhaps you will be home before I need this last.

I am so glad you are enjoying the place and its enabitants; and that your constigution (as a man said to me this afternoon) is hundergoin' a 'ealthy chinge.

I am in a perfect daze as regards the past few days. I rose (bitterly regretting I had ever promised to join such a detestable Excursion) at three o'clock; had breakfast by semi-candlelight; and issued forth in old clothes into the raw air; was taken in a wagonette to the Station; with the Boys in a van in front; and entered the compartment labeled 'Dunsden' which might as well have been ticketed Demonsden or my compartment in Purgatory itself. Such a flesh-tortured three hours did I spend in it. The Vicar perhaps had the worst time of it going—pins stuck into all his limbs paper missiles flicked at him from teeth-holden catapults—his hat snatched away—his paper bashed about and so on. It is only fair to state, however, that now and again he would grasp an urchin, and thwack, lam, hide, beat, belabour, whack, smack, flog, flail, thump, lick, and kick the creature till the tears swam round its eyes. Coming home, I was the sufferer; for I kept slipping into Lethe, and being pulled out again by the frantic behaviour of one boy—who, being quick-witted and fond of leading, managed to make everybody laugh at him—and confirmed for some two hours in a state of what would be called advanced intoxication in a man. The Vicar sat like a log through it all; and seemed to see, feel, hear and think of—nothing. Not even did he show the least sign of perturbation when the Arch-imp shrieked 'Here comes Satan! Here's the Devil!' on seeing his own reflection on the Carriage-Window.

For my part, I quite believed it, and offered no contradiction.

As for Bournemouth itself it was just enjoyable—only just. Though I have not seen the sea for more than twelve months (isn't it) I have been so often at the Sea Side in Day-dreams of late, that its Sights, Sounds and Circumstance hadn't an atom of freshness about them. I took note of this fact with surprise and regret.

I shouldn't like to say it was altogether a Sign of a stronger imagination; because Bournemouth Cliffs, Pier, Steamers, & Sands and especially the Model-Boat-Canal were positively as familiar to me as Shrewsbury is now; simply through having gazed on them so long and longingly thro' Uncle John's Stereoscopic Views ! !

As on Tuesday last, the heavens were graciously disposed to be liberal of rain, and we had it fine at short intervals only! In the afternoon I conducted a party of 18 over to Swanage, the Vicar slinking away to Bro. Lingley's[162] home. Our home-coming in the carts through the midnight roads was most romantic. Only a *Feuilletonist*[163] could do justice to it—thus—'That night, a stranger might have marked, as the midnight moon rose dimly above the woods, a carriage slowly travelling through the sleeping countryside; a carriage in which six dark forms were discernible.' One of these was a Clergyman of the Established Church, an Oxford man, of very <u>decided</u> and <u>one</u>sided religious beliefs, and one who held his <u>pedigree</u> very proudly indeed. By him, sat an Elementary School-master, of Elementary Education and elementary manners, reading, and powers of thought; a man of very orthodox religious beliefs and very ordinary income; a fellow of a sharp and quick-condemning tongue, with eyes to correspond; and one who carried his <u>petty-grievances</u> very proudly indeed. By <u>him</u>, sat a <u>Ploughman;</u> whose calling, however, could not be well made out (unless it were by a certain earthy, soddy, cloddy cast of face) for he now grinned from between the lobes of a wonderful collar, and bore upon his left chest half the floral production of his garden. Then there was a bushy-browed and horny-fisted <u>blacksmith's assistant</u>; who calls for no mention save that from his cavernous mouth rose vapours which had their origin in Burton-on-Trent.

Fifth of the company, (also suggestive, somehow, of the Roman Numeral XXX or the Clef) was a taciturn, rusty-voiced man—a <u>gardener and coachman</u> both—now uttering his annual marvel of 10 words in succession.

Lastly, that carriage held a youth—a student and a philosopher by the thoughts that ran in his head; an invalid and a poet, by the pulse that coursed in his veins; and a fellow of fine palate by the victuals that slept in his stomach. Ah, and a Lover of sleep, too, by the lead that hung on his lids. A poor youth, look you, by his clothes; yet a rich one by his hands. A Poet, again, by his economy in Barber's Bills—and by his frequent glances at the rising moon...

What brought these strangely different beings together? What sentiment allows them to converse? O Clotho, Lachesis, Atropos! How have ye brought their threads of life within so small a ring as the circle of this vehicle? [*final sheet missing*]

---

[162] The Rev. Trevor Hope Lingley, at this time living at Parkstone, Dorset. He had visited Dunsden.

[163] A *feuilleton* in French newspapers was a ruled-off space devoted to fiction, criticism, or light essays.

148. To Susan Owen

21 July 1912   *Keswick*

Dearest Mother,

I am housed here at last. I left Keswick without any definite idea of my lodging but found my way, with difficulty, to this Camp, about a mile & a half from the Town. Arrangements had been made for me, & I was shown a tent with three beds, on this level

—No other furniture whatever except <u>one</u> blanket (of stuff like sack-cloth)! We have meals in a large Marquee. The fare is very ordinary indeed; and the tea is horrid—just enough milk to make it muddy. Very different state of things from Kelso yes and Yetholm[164] too. Never mind, it will sharpen my appetite for Home.

My Camp-anion is perhaps the very one I sh'd have chosen among the arrivals so far—a divinity student from Durham.

Last night—our first—we hardly slept a wink—such was the force of the wind. Our tent thundered and creaked and shivered under the rain most frightfully; and at last we were positively nervous lest the pole sh'd come crashing down on one of our 'nuts'. All night the Captains or whatever they are called were going round; malleting & tightening or loosening cords: and on one of their rounds we heard the cry of 'tent down' next to us. We had heard not a sound of its fall; and wondered what it would be like to be struggling under a fallen canvas with no one to let us out—for the wretched bosses <u>would</u> sew—or somehow fasten—our tent door tight!

Since writing this ¶. we have had Tea; & some fifty men have now come. Some are absolute boors; downright 'dizguzders' over their meal; old blear-eyed horny-handers, some of them; but they are likely to be <u>sober</u> dogs; and men that fear Heaven, look you; which is not what I could say of my late companion, the wondrous-witty John;[165] whose sobriety, I find, is as noteworthy as that of most medical students.

I could say more on that point, but I see no use in it; unless it were to point out that a normal, manly, fellow like John or Bill,[166] might after all <u>not</u> be preferable as a son—to an eccentric being like me. I had my wits about me during the journey; and yet found that my luggage was not about me at Penrith. Some blighter of a porter put it in the wrong coach—for I saw it put in—; however it came on to Penrith by a later train. I have got Father's shoes and Cigar case; and I hope you will get the fishing rods all right. I spent 4 or 5 hours on Flodden Field; and saw the whole thing enacted to my great satisfaction—and to Blanche's[167] inward displeasure, it may be. I fancy an Englishwoman had something to do with James' weakness on the battlefield—anyhow I was not going to let a Scots girl spoil my contemplation there by dragging me to places I didn't want to see. As it was we cycled 28 miles, & walked several more! You will observe I have not a word to say about mountains or lakes or streams—Surely if Wordswth., Coleridge, Southey, Shelley, and Ruskin made it a matter of years to describe them, I cannot do so now, in this flapping, windy pavilion; with tongues, plates, piano, and such-like dinning around me.

Ever your loving Wilfred

P.S. [*top of page cut off*] as soon as you have my address.

P.P.S. I was much refreshed when seeking my luggage at the stn. to see Vera and Dorothy (and Miss F. this time upon the platform—and created quite a sensation among the Conventionists by my <u>unconventionally</u> enthusiastic greeting of them. (Except for that moment, when I was in a stew, I have been too cold rather than too warm, & simply can't understand your heat wave.)

---

[164] A village in the Cheviots, 7 miles south-east of Kelso, where the Bulmans, old family friends, had a cottage. Owen had stayed there before going on to the evangelical summer convention at Keswick. 'Aunt Nelly' Bulman, née Roderick, widow of a prosperous builder, was the daughter of the local physician in Oswestry who had supervised the birth of Wilfred Owen at Plas Wilmot. Nelly and Susan remained close friends. She lived at Pringle Bank, 'a handsome old house in Kelso' and 'discovered that the Owens' circumstances were less than prosperous, so she and her grown-up children, John, Bill and Blanche, had planned the perfect holiday for them' (DH, WOANB, p. 104). The Bulmans also had a country cottage at Yelholm.

[165] The elder of the two Bulman sons, a medical student. Later he had a general practice in Hereford, where he died in 1960.

[166] The younger Bulman son. He was killed at Gallipoli in July 1915.

[167] Blanche Bulman. Owen took a copy of Scott's *Marmion: A Tale of Flodden Field* with him on this expedition; facing the title page he drew a pencil sketch of the scene inscribed 'Among the Cheviots, July 1912'. The copy survives in Owen's Library in the Bodleian.

149. To Susan Owen

Wednesday 24 July 1912   *Penrith Road Keswick*

My own dear Mother,

I found on reading Mr. Collingwood's *Ruskin*[168] that Ruskin (my King <u>John</u> the Second) used to write elaborate (or at least full) letters to his anxious parents <u>every single day,</u> when he was once in one part of Switzerland and they in another; and that a remissness in this respect—say of three days would put Mama in a rare flutter.

Inspired by this ensample I sit me down on my tent floor, & leaning on my fair green trunk, do pencil the following. I may say that I have had to 'cut' family worship for the purpose, and that I can hear at this moment every word that is being said there; and am forced by very proximity of it, to hear another Prayer Meeting in my next-door tent; groaning at the <u>bottom</u> of its voice.

This Camp is a magnificent thing in one respect; I am thrown into the Society of just as many varieties of my species as I am capable of taking stock of during a week. Irishmen, Scotchmen, Englishmen & a German, from all parts—(including Birkenhead, Shrewsbury etc.) and drawn from all ranks.

I have 3 others in my tent now—all from different colleges in Durham University. Socially, I suppose they are the pick of the Camp, but they are really not at all interesting…We are very merry together, and agreed to have our photos taken before the tent. <u>My</u> suggestion (I believe) of having it done in pyjamas (as the Photographer was coming early in the morning) was highly acceptable to the rest, who proposed the addition of turbans (of towels). I hope it will be a success.

Of course the whole Camp has been 'done' and this has indeed turned out very well.

There is, in a tent remote from mine, a Northumberland lad who works in the pits, whose soul-life and Christianity is altogether beyond my understanding. He has absolute peace of mind; faith before which mountains not only sink, but never become visible; and most other virtues of which the Keswick Platform speaks. The watching of his conduct, conversation, expression of countenance during meetings, bids fair to speak louder to my soul than the thunderings of twenty latter-day Prophets from their rostra upon these everlasting hills.

While your sleek Thomas, Hopkins, Dixon, Holden, Scroggie,[169] and the rest of these double-barrelled guns, whose double-barrelled names I refuse to write, while they, I say, <u>preach</u> that <u>preaching</u> is no witness of a Christian Soul, your scar-backed mining-lad <u>acts</u> that acting <u>is</u> efficient. Scar-backed, I say, through running along subterranean 'roads' four feet high, and scraping against its jagged roof. And while my guide to Edinburgh would calmly send people to the Devil for no greater provocation than say having an ugly face, this youth lets no profane word pass his lips, tho' pricked with piercing pain and surrounded by the grossest human mud that ever sank to a pit's bottom.

Another interesting thing, a good antidote to student-superciliousness, is that this pit-lad is wrestling with a Class-book of Physics—and taking Correspondence Tuition in the Arts of Mining. He has no holiday and during this week, his pay is stopped.

Now I must return to myself—and chronicle that I have bathed in the lake; climbed Latrigg, seen the views from Castle Head, and Friar's Crag;[170] bought a pile of post-cards; had my hair cut (atrociously); and had my bicycle badly treated by an unauthorised borrower. It is right now; and I made the fellow pay (1s.)

I don't know what to say or think of dear Mary. I must bring her a present. Don't be anxious about me. I am feeling more energetic as the days pass. Great thanks for the parcel & letters.

Ever your loving Wilfred

[168] William Gershom Collingwood (1854–1932), Ruskin's private secretary and later his biographer, was Professor of Fine Art at the University of Reading. His home was at Coniston in the Lake District.

[169] Rev Dr W. H. Griffith Thomas, the Rev. Evan H. Hopkins, Rev Dr A.C. Dixon, Rev Dr J. Stuart Holden, and Rev Dr. W. Graham Scroggie were eminent in evangelical circles, and regular speakers at the Keswick Convention. See *Keswick's Authentic Voice: Sixty-Five Dynamic Addresses Delivered at the Keswick Convention. 1875–1957*, ed. Herbert F. Stevenson (London: Marshall, Morgan & Scott, 1959) for examples of their sermons.

[170] Three peaks in the Keswick area of the Lake District.

150. To Susan Owen

August 1912 (Alack the day!)   *Dunsden Vicarage (Alas!)*

My own sweet Mother,

I didn't bring your pre-addressed envelope; so I mean to sport a penny letter already. I have had tea, and do not feel like laying my hand to anything except a letter to your dear self…

I don't know whether it be a sign of moral decadence,* or the unsurmountable force of circumstances, or what, but I never felt so near giving vent to emotion as this morning. I know not what <u>you</u> returned to the solitary house to do; but I know that I am glad I was the only occupant of my compartment.…

> 'Tears, idle tears, I know not what they mean,
> Tears from the depth of some divine despair,
> Rise in the heart, and gather to the eyes,
> In passing by the happy Autumn fields
> And thinking of the days that are no more.'[171]

These lines might have been written for me so true to my state are they —tho' I did not think of them at the time.

But when I got here, flabby and unstable as I felt, I tried to set down verses more entirely my own. You shall see them some day.

I am getting to like railway journeys less and less. Can't understand it, but they quite upset me. I was thankful to be across my bicycle again, and gathered strength as I passed, well-loaded, along 'the sweet security of our streets.'[172]

Now it is quarter past six; a thunderstorm has just broken overhead. The feeling of pent-up grief has not left me yet—<u>not</u> altogether an unpleasant feeling, but so strange and unusual—(I am thankful for <u>that</u>).

Your provisions were over-ample; but I was glad to finish them when I arrived here at about 3.30. Only all these touching instances of your care add to my inward wretchedness of spirit just now.

I have sent a card to Mary.

Lightning & thunder and rain fill the air. (Fearfully near)

> 'When shall we two meet again
> In thunder, lightening, or in rain?'[173]

Ah when? Dunsden is already distressingly familiar; and all I love proportionately remote. I never felt so sorry to leave as this time (Uriconium has nothing to do with it) is the poor plaint

of your adoring Wilfred

* As Ch. Lamb, long 'alcoholised', would grieve to find himself involuntarily weeping, often and often.

[171] Tennyson, *The Princess*, iv, Introductory Song, l. 21.
[172] Charles Lamb (1775–1834), *The Essays of Elia*, 'New Year's Eve' (1820): 'I am in love with this green earth; the face of town and country; the unspeakable rural solitudes, and the sweet security of streets. I would set up my tabernacle here.'
[173] After *Macbeth*, I, i,1l. 1–2.

151. To Susan Owen

7.40 p.m., 14 August 1912

From the extra-specially easy chair,
In The Study
Of Dunsden Vicarage

My own dear Mother,

I wonder what you will think of these my first (complete) productions in photography?

I am certainly proud of the profile one of you. For in spite of many blemishes of background, and fogged top of plate, etc. I do think that this represents in a wonderful way your side-appearance, and if nothing else were satisfactory, the hand itself is a study.

I wonder whether you are noticing anything unusual in <u>my</u> hand-writing? Its only because I am writing without a supporting desk. The fact is, however, my left knuckles are very considerably lacerated. Just by the Well (in the P.C.'s I left out purposely for you,) I had the most violent side-slip I have yet endured. (Miss Wigan[174] badly hurt her face on this very spot from this very cause—only I didn't know till after my fall.) I was hardly off the machine 10 seconds; for no bones were broken; only the left knuckles, knee, and elbow grazed.

I soon reached the Vicarage, losing only half a dozen drops of blood from my hand, and felt remarkably unshaken. I purposed to whisk over to Alpenrose, and have first aid from one of the experts there. Meanwhile I had summoned the Temporary Housekeeper[175] to bring bandages. (The Lotts are away & Edith was out &, of course, the Vicar is away.) I was washing some of the dirt out of the wound, & had applied some of my Carbolic Ointment, when sudden twilight seemed to fall upon the world, an horror of great darkness closed around me—strange noises and a sensation of swimming under water overtook me, and in fact I fell into a regular syncope. I did not fall down however, nor yet lose all conciousness; but the semi-blindness, and the chill were frightful.

I murmured something about Brandy to Adelaide (who had little idea of what to do, & who was as white as the proverbial sheet, (in reflection no doubt from me.)

When she brought up the whiskey, I had groped right away to another room! and found myself gasping at a window, without quite knowing how I got there. I must have implored for the doctor, for Adelaide sent off the Boy poste-haste into Caversham. He had hardly gone when my senses began to return—O it was a blissful moment when the lights were turned up again in my head! And the sensation of quickening circulation & warmth was like the Return of Spring for deliciousness. I found myself indeed in an icy sweat and of a really beautiful and romantic pallor. Half an hour later I had tea, & was keenly hungry. Since then, the doctor has been, & has sent up boracic things. I got Edith to call for Dorothy when she cycled in for the Lints, and dear old D. duly came and bandaged to my satisfaction....

Now I have related everything most circumstantially, and there is nothing more to be said. You will not be able to make much of it—I had made the matter as big as it will be made. The grazes are trifling after all. And I am feeling now quite normal, and what is more, pleasantly sleepy. So I will off to bed.

Nay I will stay to gossip—that you may see how lucid my mind is, and how calm my feelings.

I had a presentiment that something of note would happen shortly.

Further, I was riding away from an old man to whom I had been reading Spurgeon[176]—and the burden of the Sermon was the fact that our lives are 'leased by seconds—not by seventy years, thirty years, five years.' 'Not more frail are flowers, more fragile moths . . . or more fleeting meteors than Human Life.'

I was even moralising on this when I tried to put it into practice!— I remember hearing that a week or so ago Kemp had an accident—& damaged his machine!

These occasional minor mishaps do a great deal of good. They make one careful for many months to follow.

By the time this reaches you I must be getting into order for the dentist. I have an appointment on Friday.

Many, many thanks for your dear letter.

Hope I have made this <u>interesting</u>, at least.

Your (but for a sq. centimetre or two) whole, safe, sound, unsuffering, cheerful

Son, Wilfred

¹⁷⁴ The vicar's sister. She did not visit her brother during Owen's stay.

¹⁷⁵ Adelaide, Mrs Lott, Edith the maid, Bray the gardener, and the boy (Frank) constituted the permanent vicarage staff.

¹⁷⁶ Charles Haddon Spurgeon (1834–92), Baptist preacher and religious writer who founded a pastors' college, an orphanage, a Christian literature society, and *The Sword and Trowel* magazine. He was pastor for thirty-eight years at the Metropolitan Tabernacle at Elephant and Castle in London, which had space for 5,000–6,000 worshippers. The building Spurgeon knew burnt down in 1898, was rebuilt, then was bombed during the Second World War. The current Metropolitan Tabernacle dates from 1956 and incorporates the original portico.

156. To Susan Owen

Monday, 9 September 1912   *Dunsden Vicarage*

My most filial-neglected Mother,

Why have I been so long in writing again? Perhaps because of the very quantity of matter to tell you.

On Sunday before last I had a Children's Service.

On Monday following, Bro. Kemp came over, & stayed till Wednesday.

His friend Morley, B.A. of Camb. has been here Wed. to Saturday. Morley, if thro' Ordination Exam, is becoming a Curate in Reading. It was rather novel to see the ins and outs of this business; to hear him telling himself he must get a Frock Coat and Top Hat even if he goes to his Cure in debt. He plays the callow Deacon very creditably, and the clerical flavour will soon be part of himself. But—(I should say—Hence) he has a very solid opinion of himself, and thinks his energy, command, erudition and such like in public speaking are wonderful, though a more stodgy, plodding, dough-faced candidate I have never met.

Good old Kemp was a delight to have here again. He says the like of being at Dunsden; but, poor fellow, a meal he had alone with the Lord Vicar of the Parish of Dunsden, was enough to remind him that all is not Elysian here.

On Wednesday, however, I had cause to feel all gratefulness to his reverence; for he remembered his promise of taking me to Town. Best of all, he gave me the leash all day.

My first move was to Watson's,¹⁷⁷ High Holborn. There I underwent the long feared test; and was told the inevitable thing—'Your eyes badly need Glasses. You have pronounced Astigmatism, Hypermetropia, and all the rest.'—Was ever

optician said otherwise to a client? Well, I had to submit, and have received spectacles to be worn reading, and walking, eating, and standing and sitting and
laughing & crying, and coughing & sneezing…I presume I may behold Dream-
Objects without them?

From Chancery Lane I looked in at the Brit. Mus. to see one or two things
I wanted to;[177] thence to the New London Museum,[179] but found it closed that
day, and so straight to Earl's Court. I was highly pleased with the reconstruction
of Shakespere's Globe Theatre.[180] I was just in time to see the very play on my
Exam. Syllabus *The Tempest*. All was conducted on rigorously Elizabethan lines,
and the effect was most instructive to a student; tho' the acting was in parts but
so so. We took an early train home—fortunately, for driving over Caversham
Bridge I spotted a Biplane, high in the Western Sky. My first sight of such craft
was as impressive as I could have devised. Scarcely a breath of wind—the calm,
yellow sunset sky, and the planes gliding smoother than wings, and so high that
the engines are perfectly inaudible…

Och! Here comes Mrs. Lott, breathless, saying Frank waits for letters.

More very soon, W

[177] W. Watson and Sons Ltd, 313 High Holborn, the scientific instrument makers and opti-
cians where Gordon Gunston was then working.
[178] 'On Seeing a Lock of Keats's Hair' was written during the summer of 1912. See *CPF*,
vol. 2, p. 446.
[179] The London Museum opened at Kensington Palace in Hyde Park in 1912 and in 1914
moved to Lancaster House, in the West End of London. Closed during the Second World War,
the Museum reopened in 1951 in Kensington Palace and in 1965 was amalgamated with the
Guildhall Museum (founded 1826) under the Museum of London Act. The Museum of London
was opened in 1976 at London Wall in the city of London. It closed in December 2022. It will
reopen as the London Museum in 2026 at West Smithfield.
[180] A model of the Globe Theatre was a feature of 'Shakespeare's England', a 1912 Earls Court
exhibition.

157. To Susan Owen

17 September 1912   *Dunsden Vicarage*

My dearest Mother,

Your letter was one of five received this morning—quite an unusual bundle.
Needless to say it was the one I opened first and shall try to keep longest. My letters
are so accumulating that I am trying to systematize their storage.

Leslie, the invaluable, has brought to my notice the *Bookman* Souvenir
Number of Keats & Shelley.[181] It has proved the best shillings-worth I have bought
for a long time. I could scarcely eat my tea for excitement when I first looked
through it. It is teeming with fascinating Pictures. I have to tell the truth, scarcely

looked at the articles yet. It is too oppressing to think how many great minds have exerted themselves for his sake, and for Shelley's.

Marie Corelli,[182] bless her, has done her best to effuse on 'Severn…lift… me…up.' But I cannot forbear quoting Lowell's[183] Sonnet 'To the Spirit of Keats'—Except for its merits of expression, I might have done it myself.

> 'Great soul, thou sittest with me in my room,
> Uplifting me with thy vast quiet eyes,
> On whose full orbs with kindly lustre, lies
> The twilight warmth of ruddy ember-gloom.
> Thy clear strong tones will oft bring sudden bloom
> Of hope secure to him who lonely cries,
> Wrestling with the young poet's agonies,
> Neglect and scorn, which seem a certain doom.'

I won't finish off this, in order to reserve your patience for a finer, By A. C. Benson.[184]

> 'Laughing, thou said'st, 'Twere hell for thee to fail
> In thy vast purpose, in thy brave design,
> Ere thy young cheek, with passion's venomed wine
> Flushed and grew pale, ah me! flushed and grew pale!
> Where is thy music now? In hearts that pine
> O'erburdened, for the clamorous world too frail,
> Yet love the charmed dusk, the nightingale
> Not for her sweet sake only, but for thine.'

etc.

The Sestette says almost what I did in Teignmouth about the 'writ in water' (alas!); and I had already, too, got the last sentiment, about the nightingale, at least in mind, if not on paper.

Last week, being thus fired afresh, I got W. M. Rossetti's *Life of Keats*,[185] and, though he is horribly crabby over the early poems, throws more light on the Life & Character than I have obtained from Sidney Colvin. I cannot read either for long without getting wound up. I have more than once turned hot and cold and trembly over the first haemorrhage scene; and sobbed over Severn's 'He is gone…'

But I never guessed till now the frightful travail of his soul towards Death; never came so near laying hold of the ghastly horror of his mind at this time. Rossetti guided my groping hand right into the wound, and I touched, for one moment the incandescent Heart of Keats.

I must not trust myself to say more on this subject now; but if you are so rash as to come near me soon, you will be in for hours of reading; both 'à bas', and also 'à haute voix' from me.

The other day I started afresh on *The Little Mermaid* and have done 19 stanzas. Would you like to hear one of the best?

IX.

> O'er this,* she set a weeping willow-tree
> To droop and mourn. Full dolefully it clung
> About his form, and moved continually,
> As if it sighed, as if it ever wrung
> Convulsive fingers, in sad reverie;
> And o'er the light blue sand it hung
> A purple shade; which hour by hour the same,
> Burned softly on like lambent sulphur-flame.

What has happened to *Little Claus and Big C.?* I meant to bring it back with me. Will you please bring it ?

I will order *Liber Studiorum*[186] & forward it within a few days.

I suffer slightly from toothache, but not acutely.

My hand shows little sign of its maltreatment; and gives (sensorarily) less.

I have not yet closed with U.C.C. but should be glad of £s when forthcoming.

Much love;   Your hopefully expectant Wilfred

* statue.

[181] *Keats–Shelley: The Bookman Memorial Souvenir* (June 1912), a miscellany of articles and poems, some reprinted and some written for the occasion.

[182] The popular novelist Marie Corelli (1854–1924) was author of *The Sorrows of Satan* (1895). By the early twentieth century, Corelli's novels were international bestsellers, earning around £10,000 each.

[183] James Russell Lowell (1819–91) succeeded Longfellow as Professor of Belles-lettres at Harvard in 1855, and was American Minister in England 1880–5.

[184] Arthur Christopher Benson (1862–1925) was Master of Magdalene College, Cambridge, and a prolific writer of poems, essays, and literary studies.

[185] Published in London, 1887. Two copies survive among Owen's books.

[186] J. M. W. Turner's *Liber Studiorum*, miniature edition (Gowans & Gray Ltd, London, 1911), containing 101 reproductions, was given to Harold for his birthday. It remains among Owen's books in the Bodleian.

[82.][187] To Harold Owen

[*late September 1912*]   First sheet missing   [*Dunsden*]

and I keep thinking

> 'Because red-lin'd accounts
> Were richer than the Songs of Grecian Years?'[188]

Indeed, I sometimes think I have fooled myself that I have not 'gone in' for red-lin'd accounts altogether—when, for instance I visit the Penny Bank, and see that its Hours are 11 to 3, and realise that the idle, loungin' clerks must look in somewhere about 10, and be absolutely Free by 4!

What time does <u>my</u> shop shut? Eleven! And <u>then</u> I merely as it were creep under the Counter to sleep, for I breathe still the same Atmosphere.

> 'I could lie down like a tir'd child,
> And weep away this life of care
> Which I have borne, and yet must bear.'[189]

I do not weep, but I snort and snuff, and quote.

I can never escape my thoughts or I would—'To France, to France…my boy'[190] with the £. Note I have in my pocket, and…

I know not what. Except that I must change my tune, if I want you to read this letter.

Saturday

Well, 'tis a fine day, to begin with.

The garden is very fine too, but the open lands are more so. I have to stop and look over the hedge every hundred yards or so of a walk.

I am trying to read Miss Mitford's *Our Village*, which village is situated just the other side of Reading.[191] Some of its descriptions are very pleasing, but I really find it difficult to read an airy-chatty collection of letters like this, when I am grappling as I never did before with the Problem of <u>Evolution</u>. I simply cannot form a Conclusion, by reading both sides of the Question, historically. The only thing to do is to make personal investigation, so it seems, into Botany, etc. But to return to the soothing side of Nature; I wished you could daub some representation of a Field which I saw, blazing with yellow charlock, backed by a Beech-woods, of a deep green so nearly black, that it puts one in mind of the colour of an ancient black coat assuming its green-old-age tints.

Leslie has been doing some remarkable bits of work with Pastels, on Art Papers [*several words illegible*] I shall never have philosophy enough to counteract the sensation that Time is increasing its velocity, in the Geometrical Progression, 1, 2, 4, 8, 16…

Except the cold, nothing is really Autumnal here, yet. Alas, tho',

> 'In the mid-days of Autumn on their eves,
> The breath of Winter comes from far away,
> And the sick West, continually bereaves
> Of some gold tinge, and plays a roundelay
> Of death among the bushes and the leaves,
> To make all bare before he dares to stray
> From his north cavern.'[192]

In case you didn't take much notice of that [*word illegible*] it may raise your interest to know that that is the metre in which I have now written 30 stanzas of

'The Little Mermaid'[193]—and not half done yet. I should to know what is the present [*word illegible*] of 'Little C. and Big C ? ?'[194]

If you have any short spasm of extra good-nature to me when you see the Turner,[195] I pray you turn it to account thus:— (thanks denied in my other form)

Find the old copy of Keats I left (with Mother?); open it at the first; begin to read. Get alone to do this; and read, as slowly as you like, say 300 lines. Then if you are not delighted <u>thirty</u> times at least, I will buy you all the Turners from the Tate Gallery for next birthday. This behest of mine must be conscientiously performed, before you write to me next. If you don't understand anything, write to me. I am sure you might ask many less capable of helping you in that way. Thus I hope this will be a '<u>red-letter</u>'[196] on your Calendar; for I don't believe that a <u>Painter</u> (of anything above houses, cheeks or sore-throats) ever existed who had not only read much, but <u>studied</u> Poetry. And a more Pictorial of Artist-souled Poet than J.K. would be hard to find. Therefore hear my words, O brother, and in proof of your loving obedience, send me <u>all</u> the lines that strike you. I wonder whether you saw the *Graphic*,[197] which contains photos of six or eight [*three lines illegible*] I think I must have seen the original; but that was in the old, happy, far-off days when (to parody Wordsworth)

> 'Two dark eyes in a maiden's head
> Two simple eyeballs were to me
>   And they were nothing more.'

(In case you don't know what W. wrote, it was

> 'A primrose by the river's brim
> A simple primrose was to him,
>   And it was nothing more.')[198]

Again, anything more [*word illegible*] than the 'Samson' picture could scarcely be put on canvas. You sh'd try and see them.

Concerning these little Turners: I have of course glanced thro' them; but I have not seen any of Ruskin's writings on them. And I have not the cheek to criticise them, even if I had the Eye, or the Tongue. I will just enumerate which took my fancy during half an hour's inspection—

5, 13, 14, 23, 38, 44, 49, 57, 78, 81, 82, 94, 97, and 101 (Page 126–7).

Now I must positively stop my ink-slinging. Keep, however, this Message, and it shall stand you in good stead when you don't know what to read, I warrant you.

Your most affectionate, Brother, Wilfred

My next shall be for Mary.

Kindly acknowledge a letter I had from Oliver,[199] begging my 2/6 sub.—if I continue an Associate.[200] I think it w'd be much more sensible for you to become the Associate, and pay for your benefits. At any rate, please instruct him at your earliest opportunity that I must be dissociated from Shrew. [*word illegible*] this year; for one reason I have not thirty pence to send him.

[187] Letter 82 in *CL* and *SL*, which give the date as June 1911, from Alpenrose, following a note in HO's hand on the MS. DH established the correct date as late September 1912, from Dunsden, because Owen refers to a book about Turner which he was sending to HO for his birthday and to the 21 September issue of *The Graphic*. See Dominic Hibberd, 'Wilfred Letters: Some Additions, Amendments, and Notes', *The Library*, 6th Series, Vol. IV, No. 3 (September 1982). It is placed in its approximate chronological order here.

[188] Keats, *Isabella; or, The Pot of Basil*, xvi.

[189] I could lie down like a tired child, / And weep away the life of care / Which I have borne and yet must bear, / Till death like sleep might steal on me. Shelley, 'Stanzas Written in Dejection, near Naples'.

[190] *Henry V*, II, iii, l. 57. Pistol: 'Let us to France; …, my boys'.

[191] Three Mile Cross, near Reading, was the original of *Our Village, Sketches of Rural Life, Character and Scenery* (1824) by Mary Russell Mitford (1787–1855). Owen's 1909 copy remains among his books in the Bodleian Library.

[192] Keats, *Isabella; or, The Pot of Basil*, xxxii.

[193] *The Little Mermaid*, based on Hans Christian Andersen's story, was completed during the course of the following year, in seventy-eight stanzas (*CPF*, p. 37).

[194] *Little Claus and Big Claus*, another long poem based on Andersen (*CPF*, pp. 17–26).

[195] *Liber Studiorum*.

[196] The letter is written in red ink.

[197] *The Graphic* was a British weekly illustrated periodical which ran from 4 December 1869 to 23 April 1932. Price: sixpence.

[198] Wordsworth, *Peter Bell: A Tale in Verse* (1819), prologue.

[199] Frederick James Oliver, brother of Harold's childhood friend Herbert Oliver of Shrewsbury.

[200] Of the YMCA.

159. To Susan Owen

6 October, 1912   *Dunsden Vicarage*

Dearest Mother,

Harvest Thanksgiving is <u>today</u>; so you will miss the inestimable spectacle of the depraved Gothic of our shanty all belittered with fowsty apples and fag-ends of the stubble-fields. Not to mention the choir and its thrills. One boy sings so flat as almost to reach two tones below his part, & sing alto. One good virtue this hath—it makes me sing imprecatory psalms with a right good will.

I can scarcely believe you will see me on Sat. <u>I</u> shall scarce see much of you unless you arrive early on account of the P.M. (Pious-Moments, 'Plainful mumblry, Pish-tush Muggery, or what-you-will.)

Sunday, too, if it's anything like this, will not permit me to come over.

I will mention your coming to the Vicar. You need not write to him. Did I tell you I was prevented from going to London, by stress of work on the Coal & Clothing Accounts?

The Vicar went on Thurs.—speaking in the Caxton Hall for the 'Protestant Woman.' He brought me home an Etching of the Nuns House, 'Cloisterham',—quite framable—as a bit of sugar after my labour—(which was not hard, but <u>so</u> trivial—complicate.)

Excuse more of a letter—(and perhaps excuse further letters)—I must reply to Mary, tho' I am about at an end of original remarks, having taken a Bible Class before Church, and having <u>prepared and deliver'd</u> a Harvest Address at the Children's Service, in addition to the Church Service.

Ever your own, Wilfred

166. To Mary Owen

16 November 1912   *Dunsden Vicarage*

My dearest Mary,

Many thanks for your letter of the 4th. About time you sent me another. I hardly think Colin has sent me more than 3 lines in as many months. Now this is too hard. And as for Harold . . . ! [*four lines illegible*] which Leslie brought for me to see?

I myself have been doing some graceful vol-planes and circuits lately. At quarter of an hour after lunch yesterday was I seized with a most dervish vertigo. I was due to start with the Vicar to a Sutton-Drawing-Room-Missionary-Reception; but I must have got 'run in' had I appeared on a public road, especially as I 'smelt' like any bacchanal, (after Edith's administration of a teaspoonful.)

So I lay down all the rest of the day, and had five hours gratis of a merry-go-round. Went to bed at 7.30. and find things slowed down this morning.

'Twas all due to (1) Cold mutton, overlayed by (2) greasy-soapy variety of Potato, overlayed by (3) Walnut Pickle, capped with (4) Stewed Apple. I will finish with an impression of the dining room at 2 o'clock yesterday.

For I won't trust myself to write more of other people and affairs, with so distorted a vision.

Your Brother, Wilfred

167. To Susan Owen

Tuesday, 10 December 1912   *Dunsden Vicarage*

My own dear Mother,

I am conscious of a glimmering sense of duty unfulfilled, after this three-weeks, isn't it? of silence; though why <u>duty</u> I cannot explain; when my half-hour of confidences and narrations to you is one I look forward to with gladness of heart, even as to a season when the righteous (dogmas) cease from troubling and the eerie (speculations) are at rest. If I must face the question, there may have been a moral reason for with-holding my speech; just that I may not speak unadvisedly.

Now, For many months, in fact ever since I have been here, the Vicar has been praying, now hotly, now coldly for <u>Revival</u>.

It has come.

At least, is coming.

Here is the Organist converted; the 'blower' and numbers of others 'under conviction'; here is Jack Dear writing to the Vicar of how he is completely healed of his backsliding, and has made a wholesale surrender of his will to God.

Here is a woman saying to our last Prayer Meeting: 'I should like help', and being 'prayed through'.

Here is a man, Bint himself, accepting Christ last night at Black's Bible Class for men.

Here is Vera Bint, the same evening at another mtg. being asked by Black whether she took Christ as her Saviour, answering Yes.

Here is a woman of the parish writing from Reading Hospital to say she has found Christ there.

Here is Willie Montague, being cornered by Black on Sunday afternoon, making his (second) profession of Christianity.

Here are women shedding tears in Church every Sunday night.

Here am I, halting between two, aye, more than two opinions, till sense deserts my mind, and strength my body.

Wednesday

Here I left off yesterday, and being in a different mood just now, it is a wonder I am letting the first Sheet pass a second reading—For already I have destroyed much more than that, earlier in the week.

Perhaps it is just as well I should send them; with the inference that I can no longer hope to do real study, amid the meetings, classes, spiritual excitements, and such like that prevail, and will prevail in this place.

With reference to my O. English, I mentioned to Mrs. Jones that I found great difficulty with Pronunciation, etc. and she very kindly referred me to Miss Morley,[201] Professor of Eng. at the College; whom I saw about two weeks ago.

She begged me to join the College, (for my sake, not the College's she was so urgent) and mentioned a scholarship[202] admitting one to the whole degree course, with residence at 'Wantage Hall'.[203] This is awarded to the person of <u>most promise</u> in the competitive exam., not necessarily the highest mark-scorer.

As to when the next scholarship is open she was very dim; but spoke as if she would like me to get it. Then she <u>invited</u> me to her remaining classes in O.E., to which I have been.

In our interview, she asked me (what prompted her I know not) whether I 'wrote'. The kindly Minerva was favourably impressed by my genuine, (and well-founded, goodness knows) self-depreciations, said they were a good sign, and pressed me to go on with attempts; adding a few words of trivial advice withal.

I wonder does Harold remember <u>Seaward</u>,[204] who was in his form, I think, at the B.I., and lived up Chestnut Grove (?) Well, Seward's aunt is a <u>great</u> friend of Miss Morley's; Miss Morley reports that S. is now the mathematical genius of the school.

Now I am dry in the head; yet my mouth waters to lick up the envelope; but two items of your letter must not remain unnoticed: (1) The assurance of a good servant sharpens my desire for Home, more than by rights such a consideration should.

and (2) The idea of meeting *'une inconnue française'*, has the same effect on your ever-mother-faithful,

Wilfred

[201] Edith Julia Morley (1875–1964) was Professor of English Language, University of Reading, 1908–40, and the first female to be appointed a professor in the United Kingdom. She was the editor of Henry Crabb Robinson's journals and the author of *Women Workers in Seven Professions: A Survey of their Economic Conditions and Prospects* (1914). She was awarded an OBE in 1950 for her work for Jewish and other refugees in the Second World War. See Edith Morley, *Before and After: Reminiscences of a Working Life,* ed. Barbara Morris (Two Rivers Press, 2016).
[202] Morley's encouragement led Owen to sit for this—unsuccessfully, as he anticipated.
[203] Wantage Hall was built in 1908 for male students, the first residential building in the University.
[204] HO did not remember Seaward from the Birkenhead Institute ('B.I.').

168. To Susan Owen

12/12/12   *Dunsden Vicarage*

Dearest Mother,

You ask for a Card, and I send you a letter: you beseech for a watered-down note, and I send you a drop of the milk of human kindness on cream-laid note-paper.

But it is well that I know I have but a short while to write it in.

I cannot put enough emphasis into my first petition: Do 'take it easy,' right on till Christmas. You little know how my happiness hangs on the assurance of your health. Suppose you were the least bit strained in the ventricles where is my Christmas joy of Homecoming.

Never have I set greater store on a holiday to brace up my nerves. They are in a shocking state, and no mistake. My breast is continually 'too full'. Just as if one had been over-long in a putrid atmosphere, and had got to the advanced stage of being painfully conscious of it. A breath of another air <u>may</u> put things right.

Maybe only Fire will clear the Cobwebs.

But I had rather kill the Spider…

I have just heard that at the Mothers' Meeting this afternoon, Milly's Mother yielded herself to God, and was brought to the point by the visible happiness of her child. Is it cowardly to be influenced by the doings of others; I mean, being willing to follow if others will lead?

That is how it strikes me, if I at this juncture, were to make <u>my</u> sacrifice—of Reason.

My time for setting out for the Club is nearly here. I press on.

I dare not give an opinion about Harold's Future. Am I his Keeper? [*two lines illegible*]

Curiously enough, both these cuttings were in *The Pall Mall* today.

172. To Susan Owen

[4 January 1913]   [Dunsden Vicarage]

First page missing

The furor [*several words missing*] now abated in the Vicarage, thank Mnemosyne; but I hope that I, who 'discovered' [his?] something over a year ago, may [*half page missing*] but the Vicar's presence (taciturn instead of wontedly gay) symbolic of my stern Destiny, sat heavy on my soul the night.[205] I have already braced myself to one important interview; the upshot of which was that he begged me to spend the next morning upon Tracts! Others will follow.

Murder will out, and I have murdered my false creed. If a true one exists, I shall find it. If not, adieu to the still falser creeds that hold the hearts of nearly all my fellow men.

Escape from this hotbed of religion I now long for more than I could ever have conceived a year and three months ago. It reminds me of that old grange in *Westward Ho!*[206] whither the priests would resort and hatch plots for the salvation of England.

To leave Dunsden will mean a terrible bust-up; but I have no intention of sneaking away by smuggling my reasons down the back-stairs. I will vanish in thunder and lightning, if I go at all.

————————————

It has just struck me that one of the occult Powers that Be may have overheard the ancient desire of my heart to be like the immortals, the immortals of earthly Fame, I mean, and is now on a fair way to granting it. This flight of mine from overbearing elders, if it comes off, will only be my version of running away from College, (Shelley, Coleridge). Only where in me is the mighty Power of Verse that covered the multitude of their sins. It is true I still find great comfort in scribbling; but lately I am deadening to all poetic impulses, save those due to the pressure of Problems pushing me to seek relief in unstopping my mouth.

Here is a Sonnet that occurred to me this morning:—

On My Songs[207]

Although on many and many a sacred time	a
Poets have spok'n as if they knew my woe;	b
Though, as it seemed, they fashioned many a rime	a
To be my own soul's cry, easing the flow	b
Of my dumb tears with Language like deep sobs,	c
—Yet there are hours when richest[208] hoards of thought	d
Hold nothing for me. <u>No</u> heart throbs <u>my</u> throbs;	c
No brain yet knew the thing wherewith mine's fraught.	d

'Tis then I voice my own, dim reveries.	e
Low croonings of a motherless child, in gloom,	f
Who fain must sing himself to sleep, are these.	e
Tonight, if Thou should'st lie in this same Room,	f
Dreading the Dark thou know'st not how to illume,	f
Listen; my songs may haply give thee ease.	e

I need scarcely explain the metaphors of the last lines. If however a conscientious '3rd Reading' fails to make it clear, I will cease talking in parables for ever.

I gave dear old E.W.M's[209] pamphlet a conscientious reading. But you know such a course of study is now quite beside the mark for me. Discussions which take it for granted the reader believes in Adam's getting outside some fruit or other; and then going off into occult matters of retributive dogma, are not what I want. They are trivial, and annoying, like the tickings of the clock that so annoyed E.W., you know, that he shelved it deep in a cupboard. Perhaps there is enough here for you to digest.

Blessings attend you, dear Mother, and the dear kindred, whose message touched me to the heart.

                                                                    Wilfred

[205] As DH notes, most of the first sheet of the letter has been cut away, and three lines that survive on a fragment have been inked out: 'The nature of the "furor" at the Vicarage is thus concealed for ever' (*The Library*, p. 279). *CL* and *SL* printed 'him' after 'discovered'; DH posits that the word could 'equally be read as "her"'; this seems to reduce the possibility which has been suggested that the commotion was over a favourite choirboy'. However, my reading is that the word could also be 'his'.

[206] A historical novel of 1855 by Charles Kingsley.

[207] *CPF*, p. 113.

[208] 'their rich' crossed out.

[209] The Rev. E. W. Moore.

176. To Susan Owen

29 January 1913   *Dunsden Vicarage*

Dearest Mother,

Tuesday Mid-day brought your very welcome letter. Things are at a standstill again with me; because the Vicar has gone away for some days to Lingley's, at Parkstone Bournemouth. (N.B. Doesn't Mrs. Corbett live at 'Lingley', Parkstone?) I had infinite labour to find 'a clergy' to take the Evening Service on Sunday. Went to about nine people in Reading about it, walking from 2.15 till nearly 10 p.m. (Not unaccompanied, however.) Got Neatby[210] eventually, and for my pains had a jolly fiery sermon, which might have been framed for my own special edification—or demolition I should rather say.

I went to the Glee Practice last night. Leslie is troubled at the idea of my leaving soon. He had some more verses to show me—astonishing!

I have also been guilty of <u>four</u> Compositions since you left! I tell you, I have no satisfaction so pleasant as the feeling of something attempted, something done, in this way. Yet it is very, very little that I have the heart to commit to writing.

I paid a visit to the School this morning. The children show no sign of missing Mrs. Hullcoop, but what signs would one expect to see?

And the other day I asked Milly if Mrs. H. were ever cross with them. 'Oh yes! I should think she was!' Did she ever punish <u>you</u>?' 'Made me "turn out" of my seat sometimes.'

'How often?' 'Oh, every day.'

'Dear me: what for?'

'Oh, I don't know.'

'Now, you must <u>know</u>.'

'Because, I read too quick, then.'

It is a mightily instructive, as well as pleasant thing to have the confidence of a child. In fact it is the only way to get at any notion of child-psychology.

Teachers in Colleges talk of studying a child. And they go about it with moral microscopes in their eyes, and forceps in their fingers. Not the way at all. All that is wanted in the hand is the child's own hand; the best lens for the eye is an earnest smile.

Children are not meant to be studied, but enjoyed. Only by studying <u>to be pleased</u> do we understand them. My opportunities of such observation are unique here. I can examine their home-influence, for I have the entrance of every house. I know their school-influence, for I know every one of their teachers. I know their spiritual influences, for I know every one of their spiritual task-masters. And I have a very good idea of their amusements.

Now is there after all some region of their natures which I shall never fathom? Is there a definite relation between them and the unseen, into which my curiosity, my jealousy may never pry? I think not.

I believe this sweet piety of theirs has reference to present environment only. Environment was the cause of it. Alter the environment and it will go. For already I grieve to say (though <u>why I grieve</u> is not very patent, considering) that 'impressions' are 'wearing off' in some cases, already. In fact I am convinced that I hold under my tongue, powers which would shake the foundations of many a spiritual life.

A week's conversation crumbles what promises to be an eternal structure.

This is speaking boldly, and terribly.

Think not I would use those Powers. Shelley scrupled not to play their whole force upon <u>his</u> young friends. But because the <u>Religion</u> he had met with was hollow, it does not follow that no religion is solid. He and all his thousand tribes may never have struck the real thing. It exists none the less, you say. Only I haven't met it—to know it—yet.

Nay, I should feel the (possibility of) the millstone tightening round my neck, and the bitter waters of the sea pouring in at my lips, if I essayed to recommend my persuasions on another. I look upon the child-lives with an eye too much like their Creator's, to play the part popularly ascribed to a malignant tempter.

By the way, when I survey a class of children in this paternal way, (for I can experience the happiness of paternity, fraternity, and amativeness all in one, sometimes) I find some excuse for the unswallowable bone of contention—the Doctrine of Election.

Nothing affords greater pleasure than singling out from a crowd. When I go through a picture-gallery I single out my favourites; when I stand in the company of the Poets, one has my enthusiasm ten-times-heated; when I live amongst a village of children, one claims seventy-times-seven-fold more affection than the others.

And this leads me—merely to the end of my letter. You won't suffer if you skip half this prosing till 'another day', and turn to the happy ending, after your manner with books: Where you will find—no expressions of devotion—but just the supplication Be strong (1) physically—(Poor Kemp lost his Mother suddenly the other day) (2) spiritually (lest through loneliness and no support I quail before the Truth of Truths).

Your own, Wilfred

[210] The Rev. George Wigram Neatby, Curate (1911–13) of Greyfriars, Reading.

177. To Mary Owen

1 February 1913   *Dunsden Vicarage*

My dear Mary,

I cannot tell you, dear sister, how glad I was to hear of your experiences in spiritual matters—because my gladness is limited by hindrances of my own. I am intensely sorry therefore that I must bid you not look to me as in any way a responsible guide in your religious life.

But be thankful that, although you have abundant 'means of grace' around you, the finest Christian spirits are those who have direct communication with Powers Unseen, and who are consequently independent of what man can do unto them, either for evil or good.

I have made the discovery that no religion is worth the having, except the vital reality just indicated. At the same time I have to acknowledge that such a religion I do not know in my own experience. That is as much as I will say to you on these points,—I should say these vast spheres—now or henceforward: till I cannot <u>but</u> speak.

Now, concerning my outer man, I must observe that I now must really own up to that objectionable title—man!—I am boy no more; that is for the greater part of my time. I have enough grey hairs to whiten the ground if they were to drop out.

––––––––––––––––––

Ha! Zooks! Something necessitates my stopping short! I will explain 'tomorrow'.

Ever your loving Brother, Wilfred

178. To Susan Owen[211]

4 February 1913   *Dunsden Vicarage*

Dearest Mother,

This morning I managed to broach the subject of my leaving, to the Vicar. He had only been waiting for me to be first in the matter. Unless I 'get right', I pack off this very week,—about Friday perhaps.[212] Tomorrow will be Ash Wednesday. How many just persons that need no repentance will sit in Ashes then! Scarcely a soul in the world will need repentance more than I.

Only <u>is</u> such a thing as repentance an actuality, or a delusion? There are left just a few hours or days for me to consider it. These days will be the intensest of my life. It amounts to finding out whether my sanest moments are really my maddest. If they are I am still—mad.

I ought to reply to Harold [*two lines illegible*] But in any case I must write again to <u>you</u> very speedily.—However much I wish to put aside immediate and circumstantial considerations, in my decision, the thought of leaving Dunsden weighs upon me terribly. Though Dunsden will contain little to attract me, if I become a religious devotee.

> '… All my pretty ones?
> Did you say all? … All?
> What all my pretty chickens
> At one fell swoop?'
> (Macbeth.)[213]

And my verse-making? O hard condition! The evidence of increasing powers of late (such as they are) is too tantalising.

I will say no more.

I <u>don't want</u> to communicate my calm frenzy to anybody—let alone you.

My allegiance to you and my Father is never to be shaken. For the rest, I have not the slightest feeling of humility for anything in existence, but the Eternal Being, the Principle of Beauty, and the Memory of Great Men.[214]

Ever your Wilfred

* * *

Notes for a letter survive from this time. 'The wildness of the writing suggests that this may have been written from the sickbed to which he retired . . . on his escape from Dunsden', Jon Stallworthy writes.[215]

'To Vicar—solely on the grounds of affection. I was a boy when I first came to you and held you in the doubtful esteem that a boy has for his Headmaster. It is also true that I was an old man when I left.... The Christian Life affords no imagination, physical sensation, aesthetic philosophy. There is but one dimension in the Christian religion, the strait line upwards whereas I cannot conceive of less than 3. But all these considerations [?] are nothing to the conviction that the philosophy of the whole system as a religion is but a religion and therefore one Interpretation of Life & Scheme of Living among a hundred and that not the most convenient.'

Owen left home in mid-April to convalesce at the Taylors' home in Torquay. He made a second Keatsian pilgrimage to Teignmouth, and was back in Shrewsbury in June to celebrate Harold's safe return from his first voyage in the Merchant Navy (it was almost his last, for the 16-year-old had barely survived an attack of heat apoplexy in Calcutta). He sat unsuccessfully for a scholarship to University College, Reading; considered going back to Dunsden to help in the village school; went up north to stay with his Quayle cousins; and succumbed to another attack of bronchitis. Acting on the doctor's comment that a winter in the South of France would do him good, he applied for a teaching post at the Berlitz School of English in Bordeaux, secured it, and arrived in France towards the end of September 1913. His father made him a small allowance to eke out the meagre salary. Harold Owen wrote: 'The pay was pathetically small, and, under the system, precarious, after working it out it seemed almost impossible that he could manage to live on it. But he was excited and keen to take it up; it was a chance to get to France, and the very nature of the work would be the best possible way to fulfil a minor ambition—to speak and think precisely as a French-born national' (JFO, II, p. 265).

[211] In this letter Owen's handwriting, normally strong and clear, is shaky and evidence of the considerable nervous stress he was experiencing.
[212] He left Dunsden three days later, the Friday.
[213] *Macbeth*, IV, iii, l. 216.
[214] 'I have not the slightest feeling of humility towards the Public—or to anything in existence, —but the eternal Being, the Principle of Beauty, and the Memory of great Men—'. John Keats to J. H. Reynolds from Teignmouth, 9 April 1818 (*Letters* I, p. 266).
[215] *WO*, p. 86.

2

Bordeaux, the Pyrenees, and Mérignac 1913–1915

199. To Susan Owen

28 September 1913   *Chez Mme. Dubo, 95 Rue Porte Dijeaux*
Bordeaux

Dearest Mother,

It seems that you had not received my 2nd letter[1] when you wrote your last card. I hope, if you have not yet got it, that you have at least had three postcards since you sent your last. I forgot exactly what I said in that letter; except that it requested you to send my Birth Certificate as soon as possible. It has just occurred to me that I forgot to write *Angleterre* on the envelope of that letter: but wrote England instead. If this has been the cause of its abortion, I renounce the French race for ever.

In reply to Father's questions I repeat that I shall be in Bordeaux till the 15th Oct. I also repeat the following points:

That my Room in Rue Castelmoron[2] cost 30 francs a month, i.e. 1 f. per day.[3]

That my present room costs only 20 francs a month.

That neither contained two beds; and the present room is very small.

But there is another room vacant on the second floor of this house, (I am on the first) which is much larger than mine; but at the same price. Hiring it by day, Father might easily get it for less than 1 franc a day.

I get very satisfactory *dejeuner* (12 o'clock) and dinner (7) for 1⅓ franc each: at a hotel not far removed from the Room and the School.

In any case it would be easy to find a cheap room near mine: and the full cost of *pension* at my Hotel is only 5 f. a day. I am lucky to have found a room which combines the qualities of cheapness, nearness to the school, tranquility and a large window, overlooking a 'garden'!!

As I indicated on a P.C. I am earning about 4 francs a night by speechifying in technical French on the subject of a Wireless Dirigible Balloon. I enjoy the business immensely, though it is often two o'clock in the morning when I get back to my Rooms. And sometimes I am teaching at 8 o'clock the same morning. Such is the influence of Climate and Environment! The demonstration is held in a Theatre (a fitter place, I take it, than the Cathedral); of course a highly respectable place; and the audience is composed of high class people almost entirely. On one occasion I had the honour of addressing the Mayor of Bordeaux—a great personage I assure you.

After all is over we usually sit drinking (syrops) in a Café till one or two o'clock. Syrops, mind, for my friend the Inventor neither drinks nor smokes and is in all respects a most amiable and estimable fellow (little older than myself, I should think.) Now, he is so pleased with the manner in which I show him off, and generally with my knowledge of French, command of English, and inklings of Wireless Telegraphy, that he has made me a proposition to the effect that if I should like to travel with him, he would give me 200 f. a month (£96. a year)—as well as travelling expenses paid. He speaks bad French and worse English, and consequently needs an interpreter and secretary while in Paris (November) and America—Mexico of all marvellous places! (next spring.)

What do you think of the idea?

One clause of the contract is that we should teach each other our languages! I feel very tempted, especially as I can only just live on the Berlitz Salary.

My 'compatriot'[4] who smokes much and saves little, has to obtain Remittances from home. He was a student of Nottingham College, but failed to pass Inter-Arts, and now at 22, is spending his time in France, awaiting a Civil Service Exam. in Spring.

I don't particularly like him. He is tall, & something of a gawk, easily enraged; and of limp principles, (I should imagine). Neither have I yet discovered that he has any interest in life.

I am fond of all my pupils—nearly. One is a doctor, and yesterday I mustered all my medical ignorance into one vast conglomeration of terms.

Another, who is preparing for the French Equivalent of Matriculation has invited me to go motoring with him over the fair lands of Médoc; but I have not yet found time.

The Doctor has also given me an infallible prescription for a pomade which cures a cold in 48 hours. (I have a slight cold—or had rather. In 2 days I have smoked it out with some Eucalyptus Cigarettes. I don't blame the weather for the Cold, but must have caught it, either from the Inventor or Langholz the Sub-Director).

I don't know whether I told you: I saw the President[5] very well when he was here last week.

During the whole of October there is to be a Fair in Bordeaux whatever that may mean.

Hydroplanes are in the habit of planing over the Garonne, but I have not yet seen any.

I sometimes promenade along the docks, and see the ships of many lands.

It would be the time of your life if you would but come over with Father. Well, well! Anyhow, I hope to hear very soon that Father is really coming.

Excuse the scraggy air of these sheets: a bad pen and a good dinner are to blame. But our communication is not wholly dependent on the 2½d post, as telegraphy is independent of wires, and I greet you night and morning as though no hundreds of miles or tens of years were between.

Ever your own Wilfred

[1] Neither this nor the first letter from Bordeaux has survived.
[2] His first lodgings, in which he stayed no more than a fortnight.
[3] The franc was worth 9½d. in 1913; he paid £1 4s. 6d. a month in his first lodgings, 16s. 3d. with Mme Dubo. His monthly salary from the Berlitz School was 130 francs, or £5 2s. 11d.
[4] His name was Tofield. DH writes that Tofield 'seems to have been away for some of the winter, working at Nantes or Angers, his place at Bordeaux being taken in November by a recruit from Merseyside, a Miss Hewitt, with whom Wilfred got on well' (WOANB, pp. 136–7). Hewitt left in April 1914 'to take over a Berlitz school elsewhere, and Tofield had apparently been brought back to replace her, but in mid-June he was mysteriously dismissed' (WOANB, p. 156). See Letter 238.
[5] Raymond Poincaré (1860–1934), President of France throughout the First World War.

205. To Susan Owen

Sunday, 2 November 1913   *Bordeaux*

PRIVATE

My darling Mother,

Last Sunday you wrote the tenderest letter of all, as if you feared all the time I might be ill; so much so that you finally say, you think you must have a fit of the blues.

It was not a fit of the blues; it was an instance of the unconfinable sympathy that exists between us.

Last Sunday I had got somewhat low, through a week's double work. Then began another week worse than the first, and I only lost my headache (beginning last Friday week) this very morning. Everything was done that was possible (except sending away pupils) to assist me; but Aumont[6] was away in Nantes, and the Sub-director found himself so very Sub under the circumstances that he would not undertake to dismiss any lessons. So, being still able to walk to the school (unfortunately) I dragged on till Friday. I took my Courses sitting in an armchair with the thick overcoat; and looked and sounded, I suppose, like a nonagenarian bishop addressing a Confirmation.

Saturday was the Feast of All Saints; and caused a holiday at the school. I stayed in bed all day, and got, with some difficulty, enough cups of milk to keep me alive. I found to my dismay that Mme. Dubo was in no disposition to get or prepare things for me; and until I actually stayed in bed I had to crawl about myself— for firewood, for instance, with which I lighted me a blaze to dry the room; for it rained heavily. I had been having nothing but milk for the last 3 days, so for dinner, I ordered some Oxo, but alas! appeared a vile salty concoction, not like the bottled Oxo, but made from a cube. Small nutriment in that; nevertheless if I had not detained her by my requests, Madame would have left me without anything to eat, (save a Siphon) and without anyone in the house (save the close Spaniard that I do not know)— and would have gone to the Fair. I was but <u>little</u> apologetic when she blustered 'it was now too late to go out!' etc.

I had long known one of my complaints, and at midnight I drank off a dose of Oil of Ricin,—French equivalent of Castor Oil. The effects are not yet entirely satisfactory. I was, however, able to eat an egg which I boiled for myself to tea today. Madame hied to the Cemetery for a large part of this day, to tend the Dead, and left the living to fend for itself. Fearing to contract more weakness, I therefore got up and dressed; and after a little promenade as far as 'the gardens' (for it was now sunny) I boiled water for my tea, and cooked egg and toast. With one knife, one plate, one spoon, and only half a stomach, imagine me taking this repast in the dismal evening gloom,—perhaps at the same time that you were round your cheerful table, and the twilight was pleasant over Haughmond, and Autumn spoke not of sadness; nor the evening bells of death. But, at this moment, are slowly tolling the most sepulchral-throated bells I ever heard. Tonight every family in France turns its thoughts to its dead.

But the melancholy of these bells! it is almost as distressing to me as the demonstration that threatened to dement me yesterday afternoon. It began with a hideous screech of 5 or ten bugles, all out of tune, and out of time. After a half-hour of this, commenced an infernal convulsion of drums—and all this seemed just below my window. Some hours of this, with intervals, (during which I doubted my senses), I abandoned the idea that it was devils, and rather adopted the theory of <u>French Soldiers</u>, practising, after dinner and wine. You know <u>just at this</u> time all men of 20 years are enlisted (for 3 years now, instead of two) Yet it did not seem like novices, either, but like old hands gone mad; & old drums gone bad.—It was in fact a concourse of some thirty miserables, who made offerings of music to the souls of the soldiers killed in 1870! And this was not all my disturbance, for in the morning I hear the people in the next room, separated only by a thin door, and in the evening a vile piano, played more vilely.

These things are not to grieve you, sweet mother, but out of the superfluity of my heart I speak;[7] How keenly I miss you I must not say; but you must not imagine that I now <u>need</u> you in an exigent sense, for I feel quite comfortable tonight, and need little but repose. You will be mad for me to see a doctor; but as a matter of fact I remonstrated with <u>Dr. Aumont</u>[8] on Friday, and he gave me Quinine. If one symptom continues, namely reddish-brown colour of urine, I shall consult Dr. Sauvaître[9] as soon as possible. I am due for a lesson at 8 a.m. tomorrow morning, but tho' I was out this afternoon, I shall probably <u>not</u> go. The School is the cause of my indisposition; it must bear a little of the consequences.

I now close the subject of my dolours with reassuring remarks. I have had no suspicion of my phantasies, a merciful provision, though it matters not whether you are here or there, for I should see you on the other side of the universe in any case;

Nor any approach to Faint.

Nor any chest affection.

I am wise, wise, wise, in the matter of clothes. On Tuesday, when you read this terrible announcement, I shall probably be quite normal, and at <u>normal</u> work, but not <u>abnormal</u> work you may be sure. As soon as two English Teachers heard of the Courses they severally fell ill, and would not leave England. The last applicant is so beautiful (in photograph) that Aumont thinks he cannot engage her. There has already been a tragedy in this very school thro' such a cause.

Your letter of today, with Father's and Mary's, came bearing great solace; even as did the brief card of Friday, seen just after having posted my briefer note (on my last journey to the School.) I wonder how much suffering the dentist has caused and will cause you! Are you yet strong enough for it? Perhaps because you fear to smile you have vouchsafed me no photo of yourself. I am delighted with all four, (& should like several more of both kinds of self); But it was cruel to find no trace of YOU!

(*Later*) I have now prepared myself Liebig in Milk.[10] The effect will be splendid; the only trouble is that these preparations have a strong psychological effect: and bring back a remembrance of your continual presence which is quite tantalising.

Still I have always the little portrait I took of you one September evening, last year.

I see the justly-proportioned face composed, yet with benignancy bright and active in the eyes; the mouth is set; and yet it ever smiles a gentle smile; With what firmness sits the head upon shoulder-throne! And lo! the arm, seemingly strong as a Titan's; and when used to succour and sustain, so strong in very truth! With the hand hanging in perfect grace, a lady's hand! And there are the four bracelets, each with its little tale and its significance not small.[11] And, on the ground behind, thrive the small plants She loveth so to grow; and the Tree is there, for she revereceth trees as if she were their daughter; and not far away, not far away, the Kitchen-room, and the whole house She reigneth in as Queen.

So do I feel, and so badly do I write, in this State!

Now please note I have made out myself worse than I really am, rather than the contrary; therefore do not say to any friend <u>or</u> relation that I am ill. I am ashamed of myself; and what is more have not had an illness. God shield you, my sweet Mother, and bring us together both stronger than when we parted.

Your devoted Wilfred x

---

[6] Maurice Aumont, Director of the Berlitz School, Bordeaux. He was also in charge of the Berlitz schools at Angers and Nantes. See Letter 235.

[7] The phrase 'I only mention *some*' was struck out by Owen in the manuscript letter.

⁸ A Bordeaux doctor, apparently not related to the Director of the Berlitz School. DH suggests Dr Aumont was the father or brother of the Director (*WOANB*, p. 140).
⁹ A Bordeaux doctor. Later he conducted Owen round a military hospital. See Letter 288.
¹⁰ Liebig's Extract of Meat.
¹¹ Bracelets made of Indian silver, one for each child, brought back from Bombay by Tom Owen before he married.

215. To Alec Paton

November 1913   *Bordeaux*

My dear Alec,

    You think me a weird bird for not answering your letter of 2 months ago. But it was natural to postpone writing until I was actually settled in France, and since I have been here I have been very, very busy. So much so that last week, just before relief came, I broke down, and had to take some days rest, which gives me leisure to remember my obligations to you.

    I got a post as Professor of English in the Berlitz School of Languages, Bordeaux. For some weeks I have been the only English Professor; but at last a lady, one Miss Hewitt (of Liverpool or Birkenhead) has arrived to share my work. I like the work well enough, on the whole. It consists in giving individual lessons to well-educated adults; who may or may not speak English. In the case of the ignorants I am obliged to act on the Berlitz Method, and teach them English without one syllable of explanation in French. This is difficult enough, and I was some time acquiring the method. At night there are Courses, and this is quite the most unpleasant part of the business.

    I hire a room near the School for only 20 f. per month, but the innumerable extras and the cost of food, contrive to make living less cheap than it is imagined to be in these parts.

    Bordeaux is a very fine town, and is of all French cities the one that most resembles Paris. The weather seems to be a regular alternation of powerful sunshine, and equally powerful rain. So far I have been rather lonely in this strange land; and it is my great regret that I scarcely speak any French; but on the contrary more English than ever in my life.

    A little time ago my Father came over to see me, and spent a few days in the same house with me. It was very pleasant for both of us.¹²

    I hardly dare ask for news of Mr. Paton. If he is capable of remembering me, I should be glad if you would convey to him my sincerest sympathies and regrets, and my thanks for the kindness that was shown to me, in the old days in Wales. And to Mrs. Paton let me offer sympathies no less earnest.

    I was glad to hear that you thought well of your new post, and that the Authorities are well-inclined towards you. I must thank you very much for suggesting to speak to your Professors. There may yet be a time when I may avail myself of your services. Meanwhile, I am looking forward to spending at least the winter in these parts. I shall envy you at home, sometimes, especially at Christmas. I hope <u>not without cause</u>, and that the season may be a happy and prosperous one to you.

Always your friend, <u>Wilfred Owen</u>

P.S. I was extremely sorry to miss seeing you, even for only a few minutes. Do write to me here: I am almost as lonely an individual as the well-known solitary, A.S.P.

[12] Owen had hinted to his acquaintances in Bordeaux that his father held a baronetcy, so during his visit in October Tom pretended to be Sir Thomas Owen of Shrewsbury. See *JFO*, III, pp. 52–6.

218. To Tom Owen

23 November 1913   *Bordeaux*

My dear Father,

I must expedite a hasty note on the Subject of the Translation.[13] I have rendered the circumlocutory French into as concise English as possible, just as would have done it if were a Task at the Berlitz School. There is no idea of <u>Signatures</u> (which have yet to be solicited) in the word *écritures*: it simply denotes the Clerical Work, Account Entries, etc. which the repayment will occasion. As for the Salutation, it can only be cooled down to the chilly 'yours truly, faithfully, etc.' or at best 'Assuring you of our careful attentions.'

The English say 'Yours truly' and mean it. The French say 'Be so good as to accept, my dear Sir, the assurance of my most cordial salutations' and mean nothing. The Italians say 'I kiss your feet' and mean—I kick your head.

I do not get <u>enough</u> Translations to do, for I find it interesting. I wrote eight pages to a man in Lord St. L'pool, the other day, instructing him how to represent a Bordeaux Firm. I little thought I came here to learn Business Methods; but I have at least learnt the phraseology and abbreviations (thro' having to translate). I have now got back into the usual swing of work, & find it going at a gallop at present: At least eight lessons tomorrow: 3 of which are Courses.

Today (Sunday), I thought it prudent not to get up till Lunch; especially as it is horribly raw and damp. In spite of this icy drizzle I stumped about the pavements during the afternoon hours for the sake of exercise. I took my dinner at the *Union Chrétienne* which is my latest discovery. It provides an ordinary table for 1 fr. 10 or 20 c. I was in hopes of getting a French Conversation, but tonight I believe every fellow was a German! The one I was presented to, having taken his fill of English for tonight, went off congratulating himself on the prospect of meeting me tomorrow. He will probably await me in vain. There is a piano, but it was monopolized by a bullet-headed German; and presently the remaining bullet-heads conceived the idea of dancing to the music. They continued to step out, and after three movements to step in again, so long that I bade them a very good night, and so here I am in my cold room. Wood for fires is fearfully expensive, and there is no coal to be had. The cheapest *Pension* I have yet discovered is the best I have yet seen. The whole house, including bedrooms, is warmed by Radiators; there is a fine bathroom, and altogether it seems a very superior establishment. It is situated by one of the Entrances to the *Jardin Public*. I got the price down to 150 f. per month including washing. I said I would decide to come if it could be done for 140 fr. but it couldn't.

The Rev. Lurton Burke[14] knows of no *Pension* whatever. It is possible to get a room in the *Union Chrétienne*, but the one vacant at present does not please me as much as Mme. Dubo's. I thank you very sincerely for the £1. When I went to the P.O. they had not yet recv'd the Mandate from Shrews. Unless I go into *Pension*, (and nothing but dangerous cold weather will drive me in) I shall now be easily able to pay my way home, supposing I stay here several months more.

I am practically righted again in Health, & have begun to eat ordinary food, and plenty of it. Hence I am visibly re-fattening day by day. I will not continue on to another page for I shall get benumbed, if I stay out of bed much longer.

Your affectionate, Wilfred

[13] Tom Owen had sent Wilfred a business letter for translation.
[14] The Anglican chaplain in Bordeaux.

225. To Susan Owen

16th [December 1913]   *Bordeaux*

My dearest Mother,

It is 10.20 P.M. But I must materialise a few of the innumerable communications which, every day, I reserve for you : Or you will cease to believe in them. I have made tonight a fire; but it is of the Alpenrose variety, both in the matter of Fuel and Intensity of Rays. One of my feet is therefore half up the chimney, & the other somewhere underneath the smouldering logs.

I was 'wistfully amused' that you should suspect the Sunday Swarry to be 'unSundaylike'. First, the *Union Chrétienne* is the Y.M.C.A.—or the French Equivalent of that Establishment. Last, the Swarry closed with Reading & Prayer. I did not play the Piano. It was a German who pressed me to; I agreed—not at once because one note is broken, & things might happen. Still it was arranged. In the course of the affair, the same German lumbered up to the Piano, sat somewhere around it, opened my *Blake's March,* & let fall his sausage-fingers, (possibly I am wrong here, & it was only the <u>thumbs</u> that were used). The Result was what a sack-race is to the March of the British Life Guards. <u>At the moment,</u> I should have <u>welcomed</u> a war with Germany. Such is the frailty of our Senses.

The same hulking fellow, (he has a neck like twenty bulls) nearly does for me every day—by the manner he eats his Soup. You know the Germans are said to be fond of saying Ach! Imagine this syllable extended over ten minutes, and you hear Herr — eating his soup.

In the morning, I take *Déjeuner* at a Restaurant where the Dishes are of wider choice, (and very good.) I have taken *cachets,* and, because I exclude wine, pay only 1 f. 10 c. per meal! This allows me afternoon tea, & a cake or so therewith. I have had to get a *service,* as Mme. not unnaturally objects to my monopolising her pot. <u>I</u> also object to the Coffee, which she usually leaves in it; for she uses it for Both. So, not wishing to buy heavy things, which I must leave behind, I have got a delightful Tea Pot, Sugar Basin, & Jug in <u>Aluminium</u>: unbreakable & portable, and elegant, & in lustre rivalling silver & surpassing all White Metals, and which I suppose, will accompany me in all my wanderings.—Such amiable concerns as tea-pots, you notice, check my wonted wanderings in letters.

This time last year—'pon my word I forget what I was going to say. Never mind! this year will do : You asked me a question? Ah yes!—I have no answer— ready :—have not the least idea how I shall spend Christmas Day, beyond that it will not be in B. School. Boxing Day may or not be in that <u>Box</u> (as the French call a 'Dirty Hole'.)

The '3rd English' was apparently a myth to keep us going strong. Fortunately I <u>am</u> going strong—but feel very troubled about one thing: I am thwarted in every serious attempt to improve my French. I cannot take lessons in the School:— Aumont says if I have <u>too many</u> lessons how can I take more? And now he has refused to make any facilities for me to follow the gratuitous Courses at the University. It appears that the Sub-Director has also asked to attend these Lectures: <u>also to be refused</u>! What is worse, with the continual drumming on English from morn to night, I have no linguistic hunger left in me and eschew 'Conversation'.

The student I met that Sunday at the Union says he himself was 'nearly a victim' of the Berlitz Schools; and is most anxious for me to find some employment where I should speak French. I shall seek for no such thing, unless I am told off the B.S. or find the work really excessive.

I do not suffer in the smallest degree from Heart.[15] I hope your inquiries were not suggested by any trouble of your own. I should forget I was not robust in that Muscle, were I not warned in a dream. For the other night (before you wrote) I was told by the people in next room that I groaned sorely many times; and I afterwards remembered having tried to impel <u>you</u> up the Cop, and of moving you about a yard an hour! Such dreams denote—Weak Heart. (Old Moore)

I have cashed the Order long ago, thanks, but have not broken into the Gold, even at my lowest moment! The Arm chair does not appear! I need absolutely nothing for Christmas & implore you to send nothing material, but a few drops of Ink, dried, after being suitably disposed over a few leaves of paper, by all your (plural) hands severally. My presents I think I must combine with Homing Gifts : but you may tell me if this is objected to. There is here no mention, no whisper of Christmas, nor ever will be. The Germans here will buy them Trees and look at them; the French will buy older wines, and gulp them, I shall buy a huge Yule Log— and feel it. And also, a few more Postage Stamps, and will lick them, all in good time.

For the Present, then, Goodbye! And fondest love

from W

<hr>

[15] Owen was later passed fit for the Army. See Letter 133. HO believed the fears over his brother's heart were imaginary, as was his incipient tuberculosis, but TB had serious consequences in those days and it not surprising that it would be feared.

226. To Susan Owen

Sunday, 21 December [1913]   *Bordeaux*

My own dear Mother,

I suddenly remembered today that if you are to hear from me 'on Christmas', I must post this very night. Today has whizzed by, and I am again sitting by my logs, and trying to render some account of myself. This afternoon I have once more been prevented from going to a 'Temple'; this time because of a Frenchman whom I have at last found to exchange lessons. I appointed him to call at two o'clock to arrange things.—He simply would not leave me. I hope to profit by this acquaintance, (arranged for me by Miss Markowsky, Professor of Russian) for the party, M. Michellet,[16](27) has been a French Master in an English Secondary School, & speaks very fluently English.

One of the Young Men, brought an elderly person to meet me one night, who had the reputation of having been a Berlitz Professor in Germany. He was willing to give lessons for 1 franc per hour, at any time, on any day. This is very convenient, & I went one day. I am doubtful of continuing, though I can't exactly say Why.—Perhaps it is the Franc!

Meanwhile the Hard Labour continues. Ten Lessons tomorrow. Christmas Day will certainly be free, tho' nothing has been said by 'the Direction'. I hardly expect any change to be made on the 24th or 26th.

I have not formed any plans for spending the 25th beyond that a portion shall be spent in Contemplation of what is going on at Mahim. May it be well and truly a day filled with peace and goodwill. As for the good tidings, the best I can give you are that I am well; and, if never gay, not often gloomy. Whatever grievances I have, I have no reason to repent having come to France. I eat (I repeat for your ease) generously and delicately, as I choose. There are many plum-puddings in the shop windows, if I needed 'em. There is even an English Grocery Shop, where if I shut my eyes to smell and listen the better, I might fancy myself in Teece's.[17] Teece's Shed is hard and hideous, and the garden thereby, barren and dismal; yet it were well if I could alight on that Garden, and witness the simple festivities; and tell ghost stories—stories of the Ghost of Christmas Past. I have no Dickens-Book with me, but the Music of the Carol is <u>remembered as if it</u> were all a memory of my own life.

I am, in a way, glad to miss <u>for once</u> the Association of Carols, Snow, Mincemeat, Presents, Holly, Stockings, Merry Christmas etc. They will have a huge interest next year.

In the same way I do not permit myself to think of Flowers, Trees, Grass, Hills, or Clouds, (No Adjectives even allowed) because I am preparing myself for a magnificent Revel one day in the Spring. Never, in all my born days, have I been so utterly towny as at this moment. Not even in Willmer Road,[18] in the old dark days; whereof, when I think, I come near tears, but not through pain. Ten years have matured those memories into Sweetness only. <u>You</u> are little changed since then; but, d'you know, Father seems more so. Mary & Harold—both little changed. Colin entirely. Alas, for Baby Colin!

If I should ever beget me a Child, he could not be more adored than was Colin in those days…In those days when I taught him the colours, showing him the Wall, the Floor, & the Carpet, <u>exactly</u> as I do at this day—to a very different type of toddler! When I begin to think how changed is Myself, I just…stop thinking.

'Tis just as well; at least in a Christmas Letter!

I have just remembered, as *à propos,* that the Spaniard is mightily anxious that I should dine with him on Christmas Day. The good Señior is very kind to desire it, but I don't relish giving Conversational Lessons without any Return. And his English is terribly jarring. However, I have to thank him for one piece of advice he gave me; '<u>If you work hardly, you must hardly eat.</u>' <u>Hardly</u> eat! He is still wondering why I smiled so loud at the remark!

Now, I break off for a while…I can only reach out my arms Northward, yearn to you, and 'wish you a Happy Christmas', aye <u>Two Happy Christmases</u>, with the intermediate days, also happy, to be thrown in…

I continue to another page [*but it is missing*]

[16] See Letter 230 for more information about him.
[17] The grocer in Cleveland Street, Shrewsbury.
[18] The Owens lived at 14 Willmer Road, Birkenhead, before moving to 51 Milton Street in 1899. In between there was a short time at another house in Elm Grove, Birkenhead.

230. To Susan Owen

Sunday, 18 January [1914]   *Union Chrétienne, Rue du Temple*
                                                                                    Bordeaux

My own dear Mother,

I found this sheet of paper, and constructed a pen from various fragments. Then I begged an envelope from the Custodian of this place, and must next buy a stamp from the Tobacconist's. Where the Ideas for a letter are coming from I don't quite know. For I am getting positively stultified by the nature of my employment.

The Cold continues still. Nothing short of a conflagration would warm my room; and that is why I am here. Water in the Jugs etc. has been frozen for several days. There has been Skating since Friday, but not for me! Garros[19] did not come to Bordeaux today, as expected; I suppose because of the weather; but is advertised for a week hence.

For the second time in life, I have met a character out of a book.[20] The Russian Professor[21] (such a wizened, little piece of womankind you never saw) found a Frenchman[22] to exchange Conversation with me. I have been several times to his house; & find him very agreeable. He is about 27, has a pleasing & handsome young *Française* to wife; and a delightful progeny, of two years' growth. He had a position as French Master in a Secondary School in Derbyshire for some years; but left England, for his wife's sake. He talks with great gusto of his life in England; boasts of talks with G. K. Chesterton; arguments with Colonel Seely;[23] and so on. He appears (only slightly) in the Book of his friend, Raymond Guasco: *John Bull's Island;*[24] which consists of a number of Sketches of English life, as it appeared to a philosophical Frenchman. Michellet (my friend) is 'the Professor', and into his mouth are put the reflective remarks, whether he actually made them or not. I enjoyed reading this book extremely; and shall buy a copy to translate to you— someday. The Author is in Paris now, making much money by his pen.

Michellet has also an Artist-friend, who has a studio in Paris. Himself has bought the Rights of Translation of Kipling's Works (some of them). Hence he is an interesting acquaintance; but, I am afraid, has an incorrigible tendency to potter. Now I must shun Potterers like the Plague. One day, he busies himself with a microscope; another day with a telescope;—and, today, it was an electric battery. Pictures, and Antiquities also interest him. In this he is so much like myself, so little more learned than myself, as to be annoying. But at least, he can help my French, if he will.

No Lessons have yet been started (in French) for us Profs. Meanwhile we have anything between 7 and 10 hours per day. One must take the good with the bad; one says; the good, so it seems, is to be enjoyed only in Summer. This is hard lines for me; and tempts me to abandon the idea of returning for a horrible exam! It would be easy to have lessons in German or other languages in the Summer, and this appeals to me likewise. If only I could dispense with the competitive Exam. and return in September, at the beginning of the term! By the way, the Sub-Director yesterday broached a 'marvellous thing' to me. Would I like to become Director of a small B. School in the N. of France? There would be plenty of work in winter; hardly any in summer; and clear profits of 4,000 francs a year. He will be pleased to tell me more when I have thought it over, and told my parents! 'But it's a marvellous thing' says he! Only I doubt my <u>business</u> capabilities.

I wonder how you have spent today. I have not been to Temple; in the week I sometimes get the opportunity of attending a Bible Class at the *Union*. I have not now space or time to make observations on the Religious Life in this Town, except to say that there is extraordinarily little of it. The Bible is unknown; especially to the Christians. I have met non-Christians who read it, however. It is indeed a sweet and precious thing to hear it read once more,—though in another tongue, yet, with the same earnest intonation as of old.

I am 'writing' just nothing; but I prosecute my Enquiries in Human Nature, and learn Philosophy, as I teach Speech, by the <u>Direct Method</u>. The B. School is a wonderful place for testing intellects. There are some pupils who, 3 months ago, knew not a word; and who now speak quite tolerably; others do not advance one bit. The <u>younger</u> and <u>busier</u> they are, the quicker they learn.

Don't forget your <u>Portraits,</u> if Uncle is so good. I shall be glad also to have the ones in which Leslie is so good. I have discovered a cheap place for my own, but the difficulty is to find the moment; as it is a long way from my usual haunts. There is a great racket going on in this room, which acts on my pen as on a Phonograph needle taking Records. Remember your Prime Object in being at Alp. is rest. Receive my fondest salutations.

x Wilfred

<hr>

[19] Roland Garros (1888–1918), a sporting pilot who invented a way of firing a machine gun forward from his Morane-Saulnier monoplane by fixing metal plates to the propeller to deflect the bullets. His name is commemorated by the Stade Roland-Garros in Paris.

[20] Mr Treacher, the geologist (see Letter 73), was probably the first.

[21] Mlle Markowski.

[22] M Michellet, first mentioned in Letter 226.

[23] John Edward Bernard Seely, 1st Baron Mottistone (1868–1947). Secretary of State for War 1912–14; he resigned office after intimating that troops would be used to enforce Home Rule in Ireland. He commanded a Canadian infantry brigade in France.

[24] J.-Raymond Guasco, *John Bull's Island: Carnet d'un reporter* (Paris, 1912).

235. To Tom Owen

Monday, 2 February 1914   *Bordeaux*

My dear Father,

I have now got more information about the 'school in the North of France'. It is none other than our Branch at Angers, of which the present director is

M. Aumont. It is the <u>Sub</u>-Director, Herr Langholz, only, who has spoken to me about it, and he does not wish me to speak to Mr. Aumont until I am certain about bidding for it.

Why does Mr. Aumont wish to part with the business?—Because, says Langholz, he is already too much occupied with Bordeaux and Nantes; and the Lady who at present manages it, is inefficient. The profits have certainly gone down in the last year; but this, I am told, is entirely due to the Lady, who speaks bad French and has no notion of how to deal with the Clients.

Langholz himself directed this school for some years;—so is worth listening to on the subject. The profits then reached 9000 f. per year. Out of this, he thinks at least 4000 f (£160) would be net gain.

I learn, however, that Aumont is asking 4,500 f as the price of its sale!

Unless, therefore, some Rich Uncle is prepared to advance some 5000 f, the thing will be impossible. Langholz says I might possibly obtain such an arrangement as this : to take the school on trial for 1 year. with a deposit of 1000 f, and pay the remainder if I found it worth continuing.

Angers is within easy reach of St. Malo; so I should not be hopelessly cut off from Home. Moreover the Summer Months are so slack, that one might well manage a month's absence! In Winter there is plenty to do, as the Director is his own English Professor under ordinary circumstances. The German Professor does the Secretary's work. Spanish & other Teachers are to be found in the town and summoned as required.

Langholz speaks in enchanting terms of the <u>premises</u>! There are three rooms for classes, an apartment for the Director's growlery and night-lair, and a Kitchen, as well as the Office. Cleaning and Personal Attention is done by Boys or Women.

I am certainly very young to take on me the Direction of a School! And unless the emoluments were really considerable, it would not be worth the Responsibility. But I should do better first to take posts as Professor in other countries, Italy for instance, in order to be capable of teaching several languages.

This is always supposing I cannot first finish my <u>English</u> studies, at College.

You were right in judging that I am not hungering for the Examination; None the less, I pine to devote two or three years to uninterrupted, unencumbered Study. If this Desire, now ten years old, be not realized, I must carry a heavy load of disappointment to my life's end!...Thus, if, considering the Angers-Box a marvellous chance, you obtained the £200 necessary for its purchase, I would still rather see the money invested in College Fees!

The more so, as an English Degree admits one to a French University, where one does a little English Instruction, while following Courses for French Degrees. Last Friday I met an English fellow (the first since I came) who is doing this. With a Double Degree, one has no mean Educational Chances. I must enquire whether the little English Teaching this man does is sufficient to maintain him.

The fact that Langholz thinks me capable of managing a school, and in a foreign element too, proves that I do not wholly live in dreams.

I have no false ideas of Business. 'Anything we do to make money is Business.' If I have shirked the idea of Shop, or Office, or Elementary School, it is only because I am more clear-sighted than another; and see that once fixed in a low-level Rut one is ever-after straightened there;—straightened intellectually and socially as surely as financially.

Neither am I under any delusions as to Literature as a means of livelihood.

But I must not wander from the purpose of this letter, which is: to ask your opinion of the Berlitz Affair; and, secondly, to state that if you find it beyond your power to supplement either of the Reading Scholarships, I willingly resign this Scheme, rather than be the least cause of adding to your worries or perplexities.

I am wondering very much what will come of all this.

I don't feel inclined to stay in Bordeaux all the summer; especially as I hear the heat is terrific (save the mark, O Harold) in July! But if the lessons are few it will be more supportable. At present they allow me little leisure: (I have been munching my afternoon refreshments while writing this letter.)

I hope you, dear Father, are fairly free of worry, and in your usual spirits.

Your most affectionate Son, Wilfred

236. To Mary Owen

Tuesday, 3 February [1914]   [*Bordeaux*]

Dearest Mary,

It was good to have some Violets in my Room that the Oxford Clays and Alpenrose Airs had nourished! I like these tangible specimens of my Motherland's sweetness, and of my Sister's Love. Many thanks for the Post Card also.

I wonder whether you are doing anything at French? My serious advice to you is not—to work hard; but to leave it entirely! Time spent on Grammars and Translations under the direction of an English Teacher is wasted. Such is the conclusion I have come to! I now realise that I must have had an abominable accent; for tho' I have made radical alterations in my pronunciation since being here, I am still a very long way from perfection. The majority of English Teachers have an execrable Accent, and what is worse, no notion of the Direct Method. If only I could give you a few lessons à la Berlitz! But I will, too, before long! We will form a French Course in the dining-room every night. I guarantee I would have you all talking good French in 3 months! At least, there are dozens of pupils who have learnt English in that time.

You must tell me if you take to my idea of your giving all your attention to English for a while! Except as a mental exercise, your laborious Translations are useless; in fact harmful! The Bertenshaw Grammar[25] has my everlasting anathema. Forgive my ardour: I yearn over your welfare.

W

[25] Owen's copy of *Longman's Illustrated First Conversational French Reader* (1904) by Thomas Handel Bertenshaw survives in his Library in the Bodleian. Some illustrations have been coloured with crayons.

238. To Susan Owen

Saturday, 14 February [1914]   *Bordeaux*

My own Mother,

I fear you will have already have got restive for the receipt of these pages tho' they are not yet written. For I haven't the faintest idea when I wrote last. It is quite by a heroic fortitude that I resist my couch this night. The week has been a whirl of lessons. However they never tire me to the point of doing me harm. There was a time when I went on till I trembled, and talked nonsense, (and finally of course lost ¾ of Life for a week) but I <u>won't do</u> that now. Yesterday six lessons following were set down for me [*three words illegible*] and <u>then 2 more</u>!

I took the list to Aumont and told him what I thought.

Strange to say, it seems to have some effect; for today I have had two lessons less than Miss Hewitt, (who goes on turning, turning, turning out lessons as a Mangler mangles hour by hour) and it is <u>she</u> (and not I) who is confronted with the enormity of Eleven Hours of it on Monday!!

I believe the Angers Box is already sold; so that is off one's mind. As it would have required much working up, and would on no account have been worth taking for less than five years or so, I am glad I am not tethered to it.

I shall write to Reading very presently, and I thank you very heartily for telling me to ! This Bordeaux business is all very well for now, but it must not be for long. I am at last beginning to sport something like an <u>accent</u>. At least those who stared when I spoke French, or answered off the point, now compliment me on my pronunciation. I consider it a scandal that such teachers as taught me French should be allowed in Schools. Dear Mary must no longer muddle her head with rules & exceptions, or corrupt her tongue with what Miss G. will teach her.

Let her study English Rules, & cultivate fluency in one language, before she undertakes to be <u>halting</u>, in <u>two</u>—for I never yet heard her compound three <u>consecutive</u> sentences within two hours. Moreover I shall need a little assistance in English when I get back, because only today I told a pupil that the preterite of 'bring' was 'brang' ! ! And, again, read '<u>Ar</u>tchangel' for 'Arkangel' and only the Blessed Ghosts of Nuttall or Webster know what spelling errors appear on these sleepy pages.

I rejoice over the photographs and their tale. You are certainly plumper; but I shall soon have to dispute the statements you make concerning your age, and consider them as a hoax, invented to hinder us from marrying young as you must have done. Keep up the game for a few more years, for I shall be young for many years yet. There is no immediate reason for Mary (or any of you) to learn French, for the countess has not yet crossed my path. In fact I was never so absolutely free of 'heart trouble' within these ten years past. This will no doubt give you immense satisfaction. But it should not....

You ought not to discourage too hard.

If you knew what hands have been laid on my arm, in the night, along the Bordeaux streets, or what eyes play upon me in the restaurant where I daily eat, methinks you would wish that the star and adoration of my life had risen; or would quickly rise.

But never fear: thank Home, and Poetry, and the FORCE behind both. And rejoice with me that a calmer time has come for me; and that fifty blandishments cannot move me like ten notes of a violin or a line of Keats.

All women, without exception, annoy me, and the mercenaries (which the innocent old pastor thought might allure) I utterly detest; more indeed than as a charitable being, I ought.

But I should not like to have seen myself in this town, two years earlier. And if you have not already spoken to Harold, I do implore you to muster courage and tell him a [? something] or two more than you told me, which was nothing.

Still, if you never had any revelations to make to me, at 14, I shall have no confession now I am 21. At least, none such as must make me blush and weep and you [? grow] pale.

But I shall perhaps continue my Reminiscences next time, according to the spirit in which you receive these present. Mistake not my spirit; if I seem joking I am really grave; (even as when my writing is most worthless my thoughts are most worthy). We say strange things in our sleep. I have been partially so for half an hour.

The enclosed is for Mary. Her photo is lovely; they are all precious, yours: though not such works of art as is Leslie's; which is quite a masterpiece, don't you think?

I have met more desirable aquaintances, (Univ. Students.) Tomorrow I am again dining with the violin boy.

I must not now depict scenes, pickle juicy bits or pick tricky characters to pieces to tickle you (witness if my wits are going)—goodnight! call me at 7 in the morning, no Sunday—*demain c'est dimanche n'est-ce pas: à 9 heures alors; oui, madame,* language—*mixé*... ah! put out the light there—ah! warm, comfortable; pillow—soft, all identity lost —save am

Mother's Son

239. To Susan Owen

Postcard

Wednesday [Postmark 25 February 1914]   *[Postmark Bordeaux]*

I don't think I asked about your headaches in my last; but I think about you most constantly—just now of all times, today a YEAR ago the pneumonia definitely appeared. It was 'to-night' I had the first phantasms.—and how have I been spending the anniversary?—Revelling! in the Carnival! I had huge success with my Costume: Nothing more elaborate than my Gown on my back a laurel wreath on my head, & a palm branch in the hand. These 3, (with of course a <u>Mask</u>—my own home-made domino) made an imposing combination! I was with a student (whom I like very much), & his friends. The crowds were enormous, & I was twice choked with confetti. Weather magnificent. But the purpose of this card is really only to thank you for your interesting & valuable letter, & Colin's also; to carry any poor comfort it can to your neuralgia, to say my throat is now tickled by nothing worse than confetti-particles; & to beg for a Standard Waverley Nib; & to ask is there any thing in the realm of France you wd. specially like for the 17th of March ? Dearest Love to All,

Wilfred

Sorry I forgot a stamp the other day—or night.

250. To Mary Owen

15 April 1914   *Bordeaux*

My own dear Sister,

Exceeding joyful was I to see your handwriting in my letter-box on Tuesday Morning; and the more so when I read of how you spent your Easter; how you thought of holy things; how you remembered me; and how you walked out, seeking the new flowers. To you then, shall I deliver such account of my own doing as is meet and right I should; hoping it will 'amuse your heart and instruct your mind'—(nay: I prefer to change the old formula, and to say 'amuse your mind, and instruct your heart.')

As soon as Rochelle scheme was impossiblised (is this English, I forget?) I told the Lems[26] I should be glad to accept their offer. I had twice met the eldest daughter of 'the Inviter's'[27] at Lem's house, and as she spoke good French, had pleasant manners, and was only good looking in a large and vague sense, I said—now here's an opportunity for two days' real peace.

I joined the Lems at 7.30 on Easter Morning, inside my old green suit, old boots, old tie, sans cuffs, gloves or hair-parting; prepared for a rare escapade in the country; so was a little abashed to find Raoul in his very best, cuffs protruding shirt-front bulging; all prognosticating that either we were going to a fine family or that some member of it had fine eyes. The first member we saw at Castelnau put me at ease—an ancient man, in wooden boots, corkscrew trousers, and a coat twice as ancient as himself. But lo! waiting for us at the station-gates, stood the young lady I already knew in costume as modern as her grandfather's were antique; and with her a superb specimen of human beauty, the younger sister of sixteen!

I walked behind them to the House feeling mighty queer. There, I was presented to the Mother, a pleasant dame of conical figure that continually put me in mind of a broody hen; and to the grandmother, who began weeping forthwith; and made me thrice welcome, as she said, for the sake of her darling grandson, who has been in Algeria six months; then, entered the father, with his dog & gun, a brown and handsome figure, with dark and terrible eyes, in rustic clothes & sabots, as scorning to appear anything but what he was, plain proprietor of vineyards. So we sat around the best room; looking at the inevitable album of postcards, while various children of the family's dependents were exhibited before us, and the grandmother, all heart and kindliness, moved round and round the room in tears, sure that the grandson must be deadly ill in that far land.

Then all but Mère & Grandmère, (who had dinner to see to) went into the woods. I took the side of the eighty-year grandfather, and we spoke of France, and of her Past. There were multitudes on multitudes of primroses & violets, gigantic marsh-marigolds, of which a little peasant boy who followed us, gathered bunches for me; which bunches Mme. Lem contrived to make me present to the right fair lady. Her name I soon learnt was Henriette—(abominable, while her sister's is so pleasing—Armande!) Knowing her beauty was of the stimulating, & quickly-effective kind, I was watching Raoul, and at dinner his restiveness began. For my part I could only sit like an Egyptian piece of Statuary, hands on knees, staring apparently into space; but seeing well enough to count how often the marvellous eyes looked in my direction, which was exactly four times per minute. Finally, Raoul made a complete ass of himself, and H. fled from the table, and locked herself up for half an hour.

In the afternoon all went to the oakwoods. Old man Lem is a merry old elephant, and in the woods ran here and there, capering and singing for pure delight. Raoul retired behind a tree and mildly sulked. I, strung up, paced along, stiff as a frightened cat. Then the blessed quiet of the woods, the subdued sunshine, the cuckoos and the nightingales worked on us all. Old man L. quieted down, I grew more at ease, Raoul returned. We reached an opening in the trees, where the oaks gave place to blossom-trees, a dance was proposed. Father L. set the time with voice and hands; but I spoilt the fun by not having the faintest notion of how to step!

In France the afternoons are long, and there was time for a second walk before the *Collation du Soir*. For this occasion, Henriette fished up a plump friend from the village, clearly to be a buffer between herself and Raoul. This time we walked arm in arm. I could scarcely have been happier. Raoul might clearly have been happier than he was ; but it was hardly my fault. And the memory of those moments will remain sweet to me, chiefly, my dear Sister, chiefly because I took no advantage of that young and ardent nature, neither even said what I thought of her 'appas', but left the compliments, with the vows, to Raoul. Perhaps I listened with too much sympathy to her plaints of captivity : how she is watched and warded everywhere: not even allowed to visit people in Bordeaux ; but has no gayer, nobler, or learned companions but the grandmother, everlastingly regretting her grandson; the little villagers; the father forever lauding his wines; and a professor who prepares her for an examination.

At dinner, Papa enjoyed himself hugely with astonishing the company by the ancient bottles of Médoc which he brought forth from time to time. The corks were opened with alarms and flourishes; and a little lecture on the harvests of the various years. Finally we got back to 1870!! It is needless to say that not one of the convivial guests overdid his proper number of glasses!

Before the dessert, Madame Poitou insisted on reading publicly the last letter from her son, (which was six times as long and circumstantial as my own) describing his adventures with some English girls in the mountains of Algeria: including such minute & numerous remarks on the character and appearance of one of them, as led to sage comments by the old people, and gave me an opportunity to exhort his sisters to learn English without delay. Afterwards they all begged me to write a message in English to the boy; which, when I translated it, delighted them beyond measure.

I shared a bedroom with Raoul. Perhaps it was the air of the pine forests (forests not woods) that made each breath a thing of joy—or perhaps it was the agitated calling of the nightingales; but I did not sleep well.

On Monday Morning, Raoul, his Father, & M. Poitou, instructed me upon the vineyards, and we spent the morning viewing the country, and picking snails from the new-budding plants.

Lunch took an immense time—and there was only time for a game of *cache-cache* about the farm before the four o'clock train. Raoul, at the last moment, got leave to stay till Wednesday; when he will come back with Armande, who will stay at Lem's for a fortnight.

Twenty minutes we waited at the window of the train, and the adieus were many. Rich masses of lilac encumbered the carriage, and the odour was carried by the inblowing breeze into my brain, to be an everlasting memory. Then those faces and those places fell away from me.

The city, at 6 o'clock, was strangely hot and empty, save of dust and glare; and back in my room, I underwent a sad reaction. But I recovered; and soon demonstrated how much I was benefited by the excursion, by writing 50 lines of poetry in as many minutes![28] (thing not attempted for 'years') ; and by getting better results out of a piano than much practice could give; and by generally soaking my specs. in that rosey liquid young blood; so that all people, all plants, all tasks, all books, appear to me far fairer than they did.

Sunday

I have kept back these pages just a little too long: but I can now acknowledge the Thursday Letter of dear Mother; and felicitate Harold on his eventually getting on *La Esmeraldas*[29]—prettier name, for one thing, than 'Carcoodoodledo'. I wonder whether Harold will have the opportunity to learn Spanish. Let him not take a S. American Spaniard; their pronunciation is bad.

Poof! here I am on 'Languages' again: a subject which gives me pain; for I am learning a hundredth part of what I teach which isn't fair!

I certainly never undertook to inculcate Slang upon my brethren; but don't thank me because you are a purist; for I have tried to make you pedants, and thank Minerva, you are not that yet.

Miss Hewitt had a day or so's notice to bundle off to—(Ha! Slang! be cheesed, vile slang!) that is to transfer herself to Angers. Another Miss has taken her place for this week but is going next week to Germany. 'The One remains; the many change and pass.'[30]

M. Aumont mentioned that he hoped I should now remain till August; but if I am given so much and so little as I have been given, I shall do no such thing. I already know several persons who would like private lessons with me....

I commend you to God who surely fends you; and to our sweet Mother who no less tends you; I, who am your devoted and very-much-elder

Brother

[26] Raoul Lem was a pupil. Later, as proposed penfriend for Colin, he stayed at Mahim. His father was a commercial traveller and the family was Protestant.

[27] M Poitou.

[28] These are part of the 'Perseus' fragments (*CPF*, pp. 467–70), a long-standing project. See also Letters 340 and 616, n. 105. For a full discussion of 'Perseus' see DH, *Owen the Poet* (Basingstoke: The Macmillan Press, 1986), pp. 42–53.

[29] HO's ship, which he joined on 22 April 1914, sailing first to Le Havre, then to South America. The ship was off Montevideo when war was declared. It reached Liverpool on 6 September 1914. See 'Harold Owen's Voyages', *WOANB*, Appendix D, pp. 475–8.

[30] Shelley, *Adonais*, LII.

253. To Mary Owen

Sunday, 10 May 1914   *Bordeaux*

My dear Sister,

Here is six o'clock on Sunday Afternoon, and unless I seize the moment and my pen and paper, you will be kept waiting for an answer to your letter indefinitely. I read your letter about 9 o'clock, and then fell back on my pillow and snored for another two hours. Then feeling I had cleared off any debts I owed to Morpheus, I made my first toilet, and collected my towels & soaps and 'clean things' and walked to my bathroom, (which is quarter of a mile away!) & paid 6d. for a few gallons of water!

Returned I made my Second Toilet, and prepared a dinner: for it is my custom on Sundays to eat in my room. On all other days I am at a Restaurant. Then I went out to read with my friend Bizardel,[31] and had a pleasant time under the chestnut-trees of his garden. This young man was until lately in the Banque de France, and now he is studying Law at home. His father is a judge.

On my way home, I noticed an imposing Funeral Service was being held in an old Church, and I went in. The gloom, the incense, the draperies, the shine of many candles, the images and ornaments, were what may be got anywhere in England; but the solemn voices of the priests was what I had never heard before. The melancholy of a bass voice, mourning, now alone, now in company with other voices or with music, was altogether fine; as fine as the Nightingale—(bird or poem). And although the chanting was Latin, yet was it more intelligible to the human soul than could be statements distinctly enunciated in the vernacular. (I hope you will at least try to understand me) So that I fell, only for a few minutes, it is true, under the spell of the Catholic Religion, and re-entered a phase of my Experience which had been buried under three or four successive and different phases of thought. The illusion soon passed and I spent the rest of the time considering this form of religion, from aloof.

There was only one fault in the Funeral Ceremony, which if it were intentional would be chiefest beauty of all. It was the Undertakers' Men. They wore imitation top-hats and kept them on in the church. What these articles were made of I cannot imagine, but their hideous shininess was most fascinating. Also, the men were noisy of foot, clumsy of hand, brutal of face. Now if these creatures had functioned in the disguise of skeletons or demons, they could not have been more abominable, and as their duties cannot be anything but abominable to the mourners, perhaps it is a stroke of real art to let them be as horrible as possible!

I suppose Grandpa is already buried.[32] I wonder where.

I was glad to have some account of your confirmation. I know who is the Bishop of Lichf'd. I remember studying his work as Rector of Liverpool, recounted in 'the Treasury' many years ago. His face also is quite familiar. I almost remember his name: something like Kempenfelt,[33] I think?

I never hear from you as to what you are reading. Circumstances considered, I am of course more pleased to hear of your industry in the house than of your much reading, and busying yourself with imaginary circumstances in which you will never be called upon to act.

But circumstances re-considered, nothing would be more painful to me than that you, most serious of sisters, were not more read and more instructed than the fast type of schoolgirl which you despise.

Therefore I hope you are serious in reading at least one genuine book per fortnight; and if the Book is Jeremiah or Jude, so much the better.

I wonder who are now your friends. Have you any bosom friend, or are they all of the arm's length variety? I have read more than once in your letters of some Miss Hilton who, you confess, is 'shoppy'.[34] Now that is distressing. The fact of being employed in a shop does not matter; but shoppiness does matter.

Do you ever write to Dorothy, or she to you?

You may ask me what friend I ever made among the living of the world; [several lines illegible] but what [? a] marvellous [one word illegible] unites me with Leslie, the proof being not that we write [one word illegible] daily, but that we write not at all, and yet understand each other perfectly.

I have half a dozen students of Bordeaux University with whom I might become intimate, but the sad pity of it is that I am as much a prisoner from social life as any wretch in the jail. Yes, and the galling part of it is that Leisure here would be so much more precious than in Shrewsbury.

Heaven knows I appreciate such leisure as I ever had, and used it, I hope, not ill; but here I could amuse myself so admirably. Thus I could any morning see the Surgical Operations of the Hospitals under the protection of a student who has invited me; or any afternoon attend the Sessions of the Law Courts, under the protection of an eminent advocate who is my pupil.

I shall have to spend here at least a fortnight living on my capital after my Engagement is done with.

(Mond.) Here follows a message to Mother: I have now received my Back-Supplements, and cashed the cheque this afternoon. I find I have more than £5. I am therefore able to pay my passage.

Now my green suit which, it will be remembered was bought, a ready-made article, about midsummer 1911, is still going strong, but I foresee a sudden collapse not far off. Thus I have only one suit left, whether for the exercise of my profession, or (as I remind myself) for garden-parties, or Royal Functions. Just when I perceive this, I find myself in a position to save 20s. by buying a suit immediately; for Monsieur Dubo through the intervention of some friend, can get stuffs <u>at Tailor's Prices</u> from Paris, and in fact a fine selection of Spring-Summer Patterns is in my room at present. The total costs would be between 50 and 60 francs. Ought I to take this opportunity? ...

I once more address myself to you, dear Sister, to beg you to understand how hastily I am writing, which makes it impossible to revise any weird things I may have said. May it be not long before I see you all again.

Adieu!

Need I add: my warmest Love for Dear Mother, Father and Childe Colin.

[31] A law student, one of Owen's pupils. On the outbreak of war in August he was working in the offices of the Prefect of Bordeaux. See Letter 284.

[32] This sentence was crossed out by Susan Owen on the manuscript, but reinstated by HO and JB. William Owen died in Torquay at the beginning of May. His widow, Martha, died in 1921.

[33] The Rt Rev. John Augustine Kempthorne (1864–1946), formerly Bishop of Hull (1910–13), Bishop of Lichfield (1913–37).

[34] Shoppy = common. HO and JB omitted the complete surname in their edition ('Miss H—'), but the manuscript names the dispenser in Boots, Shrewsbury, as Miss Hilton.

258. To Susan Owen

24 May 1914   *Bordeaux*

My dearest Mother,

I wonder what Father will have arranged about his holidays. I hope you have not been waiting since Friday to hear from me. On Thursday, as I said, I was out of Bordeaux all day; and on Wednesday all I could do between the lessons was to sprawl on my armchair, and watch through half-shut eyelids my little fingers tremblingly dropping dew on the floor.

It is a blessing that lessons can be given sitting down. And I am always cooler than my pupils, who (haven't I seen 'em from the balcony!) scorch through the streets and scramble upstairs like a mad motor-car in a Cinema, lest they should miss two minutes of their sixty. Yesterday, one pupil fell faint and couldn't go on, but needless to say, this happened exactly 4 mins. before the end of the lesson.

Today it is much cooler, after a night-thunderstorm.

I suppose now I must talk about myself or you will not consider this as a letter. Such self-expatiation makes letter-writing not only an unwholesome habit, but a distasteful task. Wouldn't it be better to invent things about acquaintances, till they seemed interesting to you; or relate weird things of pupils (no need of invention here) or even translate from local journals? Or, if I were dear ... I might note how glorious was that last Lobster-Mayonnaise; or if I were ... might specify what boats were in the docks, and how many tons each displaced; or if I were ... I might babble of Victor Hugo, and why he is the greatest possible of all the grandest, and also the highest, deepest, and thickest, and toughest.

But it happens I am full of thoughts about myself which it will be relief to expel.

It was curious you asked about my grey hairs, for just last week I noticed they were cropping up again. In winter they died down, with the grass. My face is certainly satisfactory, as regards skin & muscle, free from whelks and knobs and mud-volcanoes; but whether 'of lovely colour' as your dreams reveal, depends on the light. But I wish Dr. Carrel[35] (who startled the world by exchanging people's hearts, putting in monkey's gizzards for rhino's giblets, sausage-skins for wind-pipes, pig's tails for ladies fingers (the last operations are confined to America, I notice)) —I wish the man would put-me-in a new skull,—nothing less will help my profile. When that little job had been satisfactorily arranged, I would give in exchange my brain and heart (for they are but snares to me), for various other parts; e.g.

Pair of Eyes, which I would seek in France,
Mouth & Fittings, which I would pick up cheap in Italy;
Head of Hair, fine samples plentiful in Greece;
Chest—from Sweden;
Legs, (badly needed)—France again;
Shoulder—America, of course.

The foregoing rhapsody is only an abortive expression of a solemn enough verity: which is, that, supposing I have progeny, they must be given the maximum chance of being fair of face and limb; and that that Chance, so to speak, must be classically and romantically, generally and particularly, in sunlight and in starlight, in sickness and in health, skin, bone —; and — muscularly Beautiful. By this, must be understood that she satisfy my sense of beauty: not entirely, of course, I have gone too far in aesthetics, seen too many persons, pictures and statues, lived too long for that—but she must exhibit say 75 out of the hundred essential characters. Not every man need have even his own sense of beauty realised in order to be happy, limited and distorted as his ideal already is; but that was settled for me time and time ago. In thus laying down such exigencies I risk making myself ridiculous later on; but at least you will admit that my present mind is a safe and useful one, considering my prospects.

I was much astonished the other day to find that Tofield, *Professeur d' Anglais II*, is married, and trails a French wife about with him, from Berlitz School to Berlitz School. The young lady naturally has to be half-supported by her parents. Anyhow, though obviously happy, they are certainly not comfortable; for Tofield came borrowing 25 f. of me the other day.

I am reminded by this of another episode which I ought to have told you a time ago to give you the full effect of its suddeness. The elder Mlle. Poitou of Castelnau, the large and statuesque of bulk, during her fortnight's stay in Bordeaux, snapped up a fiancé and is to be married about August. This however is quite a usual mode of procedure in France. Another convenient French institution is the *Dot*[36] which is never missing except among the really indigent. Also the suitor invariably sends a <u>representative</u> to the lady's papa, which I think the only effective time-saving device, invented by the French.

You asked me whether I should really like to direct a Berlitz School, if Uncle Ted would raise the capital. (Perhaps the personal allusion was not your's) Certainly. I could be happy enough for a time in France, Switzerland, or Italy. And these Schools can always be sold. Compared with the ordinary teaching-post, whether private proprietor of Boys' School, or on a government staff, Berlitz Direction is incomparably more agreeable. And compared as a business with other businesses of like capital, such a School is much more profitable.

But I must cultivate more grey hairs before that.

I must study—It is among students that I feel at present the most unhappy.

Such as I teach at School respect me as a man of mature learning, and wide experience of letters & science. While by such students as meet me casually I am supposed to be a young fellow employed in a Commercial House, and am often asked which wine-business I serve!

But I am neither of these. When I ask myself <u>what</u> I am I finish my interrogations in a *crise de nerfs*. You see these self-examinations, after a year's rest, begin again. At such times the sensation of the passing of Time sharpens into agony. How much have I advanced in study since the Matriculation 1911? Enormously in some fields, but not along the marked-out high-roads, and through those absurd old toll-gates called examinations.

I sometimes wonder whether my mere Pass in Matriculation disenchanted everybody. But no one has any idea of the crushing disadvantages that I suffered through the Wyle Cop work. It was a thrice-evil system: I did what should on no account ought to be attempted by anyone under 25; I did it precisely at the moment when every precious instant should have been devoted to undivided study, and the care of my frame. And I tried to do Both under the most unfavourable of particular circumstances.

Before that time I fought with my hands free and the result was a first place on the List of my first public examination.[37] Such a result will now never be possible more; or if possible less and less probable; more and more cruelly difficult… Nothing gave me the creeps more surely than the sight of old Kemp, trying to learn his Latin Conjugations at 24! Is any scene in George Eliot more piercing-sorrowful than Baldassarre the Scholar failing to read a paragraph?[38]

But think not it is examination results which attract me, and constrain me to a manner of life much less easy than my present. It is more like the call of an Art, which, morning and evening, makes me unhappy in my unfruitful labour. What Art ? ——— Any! Where lies my happiness, there lies my usefulness! I know when I am happy. We may not know what is good for us; but we know what is good to us. (Alas for the man who deceives himself in that.) I am happy with Art. I believe in <u>Science</u> more wholeheartedly than in Art; but what good could I do in that way?

I am only conscious of any satisfaction in Scientific Reading or Thinking when it rounds off into a poetical generality and vagueness. I find purer philosophy in a Poem than in a Conclusion of Geometry, a chemical analysis, or a physical law.

But all the time, you are asking: 'What Art is the fellow driving at?'

Music? If only I dare say Yes! I certainly believe I could make a better musician than many who profess to be, and are accepted as such. Mark, I do not for a moment call myself a musician, nor do I suspect I ever shall be; but there! I love Music, Violin first, Piano next, with such <u>strength</u> that I have to conceal the passion, for fear it be thought weakness. Strange to say, I met last Thursday in the woods of the Chateau Olivier, one of my pupils, who is a student of the Conservatoire here, and has the intention of being a soloist on the piano, and of giving concerts, and takes care to remark that he has <u>no</u> idea of being a Professor of Music. But what is chiefly strange is that, though he has had the energy and endurance to vanquish a Father and wit to escape from a commercial post, I doubt if he understands Music apart from Crotchets, Rests, and appoggiaturas. When I asked whether he thought of Composition, it was clear that he considered it entirely a matter of Counterpoint Rules.

But if I were a pupil of the Conservatoire...I should not complain of overwork. What a blessed tyranny would be the tyranny of a genius of a Master! If I failed...but even the despised 'Professors of Piano', (if anything above kettle-drummers), command six and ten francs per lesson in Bordeaux; which compares well with the Profession of Tongues! But it is as extravagant of me to think of Music now as it would be for, say, Father to think of training as a sea-captain. And then a little incident has stuck in my mind like a thorn. It was quite seven years ago; I had just played one of my juvenile pieces before a 'Company' and Grandpa was so well pleased that he said quite gleefully 'He! He! But you'll make your livin' at it yet:' which remark was instantly crushed with a storm of Pooh-Pooh's! Grandma, though admitting she couldn't have done the thing herself, snubbed dear Grandpa as a mere matter of principle and habit. But everybody else was sincerely indignant. That indignation I have felt and redoubted ever since.

Failing Music, is it Pictures that I hanker to do? I am not abashed to admit it, when I realize I was never really taught even to draw: for it was evident that Miss Martin[39] who sat in our Room during Drawing Lessons, could not draw as well as the majority of the class.

But Heigh ho! If there were anything in me I should, following Legend, have covered with spirited fresco say Teece's Shed; or carved the Staircase Knob into a serene Apollo!

Yet wait, wait, O impatient world, give me two years, give me two <u>free months</u>, before it be said that I have Nothing to Show for my temperament. Let me now, seriously and shamelessly, work out a Poem. Then shall be seen whether the Executive Power needful for at least one Fine Art, be present in me, or be missing.

My Temperament I have now no right to doubt. That I believe infallible; though it remains to know which, if any, Music, Painting, Sculpture, or Verse, is the most possible.

Witness, to confirm what I believe of my composition, on one side the Tragedy of Uncle Edward Shaw,[40] torn up by the roots by a perverted appetite; and on my other side, the Comedy of Aunt Emily Owen,[41] who literally palpitates with excess of physical sensation.

These are the natures which, labouring for self-expression, produce Art; and which rolling in retrogression produce Nothing or Crime.

Are you saddened by these declarations of mine? Anyhow, you know that as Parents You have, of all the world, the least title to find fault with what I am.

You must not take for granted Bernard Shaw, when he says:

The true artist will let his wife starve, ... his mother drudge for his living at seventy sooner than work at anything than his art.[42]

Nor will I for my part put any faith in this statement, which I read in the same play;

When a man who is born a poet, refuses a stool in a stockbroker's office, and lives in a garret, spunging on a poor landlady, or on his friends and relatives sooner than work against his grain ... we make large allowances for him.[43]

The large allowance may in Wordsworthian Years have amounted to as much as £200. Today it takes the form of a large allowance of space between the poet and his father's door.

Here I must take breath. I may find more to say another day. Meanwhile I am not in a garret, and have been working for money, since I was sixteen, disguised as the fact is!

[35] Alexis Carrel (1873–1944), French-American by birth, had been awarded the Nobel Prize in 1912. Among his publications was a paper in the *Journal of the American Medical Association*, 14 November 1908—'Results of the transplantation of blood vessels, organs, and limbs'. With a medical colleague he later became widely known for work in the treatment of war wounds (the 'Carrel–Dakin Method').

[36] Dowry.

[37] Taken at the Shrewsbury Technical School.

[38] In George Eliot's *Romola* (1862–3). Owen's copy, rubber-stamped 'W. E. Owen' on the flyleaf and containing his underlining, survives in his Library in the Bodleian.

[39] The art mistress at the Birkenhead Institute.

[40] Susan Owen's only brother was an alcoholic. He left England somewhere between 1888 and 1890/1 and was last known to have been in Denver, Colorado, in 1893. Her antipathy to drink was surely cemented by her experiences with her brother, whom she often had to put to bed when he came home drunk.

⁴¹ Edward Quayle's second wife, Emily (b.1869), 'Aunt Emmie'. Emily and Susan's elder sister and Quayle's first wife was Edith. They lived at Meols in the Wirral.
⁴² 'The true artist will let his wife starve, his children go barefoot, his mother drudge for his living at seventy, sooner than work at anything but his art'; Shaw, *Man and Superman* (1903), Act I.
⁴³ Ibid.

Now it is Wednes. and I have had with delight your news. I shall hope to have an important piece of your mind on Sunday.

Your dearly-loving Son

259. To Mary Owen

Monday, 1 June 1914   [*Bordeaux*]

Dearest Mary,

Your last letter gave me very much pleasure. Mother did not remind me of your Birthday; none the less I suddenly thought of it in writing the date on Saturday. A tremendous downpour of rain prevented me from making a tour of the shops; I just dived into a Bookseller's; but found nothing fit for you except a cheap copy, (of Gowan's production) of a French Poetess. And, as yet, you are not yet fit for Marceline Desbordes-Valmores!⁴⁴ But I have a design in sending you this, viz. to keep you hungry to learn French and I hope it won't be long before you read such works 'without tears'; at least without tears due to grammatical difficulties. Don't be disconcerted by the portrait on the cover! Remember you also have had ocular attacks; and have been seen to give fifty-seven double-winks at the ceiling every three minutes. You, also, have exhibited a nose, shiny enough to read by at night. You also have worn unfortunate bodice-yokes of ancient-british design. Hence say nothing horrid of poor Marceline's picture. But regard the book as a mere rubbishy brown-paper packet, and wait for me to untie the string—gently I promise you—and then you shall find in it many 'unvalued gems, inestimable stones'.⁴⁵

Today has been Holiday.⁴⁶ The Lems earnestly invited me to go up the river with them in the afternoon: they went to visit some friends who lived in a riverside village. This family inhabits the *Mairie* or Town-Hall, the *Patron* i.e. Papa, being 'Secretary to the Mayor' = 'Town Clerk', I suppose. One of the curly-haired daughters I had seen at my famous first dance. Unfortunately there were no boys. I do really regret it, because with French girls it is quite impossible to talk soberly and intellectually, since they have the brains of linnets; and it is equally impossible to speak amorously and poetically for fear of being compromised.

It is their own fault that they are watched and warded, as is proved by this incident. The *Jeunesse* consisting of two boys and four damosels were for a short time separated from the elders. And it was not I, who was just then engaged in a

Botanical Investigation; nor yet Raoul; but one of the young ladies who suggested that now was the moment *pour s'embrasser*. I was so taken off my guard that I kissed the curly-head without so much as looking round; but I finished off the rest only with much pressure and bad grace! Clearly, it was a solemn and established custom, not a merry improvised lark!

After this I several times fell asleep conversationally, and had to be roused up by Raoul.

I now learn that Raoul is proposed for the English Scholarship, but not elected yet. I am a little bothered about him; not simply because his English sets my teeth on edge; but because he eats half his words in speaking French, and such expressions as do drivel out are in the intonation of the Bordeaux Commercial Students. I am now able to recognize four or five species of French. First the ugly accent of working-class (not peasant) *Bordelais*: which includes the Dubo Family, certain of my night-pupils, and certain of my Boy-Scout acquaintance. Next, the manner of speech of the Higher Grade Schools and School of Commerce: characterized by great rapidity and fusion of words. Next the Bordeaux University Students' French, which certainly differs from the French of Parisians, which likewise is not the Best. Such is only to be got in the neighbourhood of Tours. Hence I shut down my imitative faculties when speaking with the majority of people I have to speak with: and very regrettable it is.

I say Raoul gabbles; but I know I also once spoke as untidily and indistinctly as I write now. Father did what he could to misunderstand me, and Mother to excuse me; but now a sterner Mother, whose child is Invention, has obliged me to mend my speech; and with such effect that both pupils and director thank & praise me for fine articulation!

I don't know whether you will remark any difference in my vowel-values when you hear me again. It will be joyful to hearken to you all. How fluent you will all seem, even thyself, O Sparse of Speech! I sometimes dream of being back in England, and am always sorry! It seems to my dreaming mind too soon, that my purpose has not been accomplished; and that it is so hard to get back to France! But when I wake I think differently!

Please set about finding some pupils for French, from which I might pocket 2s. per hour!...I mean it!

And now lay to your gentle heart my gentlest Wishes for your 'Future' (as there was anything but Future for us!) Be Strong. Cherish the Cherishers of our younger lives; and lead my darling Baby Colin along gentle ways!

Wilfred

[44] *Les Chefs-d'Œuvres Lyriques de Marceline Desbordes-Valmores* (Paris, 1913). Bell and Owen noted that it featured 'an un-flattering portrait of the author on the cover'. The copy survives in Owen's Library and contains a list, in Owen's hand, of the Latin and English names of seven plants.

[45] 'Inestimable stones, unvalu'd jewels'; Shakespeare, *Richard III*, I, iv, l. 27.

[46] Whit Monday.

263. To Susan Owen

6 June 1914   *Bordeaux*

My dearest Mother,

I had your loving letter on Sunday and I think I quite well understand by now your attitude towards my Home-Coming!

But <u>now</u> I want to know your attitude towards my passing-of-next-winter.

Certainly I shall not be at the Agricultural Show.[47] For though there may be even four more weeks of maximum work, I don't doubt that July and August will be much slacker and so worth waiting for.

Now in September and October are held special Courses of French for foreigners, at the University,[48] at a very low fee. At the end of these courses, one takes an Exam. which qualifies for a Diploma, stating the holder is 'Capable of Teaching the French Language'. Such a Diploma has, I know, some sort of value in England. Anyhow I should benefit immensely by the Courses. If, then, I could maintain myself for those two months, and I think I could, ought I not to hold out against the seduction of Home yet a little longer?

What is important to note is that persons registered for these French Courses are entitled to a Reduction of 50% on French Railways! This would make it even cheaper for me to go back thro' Paris. I might even engage myself for a month or so in the Paris B. School. It would be quite a safe undertaking for in Paris, Professors are not allowed to do more than seven hours per day. I should then arrive home for Christmas, and have plenty of time for reading for the Reading Scholarship, or even for Inter. Arts itself 1915. In fact I feel the time would be too long to remain at home, unless it were certain I could get some pupils for French, (or anything else).

The Alternative would be to come home immediately I am 'told off'; and at once to pack off to some other part of the world. For I am less sanguine than ever of 'Junior Posts in Boys' School'. Both as regards amount of leisure, difficulty of work, and style of living, I should be better in France or Germany as Berlitz Prof.

But better than all would be a few hours private independent lessons a day in Shrewsbury, by which I might profit twice as much as engaged by a school whatsoever.

And with the title *Diplomé de l'Université de Bordeaux* this should be quite possible.

Raoul's people are highly anxious for me to accompany him to Eng. He should be ready in about six weeks. But I really cannot let this consideration interfere with my plans.

10.30 p.m.

Let me know what you think of these plans; and if my alternatives are not clear to you, or if you have still another alternative tell it me. I am too sleepy to make a longer letter of this.

It might seem curious that I never write to Father or hear from him: [*one line illegible*] There is no sense in my writing out again for him what I say to you; and I have no time to write more. Father has no more to say than you tell me. And tho' I suspect he reads a good part of my letters. I always make my salutations to you alone because some things I say are not meet for an audience. I had a fearful attack of mosquitoes 2 nights ago, and haven't made up the six hours of sleep then lost. I only hope I shall reach the P.O. to drop this in the Foreign Box without napping on the way. Good Courage at the Dentists! My pat-on-the-back for Mary: nasal-tweak for Tweak for not writing to me.

Your devoted Son, Wilfred x

I have sent a card to Harold.

[47] The Royal Agricultural Show was held at the former racecourse across Monkmoor Road from Mahim. Helen McPhail recounts, 'The old grandstand buildings were still in place, and in the summer of 1914 the site was graced by a royal visit, when King George V interrupted the preoccupations of that fateful year to attend' (*Wilfred Owen's Shrewsbury* [Logaston Press, 2018], p. 53; see also pp. 82–4).
[48] University of Bordeaux.

265. To Susan Owen

Picture postcard: painting of two mountaineers

[*?18 June 1914*]   [*Bordeaux*]

I have urgent news! This m'ng a pupil, Parisian lady, *distinguée*, asked me whether I would like to spend a month in the Pyrenees with her as she must speak English before October. Her husband is a 'man of letters' & professor of elocution.[49] They travel a great deal. They have a villa in the mountains, marvellous spot! Various friends from Paris will visit them. Madame has a daughter of 11: will take 2 maids.

Monsieur <u>Léger</u> came yesterday to see Aumont, not wanting me to lose my post permanently. Aumont refused to say definitely *Je verrai, je verrai*. It makes no difference whether he agrees or not!

I am in great excitement. Will tell you immediately I know more. Such as I know was communicated in an undertone during my lesson, for Aumont promised Madame to speak to me, & hasn't yet. The Tofield Affair[50] is quite a mystery still.

[49] M. Charles Léger and his wife. He was an actor-manager running an experimental theatre in Bordeaux and teaching elocution. His wife, then 31, managed his family interior-design business. They had one daughter, Nénette. A clear picture of all three emerges in Letters 277–92.
[50] Tofield had been 'suddenly dismissed' a few days earlier.

271. To Susan Owen

Friday, 8.15. p.m. [?3 July 1914]   *[Bordeaux]*

My own dear Mother,

I have no lesson at 8 tonight so I think I shall make it worth while spending 2 1/2 d on a letter! I feel comparatively energetic at this moment, having just got over a miserable stomach-ache: (the first for months), one of the effects of the renewed Heat Wave; and I always feel in a benign and docile mood on such an occasion.

Your letter & news of Harold were very welcome on Wednesday. I naturally am glad about your bit of commerce to Show Visitors,[51] that is if you didn't over-exert. I guess <u>Raoul's</u> dates will suit you. He may stay six or eight weeks, if you have him. Of course he will be glad to go to the sea. Don't worry about his English. I do not hold myself responsible in any way for what he half-knows. I repeat he has not shown linguistic talent. But that makes no difference to you. Let him <u>peck</u> up what he can. As for amusing him you mustn't think of it. Turn him out to grass with Colin once a day; and when in the house tell him to <u>study!</u> Get Doris over by all means; at least she is a study in the <u>cold</u> & colourless 'English Type'.[52]   And now, I on my part, have some Questions wanting Replies: What trains leave Paddington at decent times for R's journey: and what is the fare Padd-Shrewsbury, 3rd Class?[53]

I am really sorry you don't think of going to Hereford for a while. You don't mention any <u>reasons</u>, and I don't wonder.

Give my particular remembrances to Grandma, etc.

I heard from <u>Father Kemp</u> this morning. In how short a time has he got through his <u>Brother</u>ship. He seems cheery as usual, and talk of having preached three sermons now. His Vicar is one Tiarks; now, upon my word, I believe Mr. Robertson told me he knew of a cleric of that name in Reading.[54] And Kemp tells me his Tiarks was in Reading long ago; and mentions it as curious. Ask Mr R! How are Mr. Robertson & The Young Men, etc? The frequenters of the 'Y.M.' here are a very different set. The Shrewsbury fellowship never spoke <u>against</u> Morality ('far be it from us, etc.') but they treated 'mere morality' as a hopeless plea; a filthy rag. Here, the students, discard Morality entirely, and go without a rag. It may be an 'outsider' who has done it, but practically all my Music Sheets which I had left at the *Union* have been stolen! I am annoyed, although there was not much value in it, because there is a piano at the villa, & leisure also. Now could you find in Shrewsbury the Tuppenny Series in which I had the *Marche Funèbre* (in five sharps) and sent it me, together with any others you may select. I should be glad to have at the same time the sixpenny book containing Chapel in Mountains, etc.; and also cheap copies of Largo, Blake's March, Melody in F. and what more you will. The postage will be trifling. My copies were already in shreds, but I shall obtain some compensation for this theft from the Secretary. In any case you will draw upon my Christmas Moneys in doing this little commission. I specially should like to have what I have named, and if Mary finds any more, so much the better. I have, yesterday, bought a book for Mary which will help her French famously. It is the French equivalent of a Reader in English which has great success with my pupils.

The only news I have relating to Bagnères is that the Légers cannot go into the villa before the 20th (they wanted to go next week) because it is flooded! Owing to a great melting of snows under the late heat; a stream which divides the house from the road, has burst the bridge, so that one can't get at the house. Water has entered the downstairs rooms, and other catastrophes have happened. But it will make no difference to me I hope.

I trust you will get this on Sunday. If not I shall be sorry, but the weather & the work together are terrible enemies to writing.

Dearest Love from your own,   Wilfred

[51] Letting a room for the Agricultural Show.
[52] Doris Wharmby, daughter of a chocolate manufacturer in Mansfield. She spent a good deal of time during the holidays with the Owen children, and despite his comments here was particularly liked by Wilfred, HO recalled.
[53] '12/9d' is pencilled in here by Susan Owen.
[54] The Rev. Hope Charles Tiarks (1870–1950), Vicar of Holy Trinity, Kilburn, 1914–47, was at Greyfriars, Reading, 1906–8.

272. To Mary Owen

Le Quatorze Juillet 1914   *Bordeaux*

My dear Mary,

The first important thing I have to say is: Send me, regardless of Risks, Costs, or Pains the 'Adorable Portrait' of Colin. I imagined I had it with me, and being seized the other day with a mania to see it I plunged into my archives, but didn't find it. I was sick at heart. So you'll send me both photographs, won't you: i.e. the one with the gun and the serene, the immaculate-innocent, the noble face;[55] and other with the semi-coy, slant-smiling…face. The gap is to be filled up when the English Language shall have evolved appropriate adjectives for that Expression. As a matter of fact I can see that picture at this moment as well as I can see, (and better than I can see) the words I am scratching on this paper: and the truth is I only want the pictures to show my friends what our family can do when it tries.

P.S. Need I explain that July 14th is the National Fête, day on which Bastille was stormed. Grand military Reviews all over the country, & general holiday.

15 July

I had only got so far when I heard the fireworks beginning in the vast public square; so I dribbled round in that direction; and fell in with the most tremendous assembly of human creatures I ever saw in a public place. In Shrewsbury we like to think there is a great multitude in the Quarry at the Show, but I suppose ten quarriesful would not amount to the mass standing in the Place de Quinconces last night. The fireworks were not so pretty as 'ours' but more striking and comprehensive, they fell over the heads of the people, and embraced the whole sky. What made it the most remarkable was the lightning which sometimes blazed out at the same instant as the bursting rockets, and kept up a continual flicker in the pauses of the *feux d'artifices*. The people had hardly turned away when a ferocious storm broke. The noise of hundreds of thousands of feet and voices surging back into the town was a noise not to be forgotten. It re-awoke all the mysterious terrors which one feels for the first time in reading the *Tale of Two Cities*. And then such a pandemonium of thunder claps to finish—or rather never to finish! For they lasted till six this morning and awoke me half a dozen times in the night. Result was I fell asleep in my room after lunch, and didn't wake up till after the time for my Lesson! I had such a shock that I scuttled round to the school without waiting to awake more than half of myself; and afterwards I couldn't get more than half awake; so I sat out that lesson in a very queer mentality, very queer indeed. But I 'feel better' after a right good dinner, and no wine!

I feel quite self-conscious, the centre of observation, if, as I sometimes do, I drink nothing but water. Strange is the change.—The first time I uncorked a Claret I was in a great funk. I am glad I was; but I'm not less glad that just at the moment of my third bodily-renewing, I have been able to fortify my tissue with real Bordeaux Red & White. I am conscious of at least an appearance of robustness in my face: for when shaving I have a tight round skin to deal with now. And there are no black shadows in the corners of my eyes. Ask Raoul, though!

I am enclosing his photograph. He has just given me a larger one, but I am sending this, equally good, for lack of a big envelope.

The boy states he will arrive at Shrewsbury at 9.5 p.m. on Tuesday, July 21.

Mother was very thoughtful to ask whether I preferred him not to have my sanctum. I should certainly rather my own Colin were there if anyone.* But I don't understand whether it is a choice of one or other.

I rather suppose from recent accounts that Tweeks is at present in a state of fishy degeneration, reverting to our original aquatic habits; and, now completely amphibian, sleeps in the bathroom under water. He had better emerge and write me a letter, if he wants me to remember that he is near fourteen: How I wish the Pater would send him back with Raoul: to share my room for two months, and learn French enough to last him terms and terms without opening his Grammar. What bliss for him, eh?

I have another project for the Autumn. Herr Langholz is leaving Berlitz Schools for ever this term. After many years therein, both in Europe and America, he has got a 'name' but it brings no money. He is going to do commerce in fruit, oil and wine between Russia & Spain. But this winter he is going to Nice where he gets from 5 to 10 francs for a lesson. Now it is possible that I might go and work with him; if, as he says, I should have 3 f. per lesson for myself, I should be glad to do it. Langholz is now in Paris, but we shall talk over this when he comes back.[56]

No change in Bagnères plans. Thanks be! You will find my first visiting-card, necessitated by present circumstances, and costing 1½ franc per 100!

Give me a hint what Colin wants for 24th.

Thank dear Mother for her loving letter.

Overlook the haste-marks of these pages, but always look well into any signs you may see of my impatience to be among you.

Your fond Wilfred

* I don't mind of course Raoul having 'my room'. Certainly not. Only keep locked the Book Case, eh?

[55] Plate 3. The photograph was reproduced as Plate 111c in *CL*.
[56] The war would intervene in these plans.

277. To Susan Owen

Friday, 31 July [1914]   *Villa Lorenzo La Gayeste*
                                                          Bagnères-de-Bigorre[57]

Dearest Mother,

Getting up at half-past five on Thursday, I caught my train without any scramble. I met at the Station a pupil, young commercial student, with whom I was on good terms (Raoul knows him: Dufau); with his sister and small cousin; and I travelled with them three quarters of the way. The weather was on the change, after three weeks rain, and the country was very fair. I saw something of the vast pine forests of the Landes. The first sight of the mountains was highly exciting. They rise up with scarce any preamble in the way of spurs, hillocks, or terraces. But there was no snow. At Bagnères I found Monsieur, and outside the station Nénette holding the Donkey's head, for they have a donkey-charrette, and my green trunk was carried up therewith. The Villa is snugly placed on a hillside, not very far from the Town, but out of sight. It is very pretty, tho' not in the English style. It is not conspicuously comfortable; but the very box for an open air treatment. My room, on the ground floor, has three windows, one of which is a door. (Hem!) I have a Cabinet de Toilet (ask Raoul) where there is running-water, very-running-water: the tap doesn't act, and the water runs on for ever. 'Men may come' to repair it, but I don't expect them. I have to deaden the noise at night by a system of rags. A few yards from my door a brook keeps up the 'noise of a hidden stream, that to the sleeping woods all night, singeth a gentle song'.[58] The garden is wildish but rich in leafage. Bamboos grow prosperously. Enormous hydrangeas (hortensia) with purple inflorescences are all about... This instant I am informed that Madame is going into Bagnères, & I must go to buy my espadrilles. So shall go on with my accounts later. On arriving I went out with Mr. Léger to see the country, & did not even send a card as there is no post from here. All letters have to be taken to Bagnères. I am very content here. What Luck!

Your very own Wilfred x

[57] Ten miles east of Lourdes in the High Pyrenees. Owen misspells La Gailleste.
[58] 'A noise like of a hidden brook / In the leafy month of June, / That to the sleeping woods all night / Singeth a quiet tune.' Coleridge, *The Rime of the Ancient Mariner*, Part V.

278. To Susan Owen

Saturday, 1 August 1914   *Chez Monsieur Léger, Villa Lorenzo,*
La Gayeste, Bagnères-de-Bigorre, Htes. Pyrénées

My own dear Mother,

I was cut very short in my letter of Friday. I resume. The Villa is not ideal in plan, but pretty and practical. Only it is in a bad, bad state of repair. One ought to live here three months, says M. Léger, before it is 'anything like.' It is not, you understand, the property of the Légers but of a doctor[59] of Bagnères, who is aged and invalid, hence it is shamefully neglected. There is a largish 'property' around about, consisting of copse, meadows and a farm. There is in the garden the beginning of a *Vivier*, which I think is called in English 'stew' or 'kettle of fish' or something like that. But although two charming rivulets leap across the garden, the work is not finished. Here is a rough plan of the house:

The whole front consists of one piece—dining-room, hall, & drawing-room without separating-walls. The piano is wicked: absolutely untouchable. O la! la! Mademoiselle Levallois[60] hasn't arrived yet; comes next week.

There is a second-story to the villa, which only half-covers the flat roof.

The view is not vast, being obstructed by a near hill, very like one of the Stretton brotherhood[61]—in fact exactly like. However, we see beyond and above this, the great Pic-du-Midi, and the Mont Aigu, on which there is yet snow. I shall not attempt any arduous climbs, and none at all the first week.

Now let me speak of my excellent friends. Monsieur Léger, was educated in a Paris Engineering School, but 'abandoned the Sciences for Dramatic Art' (so saith a short notice I have read on him.) He played Comedies, I think; and the mere stamp of his countenance is enough to confirm it. He is quite small, but his bearing is notable, and his head typically dramatic: no hair on top to speak of, deep, dark eyes under prominent and moustache-like eyebrows, broad mobile mouth, clean shaven. Head beautifully poised, a little leaning-back. Voice agreeable (but I have not yet heard him recite.) There is nothing stagey about him, absolutely nothing in manner of speech, gesture, or idea; and that is remarkable considering. But the most mysterious thing is his age. In some lights, whether regarded, entire or in part, behind, before, or aside, he looks just thirty. At other times he is an old man, a grandfather. As a matter of fact, he is over fifty.

Madame is much younger. She is elegant rather than belle; has shapely features luxuriant coiffure, but is much too thin to be pretty. Probably she has been very pretty indeed. She is obviously of the same opinion herself. Her toilette, even for driving in donkey cart, is unimpeachable.

Yesterday she pointedly told me she could not stand plain people. *Je les déteste* were her words. I felt uncomfortable. You, who may take the inference in a sense more complimentary to myself, may be uncomfortable in another way. She has even confided to me that she doesn't love her husband excessively. This is all very amusing for me—and nothing else.

But I am immensely happy to be in the company of Nénette. I am enclosing a picture, with the warning that it is not very like, is not complimentary, and must be seen through a lens. Nénette, (not a nice name, <u>tant pis</u>) is perfectly a child, and, with that, is almost a perfect child. Papa prefers that she should not be educated in a town school, where they learn a great deal, but not of studies. So she goes to school with the peasants, and makes great progress. This is at the sacrifice of her accent, which is an important thing to a father like Mons. Léger. But that can be cured. The result of living out here is that Nénette's physique is magnificent. As far as I can judge, she has also more than her share of intellect. Anyhow she began to compose dramas at nine years of age. Some of her writings are astonishing. I said that our piano was atrocious: hence I don't know whether she can play with sense or not; but she goes through her exercises admirably. I made the mistake the other day, of striking the opening bars of Marche Funèbre; since when she pesters me daily for more. It is a torture to me, but I do it for the sake of her expression. We walk into Bagnères together sometimes, when we talk chiefly of armaments and what help England is giving to France!

The news of War made great stir in Bagnères. Women were weeping all about; work was suspended. Nearly all the men have already departed. Our household is one in a thousand. Mr. Leger, who doesn't look his age, and I, who look French, are objects of mark at present. I had to declare myself, and get a permit to remain here; where I must stay still under penalty of arrest and sentence as a spy—unless I get a special visa for emigrating. I don't know how this state of things will affect my Courses in Bordeaux. Our food is already much dearer, and we are all getting ready to live on bread and maize-soup. If need be, Monsieur & I will undertake the harvest between us. Nobody is very gay.

I don't know whether you will ever receive this letter. I only know everything is horribly upset, in the Post, on the Railway—everywhere. I have got your last letter & Raoul's and feel upset that Father may not get his holiday. I hope you don't feel the least anxiety about me. I escaped from Bordeaux in the nick of time. Here I am in the hands of most amiable friends, away from danger to life, and sure enough of food. I shouldn't like to be in Germany. Nor yet in Aumont's shoes. Fancy, he is now at the front; and I airing my fancies in a charming *villégiature*.[62] I finish in haste.

Shall send cards often. If I find I am a burden to the Légers, I may have to sneak home. So be prepared.

Ever your devoted Wilfred

[59] Dr Cazalas.
[60] Professional violinist, a friend of Mme Léger.
[61] The hills round Church Stretton, near Shrewsbury.
[62] This was only in Owen's imagination. In Letter 297 (CL) of 1 November 1914, he writes to Susan how Aumont managed to secure teaching extra classes at a school in Bordeaux before Owen could offer his own services: 'But what luck that I wasn't [accepted]. For if Aumont had found I had baulked him in that way, he would have been on me like a pile of bricks.'

279. To Susan Owen

Saturday, 8 August 1914   *Bagnères-de-Bigorre*

My dearest Mother,

How miserable it is not to get your letters, and not to know whether you are getting mine. I have so far had yours of July 31st: and it's a wonder I got that considering the scanty address. Fortunately Monsieur Léger is well known in Bagnères, (having at one time directed the Casino there.) I last wrote (letter) a week ago (to Aberdovey), posting the next day. Since I have sent cards. I shall with this letter forward a Card to Mahim, in case, in consequence of the mobilization you have been obliged to stay in town.

Practically all the men have now gone to join their corps. The last time we sent to Market it was empty. In villages around there is no more bread. The women pass their time knitting in the streets. Monsieur Léger spends his day tramping to and from the town, though, as a matter of fact, news only arrives once a day. All sorts of absurd stories are circulated about spies and lurking Germans. I saw a man who had the foolhardiness to call himself German (I don't think he was actually) all but killed by a mob. I never wear my spectacles now, as the Légers say they look foreign. I have received glances from knitting women which not Madame Defarge could make more menacing! It is because they think me an idle French youth, who has got himself excused! On the other hand, when Monsieur L. introduces me to his friends as English I am cordially and respectfully saluted. No one is permitted to pass out of his Commune (a very restricted area) after six o'clock in the evening!

Madame Léger has definitely offered to keep me with them as long as they remain up here, that is until the 15th of September. It is no use even discussing what I shall do then; it is yet much too soon.

I continue meanwhile to be immensely happy and famously well.[63]

I dropped into a Photographer's the day before leaving Bx.; and here is the result. Three points need to be mentioned. (1) The lop-eared-ness of the left hairs is accidental. (2) The shadow quite spoils the chic effect of the moustache. (3) I look pale, while, at present at any rate, my rich colour is a marvel to behold. The difference that has taken place in my physiognomy since the moment I was liberated from the Bordeaux Box is incredible. Bagnères is specially noted for Throat Cures, and indeed I breathe this air with as much gusto as I eat my meals.

We live very quietly. I get up about eight, and pass through the glass (!) door of my bedroom to my *déjeuner* of coffee with milk & cream, toast and butter. About nine or ten I give my lesson: not always easy, but never boring. It is often in the garden; and is usually interrupted by Nénette, who doesn't at all like this hour; and has to come for kisses and hugs at intervals.

We lunch at 12.30: have *gouter* consisting of a cup of milk at 4: and dinner at 7.30. Meals are not by any means sumptuous; for the time is a time of war. This afternoon Madame and the servant have gone with the donkey, for victuals. Mlle. Levallois, violinist, hasn't yet come: and I wish she wasn't coming: otherwise a Poet, a real live Poet, with a wife of famous beauty would have come. But in any case, the Poet has now cut his hair, and gone to war! In a few days an old lady, very distinguished, will arrive; her son is an important M.P. I shall finish my news for Mary & Colin.

Your own, happy, safe, fortnunate, and devoted Son

[63] About this time Owen scribbled out the following draft letter (Plate X; Plate XI in *CL*), which was found with his papers after his death. It carries later corrections, in a different ink (as does Letter 319, also a draft with later corrections). All the words first set down and then struck out are shown here in italics.

'In these days my present life is a lived-out book. If I have loved books it is not because they are an alternative to life, or an artificialized life, as Parson Wigan said, but because they are the *Best* Prime of life. If I seek the company *of such as write books* of *lettered* men of letters it is not because they write *books chapters thoughts* lines, but because they read things; *not because* they *alone* who compose *chapter* chapter and verse are they who discompose characters and events. So little had I *lived* been in contact with people of a mind either abundantly creative or poignantly analytic *(which I am devoutly thankful are not to be found in my family)* & devoutly thankful am I that such are not to be found in my family—so much have I lived with children, *trees, a* brothers boys and nothing more—a sister, a girl and sometimes something less, a mother who is *an* more angel than woman of the world, with *men,* such *who* as, if they read in books reaped not therefrom; and therefore had not wherewithal to sow, that I had begun to believe all romance contained between the two covers of a ballad-book; In the same way as I supposed all philosophy in the [blank], all culture at Oxford, all religion in Christ, all Poetry in J. Keats: and all love in *Miss Elsie wouldn't you like to know? little* what's her name?

Here is a typical day: last Wednesday, I think. I got up when I like: breakfast alone with Nénette, began with a *furious* tiff: and indeed with the recital of her dreams, which were *of a so* as shocking *that I couldn't listen.* as could be! Evidently there is no Censor.'

281. To Colin Owen

Monday, 10 August 1914   [*Bagnères-de-Bigorre*]

Darling Lad,—Colin,

I thought your last letter to me a very nice one. I hope at this moment you are in Camp; but I am desolated not to have had any news from Aberdovey,[64] (or from Shrewsbury either since Mother's letter of the 31st July.)

I suppose you are studying the War, with all your Patrol. Are the Scouts doing anything really useful at this time? I feel shamefully 'out of it' up here, passing my time reading the Newspapers in an armchair in a shady garden. Numbers of Bordeaux ladies are going to the Armies as Nurses. The only thing I could do, so Madame Léger says, would be to serve as stretcher-bearer, on the battlefield. After all my years of playing soldiers, and then of reading History, I have almost a mania to be in the East, to see fighting, and to serve. For I like to think this is the last War of the World! I have only a faint idea of what is going on, and what is felt, in England, as perhaps you have only a faint notion of the family affliction, the public enthusiasm, the standstill of business there is here.

Please send me a newspaper whenever an important issue appears; and keep some historical numbers, for my archives. Yes, I should honestly and solemnly like to be in Alsace at this moment! But I know your opinion at home as to such an idea; so I won't even ask for permission to engage myself as nurse, etc. What a time for the Journalists!

Meanwhile I could hardly ask for a more perfect (holiday-) existence. I have found a spot to bathe; and my daily bath is a matter of much wonderment in the family. When I proposed it, I met with all manner of opposition: stream too cold; not deep enough; people may pass: better go to the *Piscine* (Plunge Bath) (which is quite warm, ugh! and costs 1 franc.) Now I am, as you very well know, acutely uncomfortable in hot weather without a tub. So one fine morning I went forth, pretending I was going to herborise; and finding, as I knew I should, an enchanting stretch of water in an alder-glade, I was not long in 'getting in.' So now I go down every day, and I know, when I vaunt my coolness and fresh-ness, the others would be green with envy, if they were not so infernally red with heat.

Oh! certainly it is hot here at mid-day! I daren't think of what it is in Bordeaux!—or on the Continental Plains in Uniform!!!!!! But after four o'clock, just when in cities, the air begins to be intolerably *étouffant* down from the mountains comes trickling a delicious current of oxygen and we are saved. And that is why I can find Nothing the matter with me: and why I eat anything and sleep anyhow: and that is why (for a double reason) the stars are twice as brilliant than I have ever seen them before. Now, do write something for me: and say that you continue to feel my affection and respect my influence.

x Wilfred x

P.S. Down with the Germans!

---

[64] Colin was camping with his Scout troop at Aberdovey, on the west coast of Wales, at the outbreak of war.

282. To Susan Owen

Tuesday, 11 August 1914　　　　　　　　　　　　　　　　　　　*Bagnéres-de-Bigorre*

Darling Mother,

I am miserably disappointed to know, by this morning's post, that Father is kept from his holiday, and that you are not going to Wales at all. I sent a letter yesterday to Aberdovey, (with the Home Address as alternative) so you may get it at the same time or even after this—if you ever lay hands on it at all. It contained notes for Raoul and Mary, and photographs of Nénette, and of me. Your two mails of Aug. 2 and 5 I captured together this morning. I was going down to my bathe when I met the Postman on the road. Having an iron-pointed alpenstock in my hand, I made him stand and deliver. I rather suspect that my letters for England are quarantined for several days in this beastly town: if indeed they are not opened and condemned. I have sent

A Card on my arrival.
Letter on Sunday. 2nd.
Two Cards in the Week.
Letter on Monday 10.
and Cards to Torquay, Alpenrose, and various people in Bordeaux.

In case people act the goat with my Envelope at Aberdovey I here repeat that I am admirably comfortable; with people who just suit my momentary taste; and completely out of reach of the war.

I don't think I have ever enlightened you on the occupation of Madame Léger. She has an important business in Bordeaux & Paris designing and selling House Decorations, Embroideries, and so on. She goes to Canada once a year, and there makes piles of money. In six years she says her fortune will be made; and she shall sell the Business, and return to her original state of perfect lady! In two years they will remove to her dear Paris. She was not educated to be a business woman; but as Monsieur Léger had no turn for business she managed the House since the time of her marriage. She is only 31; while 'Charles' is 52. One would take her for Nénette's sister. She is a most amiable hostess, and I am as neither a guest nor a 'teacher' but as an old friend. She was once vaunting how that she could do whatever she liked with her men friends. Never did she meet with resistance. I told her that if she found me compliant to her wishes she must remember my position in her household. On which she declared that I owed her no obligations whatever. I was entirely free: in my goings-out and comings in and in the language I speak: and how I behave. So, considering the charming country and everything else, I am one of the most enviable young persons in France.

I am going to write about Nénette to Mary. This is only a supplementary Note: writ in a hurry, for in 3 mins. I must trot into Bagnères.

It makes marvellous hot in the middle of the day, i.e. at present.

I find I have no answers to attend to in your letters: but I would like to answer your anxiety on my part and grievous disappointment on your own by a Declaration of my personal Liberty, Health, Happiness, with no prospect of any immediate change.

Signed, Your Wilfred

283. To Mary Owen

20 August 1914   *Bagnères-de-Bigorre*

My dearest Mary,

Although I have very nearly written several long epistles to you, I never quite wrote one!

You understand that one or two hours of my day are taken by my 'professional duties' ; that one or two more are not less strictly taken up by Nénette, for whom I draw, play the piano, make boats, act comedy, invent stories, play hide-and-seek, bury dolls, etc. that, nearly every day I go to Bagnères for some reason or other; that when it is fine, I scramble up the hills to see 'the Chain' of the Pyrenees; and that when it is hot (remember we are more south than the N. Coast of Spain) it is a sore temptation to prostrate myself on the Verandah in the contemplation of the Peaks; the near valleys;...the silver-birches and the hortensias of the garden;...Nénette...and the end of a cigarette...

You, especially You, would be enchanted with our Villa. The name, following the inscription at the end of the Drive is Castel Lorenzo, but you might as well call Mahim a manor, as this a Castel. It is a bijou-residence: too much like a toy in appearance to please M. Léger; and indeed is a long way from being my own ideal of a country villa. This reminds me that I spent an afternoon of last summer working out my ideal of a practical English country house. I made some rough plans which I think I put in one of my stained boxes, among the pottery-collection. I should be glad if you could find those sheets (note-paper size) and send them me quietly; because Madame Léger would be interested to talk over the subject. You know her business is to set in order the houses of rich people; chiefly in Canada, where all her clients are millionaires. She sells her articles at an extremely high price; and will have made her fortune in six years hence. She works like this: inspects the house; tells the people what they want (for they never know); takes measurements, makes her designs; has these designs executed by her 30 or 40 *employées*; and makes a fabulous profit.

But you will be more interested to hear about Nénette (full name Albine)— both which names I have told her Mother are not at all pretty; and she agrees. However they belong to a very pretty Body. Her head is not without fault: there is too much recession in the line of the chin. Her hair is not at all in the manner of the photograph; but in two *macarons* on the temples, like Queen Victoria's in 1837. This gives her an air of a Russian Ballet Dancer, which she resembles in other respects also. Her dancing is said to be exquisite. I haven't seen her dance. Her voice is a continual music. But her chief feature is her eyes, which are like Margaret Quayle's[65] in colour, and richly fringed with lashes. Upon occasions they become extraordinarily alive; so that we say—she has the devil in her eyes tonight.

Her character has been a stiff problem for me. At first she was a model of obedience, meekness, and politeness; but when I ceased to be a stranger, the rebukes of *petit-papa* and *petit-maman* were differently received. Towards me she varies a good deal. We have only one subject of quarrel; and that is the superior-ity of the English nation over the French, or vice versa. She is coquette in matters of dress and is sensitive to my least remark in this respect. Everything I say to her that amuses or pricks her she repeats to her mother, when she 'sees her into bed', who duly re-repeats these tales to me. I consider I have an important rôle to play, for Madame has announced to her daughter that she desires her to marry (at 19) an Englishman, ten years older than herself, who is to be intelligent and *beau*. So I am a sort of sample. But it is difficult to know what Mademoiselle really thinks of me. *Dis donc, petit-maman* she said one night *Mais Monsieur Owen est très-joli garçon, n'est-ce pas?*—Oh! said Madame—Nothing special—'for I didn't want to put any ideas into her head; and I don't want her to suffer any chagrin when you leave!' It is only in the last few days that Nénette has been free with me: to the extent of her pulling my hair and letting me stroke hers!

And it was only this very morning that I received her confidence of confi-dences namely that she is beloved of a certain boy of her school, and loves him exceedingly; and that they have the firmest intention to get married as soon as convenient. She got this out immediately that [we] were alone after breakfast, and finding I did not laugh, but was extremely grave—having my own reasons,— ah! the days when I was eleven—she continued to relate how they contrive to exchange notes, sweets, and—even kisses; and how that her schoolmistress knows of the affair; but not her Mother or Father; and how Pierre is dressed; and that he is twelve years old. It has taken me three weeks work to win that confi-dence. But it is more than I ever won from You! Such an affair is not a proof of genius in Albine; but it is an indication; and I shall watch her future with keen interest. Very probably I shall spirit her over to Mahim for you to influence and know—if you will. Anyhow, her father said to her mother, before ever I thought of it myself, that he would like to send Nénette to my home. And her Mother asked me what would be the costs of pension in my family. Afterwards, I have shown them Mother's photograph. 'Oh, but she must be good, your Mother,' said Madame! Said Monsieur, with genuine enthusiasm: 'Why this is the face of goodness itself! This woman is goodness itself.'—So your theatrical man is the one who knows faces and character after all.

Please tell Mother she has jumped to erroneous conclusions about Madame's past: she never had any connection with the stage. The suspicions about her attitude to me, and her *Coquetterie* are more or less correct. But I don't care two pins, so let her be tranquillised, I prithee.

If it gives you all any pleasure to know that I am happy, I can tell you from the bottom of my heart that these weeks are passing like Elysian time.

Great thanks for the poems which Mother sent me and for her dear and dearly-treasured messages.

I am going to meet a great French Poet[66] in a day or two! Neither the Violinist, nor the old lady authoress are coming here it seems. Salute Scout Colin with a martial *geste!* Give my hearty condolence to Father on the suppression of his holiday. Can't be bothered to correct Raoul's letter now. In fact I don't begin another page because Nénette is at my window, stamping with impatience. Embrace sweet Mother as you would yourself—for your fondest

Brother

It is evident my letters have been detained 4 days or more in Bagnères. In fact I now know there have been no trains for Bordeaux.

[65] Margaret Quayle was Owen's cousin, daughter of Edward and Emily Quayle.
[66] Laurent Tailhade (1854–1919), French poet and man of letters, whose satirical poems were collected in *Poèmes aristophanesques* (1904). An anarchist and pacifist, his outspoken writings led to a duel with Maurice Barrés (1862–1923) and imprisonment. His pamphlets *Lettre aux Concrits* (1903) and *Pour la Paix* (1909) expounded his pacifist views. By the time he met Owen, he was 59, portly, and a vestige of the *fin-de-siècle* literary scene. However, along with Harold Monro and Siegfried Sassoon, he was one of Owen's most significant literary influences.

284. To Susan Owen

Monday, 24 August 1914   *Bagnères-de-Bigorre*

My own dear Mother,

I had yours of Sunday, Aug. 16th, on Sat. last. Tell me if you have got my budget addressed to Aberdovey, containing Photographs; and a following letter

to Raoul; and lastly, a letter to Mary. I see there is a question in one of yours:—
would I like a *Christian*? I should be strongly interested to read a Keswick
Number; and also to know what is said by prophetic students about the
Armageddon. On Sunday, if possible I go to Church with Nénette; but yesterday,
having quite lost count of the days, I was not aware it was Sunday until late in the
afternoon! It is not that one behaved in an unsundaylike fashion; but that every
day is a Sunday here. Nearly a month have I been; and perhaps have as much as a
fortnight more. We do not, however, stay till the 15th, as had been arranged, but
till the 7th or 10th. But I am to live with the Légers in Bordeaux for another month,
on the same understanding; on Oct. 10. Madame starts for Canada, if not held up
by the War. This is capital for me. I am to have Nénette's charming room, and
shall be virtually a guest. Their house is in the very best residential part, between
the vast Place de Quinconces and the Jardin Public. (rent £320.) I shall hope to
meet some interesting people, and if not too early for the season, I suppose I shall
have the run of M. Léger's Theatre. It is the only Theatre in Bordeaux where classical, literary, or decent plays are put on. Consequently it has failed four years
running. Nevertheless Léger perseveres heroically.

    You were quite wrong in supposing Madame Leger to have been an actress;
though curiously enough, most people who see her for the first time suppose it.
Most women of Paris powder and rouge; and Madame is no exception: I have
never seen her without either; but it is mild for every-day. Only once have I seen
her fully made up (one night last week for the Casino) and then, with blue-shaded
eyes, I can tell you she looked a surpassingly fair and dangerous woman. As for
her history, I only know that she was educated at one of the tip-top boarding-
schools of Paris, which she entered at the age of 3½! . . .; that she was asked in marriage at 14; and was married, at 17½ to Charles Léger, who is 20 years older than
herself; that she undertook at the time of her marriage the affairs which were previously in the family of her husband; that she is at present 31 years of age, and is
driving a commerce of enormous success.

    I am conscious that she has a considerable liking for me, both in a physical
and intellectual sense. She is now equally conscious that the former liking is
not reciprocated—not one little bit—and continues to like me for my mind's
nature. If it were not so,—I should hop it, immejit. The first week was sufficient
to enrol me a friend of the family: a talk with Monsieur in which I gave him my
views,—another with Madame when I dared to argue with her, and matched
her on her own ground (linguistic);—an inspiration to amuse Nénette by trans-
lating various people on the piano—and my position in their estimation and in
their household was assured. That translation into music—or discord—of the
characters we liked or disliked, e.g. The proprietor of the villa (discord), Monsieur
Aumont; Nénette; a little peasant, friend of Nénette; etc. was the result of a
pitch of sensation which is alas! so rare in me that I should not dream of

repeating it. I translated Nénette by the marvellous 'Rustle of Spring' of Sinding:[67] and I maintain the likeness to be perfect. The grace of the whole, the absence of any melancholy, the pretty rippling triviality of the greater portion; and the some-time sinking into a rich, rich abundance of life and earnestness—that is Nénette.

As in my letters, this child naturally occupies a good deal of room in my thoughts; but I am—alas or happily, who shall say?—too old to be in love, as you predicted. And then I see her too often… With her it is different, and my contin-ual presence has caused a commotion and an alteration which her mother per-ceives with alarm. It is true that she talks incessantly about me in my absence, and that she won't put on this or that dress for fear Monsieur Owen will not be pleased (!); and that she worries me to shave my moustache!!—But I knew the real state of affairs; and, as in self-defence, had to throw some light on the school-boy side. If petit-papa knew he would take it much more seriously, and remove her instantly from her school, and send her to goodness-knows where—England probably. Poor Pierre!—so sorry, old boy: and she had a fortune too!

On two days last week, Laurent Tailhade, the distinguished French poet, gave lectures in the Casino, for the benefit of charity. Monsieur Léger gave recitations. I was of course presented to Tailhade; and Madame invited him to lunch next Thursday, for my benefit. It is possible that Mons. Léger will be in Bordeaux all this week; but in any case I shall get at the poet alone, as I have engaged to 'fetch' him. It was interesting to see how he enjoyed being rallied in his capacity of poet, for being incapable of remembering the date or the way.

My friend Bizardel, whom I used to meet on Sunday afternoons writes to me today saying that the Prefect of Bordeaux has taken him into his Cabinet. So I am more sure of information and protection!

I also had a card from Leslie in Llandudno. I keenly regret that you didn't manage to spend a week or so with them.

Tuesday

I was writing yesterday in the nearest Thunderstorm I have ever experienced. We were right in the midst of the lightning, which I positively felt warm on my cheek.

The news of war today is decidedly bad. We understand that the Germans are over the frontier in N. Belgium,[68] and French and English losses are heavy. We are very unquiet.

But I have a piece of personal news which makes my heart bound. Madame Léger has asked me to go to Canada with her. Alas! for this voyage (Oct. to January) she says it is too late to arrange; and she would prefer the next (March–May about), which would interfere with my Exam.[69] Perhaps Nénette will go then, which I should prefer. Nothing has been agreed about fares and expenses, but, while I don't expect to gain a cent I cannot of course be responsible for any costs whatever. The entire conversation on this subject only lasted five minutes, so I have no more to tell you. But what a go!

Always your own Wilfred

[67] 'Rustle of Spring' or 'Frühlingsrauschen', Op. 32, No. 3 (1896), a solo piano piece by the Norwegian composer Christian Sinding (1856–1941).
[68] The Battle of Mons took place on 23 August; British troops fell back on the 24th.
[69] But hopes of a university were now dwindling.

285. To Susan Owen

Friday, 28 August 1914   [*Bagnères-de-Bigorre*]

Sweet my Mother,

I wonder if you'll have any difficulty in picking out your son, among the audience at the Casino, on the afternoon of Laurent Tailhade's Lecture.[70] I need scarcely tell you that on my left is Madame Léger. Nénette is a mere nebulosity. To right of me is the owner of our villa, Madame Cazalas, a weird bird, who seems to have tried to attach her left leg to me. We didn't know we were being taken; but I don't dislike my head. The radiant polish of my cheek is due, partly to happiness, partly to sunshine. I was evidently amused at the moment, and about to make a remark to Madame: possibly Monsieur Léger was reciting just then.

The Group[71] represents the poet Tailhade, on the same afternoon, posing (and proposing to the young lady who sang (infamously badly)). Monsieur Léger, behind Tailhade's left, is not at all 'like'. His mouth is never to be seen in such a pugnacious 'mug'. As a matter of fact he was furious about something when the photo was taken. The remaining people, are (obviously enough,) local johnnies who helped with the music. With these groups, I enclose two very fine views; both of which are visible—modified—from the estate. They are worthy to be framed, even for their own sake.

Tell me if you like them, and also your opinion of me & the Légers. Tailhade came to lunch yesterday; but I had very little real conversation with him. In the first place, he was suffering from his heart, precisely after your deplorable miss-fire fashion, my dear mother, and only with difficulty and opening of all windows did he sit out the meal. However—he is coming to live up here with us. At least, chiefly for my sake, Madame asked him, and he accepted. It is not yet a fact, but I don't allow myself to doubt it, although Madame says she suspects he sees some difficulty—about the distance from Bagnères, and so on. He lives generally in Paris, whence he has not yet retired into private life. The donkey-cart doesn't frighten him, because he is too Parisian to care about the amused public. A Bordeaux celebrity, so say the Légers, would never consent to go a-riding in a donkey-shandy. They beg him to attack the Bordeaux public, which they hold in merited contempt. For Tailhade is one of the wickedest satirists, and cruellest enemies that have ever used the French language as a lash. For all that he is a charming old gentleman to meet. I called at his Hotel this morning to know his mind about the day of his removal. I saw him up at his window in shirt-sleeves, mooning. He received me like a lover. To use an expression of the Rev. H. Wigan's, he quite slobbered over me. I know not how many times he squeezed my hand; and, sitting me down on a sofa, pressed my head against his shoulder. [two lines illegible] It was not intellectual; but I felt the living verve of the poet … who has fought seventeen duels (so it is said).

Quite apart from the prospect of this Friendship, I am, for quite an appreciable length of time, imbued with sensations of happiness. The war affects me less than it ought. But I can do no service to anybody by agitating for news or making dole over the slaughter. On the contrary I adopt the perfect English custom of dealing with an offender: a Frenchman duels with him: an Englishman ignores him. I feel my own life all the more precious and more dear in the presence of this deflower-ing of Europe. While it is true that the guns will effect a little useful weeding, I am furious with chagrin to think that the Minds which were to have excelled the civ-ilization of ten thousand years, are being annihilated[72]—and bodies, the product of aeons of Natural Selection, melted down to pay for political statues. I regret the mortality of the English regulars less than that of the French, Belgian, or even Russian or German armies: because the former are all Tommy Atkins, poor fellows, while the continental armies are inclusive of the finest brains and temperaments of the land. There is no exception made but for the diseased, the imbecile, and the criminal. The world is madder than—

Your own bundle of eccentricity Wilfred

[70] Plate X. This photograph was reproduced as Plate VI in CL.
[71] This photograph has not survived.
[72] He first wrote 'snuffed out'.

286. To Susan Owen

Postcard

4 September [1914]   Bagnères P.O.

Dearest Mother,

It seems quite a long time since I last heard from home—a P.C. from you— and longer since I wrote. I have been waiting for definite news to give you. Mme. L. is obliged to leave here before the 15th and Bordeaux early in Oct. She is taking a boat from Bordeaux to Havre, & thence to Montreal & would like me to go on the same boat to Havre. But if Raoul stays at Home I would rather remain at his house. The Government is at Bordeaux,[73] and as many of Parisians as can get there. Laurent Tailhade has got installed in the Villa several times and as many times retreated because of neuralgic abcess. No end of a fuss. I am dining at his hotel tonight. All serene with me. I have seen many 'Wounded' arrive here.

Fondest love. Wilfred

73 The French Government evacuated to Bordeaux on 2 September 1914.

288. To Harold Owen

Wednesday, 23 September [1914]   [12 *rue Blanc Dutrouilh, Bordeaux*]

My dear Harold,

Just a word to say how glad I am that you are safe at home: and to send you a few belated birthday wishes. One of them is that I shall see you before you start again: though this is not really my expectation. I hope anyhow that the next voyage won't be a long one. I was sorry and annoyed that you didn't send any pictures by Raoul. You might have done so without fear of damage or of criticism. Both M. and Madame Léger are artists. Monsieur had done some oil-painting, and Madame of course has a genius for Design. She employs three designers for her business, two men and a young lady. Do you know anything about styles yet? I mean the way of recognizing and imitating the Louis XV, XVI, Empire, etc? Methinks the less you know the better, for I infinitely prefer the modern manner, and, at any period of history, the English to the French.

The house where I am is spacious, rather than very large. It is not furnished as it might be. There are in the drawing-room two fine oil-paintings representing M. Léger; which have been hung in the Paris Salon. Also there is a very pretty statuette of Madame L. about six inches high, in sitting pose. Above all, they have an original bust, by a greatish sculptor, Escoula,74 of Mr. Léger in his youth. I have seen a fair number of busts and statues in my time, but I only know of one which expresses so much energy, and manliness, and feeling, as this; while at the same time it is a marvellously faithful portrait.

The photographs of Nénette are innumerable: Some of them absolute artistic perfections; not a whit below the best work Uncle John ever did. There are also plaster-casts and woodcarvings of this fair child.

The business-work of Madame L. is carried on in comparative secrecy: she won't allow me to go into the work-rooms until the articles are completed. Whether it is for fear of my cribbing the patterns or whether the work-girls I haven't well decided. Anyhow I can't inform you about either yet.

I have been living in an admirable fashion, as well in Bordeaux as at Bagnères. My friend Bizardel, who is in the Cabinet of the Prefect of Bordeaux, has two automobiles at his disposition, (all the cars are now monopolised by Government.) One day he had to make a call on all the French ministers, and he took me in his motor. I didn't see many Ministers, and nor did he; all he did was to leave the Card of the Prefect. But of course we were dressed in *grand chic*: and wore an air of tremendous diplomats. The Minister for War[75] is in the University where I ought to be having my Courses; Minister of Finance,[76] in a school; Minister of Justice[77] in the Law-Courts; Minister of Fine Arts[78] (a friend of Tailhade) in the Theatre; and so on. Poincaré is installed a few steps from my old room. Most Paris newspapers are fixed up around about this street; even money is being coined in Bordeaux. The aspect of the streets has changed a good deal. Fifty thousand extra people are here! It is easy to recognize Parisians. In certain streets pass a dream of fair women. The populace grumbles that *chic* toilets should still be worn; but if not for such gentle ladies, what on earth is the Fighting about? It is the old story of the Lists: the Princess sits in flowers, while the warriors scuffle about in the ring. As a matter of fact, there are already too many ladies offering to help with red cross work. This afternoon two friends of Madame Léger, Mlle. Levallois, (a violinist who has toured all over England, Scotland & Ireland) and another Mlle. (once a great singer) have gone out hawking copies of a new patriotic song, to get money for the hospitals.

I went with my friend the Doctor Sauvaître to one of the large hospitals one day last week, where he is operating on the wounded. The hospital is in the buildings of the Boys' *Lycée* and appliances are altogether crude. First I saw a bullet, like this ▱▷ cut out of a Zouave's[79] leg. Then we did the round of the wards; and saw some fifty German wretches: all more seriously wounded than the French. The Doctor picked out those needing surgical attention; and these were brought on stretchers to the Operating Room; formerly a Class room, with the familiar ink-stains on floor, walls, and ceiling; now a chamber of horrors with blood where the ink was. Think of it: there were eight men in the room at once, Germans being treated without the slightest distinction from the French: one scarcely knew which was which. Considering the lack of appliances—there was only one water-tap in the room—and the crowding—and the fact that the doctors were working for nothing—and on Germans too—really good work was done. Only there were no anaesthetics—no time—no money—no staff for that. So after that scene I need not fear to see the creepiest operations. One poor

 devil had his shin-bone crushed by a gun-carriage-wheel, and the doctor had to twist it about and push it like a piston to get out the pus. Another had a hole right through the knee; and the doctor passed a bandage thus:

Another had a head into which a ball had entered and come out again.

This is how the bullet lay in the Zouave. Sometimes the feet were covered with a brown, scaly, crust—dried blood.

I deliberately tell you all this to educate you to the actualities of the war.[80]

There were two Englishmen here wounded, last week; but when Bizardel & I motored out to the Hospital, they had just moved somewhere else: one having developed scarletina.

I was not much upset by the morning at the hospital; and this is a striking proof of my health. I understand that you are likewise 'strapping' and I felicitate you. It will be to me enormously interesting to hear of your voyages. If you return from Canada after a month I may just catch you at home. Of course give my dearest love to everybody: I remain here until the 12th Oct., I think!

Your affectionate, Wilfred

[74] Jean Escoula (1851–1911), the French sculptor, was born in Bagnères-de-Bigorre and was an assistant to Jean-Baptiste Carpeaux and Auguste Rodin. He won a gold medal at the Expositions Universelles of 1889 and 1900. 'Angéliques', 'La Douleur', and 'Jeunes Baigneuses' are his best-known works.

[75] Alexandre Millerand (1859–1943), French politician, Prime Minister of France in the early 1920s.

[76] Alexandre-Félix-Joseph Ribot (1842–1923), French politician, four times Prime Minister.

[77] Aristide Briand (1862–1932), French statesman, served eleven terms as Prime Minister of France during the French Third Republic and was a co-laureate of the 1926 Nobel Peace Prize.

[78] Possibly Albert-Pierre Sarraut (1872–1962), French Radical politician, twice Prime Minister during the Third Republic.

[79] A member of French light-infantry corps, originally formed of Algerians and retaining their uniform.

[80] *CL* states that HO was sailing in submarine waters at this time. DH disputes this in *WOANB*: 'Harold Owen could not resist adding the footnote…He was in fact at home when Wilfred wrote.' DH notes that the *Esmeraldas*, HO's ship, reached Liverpool on 6 September 1914. HO did not set sail on the *Esmeraldas* again until 13 October 1914. See *WOANB*, Appendix D, 'Harold Owen's Voyages', pp. 475–8.

289. To Susan Owen

Postcard

Wednesday [Postmark 30 September 1914]   *[Postmark Bordeaux]*

Your Card—both sides of which gave me a special delight—came yesterday. What a fine sensation was produced by the 'hope to hear <u>what day to expect you</u>'. Nevertheless I have seldom passed such agreeable days as these present. Dozens of interesting people defile before me. I spend my time 'looking up' friends in the town and studying French Literature. If Harold has left, I suppose you will have opened his letter and learnt that I am fixed here until Oct. 7. as Madame leaves Havre by the *Chicago* on the 12th. I have only one pupil at present. I have answered advertisements in *Schoolmaster*. French Master wanted temporarily in Birkenhead. I wonder if Father could call at Town Hall, & see Sec. R.T. Jones? Also in Chester, apply to Lovell, Educ. Off, Town Hall. I won't think of coming by Havre then. Do you know Gen. St. Nay. Co. to London is cheaper than Moss Line to L'pool. and I should prefer to land in London.

Do begin a course of Rest Cure to prepare yourself for my examination of your Health! Don't worry. The Affair Léger is 'settled'.[81] Your own W

I've received the balance from Raoul.

[81] In addition to worrying his mother, the 'affair Léger' had also disturbed Owen. See Letter 292.

292. To Susan Owen

Address your next letters till further notice:

Wednesday, 14 October 1914   *12 Cours St. Louis, Bordeaux*[82]

My own Mother,

The reading of your letter this morning was quite emotioning for me. You speak so cheerfully of yourself, you say such nice things about Harold; you tell me that dear Father approves of me yet, and will be glad—I hope gladdened—to see me; and you show me Colin, pale, and crumpled-up under Homework! I was so near booking my passage at the beginning of the week! But, all at once, three or four pupils turned up, and after all my exertions in turning 'em up, I thought it a pity to turn 'em down again.

One is a boy who began with me at Berlitz,[83] and who interested me by his intelligence. We grew friendly, and it was at his home that I spent the evening of my 21st birthday. His parents are both schoolteachers. His mother is one of the most genuine good-natured Frenchwomen existing. It was through her that I got three more pupils—girls who have done five years English already; but I haven't seen them yet. While I am still unsettled, this good lady, Madame Berthaud, has offered me a room; but as it is for the moment occupied by a wounded soldier, I may not be able to take advantage of it. For, you know, I must leave the Lems' next Saturday. They have a young lad coming to lodge with them for a matter of some years. He is entering Raoul's school; & the matter had been fixed up long ago with his wealthy parents. This youth, whom I have seen and liked, is going to receive English instruction from me, twice a week. I am glad of the excuse to leave here; for, though wondrous neat and clean, my room has no writing-table, no wardrobe, no drawers, and no armchair. The window looks on the streets, giving me advantages and annoyances. From six o'clock in the morning begins a thundering and a racketing of lorry-wheels on the stone causeway; and a growl of barrels rolling, and a clank of iron-rods flopping: above all of which, like a clarion on a battlefield, resounds the braying of Sieur Lem's ass! But the day is quieter, and at 4 o'clock I can look down on the children coming from a school close by, which never fails to make me tender and poetical. Poor children, these; for the quarter is poor but not low. Indeed I never see in France any scabby-haired, mud-stockinged arabs, hoarse of voice and hard of eye, such as breed in Liverpool muds, Birmingham cinders, and London fog-smoke.

In the *Jardin Public*, in the afternoon, gathers another type of youngsters: a great part of them are Parisians, and very *chic*. It has sometimes happened that when I have been reading there, a boy has stopped his hoop and come up to me, hat in hand, just in order to talk to me. These incidents give me hope that the Léger episodes have not taken the bloom off my innocency. I don't think I told you I have an interesting 'protégé' who would cost me dear if I had any help to give him. Before I left for Bagnères I encountered at the *Union Chrétienne* a youth of 15.[84] The first thing he said to me was that he loved Song and Music above all things; and straightway began to sing! Now his eyes, and indeed his whole countenance were the most romantically beautiful I had ever beheld. So remembered him, and having his card, looked him up on my return. I found his house in a shabby quarter. And I found his household in tears and sighing. His father was dying. Some weeks before his employer had reduced his little pittance owing to the war. The good man was so upset, that he contracted jaundice and such complications as a result of his contrariety of spirit. Now he is dead. The mother is a good soul, all heart, and, as I have seen her, never out of tears. Arriving at the moment I did, she vows I was sent by the good God. I was indeed able to do some small services; and have now won her affection, even as her son has mine. She begs and implores me to be a Counsellor to her sons. 'Oh, my dear young Sir! Give them your Advice: look after them: warn them: be their friend…Oh the poor, dears, left like this fatherless, oh! oh! oh!…'

And that was the moment when I began to realize better the seamy side of Madame Léger's cap: if you understand me. Indeed, I hope you understand the rest of this incoherent effusion: for on reading it over I scarcely make much sense of it myself. But so long as I am as wise in policy as I have proved I can be, you will let me dream and scribble as idiotically as I like!

There was no mention of Mary in your last. I hope she is mentally alive: and should like some sign of it. Let her write soon!

Ever your loving Wilfred

[82] Owen was now lodging with the Lem family.

[83] Fourteen-year-old Pierre Berthaud was in correspondence with Susan Owen after the war. He wrote to her from Bordeaux on 14 February 1925: 'Yes, Wilfred came very frequently home; he was coming every two or three days, to teach me English, and I remember that he spent his 20th [21st] birthday with us. My mother loved him. He was such a fine, a charming, a perfect fellow…I had been in acquaintance with him in 1913, or 1912, at the Berlitz School. He then lived at No. 95, rue Porte-Dijeaux. My family invited him home, and he took several times dinner with us.' An earlier letter to Susan, of 27 December 1920, conveyed his deep sadness at 'the unhappy death of my dearest friend'.

[84] André Martin. See Letter 375.

295. To Susan Owen

[Late] *October 1914*   *Chez. Veuve Martin, 31 rue Desfourniels, Bordeaux*

Dearest of Mothers,

Your loving letters never end without a prayer for my happiness. Let mine begin with the assurance that they are answered: (I mean the prayers, not the letters.) If not greatly happier than I was this time last year, I am infinitely more comfortable. And the feeling that I am under obligations to no man, is as sweet as it is new. For the moment I have neither schoolmaster nor taskmaster, neither patron nor boss. I have slain—so far as I am concerned four tyrants: first, Timpany, who taxed his subjects with grievous work; next Lightbourn, a bullying boss; next Wigan, who essayed to dominate one's entire being; next Aumont, unmercifully grinding, being goaded by avarice. These men are not my enemies (except perhaps the last); but they are not the masters I feel called to serve. Indeed, though I look up and down the world, I see no man whom I could serve without a suffocated feeling of captivity. This may turn out fortunate after all....

For the moment, my decision to throw myself on the world and live by my wits, has proved happy. I confess that, when I wrote putting off my return, I knew only two certain pupils, who would have brought me in a revenue of eight francs a week! But the pain I had to put off seeing you yet a little while pricked me so that I did a rare thing, I made an effort. And now I have every expectation of prospering—in the manner of our old friend in the *Tale of Two Cities,* the husband of Lucie Manette, (forget his name)[85] who gave lessons in Soho: and was offered the backward urchins of his friends to instruct. All my pupils are children, (thanks be); except the Viscount, who is nineteen. He is not the <u>son</u> of the General,[86] but his nephew. I like him quite well; and shall finish by a friendship, I foresee. The Consul, who sent me round to these people, spoke of a sort of <u>supervision</u> of the young spark on my part: Guide,— Philosopher, and—Friend sort of thing. His lordship is notably <u>flighty</u>, according to his aunt whom I interviewed first. Probably I showed <u>too young</u> for this business. Indeed I hinted I couldn't be bothered with his morals unless well paid. So twice a week I resort to his room—on a fourth story—and give a two hour lesson which just covers my total expenses for that day (5f.) In virtue of this, I have taken a handsome room: twice the rent of the last. But as all rents have risen lately, the difference is less real. I spent a good part of three days, hunting for a den. I nearly put up in a garret, at 15 francs. The Lems found the hole: near them: in a poky lane, behind the docks: view of thousands of roofs. Attracted by the romance of a real garret with whitewashed walls and a prospect of chimney-stacks I actually went to engage it: but the proprietor being out, the Lems made up a bed for one night more; and next day I found it would be necessary for me to have a room to receive people. For that purpose my choice is well fitted : — fine old house—looking on a little square—out of reach of tram-noises, but two minutes from trams—my rooms form a corner—a great window each way—room well carpeted—four armchairs—Louis XV (genuine) bureau—Louis XV Wardrobe—second wardrobe with mirrors modern, Louis XVI,—bed and night-table to match—fine marble fireplace—

thirty (supportable) pictures—and—a piano, out of tune, but with-out tone. A Dressing Room leads out of the Chamber: no lack of mirrors and shelves & cupboards—and even a gas-jet is fixed up for my hot-water. This window faces east as every dressing room should, and is blessed with a delightful morning sun. Suppose I help your imagination with a few lines—

The rest of the story is occupied by my widow-landlady, whose son is at the war. She takes care of me in a manner that would gratify you. The good soul, for what reason I know not, often asks if my mother and father won't come and stay with me: and as much as sends you the message that she would be glad to put you up. If only you had the <u>energy</u> to come over…!

I must run out now to a Lecture. Courses (free) are now started every evening in Raoul's College. I get up early and couch me late; but between the arrangement of my room; my lessons; my visits on & by friends; my interesting books, I don't seem to be able to succeed in Correspondence! But as for losing any modicum of desire to get home … what possessed you (to speak plainly) to pen that imagination???

Your very own, Wilfred

I had Harold's telegram: 'Not Calling Rochelle' <u>before</u> your P.C. I really think I should have started off to see him, and feel so disappointed.

---

[85] Charles Darnay, whose place on the scaffold was taken by Sydney Carton.
[86] General Louis Ernest de Maud'huy (1857–1921), first Chief Scout of Scouts de France.

296. To Mary Owen

Friday, 30 October 1914[87]   *Bordeaux*

My dear Mary,

I am upset about this malignant cold of Mother's, and hope you will keep telling me precisely how things are. For my part I have shaken of my cold in eight days.

This Nursing Training is capital for you.[88] When I saw so many French ladies busying themselves so, I meant to ask you what you were doing, and whether you couldn't join classes. I therefore am <u>ever so glad</u> to know you are tak[ing] Gardener's lectures. I confess I look for the benefit to produce itself in yourself more than for the Soldiers: and I myself shall feel a security and a comfort to know that you are able to deal with accidents and make war on microbes! I only hope you will attack the subject seriously, and get something like an orderly notion of Anatomy: and, later on, to understand the functions of the different organs. About this I am still much in the dark myself; but I used to know the names of the bones and muscles, so look out for some quizzing. If you pass your examination I shall be radiant.

I spent Wednesday morning at the oral examination of the French B.A. which is reputed to be as easy as London Matric. and is passed at seventeen years. One of my pupils for English is sitting, and I was at his elbow all the while, as well for English, as other things. I used to have a horror of the mere idea of an oral examination in anything; but having seen, I don't think the system bad. Half a dozen professors instal themselves behind tables, in odd corners of a large room: with a label above their learned noddles, telling what was in them. The candidates saunter in about eight o'clock in the morning, and if one sees an examiner unoccupied one sits down on the chair before him, and he straightaway begins to ply you with questions. Anybody may gape around, even the succeeding candidates; but 'the public' was restricted to myself and one or two anxious mothers. Five minutes after the last student has been examined the results are shown! Five minutes! and in England we wait six weeks! I recognised the professor of Latin and Ancient History, he having accompanied his daughter to my lessons at Berlitz. (This young lady was the greatest dunce imaginable, and many a time have I thumped the table, glaring at the papa, but little thought he was so erudite a pot). In the exam, I heard this Prof. telling the daughters of others what hopeless flounderers they were in Latin. To my friend, he growled—'My lad, you know nothing at all of Latin, nothing at all.' Nevertheless my friend passed.

Thus I spent all a morning; and the afternoon with my lessons, and the evening with my Free Classes finishes the day, and so finishes every day; but I don't find time to write to Mother as I should like to, or even to Colin. I have told you about his <u>double</u> who is a cousin of the pupil just mentioned. At times, I only just fail to punch the fellow's head for daring to resemble my incomparable brother and yet baulking me of the reality. Only let my incomparable brother see to it that he resembles himself, in my idea of him!

As much as I long to feel the soft caress of My Mother's hand, and to behold the hearty countenance of my Father, and as much as I long to hear the rare voice of my gentle Sister, I long to slap the shoulders of that Colin, and stroke his little chin. As for Harold I shall regard him with great astonishment for having rounded the vast mass of South America, and with ten times more admiration for having rounded off his own address.

Father's letter this afternoon, which followed Mother's of this morning, gave great pleasure. I cannot justly say that the matter of Mother's was pleasing—what with the complication of her Cold, and the miserable sketch of Dunsden—Oh my! But when I hear that Mother is on the ascending scale again, I shall be your 'most content'

Wilfred

[87] Owen incorrectly dated this letter 29 October (PN, p. 188).
[88] Mary Owen joined the VAD when war broke out. Her nursing certificate is in the Owen Archive at the Bodleian.

298. To Susan Owen

Friday, 6 November 1914   *Bordeaux*

My dearest Mother,

Many things of interest were to be found in your last envelopeful; but what most impressed me was the confession to perpetual headache. It gives to me as much uneasiness as it gives you unease. Such a state of things should be given its right name Disease, and should be treated as such. I know not what druggeries you are given, nor what semblances of rests you take, but if one thing more than another seems to me probable to clear your dear head of these distempers and infesting dreams, it would be a radical displacement of yourself, a voyage into France, bag-and-baggage into a new atmosphere, and a fresh mentality. Suppose I returned here after Ch[r]istmas, would you come? Raoul has hinted something about your having certain intentions of staying with him! What is this, pray?

I have written a card to Oliver.[89] But I don't think I could bear to live in Cambridge except in one capacity alone…yet. However, let us hear all possible about it.

And so you say Talking fatigues you to the point of irritation. I suspect it is the Talk and the Talkers that are to blame. For me, I never took such pleasure in Conversation as at this present time. The French put such an astonishing intelligence and elegance into their *Causeries,* that these equal, and supplant even, Novel-Reading. I speak now of the French represented by Tailhade, and the friends of Monsieur Léger. While, more's the pity, I think of such English representatives of Conversation as old Mrs. Williams, waddling round to waste your afternoons; or else of that loud-protesting Protestant Miss: or else of that meek handmaiden of the Lord, Mrs. Fordham, whispering prophecies, scandal, visions, prayers and shop-prices world-without-end. If this gives you a headache I feel a wicked satisfaction to know it. It ought to. To think that you are in ear-shot of Mrs Ragg…[90] What commerce hast thou with these folk? I think with sorrow of your isolation in the human world. For upon my word, if you secretly deem that your sister-in-law is living an animal life, I secretly suspect your sister of vegetating. Who shall blame 'em? The mineral state is perhaps the most preferable, after all.

But, like a Poet, thou hast thy own Creations to comfort thee, and may we, thy Works, follow thee with more consolations than the creations of art.

In any case you are less isolate than I.

I begin to suffer a hunger for Intimity. At bottom, it is that I ought to be in love and am not. Though I have abundance of acquaintance, and a thousand times more friends here than in England, (since out of the Family, I have not one in England) I lack any touch of tenderness. I ache in soul, as my bones might ache after a night spent on a cold, stone floor.

You ask about my pulsations. Now, only today I had a severe attack of palpitation: this way: in a populous street suddenly I saw bearing down on me a hard, hunting-cruel Face: Aumont! His expression alone was enough to terrify, but when that expression was worn by the very eyes one wanted to avoid...For it was the face of Sherlock Holmes gone to the bad. There is one of my 'neighbours' whom I hate as myself. There are not two: and that one is Maurice Aumont. One thing I may thank him for, and that is for providing me with a visual impression of the avaricious brothers in *Isabella*.[91] But he didn't recognize me, and no wonder, I am so much changed since the day of my emancipation. And my nerves were soon after caressed by the meeting with no less than six other faces, which were all fair in their way, and kindling with smiles. One was Master Pierre Berthaud, who bore the aspect of 'snatching a fearful joy' (as Gray put it)[92] in being out of bounds. He just had time to caution me not to remember having seen him in town, and vanished on his mysterious errand. Another was Thouverez, Colin's non-correspondent; whom I have not seen for months.

I have to signal the loss of two pupils. The Viscount de Maud'huy is going to England this week. I had a note this morning telling me of this new plan, & in which he hopes to meet me over there. In reply I opened the bars of Mahim's gates to him! For he is a fellow of some fellowship for me. My land-lady cut out the enclosed ¶. and begged me to send it to de Maud'huy 'with felicitations'. Good soul. So I send it to you in case she find it in my waste-paper basket. Och! I forgot you may not make head or tail of it. How droll! I lose also the Russian Pupil, gone to Pau, travelling in the same carriage as my landlady who went down that day to see her soldier-son, ill in hospital.

I heard that Tailhade, together with Anatole France,[93] is shouldering a rifle! Now I may be led into enlisting when I get home: so familiarise yourself with the idea! It is a sad sign if I do: for it means that I shall consider the continuation of my life of no use to England. And if once my fears are roused for the perpetuity and supremacy of my mother-tongue, in the world—I would not hesitate, as I hesitate now—to enlist.

To have the Photographs, so real and fresh, and naïf as they are, is a high pleasure for me. I think you look never so sweet. I like the attitude of Colin, and feel a special admiration for his Right Hand and there end my compliments. Mary

is so stiff, though the self-effacement of the left-arm is characteristic enough
[*remainder missing*]

[89] Frederick Oliver, a Shrewsbury friend, had gone up to Cambridge. He was ordained in 1919
and was Rector of Swithland, Leicestershire, 1925–30.

[90] Mrs Ragge's name was omitted in the *CL* and *SL*.

[91] Keats, *Isabella, or the Pot of Basil*, in which Isabella's two brothers murder her lover.

[92] 'Still as they run they look behind, / They hear a voice in every wind, / And snatch a fearful
joy.' Thomas Gray, 'Ode on a Distant Prospect of Eton College'.

[93] He was 70. Anatole France [Jacques-Anatole-François Thibault] (1844–1924), poet, novelist,
journalist, man of letters, won the Nobel Prize for Literature in 1921.

302. To Susan Owen

Wednesday, 2 December [1914]   *Bordeaux*

My own dear Mother,

You must now know all about the sinking of the English coal-boat *Prima*[94] off
Cape Cantifer, and how the crew were given ten minutes to get off into a 'whale-
boat' ; from which they were picked up by another collier. I believe this is the
third boat sunk in the Channel by German submarines. And I don't know how
many in the Atlantic. No wonder you disquiet yourself about Harold. I should
look for nothing in the papers but Atlantic shipping news; if I wasn't watching
the Channel, and practising swimming exercises. Madame Léger, who meant to
start back just at present, is not venturing yet.

Now what am I to do?

I have upset my digestion by imagining to myself that after all…after all and
after so long, so very long, I shan't, shan't be with you for Christmas!

On Saturday I consulted my Insurance-Agent-pupil who was quite settled
that the Irish Sea is mined; but that the Channel ought to be safe. So I passed a
happy Sunday, saying to myself: 'Three Weeks Today…etc.' Then I got that fright;
and everybody's saying—'Of course, you won't start now.'

I may.

I haven't bought my ticket; but I have given notice to leave my Room. It isn't,
however, let, and I have asked for a few days grace.

I was considering going round to the Consul one afternoon (Monday) when I
was handed a card from a Miss Patterson, sister of the Vice-Consul, asking if I was
'still at this address as a lady wishes someone to coach her nephews nr. Bordeaux.'[95]
I trotted round to the Vice-Consul's rooms yesterday. Found them 'having tea'
brother and sister together: as English as English could be. She a lengthy, young
lady, neck as long as a lamp-post, blond-hair, blond as dead palm-leaves. (I am
sorry to say it but Miss Patterson is <u>ridiculously</u> English). She gives lessons of
some sort to these kids, of which there are four. They were born in China where
their father remains. The aunt who takes charge of them said by the Pattersons to

be a 'charming Irish woman, of old family' is not satisfied with the education of the two elder boys who are at some Bx. School, and very much wants an Englishman to take them in hand. That was all Patterson could tell me. So this afternoon I took the tram that carries one to Mérignac in some twenty minutes. I arrived at nightfall at 'the Chalet'. I found Miss (the Aunt) out. Two boys of ten or nine were there, English thoroughbreds. We debated a bit as to when I should come again: till finally I was led by the Bonne to 'Mademoiselle'[96] whoever she may be. 'Mademoiselle' was lying in bed, being infirm and after a few apologetic words in French, addressed me in un-English English. I am no wiser about the nature of the lessons, or the number, or the terms; but, although, the people are not apparently rich, they will have to make it jolly advantageous for me, if I stay for 'em. And Miss Patterson says the boys are thick as all English boys: (for she never knew a French lad who could be so dull as the average English dummy.)

I shall go again tomorrow morning and shall let you know result immediately.

The afternoon was not lost; for the weather was Aprilic, and I had not been into the country for months. The shock was so great that I lost my memory a little while (a rare thing to lose one's sense of memory.) Indeed I am too continually revising the Past, and trying to peep over the Wall of days that separates us and which is daily higher and higher. If you give me permission to start, I shall start home. But if Father thinks it imprudent, I stay. And if you will be more flurried during the two or three days I am on the sea, than you will be regretful during the two months more that I lie low here—I stay. For me, I shall suffer more from 'ennui' in missing Christmas at Home than from nervousness on board ship.

I talked to the Vice-Consul about it. But he just hummed—and ha-'d as only a genuine well-bred Englishman can.

It is, as you say, 'a good thing Herbert Oliver has his skin.'[97] It was, as I remember, a first-quality skin; and Herbert is about the best specimen of the 'English type' I could find if asked to produce one. Where is he? Convey my personal felicitations. Wrecked survivor, is he? And here am I imagining I have some adventures while these sparks of midshipmen are hopping off sinking vessels in mid-ocean, or dodging German Cruisers! Nay, but the tables are turned for me and my English friends since last year. Now I have leisure, health, a snug retreat, many friends. And they have Military Drill, fatigue, stone floors, desperate Enemies. Now, let me talk seriously. The *Daily Mail* speaks very movingly about the 'duties shirked' by English young men. I suffer a good deal of shame. But while those ten thousand lusty louts go on playing football I shall go on playing with my little axiom:—that my life is worth more than my death to Englishmen.

Do you know what would hold me together on a battlefield?: The sense that I was perpetuating the language in which Keats and the rest of them wrote! I do not know in what else England is greatly superior, or dearer to me, than another land and people.

Write immediately what I am to do.

I should take the boat for London on Sat. Dec. 19. My greetings are almost tearful: but take good heart. Are we not still much happier than the majority of families: and safer?

Your devoted Wilfred

Friday

I went over to Mérignac yesterday morning as I said, and found the Aunt— grey-haired lady, of quiet ways, and very nice ways with the four boys. The two elder boys,[98] my affairs, arrived on bicycles from Bx. about 12.30 with a half-holiday. I am well-impressed. The eldest is thin; but it is his features rather than his health which are delicate. He is pretty rather than handsome. The second is neither; but equally intelligent, and more sensible. The third is David, who gives the appearance of fatness without being so; and bears a really close resemblance to <u>Harold</u> at his age—10 or so. The youngest[99] is temporarily crippled. One brother threw him down in play, fracturing the pelvis:— 2½ hours operation! Justifies the fragile appearance of the lads. In spite of their speaking French at will, they are all from top to toe, English schoolboys. The jargon they kept up was delicious for me to hear. The good Aunt questioned me about these weird words and their meaning, not having the faintest notion of what means 'clout', topping, etc. etc. When I got back to Bx. I seemed to be returned from a brief visit to England. We had lunch in the (Here my landlady brought in your letter: glad to know Harold's safe, and that you're expecting me don't be too benevolent to perfect strangers—shall be destitute mysel' on arriving in England.) so as I was saying—we had lunch in the garden: We boys at least—and it rained 3 times, soaking the table-cloth and our hair, and diluting the soup, and we all swore the wine tasted weaker—and Auntie let us stay out in the wet to our inexpressible delight. (I had a cold the day before—but haven't felt it since!) At lunch I put the lads through testing questions on their studies. They don't seem much advanced: but seem capable: and then the English is sound, and not only sound but elegant (lahst, get off the grahss, silly ahss! etc.) The Aunt wants me then to go to their school, and take the two aside for a special Grammar & Literature Lesson. In the Holidays she wants a Tutor to help her with them generally. The Chalet is not large—and she would take rooms in the village for the Tutor and his wards. I didn't jump at this, preferring my present mode of life: and then—I mean to start for London on Saturday, the nineteenth day of this present, towards nine in the Evening! Till—would I could state it—Till Then—

Au Revoir.

Your own Wilfred

P.S. Can you give me an address of a <u>Rubber</u> Rain-Coat Business House. A Frenchman wants to buy direct from England.

—What a mixture of things your Reply will be: But be clear on <u>one point</u>.

[94] *SS Primo,* a British cargo ship shelled by SM *U-21.* It sank in the English Channel 6 nautical miles north-west of Cap d'Antifer on the Normandy coast.

[95] The lady was Miss Anne de la Touche; Miss Patterson had been acting as part-time governess to the two youngest of her four nephews. Miss de la Touche, now 51, was a member of the old French-Irish family of which Rose de la Touche, Ruskin's pupil, was a member (see Letter 304, n. 103). From 1900 to 1909 she bad been in the household of one of the Belgian Princesses, the Duchesse de Vendôme, as governess to the young princesses. She came to Mérignac, on the western outskirts of Bordeaux, in 1910. Her sister, the Barone de Bock, lived in Bordeaux. Her brother, father of the four nephews mentioned, was in the Chinese Maritime Customs Service, and had left Charles and David, twins, with their aunt at Mérignac. The elder boys, Johnny and Bobbie, were at Downside School in Somerset; the outbreak of war found them on holiday at Mérignac, unable to get back to England. Miss de la Touche felt the need of a tutor, having tried a Bordeaux school (École Ste. Marie) for the older boys and found it unsatisfactory.

[96] Mlle Marthe de Puységur, invalid daughter of a neighbour, stayed with Miss de la Touche during her parents' frequent absences from home.

[97] Frederick Oliver's younger brother. He had gone to sea shortly after HO, his closest friend. His ship had been torpedoed in the early days of the war and he had sailed 600 miles to safety in an open boat after being marooned in the Galapagos Islands. He survived the experience, and the war.

[98] Johnny and Bobbie.

[99] Charles.

304. To Susan Owen

Wednesday, 9 December 1914[100]   *Bordeaux*

My dearest Mother,

After a day of tormenting indecision I have at last made up my mind, and have arrived at a sense of sanctified peace: I have made up my mind—Hold Tight!—to put off my voyage for <u>4 weeks</u>. In those four weeks I ought to make a haul of nearly £8. When I realised the Alternative of costing you £8. or of earning them myself: my better nature left no choice. But it was hard to refuse my poor old childish soul, the 'Christmas at Home', (though I know very well that the expression 'Merry Christmas' will not be heard in the land, or ought not to be.)

Moreover I shall be in an English family, very differently situated from a year ago: so you can be quite happy about me.

Indeed, if you want to give me a Blessing and a Christmas Wish, you can only do so by clearly saying that you completely approve, of, and acquiesce in my resolution, and admire me for it. But if, instead of saying nice things to keep up my heart, you should hint any disappointment on your part, <u>or lack of it on mine</u>: I shall not be able to bear the thing: but shall throw up my promises, and take the next train for Calais. I mean it. You have only to <u>telegraph</u>...if your self-control or your confidence in me are not strong enough to support 30 days delay—and I can yet book a bunk on the *Fauvette*.

I went yesterday to see a man, caretaker of the 'Sailors' Reading Room' (who is in touch with the crews of all English boats in here) in order to find out whether any Collier or Cargo-thing whatever would be able to take me cheap. He knew of none such: and said that Captains nowadays weren't 'tickalarly gone on that game, bein, responsible for whatever 'appened to the passenger. If the passenger 'signed on' that's another story. There certainly was a scare on in Bordeaux, by reason of the submarines: but if that Marine Insurance Agent Pupil is no more sharp-witted in his Marine Affairs than in his English lessons I ought never to have hearkened to him. So I think there is not more risk than just enough to make the trip exciting.

Two days after this scare, cropped up this other obstacle: Poverty. At present I am worth the dazzling sum of £90. a year while my expenditure merely amounts to £89.19.11³/⁴. If my board & lodging were paid for this expenditure would be reduced. Such is my prospect for the next month. I have been twice to talk things over with Miss de la Touche and have come away without settling anything. Today she stated explicitly what she wanted: Me to live out there, and look after the boys in the afternoons; terms mutual; and I to keep up as many Bordeaux lessons as I wish, tramming or bicycling in every morning. We should work about two hours a day; and amuse ourselves the rest. I took good care that, in lesson-time the boys seemed likely to work, and that in play-time, I seemed likely to amuse <u>myself</u>. It is of course only the two elder that are to work, though in our excursions we shall be half a dozen with the French comrades. Since my writing last, we went a shooting expedition, all the more enhanced for that shooting is forbidden. There were two cartridge- and one air-gun, and it might have made you creepy to see the loaded pieces in such reckless hands, but we came <u>home</u> (save the mark!), but left the game equally so. All the afternoon great guns were booming from the manoeuvring grounds, and a hovering aeroplane kept buzzing overhead. (And I thought of the thousand redeemers by whose blood my life is being redeemed. To read the Casualty List is like the twenty-first chapter of St. Luke;[101] or the last passages of *Severn's Journal*;[102] neither readable without tears.)

I think the country-month ought to repair what Bordeaux has undone of Bagnères' work on my constitution. Mérignac seems a well-wooded part; it is about half-an-hour on foot from the boulevards surrounding the city.

Miss de la Touche is of mysterious age: nearly white hair; but fresh Cousin Mayish complexion, and the evidence of very fine features. She is a cousin of the Rose de la Touche[103] whom Ruskin didn't quite marry; and who died in youth; but seems to have lived in the age of the Prophet. Will you please take down Mr. Collingwood's *Ruskin* and refer to 'de la Touche Rose' if she is mentioned therein; as I think and trust she be. If someone would copy what is said I sh'd be grateful. Miss de la Touche is in touch with the Belgian Royal Family, having in some manner fostered one of the Princesses, sister, I suppose, of the valiant King Albert, so much 'at the front' today.

The father of the boys has a Customs Post in China, where the mother still stays. Three years ago, the boys began school at the Roman Catholic College, at Downside, Somerset. The fees are extremely high, and when, in France, the operation on Charly[104] cost a formidable sum, and war reigned, the Aunt thought it best to keep them here. But papa doesn't like that; and now the Abbot of Downside writes saying that if it is only the fees that now keep them away from school, he will facilitate, etc. So, tho', last week, the Aunt thought of keeping them in Bx. next term, she now means to send them home next January. Till, then, she is frightened at the prospect of having to manage them during the holidays. and also wants someone to take them home about the middle of January. So the Consul spoke to the Vice Consul, who sent his sister to me, who have just arranged it. Now, have I done well? Yea, when I <u>do</u> enter my little room it will be ten times more snug, and my bed under the paternal roof ten times more comfortable; and when I <u>do</u> hear your voice it will be ten times more sweet. Thus only 5 or 6 more Sundays must you write! At last I tell you! Neither Love, Fear, nor Money shall prolong that:

Witness my hand Wilfred x

(If the fatted calf be already killed this letter may serve as a refrigerator.)

[100] Owen incorrectly dated the letter 8 December (PN, p. 188).

[101] Christ's prophecy of the destruction of Jerusalem.

[102] Joseph Severn (1793–1879), painter and friend of Keats, went with the poet to Italy in 1820, and attended him at his death. He kept no journal, but his letters from Rome form a record of Keats's last weeks. See Letter 157.

[103] A second cousin. Rose died on 25 May 1879, aged 27, in a Dublin nursing home, suffering most likely from the effects of anorexia. She had been Ruskin's pupil at the age of 10, and his love for the child—she was thirty years his junior—and reports of Ruskin's treatment of his first wife, Effie Gray, led Rose's parents to refuse to let them meet.

[104] A fall while playing had led three months earlier to the hip operation mentioned in Letter 302.

305. To Susan Owen

Postcard

Sunday [Postmark 14 December 1914]   *[Postmark Bordeaux]*

Your 'last' letter came yesterday night. I was glad to find that you attached small importance to 'sentiment about Christmas'. About this date next month I ought to be starting. As you love me, <u>send no material Christmas presents</u>; and expect none. We shall keep the feast on the 25th of January, about!

I don't know anything about the return of Mme. L. and don't care. Yes, I am waiting to talk over my Future, first with You; and then either with a Professor or a Recruiting Sergeant! I move to Mérignac on the 19th I think.[105] How about Mary's Exam? Fondest Love to Every-body

W.E.O

Don't write more to Raoul. He is out of my books![106]

[105] Miss de la Touche wrote to the headmaster of Downside on 15 December 1914: 'I have taken a young tutor for them for the Christmas holidays, he is giving lessons in Bordeaux preparing for Oxford. The boys will work with him at English, History, Geometry and Algebra and do some literature as well…He goes home about the 19th of January, and the boys can travel with him.' On 23 December she wrote: 'J. and B. are quite well and have begun their work with Mr. Owen. He teaches them in a most interesting way….'

[106] Probably because Raoul's behaviour whilst at Mahim was less than perfect. HO is rather scathing about him in *JFO* III, calling him 'uncontrollably disobedient, wildly emotional, and verging often towards hysteria' (p. 63) if he did not get his own way, but DH takes a more tempered view (see *WOANB*, pp. 179–80). See also Letter 308.

307. To Susan Owen

21 December 1914   *Chez Mlle de la Touche, Le Châlet, Mérignac, Gironde*

Dearest of Mothers,

So here I am; I racketed about all Saturday making luggage out of lumber; and at four o'clock, rolled away in a four-wheeler, with one box, leaving the rest with the old dame. The Châlet is not very spacious: Just a well-built bungalow, with one upstairs-room, which is mine.[107] There are four servants, one a man, who all dwell in an out-building. So all the good traditions of an English country-house are fully observed. I am more comfortable than at Dunsden, for example. I get up at 7.30, have a double-egg breakfast, with the boys and their Aunt, who have been already to Mass. Then I catch the tram and reach Bx. to start lessons about 9. Sometimes I shall not get through all my lessons in the morning, & must have lunch in town. Although two or three pupils are taking holidays, I have just been written to by two new people. The first is a doctor, mental specialist, with a Sanatorium for treating morphio-maniacs. This gentleman is, all round, an 'interesting' pupil, and what the French call 'a Brain'. Moreover his wife wants lessons too. But I just can't give them as many as they want!

The other applicant is a railway official; but as he only felt inclined to take one a week, I had to tell him to wait.

Until five o'clock in the afternoon we go out, or the boys amuse themselves as best they can. From five to seven the two eldest work with me. Today we spent the whole time on the Roman Occupation of Britain; and it was I who benefited by the lesson; for to have an attentive audience for two hours, comprehending what I said about early history was an unmixed pleasure. At other times, these fellows make a frantic noise, with lungs, feet, and every object at hand. At table they behave well, but not well enough for 'Auntie',—who having lived in a Palace and 'shaped' a Princess is naturally a stickler for correctness. She is ever so kind to me, and clearly is as fond of her nephews as Aunt could be.

I am sorry you could find nothing about Rose de la T. in Mr. Collingwood's *Ruskin*. I must make a pilgrimage to the Lakes and ask Mr. Collingwood. I must certainly make a sojourn at Alpenrose, and at Meols, and anywhere else not excepting even Scarborough.

We had three reports of that 'business':[108] the first said 'no real damage'; the second said 'a few persons killed' a third said 'more than 80 killed, 115 wounded.' When I read that a shell fell into a group of sixteen schoolboys and killed fifteen, I raved. Talk about rumours of wars and earthquakes in divers places: all that's historic now. The beginning of the End must be ended, and the beginning of the middle of the end is now.

I must be beginning to end my Christmas letter. You understand that I have every minute jammed-full of some occupation; and it is eleven o'clock when I write. The word Christmas hath lost his savour. In vain I stare at a sprig of holly and languish at a mistletoe-berry. They mean nothing. I repeat like a poor idiot 'Merry Christmas to you', 'While Shepherds watched their flocks by night'— Father Christmas—Dickens—Charles Dickens—Scrooge—Bob Cratchit—Plum Pudding—Tiny Tim—Mince Pie—Christmas Tree—Once in Bethlehem of Judah—Haunted Grange—Yule Log—no use. I can't get the atmosphere. Best to leave it, then; this year the 25th of December is the day that comes after the 24th and before the 26th: merely so. Nevertheless, all the mottoes of a million Christmas Cards could not express my Affection for You who most care for me; or tell my Wishes for You.

Know, also, that I shall be in something very like an English Home for Christmas; for I am not going with Lem, etc. where I shall be far from unhappy; but the greatest happiness of the Day and of the Season will be the Reading of your letters, and hoping for the Meeting in January

Mother's and Father's
Mary's
Harold's   } Wilfred
Colin's

---

[107] The Chalet, though small, was pleasant (it was demolished in 1964). It was set in a spacious garden, with plums, greengages, peaches, and figs, running back to a small wood. David La Touche recalls the scent of lime trees and roses; the limes provided lime tea for his aunt's frequent migraines. Accommodation was difficult. The four boys crowded into one of the four rooms, the others being drawing room, dining room, and the aunt's room. The one 'pill-box of a room' in the roof was allotted to Owen. Somehow, with a bed in the drawing room, the invalid Mlle de Puységur was fitted in. A succession of English, French, or Irish governesses came to look after the two younger boys; they did not live in. Of Owen, Charles La Touche writes:

'the only setting in which I can remember him clearly is at night prayers, when he used to stand respectfully in the background'.

[108] German battlecruisers shelled Scarborough, Hartlepool, and Whitby on 16 December 1914, killing 122 people and wounding 443.

308 (a). To Susan Owen

[First sheet missing, the remainder stained by damp and occasionally illegible]

27 December 1914   *Mérignac*

The man-servant brings me hot water for my bath every morning. I breakfast on two eggs (instead of [one] as formerly); at 12.30 I come in hungry to find a 'smashin' dinner [*two words illegible*]; at five I have tea and toast and at seven another dinner. The maids wait at meals; and the cook knows her trade. Magnificent coal-fires warm the cockles of my heart. Moreover a gold box of finest Turkish cigarettes are at my disposal; and also four 'hoards' of chocolates: for the boys had 'No Christmas present'; that is to say nothing but sweets, of which there were no lack.

I of course had a Box for me from my kindest of hostesses—<u>employers</u> is not the word. We all went to Midnight Mass on the 24th-25th: cripples included. For you know there is a lady-friend of Miss de la T. who lies on her back all her days. We made two journeys to church with the bath chair, and installed both the boys and ourselves in the very sanctuary. An interesting position for me, all mixed up with candles, incense, acolytes, chasuble and such like. If I didn't <u>bow</u>, I certainly <u>scraped,</u> for there was an unholy draught. How scandalized would certain of my acquaintance and kin have been to see me. But it would take a power of can-dlegrease and embroidery to romanize me. The question is to un-Greekize me.

It was three o'clock when we went to bed. I think the efforts of the dear, darling little acolytes to keep awake was what took most of my attention there. Johnny and Dédé both dropped asleep. 'On Christmas' then I got up somewhere about lunch-time. We spent the afternoon mostly on trams on the way to a Hospital where I accompanied three of the boys to see the Soldiers' Christmas Tree. Anyhow we spent 3 f. 80 c. on trams to get there. Then after enduring the fetid-stinking [*one word illegible*] place for 1-½ hours, we went to the boys' old school, for them to get their things, and I met their Superior. After dinner we had a few games and a lottery-thing in which everybody won [*two words illegible*]! The chief incident of the day from the boy's point of view was the smoking of a long-promised Cigarette each; and from my point of view was the turning of my thoughts to you-wards. I have not yet been able to [*one word illegible*] your Christmas Letters, but shall certainly tomorrow.

Your one mentioning my present, and containing Harold's things I read on bicycle, riding over to lunch.

You must be relieved about Harold.

Commend me to Cousin May.

I used to have the *Daily Mail* (Continental) given me; so I [*one word illegible*] English opinion.

Yes, please, keep the papers: such for example as, Annexation of [*one word illegible*] the Scarboro' affair, and, when you get it, the Fall of Berlin. Raoul merely gave me much annoyance in the Lessons I gave in the meanwhile. Not having any notions of [*one word illegible*] 'English properness' he gave me offence with his protracted drivelling, sniggering 'pleasantries'. I found I should be of service here on [*one word illegible*] so telegraphed an excuse to Preignac. I guess my Present is a down [*one word illegible*]—how 'topping'! The desire of my ten toes, for as many winters past: and having had one in my last Rooms, it will be the one thing needed.

One thinks of the 'trenches' with guilty feelings, in the midst of my surroundings; but my conscience is easily cleared by the recollection of certain happenings in my past.

I had a letter from Dunsden, expressing such a [*two words illegible*] of the Pope of Dunsden's [*one word illegible*] that I have just lain low and said nuffin.

Well done, Mary. I shall have some creepy things to tell her to 'steady her nerve, like', such creepy things that creep around and live on living men's flesh!

Now my 'mental' Doctor has sent me to yet another, whom I am obliged to refuse lessons to at present not having time. Isn't it annoying! No wonder I show signs of hurry tonight and yet all afternoon I have been sauntering, and spying sparrows in the greenwood!

My Wishes to dear Kin, and to you

Myself!

308 (b).[109] To Susan Owen

[4 January 1914]   Le Châlet, Mérignac, <u>Gironde</u>

Don't mention <u>Bordeaux</u> on Address!

Dearest Mother,

My occupations are at an end for today. It is striking ten by the village clock. I managed to get a letter off to Leslie yesterday. I forget when last I wrote. Always, when new places occupy my attention I muddle my sense of time. And here is a totally different environment to get used to from that of Bx. city. We went on Saturday to the finest Chateau[110] I ever beheld. There were the traditional 'extinguisher-topped towers'; and all the rest: a vast affair. The people are comparatively simple. The heir is a seraphic-faced, gentle little boy of eight, so I don't grudge him the possessions. There is an English governess of the conventional type, to look after this boy and his sister. The Lady of the place was one of the 'full-length portraits' in the Paris Salon. But as she was one of the miserables who this morning waited twenty minutes in pouring rain for the tram, that dignity seemed to unstiffen somewhat. I am invited to go and play tennis at the Chateau on the first fine day!! However as it will probably continue to rain until June, that proposal is not really so odd as it seems.

We also have the run of the grounds of two other rather nice estates[111] close to; and alternately invite and are invited by the boys to tea.

All the photographs are admirable, as much in execution as in pose. Father is the only one in whom I spy no change whatsoever. I am sure there is an alteration in your mouth, tho' it is not the work of Time's fangs, but of Rice-Oxley's[112] complete set. Mary is more truly youthful than she was. There is still something Ancient-British about the statuesque arms-folded one. These also are capable of caricature; (but I'm not). Father, rising discreetly into view from amid the mystical flowers, his nether parts yet confused with the background of luxuriant verdure, is most captivating. I suppose I may keep the prints with me. I am ever so pleased to have them. The Masked Lady is a joy to see; you look so well and happy. I hope Father is having a real holiday in Devon.

How decent of Fred. Oliver to blow my trumpet in Cambridge and Bournemouth. Keep him at it. One piece of news was really startling for its novelty: namely that a degree is necessary for teaching in England.

After ten years of hammering, that <u>nail</u> is beginning to give me a headache.

No doubt you know about the sinking of the *Formidable*.[113] It caused a sinking of spirits and hopes here: and Mlle. de la Touche, who for days has been hinting at keeping the boys, definitely said tonight that they should <u>not</u> go if <u>only</u> I would stay. The Principal of Downside,[114] (a Public school), her solicitor, the boys' father, their other Aunt, insist that all is safe for going over; nevertheless, and especially as the boys beg for it, Miss de la Touche would prefer to keep them here with me. I feel flattered to compete with Downside, but would rather throw it up than risk not seeing you for another batch of months. I promised her to tell you how she wishes me to stay; and you will say what you like. I can't enumerate all the pros and cons tonight. I have to get through four lessons tomorrow morning; which will make a scoop of 12 francs, not so bad seeing there are no expenses. This, however, is not a typical day, and I must beware being lured by this state of things. For tho' I am not <u>needy</u>, I am poor. Better to be poor than needy, but woe unto him that is both…

So in the meantime I am documenting myself with shipping news: and, in fault of another bust-up in the Channel, hold to my intention of starting, with courage and with love.

Yours ever, Wilfred

---

[109] JB, in *SL*, renumbered what was originally Letter 303 in *CL*, saying that Owen's 'dating seems a slip, as the letter refers to the sinking of the *Formidable* on 1 January 1915. I am assuming the date of 4 January 1915, and thus correcting the misplacing of this letter in *CL*' (p. 137).

[110] The Château du Parc, Mérignac, home of Admiral Castéjas. The boys were frequent visitors.

[111] Owned by the De L'Estapis and Piganeau families.

[112] The Owens' dentist.

[113] A British pre-dreadnought battleship torpedoed in the English Channel on 1 January 1915, with the loss of thirty-five officers and 512 men.

[114] The Roman Catholic school at Stratton-on-the-Fosse, near Bath.

309. To Susan Owen

Friday, 8 January 1915   [*Mérignac*]

Dearest Mother,

I am replying to yours of 3rd. and 4th. and am 'sitting up' to do so. I may make you 'sit up' likewise. Two days ago Miss de la Touche asked me to stay for 3 months more. I promised to, if you were agreeable, since work with these boys (in Latin especially) would do no harm to myself. Moreover, keeping on my Bordeaux lessons, my total earnings would be equivalent to £200. a year. Next day comes a telegram from China, saying 'send boys Downside', and this was a bolt from the Celestial Land which knocked us all on the head. The Aunt is more afraid of going against her brother's will than she is afraid of mines and bombs. Still people here all counsel her to continue the present arrangement, and exaggerate the dangers of crossing. On the other hand 'the Head' of Downside writes persuasively and even has the undisguised cunning to write to each of the boys personally. The boys of course have no sort of wish to go back, but are beginning to lose their appetites at the thought of it.

When I first made the necessary output of strength to carry back the date of my homecoming over three more rocky months, I was not a little jolted by the new turn of affairs.

We are not really settled yet.

I am able to preserve a strictly neutral attitude, so that should simplify the decision-problem.

It would be profitable for me to stay, and not unpleasant; whereas to start, tho' what you might call 'mighty 'greeble' would be little profitable.

The very latest report that I am able to give you is that Miss de la T. has written to Downside tonight[115] saying she means to send the boys <u>by train</u>, judging that 2½ hours on the water entails less danger than 3 days. (You know a boat that left Bordeaux early in the year went down in the Bay, the sea was so frightful.)

This is much more expensive, but the excess of the train—over the boat-fare in my case is undertaken by the de la T's. Considering how much safer it would be, I feel equal to the ennui of a land journey. We may pass a day in Paris, so that will brighten the whole business. I think you will be easier knowing I am not exposed to chances of mine or torpedo. In case I am wanted to stay, I know I have your willing consent. After all, these bogus starts bring us nearer, than a long imperturbably, settled period of sojourn.

Now follows something important.

I have long been talking to and talked at by a very 'businessy' business man, who deplores that I do not consecrate myself to Business, even as Miss Rayner did of Science, and Mr. Wigan of Religion.

Not to ramble about this good Merchant, and his impossible tenets, I want to propose that <u>Uncle Ted, that is Ed. Quayle, Esq. be approached about the possibility of doing great things with the French Government</u>. Recently, the Minister for War has asked for Tin Articles, since an enormous number of pots and pans are needed for the new recruits. I understand that it is the manufactured article that is required; but if the prospect of relations with the French Army interests in any way Uncle Ted <u>I can tackle the Minister for War</u>. What my friend advised me to do is to get price-lists and samples from England immediately. Unfortunately the *Ministère de la Guerre* left Bordeaux yesterday (the last to depart), but I still have access to the responsible officials. Mark, it is not an enterprise of my cute friend (Peyronnet), for <u>I myself, supposing I am here, would represent the Canning Tin Plate Co., if permitted</u>. Poor Peyronnet is a Manufacturer of Perfumes, and is mad that Eau de Cologne is not strictly necessary in the trenches. His friends, the Bootmaker, the Bicycle-Maker, etc. having Gov. Contracts, are making piles. Why not his friend the nephew of the English Metal Merchant. Let Father act <u>immediately</u>: repeating my words to Uncle. (On <u>no</u> account show these scrawled pages.)

Multitudinous thanks for your voluminous last letter. I keep well, very. Am seeing Dentist—paying with English Conversation! Clever Dentist, I believe.

Fondest Wishes to all, Yours ever, W.E.O.

---

[115] She wrote to the Headmaster: 'I have decided to send them by rail via Boulogne-Folkestone accompanied by Mr. Owen.... If any sea-trouble arises before the 17th, I have made arrangements with Mr. Owen who will remain here and teach the boys.'

311. To Susan Owen

Postcard

[?Early January 1915]   [Postmark Bordeaux]

All serene: bitter cold weather: pleasant: good fire: went in Prefect's motor to Antique Shop yesterday: another trip tomorrow to see Russian encampment hereabout: no 'Sunday letter':—dinner with Raoul—'Mrs. Owen not write more since one month': month hence quit France: <u>Alas! Hip-Hip-HOORAY!</u> Much health—many friends—no worry—much hope—no money—How's Yourself? God save the King—an' You-an'-Me.

312. To Susan Owen

Postcard

Wednesday, 13 January [1915][116]   [Postmark Bordeaux]

Have just had your letter: & am sending this to acknowledge it. Will write to Alpenrose for Sunday. Father may well inquire about the weather here. It is phenomenal; it has snowed on three occasions—(the first snow for some years.) One of my pupils says he does not remember such a cold for thirty years. At this moment it is snowing hard, & the snow has every sign of 'sticking' for days. I am perfectly warm, thanks, both night and days; thanks to Extra Vest & Two Mufflers by day, Dressing & Academic Gowns by night, and extra Internal Fuel, in the shape of Swiss Milk! There are excellent stoves in the *Union*—I have already said it is situated <u>almost immediately opposite</u> the door of the B. School: i.e. Rue du Temple. Best love,

W

[116] PN, p. 188.

314. To Susan Owen

Thursday, 14 January [1915][117]   [*Mérignac*]

Dearest Mother,

In consequence of the appearance of Zeppelins in the Channel, our departure is put off for a fortnight at least. That we shall stay on for three more months is by no means fixed. If I wanted I could so work it, and I think I could also bring about an early departure, if I so desired.

It was my pupil the Marine Insurance Agent who told me on Tuesday that twelve Zeppelins were careering over the Channel, while sixteen Aviatiks were about to spring across the Straits. And the announcement of this at once decided Miss de la Touche. I went to the Consul about it, at Miss T's request, and had the advice I expected: 'Really can't say; but Go if you have any reason to go.'[118]

I was gladder to know that you, considering the matter from a purely business-like standpoint, are inclined to my coming, than I should have been if you had wholly advised long-tarrying. The only thing that might make my three months tutoring expedient is that I should be obliged to work at Exam. Subjects, especially Latin, which work would be quite useful.

I wonder when and what I shall hear about my great Business Project with Fr. Gov. The good man who pointed out the affair to me is Peyronnet, the Manufacturer of Perfumes. Without offering anything definite, he interests himself in my future, mightily, and, (as I think I said) tries to convert me to 'Business'. In particular he lauds the position of commercial traveller and apparently nothing would please him better than to see me fairly launched in that line. Now, I have a most praiseworthy desire to get at the root of all evil; but it seems to me that the digging would be too long and laborious. I have every confidence that if I wholly gave myself up to fortune building, and were content to work, and working, wait,

I should 'arrive' within ten or twenty years. I consider, however, that that would be a literal losing of my soul; for that those things which my heart would put forth would then come out no more; and those things which my mind would take in, would then enter no more.

All I ask is to be held above the barren waters of want, and moving over the darkness of those waters to brood and to create. Woe is me, should I take to battling with the stream, and wet my wings of imagination!

I could never conscientiously work hard and wholeheartedly at a business. Truly, if I found myself in a fair way to becoming a London surgeon I should not, as Keats did, throw it up, and trust to the voices and visions....

And if I could devote myself to training in Music or Painting, I would take the plunge, were I never to read a book more. I halt between Professions, not between Business or Profession.

Last night I read a sentence that came as gall to me: 'It is very fortunate that Morris[119] did not lack money, or he would never have been able to afford these changes of opinion as to his career; and English Literature, and the beauty of English homes would have lost one of their most important factors.'

When I was with the Consul he suddenly interested himself in me; and, tho' I dreamed not of such a thing, said he 'wondered I didn't go in for this sort of thing' meaning a Consulship. And he straightway gave me books to read up particulars. He says it would mean a coach, and a sojourn in Spain (for another language), but that the appointments really depended on a 'Tea-Party Examination' with the Foreign Secretary or one such. Mr. Rowley[120] himself has £600. a year. This must be considered, as the age limits are something like 23-28. What must no longer be considered is the Assistant Elementary Certificated or Un-Certificated Schoolmaster. One of the wisest steps in my life was the one I didn't take (I am with Irish people) in 1911, namely hanging back from what the P.T.'s called 'College'. 'What you want' said John Bulman to me, 'Is a course in the University of Life'. I have taken that Course, and my diplomas are sealed with many secret seals....

Be more definite in your counsels to me to Come and I will come; or vice versa.

Your very own Wilfred

[117] PN, p. 188.

[118] Miss de la Touche wrote to Downside on 14 January: 'Mr. Owen went to see the Consul...who would not give him any advice about the journey ....The boys are working steadily with Mr. Owen. They have taken up English, History, Arithmetic, Geography, and Latin with him.... Greek is the difficulty, it is not taught in the same way by French teachers, and Mr. Owen says he cannot teach it.'

[119] William Morris (1834–96), poet, artist, decorator, printer, and socialist.

[120] Sir Arthur Langford Sholto Rowley (1870–1953), British Consul, Bordeaux, 1912–19, subsequently Consul-General at Barcelona and Antwerp. Knighted in 1932, he succeeded as 8th Baron Langford in 1952.

319. To Susan Owen[121]

Saturday, 6 February [1915]   *Mérignac*

Dearest of Mothers,

Your three last letters were full of charm for me, and the very last did even charm me to a tear. Which is more noble than being 'cheated to a sigh' as many things do at present, notably the 'debosched' Bosches, (By the way are They called that in England?) and my Boys. Today I first used the stick on them! Generally there is no trouble with them, but this afternoon Johnny (the-eldest-and-ought-to-know-better) got up a tree and wouldn't come down. So instead of taking a hatchet and felling the tree, I promised a caning and gave it last thing at night. A little later we go into the Orangery of the Chateau[122] (not shown in the Picture Postcard) and I give the order 'Now, don't touch the fruits.' Straightway Master Dédé begins to caress the most fattest[123] of the oranges. So I caressed his fattest parts with a great flat ruler. Only I was in an agony of laughter all the time, and all but shattered the foundations of our Government with my roars. If the poor boy had guessed what my sort of addled smile meant... but he mistook it for a sardonic frown.

The Schoolboys are to spend the Easter Holidays in England with some friends; so I quite hope to make a start at the beginning of April. Have you seen the latest declaration from the Germans, that the English waters are considered after the 18th of Feb. as being the seat of war, and no more consideration will be given to passengers and crews! God speed Harold!

I am sorry I have no photograph to bring true your recent dreams! I did take to myself a cloak at the beginning of the winter; and cold is the last thing I suffer from. And then there is the excellent breakfast before I start out every morning: and a great lunch, followed by coffee, at twelve-thirty, and a toast-and-tea at five, and a savoury dinner at seven-thirty! (Our Cook[124] was late in the service of the Minister for War; and you may know the reputation of the French Magnates) I could not bear to draw comparisons with the life of the trenches and mine; unless I felt in a manner to have suffered my share of life. And I feel I have.

I have not abandoned all idea of enlisting, but it need be discussed before I get home. My present life does not, as Father points out, lead to anywhere in particular; but, situated where I was, say in 1911, I don't think I could have done wiselier than I did. I have not struck out in any direction yet. I have made soundings in deep waters, and I have looked out from many observation-towers: and I found the deep waters terrible and nearly lost my breath there.

Of the many prospects of the world that I have spied upon, there is only one field in which I could work willingly, and would work without wage. Only, I must wait for the water[125] of many seasons before I hope to produce one acceptable flower.

If I study, I shall do so not 'to make a comfortable future for myself.' I should go about things another way for that. But suppose I missed the purpose of my life?

I talk randomly; but I think discreetly. My faith is like a weather-cock; but my hope is like a Tower, a strong and haughty Spire. And my love is as wide as the wide world. I seem without a footing on life; but I have one. It is as bold as any, and I have kept it for years. For years now. I was a boy when I first realised that the fullest life liveable was a Poets. And my later experiences ratify it.

[121] Apart from the first three paragraphs, this is a draft for Letter 330. It seems to have been received by Susan Owen, however, and was presumably enclosed by Owen with Letter 330 in error. It is in Owen's usual hand, but carries a few small corrections by him in a different ink. On this and other occasions (e.g. Letters 185 and 279 in CL) Owen worked out very carefully what he wanted to say: 'I like to think you'll keep this Letter', he writes in Letter 330. Drafts of letters were found in Owen's papers by HO after the war. An image of the draft for Letter 279 was reproduced in CL, Plate XIa.

[122] The Château du Parc.
[123] 'Anaemic' struck out.
[124] The gardener's wife.·
[125] 'Wealth' struck out.

323. To Susan Owen

Thursday, 18 February 1915   [*Mérignac*]

My own dearest Mother,

I sent off a P.C. this morning as soon as I heard of your *Grippe,* but I couldn't *say* all I should like to. I wish, now, that I had got over to England at Christmas, since the plots thicken all the time, and if Easter passes and I am still stranded, I shall be downright unhappy. At present Homesickness is not a declared malady with me; and only makes me troubled when I read your letters or definitely let my thoughts run on home. Your last news has not caused me to worry but only to spend all my spare thoughts upon you. I hope Mary has stopped her Hospital Business, and devotes her professional experience to your profit. You must indeed be wondering about Harold. (His P.C. was not in my letter). For my part, I have not—like him—touched smoking. I leave it involuntarily for days together. With me, I never produce a cigarette at fixed hours of the day. With me, smoking is not a habit. It is rather a mild mania. And be sure I prize my heart-beats more than tobacco-puffs.

There is much talk of English soldiers arriving in this region, but until they come I shall not expect them (so to say) I saw among the wounded in the Ambulances which pass along the streets every day, a wounded Hindoo.

What does R.A.M.C. mean?
What name is that along with Eric Smallpage?
Is Harry Green in the <u>Navy</u>?
Have you any news of Miles Robson's brother?[126]

What are you reading at present? I am conscious of having lost my omnivorous appetite for books. Novels, Magazines, Newspapers, Essays, bore me exceedingly. I read men now; instead of about them. Apart from pure strong Poetry; which, tho' much remains, is hard to find, I cannot savour any [*one sheet missing*] It is well. All that novelists have to tell has been told me, and by the best of them. I have even found out more. And that <u>more</u> which I had not been told I feel I ought to tell.

As for Poetry, I have let the cares of this life, Indolence, Time, and 'No-Time' do their worst. All winter, all last year and longer I have read no poetry, nor thought poetically (at least not by act of will). Neither have I reasoned seriously, or felt deeply on 'matters of faith'. Thus have I sown my wild oats, that my harvest of poppies may be the more abundant, poppies wherewith many dreams may be fed, and many sores be medicined....

I pine spiritually for need of talk with you, my dear Mother, I like no audience but either the whole world or You. There is no other, with enough sympathy or understanding. I have small affection for the people around me. I have had many affections, and shall have great ones, according to my Mood; but the only affection without Mood and without Tense is that for 'My People'.

It must be getting near the date of my pneumonia-time. I have only to think of you as you were then to me, and I immediately get into a kind of sweet anguish, an ecstasy, (very difficult to describe, but something like the effect of a great music). I hope you will think of those times, and let that memory bring its sheaves with it. The older I grow the better I understand your devotion to me, to Mary, to Harold, to Colin, to us all.

The next and nearest thing you can do for us now is to hoard, economise, bolster up, eke out, husband, spare, reserve, your own strength. Promise it to your

wholeheartedly-loving son, Wilfred

I was indeed glad to have the Hymn Words which you so lovingly copied out for me.

I shouldn't have known H. Green. Thought it one of the Cates brood.

When are Father's Photos coming?

---

[126] HO recalled Miles Robson as a clergyman in Birkenhead, whose brother entered the Navy at the outbreak of war.

330. To Susan Owen[127]

5 *March 1915*   *Mérignac*

Dearest of Mothers,

My late letters have been writ for the <u>object</u> thereof; for <u>subjects</u> I lacked. But today I have subject enough [*nine lines missing*][128]

Supposing I underwent the rigours, boredom, disgust, danger of Barracks or Camp, or saw Action on the Field, I might have better claim to a Subsidy from my Rich Uncle, which Common Sense, Common Decency, Common Charity are not quite common enough to realize. I say, it is a matter of Common Sense. Consider; I ask not for a Defence from Life-Troubles or an Excuse for not labouring, but I ask for a Weapon. I Will fight through Life; (have I not fought?) but no headway is to be made without an Arm, whether the Sword that is called Science, or the Munition, Capital. To struggle vulgarly with fist and brick-end, I do refuse. I had rather fall back among the Camp Followers of Life and mend potsherds.[129] My present life, as Father points out, is not leading to anywhere in particular; but situated where I was in 1911, I don't think I could have done wiselier than take the steps I did. True, I have not yet struck out in any direction. Since taking Soundings in Deep Waters, finding them fathomless and terrible, and all but losing my breath there, I have looked out from many observation-towers; and I have lifted the curtains from many a human secrecy.

Of the various prospects of the world which I have viewed, I found only one Field in which I could work willingly, and toil without wage. Alas, but we must wait for the waterings of many seasons before hoping to produce therefrom a single acceptable flower!

If I study, it will not be, as writes Father, 'to make a comfortable future'. A comfortable future for myself is to be provided for by other means than study. To some, I seem a fellow without a footing in life. But I have my foothold, bold as any, kept for years. A boy, I guessed that the fullest, largest liveable life was that of a Poet. I know it now; but have still to know whether it is the highest and richest: though I begin to think so. Was I born for it? Well, so far, I find myself in posses- sion of a goodly number of birth-certificates to that effect; while I can find only two or three flimsy arguments for the B.A. Craze, and half a dozen sadly unworthy ones for the 'Reverend' pretension. (In measure as I am in darkness, I keep open my ears for the Voice, should it speak. Think not I have stopped my ears to a Call, dear Mother!) But know that my prime object is not to boss a staff of school- masters, any more than it is to boom a monster business. There is one title I prize, one clear call audible, one Sphere where I may influence for Truth, one workshop whence I may send forth Beauty, one mode of living entirely congenial to me. In proof, I swear I cannot appreciate any other dignity: Headmaster of Eton; Archbishop of Canterbury; King of the English Race. My ambitions are lesser than Macbeth's and greater, not so happy, but much happier.

I said 'in proof'. I should have said 'for evidence'. The real verification is what can I write within say, a year's time? And the Crux is this—that to be able to write as I know how to, study is necessary: a period of study, then of intercourse with kin- dred spirits, then of isolation. My heart is ready, but my brain unprepared, and my hand untrained. And all,—untested. I quite envisage possibility of non-success.

My hopes rose on a tide of enthusiasm common enough in youths whose Spring is open to the Sun of Sense and Moon of Melancholy. That tide may now be about to ebb. Should it be the Tide that leads to Fortune, miserable me if I take it not at the flood! Shall Poverty leave me unlaunched? Shall my Timidity bar me? Shall my Indolence moor me to the mud?

Pray, dear Mother, that I may be loosed in time. The last two shackles are my own task; and now perhaps I shall forge levers for the First.

One more word: A Captive begs to be set free. Is his Begging contemptible? Is his supplication comparable to the whine of him who begs to eat? Better to beg boldly once, than to beg meanly all the rest of one's days.

So saying, I kiss you my own Mother, and confess I long to see you just as much as I long to see myself as you would have me.

Wilfred

P.S. I like to think you'll keep this letter; as indeed all, not, of course, megalomaniac's reason; but just because I keep no Diary; and the landmarks of one's Thoughts fade away still quicker than Events. You will impart my messages to Father. I never begin 'Dear Mother and Father' because I have the feeling of addressing an audience.

P.P.S. I keep unquiet about Harold.

---

[127] See Letter 319, n. 121.

[128] DH shows that almost three pages are missing:'Harold destroyed nearly three pages...and probably some of the draft, but enough remains of both to show that Wilfred was bitter at what he regarded as Quayle's selfishness' (WOANB, p. 190). The pages of the letter were cut.

[129] He continued, but struck out 'My meaning is (though you see it) Equipment for the front rank of a professional career, or—such a business as'.

336. To Susan Owen

le 4 avril. Dimanche de Pâques. [1915]   *Mérignac*

My own dear Mother,

It is Easter Sunday morning, and we have just come back from High Mass: real, genuine Mass, with candle, with book, and with bell, and all like abominations of desolation : none of your anglican simulacrums. On Good Friday I went also. Always I come out from these performances an hour and a half older: <u>otherwise unchanged</u>. I was going to the English Church in Bordeaux, but was snared into staying with the others. They were given Easter Eggs this morning: and I found on my Breakfast plate a Box of Egyptian Cigarettes, (which I dote on), and a leather cigarette-case, (which I don't like.)

My chief Easter Joy was your postcard: the handwriting alone, comforting and reassuring—and what a pack of matter in the mention of Harold—Dardanelles, less Danger—Submarines, Larks—swallows, your Charities—Meols. My next-best treat was a charming letter from the Poet Tailhade,[130] who is now in Paris, lecturing this week at the Odéon, on *Britannicus,* and next week on the Art of Belgium, and his personal souvenirs of that country. He, of course, advises me to travel via Paris, and talks of arranging to see me there.

On Monday afternoon (tomorrow) I'm going to a lecture by the famous novelist and poet Richepin:[131] going with the young (?) lady[132] who undertakes the French side of the de la Touche's education. About three weeks ago I met, through Miss de la T., a rather remarkable Parisian lady—'between the two ages'—whom I should like to know more. She has a Salon in Paris where many literary notables congregate. Her husband is a Ministre Plenipotentiare of some sort; but doesn't function at present. In earlier days this lady stayed in London at the French Embassy, her step-father (I think) being Ambassador before Queen Victoria, and a man whose influence is largely responsible for the *Entente Cordiale.*[133] He and King Edward seem to have fixed it up between 'em. But of all the mighty ones this lady remembers in England the chief was Burne-Jones,[134] whom she saw at work in his studio. Miss de la Touche, I suddenly found, has great talent in Life-Drawings and Oil Portraits; studied in Paris, under some great Unknown-to-me, naturally of pious memory with her. When the money gave out she had to give it up. She is, as a matter of fact, and contrary to my first ideas, badly off; and though spending irishly, spends every penny. That crippled young lady, not often referred to in my letters, being no concern of mine [*three lines missing*]

I wonder what sort of domestic you keep at present: I do hope a competent person! I will do without being considered a 'Doctor' if the creature herself needeth no physician. I feel glad you didn't pay 2 Guineas for a hum-hum-ha! [*three lines missing*]

I don't remember speaking of anything I had in mind for Harold. Well you know, and he knows, what I have at heart. That he paint, paint, paint, until his signature be known to the Rank of England, and the Bank of England. You seemed afraid [*one word missing*] Harold [*one word missing*] didn't go to church alone for Father Duncan's sake; but rather lured by the vain deceits which do lead astray etc. But can't you make as if not to see! [*two lines missing*] can't you 'deny yourselves' the fun of 'badgering' him! Badger me and I'll snap my own head off!! Do learn the importance of not being earnest.

Now, we can't have Dame Cannell at home when I land. I am indeed sorry to miss Harold again. I don't think I ever congratulated him on selling those sketches. I hope he has left plenty at home for me to see.

What Report has Colin this term? My word, I'll coach him in French. Is his body strong? How does he talk English? Does he seem to think, from what he says nowadays? What new aptitudes is he showing? Will he be 13 or 14 next birthday? Is he darker of hair now? Are his rabbit-teeth humanising? Is he 'polished' yet? And is he still tender and affectionate? Can he want to see me as much as I him? Does he give you any sort of annoyance, or provocation, or uneasiness for any cause whatever? What modifications are to be noted in

Harold and Mary also? [*one line missing*] Is Father as well as usual? Is the Gardening beginning again? What Questions! <u>One</u> I need not ask of you, nor you of me, for I am the Unchanging,

Your very <u>Childe Wilfred</u>

[130] This letter survives in Owen's Archive in the Bodleian.
[131] Jean Richepin (1849–1926), playwright and poet. A copy of his *La Mer* survives among Owen's books.
[132] Mlle Duval or her successor, Mlle Ducarpe.
[133] The French Ambassador in London 1898–1920 was Paul Cambon (1843–1924).
[134] Sir Edward Coley Burne-Jones (1833–98), the Pre-Raphaelite painter.

340. To Susan Owen

Saturday, 10 April [1915]   *Mérignac*

Dearest Mother,

Supported by a French Admiral, her brother, her sister, her solicitor, all her Friends, and the whole population of Mérignac, Miss de la Touche is now quite firm: <u>she will not send the boys.</u> She leaves me free to do what I like, always letting me understand that she would be thankful if I would stay. She can't have them unmanaged and uneducated and knows of no one to take my place. At the same time Peyronnet say I [*one word illegible*] must start during this month. So I am the Rope in a tug-of-war between Home and Business on one side and Courtesy on the other. I think I have found a compromise: to come over for, say, three weeks, and return here for the summer term and the summer holidays [*ten lines missing*]

The people in the 'Place' neighbouring ours have a ship of theirs going to London shortly. We know these people rather well, and I have asked Miss de la Touche to try and get me a passage, if the date is convenient.

Miss de la T. is frightened at the idea of having the 4 Ruffians alone even for 3 weeks and is going to try and find someone to replace me. If there could be found an Englishman who would take on the job permanently I would be glad to leave <u>for good</u>. It is scarcely worth <u>my</u> paying the fare, and I have not yet extorted a promise that Miss de la Touche will. I had cherished the hope of staying at Home until the moment of my great expedition, and devoting myself to certain writings, which I would fain accomplish. For this a month or so of seclusion is indispensable. Gardening, sketching, photography, writing for magazines may very well thrive on spare effort in odd times; but a Poem does not grow by jerks. If it is to be worth a place in Human Time, it must be worth more than fag-ends of the Poet's time. A patch-work counterpane or a ship full-rigged—in a bottle, may be perfectly fabricated off-an'-on, between-whiles, casual, like. But Poetry, 'coming naturally as leaves to a tree',[135] grows as incessantly and as delicately. And as trees in Spring produce a new ring of tissue, so does every poet put forth a fresh, and lasting outlay of stuff at the same season.

Well, well, I have not now the time to continue on paper this trend of thinking.

Let me know what your comments [*two words illegible*] you first read of my Proposition of coming back here after three weeks. I like it little, after all. I had rather coach Colin! I have no doubt his English no less than French needs it! I gather that Miss de la T. considers the boys have made immense strides in these few months. If so it is their own intelligence, not mine, that provided the seven-league-boots. I can do nothing at all with even middling pupils. The 'teaching body' should regard me as an offending mote, happily withdrawn from its longsuffering corpus.

I promise not to show shock at any of Colin's crudities of speech. (Slang, by the way, I like to hear) (And these boys swear like troopers). I will stand even dialect. Better a twang in the tongue than a twist in the eyes. By the way, does Colin's sight improve. And by the byway, let him leave off his odious goggles when he 'comes to meet me' or I shan't know him.

[*top of page cut out*] I also am sore bruised, but I am challenging many another Blow yet. Ambition may be defined as the willingness to receive any number of hits on the nose. 'There is no fiercer hell than the failure in a great ambition.'[136] (The words are sacred to me; hence you know who said them.) Ah, others also were knocked as hard as Aunt Sally…Yes, it needs a hard kick to get sent up to the stars. Perseus was a sailor lad;[137] and never, I take it, bore epaulets on his brown shoulders or gold-braid on his bare chest; but his name is written in stars, because he trusted in the armour of the Immortals [*bottom of page cut off*] I go [*several words missing*] in the early morning to buy provisions.

So Goodnight, my own dear Mother! From your very own

Wilfred x

---

[135] 'If poetry comes not naturally as leaves to a tree it had better not come at all.' Keats to John Taylor, 27 February 1818 (*Letters* I, p. 238).

[136] 'There is not a fiercer hell than the failure in a great object.' From the Preface to *Endymion*.

[137] For the projected full-scale poem on Perseus, see Letter 250, n. 28, and Letter 616.

342. To Susan Owen

Postcard

Monday [*Postmark 20 April 1915*]   [*Postmark Mérignac*]

It has just been arranged that Mr. Bonsall,[138] public school man, shall look after boys in my absence—(3 times a week—not living up here.) I had a word with him about taking the job permanently, and asked a little while to think it over; but he rather seemed to like the idea. If I start, I don't at all fancy the trebled risk of Rochelle–L'pool, nor yet the journey Bx.–Rochelle. Know no more of our neighbour's Boat, as Miss de la T. hasn't asked. So we'll leave that idea. This only I have made sure: To leave in a week or so, and for a week or so, but <u>perhaps</u> for always. That's something! Your own W.E.O.

[138] Charles La Touche recalls him as a Welshman, aged about 40, who had been left money while a law student and had spent it travelling about the world. He was now tutoring in Bordeaux. A raconteur and bon vivant and fine cricketer, with a genial, easy-going temperament, he was a great contrast to Owen and made a more direct appeal to the boys. He taught them Latin and Greek; Owen continued to take the other subjects.

349. To Susan Owen

Postcard

Wednesday [Postmark 20 May 1915]   *Cranston's Waverley Hotel, London*[139]

Did the first stroke this mng. by getting the Attaché to look up information, which will be ready tomorrow. Exhibition[140] is open Thurs. and Frid. Hence I just got my Ticket (a matter of much bus-riding and lift-climbing) then went to the great meeting in Guildhall,[141] of which you already read in papers. To hear Mr. Asquith[142] on a day like this was a unique thing! Bonar-Law[143] spoke too, and the Earl of Crewe.[144] The Archbishop hearkened, but spake not. I think I saw Rudyard Kipling! The public was not admitted but I got my ticket without trouble. I feel intensely happy in dear London!

Your W.E.O.

[139] Located at Southampton Row, Holborn, it became the Waverley House Hotel.
[140] On Monday, 3 May, Owen took the night train to Paris, where he met Tailhade, who signed a copy of his *Poèmes Élégiaques* for him. The copy survives among Owen's books. After a stay at home, Owen attended the British Industries Fair in London on behalf of his friend Peyronnet. He returned to Mérignac on 13 June.
[141] 19 May 1915, organized by the Central Committee for National Patriotic Organizations. The Lord Mayor presided; the meeting was to pay homage to the self-governing Dominions, Colonies, Protectorates, and the Indian Empire.
[142] Herbert Henry Asquith (1852–1928), Prime Minister 1908–16, was created 1st Earl of Oxford and Asquith in 1925.
[143] Andrew Bonar Law (1858–1923) was at this time Leader of the Opposition in the House of Commons. He was Prime Minister 1922–3.
[144] Robert Offley Ashburton Crewe-Milnes (1858-1945), 2nd Baron Houghton and Marquess of Crewe, was Colonial Secretary 1908–10, and Secretary of State for India 1910–15.

351. To Susan Owen

Picture postcard; colour reproduction of an oil painting, 'When I Meditate on Thee in the Night Watches', showing King Saul sunk in thought, at the side of his throne the sleeping boy David with a lyre

[*Late May 1915*]   [*London*]

Was prevented by a new turn of affairs from leaving Town today as expected. (happy turn of affairs.) Passed a joyful time at R.A. This picture is not one of the Exposed—I send it because it represents or suggests all of the dozen things I hold dear in the Universe. (but one—Home). What these are, I will enumerate when I get Home: let us say <u>Monday</u>. Many thanks for your letter. It came with a <u>nice</u> note from Peyronnet. I found a gold purse in Brompton Rd. on my first hour in London.

An Omen? Amen! So be it.

W.E.O.

356. To Susan Owen

Tuesday [*16 June 1915*]   *18 rue Beaubadat* [*Bordeaux*][145]

My very own Mother,

I'm fairly settled down to Exile, work, heat, and the rest of it; and my *bagages* both of fine apparel and of learning are well unpacked. Having given my lessons up at the Châlet, and looked up old pupils in town, I have already sealed up remembrance of this last happy month. But the first few hours in France were troubled with <u>real nostalgia</u>; and I had a lively longing for the idle, protected, loving, wholesome, hidden, intimate, sequestered Home Life of mine; I felt responsible for coming out here again, into a far different atmosphere and my first breath of Bordeaux air was a gasp, and my first step on its soil was a spiteful kick. Extraordinary how foreign everything flavoured again. But in three hours all that wore off.

I have found, not by luck, but by three hours' search, a most suitable chamber; let by most superior people. I have already said it is large & lofty, up two flights of stairs; situated in the most convenient quarter; and with high-class houses round about. There are two large windows opening on a balcony, over which the whole front of the beloved Cathedral towers tho' just before my windows is an office of some sort. The corner is haunted by a continual draught of cool air which <u>ought</u> really to raise the rent by 20 francs a month. My bed is all that could be desired; there is a wardrobe, marble mantelpiece, & handsome mirror, hanging-curtain-wardrobe, a vast writing-desk, beautiful old round table, marble washstand, two armchairs, desk-chair, etc. wall-paper an unfortunate colour; & in design like ten thousand cabbages, over-boiled, and partly digested:—clean, however. And the ornaments are all supportable, and one or two acceptable.

These are not the usual lodging-house keepers; and my room is looked after by their <u>servant</u>. The lady is a *modiste* (milliner). There are two children, boy of 9, girl of 12, but these are not likely to disturb my peace in any manner whatever.

I found it impossible to stay less than 3 days in London; first I had to obtain an Application Form for Passport, return it next day, & wait for the Passport itself; then have the thing visa'd by the French authorities in London. The voyage was delightful: marvellous clear. France was plainly visible from the train at Folkestone! The Dawn among the lovely lands of central France was an <u>experience</u> for me: the only experience of the journey.

—But I have not yet made up my back-accounts with Morpheus, and must rise early again tomorrow for seeing Peyronnet, who was out this morning. I forgot to say how gladly everybody welcomed me at Mérignac; and how undeniably pleasant it was to have to do with the dear, clever lads Johnny and Bobby. (Tell Colin). Yes, I do seem a long way off; but I also feel a short <u>time</u> off.

Your own W

By delaying to return I was saved the annoyance of a frightful storm over Mérignac on Sund. Night. The Châlet was struck[146] and a poor unfortunate in the village struck fatally. I saw the flashing from hundreds of miles away, & felt the horror of it in Paris.

---

[145] New lodgings in Bordeaux, for his room at Mérignac was wanted. But he continued his tutoring at the Chalet; he and Bonsall went out there on different days.
[146] David La Touche remembers the storm. A tree was struck by lightning.

357. To Susan Owen

[c.20] June 1915   *18 rue Beaubadat. Bx. 1er. étage*

Dearest Mother,

Notice my address. I have not gone down a floor, but find that an intermediate story between the ground & mine is not counted as a story: so, I am for postal purposes on the first floor. A week's stay has now proved that I couldn't have done better than choose this place. I have now 'touched', as they say, the reimbursement of my stay in London, from Peyronnet, amounting to 165 francs, or £6. I was all but penniless after paying my rooms on the first day, and during the day enjoyed the romantic sensation of being absolutely and literally *sans le sou*. Now if you would like me to post back some part of what I have borrowed from you, I can do so. Peyronnet received me very well, and considered I had managed the affair very properly. So he renews his proposition of an Eastern Voyage; to begin in Sept. if possible; but not until the Campaign of the Dardanelles be finished. I told him therefore that if the way were still blocked when I return home in Sept. I should try to join the Army. For I noticed in the Hotel in London an announcement that any gentleman (fit, etc.) <u>returning to England from abroad</u> will be given a Commission—in the 'Artists' Rifles'.[147] Such officers will be sent to the front in 3 months. Thus we shall watch the Dardanelles with a little more interest than before. And, in very sooth, I rather hope things there will last out as long as the war, which will be through the winter. Still more Frenchmen have been mobilised since I left France; and the outlook is not one shade brighter. I don't want the bore of training, I don't want to wear khaki; nor yet to save my honour before inquisitive grand-children fifty years hence. But I <u>now do</u> most <u>intensely want to fight</u>. In redoubting the exercises during these months of July & August I have perfectly sufficient reason for <u>not 'joining' yet</u>. But when I learnt that Peyronnet prefers me to wait until the East is more settled I felt full of peace— and of war. So the most patriotic thing I can do is to hope for non-success in the Dardanelles! In a month or so from now, forces will be as certainly lacking as munitions are now. So let us hope Lloyd George will have my shooter ready by then. Meanwhile, I lead a really enviable existence. I am adapted to the climate, and re-adapted to the mode of life. I shall play Tennis religiously.

When you were writing last Sunday I had just got in the train at the Quai d'Orsay. I shortened the Boulogne–Paris stage, by having dinner on the train; it took 1 hour and a quarter! On the Friday Night before leaving Town I was seized with a desire to see the Mile End Road, in which I had not set foot since I wore strap-slippers, at five years old. Although it was dark, I remembered the old spot perfectly; and Dr. Loughrey's[148] name is still up on red-lit glass above the door. On Sat. being now tired of the West End, I thought a little ugliness would be refreshing; and striking east from the P.O. walked down Fenchurch St. and so into the Whitechapel High Street, & the Whitechapel Road. Ugliness! I never saw so much beauty, in two hours, before that Saturday Night. The Jews are a delightful people, at home, & that night I re-read some Old Testament with a marvellous great sympathy & cordiality!

Stay long at Kidmore!

Your own W

Convey every good wish to all good people at Alp. & thereabouts & try and convey some photographs to me.

Bother Mr. Seaton's demand.[149] Refer him to the Opinion. Perhaps I'd better send him samples.

---

[147] Owen joined up in the Artists' Rifles four months later.
[148] His uncle, Dr Richard Loughrey.
[149] Unexplained.

358. To Susan Owen

Postcard

Tuesday [Postmark 22 June 1915]   *Mérignac*

Am waiting for my Train 5.30 p.m. & cannot fill my time better than by commending me to you. & wishing you a good journey tomorrow. There is an even heat, which is no longer inconvenient. —I hear my tram grinding along. So *an revoir!* W.E.O.

360. To Susan Owen

Wednesday, 30 June [1915]   *[Bordeaux]*

My dearest Mother,

   Your letters are very dear to me; but these are days when my side of correspondence languisheth like a leaf in fiery June. I cannot exaggerate the painful feelings I experienced in the first days of my change of air ; but at the same time I repeat I have nothing to grumble about here, and am therefore of an untumultuous spirit; whatever I may have of England to regret. But as the School Term seems to start about Sept. 21st, there is really a mere wisp of time to be consumed before the Return to England. Tell Leslie that the weather was astonishingly clear in the Narrow Seas that day, and I thought much of H. Belloc;[150] and have added much to my appreciation of Travel, since reading *Hills & the Sea.* Another thing: was it not Belloc's great forefinger which pointed out to me this passage of De Vigny : If any man despairs of becoming a Poet, let him carry his pack and march in the ranks.[151]

   Now I don't despair of becoming a Poet: 'Before Abraham was, I am' so to speak [*one line inked out*]

   Will you set about finding the address of the 'Artists' Rifles', as this is the Corps which offers commissions to 'gentlemen returning from abroad.'

   I certainly went a promenade with Raoul one Sunday afternoon in a 'Garden' in the Town, where choral songs were rendered by schools. I got so heartily bored that I took leave of him before the quarter of the programme was over; this was facilitated by having paid his admission [? Next Sunday I go to] Preignac with him, Philipp, his Boarder.[152]

   We have had delightful weather: gay, boisterous Rains, spasmodic, don't-care-a-hang weather; free Turkish Baths, hot, with a sensation of continually cooling, in a word delicious and sensational. Only the vines will be spoilt and a good part of the hay. Tennis has been out of the question; round the garden walks, ducklings swim. Reports come of drought, and agricultural calamity[153] in England. Is this so?

Yes, 'it pays' to be able to talk learnedly of the war; as indeed I do over the coffee, regularly every day. At home I retailed neither news, ideas, nor hopes. But here I have so many sources of information. I often see the Viscount de Maud'huy; and a Norwegian gives me items from German papers. The admiral's wife told me yesterday that his fleet bombarded a Ger: Consulate in Asia Minor,—because the Germans had dug up the ashes of Napoleon's soldiers, & scattered them to the winds!

I have just walked back from Mérignac all the way, with the boys around and upon me arriving at the Boulevard at 7. o'clock. I then hastily dined & must more hastily run to the post; for the last delivery is near; and—horror of horrors—my boots are wet! Yes, I do get Thursday-posted-letters on Sunday, so fortunate and so gratitudinous am I [one line inked out]

Yours ever and ever—Wilfred

Call to mind what pleasant impressions I gave you of Dunsden, & repeat them there. Every manner of salutation to my Cousin of Cousins and Cousine of Cousines, D.

---

[150] Joseph Hilaire Pierre René Belloc (1870–1953), essayist, novelist, poet, historian, biographer, traveller, and critic. *Hills and the Sea* (1906) does not survive among Owen's books; *Esto Perpetua* (1906) does.

[151] From *Servitude et Grandeur Militaires* (1885), the best-known work of Alfred Victor, Comte de Vigny (1797–1863), poet, dramatist, and novelist.

[152] Philippe was the current lodger at the Lems, and one of Owen's pupils.

[153] 1915 was not a bad year for farmers. The summer was fair. But the weather was dry in late August and September, with no rain in some areas for sixteen or seventeen days, which constituted a drought.

363. To Susan Owen

8 July 1915   *Bordeaux*

My dearest Mother,

[two lines inked out] but tho' I mean to cover the expenses, if permitted, I am in no hurry. Father indeed agreed that I should send back some portion of my borrowings, but now that I know not how soon I shall start home, I have changed my mind. Moreover I make no profit here these days. Mlle. de la Touche begins to despair of having money for sending the boys to the sea. Their French Lessons finish next week, and of course, they ought to have a complete rest from English work too. Mr. Bonsall goes up on certain mornings for their Latin & Greek; he is a weird, mild bird; and hath much love of Classics, and great power of Music. It is amusing to think we are rivals in Bordeaux—though not up at Mérignac; for Miss de la Touche declared once that Mr. B. 'had no manners.' He is rather lax with their discipline; and generally works under the plum-trees of the garden. Hence once or twice I have used the stick I took for Miss de la Touche, correctionally. The other day I roared: 'Dédé, I shall give you five strokes!' A few minutes later, I felt a hand smoothing my hair most caressingly. This is not an unusual pro-cedure, but it was done with such a merry gusto that I asked what it meant.— 'Oh! I'm giving <u>you</u> the <u>strokes</u> instead.'

The photographs taken the other day are not good; but the general group (in which I am) is very good: but it is not yet ready.

I went with Raoul to Preignac, & came back well pleased with the day. It can-not have been so hot here as with you. Why, at three o'clock we were dancing on the terrace, with the country maids that turned up on purpose. Then we went cycling about the country—(finest country of the Gironde)—except Raoul, who had discreet rendez-vous' in the woods. Later we tried table-turning, for the good lady, Philippe's aunt, was a great believer in the thing. We had, it seemed, marvel-lous results: the table tapped out right answers for hours. But I worked hard and cunningly to <u>prove it</u>; found certain questions wrongly answered; and suspected everybody in turn. Finally I had proof of Raoul's trickery, and made him confess it on the way home.

What is Harold's next address ? How long do you think to stay? I shall try, then to find in Bx. my Razor-blades. What does 'are having' a motor mean. Is it bought?

In the French papers today I read that Mr. Asquith in reply to a member's question said that the government had 'no intention whatever' of establishing either obligatory service or work. Yesterday, papers made allusion to fresh arrivals of Zeppelins on London [*four lines inked out*] Am I supposed to know? (I had even forgotten H's ship.) [*two lines illegible*] What is the principle of the magic waistcoat?

    [154] { Is the Quayles' new shanty[155] boxed-in, or an open tub? Who pedals? What colour is his livery? I hope you get plenty of driving at Kidmore.

                    Adieu, sweet Mother, from your Wilfred

---

[154] 'IRONY—pretty wooden too.' Written vertically here.
[155] Motor car.

364. To Susan Owen

Postcard

Saturday [*Postmark 10 July 1915*]   [*18 Rue Beaubadat, Bordeaux*]

I have nothing to report to you; if I have many things to hope for you. I have written to Artists' Rifles without address. If I don't get an English commission I should like to join the Italian Army. In any case I shall probably be out of work here in August, as the boys want an absolute holiday. So much the better! God save the King! and bless us all, said Tiny Tim.

Your W.E.O.

365. To Susan Owen

Postcard

Friday [probably 15 July 1915][156]   *P.O. Bx.*

Had your Card this mng. and what you say of Artists' Rifles is so; the Camp is at Epping. The Commission might be very long in coming. I seriously should like to join the Italian Cavalry; for reasons both aesthetic and practical. If you are too terribly opposed I will think no more of it. Certainly, I shan't join French Army. Miss de la T. now suggests I should take a room in Mérignac, to be with them during August. Can't Uncle be more precise about 'good job in War Office?'

Yours ever W.E.O.

Lord Leighton,[157] Millais,[158] Forbes Robertson[159] were in Artists' Rifles!!

[156] PN, p. 188.
[157] Frederic Leighton, 1st Baron Leighton (1830–96), President of the Royal Academy 1878–96.
[158] Sir John Everett Millais (1829–96). Originator in 1848, with Holman Hunt, of the Pre-Raphaelite Brotherhood; President of the Royal Academy in the year of his death.
[159] Sir Johnston Forbes-Robertson (1853–1937), actor and theatrical manager.

366. To Susan Owen

23 July [1915]   *Bordeaux*

My dearest Mother,

I am sorry to be niggardly of letters. It escapes my memory, the date of my last; but I hope you got my last postcard. Unless your letter of this morning had put in a claim for more of my news, I scarcely think I should be writing <u>now</u>! I have <u>no news</u> and shall have none, as I hope, before the end of next week, by which time I ought to know the manner of my departure. So far, I only am sure that I am <u>not</u> going to move up to Mérignac, again, but mean to remain <u>here</u> till about the middle of August, going up to M. for lunch and the afternoon, as now, although <u>lessons</u> stop on Aug. 1st. If a ship sails about Aug. 15 you may expect me by it. I went to Sailors' Reading Room last night, and had parley with the donkey-man of a 'Moss' Boat,—non-passenger. It would <u>not</u> be possible to make a cheap passage by private treaty with the Captain. In a delightful Liverpool brogue (delightful <u>Now</u> and <u>here</u>) which made me think of Cecil when he was Cicil, and of Tranmere, the Pier Head, Sefton Park,[160] and such like, the lad told me of the dangers of the passage! and how they carry a cannon, and were once chased by a submarine off Hormes' Ed![161] I may land at <u>London</u> on account of Peyronnet,— whom I shall next see on Monday. The 'eastern voyage' is out of the question. It will be pleasant to round off the 'Mérignac Period' of my time with a week or so of nothing but 'Ragging'. We shall go some excursions. For one, I want to visit the battlefield of Castillon, where, in 1453 Talbot Earl of Shrewsbury suffered the defeat which lost Guienne and Bordeaux to the English forever.[162] I can't understand it, but this battlefield will interest me as much as the field of the Marne;—and I am reading a tale of the Punic Wars[163] with more interest than the Communiqués. There is only one cure for me! I am already quaking at the idea of Parade; and yawning with the boredom of it. <u>Now if I could make it a real, live adventure, a real, old adventure, by flinging myself into Italy</u>...?

It will be painful now to quit Bordeaux!! I shall part with the four boys with regret,—with three of them regretfully, with two of them sorrowfully, and with one of them very sorrowfully indeed. It is an advantage of old age that <u>meetings</u> are joyful, as separations are sad; but in <u>youth</u> meetings are indifferent; youth is the time of partings, not old age [*one line inked out*] But don't expect to before the day on which I assume the role of National Hero, number million, grade Private, allowance one bob.

However I mean to run up to Meols for a day or so. When is Colin going to Torquay, and how long Holiday will Father take? (I can't help feeling the anomaly of Parliament's cajoling the Miners to work on Bank Holiday, & themselves taking six weeks holiday!) I am always annoyed to hear of your headaches; sup-posing them preventable, rather than curable. Miss de la T. has had 'migraines' continually. On such days she sits and hides in a corner of the garden, and <u>I</u> carve the joint! She has all the 'rough work' with the boys now! It takes a lot to give me a headache;—let's hope it won't need a bullet! I rejoice exceedingly in the power of the midday sun, & am strengthened by its strength:— a sure sign of being Right with Nature.

Your devoted Wilfred

Antescript [*at head of letter*]: I can't re-read these lines, but underline plentifully instead. 'Cute idea!

---

[160] All Birkenhead. WO is referring to his cousin, Cecil Quayle.
[161] Ormes Head, the North Wales headland on which Llandudno stands.
[162] The English army under John Talbot, 1st Earl of Shrewsbury (*c.*1388–1453), heavily out-numbered, was defeated and its commander killed at Castillon, 30 miles east of Bordeaux.
[163] *Salammbô* (1862) by Gustave Flaubert. See Letter 368.

368. To Leslie Gunston

25 July 1915   *Bordeaux*

My dear Leslie,

I had waited in double-daily expectation of your lines, and it was a 'high luxury' to read them in my bed, this *dimanche* morning. The only way of excusing yourself for having jilted me for my beloved friend *Icarus,* last Sunday, is to send me the 90 lines of sixty-lines-an-hour verse, non-stop-till-we-frizzle-up-in-the-solar-terminus. Couldn't you divine why 'Oxford'[164] is a banned word with me. Because it is one of my most terrible regrets. I ought to be there, not fuddling among the Vines. I ought to have been there, rather. Surely, you knew the cause of my 'flare'. Now I am going to get flary again. You say you 'hear of wars and rumours of wars'. *Vous en êtes là seulement?* You hear Rumours ? The rumours, over here, make the ears of the gunners bleed....It doesn't matter 'for my purpose' that the Dardanelles are closed; but it matters to my sentiment that Belgium is; now I don't imagine that the German War will be affected by my joining in, but I know my own future Peace will be. I wonder that you don't ply me with this argument: that Keats remained absolutely indifferent to Waterloo and all that commotion. Well, I have passed a year of fine-contemptuous nonchalance: but having now some increase of physical strength I feel proportionately useful and proportionately lacking in sense if I don't use it in the best way—The Only Way.

I was not aware that nothing remained of Cumnor, and imagined the moon still 'silvered the walls of Cumnor Hall'.[165] I believe the Black Bear still is?

Your demand for my ideal wife is too frightfully the non-limit. I have a fairly good bodily notion; but the other qualities I can only specify by negatives. However, I will make notes! I fairly roared with joy that you were taken, and taken in, by the pseudo-translation. I merely translated from some lines I had begun in French. For Gautier[166]...Zut! I never read him. No, I won't forget to give you information regarding the Author!! Kindly preserve the copy. I made no other. I can't now roll off the *Chanson de R.*[167] It is of spenserian length, and chaucerian charm. I hope you don't consider shaking hands with H.B.[168] knowing him. I meant make him a factor of your life and yourself of his. I thank God for the intercourse you and I have set up between us. I should be a sadder soul if you 'were not', or were other than you are.

'Shall you' say ever-loving, etc. I should hope so. There is no mere *entente-cordiale* between us. There is a blood-alliance. If you object to anything in me you will shout at me like a brother. I for example object to your speaking of getting 'my money's worth' of a letter! Shocking! Though I congratulate you upon trafficking in books! I still hold the violin capable of 'better' i.e. more essential, music than the organ, and shall do. while I hold Keats a more poetical poet than Milton.

I <u>have</u> read *The Prisoner of Zenda*:[169] mediocre! At present I am deciphering a monument of French literature Flaubert's *Salammbo* not that it is difficult reading, but every syllable deserves attention. Flaubert has my vote for novel-writing! Farewell, fare-very-well-indeed,

Your affectionate Wilfred

I 'started' at the idea of Llandudno; I mean, joining you there. I scarcely dare envisage such luck. I <u>could</u> get in time; but the material considerations…! Moreover, is it not an exclusive <u>family</u> holiday!

---

[164] LG was in Oxford doing measured drawings for the Intermediate RIBA examination.

[165] The Hall was demolished in 1810. Traces of the gardens can still be seen south of the churchyard. 'The dews of summer night did fall, / The moon, sweet regent of the sky, / Silver'd the walls of Cumnor Hall, / And many an oak that grew thereby.' William Julius Mickle (1734–88), 'Cumnor Hall'.

[166] Théophile Gautier (1811–72), French poet and novelist of the Romantic Movement.

[167] *Chanson de Roland*, the oldest and best known of the *chansons de geste*, French historical romances, many connected with Charlemagne. The story of Roland and Oliver and the destruction of the rearguard of Charlemagne's army at the Battle of Roncevaux in 778 was translated into English by C. K. Scott Moncrieff as *The Song of Roland, done into English, in the original measure* (Chapman & Hall 1919), with an introduction by G. K. Chesterton. A copy was inscribed for Susan Owen, 'From Charles Scott Moncrieff in endless memory of Wilfred, February 1921'. The book is dedicated to Philip Bainbrigge (see Letter 590), Wilfred Owen, and Ian Mackenzie. An early draft dedication survives in Scott Moncrieff's hand, beginning: 'To Mr. W.O. To you, my master in assonance, I dedicate part of this assonant poem: that you may cover the faults in my handiwork with the protection of your name.' For Owen's first meeting with C. K. Scott Moncrieff, see Letter 585.

[168] Hilaire Belloc. LG had been introduced to him after a lecture.

[169] The best-known novel (1894) of Anthony Hope Hawkins (1863–1933), who wrote plays and novels under the name of Anthony Hope.

370. To Susan Owen

Monday Night, 2 August 1915   [Bordeaux]

My most dear Mother,

It's only by false pretences that I am able to write to you tonight; because I am continually besieged by that Wireless Telegraphist.[170] Every single night of this week he has been inseparable from me, from the moment of my arriving in town at 7 o'clock. So this evening, to avoid a bombardment of my locked door, I have invented 'an invitation out for the evening'. So poor Thuret can swot up his lecture on Wireless, which is to be on Wednesday. I mentioned this at the Châlet, and Miss de la T. wants to send the boys to hear it. Thuret has written to his people about my staying in Rouen. He starts on the 20th; so you may take that as my definite date of leaving.

I think Colin ought to turn to thinking about such a post as Wireless Operator.

I just got your card on coming in tonight, and am indeed pleased to know Bill is supposed only taken prisoner;[171] and not less happy to think of Harold as an Officer![172] In the Artists', one is paid the usual 1s a day!

Did I tell you a Norwegian acquaintance of mine went over to Swansea, a fortnight ago, to marry an English girl. They have just got back. *Madame* was rather upset the first few hours after arriving (at the *Union Chrétienne*) but felt less lost in a strange land on meeting me. But, if uncommonly comely, she is common of speech, and I cannot introduce her into English society here. Traëmber, the hubby, is a rather *distingué* person, of 28 yrs. Miss Hall[173] is going to befriend the girl. Miss Hall leaves about a month later than I; so that will just accommodate the boys, or rather, their Aunt; for they would infinitely rather travel alone; for obvious reasons. It was Miss Hall's pupil's people who gave the Thursday picnic.

On Sunday morning I had got magnificently attired with the intention of going to the English church. Now I had refused to go in the river with Thuret for this reason, and hence Thuret must needs promise to come to my church. I agreed. But lo! instead of appearing in officer's clothes, as he ought, he lounges up in a disgraceful *déshabillé!* But, in the afternoon your good wishes for Sunday, were well realized. We had four hours of music. You have heard me speak of Richepin: one of his pieces *The Tramp*, an opera, was being played in the Open Air. The Music was by Xavier LeRoux,[174] and the Composer himself conducted the Orchestra. It was a daring opera in more ways than one; for instance, the whole thing passes between tramps and rustics, in cornfields, roads, and kitchens. The total cost of costume might be three bob, off a wholesale and retail rag-picker. The music was not particularly original; very pleasant to listen to; but there were no airs that one remembered ever after. There was very pretty work done by the drums, so much so that one listened to them rather than to the violins, sometimes. The voices, of course, were best Paris choice. Certain of the songs were marvellous touching. Anyhow I was proud to have shaken hands with the Composer—(in Paris). If anybody enjoyed himself that afternoon, it was he himself!

I think next Sunday will be spent at Lacanau,[175] that sea-side place, where the Boys are <u>not</u> going. But the Boy Scouts of the *Union* are going; and Thuret is 'in with' them. As, curiously enough, I have had no dealings yet with this group of kids, I think of going too. We start on Sunday night.

This afternoon although work is now over, I spent at Mérignac roaming the woods. The heather is extraordinarily abundant and purple. I look at it, and think of Broxton,[176] as it were, weeping; and again I examine it, and think of Doctor Rayner, and smile.

Miss de la T. gave me a pot of her plum-jam on Saturday, for my small-breakfast!

This evening I called on a Bordeaux specialist who wanted English lessons; but the time is too short. There are, in promise, a good number of pupils, for next term. Moreover, Miss de la T. would be glad to have me for Dédé & Charlie. But all this is <u>no temptation</u>: for it is not a Career. This aft. I ran, with the boys, almost a mile—significant!

We will drop the subject of Italy, though your arguments are distinctly feeble in comparison with the real objection. <u>You</u> fear I might never get into the army. Absurd! They take what they can get, even wrecks like me. The whole difficulty is <u>getting out</u>. Probably the end of the war would not liberate the volunteer as in England. He would have to perform the term of service required by the nation in question; in France it is three years! Many people are surprised that I don't join the French forces, and that I take the fag to go back to England.

It is time to look after details of travelling. I suppose I cannot use the old ticket I have kept, to 'return' from Padd? Did I mention to you that Leslie 'wants me' to go to Llandudno with them? I don't of course hold myself invited. Depends on <u>them</u>.

Betimes I have a horrible great craving to behold the Sea. But for the time, the Wind is very wild and fresh upon these moors; and not a day passes but I receive a nature-shock, such as some spend six weeks seeking and find not...

The fruit is softening in the vineyards; the muscle of France keeps resisted,—while her heart scarcely beats faster—The Emperor yet frowns imperially; and our ministers yet wear a ministerial smile.[177] And lo! the end is not by any manner of means at hand.

At least, let me end this piece of literature,

and with my lovingest x, Wilfred

What a luxury it seems to think of 'going home' again so soon!

[170] Thuret, aged 18, who worked on a French-American liner.

[171] Bill Bulman had, in fact, been killed in action at Gallipoli.

[172] Harold, formerly apprentice cadet and Fourth Officer in the Merchant Service, was now made Third Officer. In October 1916 he transferred to the Royal Naval Air Service; and to the Royal Naval Reserve, as midshipman, in spring 1917.

[173] An English governess to the Castéjas children at Mérignac.

[174] Xavier Henry Napoleón Leroux (1863–1919), French composer and Professor of Harmony at the Paris Conservatoire.

[175] On the coast north-east of Bordeaux.

[176] A village in Cheshire. Susan Owen took Wilfred there for a few happy weeks before the family left Birkenhead for Shrewsbury in 1907. 'It was in Broxton among the ferns and bracken and the little hills, secure in the safety and understanding love that my mother wrapped about him...that the poetry in Wilfred, with gentle pushings, without hurt, began to bud, and not on the battlefields of France' (JFO I, pp. 101–4). See also Letter 593. A fragmentary draft (CPF, p. 434) has these lines: 'Even the weeks at Broxton, by the Hill / Where first I felt my boyhood till / With uncontainable movements; there was born / My poethood.'

[177] These sentences turn up again in an early version of 'The Dead-Beat' (CPF, p. 144).

371. To Susan Owen

Saturday, 7 August 1915[178]   *[Bordeaux]*

Dearest Mother,

A little later on this afternoon I shall be starting for Lacanau, with the Boy Scouts. I haven't the faintest idea where I shall sleep, or what eat, or when return, or who meet, and that's why I am going. Thuret passed a 'Final' exam today, proving he can send (and receive) 30 words a minute. His brother whom he went to meet at the station at midnight has got appendicitis; but this in no way alters Thuret's plans of taking me to Rouen. Appendicitis is a fairly common complaint; Thuret was operated years ago. The brother's operation is on Sunday. It may make this oddish character 'sound all right' to you that he wanted to sing hymns for his brother last night; and I made the music.

I think I told you that 'the Boys' are going to Downside, by edict from China. Mr. de la Touche has Scarletina over there! Miss de la T. has been occupied in finding a Governess for the girls[179] (eldest 8 yrs.) She has I think met an English lady there, speaking Eng. Fr. & German, willing to go out.

Delighted to have Harold's letter, tho' you had already quoted it. Dare I hope that your project of a week in Wales and the Welsh waters, will come off? It seems a rare opportunity! Now that I have published my intentions of enlisting there is a general disapprobation among my friends. I hear through a Swiss that many of the Germans I knew there are still alive, fighting in the Vosges.

The Anglo-Norwegian couple quarrel childishly most of their time, at least at meals, where I see them. One of the girl's former adorers is called Clymo, and works in the N.W.[180] offices in Shrewsbury! I know the name. I had a voluminous letter from Leslie by the same post as your last. He hopes (speaking as it were to himself) that this will be the last 2½d worth to be torn from his pocket! Incidentally, I may point out as evidence of poor Dorothy's psychological condition: Leslie objects to my five half-penny stamps on my envelopes, and D. says I am robbing the Government of some paper by using them!—The remark was meant to be humorous; but the idea, the initial idea!—Phew!

I have just read a charming piece of fiction lent by Miss de la T.—*The Incomparable Bellairs* by Agnes & Egerton Castle.[181]

I pity you your bad weather. Here bad weather is impossible, for if it rains the nights are deliciously cool, and if the sun opens out like the mouth of a seven times heated furnace I am not incommoded. This kind of blazing heat stuns one pleasantly, like strong music.

I can't yet say the date of my arrival, and you'll be kind if you'll take me, literally, as I come, and when I come! I haven't been able to see Peyronnet, as he is on holidays.

I like to think you have been keeping pretty well these last weeks. Keep on! It has just occured to me to ask whether you prefer to avoid an inter-family party by choosing Llandudno for the holiday. I think it preferable not to join, but have you considered it?

Always your dearly-loving Wilfred

[178] PN, p. 188.
[179] There were three girls, all with their parents in China.
[180] The North-Western Railway.
[181] Egerton Castle (1858–1920) and his wife, Agnes (c.1860–1922), wrote a large number of novels and plays in collaboration. *The Incomparable Bellairs* was published in 1904 by Constable & Co.

375. To Susan Owen

Wednesday, 18 August [1915]   *Bordeaux*

My most dear Mother,

I <u>knew</u> it would be so, however hard I believed it would be otherwise —I do <u>not</u> start next Friday. Miss de la T. wants me to wait for the Boys, who go to be at school on the 15th Sept. Miss Hall is not sure when she can start, and is certain not to start in time for them; moreover the fellows don't want to travel with her. Anyhow Miss de la Touche offers me 50 f. to cover the expense of staying on in Bordeaux three more weeks. Is this a surprise? I have a bigger one over the page!

(Post Script Friday: Don't believe the following)

The Telegraphist is going to Havre & Rouen by boat on Saturday next, & has just offered me a free passage with him there <u>and back</u>. I cannot but accept. Otherwise I should not see Rouen. And what fun—shiver-me-timbers! Bay of BiscayO! By the time you read this, as I positively believe, I'll be rounding Ouessant![182] A thousand pities, you'll be saying, that I don't cross over home from le Havre. I may be tempted—must consider that tomorrow—(or later on today: it is quarter to one on Thursday mng.) After all I may have the chance of a second voyage to Havre & even to Newhaven but whether I shall take it depends rather on Miss de la Touche.

A nasty nuisance is involved by having given notice for my Room. Behold it already let to a pest who has a violent fancy for it. What a vile discord and confusing this will bring into the flourish of my Grand Finale to Bordeaux. I have to clear out on 30th Aug. Truly I should dearly love to make a scramble for it on Saturday Night—and sort o' call roun' Mahim on Wensdy Mornin! Only it might look shady to take French leave of the French. And then my Papers! Papers of Identification to prove I'm born, curl-papers—ode-and-sonnet papers, Pink Papers, (which I haven't got). I should never pack by Saturday. But to make a false start—delightful flutter! Hating decisive measures as I do, I shall taste all the sweet melancholy of leaving my endearèd Gascony, by sea—without the bitterness of the Irrevocable Finality about it. And I shall feel all the poetry of the thing, without needing to feel in my pocket if my ticket is quite safe.

I had a most memorable dinner last night with the well known Professor Devaux,[183] Botanist, who sat down to table with me at the Restaurant. Fortunately I knew him slightly before. I cleared up a lot of 'points'. The professor was very funny about his visit to England & his staying with Lubbock,[184] Darwins, etc.

On Sunday I had a pleasant two hours with a poor apprentice-tailor, formerly door-keeper of the Berlitz School. We had many a laugh over the old days, and he said many quaint things, and we rescued the boats of the little boys around the pond in the *Jardin Public*, and I earned a momentary place in the garden of boyhood, whence I am now so long banished, and that afternoon was generally very happy. Likewise also on Monday morning, strolling round the town with Bonsall who has fine—if few—wits; and an antique-flavoured—though second-hand—wit. (I think I told you such of his history as I know?)

This afternoon 10 wounded & convalescent soldiers of the Mérignac Ambulance were invited to the Chalet garden. I sort of played the host and tennis with 'em. But the wounds played the devil with my patriotism. One or two nights ago I looked up one André Martin,[185] whom I once succoured when his father died. The whole family did their level best, the Mother by producing tears, and the lads by producing bits of shrapnel horribly sharp—to dissuade me from leaving their peaceful city. Worthy souls! I threw out from the Monkmoor P. Office a card to this lad—and lo! the thing preciously preserved among the *billets-doux* and secret photographs of his pocket-book!

I think of dining with Raoul one of these evenings.

Friday

I kept back these extraordinary announcements under a presentiment that my Voyage would not come off—and, indeed, at six o'clock this evening I learnt that it can't be done. Principal reason stated—my English Nationality. The Voyage to Havre might be managed but not a Return. But, a fortnight next Saturday, I shall most undoubtedly be able to sail to Havre, & perhaps cross to Newhaven, free of charge, for I shall be returning to join the Army. Apparently, this aimless cruise makes the Cap'n suspicious. Anyhow I still believe in the 11th Sept. trip. Boys be bothered!

Your W.E.O.

---

[182] Île d'Ouessant, French island at the south-western end of the English Channel. British mariners called it Ushant. The passenger liner *Drummond Castle* sank off its shore on 16 June 1896.

[183] Unidentified.

[184] Sir John Lubbock (1834–1913), banker, author, and scientist.

[185] See Letter 292.

376. To Susan Owen

Postcard

Sunday [Postmark 19 August 1915]   [*Postmark Bordeaux*]

There is no excuse for a letter: all my news is in the future. These are the possible courses: (1) to remain in Bordeaux or France, (2) to get a 'post' in England both of which I do solemnly abjure. (2) is <u>mean</u>. Thus I shall either

  I Join Artists' Rifles
 II Work in Gov. Offices
III Join French Cavalry (?)
IV „ Italian Cavalry (?)

    For Your sake & yours only, III & IV must be queried, much to my own loss & disappointment. Answer this saying just what you think. I may get away early in Aug.[186] & shall take 'the boat' (don't know which). A. Rifles training begins in London, continues at Epping, & finishes in France.

Yours ever W.E.O.

Very many thanks for so many letters & cards.

---

[186] A slip for September.

3
The Artists' Rifles and Training
1915–1916

381. To Susan Owen

Postcard

Tuesday 11.30 p.m. [Postmark 15 September 1915]

Regent Palace Hotel, Piccadilly Circus, London W

We arrived here last night, after a not-too-troublesome journey, considering the <u>nine</u> *bagages*. The Boys[1] thought to leave for Downside tonight, & we went to Padd. but there was no train connection from Bath. I shall do my Enquiry Business tomorrow, & may not arrive Shrewsbury till Midnight, Wednes. Perhaps you are not yet home? we have come in from a walk round Whitehall & Westminster looking out for Zeps. but saw nothing in the sky & little more on earth. Behind the Admiralty there is Pitch Darkness. The Channel Crossing was uneventful. Till Tomorrow!!

W.E.O.

[1] Johnny and Bobbie. Charles and David stayed with their aunt.

383. To Susan Owen

Thursday Mng. [21 October 1915]   *Les Lilas, 54 Tavistock Square, W.C.*

Dearest of Mothers,

I left Alpenrose on Wednesday morning and attacked the day by going straight to Headquarters.[2] It was found that the Doctor had not given his signature to my papers so I was examined again—and passed. Three others at the same time were refused. One was mad about it and insisted on knowing why. 'I don't think you <u>look</u> a strong man' was the first reply. (But he <u>did</u>!) More expostulation.

Dr. 'I shouldn't like to risk you—with those teeth in your head.'

Recruit. 'They can come out.'

Dr. 'Well, if you must know, your heart murmurs sometimes.' And so on with other apparently robust fellows!

I still did not 'swear in'; but spent the afternoon hunting for Rooms. Four hours I passed on this job; and finally I chose on a French Boarding House, where Guests, Conversation, Cooking and everything else is French.

This should be quite valuable to me; but I don't know whether the price is too high—35s. a week. Bed & Breakfast at other places is 17/6 a week. I scarcely think it would come cheaper, if I took (proper) meals at A.B.C.[3] Moreover there are no A.B.C's near at hand. I am <u>two minutes</u> for the Headquarters. Only 3 minutes from Imperial Hotel, and 5 from Waverley, so I am at home in the region. Tavistock Square is a replica of every other Bloomsbury Square; wadded with fog; skeletons of dismal trees behind the palings; but the usual west-end pervasion of ghostly aristocracy. In London I cannot be unhappy in any surroundings, for what in Manchester would be dismally forlorn, is here Mysterious; What in Liverpool would be detestably sordid, is here romantically free and easy; what elsewhere seems old dinginess is here suggestive Antiquity. (I have a notion that Dickens lived in Tavistock Sq.)[4]

In the middle of this letter I was called to lunch; and then went to 'swear in'. This time it is done: I am the British Army![5] Three of us had to read the Oath together; the others were horribly nervous! and read the wrong Paragraph until the Captain stopped them! 'Kiss the Book!' says Captain. One gives it a tender little kiss; the other a loud smacking one!!

After that we had to be inoculated for Typhoid. And that is why I am in bed since four o'clock! The delightfully kind, confidence-inspiring doctor gave us full instructions. There were scores of Tommies taking the ordeal before me, and believe me some were as nervous as only fine, healthy animals <u>can be</u> before doctors. One fainted before his turn came, merely as a result of the Doctor's description of possible symptoms!

You will be glad to hear, that though it is three hours ago, I have <u>no</u> constitutional symptoms whatever! Merely a local soreness! Some will have fever & 'influenza-pains' all night! (My ink is giving out.) I quite expected such myself; but I feel so physically happy that it might have been Morphine injected! We have sick leave until Monday morning. The hours are 9.30 to 5! Jolly reasonable!

The Poetry Bookshop is about 7 mins. walk![6] There is a Reading this very night!

A Crowd of Belgian Ladies fleeing from Brussels through Holland are staying here today on their way to Paris.

There are just one or two hitches in this pleasant time in bed. First, I have broken the bridge of my specs. and can't read without risk of headache; second, I daren't smoke (Doctor's Orders); third—empty pockets!

You will like me to write again tomorrow mng. This I promise. If only you lived near London!

Fondest Love to <u>Father,</u> Mary and the <u>Dearest of Boys,</u>

From your lovingest of Boys Wilfred

[2] Of the Artists' Rifles, whose headquarters were in Duke's Road, off Euston Road, London. Owen's first medical was on 15 September 1915, according to his Army file. No. 17 Duke's Road is now the home of The Place, a centre for contemporary dance. The façade as Owen knew it remains, with the heads of Mars and Minerva in a terracotta crest over the door.

[3] Aërated Bread Company, founded 1862. By the early twentieth century, there were around 150 branches of the A.B.C. cafés, which were popular with clerks and other workers for the affordable prices, a cheaper alternative to Lyons' Corner House restaurants.

[4] Charles Dickens lived in Tavistock House, Tavistock Square, from 1850 to 1856, and there wrote *Bleak House* and *Hard Times*. The building was demolished in 1901, but a Blue Plaque marks the location, now the headquarters of the British Medical Association.

[5] HO and JB in *CL* suggest that the omission of 'in' in the sentence was 'probably intentional'.

[6] No. 35 Devonshire Street (now Boswell Street), off Queen Square and Theobalds Road, WC1. It had been opened by Harold Monro in January 1913. The building no longer exists. For a description of the 'Poetry House', see DH, *Harold Monro: Poet of the New Age* (Palgrave, 2001) and Joy Grant, *Harold Monro and the Poetry Bookshop* (Routledge & Kegan Paul, 1967).

384. To Susan Owen

Postcard

Sat. Morn. [Postmark 22 October 1915][7]   *Tavistock Sq.*

In the night the arm got pretty bad. I still feel as if a horse had got my arm between its teeth. But so long as it keeps out of the other members, I don't mind it. Those who are not right by Monday mng. will be put on Light Duty, which I believe consists of standing still and staring. The men are really 'picked men most on 'em', anything but boisterous. I am thankful I <u>did</u> put up in a Boarding House, not in a poor Bedroom without meals or attention! Looking forward to your letter tomorrow,

Yours ever W.E.O.

What is Harold's next posting address? Is your headache now quite over? I have heard that the Camp is going to move to Harrow. Pip-ip! Recruits are very numerous now—17 on Monday last! D. + Uncle want Leslie to go with me, but no thanks![8]

[7] PN notes that Saturday morning was the 23rd, but the postmark on the card is clearly the 22nd. Owen's error regarding the day.

[8] The last sentence was omitted in *CL* and *SL*.

385. To Susan Owen

Monday [Postmark 25 October 1915]   *Post Office [Postmark London]*

I had the first drill this mng. but got off this aft. because my arm is not really well. I went to Watson's, & shall have my specs. by tomorrow. I got full marks for Eyesight test at exam. On Sunday afternoon I went to Westminster Abbey: scholarly sermon on sociology and a dazzling fine Anthem. I am not yet in Khaki. The boarding house still pleases me, but I don't know if I shall like the servitude of conforming to its menu and hours of meals! The conversation at my table was all against England. I made no objections. Tomorrow I shall surprise them. Many thanks for all the kind letters received. I am quite all right again, now you know. Another injection in ten days.

Yours ever W.E.O.

386. To Susan Owen

Tuesday [Postmark 27 October 1915]   *[Tavistock Square]*

I fear I should have written my last card sooner than I did: but you can't expect to hear <u>every</u> day! I did a full day's parade today, the arm being only ticklish now. The drill is a curious compound of monotony and *qui vive*. Fortunately our Sergeant is a gentleman, and, what is more, considers us as such. As a Sergeant I admire & respect him devotedly. Harold Monro himself read at the P. Bookshop this evening, and I had a talk with him afterwards. Dorothy was impressed by his Poems which I left at Alpenrose. Please send me Tailhade: *Poèmes Aristophanesques*,[9] which is on the top shelf of the Book <u>Case</u>. Don't send the Pyjamas till I say if we are given any. It <u>was</u> so nice of Colin & Mary to give such cheery letters. The enlisting was a <u>plunge</u>, and it <u>has</u> put my wits a little out of breath.

Your own W.E.O.

[9] Published in Paris, 1904.

387. To Susan Owen

Friday Night [29 October 1915][10]   *Tavistock Sq.*

Dearest Mother,

I am dog-tired: N.B. I don't say exhausted—but stupidly, muscularly tired. I got my outfit some days ago. I have not the patience to give you a list of the contents of my Kit, but it contains numbers of footling things—toothbrush & razor-brush for example, whereas I had to buy a belt (3/6) and shall have to buy a swagger-cane. These are regulations special to our regiment, because the discipline is frightfully minute. I spent all last evening polishing my buttons. We are cautioned against appearing in the street with a single over-coat button undone: belt must be worn over the overcoat, collar never turned up (except in very inclement weather when permission is granted to do so) etc. etc. etc. There is no doubt we are as smart as anything except the Guards, whom we ape. Yesterday morning we went a Route March through Kentish Town to Highgate. I had just got my Brogues repaired in time, but those wretches who wore new service boots had to go home by tram! This morning we had 'Physical Drill' under a special Gymnastic Instructor and it is that which had so bewearied my bones. We do all this in shirt sleeves in Cartwright Gardens, a 'crescent-garden' bounded by the usual boarding houses. I have scarcely seen an officer. All our instruction is done by sergeants, who are as chummy between times as they are smart on parade. Impossible to get them out of temper. One is a rare wag, and gives plenty of exercise to the Risible Muscles. I never felt devotion, and not much respect, for any authority or individual in this world since I left the 3rd form of the Institute; but I am beginning again under these fellows. Astonishing what a changed meaning has a Captain or a Colonel for me. If a Major-General approached me I think I should fall down dead. We had to practise Salutes (on Trees) this very morning. You would be surprised how long it takes to do the thing properly.

This aft. was pay-day. Now we waited drawn up in ranks from 3 this evening, till just on 6!! And those at the rear, as I was, never got it after all. Then was the moment when you had best wad up the ears if swearing upsets them.

I spent the heavy time pleasantly enough in conversation with one who I believe will be one of my best friends. Everyone is willing to make friends, and everyone is eligible; so there is really no guide as to which one shall go for beyond the expression of his phiz. There are now five on special terms with me, one very young, another quite forty, but none artists in any sense, no enthusiasts in my line. So I am still on the lookout. I believe

Sat. morning. Here I was suddenly cut short by my bath being ready. and the arrival of a large packet of literatures from Leslie.

Today is our Second Inoculation. I must run!

Yours with dearest love, Wilfred

[10] PN, p. 188.

388. To Susan Owen

Sunday [31 October 1915][11]   *Tavistock Square*

Dearest Mother,

I have no post-cards, hence another letter, simply to say that the Second Inoculation has taken mildly enough. It was done at midday yesterday: there was enough pain to justify a morning in bed! This time one of my 'friends' did a faint. It must be pure nerves: the 'poison' can't invade the system in half-a-minute. I stayed in by the fire in the afternoon, enduring a Singing Lesson which our Proprietor gives to a Marseillais youth betimes. It seems mine host is an ancient public singer. There is generally music of a sort in the evenings which drives me up to my room. I spend a good part of my leisure polishing my buttons and badges. It is a frightful bore. Can this explain the military oath— 'Dash my buttons!'? This morning I have massaged my new boots with Castor Oil. We were told to <u>pour</u> it inside the boot! The stench resulting is perhaps the very first inconvenience I have yet endured. I have bought my swagger cane, and now feel perfectly normal in Khaki. Apart from the treasonable unlawfulness of appearing in mufti, I should feel positively ill at ease in it. No collar & tie means an economy of dressing-time; but it is paid for by the puttees, which, not being Foxes',[12] are difficult to arrange neatly. I wear the trousers bagged below the knee; but such as care to buy breeches may dress in cavalry style. In the Inns of Court no one wears the khaki provided but buys officer's stuffs, (without stripes of course.) There is a pretty general feeling of contempt for the Inns of Court among our men, that may be founded on envy. <u>We</u> are forbidden to wear waterproofs or Burberrys or mufflers or brown boots—by a special Battalion Order! So far, then, our chiefest cares have been frivolous details of this sort, but there is a stern time coming—in Camp. There is a story that three men deserted from Camp. They were not shot at dawn, but simply excluded from Commissions.

I got my Pay by going early on Sat. morning. Did I ever acknowledge the £1. you sent? It does annoy me to have to take it. Now that the Inoculations are over I am looking for a Room. If only this Life went on indefinitely I should be well pleased. It is really no great strain to strut round the gardens of a West-end square for six or seven hours a day. Walking abroad, one is the admiration of all little boys, and meets an approving glance from every eye of eld. I sometimes amuse myself by sternly contemplating the civilian dress of apparent Slackers. They return a shifty enough expression. When I clamp-clump-clamp-clumped into the Poetry Bookshop on Thursday, the poetic ladies were not a little surprised. The Readings were from Rabindranath Tagore,[13] read by a Lady without much insight into the Hindu spirit. I could not speak to Monro, but he smiled sadly at my khaki. He has a poem in his last book, which goes

> Happy boy, happy boy,
> David the immortal-willed,
> Youth, a thousand thousand times
> Slain, but not once killed,
> Swaggering again today
> In the old contemptuous way;
>
> Leaning backward from your thigh
> Up against the tinselled bar—

Dust and ashes! is it you ?
Laughing, boasting, there you are!
First we hardly recognised you
In your modern avatar.

Greybeards plotted. They were sad.
Death was in their wrinkled eyes.
At their tables, with their maps,
Plans and calculations wise
They all seemed; for well they knew
How ungrudgingly Youth dies.[14]
    etc.

Leslie talks of coming up at the end of the week. Did I tell you I got in half-price at 'the Strand' to see the *Scarlet Pimpernel*.[15] Fred Terry[16] was indisposed, but I could hardly imagine a better impersonation than was done by the Understudy. I have just read *El Dorado*, the last tale of the S. Pimpernel—not very readable. Thank Father so much for a special letter for me: It gave me good reassurance, which you must all try and do. What breed is the Dog? Ah! if Colin could share my bedroom (double bedded) for a few days one week-end! I am free from Sat. 1 o'clock to Monday mng. Just enough time to meet you at Alpenrose, one day next month, eh?

Monday. The Parcel came this morning. The handkerchiefs were just in time, and the chocs I seized with schoolboyish relish! Our drill consisted of standingat-ease and standing-easy alternately in the Drill Hall, because it has rained all day! 'Our' Sergeant has not appeared for some time. Sgt. Knight has charge of us now—the county cricketer:[17] do Father or Colin know of his renown? There is a legend that our Doctor attended the King. Certainly he belongs to a noble Order, K.C.B. or something. There seem no Artists whatever among us!! This morning I was talking to a recruit of a Henry-Irving countenance, who persists in wearing long strands of hair visible in front of the Cap. He has been 'ticked-off' four or five times for it; but is not yet shot at dawn. I am fairly close cropped.

From an Adv. in 'The Y.M.' I found a room[18] at 5/6 per week, right opposite the Poetry Bookshop!!

A plain enough affair—candlelight—no bath—and so on; but there is a coffee-shop underneath; so I have theoretically decided to go there, and shall move as soon as practicable. Indeed I gave notice this evening at this Boarding House.

There is no symptom of patri-avuncularism from Meols!

I think, if it be possible, I must beg £2 for the next remittance, on account of the Advance Payments I may have to make. This should be quite the last Allowance. If anything should turn up from Meols later be reimbursed therewith, of course. I used to think Uncle Ted's readings of Scrooge funny. I don't now. I shall move from here as soon as I have paid up.

Rumour has it that we shall be billeted for the Winter!!
Fare thee well, thou dear, dear Mother, prayeth

                                                    her Wilfred

[11] PN, p. 189.
[12] Fox, the theatrical outfitter. The store at 22 Tavistock Street, Covent Garden, was established in 1878 by Charles H. Fox (1859–93) and provided wigs, costumes, haberdashery, and make-up to London's theatrical performers.
[13] Rabindranath Tagore (1861–1941), the Indian poet. He wrote mainly in Bengali (much of his work was translated into English), but also in English. He was the first non-European to win the Nobel Prize for Literature (in 1913). Knighted in 1915, he renounced the title after the Jallianwala Bagh massacre in 1919. Susan Owen wrote to him after the war. See also Letter 482, n. 19.
[14] 'Youth in Arms' (Harold Monro, *Children of Love*, 1914). Owen omits the third and fifth of the verses that constitute Part I.
[15] By Baroness Orczy (Baroness Emma Magdalena Rosalia Maria Josefa Barbara Orczy, married name Barstow, 1865–1947), playwright and novelist. *The Scarlet Pimpernel* was published in 1905, as both novel and play, and was followed by many further books and plays about her hero, Sir Percy Blakeney.
[16] Fred Terry (1863–1933), actor, youngest of the famous theatrical family, brother of Ellen Terry (1847–1928).
[17] R. F. Knight (1879–1955), who played cricket as a professional for Northamptonshire.
[18] At 21 Devonshire Street. This building no longer exists. In a postcard postmarked 19 May 1916, Owen asks SO to 'advance 15s. to 21 Devonshire St. W.C. c/o Mr. Middleton' (Letter 436, *CL*). He kept this furnished room for some time, possibly until he went to France in December 1917.

390. To Susan Owen

Postcard

Monday [Postmark 8 November 1915]   *a Post Office [Postmark London]*

Am rejoiced to know that Father's operation[19] is well over. Surprised not to have news of him this mng. but perhaps you are saying as much of me. All my time is being given to an Author—Prof. of Lit. at Brussels, who, after 22 yrs of research has found the true Shakspere. Not Bacon but the Earl of Rutland.[20] His proofs are overwhelming. There is going to be a sensation. <u>When</u> I am convinced, I may start the propaganda in the papers. I had the registered letter. Great thanks! But I am not out of Tavistock Sq. 54, for reasons which I will explain later. I quite hope to be able to get to Alp. on Sat. What a delight!

                                                    Your W.E.O.

[19] A minor nasal operation.
[20] Célestin Demblon, *Lord Rutland est Shakespeare: le plus grand des mystères dévoilé Shaxper de Stratford hor cause* (Paris, 1912).

1. Wilfred Owen's first letter to Susan Owen, 1898. Harry Ransom Humanities Research Center, University of Texas at Austin.

2. Wilfred Owen, *c*.1915, portrait by his uncle, John Gunston. John Rylands Library, copyright of the University of Manchester.

3. Wilfred Owen, *c*.1916, portrait by his uncle, John Gunston. Bodleian Library, University of Oxford.

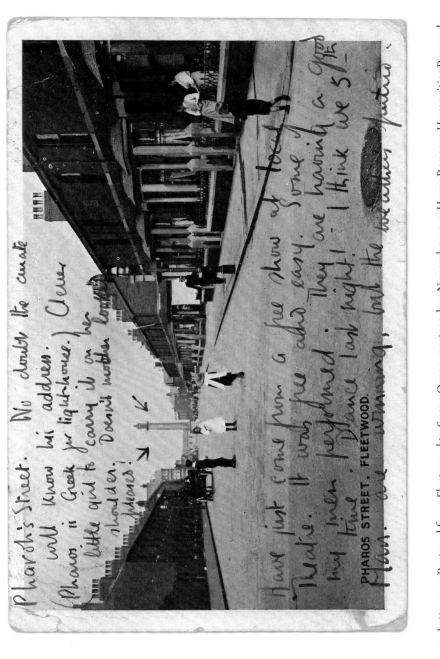

Pharoh's Street. No doubt the canals
will know his address.
(Pharos is Greek for lighthouse.) Clever
little girl to carry it in her
shoulder. Doesn't mother look
pleased!

→ ←

Have just come from a free show of local
trade. It was for this easy, some of
his men performed. They are having a great
time. Diana last night! – I think we 5½ –
Plans are simmering, but the weather spitting.

PHAROS STREET, FLEETWOOD.

4. Letter 470. Postcard from Fleetwood to Susan Owen, postmark 15 November 1915. Harry Ransom Humanities Research Center, University of Texas at Austin.

5. Letter 479. To Susan Owen, 10 January 1917. Harry Ransom Humanities Research Center, University of Texas at Austin.

6. Letter 480. To Susan Owen, 16 January 1917. Harry Ransom Humanities Research Center, University of Texas at Austin.

7. Letter 481. To Susan Owen, 19 January 1917. Harry Ransom Humanities Research Center, University of Texas at Austin.

8. Letter 488. To Harold Owen, 27 February 1917. Harry Ransom Humanities Research Center, University of Texas at Austin.

9. Letter 506. To Susan Owen, 2 May 1917. Harry Ransom Humanities Research Center, University of Texas at Austin.

10. Letter 542. To Susan Owen, 22 August 1917. Harry Ransom Humanities Research Center, University of Texas at Austin.

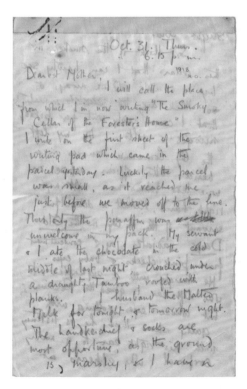

11. Letter 548. To Susan Owen, 12 September 1917. Harry Ransom Humanities
Research Center, University of Texas at Austin.

12. Letter 673. To Susan Owen, 31 October 1918. Harry Ransom Humanities
Research Center, University of Texas at Austin.

392. To Susan Owen

Postcard

Friday Aft. [*Postmark 19 November 1915*]   Y.M.C.A. [*Postmark Romford*]

Had your letter & the socks at mid-day. We have had a rough time today—up at 6 again. 3 men out of the 700 took cold Shower baths. I was one of the 3. But holding rifles frozen over with snow all day was ghastly. Sorry not to have had even the <u>bad</u> prints of my photos. We have an extra blanket now i.e. 1 blanket & 3 rugs. Food has been so-so today.

Love to all W.E.O.

393. To Susan Owen

Postcard

Friday Aft. [*Postmark 19 November 1915*]   *Railway Train* [*Postmark Watford*]

20 men were suddenly called up to do some cleaning up at High Beech. Of these am I and my two best friends. We just had time to snatch a lunch, & I managed to rip open the Parcel, & get out the socks. We may stay till Monday, but write to Gidea Park. We are carrying a sack of meat and a sack of bread. This is 'Fatigue Duty' but I am glad of the Change.

Many thanks for sending so promptly the pyjamas etc. Don't know how we shall sleep tonight. Am quite well.

Your W.E.O.

394. To Susan Owen

Postcard

[*Postmark 21 November 1915*]   Y.M.C.A. [*Postmark Romford*]

Just returned (by train) from High Beech. Worked like slaves at Transport Waggon Loading from 7.30 to 2. Thoroughly enjoyed the change, & benefited by the exercise.

Your W.E.O.

395. To Leslie Gunston

Picture Postcard

[Postmark 23 November 1915]   *[Postmark Romford]*

Here's a part of our Hut of 30. I slaved for them, all Sundays as Orderly—never thought myself capable of such strenuosities as to do skivvy's drudgery from 6.30 a.m. to 6.30 p.m.! Note the bareheaded man on my right. Shall I tell you about him and men when I can. <u>Great</u> thanks for Book. I read one page when lights went out!

397. To Susan Owen

Thursday [18 November 1915][21]

> *From Cadet W.E.S. Owen, 4756*
> *Hut 6a, Artists' Reg't. C.Coy.*
> *Hare Hall Camp Romford Essex*

I was put on Guard Duty from 9 a.m. yesterday to 9 a.m. today. Miserable time: not allowed to take off pack or boots during 24 hrs. I was Sentry from 11 to 1 and 5 to 7, etc. a. and pm. I was with fellows that I don't like—chumps all of them. We got enough to eat; and I made my toast on my Bayonnet. There was not much Challenging to do. I am one of the orderlies again tomorrow. Now that the novelty is wearing off, this Camping is beginning to get troublesome. I had a card from Stanley Webb today. I am <u>not</u> off this week end. How is everybody?

Your W.E.O.

[21] PN, p. 189.

403. To Susan Owen

Thursday [23 December 1915]   Y.M.C.A. *[Romford]*

Dearest of Mothers,

I have had no letters today. I believe there is a muddle in the P.O. this year, but I hope you will get this by Christmas Day. The certainty is absolute: I shall be here over the 25, with the majority of my Hut, and, indeed, of my Company. The latest rumour is that we shall not be allowed to get out of Camp till we have fairly eaten our Christmas Dinner under its auspices. Anyhow we shall feast rarely. Donaldson is giving us two birds, (geese or turkeys) and there will be any number of plum-puddings. We are allowed 1/6 per head extra pay for the Day, which is funded and spent on delicacies and drinks. You will be pleased to hear that no spirits will be allowed at table. The best of it is we are all pleased.

I may go to the Williams[22] later in the day, or on Boxing Day. Both Scouts have their lunch in my Hut now, instead of the Q.M. stores, where they are alone or with alien men. It is remarkable how their presence kills bad language, for the time. The Restraint is beautiful, but if the novelty wears off and usual conditions are gone back to I shall turn out the kids.

We had a lecture this afternoon on bombs, from an expert. We shall begin firing after New Year.

I am being waited for now to go into Romford and buy special provisions. One has gone to London for the Turkeys. I wonder what you will be having. It is galling to be kept away from Home for no useful reason, but it is not as if I were far away or long away. I really think to start on Tuesday or Wednesday.

Goodwill let there be; but Peace is a word that jars today and word for hushed breath. I shall write continually, but this poor sheet may be the one to carry you my dear Christmas Wishes the most ardent and solemn of any year yet.

Wilfred x

---

[22] A local, hospitable family. The Scouts were the two small Williams boys—Raymond, aged 13, and Edward, aged 11. They had two sisters—Katherine, aged 18, and Margaret, aged 8.

404. To Susan Owen

Sunday after Christmas [*26 December 1915*]   Y.M.C.A [*Romford*]

Dearest Mother,

Your dear, lovely letter reached me this morning. It was the one thing lacking yesterday to make my Christmas the happiest possible, away from Home. I had no letter, parcel or card whatsoever yesterday; but I had my consolations. The Plenty that overpoured in our Hut of good things was noised all over the Camp. In our Hut 'it snowed of meats and drinks.' One Wiggins, a noted gourmand made all manner of custards & jellies; and Donaldson's turkeys were *à point*. Healths <u>were</u> drunk; but none among us were. I had scarcely accomplished my last nut, at 3 o'clock (we sat down at 1.30!) when my Boy Scout came for me. And not long after I got to the house, we began my second Christmas Dinner, rarely good. So I made up for the Lost One in 1913! Afterwards we played Charades, exactly as we played at Home. But I shall have to tell you all about these excellent people with the live voice. There was no extension of time, last night we were all in at 9.15: but the uproar in camp could be heard afar off.

We went to Church Parade this morning as well as yesterday. The Major read the Lessons.

I have some fine Caricatures of the Colonel[23] etc. to show you which appeared in *The Tatler.*

I am sorry you don't countenance my little stay in Bath with a fair regard. Yet it is no great *détour* from London, and I am sure I could get a Permission, via Bath. But I haven't heard again from Leslie. I hope you got all my letters: a succession of 4, Dec. 21, 22, 23, 24; The pocket-book-parcel hasn't been delivered to me yet. Thanks for sending it: I hope it is safe. There seems no possibility of getting off before Wed. or Thursday.

There has been a new desertion from Camp. The boy was captured at Norwich. Two lusty ones from my hut were told off to exercise the Prisoner on Christmas Day. I have not too much spare time today, being Orderly. My Batmanship finished yesterday.

I read your dear letter many times, and <u>shall</u> read it. I quite well know how busy Colin must be.

It is fine to feel that now that Christmas is over, there is a greater treat in store. May my plans be sooner fulfilled than they were this time last year!

Ever your loving Wilfred

---

[23] Colonel W. C. Hersley (1855–1934).

406. To Susan Owen

Postcard

Thurs. [*Postmark 6 January 1916*]   [*Postmark Romford*]

I stayed with Leslie till 5, and caught a train from Liverpool St. by chance, not knowing the times. You may be surprised to know that I had a Commission offered to me today. Are you yet more surprised to know that I refused it: Lancashire Fusiliers, just going into Fighting Line. And I haven't fired my Musketry Course. I can tell you no more. A list of names was read out, and we said Yes or No according to our feelings!

So glad the Dog turned up. We had an all-day march (of course) so I haven't seen my Narks. The Gingerbreads made a warm pudding for lunch. We parade at 8.30 now!!

Yours W.E.O.

407. To Colin Owen

Sunday Evening [9 January 1916][24]   *Y.M.C.A [Romford]*

My dear Colin,

Last Wednesday seems very long ago. I suffered on Thursday from the fresh shock of discipline, cold, rough blankets and vile-tasting food; but I am habituated once more.

I had a good journey, travelling with the A.S.C.[25] men you saw, merry dogs. I got into camp half an hour before Time, but many arrived late. There are stricter Rules than ever about Boundaries, and Leave, etc. However, We find ourselves, that it my Platoon, among the veterans of the corps, and we drill and go to Lectures with the Officers' School.

Two men of my Hut offered themselves (I think that's the way to put it) for the Lancs. Fusiliers Commissions. When my name was read out I said NO! with a loud voice. We have not even started Miniature Range Firing yet.

We had Church Parade this morning. One Major read the Lesson and another played the organ. This afternoon I have been reading a book which I just received from Leslie.

Ray came for me yesterday and we had some parlour games: like Smiling Snap, which was new to them. Mr. Williams was hopelessly unsmileable.

I left my keys in the lock of my bookcase (or inside). Find them for me, dear boy, and them at once. (3 or 4 keys on a small ring.) The cake was well praised by the whole hut, and the gingerbreads by such fortunates as got any. I had no letter since Mother's first card. Love to everyone.

Your W.E.O.

[24] PN, p. 189.
[25] Army Service Corps.

408. To Susan Owen

[Postmark 14 January 1916]   *Y.M.C.A. [Postmark Romford]*

Quite impossible to write more than a card. Our Training is becoming intensive. We now finish at 6.30, and we have maps & Reports to do all evening. The Colonel gave a brilliant lecture on the causes of the War this aft. He is an expert after the style of Belloc. I had all the things you sent. Thanks, tho' only the Keys were desired: By all means let the Diary be Mary's. I must now get straight away to my Mapping. We spend the day with Note Books & Compasses in the district. I had a Card from Coz. May. I will tell you tomorrow about my coming week end.

Your W.E.O.

410. To Susan Owen

[*26 January 1916*]   Y.M.C.A. [*Romford*]

Dearest of Mothers,

I send a letter out of sheer lovingkindness, seeing there is no fact, complaint, desire, fear, regret or fancy to be addressed unto you, but only the fact of my sonship, and my greetings to the most gentlest of mothers.

I had a letter from Leslie under this same Y.M.C.A. Heading, for he was washing coffee-cups during his week-end;[26] Mars and Minerva help his soul, fingers and all the cockles of his heart.

They have now put up a chapel in the camp; 4 or 5 days ago the place where it stands knew it not; and the Bishop is coming down to dedicate (sanctify as he would say) tomorrow.

We are now—at last—on our Musketry Course. Many are falling sick about me, by reason of January, and the dead season, but I have not so much as a cold. The hours are still early and late. Still I am never tired, and often walk to Romford in the evening. An occasional Ray from the outer world visits me. I may be going in for the 5th Manchester Regiment.[27]

Did you know that no officers can be sent to the Firing Line without 5 months waiting in England.

Your lovingest of Boys Wilfred

Post Scriptum.

Give my distinguished salutations to your hosts[28] at Weston. You know Miss Ingram is at her Brother's school there. Is a school of that Name known?

[26] War work. LG had a heart murmur and after several medicals was not called up.
[27] Owen was commissioned into the 5th Battalion, Manchester Regiment, on 4 June 1916. This was the 5th (Reserve) Battalion, formed in May 1915 as a draft-finding unit for the 1st/5th and 2nd/5th (the latter, originally formed to provide drafts for the 1st/5th, having also become an active unit). It began to send out drafts towards the end of 1915. At Codford on Salisbury Plain until summer 1916, the battalion then moved to Witley, near Guildford, where Owen joined it as a newly commissioned officer. See Letter 438. All officers gazetted to the 5th Battalion reported to the 3rd/5th, or Reserve, Battalion to await posting.
[28] The Rev. William Davies, Rector of North Fitzwarren, Somerset, and Susan Owen's first cousin.

411. To Susan Owen

Tuesday [*1 February 1916*]   *Isolation Hut B11* [*Romford*]

Dearest Mother,

How frantically I wish I had complained a little louder, or been a little worse, or that you had been more touched by my groans—so that I might never have returned to this hot-bed of disease, this Quarantine, this Prison, this Charnel House. When I opened the door of the Hut in the deep midnight, and smelt the smell of Disinfectant, used wholesale,—I knew what Trap I had run into and I knew why my bones ached. But, it is nothing worse than Measles, and what is more, I don't think I've got it. But there is no doubt my system has been fighting a ferocious battle with the Germ. As usual, the Good Microbes got the best of it in me. All the same, my eyes run continually, and my brain is like a hot coal within my head. Of course I 'paraded sick', but having no rash, I just have to crouch in my Hut, now half-empty of its men, and the centre of the measles outbreak. Moreover we are refused admission to the Y.M. or Canteen, and shall not be able to leave the Camp for 16 days.

When I was going up the subway at Liverpool St. from the Underground to the G. Eastern Platform, I noticed the passages unduly encumbered, and found the outlet just closed, and Liverpool St. in complete darkness. We were corked down in those subways for close on 3 hours. This should appeal to your susceptibilities especially. There was just room to move from one Exit to another seeking an escape. After all the Zeppelins never got over the City, though we heard the guns. The result of this piece of providential by-play was that I reached Camp in the early hours of this morning. My bed had disappeared, all my belongings were hidden all over the hut, for the whole place had been emptied for disinfecting, and the things thrown back anyhow.

It was the bitterest moment of many years. I found some blankets, but all night I was persuaded I should [not] warm my limbs again in this world.

The doctor won't sign my commission papers for 3 days; supposing I may contract measles yet.

I don't think so.

What a prospect to be imprisoned in this hut for several weeks.

I hope Colin won't get it.

Nobody of my Friends knew my address, or perhaps they might have warned me.

A horrid sensation to be imprisoned with Germs. Far worse than the shutting-down under London last night.

Do not worry about my condition.

What frets me is that I ever let myself away from Home.

Do not send any things to eat. I cannot taste: and I can get by deputy something from the Y.M. if necessary.

No more of this now—at least for your ears. For me: 'Buried alive for 16 days!' I cannot bear to think of Sat. & Sunday.

                                        Farewell, Wilfred x

412. To Susan Owen

Postcard

Wednesday [Postmark 3 February 1916]   *[Postmark Romford]*

I have <u>not</u> given way to Measles, and am not going to. My cold is much less severe than yesterday: a genuine change sets in. The apparent recovery on Monday was an artificial one, brought about by deceitful drugs. Would I had taken 'Bromo-Tablets',[29] and never revived at all! About 5 men remain well in this hut; and more measley ones are carried off every day.

I was affrayed when I saw this morning that Zeppelins got into Staffs.[30] You are not so snug in Shrews. as we imagined. What local news is there of the Raid? I shall go on parade tomorrow.

Always your W.E.O.

Hope my letter was posted in London <u>yesterday</u>?

[29] Probably Bromo Quinine tablets, used to treat all manner of colds, aches, fever, congestion, and constipation.
[30] Nine Zeppelins were raiding over the Midlands on the night of 31 January–1 February 1916, making for, but not reaching, Liverpool. Fifty-nine people were killed in Staffordshire, and 101 injured. One raider came close to Shrewsbury.

419. To Susan Owen

Postcard

Saturday [Postmark 28 February 1916]   Guard Room H.Q. *[Postmark London W.C.]*

It did not occur to me, writing from so renowned (?) a place as the P. Bookshop to give you the address:

35 Devonshire St.
W.[31]

Don't put Poetry Bookshop. Tonight I am on Guard, so that my weekend is quite spoiled. But I saw Harold last night. He sailed at 1 a.m.(?)[32] We got paid today: so there is no immediate need confronting me. I stand in need of your news, but for this I have to blame myself. It goes on snowing. Shall try and write tomorrow. Tell me if you wrote to H.Q. or elsewhere.

Your W.E.O.

[31] On a ten-day course in London, Owen was allowed to find private lodgings, and stayed at the Poetry Bookshop. 'Above the shop, he [Munro] had bed-sitting rooms for poets; Wilfrid Wilson Gibson, T. E. Hulme and Wilfrid [*sic*] Owen lived there for some time…' (F. S. Flint's biographical Introduction to *The Collected Poems of Harold Monro* [London: Cobden-Sanderson, 1933]). In fact, this was Owen's only stay, and it lasted for just a few days.

[32] Harold's ship had just berthed at the East India Dock after an eventful spell at sea; he recalled spending the evening at 35 Devonshire Street, and meeting Monro. On the next day, 28 February, he sailed to Liverpool, from which port he proceeded on leave. For HO's recollections of his wartime visits with his brother, see JFO III, chs IX and X. See also Letter 459.

420. To Susan Owen

Postcard

Monday [Postmark 29 February 1916]   *[Postmark London]*

Just a card to forestall Harold with <u>my</u> Greetings: (although after all I don't think I shall go forth to post tonight, the snow is still jiggering about.) We finished work at quarter to 7 today! Lectures nearly all day, on Gas, Horses, Bombs, and such subjects. I have seen nothing of Monro, as I am out all day & he all evening. But the young housekeeper,[33] who is French, has reeled off as much information as I can desire. I had the Letter & Enclosure yesterday and thank you heartily & sadly.

Fondest love to Mary. All praise to Colin for 'washing up'. It is the most soldierly thing he can possibly do. Do keep warm. Are you at all stronger now?

Your W.E.O.

[33] Alida Klemantaski (1892–1969), later Monro's second wife. She continued to run the Poetry Bookshop, after his death in 1932, until 1935. She also worked to ensure Charlotte Mew's literary heritage. See Letter 558.

421. To Susan Owen

Postcard

Wed. Night [Postmark 2 March 1916]   *[Postmark London]*

Depressing news was announced today. All who left Camp last Wed. must return to camp in a day or two. We are too sick at heart to discuss it, even. Still it has its advantages financially. In view of leaving before Pay Day, I must beg another 10s. We are to have another month or more of 'Officers' School' Training, i.e. Lectures & Exams. Even here we work till 7 p.m. instead of 4.30! Has Harold arrived. Write here till further notice; we may extort leave to stay over Sunday. You may have noticed that the Gazettes have ceased in the Papers since some considerable time. Is the end of the war in view? There is only one consolation from this Delay, and <u>that</u> is a Coward's.

This aft. in the lecture-room I am sure I saw Ernie Hulcoop of Dunsden & Kendrick, among the "Recruits"! Ardently hoping you are getting well—

Your W.E.O.

422. To Susan Owen

Saturday [4 March 1916][34]   Y.M.C.A. *[Romford]*

My darling Mother,

Here we are again! The reason of the Remove is that all men with 'Papers in' must go through a six weeks Training in a School of Instruction before they can be gazetted. The War Office, indeed, has stated that none can have Commissions within 4 months from now. But that is sure to be changed. At the end of the 6 weeks there will be an exam. This is tiresome beyond words (tho' we <u>have</u> among ourselves certain words to fit the case.)

Our 10 days in Town were so annoying that the departure was made less galling than it might have been. Every day we 'worked', <u>doing nothing</u>, well into the evening. On Thursday the Draft left Waterloo for Southampton, and we marched with them thro' London, with several Bands, to say Goodbye. Thus we came in for a deal of cheering and staring from the windows & pavements. All day we marched about, and were recalled in the evening for Night Operations on Hampstead Heath, up to which we marched, over which we marched, and back from which we marched. I got in at 9.30!

I thought I should never see Monro; but last night at eleven o'clock, when I had strewn about my goods preparatory to sorting and packing, up comes Monro to my room, with my MSS! So we sit down, and I have the time of my life. For he was 'very struck' with these sonnets. He went over the things in detail and he told me what was fresh and clever, and what was second-hand and banal; and what Keatsian, and what 'modern'.

He summed up their value as far above that of the "Little Books of Georgian Verse". The curious part is that he applauded precisely those phrases which Prof. Morley condemned!

So then, I have gained his esteem, and a (first) handshake! I need not say that he is a peculiar being; and I doubt whether ever we shall become 'Friends'. For my own part I should prefer a Business Relation, and I believe it possible—when he re-starts his Journal *Poetry & Drama*,[35] now checked by the War.

I have quite won the heart of the Swiss Housekeeper,[36] and on two evenings she brought me up Hot Soup etc. out of human kindness. I left this morning without settling my Account, since, luckily, no Bill had been presented to me, and when I left in the early morning nobody was stirring. I have not had your letter. This is my Address now:

> Cadt W. E. S. Owen, 4756
> W. Co.—Officers' School—
> Balgores House
> Gidea Park,
> Nr. Romford, Essex.

We are crowded into large empty houses, sleeping on the floor, far less comfortable than the Hut. But we have Batmen to wash up, and a Mess Room with tablecloths, properly set out. We expect the work to be strenuous.

I am so anxious to hear when Harold arrived, and whether you have nearly reach[ed] your normal <u>health</u> (?), and withal how Mary improves.

Loving wishes for Every One, Your Wilfred

[34] PN, p. 189.
[35] Monro started this quarterly in 1913, and had published eight numbers when the war came. He did not revive it after the war.
[36] Her name was Marie Spati.

424. To Susan Owen

Monday Evening [13 March 1916][37]   *Y.M.C.A. [Romford]*

My own dear Mother,

I found your Letter on the Table where our Post is displayed this afternoon. I was twice blest to find the stray letter refound, as I was no less annoyed to think the 5s. was lost, than I was needy of it. We have been obliged to buy all manner of Note-Books for our work, and shall soon have Maps and such materials to find. I shall consider my running clothes as my Birthday Present. There is no book that I hanker after, because I can borrow anything that there is time to read; but there are some half-dozen Military Books which I ought to get, but which I can also borrow until my Gazetting.

There are probably another 8 weeks of this schooling.

We now have started in earnest; we have a lecture at 6.30 a.m. drill and field operations all day—another lecture 5 to 6 p.m., Dinner 6.30 to 7.30 and from 7.30 to 9.30 time for cleaning—preparations for next day, study, and writing up of notes. I have exactly 30 mins. of <u>my own</u> today, and 15 of those are being consecrated to these pages.

How I wish I had more, and could tell you what a merry time I had yesterday, how I ran, the moment I was free, to find my 'Nephews', and how we wandered in the Wood, and how I did the Arithmetic Homework; and what a Bath I had. (For there is no bath-room in Balgores, and no time to go over into the Camp!) So I asked for a Hot Bath, and had it! My younger nephew—of 10 years[38]—comes to pay me visits during the day, but I am always out!

I have not seen Ray, because on Saturdays I am no longer free, and even on Sunday Mornings we do the same old, insupportable drill. This last week has been enough to send crazy any thinking being—eternal inspections, parades, inspections, punishment parades, & more inspections. Every morning we alternately (1) stand and freeze, and (2) hustle around till we are blown as race horses.

Meanwhile, the Colonel himself, cursing us from the top of a Golf Mound, drills us, foaming at the mouth. Sometimes he follows at our heels, barking like a collie after straggling sheep. After this, we are at the mercy of a Coldstream Guard Sergeant, who abuses us in bad English and worse Language. I know—at last— what all this Rumpus means. Somebody very great—probably Lord French[39]—is coming down this week to overhaul us!

We had a first Exam. this evening.

There is still room for anxiety both about Mary and You. Perhaps it is as well I am so occupied, for I could easily grieve myself ill about You, if left alone to do it. I do hope Father won't get a bad cold.

What about Colin? And Harold?

Leslie is at Chelsea.

Unbounded love, Your Wilfred x x x

[37] PN, p. 189.
[38] Stanley Harper. His brother Albert ('Bertie') was four years older. Like the Williams family, the Harpers welcomed soldiers into their home. DH notes that Owen seems to have been given a standing invitation to visit the Harpers on Sundays and the Williamses on Saturday. The Harper and the Williams boys were in the same Scout troop and lived near each other at Hornchurch. Jacqui Barr has identified that Owen spent his last night in Hornchurch with the Williams family at their home, The Croft ('Wilfred Owen's Letters and the Romford District', *Wilfred Owen Association Journal* [2006], issue 1).
[39] Field Marshal Lord French (1852–1925), 1st Earl of Ypres, Commander-in-Chief, British Expeditionary Force, August 1914–December 1915, was at the time of Owen's letter Commander-in-Chief, British Home Forces.

425. To Susan Owen

Saturday 18 March [1916]   Y.M.C.A. [*Romford*]

My most darling Mother,

The Day of St. Patrick and of Saint Mother is passed and you had no note or any word from me. The thing is abominable. Excuse? Not the right word! Cause and Reason enough! You know our 'Evenings' consist of 1½ hour. On the 16th, I am obliged to rush into Romford for Running Clothes for a Run announced for the 17th. Next evening a Compulsory Lantern Lecture until after 10, so that on that day we had not so much as 3 mins. off duty, though in our Room we got up at quarter past five. We are not forced to get up till 6, for Physical Drill at 6.30, but we are punished so severely for impeachable dress that we rise in our sleep almost and begin to do our scraping, cleaning, washing, shaving, polishing, scrubbing, rubbing, brushing, oiling, sandpapering, folding, tying, tidying, cleaning up & clearing down, cleansing, ablutions, bucklings, foldings, etc. &c. Etc, and caetera. So we toil and moil.

Your Note arriving on the 17th gave me the comfort and renewing of a sacrament. Thereby I had communion with those things which are now passed behind a cloud out of sight, but which shall come to us in like manner again. Now is the winter of the world.[40] But my life has come already to its month of March…

Yes, I take and read these your words with thanksgiving.

Thanks, also, and more than thanks, I owe you for the Present of Moneys.

Previous sums having been necessities absolute for the physical fact of living in the Artists, I take them from the letter with a wince, loving not to handle them.

But a Present I can look at without fear and without reproach.

It was my Week-end, and Leave was announced for all Balgores. I promised my sore bones rest from drilling, and my sore chin rest from shaving, and my sore spirit from chafing. In my Poet[']s Room I might have lain me. There would I have lighted an incense of ten cigarettes, your own burnt offering. There would I—Thunder and the bolts of heaven confound their knavish tricks, Authorities have cancelled all Leave! Some say it is a General Order for the Eastern Command, in event of a naval Raid on the coast. I had arranged to meet Leslie, too! I have quite 'won' the Housekeeper of Monro's, for with my Washing she sent a box full of Soup Tablets, biscuits, buns, not forgetting the salt, so that I make myself suppers! I know how to value acts of this sort, though the soup is useless to me now; and I mean, one day, to promulgate my feelings in no uncertain tones, so terrible that the uttermost confines of the wirral[41] shall be shaken.

I look forward to meeting Harold again either here or in Town. Leave is cancelled 'until further notice'.

The winter is steadily drawing off; but no large trees have yet ventured to show the green flag of safety.

The Almond-trees which recall Wimbledon, are in the pink of perfection among the quaint houses of the garden city.

I am hoping that this sudden great warmth will play the angel of healing to your chest and throat.

I am quite all right, tho' a man had Influenza in our room. All those who go on sick leave are 'washed out' of the School. We are learning far more in a week here than a month of camp. The only nuisance is the Sergeant Major, Coldstream Guard, a consummate bully, amusing enough in *Punch*, but not viewed from the ranks.

The Army as a life is a curious anomaly; here we are prepared—or preparing—to lay down our lives for another, the highest moral act possible, according to the Highest Judge, and nothing of this is apparent between the jostle of discipline and jest. Again, we turn from the meanest of jobs scrubbing floors, to do delicate mapping, and while staying in for being naughty, we study the abstractions of Military Law.

On the whole, I am fortunate to be where I am, and happy sometimes, as when I think it is a life pleasing to you & Father and the Fatherland.

All the love of the whole heart of your

Wilfred

---

[40] 'War broke: and now the Winter of the world / With perishing great darkness closes in.' '1914', *CPF*, p. 116.

[41] The Wirral, the Cheshire peninsula on which Birkenhead stands.

426. To Susan Owen

Saturday Aft., 1 April [1916][42]   *Y. M. C.A.* [*Romford*]

My own dear Mother,

You have indeed written long & frequent letters, and I am not worthy to receive them. I was agitated when you mentioned visiting new Houses, but your next letter says you have not given notice. What manner of houses are these which you have seen?

It is very disappointing to know that Colin is not even trying for the Exam. I get on well enough in our Exams. having high and very high marks in Musketry, Reconnaissance, and Drill—full marks for Drill—But in Military Law I came pretty low!

I am sending you a sketch done by Muff-Ford[43] in the Canteen the other day, struck off in 10 mins. while we had our coffee. I think the resemblance to Father in youth is traced with something like divination. I find my nose growing alarmingly amorphous with my advancing years. Anyhow it is not exactly a <u>weak</u> face: and that is all I am concerned to know. (Note I wear my hair ½ in. long now.)

Muff-Ford has studied Art in many branches at the Polytechnic for 3 years. He is of German birth, and has altered his name. I like him well. As you see he has a clever eye and a cunning hand, but he is by far the slowest-mover at drill in all the Platoon. And he is punctiliously unpunctual.

Last night I saw the Zeppelin![44] <u>Lights out</u> was ordered while we were undressing. Then soon after, our room being over the Guard Room, we heard the sentry cry 'There she is! Guard—turn out!' It was larger than I thought they appeared, and just then was heading straight for us! Half a dozen Searchlights concentrated on it, & kept it lighted up, tho' it was moving fast. Suddenly a furious cannonade set up from below, and the shells burst in scores around it, but none seemed to touch the Gasbag. Some burst about 3 miles behind!! The beast looked frightened somehow; nosed about as if lost, turned eastward, inclined steeply upward, and vanished behind a 'cloud'. Now, the sky seemed cloudless & all stars of ordinary size were clear. <u>I quite think the vapour was of its own producing</u>. Anyhow the searchlights lost it, the firing ceased, and it was all over.

I can't say I saw any bombs fall tho' we thought we heard the peculiar noise of them. We 'turned out' on the Parade Ground, but were sent back to bed by the Major. About midnight I heard four more gun-shots, but nothing was to be seen. London was not touched by bombs but our brute got very near. In fact <u>we actually saw its turning-back</u>. Altogether a highly entertaining 15 minutes.

Bugles are now sounded at the proper times. We have also our Drum & Fife Band as well as the Regimental. A thrilling affair. The sound, together with the gallant bearing of the twenty fifers, has finally dazzled me with Military Glory.

The fifers are worthy to rank with the demented violins that make Queen's Hall to spin round as a top, and with the Cathedral Choir that pierces thro' the heights of heaven. Sweetly sing the fifes as it were great charmed birds in Arabian forests. And the drums pulse fearfully-voluptuously, as great hearts in death.[45]

I have hopes that you are now as well as when I was Home. Is it even so? Is Harold better than when in London? In truth, I am perfectly well, tho' during last week the cold clawed up my throat effectively, every night & morning!

Everlasting Love from your own Wilfred

No individual importance to be given to Hieroglyphics in last Letter! Shall spend week-end on Notes.

[42] PN, p. 189.
[43] Lieutenant J. W. D. Muff-Ford, 19th Battalion, London Regiment. He relinquished his command on 24 October 1923 and retained the rank of lieutenant (*London Gazette*, 23 October 1923, p. 7118).
[44] Possibly the Zeppelin raid involving the airships L14 and L16 (30 March/1 April 1916), in which forty-eight were killed and sixty-four injured in the Essex, Suffolk, and Lincolnshire areas.
[45] DH notes how in this paragraph 'The language of late Victorian lyricism is being adapted to a military subject, and Owen is accumulating a store of poetic material' that would later be used in his war poems such as 'Anthem for Doomed Youth' and 'Greater Love' (*Owen the Poet* [Macmillan, 1986], p. 60).

428. To Colin Owen

Sunday Night [2 April 1916] [46]   *Romford*

My dear Colin,

[*six lines cut out*] last I wrote: but I may mention that neither on Sat. did I go to Williams', nor today to Harper's because I had such a Mass of Notes to write up. We were made to dig trenches on Sunday Morning…!!††§?? !!!

When a barrel is full of nuts there is yet room to pour much oil therein, say the Arabians. It is only by combining systematic physical [*six lines cut out*]

I hear you are applying yourself to some solid study for the J. Oxford.[47] I am bucked to hear it. I am sure that 3 months of this kind of work will get you through.

Let it be a time of worry—only don't worry <u>yourself</u> but your <u>subjects.</u>

It is the only way, not only for average brains like you & me, but for the best of them.

Now approach the days when the evening light draws out seductively: tempting all such as have moveable hearts and moveable bodies to stray forth and behold clouds, games, lamps, starts, riversides, swallows, and the daughters of men.

But the Student longeth after none of these things.

I have discovered two young men of letters in this House.

1. King, who seems well versed & well-connected, in modern literature. For instance his sister knows Bernard Shaw, and Yeats.

2. Denny, who is an old Reading student, still under the wing of Prof. Morley!

Do write me a rough note with plenty of wild talk about your intentions, and some <u>accurate information</u> upon dear Mother & dear Mary.

Be full of thanks nightly for a Fire, a Chamber, and a Bed, not to mention a loving Father Mother Sister about you.

Not to mention 2 Brothers.

The Lord loveth not the speed of an horse, nor delighteth He in any man's legs.

Prov. Ch. — V. —

Your devoted Brother Wilfred

[46] PN, p. 189.
[47] The Oxford Junior Examination.

430. To Susan Owen

Wed. [*12 April 1916*][48]   [*Romford*]

Dearest Mother,

I have a few minutes. They shall be Yours.

Yesterday we had an Oral Exam. in the form of an Interview with a no. of Officers. Apparently I made a satisfactory impression. I answered successfully the 3 Questions put to me. We also had another Written Exam. in which I have done pretty well, being above the average, and top of my Room. I can never beat a young blood of 17, but as he is going into the Scots Guards, and the Army is his family profession I am not annoyed. I have frequent tiffs with this Johnny, and call him the Scarlet Cockatoo, and the Crimson Toucan variously.

I was suddenly struck the other day to realize that my Section, thrown together by pure chance, contains some desirable fellows. First Muff-Ford, Artist: then a Journalist & Reporter, then an Actor, now well established, tho' quite young, and taking no end of money. He has promised me a job after the War, at £5. to £6. a week! He is a gentleman, and loves his profession. I wonder?[49]

Then Briggs,[50] of the 5th Manchester, chemical student at Leeds. He is quite my closest chum: a boy of admirable industry in work, inquiring mind, a hater of swank, malice, and all uncharitableness, and very Provincial.

This spark King, poetical aspirant, Public School Exhibitioner in Classics, sportsman, gamester, wag, has something of a 'Set' about him. I am partly of them, but my variable moods, and relapses into solemnity, won't do for them.

There are rumours of Week-end Leave.

I am anxious to know Harold's movements. Are you going to take Mary to Manchester? Now, have you quite got over the Chest Troubles, and is the weakness nearly gone? Nothing could possibly have put me into so fit a state as this Army Trade. You must be duly glad; Father should indeed crow. Is he quite well? Would Mary write?

All my love. Wilfred x

48 PN, p. 189.
49 Later, at Craiglockhart Military Hospital, Owen took part in theatrical productions.
50 Lieutenant H. B. Briggs, Manchester Regiment, was wounded on 17 September 1918.

433. To Susan Owen

Sunday Evening [7 May 1916][51]   *Canteen—Romford*

My own dear Mother,

I safely received, first the Letter containing 10/- then the Parcel with Key, Frankincense of Araby and the Mexic Nutriment. Hearty & true thanks for all.

We had our Final Exam. on Friday, and I am sending the Papers together with the Syllabus, which Father will be interested to read—and which Colin may be, may not. I am confident enough of a Pass: and although the Time was too short (2 hrs) for so very extensive questions, I 'got in' something for every one of the 10 Questions, which is more than certain men did.

When you have seen them, please drop the Papers in my Desk or thereabouts.

I didn't know the Seatons were moving, emigrating, Simple-Life-Campaigning, absconding, or whatever is it?

Very distressing about the Lawrences.[52]

What of new about Childe Colin? I fear the needle of his Ambition, having no Pole, must be sought in a Haystack.

We have to go back to Camp on Monday! There are a number of Tents now standing: perhaps for us! I have not been to Hornchurch this Afternoon, but finding a well-furnished Room over a Tea Shop here vacant (of all but <u>sleeping</u> Artists), there remained; and, on the strength of Coffee, read, the whole afternoon. Yesterday aft. Briggs took me to the Romford Baths. There I proved two things: first that there is no ill effect of cold water within 20 minutes of a big meal; second that one touch of Nature's garb makes the whole world kin:— Since, the Entrance being twopence, the place was beswarmed with swart pestiferous brats: at the same time there were two Guards Officers (potential) and one gilt youth with £2000 a year of his own: from which I deduce that there are two things, and no more, which cause distinctions to disappear from between men: they are Animal <u>Sports</u> and Mortal <u>Danger</u>. And neither Religion, nor Love, nor Charity, nor Community of Interests, nor Socialism, nor Conviviality can do it at all.

Knowing well how well you are remembering me tonight, I say Goodnight, with all my love, and many prayers.

Your Wilfred x

---

[51] PN, p. 189.
[52] Shrewsbury friends. The father had a stroke about this time; the son, Keith, was delicate and in declining health.

438. To Tom Owen

Monday 10 p.m. [12 June 1916][53]   *Manchester Regiment 5th Battalion*[54]

My dear Father,

I got everything done in London in good time. I even got the strap changed at Gamages.[55]

Got a car from Milford to the Camp 2 or 3 miles off: a vast affair on the top of a hill with Pines interspersed among the Huts. The Officers' Huts form a big settlement apart. I was introduced by Briggs to the Adjutant, who shook hands and left me to my own devices.

Supper was an informal meal today. I was helped to an enormous portion of pies and things. The Band meanwhile played outside. I need Camp Tackle, but have been provided for tonight.

I know nothing of the officers, other than our Set of 'Artists', and nothing of my duties. The men seem a fairly superior crowd.

The site is delightful for a Camp; but we are all confined in it.

My fellow-traveller the Sculptor saw me in the Train at Wolverhampton and moved to my Compartment for the rest of the journey.

I shall have more time and more impressions in a few days. Tonight I feel as if I had left Home about 7 days ago!

Fondest love to all,

Your W.E.O.

[53] PN, p. 189.

[54] The battalion was stationed at Milford Camp, near Witley, 5 miles south-west of Guildford, Surrey.

[55] Gamages, founded in 1878 by A. W. Gamage, was a department store at 125–9 High Holborn, London. Its enormous range of merchandise included everything from hardware and toys to furniture and fashion. During the First World War, Gamages manufactured the Leach Trench Catapult. It closed in 1972.

439. To Susan Owen

Saturday [17 June 1916][56]

Manchester Regiment
5th Battalion
My Room

My own dear Mother,

I quite hope for your letter tomorrow morning. I am an exile here, suddenly cut off both from the present day world, and from my own past life. I feel more in a strange land than when arriving at Bordeaux! It is due to the complete newness of the country, the people, my dress, my duties, the dialect, the air, food, everything.

I am marooned on a Crag of Superiority in an ocean of Soldiers.

I have had chiefly General Duties so far, such as Supernumerary Officer to the Battalion, Company Orderly Officer (today) etc.

The generality of men are hard-handed, hard-headed miners, dogged, loutish, ugly. (But I would trust them to advance under fire and to hold their trench;) blond, coarse, ungainly, strong, 'unfatigueable', unlovely, Lancashire soldiers, Saxons to the bone.

But I don't know the individuals of my platoon.

Some are overseas men who have seen fighting.

Had to assist inspection of kit, this morning.

I see a toothbrush and a box of polish missing. I demand in a terrible voice 'Where's your Tooth-Brush?' and learn that the fellow has just returned from 'overseas'! 'Somewhere in France' is never heard here. All our draughts go to Egypt; thence to Mesopotamia. I am glad.

One of our officers at Mess has been wounded.

There is none of that Levity amongst us which prevailed in the Artists'.

The Sub. has a stiffish day's work: has to do the 'Third' Physical Training (i.e. most strenuous) at 6.15, carries pack on parade & march, and has a good deal of responsibility, writing, and ceremonial to fetter him. I had the misfortune to walk down the road to some Camp Shops when the men were 'at large': and had to take <u>millions</u> of salutes.

I have nearly got together my Camp effects, Bed, chair, washstand, etc. all necessary here.

Shall be glad of socks as soon as you can send them. Would you include my enamel <u>mug</u>, left on my dressing table.

My servant has nothing else to do but serve, so that is satisfactory.

If I am not pleased, say with my bed, I send him to change it at the shops. He is indispensable for taking my messages & reports to the Orderly Room.

Frankly, I don't like the C.O.[57] nor does anybody, except one major, his sole friend. But never fear, we shan't '<u>go out</u>' under him.

I like my Company Commander, a Lieut., and nearly all the rest.

The doctor cured my deafness, by syringing, yesterday.

Five of us, how chosen I don't know, took the Army Exam. to qualify for Service, yesterday. There is more on Monday. Briggs did not take it.

I am staying in this week-end, in my new chair, having no pocket money whatever.

Cox's[58] were 6 weeks in opening their account with the fellows in my room!

My most irksome duty is acting Taskmaster while the tired fellows dig: the most pleasant is marching home over the wild country at the head of my platoon, with a flourish of trumpets, and an everlasting roll of drums.

Your own boy Wilfred x

How I miss the delightful time you gave me at home is not for me to think of now.

---

[56] PN, p. 189.
[57] Lieutenant Colonel W. H. Ridge.
[58] Cox's was a military banking agent, established in 1758. The Charing Cross office was open all day every day during the war, cashing cheques around the clock for officers returning from the front. The branch had around 250,000 men on its books. At the height of the conflict 50,000 cheques a day were cleared. The firm's Insurance Department could arrange to insure the officer's kit; the Income Tax Department could deal with his tax returns; and the Standing Order Department would ensure that his tailor was paid regularly. Cox's also sent a cashier with a supply of money to every hospital ship as it arrived, to enable wounded officers to cash cheques.

440. To Susan Owen

Sunday Evening [18 June 1916][59]   *Manchester Regiment*
5th Battalion

Dearest Mother,

Your Thursday Parcel arrived only this morning. Many loving thanks for the Chocs. But you really mustn't send any more. I fare sumptuously every day.

This afternoon I borrowed a (very groggy) bicycle and rode through Godalming to Guildford, in perfect weather. I accomplished <u>being alone</u>, and conversed with no creature all the five hours. Guildford is an old town of great charm, with suggestions of Shrewsbury. I had tea in an old casement overlooking the High Street: a real old lattice Bay, no shams: I remained there an hour longer so pleasant was the place.

One of the dear old Houses took fire yesterday, and the ruins were still smoking.

I thought of you at tea in the Garden, scarcely able to believe I was with you seven days ago.

Alas! I <u>feel</u>, as well as appear, a different being, here & in uniform, from the lounger on divans, the reader of verse, the runner of dogs on racecourses, the midday riser…

Guildford seems to exist in another age than Buildwas & Much Wenlock.[60]

It is a rather peculiar type of country, neither mountain nor plain. There were some lovely bits of road, field, cottage, and street. As I was coming back the footpaths undulated with saluting arms.

I am Orderly Officer tomorrow, and intend to make a rumpus about untidy huts. 'My' Sergeant-Major is a young fellow, of capacity. He marches at my side, & very priceless he is.

I am perfectly well, not a bit worried or overworked: though I trod on knife-edges at the first.

Your very own W.E.O.

I don't yet want Pyjamas, but shall I think. There are rumours of moving Camp to Formby Lancs!

[59] PN, p. 189.
[60] Buildwas Abbey, Shropshire, whose ruins Owen had visited on leave, and Much Wenlock, a market town in Shropshire.

442. To Susan Owen

Sunday [2 July 1916][61]   *Manchester Regiment, 5th Battalion*

Dearest of Mothers,

I could have gone to London from Sat. Evening to Monday Morning, but <u>having nothing in particular to go for</u>, didn't. I made my usual sally into Guildford, however, and had a happy enough ramble around Thorpe's Bookshelves,[62] and the Town and the little River, where there are Punts and Canoes. It is hardly wide enough for sculls.

I think I told you about my Course at Aldershot, beginning on the 11th. It may be postponed, for another course which a party of officers & men have to go to somewhere else. I have had both parcels. No hurry about the Music. I shan't be able to play till next Sunday now! (I may get a long week-end, starting next Friday.)

I am sending the Cheque to what's-is-name, in Coventry.

I am glad you are able to realize my signature in Shrewsbury. I shall try to send one weekly.

I have now enough Socks till Winter thanks! They fit very parfitly.

I am glad you sent on D.G's appreciation. There is no doubt about the craven-heartedness of <u>both her brothers</u>: at the same time I would rather my cousin Leslie did not perish, or become as the generalty of men.[63]

(The way they have in the Army is not My way, saith the Lord of Hosts.)

I am 'commanding' numbers of wounded men, now restored. It gives me a great deal of pain to speak severely to them, as now & again need is.

I am beginning to pick out the Intelligent, and the Smart 'laads' from amongst the uncouth and ungainly. But I have no individual dealings. My Servant is a Grandfather, with medals of old wars, and sons fighting. I had the Leave Party to conduct to the Station the other day. Poor old man, my servant, had to fall out of the march! Waiting for the train I had more individual dealings, & was wondering whether it would be unwise to give my men some cigarettes, but deciding not to, when one of the 'Underage' came to me with an offering of apples!! Poor penniless school boy! But you must not think there was anything but ingenuousness. These Lancashires are extraordinarily open, honest, and incapable of strategy. I often have a Platoon completely to myself on the Moors.[64] Red-Hats gallop up to us at startling speed, or sometimes whizz up in Motors, but they never stay long, or criticise. We have been expecting the King to visit our trenches, and have worked overtime every day this week. Our anxiety begins again tomorrow! I give an extra ten minutes to shaving every morning in consequence. It is most annoying.

It seems to me many months since I left Shrewsbury. I am tempted to run up for a week-end, but don't really think of it next week. I was so happy to learn that your motor-smash came to no harm, and the imagination of what might have taken place was <u>so intolerable</u> that I dismissed it from my mind effectively. I am now given to think that I shan't go out for <u>several months</u>.

Your very own Wilfred

---

[61] PN, p. 189.

[62] T. Thorpe, Bookseller, Guildford High Street. Although the shop closed in 2003, the premises remain a Grade II listed building.

[63] This paragraph was omitted in *CL* and *SL*.

[64] The Surrey Downs.

443. To Susan Owen

[7 July 1916]   2nd. Lieut. W. E. S. Owen
                                              attached to 25 Middlesex Regt.,
                                                  Talavera Barracks, Aldershot

Dearest Mother,

I have just arrived. It is an old style Barracks, about as old as the Battle of T! And the regiment is a Regular. This with the mere name of Aldershot makes it quite like my old ideas of A R M Y. It is the finishing touch in my transformation into a Soldier.

I share a room with a Lt. from Witley who travelled with me, but is not from the Manchesters.

I returned from London [*remainder missing*]

444. To Colin Owen

11 July 1916   Aldershot

My dearest Colin,

Just a page to show you where I am living, and that I am living, still. I am here for a Course of Musketry.

It is the first time I have set foot in an English Barracks! It is an old place, used by the Regulars in the old days. But we are not so comfortable or so well messed as in our Witley Huts.

Residentially, Aldershot is a hateful little place. As a soldier I am glad to be here.

I have bought a miniature rifle and some cartridges. It won't shoot sporting shot, but is very accurate with its lead bullet at close range. Is it any use to you?

I wish we could meet at Alpenrose or something.

Write always to Mother, and some time to me.

Among so many fellows that I must know and 'care for', I don't forget the only chap I really <u>care for</u>: the Shropshire Lad.

The man sharing my room now, a stranger, is a budding High Church Parson and the most insupportable bore I have ever been quartered with!

My What-yer-call 'ums to the Jones'.[65] (don't say that).

                                                       Your own Wilfred

[65] Colin was spending the summer working for a farmer, Mr Jones, of Oakengates, near Shrewsbury.

445. To Susan Owen

Wed. [12 July 1916][66]   *Aldershot*

Dearest Mother,

Brief Note (wish my Musketry Notes were as brief) with
(1) My Love.
(2) Request that you will rout out my Musketry Note Book from the Cupboard
of the Bookcase. It is a shiny black book with purple edges.

Include a letter to save your stamps and my disappointment.

I am anxious to be told 'truthly' that your rheumatism is once again gone
from you.

We are having horrible cold wet times.

I was so annoyed with the High Church Divinity Student who shared my
Room, not because of his Divinity, but by reason of his dogmatic, pig-headed,
preachifying, self-sufficient manners and domineering tone, that I gave instructions to my servant this morning to move all my furniture into another Room,
which I discovered in the Barracks.

I am now alone and in peace.

I could tell by the shape of the man's head that he was a dogged dogmatic dog.

A Parson is a Lamb in a drawing room, but a Lion in the Vestry, said Keats.[67] In
a Bedroom and arrayed as an Officer, he is an Ass in Lion's Clothing.

(The origin of our Quarrel was his insistence on singing Rag-Times, and my
commanding him to shut his mouth.)

Always your Wilfred

---

[66] PN, p. 189.
[67] John Keats to George and Georgiana Keats, 19 February 1819 (*Letters* II, p. 63).

447. To Susan Owen

[24 July 1916][68]   *Manchester Regiment, 5th Battalion*

My dearest Mother,

Monday evening, so this should get to you by Wed. I had a shock on arriving.
Three of 'the Artists' are now in France ! ! ! But Briggs is left in Aldershot, and my
happening to be there was the reason, I suppose, that I was not sent. I think it is
necessary to tell you this, in case you should be too surprised if I went next week.
Mind, I haven't the slightest intimation, but this disappearance of Foster,[69] Jubb[70]
and Crampton[71] is a warning.

At present I parade as Company Commander of B Company, a Captain's job! I
am also in tonight's orders as Fire Officer of the Battalion. Fortunately two fires

which raged in the scrub last night were just too soon to bother me. I am also detailed for some Lectures on Gas, in which certain officers are initiated into many secrets. I <u>may</u>, thus, become Gas Officer.

I can't promise anything about next week-end.

In the train from Aldershot, (I did <u>not</u> taxi) I met Walthew[72] the man from my Room who has just married. His wife insisted that I should go to supper with them in their cottage, near the Camp. The mad thing doted over me all evening. I shall never go there again. Poor Walthew!

I might have taken a later train from Reading, for no one looked for me till Sunday Morning, when I led my Company to Church Parade [*remainder missing*]

[68] PN, p. 189.
[69] Lieutenant W. A. Foster, Manchester Regiment.
[70] Lieutenant Norris Jubb, Manchester Regiment.
[71] Second Lieutenant Hubert Crampton, MC, Manchester Regiment.
[72] Name originally omitted in CL and SL.

449. To Susan Owen

[*Early August 1916*]   *Manchester Regiment, 5th Battalion*

Dearest Mother,

Most desperating! No help! <u>Must</u> go and fire a Course near Aldershot! There are a number of men, N.C.O's and two Officers, of whom I am the Senior. We have to march there, a performance which I grow weak to think of. But it will be some solace to know that the Halts and Halting Places are of my own sweet choice.

166 men are going on Draft tomorrow, but the two conducting officers are coming back. There will be scarcely any men left to us!

I am now as well up in <u>Gas</u> Warfare as can be. It is some satisfaction to feel knowing in these matters, because I am sure it will be used more and more.

Gregg[73] and I have devised a slight improvement in the P.H. Helmet,[74] but it is not worth noising abroad since the Helmet is really out of date now, displaced by—But, here I am beginning to 'leak information', (when I have to read daily a solemn W.O. Letter, saying that no talk of the War is ever to be indulged in, even in private letters and so on!)

I had command of a Party firing on the Range with Gas Helmets on. One old blitherer let his bullet off by accident, but as it hit no one, I was not interested to follow its course.

We had a Concert for the men yesterday, and the gay ladies could not be got out of our Mess Room till 12.30 a.m! And we set out on our march every morning at 7.

We had a fearful field-day yesterday, too. Luckily we 'attacked' a Lake, where there was bathing afterwards. I found a sandy cove for myself, inhabited only by a solitary, mysterious kind of boy. It turned out he was Portuguese, a noble, whose father is in the suite of the exiled King.[75]

There was something in our Orders about a bicycle stolen from a P.O. I did not heed it, but perhaps it was Leslie's!

I search your envelopes in vain for ⟨ W.O. ⟩ s![76]

I have long ceased to look for Colin's letter, tho' certain smudges on the envelope aroused my suspicions of his handwriting.

Do be careful to 'avoid unnecessary movement' as the military phrase goes.

The adjutant encourages me to believe in Long Leave next Fortnight.

I don't know my address, but it won't be Talavera.

Your lovingest Wilfred

[73] Second Lieutenant Reginald Arthur Gregg, Manchester Regiment. DH has shown how this is not the same R. Gregg Owen reports as having died of wounds in Letter 667 (WOANB, p. 516, n. 17).
[74] An anti-gas helmet, taking its initials from the phosgene and hexamine with which it was impregnated. When goggles were later incorporated, it was known as the PHG helmet.
[75] Manuel II (1889–1932), ex-King of Portugal, succeeded to the throne 1908, fled his country at the Revolution (1910), and took refuge in England, settling in Twickenham.
[76] Owen had asked SO for initial-tapes.

452. To Susan Owen

Sat. Night [12 August 1916][77]   *Mytchett Musketry Camp*

Dearest of Mothers,

Just had your Letter which came, as you designed, tonight. It came refreshingly, comparable to the cool rain that broke over this desert this evening.

I have just been to Aldershot for my bicycle only to find it was waiting up here, 200 yds. from Camp.

For having displeased the Brigade Musketry Officer, all officers were confined to Camp till 6 this evening. Chief cause of our Strafing: bad Marking behind the Butts. But I am not concerned with marking.

I am well punished, because I gave my men 2 hours extra drill this morning; not in punishment, but because they have been detailed for Guard tonight, and most have never fixed Bayonets in their life.

My own shooting, alas, is the least of my cares. But it is a bit of a worry, because, in duty bound, one strafes the men for bad shooting, and is never sure of not doing worse than the worst of them. They keep a relentless watch on my Target. I have so far got a Pass every day, but I only do well in Rapid! I can get off

5 rounds in 30 secs. scoring 3 bulls and 2 inners, <u>17 marks out of 20</u>. If allowed more time I do less well. It is an interesting point of my psychological 'erraticness'.

There is no chance of next week-end. Excellent news of dear old W.H.O.[78] No more now but this x.

W.E.O.

[77] PN, p. 189.

[78] HO (he was christened William Harold Owen) had been selected to train as a pilot. See letter 488.

453. To Susan Owen

Tuesday [*15 August 1916*][79]   [*Mytchett Musketry Camp*]

Dearest My Mother,

Just a scrap to thank for your letter just arrived tonight. I was so busy that I scrawled notes over the envelope before ever I opened it! This Napoleonic Work will stop on Sat. Meanwhile I have just scraped enough points to be a 1st Class Shot.

Most of the <u>men</u> are 2nd Class and more are 3rd.

But then 9 of them have defective eyesight.

We were caught in Monsoonal Rains this afternoon, and my poor troops were wet to the bone. (But I had my Trench Coat.) It was the first time I had seen these men <u>really</u> cheerful. British troops are beyond my understanding. On a bright warm day they are as dull and dogged as November.

There is a Rumour[80] that <u>all</u> the Manchesters move to Newhaven on the 28th.

Yours ever W.E.O. x

[79] PN, p. 189.
[80] Without substance.

454. To Susan Owen

Monday Evening 9 p.m [*21 August 1916*][81]   [*Manchester Regiment, 5th Battalion*]

My own sweet Mother,

What an age since we were at supper yesterday!

At Tamworth there was an hour to wait on the miserable little Station, so I wandered into the old Town to try and look up my old friend Lord Marmion.[82] There was a low, glamorous Moon and to see any strange place by a vague moon, for an hour, is better than a week's stay there; and I was already tuned up to an emotion not pitched in keys of moon or castles....

Sure enough I found Tamworth Castle, and was informed by the policeman that Lord Marmion had lorded it there. I was an event of much perplexity to the Bobby, and he shadowed my rubber heels all the way back to the station.

I was conscious during all this venture of a very peculiar odour following me and was so sure I had never smelled it before that I began to seek about for some local phenomena.

But it was only that Quinine uncorking itself in my pocket!

We were <u>an hour</u> late at Euston, so I was a bitter mixture of sleep, quinine, and panic.

There were no taxis.

At last I held up a Growler[83] and pushed on for Waterloo.

The dawn broke as I crossed the Bridge, and the Dome, and the East End showed so purply against the orange infinite EAST that in my worship there was no more care of trains, adjutants, or wars.

Thus I caught that train by 1½ mins. From Milford, I pushed on to the Camp by motor miraculously waiting at the station; and had plenty of time for a second breakfast and shave.

I was on Bomb Throwing with real live Mills Grenades.

I went to sleep in a safe spot when I had thrown my own; but the noise was too frightful to go on. After lunch I fell asleep; and remained so long after the rest had fallen in! But none noticed me! Arriving back in Camp I was called upon suddenly to lecture on Discipline. I was now feeling 'rotten'; but I thought obedience in this case would make a good opening verse for the Lecture; and so it did.

I am Orderly Officer tomorrow, which means work up to midnight.

Father please excuse. I had plenty to breakfast on in the train, and am sorry I panicked about the drinks.

As you may know, there was a General Mobilization on Sunday, and a longer leave would have been cut short in any case! Their Sunday was spoilt here: they were in perfect readiness to march off: officers snatched rifles for themselves, and packed their pockets with Rations. All for the N. Sea Bubble.[84]

No more now!

Your Wilfred

---

[81] PN, p. 189.

[82] 'They hailed him Lord of Fontenaye, / Of Lutterward and Scrivelbaye, / Of Tamworth tower and town.' Sir Walter Scott, *Marmion*, Canto I, ll. 157–9.
Owen may have been recalling a visit to Flodden with Blanche Bulman in the summer of 1912. See Letter 148.

[83] Slang term for a horse-drawn, four-wheeled cab.

[84] On Saturday, 9 August, the Grand Fleet, concentrated near Long Forties in the North Sea with the battlecruiser fleet 30 miles ahead, was attacked by U-boats. Zeppelins were sighted, as well as the German High Seas Fleet. HMS *Nottingham* and HMS *Falmouth* were sunk by torpedoes.

455. To Colin Owen

23 August 1916   *Manchester Regiment, 5th Battalion*

Dearest Colin,

I was frightfully disappointed to miss you: and I spent all the time scheming to get you over. Somehow my plans found no favour with Father or Mother.

There is none else can thwart me.

I noted all you said in your last letter and remember those words before the best things I have read.

There are changes happening daily, but I remain. Briggs went this morning to be attached to another Regiment; no choice of his.

One or two are trying for the R. Flying Corps. Shall I? I think so.

Of the last Draught that went out, men I had helped to train, some are already fallen. Your tender age is a thing to be valued and gloried in, more than many wounds.

Not only because it puts you among the Elders and the gods, high witnesses of the general slaughter, being one of those for whom every soldier fights, if he knew it; your Youth is to be prized not because your blood will not be drained, but because it <u>is</u> blood; and Time dare not yet mix into it his abominable physic.

Only, all bright mettle rusts in the open air.

Don't rust rustically.

Love Nature more than the Country, and know that to be natural is not to be countrified.

False men grow in the country more commonly than in the Town, for they are often turnips in disguise.

Your farmering is not without its dangers.

For me, Germans, Turks, and mysterious spiritual devils, For Harold, Torpedoes and dark deeds in evil ports, For You, the hob-nobbing with cattle and carrots, and the deep sleep after over-labour.

Meanwhile, however, get the highest profit of happiness out of your present job.

Let your hands be gloved with the dust of earth, and your neck scarved with the brown scarf of sunshine.[85]

This is not poetry which I write, but the Sun is, and the earth may be.

Write very soon.

Look to me for counsel in all affairs of thought and learning; but look to your early self for a prototype of sweetness and good living.

This is no sermon, but a substitute.

If you should straitway go and be baptised in your Bethel or Ebeneezer Place,[86] I would never wash my beard more.

Cheery-ho!

Your own, Wilfred

[85] The earlier of two drafts of 'Disabled' gives a stanza, later cancelled, between the present stanzas 2 and 3: 'Ah! He was handsome when he used to stand / Each evening on the curb or by the quays. / His old soft cap slung half-way down his ear; / Proud of his neck, scarfed with a sunburn band, / And of his curl, and all his reckless gear, / Down to the gloves of sun-brown on his hand.' *CPF*, p. 353.
[86] Jones the farmer was a strict Baptist.

456. To Susan Owen

Sunday 27 August [1916]   *Manchester Regiment, 5th Battalion*

My dearest Mother,

Your letter came on Sat. Night. We do have a Sunday Post.

You need not be anxious about Final Leave coming yet.

The C.O. himself told me on Thursday that he was putting me down for the New Battalion, so that I am not being kicked out of the Manchesters, whatever happens. The C.O. appears to have found my work—or my person—not too offensive to him.

There is only one other of the Artist Batch now left, and he has not been told he is to remain on the New Staff. Briggs awoke one morning and found himself gone. He is attached to some Lancashire Regt. and 'goes out' in a month's time.

I was on the point of sending in an application for the R. Flying Corps, when, at tea, the C.O. spoke to me about being kept on.

I said 'I thank you, sir', being an Englishman.

But I still have a big idea of turning to Flight.

It is not quite a determination, or I might say it would certainly come about.

There are ways and means, and I will work them, if I decide to.

On Tuesday I am going up to London, on Dental Leave, in order to see a high official at the War Office. Nothing succeeds in Aerial Matters without some boldness. So I am starting well.

I have not sent in my application for Transfer, as, once I did so, I should commit myself to the C.O's eternal displeasure.

Now what do you think about it?

Flying is the only active profession I could ever continue with enthusiasm after the War.

Once a certified pilot, the pay is £350. The Training lasts three months.

By Hermes, I will fly. Though I have sat alone, twittering, like even as it were a sparrow upon the housetop, I will yet swoop over Wrekin with the strength of a thousand Eagles, and all you shall see me light upon the Racecourse, and marvelling behold the pinion of Hermes, who is called Mercury, upon my cap.

Then I will publish my ode on the Swift.[87]

If I fall, I shall fall mightily. I shall be with Perseus and Icarus, whom I loved; and not with Fritz, whom I did not hate. To battle with the Super-Zeppelin, when he comes, this would be chivalry more than Arthur dreamed of.

Zeppelin, the giant dragon, the child-slayer, I would happily die in any adventure against him. . . .

But I am terrified of Fritz, the hideous, whom I do not hate.

Fondest wishes for a fine old Aberystwithian Holiday.

Your own Wilfred x

The 5th. won most points of all the Regiments; and so gains the Cup, in Saturday's Sports.

---

[87] *CPF*, pp. 92–4.

457. To Susan Owen

Friday [Early September 1916]   *Witley*

Dearest Mother,

I feel myself to be in a Passage when to think much about you in your merry days at the mouth of Ystwith would be more than I could cope with. I am harassed with events.

I went to London on Tues. saw the Authorities and had my name put down with certain particulars. I was told by the Major that I had every chance, but the regular Transfer Papers (almost as exciting as those sold at 4 a penny) must go through my Division. My C.O's signature is necessary. The Adjutant said he would sign it on Thursday. At tea the C.O. severely refused, on the ground that I could not be spared from the Regiment. And indeed he had put me down on the Posted Staff, a favour shared by none of the Artists and only half of the old officers. I am on the Musketry Company, so my 'D' did it, and your earnest behests are now fulfilled. I am even as your 'Type', Fred Oliver.

On the strength of my good success at the R.F.C. H.Q. I had that old vicious tooth drawn by my kind dentist; saving half a guinea.

At tea today I was alone with the C.O. and succeeded in making him promise to sign my application for Transfer, and that without losing his favour ! ! He was frightfully decent about it. I was tickled at the idea that you & Father required time to consider: that it came as too great a surprise to be grasped. But the whole thing in modern public (I won't say Business) life is <u>instant</u> adaptation to the Fittest Environment. I have not gone about this affair without a great deal of strain of mind, & the more so that everything in the Battalion is upside down. The 6 & 7 Manch: are amalgamated with us today. You can't imagine what a panic it causes. But for one thing let us be proud. The old Fifth keeps its name, & is the nucleus of the whole new Battalion. Alas some of my men, whom I know, and who know me are sent to another Regt. to be drafted to France immediately. It is most disheartening. The Rumpus will soon settle down. Leave should then be more frequent.

G. Thomas sent me this tonight.[88]

Leslie is likely to get a Sedentary Flying Commission.

Goodbye, Darling Mother. Have a good time.

Your very own Wilfred x

---

[88] Probably the copy of *The Voice of Peace: Poems* by Gilbert Thomas (Chapman & Hall, 1914) that survives among Owen's books. It is inscribed 'W. E. S. Owen, with all good wishes from Gilbert Thomas'.

459. To Susan Owen

Wednesday [13 September 1916][89]   *Witley*

Dearest Mother,

News! The Battalion moves North next week:—the Advance Party on the 19th, the Main Body on the 20th. It is supposed that the place is near Conway N. Wales. What luck for us.

Harold came over yesterday afternoon in response to my telegram. He came out with me on my Afternoon Work, and we had a little supper in Guildford. He stayed the night in my Hut, where I am now writing at present. He looked many tints and pounds healthier & stronger than last Winter: and we had a jolly time.[90] If he were sure to be in London this week I would go to him on Friday, but expect Leslie and Winchester will have it! Why, from Conway I can come over on Sunday Afternoons!

I find that by today's orders I am detailed for a Sniper Course at Aldershot on the 19th. I shall probably have to go, and move North independently of all the Rumpus.

This will be quite decent and in order, especially if I travel via Shrewsbury!

I hope my last Note was forwarded from Wales.

I believe there lies in my Drawers a medium-thickness vest. Could you send it <u>at once</u> here?

Of course I tell you all I know as it leaks out. I only heard this bit of news quarter of an hour ago.

Your own Wilfred

Please include in Parcel Keats's *Letters*. (Vol. IV & V) (in Book<u>case</u>)

<hr/>

[89] PN, p. 189.

[90] Their meeting is described in *JFO* III, pp. 151–8. HO recalled, 'What a memorable afternoon that was for me. Here I was with a different Wilfred, or was it me that was different? We neither of us I think really knew' (p. 152).

466. To Susan Owen

[Early November 1916]   *Queen's Hotel, Southport*

Dearest Mother,

I <u>shall</u> be going to Fleetwood, on Sunday at 10 o'clock as O.C. Firing Party. I am glad to see a bit more England. I am still trying to understand the English. We shall be in easy reach of Blackpool, but I don't expect to find much time for that.

Now I most urgently want good Field Glasses—part of my Equipment. <u>Do</u> let me have the Zeiss[91] (for this fortnight only.) I shall first need it on Monday, but don't think you had better send it here—but you could quite safely as a Registered Parcel to Fleetwood Post Office.

Please do!

Or could Father come over to Fleetwood with it?

I am, compared with my 'situation' this time last year <u>very</u> comfortable here. I think I was inoculated about now? [*three lines inked out*]

Your lovingest W.E.O.

<hr/>

[91] A pair of Zeiss field glasses was lying unclaimed in the lost property office at Shrewsbury Station. Against his better judgement, Tom Owen agreed to lend them to Wilfred for use on the firing range at Fleetwood, arranging to telegraph for their return if the owner turned up. The owner did appear, and Owen returned the glasses (see Letter 469); but Tom Owen had to extricate himself from what might have been a serious predicament. The field glasses case was damaged in transit (see Letter 473), and Tom Owen had to pay for repairs.

467. To Susan Owen

Sunday [5 November 1916][92]   *111 Bold Street, Fleetwood*

Dearest my Mother,

My good comrade is using my pen, so I profit by the moment of silence to pencil my Address, and my self-congratulations on being in so snug a Lodging.

We are two in these 'Apartments' as the vulgar call them. I should have chosen Rickard[93] before all the Battalion as it now is. But, then, I am in a Position to choose. I am O-in-C. of the Brigade Firing Point ! ! Long ago, I left the Platoon for the Company, then the Company for the Battalion, and now if you please the Battalion for the Brigade ! ! ! I shall at the Firing Point be responsible for the discipline of the 5th Manchesters, 8th Man: and all the various Lancashire Fusiliers and their officers. I have handed over the command of our own party of 120 to Rickard. I'm far too important for these petty administrations ! !

But it was interesting to see to their billeting when we arrived. We made the journey without worse mishap than the loss of our oil, which was certainly pinched by another Regiment.

I must have Field Glasses, (was told so by the Staff Officer at our Meeting this afternoon.) So I hope I shall find von Zeiss at the P.O. tomorrow. Anyhow I have done my best to persuade you on what dazzling an eminence they shall be worn.

Our own Major Eaton[94] (whom you saw) is in supreme command. He is an imposing warrior, and things will go well under him. He has promised £5. (from our Funds) to be distributed to Marksmen.

Has the chair arrived? Are you any better?

I like this Digs far better than the Queen's Hotel life.

It is the first time I ever shared rooms, in the Keats–Brown manner.[95] I confess Rickard is not kin spiritually or literarily, but actually and personally and militarily we agree famously. He has more than once been mistaken for me.

I like Fleetwood.

Have finished tonight a fine novel by Wells:[96] which I must shake off before tomorrow. I shall go and inspect the men's billets to see if they are comfortable now.

Goodnight, dearest Mother! W.E.O. x

---

[92] PN, p. 189.
[93] Second Lieutenant A. R. Rickard, 5th Manchesters.
[94] Major T. R. Eaton, 7th Manchesters, later joined the 2nd/5th in France.
[95] Charles Brown, friend of Keats. 'With Dilke and Brown I am quite thick—with Brown indeed I am going to domesticate—that is, we shall keep house together—I shall have the front parlour and he the back one...'; John Keats to George and Georgian Keats, 16 December 1818 (*Letters* ii, pp. 4–5).
[96] Herbert George (H. G.) Wells (1866–1946). Owen met him on several occasions in 1917 and 1918. See Letters 559 and 565.

468. To Susan Owen

Picture postcard: Fleetwood, St. Peter's Church[97]

[*Postmark 13 November 1916*]   [*Postmark Fleetwood*]

To this Church I took my little Family today. Lofty service, elevated singing &, the complement, a flat sermon. Have stayed in all day. H. G. Wells has a book (which you shall soon read) with an Oliver twist about it,[98] but which for me knocks *Oliver Twist* back to workhouse readers. None of the best news from you. But it is good news of Alpenrose! Decidedly!

W.E.O.

Yes, tell Meols.

---

[97] An advertising sign attached to a passing tram also visible in the picture declares: 'ASK FOR SLATTERY'S IRISH BACON', which Owen annotates with the words 'Local Colour!'.

[98] Possibly H. G. Wells's *The Passionate Friends* (Macmillan & Co., 1913). See Letter 512, n. 2.

469. To Tom Owen

Picture postcard of Fleetwood, the promenade and ferry

[*Postmark 14 November 1916*]   [*Postmark Fleetwood*]

I return the Parcel 3 as it came. Certain, is it? What a blow! I had the telegram on the Range this afternoon. The only consolations are the good scoring of the men, and this sentence which Major Eaton showed me from a letter from the General: 'Owen should be of great assistance to you.' Didn't know he suspected my existence!

W.E.O.

470. To Susan Owen

Picture postcard of Fleetwood, Pharos Street, the lighthouse in the background. A child is posed in the foreground to give the impression that she carries the lighthouse on her shoulders. The photograph is superscribed:

'Pharoh's Street. No doubt the curate will know the address. (Pharos is the Greek for lighthouse.) Clever little girl to carry it on her shoulder. Doesn't her mother look pleased! Have just come from a free show at the local Theatre. It was free and easy. Some of my men performed. They were having a good time. Dance last night! I think we 5th Man. are winning, but the weather's putrid.'

Tues. [*Postmark 15 November 1916*]   [*Postmark Fleetwood*]

Please do send your Glasses[99] if you will. Thanks for the letter this morning. Is it an Officer at Kimmel Park, who claims. Are you quite sure it is genuine, & that no one has wind of the thing? Do not send parcel later than Thurs. Tho' I may have to stay another Fortnight.

Your W.E.O.

---

[99] Susan Owen's opera glasses.

471. To Susan Owen

Wednesday [22 November 1916][100]   *111 Bold Street, Fleetwood*

Page 1 (evidently enough)
My own dear Mother,

It must be more than the limit of a week since I wrote. The time begins to speed now that I am used to the Place, and engrossed in my work. I have a good deal of writing in the evenings. Only twice I have been to Blackpool. The first, I was utterly bored, having nothing to do. The second, (yesterday) I scuttled about so fast that I nearly got warm. It has been icily cold here as well as with you. The sea had not a chance of modifying influence. The east wind had the influenza. It was a draught blowing straight from continental Germany.

As I was saying I went to Blackpool with a business; to find a Trench Coat for your entreaties helped me to decide. I stand glued to one spot for just 6 hours. Luckily my attention is also glued, or I should gnaw my head off. I can of course always gnaw my lunch; and no man smiles when I shout Sheesh Fire !! ! and score a bull with explosive crumbs. Major Eaton and I tried a shot ourselves this morning, each pretty nervous of the other. We both scored dead central Bulls with five shots in a 4 in. group! ! (a 12 in. group would Pass). So if we didn't <u>wink at each other</u> exactly, we certainly smiled in our innards.

Whittaker[101] turned up to see us this morning. I was very glad to see him. He says the Egyptian Draft is washed out. Did I tell you my name was down as a Candidate? There is a rumour of <u>India for the whole Brigade</u>. Whittaker has been offered a (real) Staff Job at Altcar School of Instruction. Before I left, several wounded but fit officers went on a Course to Altcar, and I thought they might have returned to take my old place. But it hasn't happened yet. Meanwhile I am snug enough at Fleetwood, (barring the day-time!) Major Eaton is awfully decent to me. The cooking improves with encouragement. I have a practically perfect orderly, and another willing body-servant on the Range. Best of all I have your letters unfailingly, and feel a sort of desperate joy in delaying answers without being scolded. I feel sick of any sort of prose. On the other hand, I have suddenly seen what I wanted to do with that War Ballad,[102] and indeed finished it on Sunday to my content. You shall have it in our next. I haven't seen 'L'Amour' in print. I don't like Print, now that I see what a dead letter it is to all these living men about me. You shall rather send my stuff to Helen Bowick, for Recitation. They would not have it in Y.M. They'd find it blasphemous, I not doubt. I want to see Leslie's last, but can't get 'Young Men' here. Young men nowadays don't exist, quite right too. We are youths, lads, fellows, pals, chaps, comrades, boys, blokes if you will, but not your Young Men.

I have quite a veneration for Charles Chaplin by the way. Made me laugh almost as much as H. G. Wells. I have not read the books you mention.

Am so glad you quite like the Chair.

If I had missed the S. of France by having a chill I would wear Jaeger's sack-cloth ever after. I did indeed venture to put on a rough vest, 6 ins. thick which I rashly bought in Guildford. (Rashly indeed.) I was quite unnerved by it. It seemed to draw the blood to the head.

I am perfectly well, as you have had ample assurance from the post-man's back lately.

Your veriest own lovingest Wilfred x

I do not enquire after you, like a next door neighbour. Nor after our sick neighbours for they are not of my generation, even as Keith Lawrence[103] is not.

---

[100] PN, p. 189.
[101] Major L. A. Whittaker, MC, Manchester Regiment.
[102] Possibly 'To a Comrade in Flanders' (CPF, p. 148), dated September 1916. 'L'Amour' by LG was printed in The Red Triangle, the YMCA magazine, and subsequently in E. Leslie Gunston, The Nymph and Other Poems (A.H. Stockwell, 1917).
[103] See Letter 433.

472. To Mary Owen

[Late November 1916]   111 Bold St, Fleetwood

Dearest Mary,

I have seen in Southport a jolly silver Teapot & Sugar Basin & Cream Jug. For the Silver-Wedding Present, must be a Silver Wedding-Present.[104] Don't you think this sort of thing would be the best? Harold is halving the moderate cost with me, if you think it's a good idea. You shall provide the Indigo or Prussian Blue Ribbon which must be arranged for to give its full éclat. (Not as an indication that the teapot is for Temperance use only)[105]

Write soon, dear, letting me also know how you & Mother are.

Your lovingest Brother Wilfred

---

[104] The Owen family still has the teapot. According to HO, the sugar basin and cream jug could not be afforded.
[105] A blue ribbon was a symbol of the Temperance Movement, sometimes referred to as the 'Blue Ribbon Fellowship' or the 'Blue Ribbon Army'.

473. To Susan Owen

Monday [11 December 1916][106]   *Queen's Hotel, Southport*

We all came down on Sunday Morning. I am back at the Queen's in a rather poor little room at the top.

I am stuck on the new Musketry Party, firing at Crossens, where we march out every morning, about 3 miles, starting at 7.15. It is a bitter change from the good times at Fleetwood. Major Eaton is not our Commandant, but Major Melville,[107] a snotty, acid, scot, impatient, irritated wretch. Nothing will run smoothly while his voice files the air. He is Melville's Scotch Whiskey.

On Sunday I was very miserable for some reason, but I went round to Averys[108] to tea: and amused myself not badly with their pianola. It is an amusing toy, but not worth a street fiddle for melody.

Mrs. Avery is the type of woman who interests herself in the amatory welfare of her young friends. She has <u>by her own suggestion entirely</u>, arranged a meeting with two girls on Thursday.

All Leave except under exceptional circumstances is stopped by the Brigade until further notice. It may mean a move of the Brigade .... abroad ? ?

There is also a rumour of 7 days work a week. Sickening!

Really, you might, some of you come up here for a week-end. Considering how little you are deterred by travelling expenses, the one nuisance with most People, I can't understand why you don't. Stay at the Averys', hospitable folk! 'Sno good, <u>I can't come.</u>

I have Pharyngitis again to a ticklish extent, tho' my throat is not in any way painful or 'swollen'. I am to have it cauterised.

I am sad these days for some reason.

Am I getting fed up with England?

I was today!

Saw Col. Ridge yesterday. He was very nice, and is going to mention the R.F.C. Transfer to the Brigadier.

I knew Father would strafe me about the mutilated Case. I can get a <u>new</u> Revolver at that Rogue's price, in my own Armoury.

Dearest loves to all, Your W.E.O. x x

---

[106] PN, p. 189.

[107] Major M. G. D. Melville, MC, became Commanding Officer of the 2nd/5th Manchesters on 4 November 1917.

[108] Friends of Susan Owen who lived locally.

474. To Susan Owen

[*29 December 1916*]   *Hotel Metropole, Folkestone*

Just put up here. Train was wickedly late. I travelled[109] in Guard's van. Sitting in the Guard's Nook I narrowly escaped being smashed by a passing Goods' train. Some loose timber hit the coach just above my head.

It awoke me with a big shock. This caused our train to stop a long while: I believe in order to telephone about the dangerous goods' train.

I got the Hat Cover and spent half-an-hour finding a suitable pen at Waverley House.

I went an hour early to Charing Cross, in case Harold should be there. He came quarter of an hour before we started, and made the journey as far as London Bridge.

It was a fine thing to see him. He is translated utterly from the being he was five years ago.

'Tis a glorious fellow.

At Folkestone here I met a Canadian Doctor who seems to be the only other on the train reporting tomorrow. He took me to the best Hotel, where we are sharing a magnificent room.

There is a Boat at 11.30 a.m. More I know not.

Your W.E.O.

---

[109] After embarkation leave.

4
The Somme and Craiglockhart
1917

475. To Susan Owen

1 January 1917 [*France*]

My own dearest Mother,

1.30 p.m. I have just received Orders to take the train at Étaples, to join the 2nd Manchesters. This is a Regular Regiment, so I have come off mighty well. The original Party from the 5th has in the last 2 days got completely dissolved, and as far as I know I am the only one for this Regt. It is a huge satisfaction to be going among well-trained troops and genuine 'real-old' Officers.

I don't pretend it was more than hazard that detailed me to this Battalion; but it is all very mysterious.

I got my Baggage before bed-time.

I have not alas! had any letter from you or anyone.

I <u>think</u> 1/2nd Manchester should find me. But don't send any goods yet.

This is a sort of Hotel Camp where none stay more than 2 or 3 days! I have not been uncomfortable so far, with a tent to myself, and with a diligent Orderly.

This morning I was hit! We were bombing and a fragment from somewhere hit my thumb knuckle. I coaxed out 1 drop of blood. Alas! no more!!

There is a fine heroic feeling about being in France, and I am in perfect spirits. A tinge of excitement is about me, but excitement is always necessary to my happiness.

I don't think it is the real front I'm going to.

If on my Field Post Card I cross out 'I am being sent down to the Base' with a double line ══════════ than I shall actually be at the Front.

Can't believe it.

Nor must you.

Now I must pack.

Your own Wilfred xx

476. To Susan Owen

4 January 1917   *Address. 2nd Manchester Regt B.E.F.*

My own dear Mother,

I have joined the Regiment, who are just at the end of six weeks' rest.[1] I will not describe the awful vicissitudes of the journey here. I arrived at Folkestone, and put up at the best hotel. It was a place of luxury—inconceivable now— carpets as deep as the mud here—golden flunkeys; pages who must have been melted into their clothes, and expanded since; even the porters had clean hands. Even the dogs that licked up the crumbs had clean teeth.

Since I set foot on Calais quays I have not had dry feet.

No one knew anything about us on this side, and we might have taken weeks to get here, and <u>must</u> have, but for fighting our way here.

I spent something like a pound in getting my baggage carried from trains to trains.

At the Base, as I said, it was not so bad. We were in the camp of Sir Percy Cunynghame,[2] who had bagged for his Mess the Duke of Connaught's chef.

After those two days, we were let down, gently, into the real thing, Mud.

It has penetrated now into that Sanctuary my sleeping bag, and that holy of holies my pyjamas. For I sleep on a stone floor and the servant squashed mud on all my belongings; I suppose by way of baptism. We are 3 officers in this 'Room', the rest of the house is occupied by servants and the band; the roughest set of knaves I have ever been herded with. Even now their vile language is shaking the flimsy door between the rooms.

I chose a servant for myself yesterday, not for his profile, nor yet his clean hands, but for his excellence in bayonet work. For the servant [is] always at the side of his officer in the charge and is therefore worth a dozen nurses. Alas, he of the Bayonet is in the Bombing Section, and it is against Regulations to employ such as a servant. I makeshift with another.

Everything is makeshift. The English seem to have fallen into the French unhappy-go-lucky non-system. There are scarcely any houses here. The men lie in Barns.

Our Mess Room is also an Ante and Orderly Room. We eat & drink out of old tins, some of which show traces of ancient enamel. We are never dry, and never 'off duty'.

On all the officers' faces there is a harassed look that I have never seen before, and which in England, never will be seen—out of jails. The men are just as Bairn[s]father[3] has them—expressionless lumps.

We feel the weight of them hanging on us. I have found not a few of the old Fleetwood Musketry party here. They seemed glad to see me, as far as the set dog- gedness of their features would admit.

I censored hundreds of letters yesterday, and the hope of peace was in every one. The *Daily Mail*[4] map which appeared about Jan 2 will be of extreme interest to you.

We were stranded in a certain town one night and I saved the party of us by collaring an Orderly in the streets and making him take us to a Sergeants Mess. We were famishing, and a mug of beer did me more good than any meal I ever munched. The place was like a bit of Blighty, all hung with English Greetings and Mistletoe.[5]

As I could I collected accoutrement, some here, some there, and almost am complete: Steel Helmets, & Gas; improved Box Respirator, and cetera.

The badge of the Regt. is some red tabs on the shoulder thus ◊ I scarcely know any of the officers. The senior are old regulars. The younger are, several, Artists! In my room is an Artist of the same school as I passed. He is also a fine water-colour sketcher. I may <u>have</u> time to write again tomorrow. I have not of course had anything from you.

I am perfectly well and strong, but unthinkably dirty and squalid.

I scarcely dare to wash.

Pass on as much of this happy news as may interest people.

The favourite song of the men is

> The Roses round the door
> Makes me love Mother more.'[6]

They sing this everlastingly.

I don't disagree.

Your very own W.E.O. x

---

[1] The 2nd Manchesters were at Halloy, near Beaumont Hamel, where they had been resting for six weeks after severe fighting. In the meantime drafts or reinforcements of 527 officers and men had joined, in readiness for an assault on the German salient between the Scarpe and the Ancre Rivers by the British Third and Fifth Armies.

[2] Lieutenant Colonel Sir Percy Cunynghame (1867–1941).

[3] (Charles) Bruce Bairnsfather (1887–1959), artist and journalist, whose war cartoons featuring 'Old Bill' Busby with his walrus moustache were published in *The Bystander* and in eight separate collections, including *Fragments from France* (which sold more than 250,000 copies in 1916 alone), *The Better 'Ole, Bullets and Billets,* and *From Mud to Mufti.*

[4] The map showed the St Quentin front, the British line on the Somme, extending from Gommecourt to Beaumont Hamel to Grandcourt to Le Transloy.

[5] DH identified 'Mistletoe' as a code word ('Concealed Messages in Wilfred Owen's Trench Letters', *Notes and Queries,* Vol. 27, No. 6, December 1980). Susan Owen wrote to Edmund Blunden that she agreed with her son that, after 'Mistletoe' occurred in his letters, she was to take the second letter of each line and so read the name of the place from which he was writing, since it was forbidden for soldiers to include their whereabouts in letters home. It is only possible to make out the location by viewing the manuscripts because line breaks in published versions are different. Thus, in this letter the line breaks in the manuscript are: 'As I could I collected

accoutrement, / some here, some there, and almost / am complete: Steel Helmets, & Gas; / improved Box Respirator, and / cetera.' SOMME.

⁶ From 'Just Try to Picture Me Back Home in Tennessee', 1915, words by W. M. Jerome, music by Walter Donaldson.

477. To Susan Owen

Sunday, 7 January 1917   *[2nd Manchester Regt., B.E.F.]*

My dear dear Mother,

It is afternoon. We had an Inspection to make from 9 to 12 this morning. I have wandered into a village cafe where they gave me writing paper. We made a redoubtable March yesterday from the last Camp to this.⁷ The awful state of the roads and the enormous weight carried, was too much for scores of men. Officers also carried full packs, but I had a horse part of the way.

It was beginning to freeze through the rain when we arrived at our tents. We were at the mercy of the cold, and, being in health, I never suffered so terribly as yesterday afternoon. I am really quite well, but have sensations kindred to being seriously ill.

As I was making my damp bed, I heard the Guns for the first time. It was a sound not without a certain sublimity. They woke me again at 4 o'clock.

We are two in a tent. I am with the Lewis Gun Officer. We begged stretchers from the doctor to sleep on. Our servant brings our food to us in our tents. This would not be so bad but for lack of water, and the intense damp cold.

I have had to censor letters by the hundred lately. They don't make inspiring reading.

This morning I have been reading Trench Standing Orders to my Platoon. (Verb. Sap.)⁸

Needless to say I show a cheerier face to them than I wear in writing this letter; but I must not disguise from you the fact that we are at one of the worst parts of the Line.

I have lost no possessions so far; but have acquired a pair of boots and a map case (presents). And of course my valise is heavier by much dirt.

I want a Compass really more than Field Glasses.

My address is

2nd Manchester Regt.

B.E.F.

I have not a word from England since I left.

I can't tell you any more Facts. I have no Fancies and no Feelings. Positively they went numb with my feet.

Love is not quenched, except the unenduring flickerings thereof. By your love, O Mother, O Home, I am protected from Fatigue of life and the keen spiritual Cold.

Your own W.E.O.

7 The battalion left Halloy on 6 January, marching to Beauval and moving thence by motor bus to Bertrancourt.
8 Latin *verbum sapienti est*: enough said.

478. To Susan Owen

[9 January 1917]   [2nd Manchester Regt., B.E.F.]

My own dear Mother,

I forget both the day and the date. It is about the 9th. We moved further up yesterday, most of the way on 'Buses.

I have just had your long-looked-for letter. It seems wrong that even your dear handwriting should come into such a Gehenna as this. There is a terrific Strafe on. Our artillery are doing a 48 hours bombardment.

At night it is like a stupendous thunderstorm, for the flashes are quite as bright as lightning.

When we arrived at this deserted Village[9] last night, there had been no billets prepared for the Battalion—owing to misunderstanding. Imagine the confusion!

For my part I discovered, or rather my new chosen and faithful Servant discovered a fine little hut, with a chair in it! A four-legged chair! The Roof is waterproof, and there is a Stove. There is only one slight disadvantage: there is a Howitzer just 70 or 80 yards away, firing over the top every minute or so. I can't tell you how glad I am you got me the ear-defenders. I have to wear them at night. Every time No. 2 (the nearest gun) fires, all my pharmacopæia, all my boots, candle, and nerves take a smart jump upwards. This phenomena is immediately followed by a fine rain of particles from the roof. I keep blowing them off the page.

From time to time the Village is shelled but just now nothing is coming over. Anyhow there is a good cellar close to.

I am Orderly Officer today and stamp all the Battalion's letters. This has taken an age, and I have only a minute or two before I must despatch the Post.

I chose to spend an hour today behind the guns (to get used to them). The Major commanding the Battery was very pleasant indeed. He took me to his H.Q. and gave me a book of Poems to read as if it were the natural thing to do ! !

But all night I shall be hearing the fellow's voice:

Number Two—FIRE!

Please send the compass: 2 Manchester Regt. B.E.F. I also need 50 Players Cigarettes & some plain chocolate. There is nothing in all this inferno but mud and thunder.

I am quite incapable of reading anything but your letters; and as you see nearly incapable of writing. Tell me every detail about Colin & Harold that you can; and of course, I long to know everything that happens—or does not happen—at home.

Please tell Leslie & everybody that I really have not time nor wits to write to them from under the cannon's mouth.

But it will lull shortly. I am quite well, and have plenty to eat.

I get more and more used to the cold and wet.

Dearest love, my sweet Mother, from your Wilfred

I want a large, soft sleeping helmet and refills for the lamp.

s.v.p.

⁹ Bertrancourt.

479. To Susan Owen

10 January 1917   [*2nd Manchester Regt., B.E.F.*]

My own Mother,

I was censoring letters all afternoon. After tea commenced a big commotion among my friendly neighbours the Howitzers, in the midst of which I wrote a distracted note to Leslie, but the concussion blew out my candle so many times that I lost heart.

I am kept pretty busy, tho' there is only a short 'parade'. The men do practically nothing all day but write letters; but officers have frequent meetings over schemes, maps, instructions, and a thousand cares.

Yesterday I took a tour into the Line which we shall occupy. Our little party was shelled going up across the open country. It was not at all frightful and only one 4.7 got anywhere near, falling plump in the road, but quite a minute after we had passed the spot. I tell you these things because afterwards they will sound less exciting. If I leave all my exploits for recitation after the war without mentioning them now, they will be appearing bomb-shell-bastic.

Now I am not so uncomfortable as last week, for my new servant who has been a chemist's assistant, has turned out not only clean & smart, but enterprising and inventive. He keeps a jolly fire going; and thieves me wood with much cunning.

My Company Commander (A Company) has been out here since the beginning : 'tis a gentleman and an original (!)¹⁰

Next in command is Haydon,¹¹ whom I greatly like, and once revered as the assistant Adjutant at Witley & Oswestry.

Then come I, for the remaining subalterns are junior. I chose no. 3 Platoon. I was posted to 2, but one day I took No. 3 in tow when its officer left, because I liked the look of the men.

Even as they prophesied in the Artists, I have to take a close interest in feet, and this very day I knelt down with a candle and watched each man perform his anointment with Whale Oil; praising the clean feet, but not reviling the unclean.

As a matter of fact, my servant and one other, are the only non-verminous bodies in the platoon; not to say Lice-ntious.

Today's letters were rather interesting. The Daddys' letters are specially touching, and the number of x x x to sisters and mothers weigh more in heaven than Victoria Crosses. The Victoria Cross! I covet it not. Is it not <u>Victorian</u>? yah! pah!

I am not allowed to send a sketch, but you must know I am transformed now, wearing a steel helmet, buff jerkin of leather, rubber-waders up to the hips, & gauntlets. But for the rifle, we are exactly like Cromwellian Troopers. The waders are of course indispensable. In 2½ miles of trench which I waded yesterday there was not one inch of dry ground. There is a mean depth of 2 feet of water.

It seems an era since Christmas, Day, and Goose, Carols, Dickens & Mistletoe.

Assuming the war lasts another year I should get leave twice, or three times, for we get it, or should get it every 3 months. Be sure to have no Chloride[12] of Lime in the house. Our water is overdosed with it enough to poison us. But in the Mess we can get Perrier fortunately.

You need not ask where I am. I have told you as far as I can.

These things I need

(1) small pair nail scissors
(2) celluloid hair-pin box from Boots (<u>9</u>d.) with <u>tightfitting lid</u>, & containing boracic powder.
(3) Players Navy Cut
(4) Ink pellets
(5) Sweets (! !) (We shall not be in touch with Supplies by day)

Have no anxiety. I cannot do a better thing or be in a righter place.

Yet I am not sainted therefore, and so I beg you to annoy Gordon Gunston,[13] for my wicked pleasure.

W.E.O. X X X

---

[10] Captain (later Major) H. R. Crichton Green (1892–1963), Manchester Regiment. In 1939 he rejoined, and was Camp Commandant at Le Mans until the Dunkirk evacuation. Later he commanded the regimental depot of the Manchester Regiment.

[11] Lieutenant Arthur Heydon was a chartered accountant from Stockport before joining up in August 1914. Wounded in the arm at Gallipoli, he was later commissioned. Heydon did NOT die of wounds. See Letter 503, n. 79.

[12] 'Not so bad' is written in the margin against these lines. Another use of the Mistletoe code. 'Assuming the war lasts another / year I should get leave twice, / or three times, for we get it, / or should get it every 3 months. / be sure to have no Chloride': SERRE. The rest of the paragraph continues over the page.

[13] Leslie Gunston's elder brother, six years older than Owen, who was working as an optician in London. His name was omitted from this paragraph in CL and SL.

480. To Susan Owen

Tues: 16 January 1917   [*2nd Manchester Regt., B.E.F.*]

My own sweet Mother,

I am sorry you have had about 5 days letterless. I hope you had my two letters 'posted' since you wrote your last, which I received tonight. I am bitterly disappointed that I never got one of yours.

I can see no excuse for deceiving you about these last 4 days. I have suffered seventh hell.

I have not been at the front.

I have been in front of it.

I held an advanced post, that is, a 'dug-out' in the middle of No Man's Land.

We had a march of 3 miles over shelled road then nearly 3 along a flooded Trench. After that we came to where the trenches had been blown flat out and had to go over the top. It was of course dark, too dark, and the ground was not mud, not sloppy mud, but an octopus of sucking clay, 3, 4, and 5 feet deep, relieved only by craters full of water. Men have been known to drown in them. Many stuck in the mud & only got on by leaving their waders, equipment, and in some cases their clothes.

High explosives were dropping all around out, and machine guns spluttered every few minutes. But it was so dark that even the German flares did not reveal us.

Three quarters dead, I mean each of us ¾ dead, we reached the dug-out, and relieved the wretches therein. I then had to go forth and find another dug-out for a still more advanced post where I left 18 bombers. I was responsible for other posts on the left but there was a junior officer in charge.

My dug-out held 25 men tight packed. Water filled it to a depth of 1 or 2 feet, leaving say 4 feet of air.

One entrance had been blown in & blocked.

So far, the other remained.

The Germans knew we were staying there and decided we shouldn't.

Those fifty hours were the agony of my happy life.

Every ten minutes on Sunday afternoon seemed an hour.

I nearly broke down and let myself drown in the water that was now slowly rising over my knees.

Towards 6 o'clock, when, I suppose, you would be going to church, the shelling grew less intense and less accurate: so that I was mercifully helped to do my duty and crawl, wade, climb and flounder over No Man's Land to visit my other post. It took me half an hour to move about 150 yards.

I was chiefly annoyed by our own machine guns from behind. The seeng-seeng-seeng of the bullets reminded me of Mary's Canary. On the whole I can support the canary better.

In the Platoon on my left the sentries over the dug-out were blown to nothing. One of these poor fellows was my first servant whom I rejected. If I had kept him he would have lived, for servants don't do Sentry Duty. I kept my own sentries half way down the stairs during the more terrific bombardment. In spite of this one lad was blown down and, I am afraid, blinded.[14]

This was my only casualty.

The officer of the left Platoon has come out completely prostrated and is in hospital.

I am now as well, I suppose, as ever.

I allow myself to tell you all these things because I am never <u>going back to this awful post.</u> It is the worst the Manchesters have ever held; and we are going back for a rest.

I hear that the officer who relieved me left his 3 Lewis Guns behind when he came out. (He had only 24. hours in). He will be court-martialled.

In conclusion, I must say that if there is any power whom the Soldiery execrate more than another it is that of our distinguished countryman.[15] You may pass it on via Owen, Owen.

Don't pass round these sheets but have portions typed for Leslie etc. My previous letter to you has just been returned. It will be too heavy to include in this.

Your very own Wilfred x

---

[14] This incident became the subject of 'The Sentry' (*CPF*, p. 188).
[15] David Lloyd George of Dwyfor, 1st Earl (1863–1945), Minister for War before becoming Prime Minister 1916–22.

481. To Susan Owen

Friday, 19 January 1917   [*2nd Manchester Regt., B.E.F.*]

We are now a long way back in a ruined village, all huddled together in a farm. We all sleep in the same room where we eat and try to live. My bed is a hammock of rabbit-wire stuck up beside a great shell hole in the wall. Snow is deep about, and melts through the gaping roof, on to my blanket. We are wretched beyond my previous imagination—but safe.

Last night indeed I had to 'go up' with a party. We got lost in the snow. I went on ahead to scout—foolishly alone—and when, half a mile away from the party, got overtaken by

GAS

It was only tear-gas from a shell, and I got safely back (to the party) in my helmet, with nothing worse than a severe fright! And a few tears. some natural, some unnatural.

Here is an Addition to my List of Wants:

Safety Razor (in my drawer) & Blades

Socks (2 pairs)

6 Handkerchiefs

Celluloid Soap Box (Boots)

Cigarette Holder (Bone, 3d. or 6d.)

Paraffin for Hair.

(I can't wash hair and have taken to washing my face with snow.)

Coal, water, candles, accommodation, everything is scarce. We have not always air! When I took my helmet off last night—O Air it was a heavenly thing!

Please thank Uncle for his letter, and send the Compass. I scattered abroad some 50 Field Post Cards from the Base, which should bring forth a good harvest of letters. But nothing but a daily one from you will keep me up.

I think Colin might try a weekly letter. And Father?

We have a Gramophone, and so musical does it seem now that I shall never more disparage one. Indeed I can never disparage anything in Blighty again for a long time except certain parvenus living in a street of the same name as you take to go to the Abbey.

They want to call No Man's Land 'England' because we keep supremacy there.

It is like the eternal place of gnashing of teeth; the Slough of Despond could be contained in one of its crater-holes; the fires of Sodom and Gomorrah could not light a candle to it—to find the way to Babylon the Fallen.

It is pock-marked like a body of foulest disease and its odour is the breath of cancer.[16]

I have not seen any dead. I have done worse. In the dank air I have <u>perceived</u> it, and in the darkness, <u>felt</u>. Those 'Somme Pictures'[17] are the laughing stock of the army—like the trenches on exhibition in Kensington.[18]

No Man's Land under snow is like the face of the moon chaotic, crater-ridden, uninhabitable, awful, the abode of madness.

To call it 'England'!

I would as soon call my House (!) Krupp Villa, or my child Chlorina-Phosgena.

Now I have let myself tell you more facts than I should, in the exuberance of having already done 'a Bit.' <u>It is done</u>, and we are all going still farther back for a long time. A long time. The people of England needn't hope. They must agitate. But they are not yet agitated even. Let them imagine 50 strong men trembling as with ague for 50 hours!

Dearer & stronger love than ever. W.E.O.

[16] 'The Show' (*CPF*, p. 155) is foreshadowed in this letter.

[17] Owen is probably responding to the film *The Battle of the Ancre and the Advance of the Tanks*, which was released in January 1917. See Mark Connelly, 'Visualization of Violence', *1914-1918-Online. International Encyclopedia of the First World War*, ed. by Daniel Ute, et.al., issued by Freie Universität Berlin. DOI: 10.15463/ie1418.10169.

[18] The Camouflage School, established by Solomon J. Solomon, RA (1860–1927), fine artist and pioneer of camouflage techniques, was sited at Kensington Gardens in West London. Trenches were constructed to train soldiers for warfare on the Western Front. These were open to public viewing. During the centenary of the First World War in September 2017, a specially constructed trench was once again open to the public as part of an immersive interactive tour by the 10th Essex Living History Regiment (https://www.10thessex.uk/2017/10/kensington-gardens-trench-2017/).

482. To Susan Owen

Sunday, 4 February 1917   [*Advanced Horse Transport Depot*]

My own dear Mother,

I am now indeed and in truth very far behind the Line; sent down to this old Town[19] for a Course in Transport Duties. The Battalion did <u>not</u> get out for a rest, and since my last letter I have had another strong dose of the advanced Front Line.

To begin with, I have come out quite unhurt, except for a touch of dysentery, which is now passed, and a severe cold and cough which keep me in bed today.

I have no mind to describe all the horrors of this last Tour. But it was almost wusser than the first, because in this place my Platoon had no Dug-Outs, but had to lie in the snow under the deadly wind. By day it was impossible to stand up or even crawl about because we were behind only a little ridge screening us from the Bosches' periscope.

We had 5 Tommy's cookers between the Platoon, but they did not suffice to melt the ice in the water-cans. So we suffered cruelly from thirst.

The marvel is that we did not all die of cold.[20] As a matter of fact, only one of my party actually froze to death before he could be got back, but I am not able to tell how many have ended in hospital. I had no real casualties from shelling, though for 10 minutes every hour whizz-bangs fell a few yards short of us. Showers of soil rained on us, but no fragments of shell could find us.

I had lost my gloves in a dug-out, but I found 1 mitten on the Field; I had my Trench Coat (without lining but with a Jerkin underneath). My feet ached until they could ache no more, and so they temporarily died. I was kept warm by the ardour of Life within me. I forgot hunger in the hunger for Life. The intensity of your Love reached me and kept me living. I thought of you and Mary without a break all the time. I cannot say I felt any fear. We were all half-crazed by the buffetting of the High Explosives. I think the most unpleasant reflection that weighed on me was the impossibility of getting back any wounded, a total impossibility all day, and frightfully difficult by night.

We were marooned on a frozen desert.

There is not a sign of life on the horizon and a thousand signs of death.

Not a blade of grass, not an insect; once or twice a day the shadow of big hawk, scenting carrion.

By degrees, day by day, we worked back through the reserve, & support lines to the crazy village where the Battalion takes breath. While in Support we inhabited vast Bosche dug-out (full of all kinds of souvenirs). They are so deep that they seem warm like mines! There we began to thaw. At last I got to the village, & found all your dear precious letters, and the parcel of good and precious things. The Lamp is perfect your Helmet is perfect, everything was perfect.

Then I had the heavenly-dictated order to proceed on a Transport Course. Me in Transports? Ar[e]n't <u>you</u>? When I departed, the gloom among the rest of the Subs. and even among Captains, was a darkness that could be felt. They can't understand my luck.

It doesn't necessarily mean a job as Transport Officer straight away, but here I am, in a delightful old town billeted in a <u>house</u> with a young Scotch Officer.

True, we can get no fuel and the very milk freezes in the jug in a few minutes. True, I am sorely bruised by riding. True, this kind of Life is expensive. But I have not been so full of content since the middle of November last.

Tell Colin how we have to ride all manner of horseflesh in the School, cantering round & round for hours, without stirrups, and folding arms and doing all kinds of circus tricks.

It is very amusing—to watch.

Tomorrow I shall send a P.C. of this Town which I must not name in a letter.

Address : R.E. Section
Advanced Horse Transport Depot
A.P.O. S1.
BEF France.
Hope you had numerous Field P.C.'s which I dropped *en route* to here.
The Course should last 1 month !!
Alas! I have missed your last letters. It has taken 3 days to get here.
Fondest love to all, & thanks for all their letters,

Your own Wilfred x

P.S. I don't at all deserve the spirited approbation which Father gives me. Though I confess I like to have his kind letters immensely. I shall read them less shame-facedly in dug-outs and trenches, than I do here in this pleasant peaceful town.

Quite 10 years ago I made a study of this town & Cathedral, in the Treasury. It is all familiar now!

Auntie Emma fairly hit it when she 'perceived the awful <u>distaste</u> underlying' my accounts. Dear Aunt was ever a shrewd Doogie.

I suppose I can endure cold, and fatigue, and the face-to-face death, as well as another; but extra for me there is the universal pervasion of <u>Ugliness</u>. Hideous landscapes, vile noises, foul language and nothing but foul, even from one's own mouth (for all are devil ridden)—everything unnatural, broken, blasted;

the distortion of the dead, whose unburiable bodies sit outside the dug-outs all day, all night, the most execrable sights on earth. In poetry we call them the most glorious. But to sit with them all day, all night ....and a week later to come back and find them still sitting there, in motionless groups, THAT is what saps the 'soldierly spirit'...

Distaste ? Distaste, Quotha?

I used to consider Tankerville Street[21] ugly, but now...

Well, I easily forget the unpleasant, and, look you, I even have to write it down for the sake of future reminders, reminder of how incomparable is an innocent and quiet life, at home, of work creative with books or without books, moneyed or moneyless, in sunshine or fog, but under an inoffensive sky, that does not shriek all night with flights of shells.

Again I have said too much. But let me repeat that I am mighty snug here, and have a goodly prospect before me now.

I am not sorry you keep in bed from time to time, but I do hope you'll soon get some sunny walks. Are you painting?

The Letter from Lancs. was from Bobby. All the brothers are in college there.[22] Miss de la Touche is as Bobby says 'supposed to be boss' of a Belgian Hospital in London.[23]

Again, dearest love to all. W.E.O.

[19] Abbeville. The instruction to report to the Advanced Horse Transport Depot there survives in Owen's archive in Oxford. On the back of the message form Owen pencilled some lines from Rabindranath Tagore's *Gitanjali*, beginning: 'When I go from hence let this be my parting word, that what I have seen is unsurpassable.' He quoted these words to Susan Owen in August 1918, the day before his last embarkation leave was over.

[20] 'Exposure' (*CPF*, p. 185) stems from the experience described here.

[21] In Shrewsbury.

[22] Bobbie and Johnny de la Touche left Downside in July 1916 and transferred to Stonyhurst College, near Blackburn, Lancashire, where Charles and David had already arrived as pupils from Mérignac.

[23] Miss de la Touche was then in charge of a hospital for Belgian refugees in Surbiton, Surrey.

483. To Susan Owen

[9 February 1917]   [*Advanced Horse Transport Depot*]

My own dear Mother,

Your last letter is not numbered—dated Jan. 31. No doubt you have mine from here. No parcel yet. The back of it is all covered with Veterinery Notes which I must try to copy out. The cold almost freezes my eyelids together.

I am in a hut now, because the Scot disturbed me by rolling in every midnight, and when at last he got into our bed, his three sheets did not somehow add to the warmth.

Last night I burnt a petrol lamp under my bed !! I don't know what <u>Risk</u> is, now.

In the morning, the top blanket was stiffish with frost. Don't think I suffer. Every detail of this blessed Life is sweet and precious. 3 more weeks of it yet!

I am putting Colin's letter herein. I'm sorry I was so pretentious as to ask for a typing of my letters. But I really am ashamed of sending such scrawl to Colin. <u>Do</u> have it copied!

I don't think I have told you that I am Mess President of the School Mess! It means a good deal of work. But I am honoured to have it. In the evening I go shopping with the Mess Cart. I am certainly a suitable person to hold the key of our Whisky store! I have fixed the charge of Messing at 25f. per week!

Sorry I am so busy—for your sake, but no more now but my perfect Love to you.

W.E.O. x x x

484. To Susan Owen

Monday [12] *February 1917*   [*Advanced Horse Transport Depot*]

My own dear Mother,

I thought to write yesterday, but we were working all day; sick animals in the morning, and riding in the afternoon. In spite of the hard ground we went out into the country. I had a horse with a reputation of 'warming up'. Sure enough, he would not let me remount after a halt. When at last I swung over, and before I could get the reins properly gathered, he bolted. It was not so much a gallop, as a terrific series of ricochets off the ground, as if we had been fired from a Naval Gun. But the worst part was the sudden checks. Once I found myself with my hands in the brute's mouth; but I was still on top of him somewhere, and never actually touched ground. I was only thoroughly shaken.

Your 3 parcels came within 2 days of each other, 2 actually together. It is so unlucky that they did not reach me up the line, where everything has a tenfold value. Still nothing can take from the preciousness of the presents you send me.

The Cigarettes are the most essential of all, because the stuff sold out here is abominable: except Turkish, which are cheap & good. The Cigarette-holder is the finest imaginable. I am e'en champing it now.

The socks have almost exceeded my need. Withhold Socks for another month or more.

Gingerbreads arrived in fine condition—both lots. They are the most home-like bits in all the parcel

You made a very cunning choice of Biscuits. You overwhelm me with Chocolate. I am keeping it, like most of the sweet-stuff, for going up the Line. Now the potted meat is much too heavy an article, don't you think, especially as it is plentiful, and, even, <u>a Ration</u>. Munchie[24] of course is one of the very best things you could send. Handkerchiefs A.1.

I have not yet come to use the first Lamp Refill. The Lamp is admirable.

Thanks for the Boracic Box, exactly what I desired.

I forget how to use the Quassia.[25] But have had no need.

I get a bath for 1 f. 50. at the Officers' Club, a sumptuous place. But the meals are rather dear. My Mess is succeeding, but the shortage of coal is a terrible nuisance for me.

We have a Canadian, an Australian, various M.G.C's,[26] a S.W.B.[27] a Scot, etc. etc. The S.W. Borderer is in the same Battalion as Merrifield,[28] the 'Artist' who mimicked the Colonel at the Holborn. We are all fairly near together on the Line.

What a curious thing about H. Kent! If you care to get the *Morning Post* of Feb. 8 you will see on P. 8 a map[29] (which I should like kept.) The dotted lines represent the exact posts where we lay freezing. I could almost pick out the identical dot where I was. I can't get any news of the Battalion, but the Advance was certainly from the place where I left them.

I brought my servant with me. It is a soft job for him here. I don't know that he is quite worthy of such a holiday. I am not fond of him, because he does nothing off his own bat, and doesn't always 'jump to' my orders!

I must write at once to that lad Browne to go and see you from Wrexham if he can. I think I told you how he stood by me when I was stranded somewhere in F. He had been out over a year and was then on his way home sent back for being under age! He was a Rly. clerk.

I am settling down to a little verse once more, and tonight I want to do Leslie's subject 'Golden Hair' and O.A.J.'s[30] 'Happiness'. Leslie tells me that Miss Joergens considers my Sonnet on 'The End'[31] the finest of the lot. Naturally, because it is, intentionally, in her style! It is in Leslie's possession now. I think hers on 'Golden Hair' very fine indeed. I have lost a bundle of my MSS, together with all the photographs I brought out. They were left out of packing. That's the sort of servant I've got. <u>Please send some photographs</u>. Also would you mind getting an Army Book *Animal Management* pub. by Gale & Polden, Aldershot.

Please thank Mary specially for her dear letters which I read constantly. As for yours, I live by them.

Ever your loving W.E.O. x

[24] The family name for nut, raisin, and chocolate blocks.
[25] Quassia chips, dissolved in water as a disinfectant.
[26] Machine-gun companies.
[27] South Wales Borderer.
[28] HO and JP in CL identify Merrifield as Lieutenant S. H. Merfield, but it is not clear how they came to this conclusion or whether their spelling or Owen's is correct

²⁹ It showed the Beaumont Hamel–Beaucourt area of the front before Grandcourt, just evacuated by the Germans.

³⁰ Olwen Joergens, daughter of an artist friend and neighbour of the Gunstons at Kidmore End. She, LG, and Owen exchanged poems on set subjects.

³¹ Poems were still being exchanged between the three. 'The End' (*CP*, p. 159); 'Happiness' (*CP*, p. 88); 'Purple' (*CP*, p. 117); and 'Golden Hair' (*CP*, p. 497). LG's *The Nymph* includes *his* poems 'Happiness', 'Golden Hair', and 'Purple'. For Owen's further opinion of his own 'Happiness' see Letters 487–8. Olwen Joergens did not include any of these 'set subjects' in her collection, *The Woman and the Sage* (Erskine MacDonald, 1916).

485. To Mary Owen

Wed, [14] February 1917   [*Advanced Horse Transport Depot*]

My dear Mary,

Your letter was one of six, three of mother's, one from Leslie, and one from Kemp, who is now Curate at Watford. He believes it is more than 4 years since we met in his study at Highbury.

I have just come in from driving G.S. Wagons with 4 horses. This hour's work is about all we do in the morning, and this afternoon we are driving out to a Horse Hospital. I tell you, these days are the best I've ever had in the army. What a pity about the brooch! but if you saw the enormity of the destruction and loss that goes on out here you would think less seriously of your little breakages.

Do you need a Brooch? I saw an Egyptian one, rather huge, but I am afraid you wouldn't like it.

and an Assyrian. No they wouldn't do since you no longer wear your Ancient British frocks. All the others in this town are either Romish, or nondescript.

One of the officers with me is a lace-designer by profession. You would never guess he spent his days concocting Insertions & Counterpoint, for he is one of the most dashing fellows with the horses.

Do you remember how the Bishop of London said he thought it 'disgraceful for any young man to be fingering lace over a counter, in peace-time or war-time.' Hum-hum! I wonder who loves to wear fine lace about him more than milord Winnie Ingram?³²

I am so glad you had such good skating. There are no skates of any sort to be had here, so we had no thought of it.

Yesterday we rode not far from the field of Crecy! It was a gallant ride, until we got on some slippery roads where several horses fell. One chap got underneath his beast, but after a modest attempt at fainting, recovered.

I am annoyed that my letters faint so long by the wayside. It is a marvel to me that your parcels come. A very blessed marvel.

Goodbye, sweet sister. I go to preside at Lunch.

W.E.O.

---

[32] Arthur Foley Winnington-Ingram (1858–1946), Bishop of London 1901–39. He was a tireless and outspoken advocate of Britain's 'great crusade' in the First World War. H. H. Asquith accused him of peddling 'jingoism of the shallowest kind'. See Jeremy Morris, 'Ingram, Arthur Foley Winnington (1858–1946), bishop of London', *Oxford Dictionary of National Biography*, https://www.oxforddnb.com/view/10.1093/ref:odnb/9780198614128.001.0001/odnb-9780198614128-e-36979.

486. To Susan Owen

Sunday, February? [18] 1917   [*Advanced Horse Transport Depot*]

My own dear Mother,

So little happens that I can't keep up my instalments of blood-and-thunder literature.

I'm glad you got the Picture Post Card. My last letter was to Mary, I think. The Gloves came only yesterday, in an opened envelope, but still containing the ribbon, which is not needed yet. I have now <u>three</u> Sleeping Helmets, but can't make up my mind which to give away. I may need one for <u>waking</u> wear. I found the first one—your make—of great use on a 'Working Party', the very day it came. After a day's work in reserve, Heydon & I were suddenly called to take a fatigue party up to the front. We hadn't time to snatch a cup of tea, but I remembered the Wool Helmet, and after dusk wore it under the steel, which was again reinforced with a layer of ice. We marched, about 10 miles, up to the front and there the men had to dig trenches in ground like granite:—the same men, or rather the survivors of them, who 2 days before had been holding the advanced posts ! ! The shells were wonderfully few, and we all reached 'Home' about 2 in the morning. They can all march <u>back</u> from the line somehow, I say <u>march</u>, but of course there is no Left-Right-Left, and we got on miserably slowly, because some of the men could not wear boots, but wound their puttees round their frost-bitten feet. It is a good thing no photographs can be taken by night. If they could they would not appear in the *Daily Mirror,* which I see still depicts the radiant smiles of Tommies 'well behind'.

I really thought that night that my Dysentery would soon be bad enough for Hospital, and so it would if next morning I had not been starting for A. By the way Dysentery is not just a polite name. I really had it, but civilised life has soon cured it. I should not have eaten so much Snow. But I still think it better than 'Shell Water'.

Didn't I tell you how I came here? There being no trains at all, I was not likely to go back and wait in the Orderly Room. No! I stopped the first Motor Lorry that came along, without bothering about its direction, and so got a respectable distance from the Battalion. That was a good start. Moreover no shell-holes any more appeared anywhere. That was a very good start. After I had taken 5 different 'buses, I found myself 1/3 of the way here, and in quite a nice little Town, where I stopped the night and had a bath, the first since Shrewsbury. The rest of the distance I was lucky enough to cover in one Bus. only. I put up, the first night, in a cafe, the Officers' Club being both costly and crowded. Then I billeted with the Scot, canny, and sometimes uncannily 'canned', in the house of a (very) retired old English gentleman, come down in the world.

I did not stay long in the Hut, but soon found a cosy room just outside the camp.

Wed, February ? [21] 1917

I kept back the Sunday Letter because the Mails have been held up for 5 days. So that all your letters since the Glove Packet came together this morning.

I am glad enough of the 2 Photographs but should like some more, not excluding one or two of the last of myself. Photography is dear here, but tomorrow we are having a group taken.

I'm jolly glad you have rolled out the Beer-Jug-and-Barrel, and it will be interesting to hear how the next curio behaves.

The Course should end next Sunday. I shall surely be with the Battalion by March 1. I hear from a Staff Officer who came into this Billet last night that 'during Operations' two [*one page missing*] procedure to open any fellows' letters from Paris.

Yes, I <u>was</u> using an Essence last week on my handkerchief, on account of the stenches from the Sick Horses Lines. Certain cases of Thrush, Quitter,[33] and such suppurations go one worse than the battlefield-exhalations.

Yes, once again I shave meticulously, and have re-established a Parting. For in another week I shall again be cleaning my teeth on my sleeve-cuffs and washing my face in my damp pillow.

All the school are desperate nuts in dress: as befits our calling, and immemorial custom of all gallants in a safe place. It is a favourite 'Flash' to trail a violet silk handkerchief! but for my part I consider the colour too noble for such an article.

I hope your next parcel will not reach me until I am up the Line. All I really want is Cigarettes, Munchie, and <u>plain Cadbury's</u>.

I have only received <u>one</u> Identity Disc so far!

I have had all the parcels you made a list of.

You say Father was going to enquire after Brown at Wrexham Stn. but he is still a soldier—in Wrexham Barracks.

No more now, but some more tomorrow.

Your very ownest Wilfred x

[33] Thrush—a common bacterial infection of a horse's hoof; quittor—a septic condition of a horse's lower leg.

487. To Susan Owen

Sunday, 25 February 1917   [*Advanced Horse Transport Depot*]

Mine own Mother,

Just had your letter of Tuesday 20th, enclosing Denny's.[34] I believe it sincere, and value it a good deal more than an acceptance of our proposal. The Salopian applause would be directed to the fine reciter, but here we have the fine reciter applauding. Very thoughtful of you to copy it out for me. Yes, I think Leslie might well see the original. If you write to him you will ask him for my 'Golden Hair'[35] (not a sonnet). It contains about five consecutive lines which I leave as final! My 'Happiness'[36] is dedicated to you. It contains perhaps two good lines. Between you an' me the sentiment is all bilge. Or nearly all. But I think it makes a creditable Sonnet. You must not conclude I have misbehaved in any way from the tone of the poem (though you might infer it if you knew the tone of this Town.) On the contrary I have been a very good boy [*one sheet missing*]

I don't need any more ear-defenders. I don't use these now. The only other thing for Parcels would be some more of those coffee & cocoa cubes. They are A.1.

To demonstrate in concrete form that I am still of my old vain mind, I am going to send over a parcel to you of a cheap copper vase (not 'cheap tin trays')[37] & pot. For cheap modern work, I 'specially approve of this vase. When the field-flowers appear, I foresee that you will fill it with them unto the day of my returning.

The souvenirs which sell in millions to the soldiers are artistic atrocities: fit signs of the times. This Aluminium Letter Opener which cost 8d. is probably German, judging from the Gretchen-plaits. It is not a souvenir; and I have no intention of collecting souvenirs of any description.[38] What England will need will be an anti-souvenir. I shall have to send my parcel as if from the landlady of this house!

As regards your botanical enquiries concerning the prevalence of parasitic shrubs on apple and oak trees[39] I shall give you information as the data is acquired.

I have been to the dentist here (Army) and also the Doctor. I have not much of a cough, but produce an extra-ordinary amount of phlegm, brown, black, & grey. Fortunately or unfortunately, I feel perfectly well on it.

Nothing keeps me so cool of mind as knowing you are normally well, and I keep hoping from all accounts supernormally so.

Goodbye now, sweet Mother. I am like to be 4 or 5 days journeying.

Fondest love to all

Your very own, Wilfred x

[34] It is unclear whether this is the same Ernest Denny mentioned in Letter 428 to CO (*CL*), who was a poet and former student of Edith Morley's at Reading and who trained with Owen at Romford in 1916. Second Lieutenant Ernst Denny (London Regiment, Prince of Wales' Owen Civil Service Rifles, 15th Bn.) was killed on 4 August 1917, age 29, and is buried at Dozinghem Military Cemetery in Belgium. His poems were eventually published in 1978 as Triumphant Laughter (Bentham Press).

[35] *CPF*, p. 497.

[36] *CPF*, p. 88.

[37] The reference is to John Masefield's poem 'Cargoes', in *Salt-Water Poems* (1904). The 'Dirty British coaster' carries a 'cargo of Tyne coal, / Road-rails, pig lead, / Firewood, iron-ware, and cheap tin-trays'.

[38] See, however, Letters 502, 504, 510.

[39] A reference to the Mistletoe code from Susan Owen. As DH noted, 'on one occasion at least' she 'clearly enquired when she was to hear more about "parasitic shrubs on apple and oak trees"'. (*Notes and Queries*, December 1980)

488. To Harold Owen[40]

[*27 February 1917*]   [*2nd Manchester Regt., B.E.F.*]

My dear old Harold,

I think I have had more joy from Mother's news of You than chagrin. <u>Certainly</u>. You are entire. Let all the machinations of the Army crash, bang, and utterly spiflicate themselves: I rejoice; you are whole[41] [*three lines inked out*] yourself to the point of insomnia. I know what insomnia is. So I won't ask you to write 'all about it' to me yet. How I admire, & understand, [*four lines inked out*] stand as an excuse for you, no other excuse for any wounds going septic in England! [*one line inked out*] Did you carry First Field Dressing? NO!

[*four lines inked out*] with quiet, and a little designing—and HOME.

I think less and less of applying to R.F.C.... loops and circuits [*one line illegible*] and easy soarings of [*one word illegible*]. Answer me one question. Did [*one line illegible*] a sinister attraction on you [*one word illegible*]? I hope anyhow you will soon feel right [*one page inked out*] As I said, I have no room for commiseration. It is swallowed up in Congratulation.

I believe I said something nasty about <u>the Navy</u> [*two words inked*] I had no notion of what had happened, or was to happen! [*one and a half pages inked out*]

It is 10 o'clock; and I must now be turned out of the Café, and will go and doze on my luggage, probably until Dawn.

I shall dream happily of you at home, where the same Voice that gave us ease when we broke a window, will give you the same ease, always.

I think it was your disconsolate mind that wrote my last Sonnet 'Happiness'. You will see.

[*several words inked out*]

Your affectionate, Wilfred

---

[40] This letter survives in fragments only.

[41] HO had just survived an aeroplane crash. He was under training as a pilot at the Royal Naval Air Station, Chingford, Essex, from October 1916 to March 1917. Two crashes were allowed in training; HO crashed a third time and was sent back to sea service.

489. To Susan Owen

1 March [*1917*]   *My Dug-Out*

Dearest Mother,

Have just reported at B.H.Q. Dug Out. Find myself posted to B. Coy. of which the Captain is poet Sorrel.[42] There is small chance of doing Transport for a long time if ever. Howsoever, this is a glorious part of the Line,[43] new to us, and indeed, to the English (sh!) Most comfortable dug-outs, grass fields, woods, sunshine, quiet. True we are in reserve today, but I hear the very front line is a line, and a quiet one.

My letter to Harold left yesterday by the Army Post. It was in an astonishing way I had your parcel. A man rose up from a hole in a field holding it above his head. It was a fine moment. I soon rushed down & tore it open. Socks most specially valuable, as my servant forgot to put any spare in my Trench Kit. Likewise, I took no Cigarettes, hoping to find 50 in the Parcel. Lo! here are thousands! How good of you all. I smoke Harold's with reverence.

I shall not touch the goodies until the very front line is reached.

The Post is waiting to go.

Yours as ever, but slightly happier than usual.

W.E.O.

---

[42] Lieutenant Sebastian Sorrell, MC, Manchester Regiment, was invalided home a few weeks later with shell shock. In March 1918 he was a Staff Captain (Assistant Military Landing Officer), and was listed on the Army Reserve in August 1918. DH refers to Sorrell as 'a poet and aesthete; who had been a private secretary before the War and lived with his mother in Kensington'. Like HO and JB, DH could find 'no trace of his poetry' (WOANB, pp. 282–3).

[43] On 25 February the brigade of which 2nd Manchesters formed a part had taken over the line from the French near Fresnoy, occupying dugouts at Bouchoir and billets at Beauvois. They were still on the St Quentin front. On the same day the Germans were found to have evacuated their positions in front of the Le Transloy–Loupart line and north of the Albert–Bapaume road.

490. To Colin Owen

2 March 1917   *B Coy Dug-Out*

My dearest Colin,

    This is the first time I have written from a Dug-Out. I am in a French one now. We have straw to sleep on, but it is pretty lousy—after the poilus!

    There is a gas-alarm on just now, but I don't really expect it. The air is too still. Just this moment, and since I sat down, a tremendous artillery strafe has opened up. We all remark to each other that it seems there is a war on. I went up to the Front Line with a Fatigue Party for digging. Let me tell you in confidence that I was for the first time a <u>Target</u>.* I ran over the top to get to the head of the Party in the Trench, & stood a moment to shout an order, when a bullet went Ping, a good 5 ft. over my silly head.

———————————————

    Next day. Where you see the * I left off because the order came 'Stand to Arms!' What a commotion! We half expected an attack, but nothing happened. I have no paper to write more, but this letter should be interesting circumstantially.

    Dearest love to you, sweet my Brother.   W.E.O.
You <u>must</u> disinfect your hands, whether sore or not, after stables.

491. To Susan Owen

2 March 1917   *B Coy's Dug-Out*

My dearest Mother,

    I am in a good warm Dug-Out, decorated with French postcards, picturing embraces, medals, roses and mistletoe![44]

    Is it possible I was living civilly no more than 2 days ago? From letter of last night I hear you have seen the illusory War Films.[45] However, they must hint at the truth, and if done anywhere on <u>this</u> Front, would not be quite devoid of realism. But, as you know, a just idea of the First Place could best be got by a tour around Purgatorio.

    Did you see any Shell-bursts?

    And did they bang tins or whack drums?

    Did you see any Red X at the front?

    Under no circumstance do we! A good half of their work is done by S. Bearers of our own Coys. You don't mention Dug-Outs or snipers. I was marked by one of the Pests yesterday. His 'Direction' was good, only his 'Elevation' slightly high. A curious thing was who first hissed 'Get down, Sir!'?

One of my old Fleetwood Musketry Party! Quite a few are with me. One of those to whom I swore I would never tolerate near me at the Front. I remember his total score was 5!! One of the servants of this Dug-Out remembers <u>me</u> at Thursley Common, (Witley), and has photographs of lads <u>I</u> remember, who are now in Egypt, bless 'em.

The Corporal who shared my Coat in the last dug-out (before my Course), & who was one of them who fell out by the wayside, is now in hospital, his dysentery having taken a serious form.

I have almost cleared away my cold by means of douches. Thanks however for the Formamin. Do quick tell me how to use 'Quasha'. Do I chew it? or suck it? boil it? burn it? or rub it? well in the part affected? (I have parts affected since last night.)

'Colin's' socks are splendid things.

The Rice fluffy-fluffy makes excellent packing-material.

A Prize for who first solves my conundrum.[46]

<u>No knowledge of French required</u>. I wrote to Harold 3 days ago, & to Colin this afternoon.

Ever your fondest Wilfred x

[44] The Mistletoe code. 'Is it possible I was living civilly no / more than 2 days ago? From letter / of last night I hear you have seen the / illusory War Films. However, they must / hint at the truth, and if done anywhere / on <u>this</u> Front, would not be quite / devoid of realism. But, as you know, / a just idea of the First Place could best be / got by a tour around Purgatorio. / Did you see any Shell-bursts? / And did they bang tins or whack drums? / Did you see any Red X at the front? / Under no circumstance do we! / A good half of their work is done by S. Bearers / of our own Coys. You don't mention Dug-Outs / or snipers. I was marked by one of the / Pests yesterday. His 'Direction' was good, / only his 'Elevation' slightly high. / A curious thing was/ who first hissed 'Get down, Sir!'? SOFLINEJOININGFRENCH.

[45] At least 240 official war films were released between 1915 and 1918, the most famous being *The Battle of the Somme* (1916). See Nicholas Reeves, 'Film Propaganda and Its Audience: The Example of Britain's Official Films during the First World War', *Journal of Contemporary History*, Vol. 18, No. 3 (July 1983), pp. 463–94.

[46] The Mistletoe code on the previous page of the letter: 'south of line, joining French'.

492. To Susan Owen

Sunday, 4 March 1917 [*2nd Manchester Regt., B.E.F.*]

Dearest Mother,

Just a line at 5.30 today, while you are at Tea. Until I came in from work at 4 o'clock I had no idea it was Sunday. It often happens so. The work was the usual Digging. If anything could give a touch of interest to the work, it was that many of these diggers dug the show-trenches at Thursley,[47] in the days when my stars were bright from their creation by Pope & Bradley.[48]

Some chaps even fired their Course with me at Mytchett. I felt very tempted to take a rifle & do a bit of snapping, but it is forbidden to officers. On bright days like this I begin to be glad of your khaki covers.

For lunch, I had bully-beef, munchie, and flatulent rice. I like this stuff very much.

When I came in, Capt. Sorrel gave me the choice of writing a Sonnet before 7.30. or going with the next Fatigue Party !! I am ever so happy to be with him. He chokes filthiness as summarily as I ever heard a Captain do, or try to do. He is himself an aesthete, and not virtuous according to English standards, perhaps, but no man swears in his presence, nor broaches those pleasantries which so amuse the English officer's mind.

He seems to be one of the few young men who live up to my principle: that Amusement is never an excuse for 'immorality', but that Passion may be so.

I find this Company in a far better state than A, partly, of course, because of good sergeants, but Sorrel has a fine control.

My important letter written yesterday[49] left today, as today's will go tomorrow. How long do they take. It is so quiet here that we have our meals in a shallow dug-out, and only go down deep to sleep.

I sleep well; I eat well; I am well. Surely better than any of you at home. Dear old Harold has not written yet? Did I not warn Colin about his dirty hands? Has the new servant had any effect on your strength? I hope so.

Fondest love to all, Your W.E.O. x

---

[47] Owen had his men dig trenches at Witley. See Letters 439 and 442. As with those in Kensington Gardens (see Letter 481), extensive practice trenches were dug by troops in training before they were sent to the Western Front. Many still survive as archaeological earthworks, under the care of English Heritage.

[48] Military tailors, in Bond Street, W1 (now 35 Dover Street).

[49] Although HO and JB stated that this letter 'has not survived' (CL), DH surmised that this is the March 2 letter with the 'conundrum', 'despite the slight inconsistency of date.'

493. To Susan Owen

9 March 1917   *Deserted Village*

My own dearest Mother,

I had no idea your throat was so seriously bad when I last wrote, 3 or 4 days ago from the Dug-Out. But your 2 letters and Mary's came a few hours after dispatching my mail. During these last few days, I have not been able to write at all, nor had I any Field Cards to send. And nothing has come from you since the one telling of how you were sitting up for tea, being a little better. How I hope that by now the pain at least and the Malady of it are gone; and that there is a fair sun healing you!

We have gone back to severe cold and snow. This Village is half destroyed and our billets are not half so cosy as dug-outs.

Another Place

11 *March*   *More Deserted Village*

No sooner had I set out my Kit and done a page for you, than I was boosted back nearer the Line on a special job: in charge of a party of Dug-Out Diggers. It is a soft job. I take the men up sometimes by day, sometimes by night, so that (as today) I lie snug in my blankets until lunchtime. We are 4 officers living in this cellar; our servants cook for us. It is a relief to be away from the Battalion for a while. How I hope it will last. It <u>may</u> spin out 3 weeks.

I have just been sweating along a dangerous road to a factory where there is a shower bath. There was no water today! I sweated some more coming back. (Methinks I am becoming something crude in my speech.) 'Tis a crude, vaga-bondage of a life. While Leslie is theorizing over the art of building, here am I watching a fair old village toppling about my head. I think the wreckage will look even sicklier when the orchard-trees break out, like the souls of infants in Limbo. I am able to read here, but have nothing left now. I receive your *Red* Δ[50] with grati-tude, but do you think, now, that I am going to read the <u>war-impressions</u> of home-editors? If, here & there, you get a true version of the business—so much the more unreadable. *Punch,* on the other hand takes humour too seriously. From *Punch* you would take a <u>Sentry</u> to be the laughing-stock of Europe.

Spleen!

No, I still tipple *Punch* as hilariously as ever. But don't send any, for some one or other is bound to have one.

What I should like would be a current *Poetry Review.*[51]

Please don't send anything special for my Birthday. You have sent so many specialities lately. For instance, expensive chocolate!

I hope to be able to write again tomorrow, but I have an unwonted amount of official letters to do.

It's now nearly ten days since your Throat started bettering. Surely it is passed off now?

Longing unspeakably to see you, dear Mother, I look forward to Leave in about 3 more months ! !

Your own Wilfred x x

---

[50]   *The Red Triangle*, the journal of the YMCA 1917–23.
[51]   *Poetry Review*, the journal of the Poetry Society, founded 1912.

494. To Susan Owen

Sunday, [18] March [1917]   *[13th Casualty Clearing Station]*

My dearest Mother,

I am in a hospital bed, (for the first time in life.)

After falling into that hole[52] (which I believe was a shell-hole in a floor, laying open a deep cellar) I felt nothing more than a headache, for 3 days; and went up to the front in the usual way—or nearly the usual way, for I felt too weak to wrestle with the mud, and sneaked along the top, snapping my fingers at a clumsy sniper. When I got back I developed a high fever, vomited strenuously, and long, and was seized with muscular pains. The night before last I was sent to a shanty[53] a bit further back, & yesterday motored on to this Field Hospital, called Casualty Clearing Station 13.[54] It is nowhere in particular that I know, but I may be evacuated to Amiens, if my case lasts long enough. For I began to get right again immediately after getting into these sheets 'that soon smooth away trouble.'[55] The physician handed me over to the surgeon. But my head is not broken or even cut in any way. My temperature etc. <u>may not</u> have had any relation to the knock, and the first doctor said he only hoped it had. Anyhow it was normal yesterday, and below today, and the only abnormal thing about me now is that I don't want a cigarette. That, then, should not worry you. I have now told you everything, and I hope, dear Mother, that you are duly grateful —to me, and concerning the whole circumstance.

Sometimes a Sister blows in to this ward, and flutes a bit on a high voice, or pegs around on a high heel, but we are really attended by orderlies, who are fresh & clean, and much preferable, being not only serener and sensibler, but also private soldiers with no airs of authority about 'm. Rather the other way.

All my kit and belongings have come down with me, including 55 francs, much mud, and Pte. Heath.

Alas! I've had no letter for about 5 days when I had 3 together, and am not likely now to have any for quite a week. I think that for a few days: 2 Man. Regt. with 'Please Forward' will be the best address

[*six lines cut out*]

ever, Wilfred x

---

[52] At Le Quesnoy-en-Santerre, according to Edmund Blunden. A letter dated 14 March 1917—which has not survived—was seen by Blunden when he was writing the Memoir to his 1931 edition of Owen's Poems. Blunden quotes from the letter as follows: 'Last night I was going round through pitch darkness to see a man in a dangerous state of exhaustion. I fell into a kind of well, only about 15 ft., but I caught the hack of my head on the way down. The doctors (not in consultation!) say I have a slight concussion. Of course I have a vile headache, but I don't feel at all fuddled.' See also JS, WO, p. 171. Subsequent letters refer to the well as a cellar.

[53] The military hospital at Nesle. See Letter 607.

[54] This was at Gailly. See Letter 556.

[55] Rupert Brooke, 'The Great Lover', ll. 35–6.

495. To Colin Owen

Monday, 19 March   *13th Casualty Clearing Station*

My dearest Colin,

I am still kept in bed, though I feel fit for a walk.

Yesterday I wrote to Mother without knowing it was my birthday! I found out in the evening. It is too bad to be without letters of any sort. It must be a week since I had any. But I lost count of days in that cellar, & even missed the passing of night & daylight, because my only light was a candle.

I know something of the Advances.[56] You will be glad to hear that there has been no undue influx on the hospitals, at least in this area.

Have you met that mighty horse-tamer at Underdale? His picture was in a *Sketch*[57] I saw yesterday.

Always your loving W.E.O.

[56] By 10 March it had become clear that the Germans were planning withdrawal to the new positions in the rear known as the Hindenburg Line, and Allied pressure was increasing.

[57] *The Sketch*, an illustrated weekly British periodical, sister paper to *The Illustrated London News*, founded 1893.

496. To Susan Owen

21 March [1917]   *13th Casualty Clearing Station*

My dearest Mother,

I am getting up today, and perhaps by the time you receive this I shall be starting back to overtake my Battalion, if it is not chasing along too fast.

One of the villages mentioned in the *Daily Mail*, thus: 'we captured a farm so many miles North East of Q[58] ...' was the one to which I have been going every day or night last week.

We knew what was happening weeks ago, and I saw the smoke of burning behind the Bosche Line on the last day I was up.

I am not moving down to a Base—fortunately, perhaps, because anyone going further back than here becomes detached from his battalion, and is returned somewhere else.

There is no proper village here, and I am miserably in want of Books, not to say Letters. It is not worth writing to the Battalion, which for all I know may be openly warfaring, or perhaps is now already clean wiped out.

One of the sisters brought me some novels, about as palatable as warm water to a starving jaguar. Your remarks on Crocketts' last,[59] remind me that I once said his books were like sawdust—on which an ox has just been slaughtered.

I suppose you did not see Bernard Shaw's accounts of his visit to the front, appearing in the *Glasgow Herald*. He says he put black things like collar-studs into his ears. So very like collar-studs that I have been using mine as such for some time![60]

Yes, I have long missed my Pen, and don't want another. My watch has disappeared since I left the cellar. Left there I think. I was too blind sick to notice anything. In my next parcel I should like some Harrison's Pomade & some more Paraffin.

Fondest Love, Wilfred x

[58] Le Quesnoy-en-Santerre.
[59] Samuel Rutherford Crockett (1959–1914), whose romantic novels included *Princess Penniless* (1908) and *Old Nick and Young Nick* (1910), is associated with the Kailyard School of Scottish literature, characterized by sentimental, old-fashioned tales of Scottish rural life.
[60] A light-hearted article by Shaw in *The Glasgow Herald*, 5 March 1917, entitled 'Joy-Riding at the Front', described his visit as *Daily Chronicle* correspondent to Arras, Ypres, and the Somme front. At Ypres he wrote, 'I stuck into my ears a pair of seeming black collar-studs, which did not prevent my hearing anything, but did prevent me from overdoing it.'

497. To Mary Owen

Wednesday Mng. [21 March 1917][61]   *13th Casualty Clearing Station*

Dearest Mary,

I am now really quite well, but am not getting up yet, as it is snowing and I couldn't go out if I did dress. But we sit round the stove in Kimonos, padded with cotton, very pleasant wear. We are now about ten in the ward. One is an old Artist Rifle, but I never knew him, nor ever want to. They are none of them interesting, from any point of view whatever.

I amuse myself with drawing plans for Country Houses and Bungalows, especially Bungalows. I worked my wits all day on one, and, within the prescribed limits, it is about perfect, for the intended occupant —solitary me.[62]

You see I am thinking of sitting down under my own vine and living for use, some day, and a concrete presentment of the Vine should be incentive.

This passage rather winded me, yea wounded me. Mistress Browning:

> Many fervent souls
> Strike rhyme on rhyme, who would strike steel on steel,
> If steel had offered, in a restless heat
> Of doing something. Many tender hearts
> Have strung their losses on a rhyming thread,
> As children, cowslips. The more pains they take,
> The work more withers. Young men, ay and maids,

Too often sow their wild oats in tame verse,
Before they sit down under their own vine,
And live for use.

      Alas, near all the birds,
Will sing at dawn, and yet we do not take
The chafering swallow for the holy lark.[63]

Or words to that effect.

Adieu, sweet sister.

                       Your ever loving W.E.O.

---

[61] PN, p. 189.

[62] According to a note in *CL*, 'HO saw this after the war, and remembers it as a detailed and loving piece of work' (p. 445).

[63] From *Aurora Leigh*, by Elizabeth Barrett Browning (1806–61). A copy of *The Poems of E B Browning* (vol. 2, George Newnes, Ltd., London [1904] n.d.), inscribed on the fly-leaf 'WEO/ Bouchoir, Somme/March: 1917' and containing Owen's marginal notes, survives among his books in the Bodleian.

498. To Colin Owen

24 *March* [1917]   *13th Casualty Clearing Station*

My dear Colin,

In my walk this afternoon, considering at leisure the sunshine and the appearance of peace (I don't mean from the news) I determined what I should do after the war.

I determined to keep pigs.

It occurred to me that after five years development of one pig-stye in a careful & sanitary manner, a very considerable farm would establish itself.

I should like to take a cottage and orchard in Kent Surrey or Sussex, and give my afternoons to the care of pigs. The hired labour would be very cheap, 2 boys could tend 50 pigs. And it would be the abruptest possible change from my morning's work.

If any man mocks me, Remember Paderewski![64]

What do you think of this?

I wonder you do not start with a sow <u>of your own</u>, this year.

Perhaps you will think me clean mad and translated by my knock on the head. How shall I prove that my old form of madness has in no way changed? I will send you my last Sonnet, which I started yesterday. I think I will address it to you.

Adieu, mon petit. Je t'embrasse.

                            W.E.O.

SONNET—with an Identity Disc[65]

If ever I had dreamed of my dead name
High in the Heart of London; unsurpassed
By Time forever; and the fugitive, Fame,
There taking a long sanctuary <u>at</u> last,

—I'll better that! Yea, now, I think with shame
How once I wished it hidd'n from its defeats
Under those holy cypresses, the same
That mourn around the quiet place of Keats.

Now rather let's be thankful there's no risk
Of gravers scoring[66] it with hideous screed.
For let my gravestone be this body-disc
Which was my yoke. Inscribe no date, nor deed.

But let thy heart-beat kiss it night & day…
Until the name grow vague and wear away.

This is private.

I stickle that a sonnet must contain at least 3 clever turns to be good. This has only two.

---

[64] Ignacy Jan Paderewski (1860–1941), the pianist and composer who was prime minister of Poland in 1919.
[65] An early draft of 'To My Friend (with an Identity Disc)', *CPF*, p. 96.
[66] 'notching' struck out.

499. To Mary Owen

25 March 1917   *13th Casualty Clearing Station*

My dear Mary,

I went a joy ride on a Motor Ambulance, a Daimler (as pictured in the *Sketch* last week) and so passed a vivid afternoon. The car was going in the direction of the Front, and I stopped at a certain village where refugees from the regained area were just arriving: all hags & children. I had a long talk with a boy of 14, who if he had been 15 would not have been liberated. He could not spell his name, since he has worked on the fields since he was 11. He did not look by any means starving, but had known nothing but scanty food for 2½ years. I plied him with chocolate, and drew the following information. That the Germans carried off all men over 15; left 5 days bread rations for the remainder, set fire to almost every building, choked up the wells with farmyard refuse and disappeared.

Our guns have begun strafing heavily this morning. I can hear, from my bed, the continuous growling.

We are by a Canal, much used by the Army. It looks funny to see a Sergeant Major commanding a Tug, and a Corporal at the helm of the barge.[67] A pleasant life for khaki. Why doesn't Harold try it! The Inland Water Transport Service.

The surgeon says there is no hurry to send me back! I want to go—because of the letters!

Your own W.E.O.

---

[67] See Letter 509.

500. To Susan Owen

Wed. Mng., 28 March 1917   [13th] *Casualty Clearing Station*

My own dear Mother,

They still keep me here, though I go out every afternoon. I have no letters, but have been able to get a few books from a small town where I motored on Sunday. I also got a cheap watch,—pocket size. I think the usual penalty of loss of property on coming to hospital has been small in my case: my watch. Not the original Brummagem of Clarke's, but a better one which I exchanged for it at a shop in A.[68] I left Colin's there for repairs. It is probably with the Battalion now.

At C.[69] I went into the great Gothic Church, and listened under the nave, as Belloc says, for the voice of the Middle Ages. All I could hear was a voice very much beyond the middle age. However I stayed to vespers; and after leaning my hat and stick up against a piece of the true Cross, I sat and regarded the plants (with their paper flowers wired on them), and St. John in bathing costume looking ruefully at another saint in a gold dressing-gown; and the scarlet urchins holding candles and chewing,—probably the grease. Indeed it is enough to set the Wykliffe's[70] howling.

I hear that young Boultbee, son of Father Boultbee,[71] one of the prophets, is missing. He was in the R.F.C. and I am told a very wild fellow!

The man in the next bed told me this. We have two cases, pilot & observer, who are terribly smashed. They will both recover, but the pilot has both arms broken, abdominal injuries, both eyes contused, nose cut, teeth knocked in, and skull fractured. It makes me ashamed to be here. But I help to look after him at night. The sister has a wonderful way with him. I like her very much. Constitutionally I am better able to do Service in a hospital than in the trenches. But I suppose we all think that.

Yours as ever W.E.O.

---

[68] Probably Amiens. Owen sent SO a picture-postcard depicting 'AMIENS. –*Le Marché sur l'eau et la Cathédrale*' (postmarked 30 March 1917) without an accompanying written message on the reverse, but with the word 'Amiens' in the caption underlined. This is Letter 501 in *CL*.

[69] Probably Corbie.

[70] i.e. the Protestant reformers.

[71] Lt. Arthur Elsdale Boultbee, 25th Sqdn., son of the Rev. Frederick Croxall and Henrietta Boultbee, is buried in the Canadian Cemetery No. 2, Neuville-St. Vaast. He was 19.

502. To Susan Owen

4 April 1917[72]   [*2nd Manchester Regt., B.E.F.*]

Dearest Mother,

Know that I have cut my forefinger with a tin of Lobster, and that is why I write shaky. I have been 4 days caravanning from the CCS, & have just found our H.Q. Journeying over the new ground has been most frightfully interesting. The Batt. has just done something great[73] which will find its way into the Communiqué. I am going up to join them in an hour's time. They have lost one officer & many are wounded, Heydon among them.[74] I shall no doubt be in time for the Counter Attack. I have bought an automatic pistol in the town (from which I sent a P.P.C.) By the time you get this we'll be out of the line again. Tonight will be over....

My long rest has shaken my nerve. But after all I hate old age, and there is only one way to avoid it!

Last night I bedded down with a family[75] of refugees, 3 boys, 2 tiny girls: a good class socially, and of great charm personally. I was treated as a god, and indeed begin to suspect I have a heart as comprehensive as Victor Hugo's, Shakspere's, or your own. In 24 hours I never took so many hugs & kisses in my life, no, not in the first chapter even. They took reliefs at it. It would have astounded the English mind.—While, just the night before I was in blues as deep as the Prussian Blue—not having heard an affectionate spoken word since I left you—or rather since I left A. I am now in the Pink.

No need to tell you where I am going up to fight. It is the town on which the hopes of all England are now turned.[76] I must now dress up in Battle Order.

Your own W.E.O. xxxxx

I find no letters here. Your parcels did not take part in the advance—Too heavy! Without your Letters I should give in. What to I know not, but I 'sorter' feel I should 'give up the unequal contest!'—without a definite object for carrying on. And that object is not my Motherland, which is a good land, nor my Mother tongue, which is a dear language, but for my Mother, of whom I am not worthy to be called

The Son x x x

I hope this bit of paper is not incriminating[77] to send over but it is all I can find. I must write to Colin & send him some small souvenirs tomorrow. Ah my poor angel! He wants to be with me. He would not live three weeks in this sector of Hades.

⁷² Corrected by Susan Owen from the original 4 March.
⁷³ A successful but costly brigade attack had been mounted on Savy Wood on 2 April with Selency as its objective. Thereafter A Company (which had suffered heavy losses) probed forward to the outskirts of St Quentin. See Letter 503.
⁷⁴ Altogether, two officers and twelve other ranks were killed, seven officers and fifty-two other ranks wounded.
⁷⁵ Perhaps the Lemaire family mentioned in Letter 504.
⁷⁶ St Quentin.
⁷⁷ The last sheet is written on the back of a scrap headed:

AMENDMENT
S.S.143. 'Instructions for the
Training of Platoons in Offensive Action'
Appendix I. NOTES. LINE 6. After 'No. 1' add 'and No. 2'.

503. To Susan Owen

6 [?8] April [1917]   [2nd Manchester Regt. B.E.F.]

My own dearest Mother,

We are 'in rest.'⁷⁸ I arrived at the Battalion a day too late for the stunt: I am therefore not in the 'we' when I say we captured 6 guns, numerous machine guns, and of course, the Position.

But I am still ME.

I am afraid poor Heydon will not live,⁷⁹ and other officers, one of my company, fell on the field. It is interdicted to give any figures at all, but a good number of us are (agreeably) wounded.

When I turned up I went back to A. Coy, where Captain Green was hanging on with only one officer. We stuck to our line 4 days (and 4 nights) without relief, in the open, and in the snow. Not an hour passed without a shell amongst us. I never went off to sleep for those days, because the others were far more fagged after several days of fighting than I fresh from bed. We lay in wet snow. I kept alive on brandy, the fear of death, and the glorious prospect of the cathedral Town⁸⁰ just below us, glittering with the morning. With glasses I could easily make out the general architecture of the cathedral: so I have told you how near we have got. The French are on the skirts of the Town, as I could see. It was unknown where exactly the Bosche was lying in front of us. The job of finding out fell upon me. I started out at midnight with 2 corporals & 6 picked men; warning other Regiments on our flanks not to make any mistake about us. It was not very long before the Hun sent up his verilights, but the ground was favourable to us, and I and my Corporal prowled on until we clearly heard voices, and the noises of carrying & digging. When I had seen them quite clearly moving about, and marked the line of their entrenchment it might seem my job was done; but my orders were to discover the force of the enemy. So then I took an inch or two of cover and made a noise like a platoon. Instantly we had at least two machine guns turned on us, and a few odd rifles. Then we made a scramble for 'home'.

Another night I was putting out an Advanced Post when we were seen or heard and greeted with Shrapnel. The man crouching shoulder to shoulder to me gets a beautiful round hole[81] deep in his biceps. I am nothing so fortunate, being only buffeted in the eyes by the shock, and whacked on the calf by a spent fragment, which scarcely tore the puttee.

One day I hung my Trench Coat (which you used to button up for me at Southport) on a bush, & had just jumped down into my hole when a splinter ripped a hole through the chest & back. The tears are not big enough to spoil it for Field use.

I found your Parcel waiting for me here, when we got in at 3 in the morning (all half dead with fatigue & some quite, poor lads.) It was like a look in at Home to burrow into that lovely big box and examine all the loving presents. I opened it in bed (for I found my blankets ready laid out in this cosy cellar) and before I had opened all the boxes fell fast asleep. I am not awake now properly and my letter may appear disjointed. But then I'm not disjointed. I learned with astonishment that you had measles, and selfishly speaking am glad enough I only know it now you are better of it. O darling Mother you can't think how you could secure my peace of mind by being able to tell me you are well. Look at me I am nearly screwed to death with cold and nerves one night. Two days later I am in perfect, glowing, brilliant Health.

Tell Mary that Captain Crichton Green is immensely complimentary about her gingerbread.

I will write again tomorrow. Just had yours of 27th. Found Mar. 31st waiting for me. Be sure we shall not go into action again for a long time. It couldn't be done.

Still, always, and ever your very own

Wilfred x x x

[78] The battalion was relieved on 8 April and withdrew to billets in Beauvois till 12 April, when it returned to Savy Wood. This letter seems to be predated by some two days.

[79] Although severely wounded in the thigh, Heydon did, in fact, survive. DH notes that he was later assigned to a job at the Ministry of Munitions (WOANB, p. 291 and p.503, n. 10).

[80] St Quentin.

[81] The uncompleted poem 'Beauty' (CP, p. 489) may have been recalling this event, where a wound is called a beauty because it was serious enough for the sufferer to be sent back to England, 'Blighty'.

504. To Colin Owen

Monday, 9 April 1917   *[2nd Manchester Regt., B.E.F.]*

My dear Colin,

You want Souvenirs? There were plenty of Helmets, Bayonets, Caps, Coats, Shirts, Handkerchiefs, Tobacco, Bread, Soap, Needles & Cotton left by the Hun in the place we took and were holding last week.

I took a Name Patch out of a Coat for you, and a Mark Note, which is specially interesting by reason of its date. 12 August 1914. It looks as if the plant for issuing these war notes was ready before the Declaration of War.

There was nothing of value that I could lay hands on. For I was too occupied with my heavy duties to go scratching around for souvenirs.

Yesterday afternoon, Easter Sunday, we were finishing tea in this Cellar with something like Sunday peace & serenity when we were roused by the unexpected shattering sound of machine guns. I rushed up just in time to see a German Aeroplane come shuddering down the sky. With my little pistol in my pocket I dashed over the fields as fast as my sore feet would carry me.

The Machine was a new Albatross[82] No 2234. The Pilot—well I need not horrify you without need. But I took his handkerchief—a rather touching souvenir. You need not show them at home the spatter of blood in the corner. I rather want this handkerchief kept for me. The 3-ply wood is a bit of the body (of the machine).

I could not stay to see the engines & guns dug out of the soil, because I am so frightfully busy. The only other officer of A. Coy has gone sick, and Capt. Green is always in the Battalion Orderly Room fighting so to speak, for V.C.'s, D.C.M.'s etc. for our men. At least one of our Coy. is put in for V.C. and many others for the D.C.M.[83] I think Capt. Green, though not in the action before myself, will get a Military Cross,[84] which he has long deserved—for 2½ years active service.

Between us we are pulling the Company together for we 'go in' again tomorrow! It is rather strange to feel that these heroes feel me as their boss!

We had congratulatory Telegrams from the Commander in Chief downwards. He himself came[85] ... sh! 'Ware Censor!

I suppose things were done so well that we are needed again. I had hoped to get down the line as far as V[86] ... to see my sudden great friend André Lemaire, with whom I lodged on my way up. He has done more damage to the Boche when his fiery soul was under their hated domineering than I ever managed to do:— stretched wires across the high road at night, & upset a Staff Motor Car, threw hundreds of bombs [letter posted unfinished]

---

[82] German scout plane from the *Jagdstaffel* 6 unit. Nigel Wood has identified the pilot from unit records as Leutnant de Reserve Roland Nauck, born in Iserlohn, southeast of Dortmund in February 1893, and thus 'a very near contemporary of Owen'. Wood also identified the French pilot who brought down Nauck's plane, Lieutenant Alfred de Laage de Meux of the *Escadrille Lafayette*. See Nigel Wood, 'Owen's Airman: Who was the victim of the crash witnessed by Wilfred Owen on 8 April 1917?', *Wilfred Owen Association Journal*, Winter 2013.

[83] Four Military Crosses were awarded for the Savy Wood action, and one DCM (to Private Overton, A. Coy signaller, who had been recommended for the VC).

[84] But he did not.

[85] Field-Marshal Douglas Haig, 1st Earl Haig (1861–1928), Commander-in-Chief of the British Expeditionary Forces in France and Flanders 1915–19.

[86] Perhaps Villers-Bretonneux, between Amiens and the front.

505. To Susan Owen

25 April 1917   *A. Coy., My Cellar*

My own dearest Mother,

Immediately after I sent my last letter, more than a fortnight ago, we were rushed up into the Line.[87] Twice in one day we went over the top, gaining both our objectives. Our A Company led the Attack, and of course lost a certain number of men. I had sonic extraordinary escapes from shells & bullets. Fortunately there was no bayonet work, since the Hun ran before we got up to his trench. You will find mention of our fight in the Communiqué; the place happens to be the very village[88] which Father named in his last letter! Never before has the Battalion encountered such intense shelling as rained on us as we advanced in the open.[89] The Colonel sent round this message the next day: 'I was filled with admiration at the conduct of the Battalion under the heavy shellfire... The leadership of officers was excellent, and the conduct of the men beyond praise.' The reward we got for all this was to remain in the Line 12 days. For twelve days I did not wash my face, nor take off my boots, nor sleep a deep sleep. For twelve days we lay in holes, where at any moment a shell might put us out. I think the worst incident was one wet night when we lay up against a railway embankment. A big shell lit on the top of the bank, just 2 yards from my head. Before I awoke, I was blown in the air right away from the bank![90] I passed most of the following days in a railway Cutting, in a hole just big enough to lie in, and covered with corrugated iron. My brother officer of B Coy, 2/Lt Gaukroger[91] lay opposite in a similar hole. But he was covered with earth, and no relief will ever relieve him, nor will his Rest will be a 9 days-Rest. I think that the terribly long time we stayed unrelieved was unavoidable; yet it makes us feel bitterly towards those in England who might relieve us, and will not.

We are now doing what is called a Rest,[92] but we rise at 6.15 and work without break until about 10 p.m. for there is always a Pow-Wow for officers after dinner. And if I have not written yesterday, it is because I must have kept hundreds of Letters uncensored, and enquiries about Missing Men unanswered [*remainder missing*]

---

[87] The battalion had returned to the front at Savy Wood on 12 April to support a new French attack on St Quentin.

[88] In Letter 536 Owen refers to 'the barrage at Feyet', but, as JS notes, 'Contemporary maps of that district show no place of that name. There is, however, a village of Fayet, half a mile northeast of Selency, and it may well have been there that WO experienced the bombardment described' (*WO*, p. 181).

[89] Thirty men were killed in the barrage. See Letter 510. It was the inspiration for Owen's last poem, 'Spring Offensive' (*CPF*, p. 192).

[90] This experience (enlarged on in Letter 508) resulted in Owen's shell shock and being invalided home.

[91] Second-Lieutenant Herbert Gaukroger, 1st Battalion Manchester Regiment, was born in Didsbury, Manchester, and was a fruit-grower before the war. He enlisted in the ranks in August 1914 and was commissioned into the Manchesters in 1915. According to his Army file, he was buried in the vicinity of Savy and later moved to the Savy British Cemetery outside the village. The inscription on his headstone reads, 'Thy Will Be Done'. He was known in the battalion as 'Cock Robin'. See Letter 508.

[92] The battalion was relieved on 21 April, and moved to cellar quarters in Quivières. The only draft of 'Le Christianisme' (*CPF*, p. 126) is annotated 'Quivières', but, as *CPF* points out, Quivières has no church.

506. To Susan Owen

2 May 1917   *13th Casualty Clearing Station*

Dearest Mother,

Here again! The Doctor suddenly was moved to forbid me to go into action next time the Battalion go, which will be in a day or two. I did not go sick or anything, but he is nervous about my nerves, and sent me down yesterday—labelled Neurasthenia. I still of course suffer from the headaches traceable to my concussion. This will mean that I shall stay here and miss the next Action Tour of Front Line; or even it may mean that I go further down & be employed for a more considerable time on Base Duty or something of the sort. I shall now try and make my French of some avail... having satisfied myself that, though in Action I bear a charmed life, and none of woman born can hurt me, as regards flesh and bone, yet my nerves have not come out without a scratch. Do not for a moment suppose I have had a 'breakdown'. I am simply <u>avoiding</u> one.

At the first Ambulance I arrived at in the Car, a Corporal came up to me with a staid air of sleepy dignity that seemed somehow familiar. And when he began to enter in a Note Book my name & age, we knew each other. It was old Hartop of the Technical![93] Bystanding Tommies were astounded at our fraternity. For the Good old Sort brought back in an instant all the days of study in Shrewsbury, and the years that were better than these, or any years to come. Although married, as you may know to one of the girls who acted with me at the Socials, he has not grown up any more since the last term at the P.T.C. He was reading the same old books that we 'did' there. I was jolly glad to see them again, & to borrow. For he has nothing particular to do but read on his present job of Pack Store Corporal in the R.A.M.C. Davis also is married. How fortunate is Stanley Webb, (not speaking of his engagement, but of his Blighty.)[94]

If I haven't got a Blighty in this war, I will take good care not to get a <u>Blight</u>, as many have done, even from this Regiment. I should certainly have got a bullet wound, if I had not used the utmost caution in wriggling along the ground on one occasion. There was a party of Germans in a wood about 200 yds <u>behind</u> us, and his trench which we had just taken was only a foot deep in places, & I was obliged to keep passing up & down it. As a matter of fact I rather enjoyed the evening after the Stunt, being only a few hundred yds. from the Town, as you knew, and having come through the fire so miraculously: and being, moreover, well fed on the Bosche's untouched repast ! ! It was curious and troubling to pick up his letters where he had left off writing in the middle of a word! If we had gone down from the line next day all would have been very well, but we were kept up (in another part of the line) for 9 days after it: under incessant shelling.

I am so glad you got the one Field Card which I was able to work down from there. Your last Parcel has arrived, and I enjoyed the Munchoc right well. I had some compensation for lost parcels in being given a parcel sent to an officer who was wounded the <u>first day</u> he joined us. It is a regimental custom never to send Food Stuffs back after Officers who go down to Hospital! I shall soon want some more Players. <u>Nothing else yet!</u>—Don't omit to address C.C.S.13.

I am more glad than I dare say to know that dear Mary is now all right. I try to imagine that you are really well. How strange that the fact that I am in Hospital means that all cause of uneasiness about me is removed from you! Do not hawk this letter about! Nay, I would rather you told no one I am a Casual again!

Your very own Wilfred

[93] Fred Hartop, who attended the Shrewsbury Technical School during Owen's time there.
[94] Stanley Webb was wounded at Monchy-le-Preux. He enlisted in the RAMC in 1914 and was commissioned Second Lieutenant in the East Surrey Regiment in November 1916.

507. To Susan Owen

4 May 1917   *13th Casually Clearing Station*

My own dear Mother,

I have been expecting every day to be moved from here, but nothing happens; only a great calm happiness. We are a cheery crowd here this time, and I like everyone as a great & interesting fellow. <u>Some</u> of us have been sent down here as a little mad. Possibly I am among them. One man in particular is supposed to be a Brain Case. He is a Trinity College (Oxford) boy, and a nephew of Sir Frederick Treves;[95] and is going to get damages from his C.O. for libel or something of that sort; with Sir Frederick & F. E. Smith[96] to back him up!! The chief arguments of his denouncers are (1) that he had an original Scheme for making a haul of German Prisoners, and (2) he happened to read the Bible. He is, of course, perfectly sane, but may be sent to England!

I have just been writing in French some letters for one <u>Barlow</u>[97] of Typewriter fame, who has given me a personal introduction to old Erskine Macdonald,[98] whom he treats to dinners in Town in return for the literary chat which old Skinny can give him. Also, I shall now have no trouble about Typewriting!

I have no news, but that it has been splendidly hot lately, & we have been living the lounging, irresponsible life of a hydro. It will not last long for some of us. I don't care at all if I am not sent back to the same Batt. since the C.O.[99] is leaving, & Sorrel is in England: and I believe we are going to be a Flying Column, rushed about to wherever there is scrapping to be done.

I have, before coming down here, made proper arrangements for your letters to be sent on. Please address everything to 13 C.C.S. who will also send things after me.

Players & the thin Viyella Shirt left in the Drawer are all I want. If you haven't got the Viyella, I must needs have a new one.

Always your lovingest   W.E.O. x

(Leslie has my 'Sunrise'[100] just done here.)

[95] Sir Frederick Treves (1853–1923), Sergeant-Surgeon to King Edward VII and famous for his friendship with Joseph Merrick, the 'Elephant Man'. He was also noted for his field hospital work in the Second Anglo-Boer War (1899–1902).

[96] Frederick Edwin Smith (1872–1930), 1st Earl of Birkenhead, British Conservative politician, who was Attorney General 1915–19.

[97] Unidentified.

[98] London publisher of *The Little Books of Georgian Verse, The Poetry Review* (edited by Galloway Kyle), and the XXth Century Poetry Series. Macdonald and Kyle were one and the same person. See DH, 'A Publisher of the First World War Poetry: Galloway Kyle', *Notes and Queries* (June 1986), pp. 185–6.

[99] Lieutenant Colonel L. Luxmore, DSO, commanded the battalion throughout the Somme battles of 1916 until May 1917; he was succeeded as CO by Lieutenant Colonel Whittaker, MC, Dorsetshire Regiment. In November 1917 Lieutenant Colonel E. Vaughan, DSO, Manchester Regiment, took over.

[100] See Letter 509.

508. To Mary Owen

8 May 1917   *13th Casualty Clearing Station*

My very dear Sister,

I have just re-read your last letter of April 22, which I carry about with me in my Pocket Folio of most valuable papers. Such letters are not received every day—except only from Mother. These papers have had an addition which may be useful—an introductory note to Erskine Macdonald, who edits the

Georgy-porgy Verse Books. My new acquaintance Barlow seems to have old Erskine at his beck & call. This Barlow is a Yorkshire man, & knows the Jobsons. Which is more than I do. But I have begun to find that everyone I meet knows someone that I know. There is a 'Neurasthenia Case' here that I remember at H.Q. of the Artists Rifles. He was Mark Hamburg's[101] father's pupil, & Boris Hamburg's secretary. There is an officer of the Welsh Guards who also has news of old friends. I told you how I met old Hartop.

I have also found among French Officers relations of people I knew in Bordeaux!

I saw in the Casualty List about May: Major W. Forrest,[102] KOSB International Footballer. I could find no room for doubt about poor old Walter.

I had a most characteristic lovable letter from Dorothy about a week ago. I cannot bear to read the exalted things she exclaims, while I am here, so indolent, & well-looked after.

The Nerve Specialist is a kind of wizard, who mesmerises when he likes: a famous man. He is a friend of Dr. Keeble[103] and the Reading Botany People!

You must not entertain the least concern about me because I am here. I certainly was shaky when I first arrived. But today Dr. Browne[104] was hammering at my knees without any response whatever. (At first I used to execute the High Kick whenever he touched them) i.e. Reflex Actions quite normal. You know it was not the Bosche that worked me up, nor the explosives, but it was living so long by poor old Cock Robin (as we used to call 2/Lt. Gaukroger), who lay not only near by, but in various places around and about, if you understand. I hope you don't!

I have no intimation at all about my next move.

Meanwhile I have superb weather, sociably-possible friends, great blue bowls of yellow Mayflower,[105] baths and bed *ad lib*. Soon I shall have Letters from Home.

Your own W.E.O. X

It is absurd for me to keep saying 'I hope you are well' or even to enquire about Mother. What do you take me for ? ? ?

---

[101] Mark Hambourg (1879–1960), pianist and composer.

[102] Walter Torrie Forrest, MC, 1st/4th Battalion, King's Own Scottish Borderers, Blanche Bulman's fiancé, was killed in action at Gaza, Palestine, 19 April 1917, aged 37, and is buried at Gaza Military Cemetery.

[103] Professor Sir Frederick William Keeble, CBE, FRS (1870–1952), botanist, was Director of the Royal Horticultural Society's Garden Wisley at this time, in addition to being Controller of the Horticultural Food Production Department, Board of Agriculture. His *Practical Plant Physiology* survives among Owen's books.

[104] DH identifies him as William Brown, an eminent psychiatrist and later Reader at Oxford (*WOANB*, p. 309).

[105] 'His fingers wake and flutter; up the bed. / His eyes come open with a pull of will, / Helped by the yellow may-flowers by his head.' 'Conscious', *CPF*, p. 138.

509. To Susan Owen[106]

10 May 1917   13th Casualty Clearing Station

Dearest Mother,

I sent a card yesterday of a place I know very well.[107] When I was with the Dug-Out Making Detachment, we used to pass this village, and every night the whiz-bangs & machine guns exacted their Toll. This card I found in a shop in Corbie,[108] with the enclosed, a picture taken in Summer 1915, so you can imagine what sort of a billet it made in the Feb. of 1917! It was in this village that I fell, & knocked the good old Nut.[109] I hope you will keep these safe!

I sailed in a steam-tug about 6 miles down the Canal with another 'inmate'.

The heat of the afternoon was Augustan; and it has probably added another year to my old age to have been able to escape marching in equipment under such a sun.

The scenery was such as I never saw or dreamed of since I read the *Fairie Queene*. Just as in the Winter when I woke up lying on the burning cold snow I fancied I must have died & been pitch-forked into the Wrong Place, so, yesterday, it was not more difficult to imagine that my dusky barge was wending up to Avalon, and the peace of Arthur, and where Lancelot heals him of his grievous wound.[110] But the Saxon is not broken, as we could very well hear last night. Later, a real thunderstorm did its best to seem terrible, and quite failed.

The next book for you to read is *A Knight on Wheels*.[111] It is great.

I, with the inherited diffidence of my distinguished Grandma, must say I could never do anything like so great.

I suppose in the million eyes of the Empire I have already done a thing greater than this merry book; but, then, more fools the million eyes...

I think it is about time your letters addressed here were turning up. None have been sent down from the Line.

How are you rationing? The French hereabouts subsist chiefly on Dandelion Salad. I am not joking. The young leaves with oil make an excellent supper. Tell me how you find it.

I live mainly on Pine Apple Chunks. There are going to be certain things Afterwards which will be held by all who love me in everlasting TABOO,

One of these is Pine Apple Chunks.

Another is a lead pencil on bad paper.

Another is the smoke of a damp wood fire.

Post is now being cleared.

All Love from your very own   Wilfred x

---

[106] With this letter Owen enclosed a first draft of 'Sunrise' (*CPF*, p. 526).
[107] The card has not survived.

108 Near Amiens.
109 This card, too, is lost. It probably pictured Le Quesnoy-en-Santerre.
110 This afternoon on the canal inspired 'Hospital Barge' (*CPF*, p. 127).
111 *A Knight on Wheels* (Hodder & Stoughton, 1914), by Ian Hay (Major General John Hay Beith, 1876–1952), novelist and playwright.

510. To Colin Owen

14 May 1917   [*13th Casualty Clearing Station*]

Dearest Colin,

Here is some Loot, from a Pocket which I rifled on the Field. I was thinking of you when I was unbuckling the Bugle from the equipment, and being then in a particularly noble frame of mind, meant to present it to you some day. But now I have got too fond of the thing to part with it![112]

The sensations of going over the top are about as exhilarating as those dreams of falling over a precipice, when you see the rocks at the bottom surging up to you. I woke up without being squashed. Some didn't. There was an extraordinary exultation in the act of slowly walking forward, showing ourselves openly.[113]

There was no bugle and no drum for which I was very sorry. I kept up a kind of chanting sing-song: Keep the Line straight!

Not so fast on the left!

Steady on the Left!

Not so fast!

Then we were caught in a Tornado of Shells. The various 'waves' were all broken up and we carried on like a crowd moving off a cricket-field. When I looked back and saw the ground all crawling and wormy with wounded bodies,[114] I felt no horror at all but only an immense exultation at having got through the Barrage…We were more than an hour moving over the open and by the time we came to the German Trench every Bosche had fled. But a party of them had remained lying low in a wood close behind us, and they gave us a very bad time for the next four hours.

When we were marching along a sunken road, we got the wind up once. We knew we must have passed the German outposts somewhere on our left rear. All at once the cry rang down 'Line the Bank'. There was a tremendous scurry of fixing bayonets, tugging off breach-covers & opening pouches, but when we peeped over, behold one solitary German, haring along towards us, with his head down and his arms stretched in front of him, as if he were going to take a high dive through the earth (which I have no doubt he would like to have done). Nobody offered to shoot him, he looked too funny; that was our only prisoner that day!

Did I tell you that on Easter Sunday evening we brought down a Hun Plane, I took the aviator's handkerchief as a souvenir! It is not permitted to take anything belonging to the machine.

Now write soon something about your new Farm. Sketch me a plan of it. Have you a pleasant room of your own? Most of the gentlemen here seem keen on farming after the war. The musician is going to farm, having not practised the piano since 1914; the aviator is going to farm; the undergraduate is going to farm. Some day I will arise and go unto Mr. Bather,[115] and will say unto him 'Bather, I am no more worthy to be called thy son than Colin; but make me as one of thy hired servants.' But his brother was wrath and would not let him in, and began to beat him and entreat him shamefully. But this Bather came out and said unto him 'Why beatest thou the ass? Be gentle with my servant, lest he fall on good soil, and make it like the wilderness of Judea, which is a great wilderness.'

So he departed unto Some Area, and seeing a tree, he also pruned it that it might bring forth more fruit.

After that the tree died also, and he lay down, and slept under the shadow thereof forty days and forty nights; and gathered in his ears in due season, the mustard seed, which is the smallest of all seeds, yet brought forth ten fold, fifty fold, and an hundred fold.

And with the price thereof he bought a field, which is called the Potter's Field, because he pottered there day and night and wrought nothing.

But dined sumptuously every day of locusts and wild asses' milk.

And it came to pass that a woman besought him saying 'Give me, I pray thee, a little water to drink.' Instead of water he gave her the milk. And the same woman was bent double for eighteen years. And went out sorrowful, and wept by the river of Babylon. And all fish that were in the river died.

And he knowing that the time of harvest was near at hand, and of the creeping things that creep upon the earth, went down into that water and washed seven times.

And he was covered with boils from head to foot.

And they put him upon his own ass and took him to an inn.

And in the process of time, he saithe unto him that kept the inn 'I will drink a little wine for my stomach's sake. Fill me seven barrels full.' And they filled them unto the brim.

And there was silence for the space of half an hour.

And when he understood the meaning of the seven stars, he lifted up his voice, and cried 'Fill them a second time.' So they filled them a second time. Till there was no room for him in the inn.

And his face shone with the brightness of the sun.

And they all looking steadfastly upon his face, said one to another, 'Peradventure he sleepeth.' But he began to belabour them with staves of a new song, so that they all with one accord fled violently down a steep place into the sea.

And there arose a great storm.

For a third part of all the dwellers upon the earth fell into the sea.

But he was asleep.

And he, when he came to himself, saw the stars falling in heaven, like a fig-tree when she casteth her untimely fruits.

But in process of time the devil departed from him, and he arose, and girt up his loins, and sneezed three times, so that the fool said in his heart: It is the coming of a great rain.

But he, stooping down, began to tie the latchet of his shoe. Now because of the new wine and the old leather, it came to pass that the same was rent in twain. And he stood up and cursed them.

And hell followed after.

Then cometh he that kept the inn, grievously tormented, seeking goodly pearls.

But he turned and saithe unto him: Go to! and when I come again I will pay thee.

And he answered and saithe: 'Peradventure thou wilt not return. I will follow thee whithersoever thou goest.'

And he led him up to a pinnacle of the temple; and let him down vehemently through the roof: so that even the stones cried out. And they that saw it were astonied supposing the clouds had dropped this fatness upon the earth. And looking up they beheld the husbandman upon the head-stone of the corner.

And he shook the dust off his feet, and they were all smitten with blindness, because of the things that fell upon the earth.

And he went on his way, rejoicing, and grinning like a dog that licketh the crumbs that the swine would fain have eaten.

And the ass leaped like the hills, even the hill of Basan, which is an high hill. Selah.

CUM PRIVILEGIO.

You can send this to Harold: to be returned to me! I have let my imagination run riot. You must not show these sheets at home. But I hope you will get an innocent laugh out of 'em. I have. It has passed an afternoon very well.

Best love, dear boy. W.E.O. x

[112] The bugle is still in the possession of the Owen Family. It was played at Owen's graveside during the Centenary commemorations at Ors, 4 November 2018.

[113] The action at Fayet described in Letter 505.

[114] This image is expanded in 'The Show' (*CPF*, p. 155).

[115] The farmer for whom Colin was now working at Cressage, 10 miles south-west of Shrewsbury.

512. To Susan Owen

[?16] May 1917   41st Stationary Hospital[116]

My own dear Mother,

Just had yours of Sat. Evening and was astonished to apprehend that the Great Shadow is creeping on towards Colin. What will he be next birthday, seventeen?

I wrote him a wholesome bit of realism in that last letter, as well as a fantasy in the language of the Auth: Ver: of 1611. I have changed my mind and see no reason why you should not have that letter and that fantasia. It was on the model of Leslie's 'Throw her down. So they threw her down. And he said Throw her down again. And they threw her down again. And they gathered up of the fragments that remained etc.'

I did it without any reference to the Book, of course; and without any more detraction from reverence, than, say, is the case when a bishop uses modern slang to relate a biblical story. I simply employed seventeenth century English, and was carried away with it.

Incidentally, I think the big number of texts which jogged up in my mind in half-an-hour bears witness to a goodly store of them in my being. It is indeed so; and I am more and more Christian as I walk the unchristian ways of Christendom. Already I have comprehended a light which never will filter into the dogma of any national church: namely that one of Christ's essential commands was: Passivity at any price! Suffer dishonour and disgrace; but never resort to arms. Be bullied, be outraged, be killed; but do not kill. It may be a chimerical and an ignominious principle, but there it is. It can only be ignored: and I think pulpit professionals are ignoring it very skilfully and successfully indeed.

Have you seen what ridiculous figures Frederick & Arthur Wood[117] are cutting? If they made the Great Objection, I should admire them. They have not the courage.

To begin with I think it was puny of Fritz to deny his name. They are now getting up a petition, mentioning their 'unique powers' invaluable work' and so on, and wish to carry on their work from 82 Mortimer St. W. as usual. I do not recollect Christ's office address in Jerusalem, but in any case I don't think He spent much time there.

St. Paul's business premises, if I remember, were somewhat cramped, not to say confined.

But I must not malign these Brethren because I do not know their exact Apologia.

And am I not myself a conscientious objector with a very seared conscience?

The evangelicals have fled from a few Candles, discreet incense, serene altars, mysterious music, harmonious ritual to powerful electric lighting, overheated atmosphere, palm-tree platforms, grand pianos, loud and animated music, extempore ritual; but I cannot see that they are any nearer to the Kingdom.

Christ is literally in no man's land. There men often hear His voice: Greater love hath no man than this, that a man lay down his life—for a friend.

Is it spoken in English only and French?

I do not believe so.

Thus you see how pure Christianity will not fit in with pure patriotism.

I am glad you sent that cutting from Wells' Book.[118] I hope you understood it. I did not. Not a word of it can I make sense of. I would rather we did not read this Book. Now *The Passionate Friends*[119] I found astounding in its realism but like all the great terrible books it is impossible to 'take sides'. It is not meant to be a comfortable book; it is discussional; it refuses to ignore the unpleasant.

(This practice of <u>selective ignorance</u> is, as I have pointed out, one cause of the War. Christians have deliberately <u>cut</u> some of the main teachings of their code.)

At present I am deep in a marvellous work of Hugo's *The Laughing Man*.

By the same post as your letter came two books from Leslie, by O. Henry.[120]

So I am well set up.

I am marked <u>for the next Evacuation</u> ! !

So glad my Oak Seedlings are growing. How many are there likely to thrive, out of how many acorns? They have been 'dry', you know, for 6 years. Give them every chance.

This countryside is now superb. But from this we are no longer allowed out of the hospital bounds.

Many thanks for *Punch*. Yes Colin has been very good in writing to me. Keep him up to it. It will do <u>him</u> good, don't-you-know! And as for me: they bring me Shropshire, even as yours bring me Home.

Expect me—before Christmas.

Your—one and only—Wilfred x

[116] 13th Casualty Clearing Station was restaffed at this time (see Letter 514, para. 2) and renamed 41st Stationary Hospital.

[117] The travelling evangelist brothers noted in Letter 111. Fritz anglicized his name to Frederick, and both brothers avoided military service by asserting that their services in spiritual healing were crucial to the war effort in the community. See Jennifer Breen, *Wilfred Owen: Selected Poetry and Prose* (Routledge, 1988).

[118] H. G. Wells's *God the Invisible King* was published on 10 May 1917.

[119] By H. G. Wells, London, 1913.

[120] William Sydney Porter ('O. Henry'), 1862–1910, American journalist and prolific writer of humorous short stories.

513. To Susan Owen

18 May 1917   [*41st Stationary Hospital*]

Dearest Mother,

I had the Parcel (Shirt) last night. Have just awakened—too late to write before the post leaves. Your two letters, with enclosures from Paris, came at the same time. The flowers were quite fresh; & I was very refreshed with them.

No more now. They have just awakened me to know if I have any letters for Post!

Your W.E.O. x

514. To Susan Owen

23 May 1917   [*41st Stationary Hospital*]

Dearest Mother,

I wondered why it was such an effort to write the short notes of a day or two ago. I have discovered that I had a temperature of 102.9, so it was not surprising. I am still feverish but on the right side of 100°. I suppose it is Trench Fever, which has been incubating all this time, but they don't say what it is and I don't think they know.

I have had a wretched enough time, <u>not from the fever</u> in myself but from the stew that the whole hospital has got into. A completely new staff from England has taken over. The old people cleared off bag and baggage, bed & bedding, before even the new things arrived. They <u>did</u> put us in some sort of beds, but otherwise they stripped the ward stark, taking even the drugs. There was not left one chair, one mug, one teapot, one rug, one screen. They took the very ashtrays to which indeed they were welcome, for they are not worth a farthing, and I don't smoke.

No, I could no more smoke a cigarette than any unborn chicken. My servant informed me that I had some Mangee* as he calls it—in my valise. But it does not tempt me at all.

He will not follow me to the Base when—or if—I go.

I repeat the new address of this place:

41st Stationary Hospital.

It is quite likely that I shall appear in the Casualty List, as Neurasthenia is marked W(ound) not S(ick)—not wrongly I think. I know that Capt. Sorrel was mentioned for Shock, and that some persons wear gold stripes for neurasthenia!

Many more are worn for bullet grazes which did not more harm than a needle-scratch.

I am afraid it is quite out of the question to find anything for Mary or even to write for today's post.

Yours ever W.E.O. x

The new staff of the hospital will no doubt start unpacking today.
But I shall never get over my indignation at the manner of the Relief!
* Pronounced Mŭnjy (Lancashire 'u').

515. To Susan Owen

24 May 1917   *41st Stationary Hospital*

My own dearest Mother,

I feel normal today. Am sitting on the bed in the one Kimono left in this Rag Time Hospital. Have just had your Sat. evening (May 19) Letter, full of gracious truths: the most pleasing being the tales of your gardening. I am sure it will do you good, and I may indeed get Leave before the Summer falls, now that it is likely I am out of the 'Area' of the 2nd Battalion. Some regiments get leave for every officer regularly every 5, 4, or even 3 months, but in the 2nd Man. the <u>minimum</u> seems to have been 7!

*   *   *

The M.O. has just been round—leaving me 5 mins. before the Post goes.

I am astonished at my Balance at Cox's, but not so astonished as you, knowing it is deceptive. There have been a number of Mess Bills, & other cheques drawn lately which are <u>not yet entered</u> at the Bank. Moreover my Military Wardrobe will want renewing if there is another winter campaign.

On the other hand I confess—I mean I profess with pride—that I have not run into any kind of danger of losing moneys. My first Mess Bill for Jan. was £6: which I consider disgraceful for the kind of stuff we got.

I think it will be safe if you send both Cheque Book & Pass Book in registered envelope to <u>41st Stationary Hospital</u>: (by return)

It is evidently Trench Fever I had, but I feel fine today. I shall send this note & go on writing for tomorrow's post.

Your own W.E.O.

516. To Mary Owen

25 May 1917   *41st Stationary Hospital*

My dearest Mary,

I hope this little note will arrive in time for the Birthday Morning.[121]

I am writing in bed, after an awful breakfast. Enough of those who profess and call themselves Sisters. I have a real sister, and I want her with me!

On one's 21st Birthday, it is better to look forward than back, because that way one cannot see anything at all. It is a good thing—for Father's ethics, and the Bunting, the Majestic One, and the rest—that on my 21st Birthday, when I looked into the Future, I did not see the War coming. I did not. But if I had, I should certainly have borrowed sixpence and bundled over into Spain. In August 1914, when the moon was red, I used to go up at night to a hill-top, and look at Spain. I still do that in dreams. You have your battlefield, my dear sister, to look back upon. You too have walked slowly through many barrages; you have taken trench after trench from resisting Life; and no terror has halted you. You have taken your objective: all that remains is to consolidate....

I've now had all your letters from Alpenrose; they were full of atmosphere. Glad you saw & liked Miss O.A.J.[122] Without wishing to see her myself, I may say that this lady is much to be admired. She has extraordinary power over words. Her power alas sometimes degenerates into tyranny. But she is a woman who has as much poetic worth as Madam Wilcox,[123] the hussy.

It grieves me that I can't send you any present at all yet. I am a prisoner. If they would send me to a Town of some sort I should be cured in a week. Here is the list of places & the amt. of time required to effect complete cure, showing average temperature & pulses.

Place.	Time Req'd to effect Cure.	Temp. Normal (98.4)	Pulse. Normal 80
St. Q.[124]	10 years after 'Duration'	107° (in the shade)	150
Bordeaux	6 months	98.4	90
Paris	3 months	do.	100
Cressage[125]	10 minutes	do.	normal
H.M.S. *Zealandia*[126]	20 mins.	do.	rather erratic
London	1 hour	perfect	
Alpenrose	1/2 Hour	90°	50
Mahim (Europe)	.01 second	perfect	200 (1st minute only)

There are too many officers here who are quite well. For the last 3 nights the ward has been a midnight pandemonium. It makes me in such a stew that a thermometer if put in my mouth would at once explode. Fortunately, last night an Artillery Colonel came to sleep here. The racket awaked him. He coughs a bit, and kicks the bedclothes up and the mattress down, and the flies all around and about. Then he sits up and opening his eyes to the full extent, bellows: 'Are there NONE in this ward who wish to sleep.' 'There are, sir,' says I, 'and I am glad you mean to stop the din.' With that he leaps off the bed, & runs out of the ward for the Sister, brings in a wretched trembling maiden just out of England: and cries: 'Look! Madam! Is this a hospital or is it a _____ _____ _____ ? ? ?' And flaps his pyjamas, and tries to stamp, but his bare feet made a poor enough noise. I wonder what kind of men you get in your wards. I hear that the sisters & nurses are nice people. Did you see anything of 'Missis Gordon'[127] when at Alpenrose?

No more nonsense now, but just my very dearest wishes for the best years of my darling sister. May they be without cloud or ruffle of storm. May they each be long years, that is to say, full, and may they be full of good, filled from Heaven. You will speak for me when you look up to God; and I will stand by you and for you as long as we move among men. In other words, I am, gentle Sister, always your Brother,

Wilfred

[121] Mary's twenty-first birthday, 30 May 1917.
[122] Olwen Joergens.
[123] Ella Wheeler Wilcox (1850–1919), a popular American poet and journalist.
[124] St Quentin.
[125] Where Colin was farming.
[126] The battleship on which Harold was then at sea.
[127] Gordon Gunston had got engaged.

517. To Susan Owen

Monday, 28 May 1917   [*41st Stationary Hospital*]

Dearest Mother,

Just a note. I was down on the list for evacuation all last week & up to last night. This morning the evacuation takes place—I and another, a Major, are crossed off the list at the last moment. It is sickening, more especially as this place becomes less and less pleasant. I suppose I shall wait for the next batch, but before that I may be turned out elsewhere—to some Line Battalion.

These are the days when last year the army was good to me. The same dreadful uncertainty overhangs me here as on that 'Leave pending Gazette.' Would I had to report at Witley Camp on June —. I came across an old 5 Man. lad a day or two ago. Some of the Witley officers are out near here with the 1/5th. I wish I could rejoin them. I hear that the horrid old Major[128] is now commanding the 2nd Batt. It is not likely that Sorrel will be back for a long time. Hence I hope that I am clear of them, and shall try to avoid rather than find them again. As you may have seen they charged me £6. for my January Mess Bill. I scarcely had anything for it.

I am feeling quite well now, but I keep a sub-normal temp.! Useful enough in this weather.

I hope you will have plenty of picnics in the hay. Have you been to Cressage? P.R.[129] arrived last evening before I went to Church. Rather a 'footy' paper as Leslie says. There is a rumour you are going to Alpenrose. Go!

Your lovingest W.E.O. x

[128] Major, later Lieutenant Colonel, J. F. Dempster, temporarily assumed command of 2nd Manchesters on 18 May 1917. Owen encountered him again in London. See Letter 528.
[129] *The Poetry Review.*

518. To Susan Owen

Picture postcard: Amiens,[130] La Cathédrale vue de Saint-Maurice

5 June 1917   [*41st Stationary Hospital*]

Am not here—no move yet—quite happy—you have some erroneous ideas about my state of health! I have a chum here—glorious in my eyes for having hob-nobbed with Ian Hay. You sh'd keep the *Chambers*[131] in which *Knight on Wheels* first appeared. Last evening had your dear letter of May 31.

Things are vastly improving now in the management of this Hydro! Poor Mawkie Morgan! Poor Ragge[132] & no Bones

[130] Against the name is written 'I am not here'.
[131] *Chambers's Edinburgh Journal*, established 1832, regularly taken by Tom Owen.
[132] John Ragge had been invalided home. He later returned to France, where he was killed, aged 19, on 22 September 1918. He is commemorated on the Loos Memorial, Pas-de-Calais.

519. To Susan Owen

6 June 1917   *41st Stationary Hospital*

Dearest Mother,

I go down today. Where to?—Nobody knows. May be in the Hosp. Train for days.

Health: quite restored.
Mood: highest variety of jinks.
Weather: sub-tropical.
Time: 11 a.m.
Appearance: sun-boiled lobster.
Hair: 8% Grey.
Cash in hand: 5 francs.

Size of Socks: same as previous consignment.
Sole Complaints: Nostalgia
                    Mosquito Bites
Last Book Read: *A picked Company* by Belloc.[133]
Clothing: sparse, almost <u>faun</u>.
Religion: Primitive Christian.
Aim in War: Extinction of Militarism <u>beginning</u> with Prussian.
Aim in Life: Pearls <u>before</u> Swine.
Medicine: Iron
Nerve: Iron—(over ?–) wrought.
Favourite Metal: Silver.
Favourite Colour: Sky- violet.
Favourite Drink: Natural Lemon Juice.
Favourite Animal: Children.
         „ Haunt and which?: Moor —Monk.
Pet Aversion: Pets.
Blood Relations: Unbleedable.
Address of same: Temporal only.
                    Permanent: Unknown & doubtful.
My address: as usual; i.e. unfixed.
Affection: Yours.
Name: W.E.O. or words to that effect.

[133] *A Picked Company: being a selection from the writings of H. Belloc* (Methuen, 1915).

520. To Susan Owen

8 June [1917]   *41st Stationary Hosp!*

Dearest Mother,

Two days ago we started forth in motors for the Railhead: The Train was there, but no accommodation for Officers. The O.C. Train a mi<u>nute</u> doctor, with many papers and much pince-nez, refused to let us board: especially as a Major who was with us expressed himself thus: 'Aw I decline. I <u>ab</u>solutely decline, to travel in a coach where there are—haw—<u>Men</u>!'

This Major is an unconscionable snob, and consequently suffers something from my humour.

It was slightly too hot that afternoon: they put some twenty Germans into this sumptuous train, and left us stamping on the platform: some indeed lying on stretchers in blankets under the staring sun. When we got back to the Hospital we were the objects of some very ungratifying applause from the unlucky ones left behind. I am still on the List, & the thing may come off more successfully tomorrow or on Monday.

I have not written yesterday, because it is just as well that you should not address any more to the 41st as from the date you heard of my departure. Thus I am getting all you send here up to the last and none will be lost. On the evening we[134] were brought back to this place, all thick, as it was, with the dust we had shaken off our feet. I had the blessed compensation of your parcel. The Cake travelled perfectly: and the gingerbreads likewise have journeyed yet further to their appointed place. The destiny of the cake is now half accomplished.

I wonder if its nutriment went to succour the white corpuscles so put about by insect-bites, or whether it went to swell the grey matter so diminished by the war.

There is an excellent article on Nerves in the *Daily Mail*, June 5th 6th or 7th; 6th I think.

You need study to observe none of these precautions concerning me: except to respect my strange solitude when I resort to it, and stranger friends if I resort to them. And except the following:—

Preserve me scrupulously from old women without dignity, wit, or wisdom.

Preserve me from young women with gush and no beauty.

Preserve me from women of beauty and no charm; but take not measures against women of charm and no beauty, for they are the sugar of the earth.

Preserve me from dogs.

Preserve me from ugly children.

Preserve me from varnished wood, powdered women, dusty plants, plated silver, antimacassars, wigs, and all false hair.

Preserve me from men in waistcoats shirt cuffs and braces of a Sunday afternoon; (and preserve them from me for I would tear their waistcoats from them, and cut their throats (open at the neck) and belt them into noble creatures.)

Preserve me from the man who sits in stocking feet of an evenin', and scratches his big toe with his heel.

Preserve me from the youth who carries a pencil on the lobe of his right ear; (but preserve the cigarette in the ear of a Tommy for it is his last.)

Preserve this letter.

Preserve me from irritant underclothes.

Preserve me from the unclean bath.

Preserve me from billiards, whist, and football, and all talk of the same.

Preserve me from people who eat eggs when I don't want any.

Preserve me from the person who sneezes like a bomb bursting in water.

Preserve me from the player who in the same chord strikes the bass before the treble.

Preserve me from all rag-time.

Preserve me from *Answers,*[135] *Pearsons,*[136] and all but Page 1 of *Tit-Bits*[137]

Preserve me from Pennyman.[138]

Preserve me from Morris.[139]

Preserve me from the exposition of all instruments of war in chambers, all ships in glass-bottles, plush chairs, group-photographs, flowers under glass-shades, shell-pictures-frames, scene-painted boulders, and all the arts and deceitful devices of Victoria.

This will be as much as you can memorize for the moment.

I have not finished.

Your very own W.E.O.

Great thanks for Book: *Barbe*[140] which I had read in ancient days—in Torquay—borrowing from the library: but have quite forgotten & shall be so glad to read again.

[134] DH demonstrates that Letter 628 (*CL*) is in fact the missing half of this letter, 'one of a series of flippant epistles...to cheer himself and his family during the early stages of recovery from shellshock' (*The Library*, p. 284). It is reinstated here.

[135] A light weekly journal containing fiction, topical articles, and competitions. Founded in 1888, it continued, in a modified form, until 1956.

[136] *Pearson's Weekly* contained articles on general topics, fiction, and humour. Founded in 1890, it was incorporated into *Tit-Bits* in 1939.

[137] The first page of *Tit-Bits* was composed entirely of jokes.

[138] The Rev. William Geoffrey Pennyman (d.1942) was Vicar of St Mary the Virgin, Shrewsbury, 1910–13, and author of *The War's Challenge to the Church*—possibly the cause of Owen's antipathy.

[139] Based on the condemnation in the next paragraph of 'all the arts and deceitful devices of Victoria', possibly William Morris (1834–96), poet, textile designer, socialist activist, and leader of the Arts and Crafts Movement.

[140] *Barbe of Grand Bayou* by John Oxenham. See Letter 521.

521. To Susan Owen

Sunday, 10 June 1917   [*41st Stationary Hospital*]

Dearest Mother,

We make another sally this day. On the whole, the rout of our last sortie was fortunate for me, as I have the parcel, and the letters and J. Oxenham's Books.[141]

The *V. Splendid* contains several real poems: those indeed which you have marked. But the majority of the things have no <u>poetic</u> value at all.

The 'Cross Roads' is very very good. Otherwise the work has little <u>Pacific</u> Value, if you understand me.

Except to individual troubles: for he evidently holds the Moslem doctrine—preached by Horatio Bottomley,[142] but not by the Nazarene—of salvation <u>by death in war.</u>

Barbe of Grand Bayou[143] seems a little too idyllic so far. Oxenham's aim seems to be to unsophisticate the reader. It is very pleasant to be reminded of Brittany, which seems not to be of this continent at all.

The book is at the opposite pole from the O. Henry books which Leslie sent me. Impossible to read them together.

At the same time I am at p. 50 of A. & E. Castle's recent book : *The Hope of the House,*[144] which promises well, and which I can recommend.

My man has gone to the neighbouring Town today, so I am in haste to pack. I shall think especially with you this Evening. I crave Travel and shall be pleased like any infant to get into a puff puff again. Have your letter writ, and post it as soon as you get my address ! !

Your W.E.O. x

[141] John Oxenham (1852–1941), novelist and poet. *The Vision Splendid* (verse, 1917) contains a poem entitled 'Cross Roads', first published separately in 1903.

[142] Horatio Bottomley (1860–1933), journalist and financier who founded the *John Bull* periodical in 1906. Liberal MP 1906–12, Independent MP 1918–22. Twice bankrupt, twice acquitted on fraud charges, he was imprisoned 1922–7. For an example of his style see Letter 667, n. 187.

[143] Published 1915.

[144] Published 1915.

523. To Susan Owen

Picture postcard: Étretat,[145] Les Roches

[*Postmark 12 June 1917*]   [*No. 1 General Hospital*]

I am sending by same post a Panorama of the Bay. I seem to be in America: the Hospital is staffed with the Amer[n]. Doctors, Orderlies, and Sisters. This is the Officers' Quarter. I live in a Marquee on the front lawn. We are free to walk away thr' this delicious Norman Coast. But so far—all yesterday—and this m'ng we are hanging around waiting for the M.O's interview. I have no idea how long I shall be kept here. Not worth your coming over ! !

W.E.O.

P.S. (later) Shall soon be home on Sick Leave. Vive !

[145] On the Channel coast, 5 miles north of Le Havre.

524. To Susan Owen

June 1917   *No. I General Hospital*

My dearest Mother,

I think it is very likely that the Americans will send me to England, but we must permit ourselves no jubilations yet. I shall believe it as soon as I find myself within swimming distance of the Suffolk Coast. The usual thing on arrival is a fortnight or more of genuine leave at home!

I am sorry! I can think of nothing else to write about, and if I went on about my expectations this letter would end in a scream. If I go bathing this afternoon it will be to practise swimming in Channel waters.

If I looked all morning at the Northern Horizon it was not because of its infinity of sea, but because of its boundary of cliffs, and the starting of the firm home road.

If I enjoy this place and make the most of it, it is because I believe I am to leave it very soon.

If I seem to be writing a matter of fact letter, it is because I am not too sure that what I am writing about will realize into matter of fact.

I will let you have a card the moment we leave. Don't expect Telegrams. I may be kept some time in London or elsewhere.

                                                  Always your W.E.O. x

525. To Susan Owen

Postcard

Sunday Mng. [Postmark 17 June 1917]   *Welsh Hospital, Netley*[146] *Hampshire*

I shall have to stay here a week or so. Visitors are allowed in the afternoons, but you will of course wait till I get my 3 Weeks at home. We are on Southampton Water, pleasantly placed, but not so lovely a coast as Etretat. The Town is not far off, & we are allowed to go in. Hope you had my Telegram. Nothing to write about now. I am in too <u>receptive</u> a mood to speak at all about the other side the seamy side of the *Manche*. I just wander about absorbing Hampshire.

                                                            W.E.

---

[146] The Royal Victoria Hospital, with its imposing faççde on Southampton Water, was built in 1863 and demolished in 1966. It was a quarter of a mile long, the world's largest military hospital at its inception. See Philip Hoare, *Spike Island: The Memory of a Military Hospital* (Fourth Estate, 2001).

526. To Susan Owen

Monday [?18 June 1917]   *Welsh Hospital, Netley*

Dearest of Mothers,

I had your letter this morning—a great delight. This place is very boring, and I cannot believe myself in England in this unknown region. I have just written to Leslie asking him to come and convince me.

It is pleasant to be among the Welsh—doctors, sisters, orderlies.

And nurses.

They kept me in bed all yesterday, but I got up for an hour & went out today, only to be recaught and put back to bed for the inspection of a specialist. He was very nice, and when I said my home was in Shrewsbury he asked if it were in the Town itself or in the country.

I said it was nearer the country. To which he gave the usual specialist reply 'Ha!' I also inwardly said 'Ha!'

There was no choice of Hospitals when we were detailed off from Southampton, tho' I tried to get the Birmingham Train, which those officers who lived hereabouts had to take!

When I get away I shall try to journey through London. There are new clothes I want.

The Voyage was in a luxurious West Indian Liner. I had a cabin to myself, and fared sumptuously at Table.

Here also we fare much better than anywhere in France. I sleep well and show every sign of health, except in the manipulation of this pencil.

                                                         Your own W.E.O. x

You may as well prepare Mr. Bather gently for an agricultural slump in labour.

528. To Susan Owen

26 June 1917   *Craiglockhart War Hospital,*[147] *Slateford, Midlothian*

My dearest Mother,

We left Netley at 11 on Monday Morning, & I separated from Captain Robertson at King's Cross about 3 p.m. I got a new hat at Peter Robinson's,[148] and changed into new collar, tie, & pin. I entrusted Peter Robinson to send my old hat to a Cleaner's. It should turn up at home in a week or so. Then I made for

Burlington House. This year's show is nothing so good as the last; and I didn't spend very long there. I had tea at the Shamrock Tea Rooms, perhaps the most eminently respectable exclusive and secluded in Town. There was the usual deaf old lady and her Companion holding forth upon the new curate. I happen to know that a few stories higher in the same building is an Opium Den. I have not investigated. But I know. That's London. I met few faces I knew. <u>But</u> Strolling down New Bond Street, I ran into the last person on earth or under the earth that I wished to meet: Major, now Colonel, Dempster, of the 2nd Battalion. We stopped, of course, and he pretended to be very affable and cordial. Yet I know a more thorough-bred Snob does not exist—even in the imagination of Thackeray. To meet him in my first hour in town. Alas! This, also, is London!...

I had time to get measured for new Slacks at Pope and Bradley's.

A cheap dinner, and so to King's Cross an hour early to get a Corner Seat.

I read some Israel Zangwill[149] as far as the Midlands. Then wondering how few miles I was from You, slept. I woke up as we were rounding the Coast by Dunbar. I saw nothing waiting to meet me at the Waverley Station, so I went into the Hotel and breakfasted hugely. I then walked the lovely length of Princes Street. The Castle looked more than ever a Hallucination, with the morning sun behind it. Or again it had the appearance of a huge canvas scenic device such as surrounds Earls Court.

A Taxi brought me up here about 2½ miles from the Town.

There is nothing very attractive about the place, it is a decayed Hydro,[150] far too full of officers, some of whom I know.

I shall not see the M.O. till Tomorrow: I am going out now to take the lie of the land.

Has my watch turned up? (Colin's I mean.) It was at a Repairer's when I was called away, but I did not forget it, & an American girl promised to mail it across home right then. Always your lovingest of all,

Wilfred x

---

[147] At the time that HO and JB published *CL*, the Craiglockhart building was the Convent of the Sacred Heart, a College of Education. It now houses the Business School of Edinburgh Napier University as well as the War Poets Collection, including a permanent exhibition of its tenure as a war hospital.

[148] A department store in Oxford Street.

[149] Israel Zangwill (1864–1926), Jewish novelist, playwright, and lecturer; *Children of the Ghetto* (1892) was his best-known work.

[150] Siegfried Sassoon describes Craiglockhart in similar terms in *Sherston's Progress* (Faber & Faber, 1936, pp. 86–8), where he calls it Slateford (after the nearest railway station): 'the War Office had wasted no money on interior decoration; consequently the place had the melancholy atmosphere of a decayed hydro, redeemed only by its healthy situation and pleasant view of the Pentland Hills.'

530. To Mrs Nelly Bulman

1 July 1917   *Craiglockhart*

Dear Mrs Bulman,

How exceedingly kind of you to send Miss Henderson[151] to see me, and with such a goodly present! A good friend might have sent me strawberries, but only a very special friend could have remembered the cream!

I have also to thank you for the encouragement of your Letter received in France when encouragement was most needed; but when to answer letters was a physical impossibility. Unfortunately, if I delay an answer for a month, it becomes a moral impossibility! Even this I might have written two days ago; but you will forgive me, my Auntie Nelly, and charitably put it down to my distraught state of mind? (For you are all Charity, and I am beginning to discover the sources of my own Mother's sweetness.)

I am not able to settle down here without seeing Mother. I feel a sort of reserve and suspense about everything I do. Otherwise I am quite well—far better than, say, in the good days at Kelso.

I have endured unnameable tortures in France; but I know that I have not suffered by this war as you have and are suffering.[152] I felt your sympathy with me out there; but now, my dear Auntie Nelly, it is all on my part.

Believe me, very sincerely, and, may I not say affectionately, yours,

Wilfred Owen

---

[151] See Letter 532.
[152] Her son Bill and her daughter's fiancé, Walter Forrest, had been killed in action. See Letters 370 and 508.

531. To Leslie Gunston

1 July 1917   *Craiglockhart*

Dear L.

> Worde is comen unto Edenburrowe
> That you are in Londonne Towne.

You give no address so I forward the *Morals*[153] to Alpenrose. You will like to read it in London. I feel rather limp this morning—couldn't sleep —so read Locke until 3 a.m.

I noticed it never grew quite dark all night; Daylight glimmered through my Northern window even at 2 o'clock.

I have to meet Blanche Bulman in Edinburgh this afternoon.

A pleasaunte streme of letters is flowing in to me: but it must be fed by my own showres swoote.

My Ballad[154] is going strong, finished Fytte 1 at the second sitting. Late last night I very hastily draughted a Fate sonnet.[155] I had an Idea—which is almost my Gospel. Can you get it from this? If so, how would you express it in prose?

Don't omit to enquire about H. Monro. Your own W.E.O.

The Fates. (2nd Draught.)

They watch me, shadowing, to inform the Fates,
   Those constables called Fortune, Chance, and Death;
G. Time, in disguise as one who serves and waits,
Eternity, as women that have breath:

I know them. Men and boys are in their pay,
And those I hold my perfect friends may prove
Agent of theirs, to take me if I stray
From Fatal[156] ordnance. If I move, they move…

_____

Escape? There is one unwatched way: your eyes,
O Beauty! Keep me good that secret gate.[157]
And when the cordon tightens of the spies.
Let the clear iris of your eyes grow great!
Bad So I'll evade the press-gang raid of age
G. And miss the march of lifetime, stage by stage.

June 2. '17[158]

Your W.E.O.

[153] *The Morals of Marcus Ordeyne* (1905), a novel by W. J. Locke (1863–1930). Locke was Secretary to RIBA 1897–1907. Another of his novels is mentioned in Letter 535.

[154] 'Ballad of Lady Yolande', an unfinished ballad in the manner of Sir Walter Scott (*CPF*, p. 472).

[155] 'The Fates' (*CPF*, p. 87).

[156] 'Fate's old' struck out.

[157] 'O Beauty! Keep me ever good that gate' amended to read as above.

[158] A slip for 2 July, the poem being drafted 'late last night'.

532. To Susan Owen

Sunday [1 July 1917][159]   *Craiglockhart*

My dearest Mother,

Your last news was the Note of the 29th. I can't even tell you how long I shall be kept here. I feel pretty sure of another fortnight; but in any case it would be of no interest for you to come just before I am able to get home.

My own plan would be for you to come this week to a lodgement in Edinburgh. (Hotel, Boarding House, Pension, what you will) for two days. Then stay with Mrs. Bulman for a Holiday. It will be very difficult for me to get to Kelso. I should not manage it more than once. I could as easily get right home, I think.

I fancy that having once dislodged you as far as Southport I must not exert you so soon again.

The Stunt Magnificent would have been a semi-surprise expedition to Netley—you and Colin.

I don't want you to travel up alone: taxis & porters require to be hailed with exceeding heavy hailstorms of sticks, bags and umbrellas, nowadays. What about Father? Couldn't he come alone if not with you? Last of all, Send Colin with Tydynges of you all. I will find him a room in the village here, and give him a thundering good time, and he can have my heather suit to come in, and he shall stay four days, and (huf)* I will show him Edinburgh and (huf) the Castle (huf) and Holyrood and (huf) the Zoo, and the fertile fields of Midlothian, and he shall be the incarnation of you all. So shall I be more at rest. For I feel a kind of reservation about all pleasant things I do here. I have made no friends in this place, and the impulse is not in me to walk abroad and find them.

Send therefore Benjamin and inform yourself of me.

I won't write letters. It seems too absurd.

It was good of Leslie to write to you.

Mrs. Bulman sent an ambassadress with strawberries & cream on Friday afternoon: a Miss Henderson, a pleasant young lady, from what I could make out of her Scotch; a trifle nervous of me at first; but I did my best: and was sorry I called her Miss Ferguson so often. We have a fool of a butler-orderly, who comes up to me & says 'Young Lady to see you, Sir!'—no card—no name. So I says 'I don't think, but what's it like?' about a yard from where she was round a corner.

Because the middle of the night before I was wakened up by a kind of monotony in my room, which proved to be an orderly expounding a telegram to me about meeting you or somebody at a certain station next morning. And when I had given thanks, I perceived the telegram was for somebody else.

I therefore turned my face to the wall. But I have yet to deal with that Orderly.

If any of you should just look me up out of friendliness—just a fren'ly aft'noon call—when there's nothin' much doin' at home—please bring plenty of room in your baggage for taking back my surplus stuff.

Personally I don't see what Auntie Bobs[160] has got to do with my seeing my Mother on my return from war. If I had foreseen Auntie Bobs when I was sinking in the mud or coming-to after the Embankment-Shell-Shock it would have been the last straw.

I went to a United Free Church this evening, giving up my dinner to do so. It gave me the indigoes, not half.

Really I am looking so well as to cause remarks to be made as I pass the guid wives in the town. I want you to see me now.

Oh Mother!

x W.E.O.

* Take breath vehemently.

159 PN, p. 189.
160 A friend of Mrs Bulman at Kelso.

533. To Susan Owen

Saturday, [probably 14] July 1917[161]   *[Craiglockhart]*

My dear, dear Mother,

So good of you to send a note from Yetholm.[162] I had not expected anything before. I am full of activities now. We founded last night a Natural History Club after a first Lecture on the Mosses of the District. I suppose I shall have to revive my Plants, for a Talk on Physiology or something. Few seemed to know what you told me about Sphagnum!

I have done an Essay on the Outlook Tower,[163] to be delivered in privacy to Dr. Brock[164] this afternoon!

On The Hercules–Antaeas[165] Subject—there are only 3 or 4 lines in the Dictionaries. So I shall just do a Sonnet.

I have not seen Dr. Brock's ladies[166] since. The Ballad came 2 days ago. I had even forgotten the title, and had so far forgotten the text that I was deceived in thinking it suitable for the Entertainments Programme.

I went down to Leith as arranged on Thursday. Alas! I had said I must be back by 5.30. The Newboults[167] found it wd. be impossible, unless we started immediately after lunch. So I am to go down to lunch one day next week.

That afternoon I went over the Factory and after that over Munition Works and Brass Foundries.

I am glad you were eye-witness to the instant gravitation of Chubby Cubby[168] into my Spheres. You notice it happened before the Lure of the Sweets came on the Scene. It may be the soldier's clothes: 'that the sweit bairn did win'[169] as the old Ballad says. But I hae me douts.

I spent yesterday morning beating out a plate of Copper into a bowl. That is as near as I can get to those summits of virtuous pursuits: Fretwork, and the taming of Mice.[170]

Leslie is at Hazely Down,[171] not Haslar.

Don't hurry back. There is a difference of environment between Pringle Bank and Somerside Road which must prove a severe trial to your adaptability when you have to return.

Looking forward to some privately conducted tours with you when you get back. Now which of us shall meet you? Tell me the times, & only me.

W. E. O.

Best messages to Auntie Nellie.

---

[161] PN, p. 189.

[162] Susan Owen had responded to the plea in the previous letter and come to Edinburgh. She had travelled on to stay with Mrs Bulman at Yetholm.

[163] A building near Edinburgh Castle, the centre for the eminent Scottish polymath Patrick Geddes to elaborate his sociological theories.

[164] Captain Arthur J. Brock, MD, RAMC (1879–1947), classicist and sociologist, was the doctor in charge of Owen. Brock admired and translated the work of the ancient physician Galen, who believed in treating the whole man and whose writings were the foundation of Geddes's theories. Brock put his mentor's therapeutic ideas of 'Faith—Work—Folk' into practice at Craiglockhart, under his own vocabulary, 'organism—function—environment'. The isolated man was an unhealthy man—he can only function when integrated into his environment. The neurasthenic was the embodiment of the dissociation between organism and environment. Thus Brock's main form of treatment was not a rest cure but a work cure, or 'ergotherapy'. See Dominic Hibberd 'A Sociological Cure for Shellshock', *The Sociological Review*, Vol. 25, no. 2 (1977); David Cantor, 'Between Galen, Geddes, and the Gael: Arthur Brock, Modernity, and Medical Humanism in Early-Twentieth-Century Scotland', *Journal of the History of Medicine* (Vol. 60, Jan. 2005), pp. 1–41; and Meredith Martin, 'Therapeutic Measures: *The Hydra* and Wilfred Owen at Craiglockhart War Hospital', *Modernism/Modernity* (Vol. 14, No. 1, Jan. 2007), pp. 35–54.

[165] 'The Wrestlers', CPF, pp. 520–5. JS describes how Owen 'began another long poem…in blank verse, on a subject of Dr. Brock's suggestion: the mythic encounter of Hercules and Antaeus, the giant who derived invincible strength from contact with the earth. The moral for the lapsed botanist in the shell-shock hospital is clear enough' (WO, pp. 195–6).

[166] A group of Edinburgh women who interested themselves in the rehabilitation of Dr Brock's patients. See Letter 546.

[167] A Leith family, old friends of the Owens and of Mrs Bulman. They lived at Bangower, 8 Summerside Place, Leith. Susan Owen had stayed with them for almost two weeks in July. Mary Newboult's recollections in a letter to HO and JB of 26 February 1967 were published as part of an appendix to the CL. She remembered Owen as having 'the gift of drawing people out of themselves' and that he had '*deep compassion* for other people'. When he read his poems aloud, 'the beautiful cadence of his voice held me spellbound' (CL, p. 594).

[168] Arthur, the small son of the Newboults. See Letter 553. Arthur Newboult's recollections (dated 1 February 1967) were printed along with those of his sister Mary in an appendix to the CL. Despite these being 'rather dim now', Newboult recalled Owen purchasing for him his first penknife, taking him on a visit to Edinburgh Zoo, and picking him up and swinging him 'round and round to my great delight' in the kitchen of their Edinburgh house. The grief when the family learned of Owen's death remained vivid: 'I can see my mother now standing in the kitchen crying when she heard either by letter or wire that he had been killed in action' (CL, p. 594).

[169] Bishop Percy's *Reliques*, 'The Jew's Daughter', and stanza 3, l. 4.

[170] Colin's two indoor pursuits.

[171] Near Winchester, where Owen later visited LG (who was working at the YMCA there). See Letter 561.

534. To Susan Owen

Tues. [17 July 1917] *Craiglockhart*

Dearest Mother,

Yes: if you came on Friday Morning we would lunch, & have an hour on the Tower: given a fine afternoon.

I have found myself obliged to order a new tunic, to have this old one cleaned, and the other one enlarged by Pope & B. and the longer I leave it, the more extortionate the cost. Already this will be £5: 10! am to be fitted on Thursday aft. But no reason you sh'd not come on Thurs. if more convenient.

Dorothy's letter aches with fine-feeling. I hope Mary will never write like that. It is too disturbing. Her thoughts are too shockingly unveiled. I mean to write to her, but not as I 'mean' to write to the hundred and one expecters of my letters. I give myself three days to fit it in and no more.

My tiny Notice of the first meeting of our Field Club has gone to press.[172] Old Brock is supposed to have written it. It was better paid than by a pukka Editor's best guineas. He will probably pay me in terms of Months, which is more than Money.

Here is the opening of Antaeas:

'So neck to stubborn neck, and obstinate knee to knee,
Wrestled those two; and peerless Heracles
Could not prevail, nor get at any vantage…
So those huge hands that, small, had snapped great snakes,
Let slip the writhing of Antaeas' wrists;
Those hero's hands that wrenched the necks of bulls,
Now fumbled round the slim Antaeas' limbs,
Baffled. Then anger swelled in Heracles,
And terribly he grappled broader arms,
And yet more firmly fixed his grasped feet.
And up his back the muscles bulged and shone
Like climbing banks and domes of towering cloud.
And they who watched that wrestling say he laughed,
But not so loud as on Eurystheus of old.'
                    Wilpher d'Oen (! !)

About 50 lines are now done.

[172] It was written for *The Hydra*, the journal of the Craiglockhart War Hospital, published fortnightly, and appeared in the 21 July issue—by which time Owen had become Editor. For the next few months he wrote articles and reviews, as well as editorials—all anonymously. His most distinguished contributor was Siegfried Sassoon, who arrived at Craiglockhart in late July 1917.

535. To Leslie Gunston

Wednesday, [25] July 1917[173]   *Craiglockhart*

Dear L.

Thanks for yours of this morning. I hope you have had my card posted last Monday.

On Mond. next I lecture the 'Field Club'—a Nat. Hist. association, on the lines of our old Society[174]—Geological, (you & me) & Botanical (Vera). Do you remember: you old Black Moth? Well, the days have come when I am one of the founders of a real learned society.[175] My subject has the rather journalese Title of 'Do Plants Think?'—a study of the Response to Stimuli & Devices for Fertilisation, etc. I have no books yet, but I remember a number of useful points from your big Cassell's (I think it was Cassell's) studied in 1911. Meanwhile I'm beastly bothered with our Mag.[176] (herewith) <u>and</u> I'm [to] take German Lessons at the Berlitz, Edin. Last week I wrote (to order) a strong bit of Blank: on <u>Antaeus v. Heracles</u>. These are the best lines, methinks: (N.B. Antaeus deriving strength from his Mother Earth nearly licked old Herk.)

  ... How Earth herself empowered him with her touch,
  Gave him the grip and stringency of winter,
  And all the ardour of th' invincible Spring;
  How all the blood of June glutted his heart.
  And all the glow of huge autumnal storms
  Stirred on his face, and flickered from his eyes.

I had seen your Song. May the music be equally happy. You <u>are</u> lucky! You shall have my Locke's *Usurpers*[177] if you will. Its now at home.

I see Swinburne also wrote a number of replicas of the olde Ballad! Heigh ho!

                Ever Your W.E.O.

---

[173] PN, p. 189.
[174] The Astronomical, Geological, and Botanical Society (AGBS). See Letter 35. LG was known as Black Moth, Owen as Carnation.
[175] The Craiglockhart Field Club.
[176] *The Hydra* magazine.
[177] W. J. Locke, *The Usurper* (1901).

536. To Susan Owen

Monday, 30 July 1917, 11 p.m.   [*Craiglockhart*]

My own dear Mother,

The Lecture[178] was a huge success, & went on till 10.20 !! At least I was answering cross-questions until that time. My swotting & pottering of the good old

Matric. days, and my laborious escapes from Dunsden Vicarage to Reading College have been well crowned tonight. I have <u>only once</u> since getting through the Barrage at Feyet felt such exultation as when winding up to my peroration tonight! The peroration was a [*three words struck out*] (I'm tired) bit from Mrs. Browning which I remembered reading at Gailly:[179]

> 'Earth's crammed with Heaven
> And every common bush afire with God;
> But only he who sees takes off his shoes;
> The rest sit round it and pluck Blackberries,
> And daub their natural faces unaware,
> More and more from the first similitude.'

The 'only once' was when I saw you gliding up to me, veiled in azure, at the Caledonian. I thought you looked very very beautiful and well, through the veil, and especially on the night of the concert. But without the veil I saw better the supremer beauty of the ashes of all your Sacrifices: for Father, for me, and for all of us. (Even, methought, for Mowgli-Mowlgi of Fiji, or whoever it be that will receive the much fine gold of Israel's literature through your hands.)

Formerly, I should have said I had not time to write to you before. I now (with ever increasing mental vigour) perceive it was that I lacked <u>energy</u>. Not culpably, at all, or lazily. I cannot write to you without intensity, or without all my mind, my soul and heart and (yes, I forget the Catechism as thoroughly as I remember: 'To him that overcometh, I will give the bright and morning star'. O exquisite words!)

I saw a 1st Edition of Keats' third book[180] this morning. The present price was pencilled on the cover: £56. (I will tell you what dear Mrs. Browning says of Keats next time.)   This is a letter of parentheses. It is itself a parenthesis between my work. I must have the Magazine ready by tomorrow morning.

Your own W.E.O. x

P.S. The Concert was a great success. Far better than the one you saw. (I simply made faces.) I looked so sympathetically at poor Antonio by thinking of Portia, who broke down. I <u>was</u> so sorry. She is an old Bensonian,[181] like her husband, who played Shylock. Mrs. Pockett,[182] <u>fresh from the vast London stage</u>, prompted her <u>at the top of her voice</u>! To make a last parenthesis I will add that both these ladies are model wives, no less than model women. And how they love their profession!

---

[178] Lecture to the Field Club: 'Do Plants Think?' The paper survives among Owen's papers in the Bodleian.

[179] 13th CCS, from where he had written to Mary (Letter 497) quoting from Mrs. Browning's *Aurora Leigh*. He now quotes from the same poem again.

[180] *Lamia, Isabella, The Eve of St. Agnes, and other poems* (1820).

[181] A member of Benson's company. Mrs Isaacson played Portia; her husband, Second Lieutenant John Leslie Isaacson, RFC, was Shylock. See Letter 598.

[182] Mrs Pockett had acted a fortnight earlier in Alfred Sutro's *The Bracelet*, produced by her husband, Lieutenant J. W. G. Pockett. The Pocketts, like the Isaacsons, were professional actors.

537. To Susan Owen

Friday, 3 August 1917   [*Craiglockhart*]

Dearest Mother,

We Field Club were to have excursed to the Pentland Hills this afternoon, but rain prevented it.

By some means, chiefly by swimming in the Public Baths really religiously, for it never fails to give me a Greek feeling of energy and elemental life; by some means, I say, I have managed to have the Magazine out in plenty of time. You will have your Copy no later than the moment of publication, which is when I plunk the copies outside the Breakfast Room Door tomorrow morning, where they will be given away to all the Club. I am glad my motion has been adopted by the Committee.

The Editorial, with its satires on Trams, the abolition of evening refreshments, the Field Club, a malcontent who sent a letter of evil 'gas' to a previous issue, and so on may read all rubbish to you. In the ¶. beginning 'For our part' there are six awful puns. But you need to know Musketry, or they will misfire.

I have a hand in the Notes & News, but no finger in the pie Peas Blossom has made of the Concert Critique. It was handed to me just as I was dashing away 'to Press'. There is an innuendo about Pockett which I don't like, even if it is unintentional.[183] Had I made the simple change <u>Gratiano</u> instead of <u>Pockett</u>, it would not have carried any innuendo. It is too late.

Thus I learn the awful finality of a corrected proof.

I have had so far one poetical contribution—from a Guards Officer—which he timidly brought up to my room with his own towering person. I was trotting around the room talking to the furniture in German at the moment; but I affected what dignity I could, and tried to look as if I had 10/6 in my pocket, and fifty more contributions on my desk.

Many many dear thanks for your Dorothean letters. This lumbago is a pitiful anticlimax to your holiday and to my Letters. Care should ward it off. You have an infinite capacity for taking Pains! Tut! (or words to that effect) I'm talking like a nasty incapable Doctor! But really I am fretted to hear this trouble, when I imagined you were bettered by being up here.

How is everybody else?

x W.E.O.

---

[183] 'Mr. Pockett thoroughly convinced us that he was annoyed by the whole business.' *The Hydra*.

538. To Susan Owen

Tues. Night [7 August 1917][184]   *[Craiglockhart]*

Dearest of Mothers,

So pleased to have Father's letter & your note this morning. Letters have been scarce lately. Last week passed unmercifully quickly. The only way to lengthen time is to add more miles to the roads of our journeys. And the only way to lengthen life is to live out several threads at a time and join them up in crucial moments.

At present I am a sick man in hospital, by night; a poet, for quarter of an hour after breakfast; I am whatever and whoever I see while going down to Edinburgh on the tram: greengrocer, policeman, shopping lady, errand boy, paper-boy, blind man, crippled Tommy, bank-clerk, carter, all of these in half an hour; next a German student in earnest; then I either peer over bookstalls in back-streets, or do a bit of a dash down Princes Street,—according as I have taken weak tea or strong coffee for breakfast.

This afternoon I spent with a *Daily Mail* sub-editor, Salmond,[185] and writer to the B.O.P.[186] (who is going to talk our Printer into shape.) When we had discussed together many mighty things and men, and an Emersonian silence fell between us, we went upstairs to the Cinema, & so finished a very pleasant afternoon. Tonight Pockett enrôled me as Mr. Wallcomb, in *Lucky Durham*[187]: a fashionable young fellow, whose chief business in the play is introducing people.

Thus I need at once:

1) 1 Green Suit.
2) 2 or 3 Green Shirts.
3) Green Collars (if any)
4) Green Cap.
5) Green Glass Cuff-links: —(on second thoughts, I think one of these lies somewhere in the purlieus of Bordeaux.) But didn't Father give me an Indian Silver Pair?
6) The Oil-cloth raincoat.
7) Straw Hat (if any—I think not!)

Pockett, and Mrs. Pockett, Isaacson and Mrs. Isaacson (Portia) are all in it, so I shall know what it really feels like to be 'on the stage'. Only the first 2 Acts are being done next Sat., finishing the following week.

Salmond, the journalist, by the way, knew Walter Forrest, and often wrote his fame; knows also 'Jack' Bulman, the medico![188]

Yes, you will like to read Mrs. Browning. Having listened so long to her low, sighing voice (which <u>can</u> be <u>heard</u> often through the page,) and having seen her hair, not in a museum case, but palpably in visions, and having received kindness from a boy to whom she was kind (M. Léger—he is still a boy); for these reasons, I say, the Flapper flaps in vain.

The other day I read a Biography of Tennyson, which says he was unhappy, even in the midst of his fame, wealth, and domestic serenity. Divine discontent![189] I can quite believe he never knew happiness for one moment such as I have—for one or two moments. But as for misery, was he ever frozen alive, with dead men for comforters. Did he hear the moaning at the bar, not at twilight and the evening bell only, but at dawn, noon, and night, eating and sleeping, walking and working, always the close moaning of the Bar; the thunder, the hissing and the whining of the Bar?

Tennyson, it seems, was always a great child.[190]

So should I have been, but for Beaumont Hamel.

(Not before January 1917 did I write the <u>only lines</u> of mine that carry the stamp of maturity: these:

But the old happiness is unreturning.

Boys have no grief so grievous as youth's yearning;

Boys have no sadness sadder than our hope.[191])

Mayes[192] has just been in, and it is now quarter to one on Wednesday. There is this advantage in being 'one of the ones' at the Hospital, that nurses cease from troubling the weary who don't want rest.

I have a sort of suspicion your note was written in bed; but perhaps it was before nine in the morning.

It is worthy of mention that we have been in mist for 3 days: a gloriously luminous mist at times. I saw Holyrood on Sunday Afternoon (being alone on Salisbury Crags), a floating mirage in gold mist. A sight familiar enough in dreams and poems, but which I never thought possible in these islands. It was the picture <u>of</u> a picture; if you understand. I don't.

It's too late o'night to talk like this. Time I snuggled myself away.

Goodnight, dear Mother.   x W.E.O.

[184] PN, p. 189.

[185] Second Lieutenant J[ames] B[ell] Salmond (1891–1958), 7th (Fife)Battalion (Territorial), Black Watch (the Royal Highlanders). He took part in the attack at Beaumont Hamel during the Battle of the Somme in 1917 and was admitted to Craiglockhart in June 1917. After the war he joined the staff of the *Dundee Advertiser* and then in 1927 became editor of *The Scots Magazine*, a post he held for twenty years. He wrote histories of the 51st (Highland) Division and the Royal & Ancient Golf Club. In 1948 he became Keeper of Muniments at the University of St Andrews. His poems in Scots and English were collected in *The Old Stalker and Other Poems* (1936). See also Patrick W. Anderson, 'J. B. Salmond', *Wilfred Owen Association Journal*, Summer 2014.

[186] *The Boy's Own Paper.* A scribbled sheet survives from this time outlining an idea for a short story. The heading is *'B.O.P. Stories for magazines'.*

[187] A comedy by the actor-manager Wilson Barrett (1847–1904), first performed at the King's Theatre, Hammersmith, 28 August 1905. Owen's interest in the theatre was considerable and it was known in the family that he drafted a full-length play at Craiglockhart. The MS was never seen, but the following note survives, on headed Craiglockhart paper:

Two Thousand

Act I Scene I   The Lord of Europe's Dining Room, London
    Scene II Schoolroom
Act II (2 days later)
Act III Secret Meeting House under The Atlantic: reached by private submarine

----

Purpose: To expose war to the criticism of reason.
Plot: The federation of America with Europe by personal violence to the American Emperor.
Interest: Dress: Manners, Machines, References to men of this century.
    e.g. who was Lloyd George?

[188] See Letter 323.

[189] Echoing Tennyson's 'Tears from the depth of some divine despair' (*The Princess*, iv, Introductory Song, l. 21).

[190] DH cites A. C. Benson, *Tennyson* (1912), p. 79. Coventry Patmore is quoted: 'Tennyson is like a great child, very simple and very much self-absorbed', a comment on the man, not the poet.'

[191] From 'Happiness', *CPF*, p. 88.

[192] Charles Mayes, 19-year-old artillery subaltern, who had been at Craiglockhart since March 1917, and who was often paired with Owen during treatment sessions. Mayes never returned to active service, but went to work for the Ministry of Munitions in 1918.

539. To Susan Owen

Friday Night [10 *August* 1917][193]   [*Craiglockhart*]

My own dear Mother,

  The Field Club went a long walk over the Pentland foot-hills this afternoon.[194] The Party was:

1) Dr. Brock
2) Mr. Chase, learned (?) in Mosses,
3) „ Quayle, „   „ Bees,
4) a Shropshire man, „ „ Birds
5) Capt. Mackenzie, electrician.
6) his son, aetat 13, learned in nothing.
7) A padre,   „ „ ditto.
8) Me   „ „ very much ditto.

  Thus it was a representative body, and between us we managed to observe and philosophize the country to about half the extent that say Belloc would have done, had he taken that walk.

I held my own in the matter of Water Plants, and my ancient chippings at Geology came in useful, not to mention the physical geography I learnt from Miss Jones. (For which lady a fee of fifty guineas would not repay the tuition she gave.) But it is very kind of the Army to provide this free-and-easy Oxford for me. It was a unique walk. We had lunch on the roadside, and tea in a cottage.

But we stayed too long, or went too far, and arrived ¼ hour late for dinner, and very fatigued. And immediately after dinner I had to do the last rehearsal of *Lucky Durham*. It is done now, & I must get to bed. I read your letter by a waterfall. The Parcel has not yet come. Many thanks for the considerable trouble of packing it off. Where then is my green cap? So glad you thought of socks. The Expense will be refunded by the Club. I forgot to tell you this.

Yes, I really do wish you could be here tomorrow, for I am fairly confident of my part, and the more so, being with professionals, who can't let one down by any false cues or anything.

Glad you have been to Cressage.

I laughed at your hoping I should learn German during my stay in Edinburgh. It's a vile language to learn. I'm overjoyed that you think of making bandages for the wounded. Leave Black Sambo ignorant of Heaven. White men are in Hell. Aye, leave him ignorant of the civilization that sends us there, and the religious men that say it is good to be in that Hell. (Continued, because important) Send an English Testament to his Grace of Canterbury, and let it consist of that one sentence, at which he winks his eyes:

'Ye have heard that it hath been said: An eye for an eye, and a tooth for a tooth:

But I say that ye resist not evil, but whosoever shall smite thee on thy right cheek, turn to him the other also.'

And if his reply be 'Most unsuitable for the present distressing moment, my dear lady! But I trust that in God's good time… etc.' —then there is only one possible conclusion, that there are no more Christians at the present moment than there were at the end of the first century.

While I wear my star and eat my rations, I continue to take care of my Other Cheek; and, thinking of the eyes I have seen made sightless, and the bleeding lad's cheeks I have wiped, I say: Vengeance is mine, I, Owen, will repay.

Let my lords turn to the people when they say 'I believe in… Jesus Christ', and we shall see as dishonest a face as ever turned to the East, bowing, over the Block at Tyburn.[195]

I fear I've written like a converted Horatio Bottomley.

And to you who need no such words.

That is why I want you not to destroy them; for I write so because I see clear at this moment. In my eye there is no mote nor beam, when I look through you across the world.

There is a mote in many eyes, often no other than a tear. It is this: That men are laying down their lives for a friend. I say it is a mote; a distorted view to hold in a general way.

For that reason, if no other, I won't publish in any way the 'Kings and Christs.'[196]
Saturday
Have just got the parcel up from Slateford Station by an Orderly. The Rly. sent me a notification this morning. The suit is not crushed. Everything in order. Wish I were. Shan't wear the ring, or the Emerald!

Have not re-read last night's copy, lest I should cancel it, and you be without a letter of any sort.

Your own W.E.O. x

---

[193] PN, p. 189.
[194] The expedition is described in Owen's (unsigned) Field Club article in *The Hydra* for 18 August 1917, in which he also gives an anonymous account of his own paper (read on 31 July), 'Do Plants Think?'
[195] Tyburn at the southern end of Edgware Road, London. It was the principal place of execution of criminals, traitors, and martyrs until the late eighteenth century.
[196] 'The Women and the Slain', *CPF*, p. 500.

540. To Susan Owen

15 August 1917   *Scottish Conservative Club, Edinburgh*

Dearest Mother,

I am going to Leith this afternoon; am on the way now. Got up rather late this morning, having had some very bellicose dreams of late.

I really felt most delightfully <u>at ease</u> *en scene* on Sat. Night. The whole Concert was the biggest success our stage has seen. I will send you the Magazine in good time. Mayes wrote 'The Concert' but I rewrote parts and cancelled the reference to myself. I have also had to re-write the field club account of my lecture.

I was very proud of my 'straight make-up' which Isaacson did for me.

How I hankered, a boy, to know the secrets of the glamour of the Shakesperian actors. Well, so it has come about that my first make up was done with the real Bensonian touch. (By Isaacson.)

(Friday)

I found the Newboults out on Wednesday. I thought Wednesday a likely day for a family excursion.

I received a card this morning, which should nerve me for a further attempt at aimless visiting.

I have just been reading Siegfried Sassoon, and am feeling at a very high pitch of emotion. Nothing like his trench life sketches has ever been written or ever will be written. Shakespere reads vapid after these. Not of course because Sassoon is a greater artist, but because of the subjects, I mean. I think if I had the choice of making friends with Tennyson or with Sassoon I should go to Sassoon.

That is why I have not yet dared to go up to him and parley in a casual way. He is here you know because he wrote a letter to the Higher Command which was too plain-spoken. They promptly sent him over here![197] I will send you his book, one day, and tell you what sort of pow-wow we've had.

Your own W.E.O. x

Friday aft. Just had yours. Haven't given it close attention yet.

---

[197] Second Lieutenant Siegfried Lorraine Sassoon, on convalescent leave from France earlier in the summer, had drawn up and deliberately publicized, through arranging a question in the House of Commons, a statement containing the following key sentence: 'I believe that this war, upon which I entered as a war of defence and liberation, has now become a war of aggression and conquest.' Robert Graves helped to engineer Sassoon's medical board in lieu of a court martial, the outcome of which was Sassoon's treatment at Craiglockhart. As Sassoon wrote in his memoir, 'The Under-Secretary for War told the House of Commons that I was suffering from a nervous breakdown' (*Siegfried's Journey, 1916–1920* [Faber & Faber, 1945], p. 56). His first collection of poems, *The Old Huntsman and Other Poems*, had been published earlier in the year.

541. To Leslie Gunston

22 August 1917   *Craiglockhart*

My dear Leslie,

At last I have an event worth a letter. I have beknown myself to Siegfried Sassoon. Went in to him last night (my second call). The first visit was one morning last week.[198] The sun blazed into his room making his purple dressing suit of a brilliance—almost matching my sonnet! He is very tall and stately, with a fine firm chisel'd (how's that?)[199] head, ordinary short brown hair. The general expression of his face is one of boredom. Last night when I went in he was struggling to read a letter from Wells; whose handwriting is not only a slurred <u>suggestion</u> of words, but in a dim pink ink! Wells talks of coming up here to see him and his doctor; not about Sassoon's state of health, but about *God the Invisible King*.[200] After leaving him, I wrote something in Sassoon's style, which I may as well send you, since you ask for the latest.

<u>The Dead-Beat</u>[201] (True—in the incidental)

He dropped, more sullenly, than wearily,
    Became a lump of stench, a clot of meat,
    And none of us could kick him to his feet.
He blinked at my revolver, blearily.

He didn't seem to know a war was on,
    Or see or smell the bloody trench at all…
    Perhaps he saw the crowd at Caxton Hall,
And that is why the fellow's pluck's all gone—

———————————

Not that the Kaiser frowns imperially.
    He sees his wife, how cosily she chats;
    Not his blue pal there, feeding fifty rats.
Hotels he sees, improved materially:

———————————

Where ministers smile ministerially.
    Sees Punch still grinning at the Belcher bloke;
    Bairnsfather, enlarging on his little joke,
While Belloc prophecies of last year, serially.[202]

———————————

We sent him down at last, he seemed so bad,
    Although a strongish chap and quite unhurt.
    Next day I heard the Doc's fat laugh: 'That dirt
You sent me down last night's just died. So glad!'[203]

———————————

Next day
I am going to send you *The Old Huntsman*[204] as a festive gift for the occasion of your First Publication.[205]

'The Death Bed' is the finest poem. I told him my opinion. It is his own. This poem is coming out in the Georgian Anthology. He was struck with the 'Dead Beat', but pointed out that the facetious bit was out of keeping with the first & last stanzas. Thus the piece as a whole is no good. Some of my old Sonnets didn't please him at all. But the 'Antæus' he applauded fervently; and a short lyric which I don't think you know 'Sing me at morn but only with thy Laugh'[206] he pronounced perfect work, absolutely charming, etc. etc. and begged that I would copy it out for him, to show to the powers that be.

So the last thing he said was 'Sweat your guts out writing poetry!' 'Eh?' says I. 'Sweat your guts out, I say!' He also warned me against early publishing: but recommended Martin Secker[207] for a small volume of 10 or 20 poems.

He himself is 30! Looks under 25!

So glad your proofs are done. How long now before I have my copies? That 'Farley Down' occasional verse did not impress me, I am longing to re-read *The Nymph*, & give it to Sassoon!

Would you mind sending me all the MSS verse of mine in your keeping as soon as you can get at them? How I want a confabulation with you in my Room with everything at hand!

Sassoon admires Thos. Hardy more than anybody living. I don't think much of what I've read. Quite potatoey after the meaty *Morals*.

You'll have had enough of Sassoon, what? Just one more tit-bit. Wells said in his last letter: hope you will soon 'devote yourself to the real business of your life, which is poetry only by the way.' Poor Wells! We made some fancy guesses as to what he meant:—Tract-writing? stump-oratory? politics? what?

Cheero! I'm well enough by day, and generally so by night. A better mode of life than this present I could not practically manage.

Yours, with affection, ever, W.E.O.

[198] SS has also described this first meeting, in *Siegfried's Journey*, ch. VI.

[199] DH notes how this is 'a teasing allusion to a phrase of LG's, "a white chiselled nose"' from *The Nymph* (WOANB, p. 507, n. 2).

[200] Published in London, 1917.

[201] *CPF*, p. 298. A version of verses 3 and 4 appeared in Owen's editorial in *The Hydra*, 1 September 1917. The same issue also prints SS's 'Dreamers' and (unsigned) 'Song of Songs' (*CPF*, p. 89).

[202] Vertically alongside these four lines Owen wrote, 'These lines are years old!!'

[203] Vertically alongside these final two lines Owen wrote, '<u>Those</u> are the very words!'

[204] *The Old Huntsman and Other Poems* (William Heinemann, 1917).

[205] *The Nymph and Other Poems* was published by the firm of Arthur H. Stockwell. It is dedicated to Wilfred Owen, 'with affection'.

[206] 'Song of Songs' was later published in *The Bookman* in May 1918. *CPF*, p. 89.

[207] Martin Secker (1882–1978), London publisher noted for publishing D. H. Lawrence, Thomas Mann, Henry James, and George Orwell, among others. His firm was taken over by Fredric Warburg and Roger Senhouse in 1935 to form Secker & Warburg.

543. To Tom Owen

26 August 1917   [*Craiglockhart*]

My dear Father,

I think this work of Sassoon's will show you to the best possible advantage the tendencies of Modern Poetry. If you don't appreciate these then it's Na-poo.[208] There is nothing better this century can offer you. I've marked the pieces for first reading, and those underlined are specially good. The Old Huntsman was put in as a title piece, to catch the hunting-people, and make 'em read the rest.

'The Death-Bed' is a piece of perfect art.

'Morning Express', page 56 is the kind of thing that makes me despair of myself; everyone says 'I could have done that myself!'

Only no one ever did.

Please send me your Criticisms.

I am beginning to feel uncomfortably editorial again after a fortnight's rest. Nobody is willing to write about our last Concerts, and it looks as if I shall have to fill half the Mag. myself, between now & tomorrow.

I <u>am</u> glad Colin is with you.

Realizing how impossible it is for me to be there has spoilt my holiday here. I was make-believing that I was a free creature here, but it is only that my chain has been let out a little. I should only hurt myself with tugging at it.

Fondest love to all,

Your W.E.O.

[208] Napoo: World War I slang, a corruption of French 'il n'y a plus', meaning 'there is no more' or 'finished'.

544. To Mary Owen

Thursday, 30 August 1917[209]   *Craiglockhart*

My dear Mary,

I was grieved—almost aggrieved—to hear you had had some bad days at Aberystwyth, and I am still waiting to hear you are all right. This cloud, and a great many other real ones messing about in the heavens and sometimes moon-ing around the building itself, and generally behaving unbecomingly on the top of us all—and the Russians panicking, and getting out of the war, and ourselves getting deeper and deeper into it, these things, I say, do not make one (eider)—downhearted. So it is not to be wondered at that I was a bit snappy in my Editorial, which you shall have in a day or two.

But a word from Sassoon, though he is not a cheery dog himself, makes me cut capers of pleasure.

My dear, except in one or two of my letters, (ahem!) you will find nothing so perfectly truthfully descriptive of war. Cinemas, cartoons, photographs, tales, plays—Na-poo.

Now you see why I have always extolled Poetry.

The 'Redeemer', I have been wishing to write every week for the last three years.

Well, it has been done and I have shaken the greater hand that did it. 'The Death-Bed', my dear sister, should be read seven times, and after that, not again, but thought of only.

Here is a very good brooch, a very good brooch. Unless you like it much, I shall very likely sneak it again for a model of latter-day design! There is no hint of a Board for me yet! I'm going down to make my Evening Tea now. Just a card will tell me how you & dear Mother are.

Your loving Wilfred

[209] PN, p. 189.

545. To Susan Owen

Monday [3 September 1917][210]   [*Craiglockhart*]

My dearest Mother,

It seems you have had unmerciful weather. You will be all the more glad, according to your custom, to be Home again.

Mayes introduced me to some 'modern' people, and I went there yesterday afternoon:—two men and their wives, who share a big house in a fine Georgian Crescent in Edinburgh.[211]

The ladies wear short hair and decorative gowns, and think themselves artistic. But yesterday they had to mind their babies, which being self-centred, unmannerly blobs of one to three years bored me utterly.

The drawing room was worth seeing with its black carpetless floor, white walls, solitary superb picture, grand piano, Empire sofa and so on.

I think they are genuine people—the more so because they adore their progeny than because they profess to admire my poetry.

Their picture—a loan—is an Academy Exhibit by the painter of the finest picture now in the Edinburgh Gallery, which you did not see. This last is called Avatar. Bibby[212] of the *Annual* wrote to the artist[213] asking for the same canvas with additions (a wounded soldier). The Artist (forget his name) wrote back: accepted—fee £500. Thus I am specially anxious to see *Bibby's*. Has Father got it? If not I must buy one.

Many thanks for Father's Views (of Aberystwyth). Wish I had his views of S.S. I will copy out one or two of my recent efforts in Sassoon's manner.[214]

I have been doubtful whether to [?confirm] the 'Song of Songs' as mine. But now I find it well received by the public and praised by Sassoon with no patronizing manner but as a musical achievement not possible to him. He is sending copies of the *Hydra* to Personages!

Last night I had a consultation with Dr. Brock from 11 to midnight!

I asked him (for the first time) when he meant to have me boarded. He said there were no instructions given to him yet; and wasn't I quite happy where I am? Very well...

I still have disastrous dreams, but they are taking on a more civilian character, motor accidents and so on.

The Concert last Sat. was nothing very notable. What took the applause of the Faery Mustard Seed was some charming dancing by a girl of 13 or 14. When I see a Ballet Dance, I surrender half my kingdom, lose my head, and put it on a charger. Thus at least I forget the war.

The Field Club Tonight was some stories of Sea-Fishing off the Waterford—Cork Coast—some good yarns.

Nothing more to tell, I think. Horrid weather continues.

Ever your own W.E.O. x

P.S. (1) I should rather like some Typed Copies of these verses.

(2) Please return at once all MSS. you have—such as were sent on by Leslie.

---

[210] PN, p. 189.

[211] The Grays and the Steinthals; Bernard Crescent. Maria Steinthal, née Zimmern, was a sculptor (see Letter 546). Leonard Gray was a captain in the Royal Scots Guards and managed the family foundry firm. He married Mary 'Maidie' Rachel Scott in June 1916. Maidie Gray was one of 'Dr Brock's ladies' and was particularly enamoured with Owen (see Guy Cuthbertson, *Wilfred Owen* [Yale University Press, 2014], pp. 1–2, 209, 210, 211, 212–13).

[212] Joseph Bibby (1851–1940), founder of J. Bibby and Sons Ltd, soap manufacturers, writer on economic subjects, and editor of *Bibby's Annual* 1906–22 and 1936.

[213] Henry John Lintott (1877–1965), ARSA, RSA, painter of figure subjects and portraits. See also Letter 549.

[214] The 29 September issue of *The Hydra* carried (anonymously) 'The Next War' (*CPF*, p. 165).

546. To Susan Owen

7 September 1917   [*Craiglockhart*]

My dearest Mother,

These last two days Thursday and Friday have been the very fullest-happiest of the year—excluding only one or two of the days when you were up here. Went with Mayes to a perfect little dinner at the Grays' and passed an evening of extraordinary fellowship in All the Arts. The men are not of the expansive type—one is a History Honoursman at Oxford,[215] the other owner of a large Munition Works.[216] The ladies have more effusiveness, but are genuine. One is really witty[217] and the other is a sculptor of great power.[218]

They showered books upon me on leaving; and on Monday I am to escort Mrs. Gray on an expedition into the slums to see an old Italian—a street-singer whom she 'took-up' and who says he was once an operatic star![219] He is probably a fraud, but we shall see that—and we shall see his many children.

Mayes and I crept in at a late hour last night. This is known to the C.O. but he has said nothing to me. Mayes talked it over with him this morning. At midnight, however, a nurse came to me very austerely: 'Dr. Brock will see you at once Mr. Owen!' I went: in pyjamas and perspiration. He said a lady in Edinburgh expected me to lunch today to show me around the Slum Gardens. Goodnight! I retired in stupor.

So I went to lunch at their palatial house with two maiden sisters, The Misses Wyer. One of them took me over the Gardens[220] and I gave my opinions and views. (Dr. Brock is trying to get me in touch with the Edinburgh submerged tenth.) It will never come off while I am in uniform: but I can't tell him that. I went back to a marvellous pleasant Tea with the other Lady, who has travelled far and wide over the continents and the literatures. Then in sailed an enormous old lady of the type of old lady I have but once or twice met—outside Thackeray—intellectual, witty, vigorous: told some good stories and eat a huge tea; an admirer of Alec Waugh's book *Loom of Youth!*[221] Waugh wrote this at 18. But more of this book later. The touches of what I can only call 'kultur' in its universal sense, not English French or German but universal, and the discovery of my own—almost secret—views of such things as sculpture, state-craft, ethics, etc. etc, in these strange beings and places were enough to make the day memorable in itself.

But tonight Sassoon called me in to him; and having condemned some of my poems, amended others, and rejoiced over a few, he read me his very last works, which are superb beyond anything in his Book. Last night he wrote a piece which is the most exquisitely painful war poem of any language or time.[222] I don't tell him so, or that I am not worthy to light his pipe. I simply sit tight and tell him where I think he goes wrong. He is going to alter one passage of this very poem for me.

No wonder I was happy last night, and that tonight I must get it off my chest before I sleep.

The Field Club of 12 members went to the Observatory[223] this afternoon. I forgot I was missing that. But Sassoon as it happens has just asked me to go to tea with the Astronomer Royal tomorrow. So I shall see much more than what I missed! How I shall get a Magazine out this week-end I don't know.

Will you do a sacred task for me? Wrench open the Cupboard of my Desk and withdraw from the top-shelf right-hand side, three port-folios—two are khaki, one is Harold's gilt-stencilled velvet blotter. Upon your unimpeachable honour do not inspect the contents either of the cupboard or of the portfolios. But promptly pack off the portfolios under secure wrappings and plain address. I don't care if you damage the cupboard-door. But don't damage the hinges of your mind by wrenching the secrets of my portfolios. This sounds mysterious; but I am serious. Some of these verses will light my cigarettes, but one or two may light the darkness of the world. It is not a question of wheat and chaff, but of devils and angels.

Sassoon considers E.L. Gunston not only flatulent, but hopeless. But he has not seen much of it.[224]

I have written to Harold. I hope I am not 'feeding' you with this kind of talk, but I write straight from my experiences and heart.

Do thou likewise.

Your own W.E.O. x

215 Francis Steinthal.
216 Leonard Gray.
217 Maidie Gray.
218 Maria Steinthal.
219 His name was Tomaso. See Letter 548.
220 Miss Wyer had taken over Dr Brock's peacetime chairmanship of the Open Spaces Committee at the Outlook Tower. These 'Slum Gardens' were cultivated with and for the residents. See also Letter 551. She was on Owen's draft list of recipients of his first collection. See Letter 634, n. 128.
221 Published by Methuen, London, 1917, when Alec Waugh (1898–1981) was 19. Waugh served with the British Army as an officer in the Dorset Regiment and saw action at Passchendaele. He was captured by the Germans in March 1918, near Arras, and spent the rest of the conflict as a prisoner of war at Karlsruhe and the Mainz Citadel. He was the elder brother of the novelist Evelyn Waugh (1903–66) and the son of Arthur Waugh (1866–1943), managing director of the publishing firm of Chapman & Hall (1902–30).
222 SS thought this must have been 'Dreamers' (Siegfried Sassoon, *Collected Poems 1908–1956* [Faber & Faber, 1961], p. 71). But DH points out (*Notes and Queries*, August 1982) that 'Dreamers' had already been published in *The Hydra*, and argues for the last stanza of 'Prelude: The Troops' (*Collected Poems*, p. 67).
223 This visit to the Royal Observatory, Edinburgh, is recorded in *The Hydra*, 15 September 1917. Professor Ralph Allen Sampson (1866–1939), Astronomer Royal for Scotland 1910–37, showed the party round and gave them tea. See also SS, *Sherston's Progress* (1936), pp. 62–7.
224 This sentence was omitted in *CL* and *SL*.

547. To Susan Owen

*Sunday Evening [9 September 1917]*225   [*Craiglockhart*]

My dearest Mother,

My pen is wet from an amusing contribution to myself: Extracte from the Chronicles of Wilfred de Salope, Knight:226 describing the Hospital Life in mediæval jargon. I am still 'worried' by lack of matter for my Mag.

Yesterday I lunched with Sassoon at his Golf Club.227 My discipleship was put to a severe fleshly trial. I had had no breakfast (quite right if invited out to lunch!) choosing to stay in bed till 10; and he did not come in from the Course till quarter past two.

Afterwards I put him to the trial of writing a poem in 3 minutes in the manner of those in the *Graphic*, etc. He produced 12 lines in 4 minutes. Absolutely undistinguishable from the style of thing in the Magazines.

Then we walked over to the Observatory, and had a most interesting tea with the Astronomer, his wife and children. The children were dumbfounded with boredom. The only star we talked about was Sir H. Tree,[228] and the only stars Sassoon saw were in the electric-blue eyes of little Tom when I took courage and spoke to him.

S. & I had made a plan to pull the Astronomer's leg, but it didn't come off.

He is a parlous clever man.

There was a pretty good concert that evening.

Tomorrow is the great performance (hinted at by Mustard Seed)[229]

I shall have a busy day with various appointments & am glad I kept out of further play-acting.

Brock wants me to get busy with Scouts now!

Chase wants a Lecture on 'Soil' for the Field Club.

I just want to get home. Would you send around your next letter Poèmes Elégiaques,[230] Laurent Tailhade, high shelf of book-case, yellow-backed.

Your lovingest W.E.O.

S. wants to get me a green-tab job[231] in England. I think he could. Fondest love & wishes for Mary, and thanks for her long letter.

[225] PN, p. 189.

[226] In the 15 September issue of The Hydra.

[227] Neil McLennan has established that this was the Baberton Golf Club, Juniper Green, Edinburgh (https://www.bbc.co.uk/news/uk-scotland-edinburgh-east-fife-39567320). A plaque on the site of the old clubhouse now commemorates the meeting of Owen, Sassoon, and Graves on 13 October 1917. See Letter 551.

[228] Sir Herbert Beerbohm Tree (1853–1917), actor-manager and brother of Max Beerbohm. He had died a few weeks earlier, on 2 July.

[229] Owen's pseudonym (and that of his predecessor) as theatrical and concert critic in The Hydra.

[230] Third edition, Paris, 1907. This copy survives amongst Owen's books, with the inscription: 'À Wilfred E. S. Owen, en souvenir de nos belles causeries et des beaux soirs à La Gailleste. Laurent Tailhade, Paris, le 4 Mai, 1915'.

[231] In Military Intelligence.

548. To Susan Owen

Tuesday [11] September 1917[232]   [Craiglockhart]

My own dear Mother,

Many true thanks for your long letter. I have read it many times. You also find letter writing a fitter mode of intimate communication than speaking.

The enclosed came out of my Parcel of Portfolios rec'vd this evening, together with a stamped letter addressed to Langley, Worcester, which I have duly posted. They had slipped right inside the parcel! Was it a trick of some urchin of Cleveland Street?

The MSS. arrived in perfect order. Did I classify them as Angels & Devils? I meant simply: Live Ones and Duds. I have written no Barrack Room Ballads! You may be a little shocked by Sassoon's language. He is of course, with W.E.O. practically the only one in the place who doesn't swear conversationally. He is simply honest about the war.

Your questions concerning him are searching. You will do well to put them on all similar occasions.

For it is very true there are not a few whom I like, say, as a poet only, as an actor only, as a table-companion only, as a trench-mate only, as a servant only, as a statue only, as a marble idol only.

Sassoon I like equally in all the ways you mention, as a man, as a friend, as a poet.

The man is tall and noble-looking. Before I knew him I was told this and by this much only I spotted him! I quote from a publication:[233] 'very slim and shy, with eyes which may be blue or brown when you come to examine them closely.'

He is thirty-one. Let it be thoroughly understood that I nourish no admiration for his nose or any other feature whatever.

The Friend is intensely sympathetic*, with me about every vital question on the planet or off it. He keeps all effusiveness strictly within his pages. In this he is eminently English. It is so restful after the French absurdities, and after Mrs. Gray who gushes all over me. But there is no denying to myself that he is already a closer friend than, say, Leslie. Just as this assertion is not the result of having been with him so much lately, neither is it derogated by the shortness of our acquaintance-time. We have followed parallel trenches all our lives, and have more friends in common, authors I mean, than most people can boast of in a lifetime.

As for the Poet you know my judgement. What's your's? If I ever said anything so ambiguous as 'I wish I had Father's views' I meant 'I wish I knew Father's views' and had them before me. By the way S. has written two or three pieces 'around' chance things I have mentioned or related! Thus the enclosed scribble[234] is a copy of what he wrote after I had read three Sonnets on 'Beauty' (subject) by E.L.G., O.A.J., and me. He was appalled by Leslie's verbiage![235] I do think it a pity Leslie is in such a hurry.

I had a jolly afternoon with Mrs. Gray on Saturday. We got ourselves admirably stared at in Lower Edinburgh. I wore a hooligan manner and cap, but unimpeachable gloves, boots and tie. Mrs. Gray wore weird clothes and some priceless rings. Tomaso[236] was out. We left the macaroni, the toffees and so on, in the wrong house at first. We thought the stupefaction of the good woman 'part of the day's work'. However she discovered our mistake and came after us. We were by then mingling with a crowd following a poor (sober) woman who was being arrested. Tomaso was out, but we found a suitable object of compassion in his (unmistakably Italian) boy who had impaled his leg on a railing-spike. We did not inspect the leg. The smell of carbolic was strong enough under the clothes. Then we rummaged over a delightful dark and filthy curiosity-shop, and I discovered a real Roman Vase which I got for a shilling. But Mrs. Gray bought a real bronze, doubtful Roman—lamp for 1/6 as a present for me. So I had to give her the vase! For I had another little dinner with them and came up to the Concert in their taxi. Mrs. Steinthal[237] is a mighty clever sculptress. We had great fun in Princes St. buying a laurel-wreath for Mayes for presentation after the play. Poor Mayes overdid himself and has lost his speech. Came up to my room and woke me up this morning with appealing eyes and curious gesturations. I thought he was mad and have yet to get over it! He has been often seized thus, and will soon get right again.

Surely you have some more MSS.—'Purple' for instance. If not, many are lost. I hate losing trifles;—and because they are my only diary, I humbly desire you to keep these letters.

Your very own W.E.O. x

How is Mary?
* sym-pathy = feeling with (Greek)

[232] PN, p. 189.
[233] Saul Kain, *The Daffodil Murderer* (John Richmond Ltd, 1913), a skilful parody of Masefield (and an interesting poem in its own right) by SS. Owen is quoting from the preface by 'William Butler' (in fact T. W. H. Crosland). The whole paragraph reads: 'I have only to add that Mr. Rain is still a young man, between four and six feet in height, very slim and shy, with eyes which may be blue or brown when you conic to examine them closely.' The Preface opens: 'I have read the "Daffodil Murderer" nineteen times. It is, without doubt, the finest literature we have had since Christmas.' Owen's copy survives amongst his books, with an inscription by SS. For a discussion of the poem see Michael Thorpe, *Siegfried Sassoon: a Critical Study* (Oxford University Press, 1966).
[234] This has not survived.
[235] This sentence was omitted in *CL* and *SL*.
[236] The Italian singer.
[237] Another of Dr Brock's ladies. See Letter 552.

549. To Susan Owen

Tuesday Aft., 25 September 1917   *Craiglockhart*

My own dear Mother,

Last week has been a pretty full one. I might if I wanted become mildly 'lionized by Edinburgh Society'. The best visit I made was to John Duncan:[238] a pretty great artist, living near the Grays. He is 'one of the ones' in the Academy;

but didn't sell his picture this year. It is a thing of many beauties.[239] I have been made very sad by the extreme beauty of the eyelids of one of his Faces. But he used no model for her. It is a sad thought that Nature can't grow a face as old Duncan can. I was to go on to see Lintott, of the Avatar, but I got so comfortable at Duncan's that Mrs. Gray couldn't get me away.

I hear that Lintott's bargain with Bibby took the form of a dying English soldier and four angels carrying off a crystal! Something like that.

One night we had a jolly dinner at the Caledonian Hotel. One of the party was the Librarian[240] of the University, who would be delighted to teach me German. My Berlitz Lessons are now finished. I have learnt enough not to be a nuisance of a pupil to him. I had the first lesson in the University last Friday.

On Sat. we had a Field Day for Boy Scouts.

This morning I gave my first lesson of course of English Literature in a big school[241] in Edinburgh! I had 39 boys, who seemed most intelligently attentive.

I am to be boarded today, and am waiting to be called in at any moment. Dr. Brock says I shall be given an extension.

I had one horrid night since I last wrote.

I send you my two best war Poems.

Sassoon supplied the title 'Anthem':[242] just what I meant it to be. Harold might have them after.

Will write soon again.

Your very own Wilfred x

---

[238] John Duncan (1866–1945), painter and illustrator. An artist of the Celtic Twilight, Duncan's work focused on the movement's characteristic themes of myths, legends, and fairy tales, including *The Awakening of Cuchulain* (1896), *St Bride* (1913), and *The Children of Lir* (1914). He was a close friend and follower of Patrick Geddes (see Letter 533, n. 163) and a member of the Edinburgh Theosophical Society. At the time he met Owen, Duncan was an associate member of the Royal Scottish Academy, but was made a full member in 1923. See Clara Young, 'Duncan, John (1866–1945), painter and illustrator', in *Oxford Dictionary of National Biography*, https://www.oxforddnb.com/view/10.1093/ref:odnb/9780198614128.001.0001/odnb-9780198614128-e-94434, and Guy Cuthbertson, *Wilfred Owen* (Yale University Press, 2014), pp. 190–3.

[239] Guy Cuthbertson identified the painting as *The Coming of Bride*. 'The painting portrays the ancient Scottish folk-tale about the arrival of spring.... Originally, in the winter and spring of 1917, the picture was called "Spring Song" and Duncan may have referred to it by that name when he showed it to Owen, who had himself been one of the March-born. Owen wrote a song called 'Winter Song' at Craiglockhart in October' (GC, *Wilfred Owen*, p. 191). For 'Winter Song' see *CPF*, vol. 1, p. 101.

[240] Frank Nicholson, whose recollections of Owen, given to Edmund Blunden, were printed as an Appendix to *The Poems of Wilfred Owen* (Chatto & Windus, 1931). See also Osbert Sitwell, *Noble Essences* (Macmillan, 1950), pp. 95–6.

[241] Tynecastle School. See Letter 550.

[242] 'Anthem for Doomed Youth' (*CPF*, p. 99). The other poem was 'The Next War'. See Letter 550.

550. To Susan Owen

Thursday, 70 p.m. [27 September 1917]   [*Craiglockhart*]

My own dear Mother,

Glad to have your reproach this morning & to think my letter could not arrive long after your posting. The Result of the Board has not been officially announced, but before it Dr. Brock said I should be kept on. In a few minutes I must go down to a special meeting about the Magazine. We have a new House President now, who is willing to lay out more money for it. At last, moreover, there seem to be people capable of helping to it. Sassoon is too much the great man to be bothered with it, and I wish I had back again the time I have wasted on it. I was cajoled into promising to act in the next big play, but had the fortitude to get out of it again.

I think one of the most humanly useful things I am doing now is the teaching at Tynecastle School.[243] Did I tell you what a great time I had on Tuesday with the 39 boys. Their 'Teacher'[244] is a charming girl,—wife (of course) of an Army Doctor. She had the exquisite tact to offer to leave me alone, but I requested her company for the lesson.

They also have a School Magazine. I was rather struck with this:

'Mr Seaton bought a motor car,
     And had it painted yellow.
In goggles and a big fur coat,
     He looked a handsome fellow.'

Observe the astonishing conciseness of the thing. Three things conjure the complete picture: yellow paint, goggles, big fur coat! And the irony of the last line!

I called for the poet—a wizened little pinch-face, about two feet high! The international idea has already got hold of some of their little imaginations.

Tues. Aft.
2 October 1917

I have rescued these sheets from under a few feet of later accumulations.

I have been quite well all week save for a cold. Nothing has been announced about my Board. Clearly I have another 3 weeks yet—before leaving—or having another board.

Have been to School again. Am going to do *Hiawatha* with them now.

On Friday last I went with a party over the Fleet: inspecting in Detail the longest fighting ship in the world.[245]

Midshipmen showed us round.

Most people knew the *Zealandia*, but I had forgotten the name of Harold's present ship. The officers' cabins are marvels of size & comfort. In the 'Mess Room' an asiatic creature in frowsy livery was hovering behind the table. For a long time I thought it was some waiter or steward, & was astonished when it sat down beside me. It was some Japanese dignitary.

I have been to see the Lintotts. He seems an excellent gentleman, blessed by nature with a clubbed foot, for he is still 'of age', and a boy of about 12.

On Monday I lectured on 'Soil', out of Sheer light-heartedness!

This afternoon I was booked by the Mackenzies to go with them to their son's school. A merciful rainy day and my cold have been my excuse. I think they only want me to see what a magnificent school their kid—a wash out—attends.

Saturday's Concert consisted for me of a series of manoeuvres with the Dancer portrayed on Page 14. It was fluttering about the doors unattended so long that I invited it in. When the lights went up, I thought worse of it; and after a little furious thinking, contrived to steer it safely out of the building, and return to see the Play in peace.

I have before me a letter, (as the novelists say,) from Lady Margaret Sackville[246] to Sassoon, shyly presenting him with her war poems—some of them very fine. She is the great Patroness of Literature, and I am going to ask her for something for the Magazine.

I included my 'Next War' in order to strike a note. I want Colin to read, mark, learn etc. it. This is wretched news of him. If he joins as a private in the R.F.C. very well. But he will never fly with advantage to his Country.

Read Wells' article in today's *Mail*. Most important. I enclose it.[247]

As for myself, I hate washy pacifists as temperamentally as I hate whiskied prussianists. Therefore I feel that I must first get some reputation of gallantry before I could successfully and usefully declare my principles.

I may as well (to make up for so little letter-stuff lately) send you my most lurid war-episode.[248] It is not in a finished state. You had better keep it strictly to yourself, & send it back before you have marked, learnt, & inwardly digested it.

I have been rendered an apathetic maudlin by a cold last week, but it is clearing up now.

Always your own Wilfred x

The figure of the Caliban at Somerside Place affects my imagination even more than the dainty Ariel. I have not been round.

---

[243] Founded in 1912 and located in McLeod Street, Edinburgh, Tynecastle High School offered an innovative teaching environment that combined traditional and technical education. Owen was among a group of four officers that taught at the school, an activity that helped their own rehabilitation. See Neil McLennan, 'A Very Special English Teacher: Wilfred Owen and the "Lost Boys" of Tynecastle High School', *Stand To! Western Front Association Journal*, vol. 88 (2010), pp. 34–9.

²⁴⁴ Mary 'Mamie' Knox Fullerton, née Howie. She married Lieutenant Edward Fullerton, RAMC, on 29 October 1915. She was 23 years old in 1917 (see Letter 555). HO met her after the war and she presented him with a copy of Longfellow's *The Song of Hiawatha*, which she originally meant for Wilfred and had earlier inscribed: 'In memory of the / reading of Hiawatha / Autumn 1917. Edinburgh / M.K. Fullerton / Alnwick / Autumn 1918'. The book survives in Owen's Library at the Bodleian. Mamie Fullerton was also one of the proposed recipients of Owen's planned first volume of poetry.

²⁴⁵ Probably HMS *Repulse* (794 ft. overall length), with the Grand Fleet in 1917.

²⁴⁶ Lady Margaret Sackville (1881–1963), poet and children's writer, was the daughter of the 7th Earl De La Warr, Reginald Windsor Sackville, and a second cousin of Vita Sackville-West. Her brother, Gilbert, the 8th Earl, was killed in action in 1915. A pacifist, she was a member of the anti-war Union of Democratic Control, a supporter of women's suffrage, and a member of the British Committee of the International Women's Congress. She was the first President of the Poetry Recital Society (later the Poetry Society). A copy of her war poems, *Pageant of War* (1916), inscribed by her, survives among Owen's books. See Letter 552.

²⁴⁷ H.G. Wells had written an article asking for peace between pacifists and belligerents, which had aroused opposition. In an article on 22 August 1917 he replied: 'I have always insisted that this war must end not simply in the defeat but in the disappearance of militant imperialism from the world…however difficult international controls may be, we have to solve these difficulties.… The alternative to the United States of the World is the periodic blood-bath of the world.'

²⁴⁸ It is unclear which poem Owen is referring to.

[552.]²⁴⁹ To Susan Owen

Tuesday [9 October 1917]   [*Craiglockhart*]

Dearest Mother,

I went with Blanche to her Uncle's this evening. As you have been I need not describe. They were extremely pleasant, [*half sheet cut out and missing*] to see the case tomorrow. Here is a gas poem,²⁵⁰ done yesterday, (which is not private, but not final).

The famous Latin tag means of course It is sweet and meet to die for one's country. Sweet! And decorous! [*half sheet cut out and missing*] boys to Swanston Cottage—Stevenson's you know. We are reading *St. Ives;* many scenes occur there,²⁵¹ and in the Castle, & even on the road just outside the Hydro!

It is horribly cold in my room, but what like out There?

I will enclose this in *The Pageant of War*.²⁵² I don't know why Lady Margaret has put all those + +

Colin might join the Artists' Rifles with about a year's certainty of life; or as a private in the R.F.C. with no danger.

Sassoon came up to me the other night & confessed he didn't know what to do next about his 'show'. He is to be boarded soon, and is getting in a tighter fix than ever.

Wednesday

Here Mayes came up & pow-wowed till after midnight. This afternoon instead of going to Bangower I went to St. Bernards' Crescent,[253] & had my first sitting—about an hour. The charcoal outline was finished in 5 minutes, & before tea the complete rough likeness was done in oils![254] I think it will be a great success—impressionistic rather than finicky. Mrs. S's mother-in-law was there, & did at the same time a small water-colour; it turned out a failure in my opinion.

I proudly record that Pixie, (aged one exactly, & the most exquisite bit of protoplasm of that age I have handled) much preferred me to her grandmother; and would not be taken away from me. I enclose her photograph with her Mother. The fat boy is Martin, Mrs. Steinthal's.

I will help Colin to a motor bike if he will come up here on it.

Ever your lovingest—by many years—of Sons,

Wilfred x

[249] Originally dated [? 16 October 1917] in CL and SL, but PN (p. 187) established that 'It must have been written the previous week: begun on Tuesday 9 October—with the "gas poem, done yesterday" on the 8th, as recorded on the MS—it was completed on Wednesday 10 October.' It is here placed in correct chronological order.

[250] 'Dulce Et Decorum Est' (CPF, p. 140).

[251] St. Ives, by Robert Louis Stevenson (1850–94), was published in 1898. (Thirty chapters had been written at his death; the six final chapters were written by Sir Arthur Quiller-Couch.) The house in which the heroine, Flora Gilchrist, lived is closely described from Stevenson's memories of Swanton Cottage, a farmhouse on the slopes of the Pentlands, the lease on which his father took in 1867. Family summer holidays were spent there until 1881.

[252] See Letter 550, n. 246.

[253] Home of the Steinthal family.

[254] Susan Owen did not like Steinthal's portrait and she destroyed it after the war.

551. To Susan Owen

Sunday, 14 October [1917]   *Craiglockhart*

My own dear Mother,

It's getting time I saw you again. Three months without leave would seem long with a Regiment, longer perhaps than it does here; where I am kept amused.

This afternoon, after lunching with Miss Wyer, and a scholastic lady-friend of hers, we went up to Colinton, a village close to here, to see Mr. Blaikie, one of the heads of Constable's, Printers.[255] I was not long discovering that he was a friend of Stevenson's from boyhood. Stevenson's famous old nurse was Blaikie's first. So it was an interesting afternoon; tho' old Blaikie affects a contempt for R.L.S. It is a beautiful thing that children of Tynecastle School,—or of the Birkenhead Institute are able to get nearer to the romantic heart of Stevenson, and really know him in a better way, than this person who played with him before even *Treasure Island* was dreamed of.

On Friday I went to the Lintotts again. Lintott has reason to be proud of his work, which he is not—particularly—; and the beautiful Mrs. Lintott has reason to be proud of her boy, which she is. From there I went to see Mrs. Scott, Mrs. Gray's mother, and her daughter, who has just given up work in the War Office. Miss Scott was out.

On Sat. I met Robert Graves (see last poem of O.H.)[256] for Sassoon, whom nothing could keep from his morning's golf; & took Graves over to the Course when he arrived. He is a big, rather ugly[257] plain fellow, the last man on earth apparently capable of the extraordinary, delicate fancies in his books.

No doubt he thought me a slacker sort of sub. S.S. when they were together showed him my longish war-piece 'Disabled'[258] (you haven't seen it) & it seems Graves was mightily impressed, and considers me a kind of <u>Find</u> ! ![259] No thanks, Captain Graves! I'll find myself in due time.

I think it a rather precious exhibition of esteem that S.S. lends me the MSS. of his next book. On the other hand, when I pointed out a quotation from Shakespere that I intended for my Frontispiece, he collared it by main force, & copied it out for himself!

I don't think of anything else of interest to tell you—even if the above is so. My next board should be a week next Tuesday. They may cast me out the same day,—or give me another month. Both issues are acceptable. I could do a lot with another month here; but I feel a growing homesickness.

I am no longer neurasthenic, though I may be neurotic.

It is high time you started a special course of <u>getting fit</u> so that I may find you all bonny, & so that the exertion of my company may not fatigue you. Time also to get the house swept and garnished, not of dust and cobwebs but of the Webby people that come to spin their yarns there.

Dearest love all round and round   From Wilfred x

---

[255] Walter Biggar Blaikie (1847–1928), Chairman of T. and A. Constable Ltd, University Press, Edinburgh. He lived at Bridgend, Colinton, Midlothian.

[256] *The Old Huntsman and Other Poems.* The last poem (p. 96) is 'A Letter Home; to Robert Graves'. Owen used the last two lines to preface his own poem 'The Next War'. They run: 'War's a joke for me and you / While we know such dreams are true!'

[257] 'ugly' is scribbled out in ink, not by Owen, and was omitted in *CL* and *SL*.

[258] *CPF*, p. 175.

[259] Robert Graves wrote to Owen about the poem. In a letter to HO and JB (22 February 1966), Graves writes: 'I met Owen at Craiglockhart when I "escorted" Sassoon there—actually I missed the train and Sassoon got there first; but only occasionally later. Owen came to my wedding, Jan 23 1918, at St. James', Piccadilly & brought me a present of 11 Apostle Spoons. He said the twelfth had been court-martialled for cowardice & was awaiting execution. He sent me a Field Service Postcard from France the day before he was killed.' (*CL*, p. 499)

553. To Susan Owen

Thursday, 18 October 1917   *Craiglockhart*

My own Mother,

I think I described to you my meeting with Robert Graves, and how S.S. said of him: he is a man one likes better <u>after</u> he has been with one.[260]

So it turns out with my case. You will be amused with his letter.[261] He carried away a Poem, or was carried away with it, without my knowledge. It was only in a <u>Draft</u> State, & I was perfectly aware of all the solecisms.

Yesterday I did go to Newboults—an event you will no doubt hear of. Chubby Cubby had grown, and his face altered. But the old gold and olive ensheath him as in Summer.[262] I should like to pickle his hands for the benefit of mankind in the future.

From there, I went to a *tête-à-tête* dinner with Miss Scott, Mrs. Gray's sister. By the way, you have mixed up the babies of these families—as fairy-godmothers often do. Miss Scott, whose financial means of support are considerable, but whose physical means of support are inadequate, she being some four feet high, became very personal during the meal, & I had hard work to keep the talk on R.L.S. and not L.S.D.[263]

What is the name of Harold's ship? Blanche B. mentioned the Motor Cycle, & I hope to ride home on it. To hear Margaret Bickerton[264] talk physiology gives me the sky-blue shakes. I naturally forget whatever she said except this, that she likes the negro students. Mrs. B., I remember, was kind of pink negress.[265]

Always your W.E.O. x

Friday

I forgot to mention that yesterday I bought a £5. National Bond; and a Wrist Watch.

Called on Lintott's this afternoon. I notice your last letter wilfully misplaces the adjectives. It is only Lintott's <u>wife</u> that is beautiful, which I say ungrudgingly.

I think quite the best picture in B.'s -*Annual* is Lee Hankey's[266] 'Madonna'. Look at it at once!

Good old Lee Hankey. One day when the morning after a night-talk with Harold Monro in the Bookshop Days I turned up on parade in Regent's Park without my belt. Lee Hankey gave me an hour's penal drill for this!

I am to meet Lord Guthrie[267] on Sat. at Swanston.

Somewhere in my Bookshelves, perhaps near the Dressing Table, there is a large boy's-book, pub. by R.T.S.[268] about West Indian Missions. It contains a number of fine photographs of Red Skins. I want all these photographs, if you would please find them and cut them out, and send them. Thanks!

W.E.O.

[260] Two words—'and left'—were crossed through in ink by Owen.
[261] Graves's letter, dated *c.* 17 October 1917, begins, 'Do you know, Owen, that's a damn fine poem of yours, that "Disabled". Really damn fine.' See *CL*, Appendix C.
[262] 'Sonnet: to a Child' (*CP*, p. 129) and 'Winter Song' (*CP*, p. 101) are both addressed to Arthur Newboult. 'Winter Song' is inscribed October 18, 1917, and 'Sonnet: to a Child' is likely to have been written at the same time. 'The old gold and olive ensheath him as in summer' is echoed in 'Sonnet'—'For earlier suns than ours have lent you gold'—and in 'Winter Song': 'The browns, the olives and the yellows died … / From off your face … / The sun-brown and the summer gold are blowing.'
[263] R.L.S.: Robert Louis Stevenson (Owen crossed out 'Stevenson' before the initials). L.S.D.: possibly, given the context of Miss Scott's finances, 'pounds (£), shillings (s), and pence (d)' in predecimal currency.
[264] One of the two daughters of a Shrewsbury builder. See *JFO* II, pp. 8–13, where she is mistakenly called Kathleen.
[265] The final eighteen words of this paragraph were omitted in *CL* and *SL*.
[266] William Lee-Hankey (1869–1952), ROI, RWS, painter and illustrator. Gazetted lieutenant, Artists' Rifles, November 1916.
[267] Lord Charles Guthrie (1849–1920), an eminent lawyer and antiquarian. He lived at Swanston Cottage; among his publications was *Cummy, R. L. Stevenson's nurse, an Appreciation* (1914).
[268] The Religious Tract Society.

554. To Susan Owen

Sunday, 21 October 1917   *Craiglockhart*

My dearest Mother,

It was a puzzle and a mystery to many, the party of six that assembled this afternoon at the Braid Hills Tram Terminus, and began a saunter into the Pentland Hills. People saw a married lady, an obviously unmarried young man in a reckless soft-cap, a well-dressed boy with violet eyes and tie, (wonder where his mother learnt that?) an ill-dressed thin boy, with an intellect behind his parchment forehead; a fat little knave apparently with a large apple stowed under each cheek in case of emergency; and a tall awkward boy, very nervous of himself. What spirit drove us together? The spirit of Stevenson it was; and he was with us at his gayest all the time.

He caused the finest wind the Pentlands can produce to come and play with us; and October spared us the last of her sun-remnants. When we beheld the Cottage to good advantage, we sat in the lee of a haystack and ate sandwiches. We then sang songs, and told tales, every now and then leaping about and prancing for joy.

It was already darkening when we reached Colinton and had tea, and quite dark when we took the Edinburgh road; and so we took it in good style with songs and dancing, whistling and holloing. Until the meteors showered in heaven; and we fell calm under the winter stars, and some of us saw the pale pathway of the Spirits for the first time.

And seeing it so far above us, and feeling the good road so firm beneath us, we worshipped God in our hearts; and knew we loved one another as no men love for long.[269]

That was my way of spending Sunday.

The boys had each been to church in the morning, and I had been at my travail, for I am not ordained a listener in the temple of life.

Monday

On Sat. I went to Swanston, & fell into a trap. Lord Guthrie wants me to do some historical research work for him in the Edinburgh Libraries. I was not at all keen, & pleaded in vain my ignorance & my hatred of legal matters. But I had to meet him this morning in The Advocates' Library,[270] & have now my work cut out.

In person he is my old idea of a judge, tall, long-faced, with solemn hanging jowls, scrupulously shaven and dazzlingly clean in his tall collar; blue clothes, cravat, and tie-pin.

A most courteous gentleman withal, and no lady has ever given me tea in so fine a manner. We had tea alone in Stevenson's room; but scarcely a word was spoken of him!

I would like you to get his *St. Ives* for 1s. (or 1/3 if you are weak) for I haven't a copy of my own: and read it as quick as you can.

I wrote quite six poems last week, chiefly in Edinburgh; and when I read them to S.S. over a private tea in his room this afternoon, he came round from his first advice of deferred publishing, and said I must hurry up & get what is ready typed. He & his friends will get Heinemann[271] to produce for me. Now it is my judgment alone that I must screw up to printing pitch.

Tell me the date & contents of yr. last letter. Saturday's post didn't arrive owing to the Raid in the South!

I heard from Harold yesterday.

Looking out for the Redskin Photographs, and hoping you will read *St. Ives*,

Yours ever W.E.O. x

You must be prepared for a long period of Post Cards! I find I have put some poetic material on p. 3 for instance which ought to have been economized for my serious workshop.

[269] These sentences appear again, more or less verbatim, in Letter 557.
[270] The Advocates' Library, Parliament House, Edinburgh, was founded in 1682, and became a copyright library under the Statute of Anne in 1709 with a right to claim a copy of every book published in the British Isles. By the 1850s it had become in effect Scotland's national library, until 1925, when the National Library of Scotland was founded and the Faculty gifted its non-law materials to the nation. The Advocates' Library still holds a historical collection of early modern legal books, manuscripts, and special collections.

[271] William Henry Heinemann (1863–1920), British publisher of Sassoon's work. His firm, located at 21 Bedford Street, London, published other important First World War texts including Philip Gibbs's *The Soul of the War* (1915), Enid Bagnold's *A Diary without Dates* (1918), and Mary Borden's *The Forbidden Zone* (1929). It was noted for lists that included R. L. Stevenson, Rudyard Kipling, and Joseph Conrad, as well as Constance Garnett's translations of Russian writers and the Loeb Classical Library.

555. To Susan Owen

Sat. [27 October 1917][272]   *Craiglockhart*

My own dearest Mother,

So relieved by your Card this morning. How good of you to report instantly of your <u>palatial</u>-<u>gorgeous</u> sickness. But it was not a joke to me yesterday.

I hear this morning that I am to be boarded <u>next</u> Tuesday—and sent away. It is not absolutely certain, but Dr. Brock thinks that will be the issue this time. I am rather upset about it. Especially as I am so happy with Sassoon. Spent all day with him yesterday, Breakfast, Lunch, Tea & Dinner, chiefly at the Conservative Club. Hence no letter yesterday!

Today, since 3 o'clock High Jinks reigned at Mrs. Fullerton's Apartments; we gave the boys Tea & Supper; Mrs. F. says she never enjoyed so much any party in her 23 years experience. I can say almost as much. We left the House at 9 p.m. & I have just arrived here.

Strange, if you like, but I am seriously beginning to have aching sensations at being rooted up from this pleasant Region. I wanted to arrange my 3 Weeks around Christmas; but now I can only think of spending the 25th in a detestable Mess Room.

However you will be none too well by Wednesday next, & I may cheer you up, my precious Mother, whose little finger will break all the charm of Edinburgh, and all the love that it has thrown about me.

No more news—or I shall have not enough to gabble about around the Home Fire.

I may not arrive till Thurs. or Friday. Or again I <u>may</u> not come till next year!

S.S. has come in since I started this (2 mins. ago) & is deeply annoyed about this news, and is going to siege his Dr. Rivers about me![273]

Ever your own W.E.O.

[272] PN, p. 189.

[273] Dr W[illiam] H[alse] R[ivers] Rivers (1864–1922) FRS, RAMC, physician and anthropologist, was Sassoon's doctor at Craiglockhart. He was already recognized as an important scholar of anthropology by the time of the First World War for publications that included *The Todas* (1906) and *History of Melanesian Society* (1914). *Kinship and Social Organisation* was published in 1915. A proponent of the work of Freud and Jung, Rivers favoured psychoanalytic methods of treatment for shell shock. He is remembered warmly by Sassoon in *Sherston's Progress* (1936) and features prominently as a character in Pat Barker's *Regeneration* trilogy (1992, 1994, 1996).

556. To Susan Owen

Postcard

Monday [Postmark 29 October 1917]   *[Postmark Midlothian]*

It seems really likely that I shall be evacuated on Tuesday. Some time ago the Grays made me promise to stay 2 or 3 days with them before leaving Edinburgh. I am going there this afternoon, & if they ask me again, I may stay <u>one day</u> in order to get my picture done. Sassoon is anxious for me to spend a day or two of my 3 weeks with some people at a Manor near Oxford.[274] I have not made up my mind. We went to the Astronomer's yesterday, & saw the moon.

I wonder how I shall find you all. I shall be in a desperate excited state when I arrive. Make due arrangements for Colin's presence!

So, then, I may turn up on Tues. Night, or Wednesday Morning, or any day until Sat., for I want to stay on here a few days (if it won't shorten the 3 weeks) to be able to return all my borrowed books, & make a graceful exit from these scenes.

W.E.O.

[274] Garsington Manor, home of Philip Morrell (1870–1943), Liberal MP for South Oxfordshire, and Lady Ottoline Morrell (1873–1938). SS had first been there in 1916 (see Sassoon, *Siegfried's Journey, 1916–1920*). Owen never got there.

557. To Siegfried Sassoon

5 November 1917   *Mahim, Monkmoor Road, Shrewsbury*

My dear Sassoon,

When I had opened your envelope[275] in a quiet corner of the Club Staircase, I sat on the stairs and groaned a little, and then went up and loosed off a gourd, a Gothic vacuum[276] of a letter, which I 'put by' (as you would recommend for such effusions) until I could think over the thing without grame.[277]

I have also waited for this photograph.

Show some rich anger if you will.[278] I thank you; but not on this paper only, or in any writing. You gave—with what Christ, if he had known Latin & dealt in oxymoron, might have called Sinister Dexterity. I imagined you were entrusting me with some holy secret concerning yourself. A secret, however, it shall be until such time as I shall have climbed to the housetops, and you to the minarets of the world.

Smile the penny! This Fact has not intensified my feelings for you by the least—the least <u>grame</u>. Know that since mid-September, when you still regarded me as a tiresome little knocker on your door, I held you as Keats + Christ + Elijah + my Colonel + my father-confessor + Amenophis IV in profile.

What's that mathematically?

In effect it is this: that I love you, dispassionately, so much, so <u>very</u> much, dear Fellow, that the blasting little smile you wear on reading this can't hurt me in the least.

If you consider what the above Names have severally done for me, you will know what you are doing. And you have <u>fixed</u> my Life—however short. You did not light me: I was always a mad comet; but you have fixed me.[279] I spun round you a satellite for a month, but I shall swing out soon, a dark star in the orbit where you will blaze. It is some consolation to know that Jupiter himself sometimes swims out of Ken!

To come back to our sheep, as the French <u>never</u> say, I have had a perfect little note from Robt. Ross,[280] and have arranged a meeting at 12.30 on Nov. 9th. He mentioned staying at Half Moon St., but the house is full.

I have ordered several copies of *Fairies & Fusiliers*,[281] but shall not buy all, in order to leave the book exposed on the Shrewsbury counters! I'm also getting Colvin's new *Life of Keats*,[282] no price advertised, but damn it, I'm to enjoy my Leave!

I am spending happy enough days with my Mother, but I can't get sociable with my Father without going back on myself over ten years of thought.

What I most miss in Edinburgh (not Craiglockhart) is the <u>conviviality</u> of the Four Boys (L. *vivere*—to live). Someday, I must tell how we sang, shouted, whistled and danced through the dark lanes through Colinton; and how we laughed till the meteors showered around us, and we fell calm under the winter stars. And some of us saw the pathway of the spirits for the first time. And seeing it so far above us, and feeling the good road so safe beneath us, we praised God with louder whistling; and knew we loved one another as no men love for long.[283]

Which, if the Bridge-players Craig & Lockhart could have seen, they would have called down the wrath of Jahveh, and buried us under the fires of the City you wot of.

To which also it is time you committed this letter. I wish you were less undemonstrative, for I have many adjectives with which to qualify myself. As it is I can only say I am

Your proud friend, Owen

---

[275] SS recalled that in saying goodbye at the Conservative Club he gave Owen a sealed envelope. It contained a ten-pound note and Robert Ross's address in London.

[276] For a vivid and joyful recollection of SS and Owen's final evening in Edinburgh, see *Siegfried's Journey 1916–1920*, pp. 64–5. The volume of verse that 'convulsed' them with laughter was *A Human Voice* by Aylmer Strong (1917). It survives among Owen's books, inscribed to him by SS.

[277] SS could not explain this word; but DH notes that Aylmer Strong uses it (*WOANB*, p. 351).

[278] Keats, 'Ode on Melancholy': 'Some rich anger shows.'

279 See ll. 25–8 of 'O World of Many Worlds' (*CPF*, p. 71): 'To be a meteor, fast, eccentric, lone, / Lawless; in passage through all spheres, / Warning the earth of wider ways unknown / And rousing men with heavenly fears.'

280 Robert Baldwin Ross (1869–1918), Oscar Wilde's editor and loyal friend; critic, authority on art, and patron of young writers. He published Wilde's *De Profundis* in 1905 and *The Collected Works of Oscar Wilde* (14 vols.) in 1908. Through him Owen met Osbert Sitwell, Arnold Bennett, H. G. Wells, and others. He lived in an apartment at Half Moon Street, Mayfair, London, which 'became a sanctuary for war-weary young men [....] In Ross's delightful and witty company, for a few precious hours, they could forget the horrors of trench warfare' (Maureen Borland, 'Ross, Robert Baldwin (1869–1918), journalist and gallery owner.' *Oxford Dictionary of National Biography*, https://www.oxforddnb.com/view/10.1093/ref:odnb/9780198614128.001.0001/odnb-9780198614128-e-37915.

281 Robert Graves's second book of poems (William Heinemann, 1917). The first was *Over the Brazier* (The Poetry Bookshop, 1916).

282 *John Keats, His Life and Poetry* (Macmillan, 1917). Sir Sidney Colvin (1845–1927) had published an earlier life in the English Men of Letters series (*Keats*, Macmillan and Co. Ltd, 1887). Owen's copy of the 1909 impression is inscribed 'Torquay, Spring, 1911'.

283 See Letter 554.

558. To Susan Owen

Postcard

Thurs. Night [Postmark 9 November 1917]   *Regent Palace Hotel,*
Piccadilly Circus, London W.1

Woke up at Padd. arriving an hour sooner than expected. Had no difficulty in getting a good room. Looked in at Poetry Bookshop, where I was informed by Miss Klematanski284 that I had met a friend of hers in Edinburgh. I couldn't recall this friend for some minutes, so shocked at being recognized myself. Monro is in England, but ill.

Your W.E.O.

284 Alida Klemantaski. She married Harold Monro in 1920, his first marriage having been dissolved in 1916. See Letter 420.

559. To Susan Owen285

Sunday Mng. [11 November 1917]286   *Regent Palace Hotel*

Dearest Mother,

I have just lunched with Ross, H. G. Wells, & Arnold Bennett. Wells talked exclusively to me for an hour over the coffee, & made jokes at the expense of the Editor of the *Daily News*,287 who joined us.

I think I can't honestly put more news under one penny stamp!

Your W.E.O.

P.S. Just going up to Gidea Park. I am to have dinner with Ross tomorrow.

[*Later*]

Had a memorable dinner at the Reform[288] last night, & stayed talking with Ross till one A.M. I and my work are a success. I had already sent something to the *Nation*[289] which hasn't appeared yet, but it seems the Editor[290] has started talking of me, and Wells told me he had heard of me through that Editor! H.G.W. said some rare things for my edification, & told me a lot of secrets. I only felt ill at ease with him once, and that was when he tried to make me laugh at Arnold Bennett. Wells is easily top dog when it comes to jests, and I'm afraid I took his side, and told Bennett I disapproved of his gaudy silk handkerchief!

Bennett had just had a look round in Ireland, but he had nothing to say outside his *Daily News* Article,[291] which I suppose you read. I didn't. I got Bennett into a corner about Sassoon. I think they 'noticed' me because I <u>stood up to them</u> both politely when they shook hands to go, <u>and argumentatively</u>.

W.E.O.

I've had an imploring card from Leslie, received in a weak moment, namely in a hot bath, and so resolved to go down this afternoon.

---

[285] DH demonstrated that the two parts of this letter were printed in reverse in *CL* and *SL*. The order has been corrected here.

[286] PN, p. 189.

[287] Alfred George Gardiner (1865–1946) was Editor of *The Daily News* 1902–19. He wrote regularly under the pseudonym 'Alpha of the Plough'.

[288] The Reform Club, 104 Pall Mall, London. Founded in the wake of the Reform Bill of 1832, its members included writers, politicians, doctors, lawyers, and business people. In 1981 it was the first London club to admit women on an equal basis with men.

[289] 'Miners' (*CPF*, p. 135). Published in *The Nation*, 16 January 1918.

[290] Henry William Massingham (1860–1924) was Editor of *The Nation* 1907–23.

[291] Arnold Bennett's three pieces on Irish Home Rule were published on 8, 12, and 15 November 1917.

561. To Leslie Gunston

16 November 1917   [*? Shrewsbury*]

My dear Leslie,

I did not think to send back a driblet of your Ink so soon, but I have indeed carried off the key.

Had it been the key of my box I should surely have left it with you. As it was I left you the key to many of my poems, which you will guard from rust or soilure.

As I said, if Hilda herself had any feelings for you, she would devise means of communication. I hope your plan succeeds.[292]

Good of you to send me the Lyric of Nov. 14th. I can only send my own of the same date,[293] which came from Winchester Downs, as I crossed the long backs of the downs after leaving you. It is written <u>as from</u> the trenches. I could almost see the dead lying about in the hollows of the downs.

I called at the Bookshop during my 3 hours in Town, & had a good chat with Monro, not forgetting to ask him about the *Nymph*. Graves' book just came in while I was here. Haste thee, *Nymph*, and bring with thee Jest & youthful jollity!

Your W.E.O.

[292] This sentence was omitted in *CL* and *SL*.

[293] 'Asleep' (*CPF*, p. 152).

5

Scarborough and the Return to France
1918

563. To Susan Owen

23 November 1917   *5 (Reserve) Bn. Manchester Regt.,*[1]
                              Northern cavalry Barracks, Scarborough

Dearest Mother,

I have been put on a species of Light Duty which I little expected: I am Major Domo[2] of the Hotel. There is a Mess President, the Doctor, Capt. Mather,[3] whom I knew at Witley, and like very much; there is also a Food Specialist: under him like me. Capt. Mather then has the responsibility, but will do little but sign his name. I have to control the Household, which consists of sonic dozen Batmen, 4 Mess Orderlies, 4 Buglers, the Cook, (a fat woman of great skill,) two female kitcheners, and various charwomen!

They need driving. You should see me scooting the buglers round the dining-room on their knees with dustpan and brush! You should hear me rate the Charwoman for leaving the Lavatory-Basins unclean.

I am responsible for finding rooms for newcomers, which is a great worry, as we are full up. This means however that I have a good room to myself, as well as my Office!

I keep two officers under arrest in their rooms; & spent a dismal hour this morning taking one of these for exercise.

I get up at 6.30. to see that the breakfast is ready in time.

I spent this morning in Correspondence, and Inspection of rooms: working from 8 a.m. to 12. This afternoon I ordered from the Grocers and the Greengrocers vast quantities of food.

I do no parades, and can go out when I like. (This by special ruling of the Colonel.)[4] —Who is not liked among his 70 officers.

I am specially busy at present. There was a guest night yesterday, which meant a gorgeous meal, whose menu I am ashamed to give you. It kept my house-lads sweating till after midnight.

And the Food Expert has gone away for a time.

I am also in charge of the Wine & Tobacco, and took stock in a most business-like manner this afternoon.

It is interesting work but hardly 'lighter' than a Platoon Commander's.

I am pestered by these new officers who are in the first flush of commission-hood, and need to be suppressed.

I shall soon be putting up another pip.

I beg to acknowledge your letter of the 22nd inst. and have noted the facts. Confound this business mood which possesses me! It, as much as the busy-ness of my hours, will prove disastrous to my poems. But things will slack down next week, and so shall my temper.

The C.O. is a terrible old 'Regular', and I am in mortal terror lest one day his bath-water should be cold, or his plates too hot.

There was a Mess Dance the first night I arrived, and I was glad to see several of the old Witley N.C.O.'s. Some had been out & wounded. It was strange to see the change in their expressions. They had been told I was killed. I <u>think</u> I am marked Permanent Home Service:

Always your own

W.E.O.

---

[1] Owen had left the battalion at Southport in December 1916 to go to France. Shortly after, 3rd/5th, 3rd/6th, and 3rd/7th Manchesters were amalgamated into the 5th (Reserve) Battalion, which moved to Scarborough in the summer of 1917. The officers were in the Queen's Hotel and Clarence Gardens Hotel, the men in the large cavalry barracks at Burniston, outside the town. The battalion was filled up in 1918 with boys under 18 who continued training until the Armistice. The Clarence Gardens Hotel is now known as the Clifton Hotel. Owen's stay is marked by a blue plaque.

[2] Camp Commandant, but probably not an official title (see WOANB, p. 510, n. 1).

[3] Captain J. de V. Mather, RAMC.

[4] Lieutenant Colonel Spencer Mitchell, Manchester Regiment.

564. To Leslie Gunston

Sunday, 25 November 1917   *Clarence Gardens Hotel, Scarborough*

My dear Leslie,

Received the Books last night, and spent an exciting few minutes looking through <u>the poems</u>.[5] I congratulate you on the Binding & Type. The Dedication Page & the Prefatory Note are set perfectly. Yes, it is rather disappointing to have no Back Lettering. I still think many of the Pieces might have enriched themselves with Time. I like best

(1) <u>The Caradoc</u>. How much better than a photograph does it souvenir that day! I remember talking about the Croziers,[6] and plucking them & uncurling them. What was the date of this June?

(2) <u>Golden Hair</u>. This is your very best.

(3) <u>Sestet of Attar Roses</u> 'red as the dawn of doubtful days' is the best thought in the book.

(4) Ode for A.C.S.

(5) Chopin

(6) The Colloseum!!

I don't like 'Hymn of Love to England', naturally, at this period while I am composing 'Hymns of Hate'.

I wonder you did not include the Bluebottle thing. I liked that ever so well.

And why omit certain Rose Poems which I remember?

It struck me that there was a little too much osculation throughout the book. People will not know that poetry is your only manner of satisfaction, and may draw wrong conclusions.

I think every poem, and every figure of speech should be a <u>matter of experience</u>. That is why I like the first verse of 'Song', and should have omitted the second!

Am looking out for mentions & reviews, and anxious to hear what you know of the Sales.

I am wickedly busy and businesslike now, being Boss of the Hotel, Accommodation, Food, Fires, Lighting, Service, etc. etc. I do no parades, but have not yet allowed myself any free time for walks or reading.

I have no table, & am writing on my knee.

Yours always W.E.O.

⁵ *The Nymph and Other Poems* (Arthur H. Stockwell, 1917).

⁶ A description of bracken: 'Like carven croziers are the curled shoots growing / To bless me as I pass.'

565. To Siegfried Sassoon

27 November 1917   *Scarborough*

I sit alone at last, and therefore with you, my dear Siegfried. For which name, as much as for anything in any envelope of your sealing, I give thanks and rejoice.

The 5th have taken over a big Hotel, of which I am Major Domo, which in the vulgar, means Lift Boy. I manage Accommodation, Food, and Service. I boss cooks, housemaids, charwomen, chamber-maids, mess orderlies and— drummers.

There were 80 officers when I came, or 800 grouses daily.

I had a Third Heaven of a time in London, and should have got into a Fourth or Fifth if I had not missed you on Wednesday. Were you there for a 'Reading?' I know nothing of it to this day.

After London, I went to Winchester to see my Cousin, whose fine Book cover with its enclosed pages I dare to send you herewith. ('Herewith' is the staple of my morning's letters, <u>re</u> this and <u>per</u> that.)

In Town, then, R.R. gave me a glorified morning at the Reform, & evening at Half Moon St.—When he had steered me to a lunch-table I found beside me an upstart rodent of a man, who looked astonished to find himself there. But dear Ross sang out with blessed distinctness 'Mister Arnnoldd Bennnettt'. So I stood up and shook hands. Presently I became aware of a pair of bayonet-coloured eyes, threatening at me from over, as it were, a brown sandbag. 'H. G. Wells!' So I stood up and shook hands. I think these men noticed me because I stood up to them—in two senses. Anyhow I got A.B. into a corner about you, as I will tell you someday. And H.G. talked to me exclusively for an hour. I was only ill at ease with him once, and that was when he tried to make me laugh with him at Bennett's gaudy handkerchief.

What sport for my imagination is the idea of your Meeting with R. Nichols.[7]— He is so self-concerned & *vaniteux* in his verse that I thought he must efface himself in a room : even as you who write so acid are so-unsoured; and me, who write so big, am so minuscule.

What is Nichols up to now?

I called at the P. Bookshop the Wednesday you were in Town. A lady was badgering H Monro, trying to discover your age and whereabouts, and so on. Monro proved himself as reticent as his books. But we exchanged some delicious winks. R.G.'s book[8] came in during the hour I was there. I should never stop if I started to rejoice over these poems.

You read many to me: but, wisely, not the best:—or the most charming.

The 'Legion' is too glorious. I tell you I can <u>not</u> believe I rode in a taxi with the man Gracchus. But I did, and he has cursed, battered on the table, over a poor word of mine.[9] Oh! world you are making for me, Sassoon!

I think I liked reading his Letter[10] to you more than yours to him,[11] but for no better reasons than that I like the future better than the past, and hope you <u>will</u> learn the piccolo. If These tetrameters aren't enough to bring you to your senses, Mad Jack,[12] what can <u>my</u> drivel effect to keep you from France?

Have you been very sat upon by this Board? Do tell me quick what your movements are.

I have studied and expanded every sentencience of your sole letter to me; until I can make no more out of it, and want some more, please.

Concerning Gunston's book: you might, of your charity, read (1) page 41,[13] because it is the best.

(2) page 49,[14] the sextet, because I asked him to write, on this subject, and because his every mention of a kiss is pitiable in itself, since he has osculated nothing better than a love token in his born days! This is a solemn fact, and indeed obvious enough from the other verses.[15]

(3) Page 11. There is a conceit in v. 3,—a poor thing, but mine own.[16]

My 'Vision'[17] is the result of two hours' leisure yesterday,—and getting up early this morning! If you have objections to make, would you return it? If not, pass it on to R.R.

I trust you'll like the 'Soldier's Dream'[18] well enough to pass it on to the *Nation* or *Cambridge*?

This was the last piece from Craiglockhart.

Winchester Downs gave me 'Asleep.'

As I do no parades, I shall presently be able to make time for seclusion. There is no one here whose mind is Truth, or whose body Keats's synonym for Truth.

I'll mind my business, I'm a good worm.[19]

Could you get me another portrait for my room here? I framed the one, and could not pack it.

But don't make it an excuse for delaying a letter.

I hope you will read through this, twice.

I hope you read Graves's Letter to S.S. twice a day, <u>till war ends</u>.

We have had some strong sunshine; and when it strikes anything blue I see you sitting by the bedside as on That Morning in September. You look round,—over my head, which annoys me, so that I go down and rate the kitchen staff of the Hotel, and insult the new subalterns.

> I am Owen; and I am dying.
> I am Wilfred; and I follow the Gleam.[20]

---

[7] Robert Malise Bowyer Nichols (1893–1944). He had been invalided home from France (Second Lieutenant RFA) and was about to join the British Mission (Ministry of Information) to the U.S.A. At this time he had published two collections: *Invocation: War Poems and Others* (Elkin Mathews, 1915) and *Ardours and Endurances* (Chatto & Windus, 1917).

[8] Robert Graves, *Fairies and Fusiliers* (William Heinemann, 1917).

[9] 'The Legion' (*Fairies and Fusiliers*) ends with Gracchus speaking: 'The legion is the legion while Rome stands, / And these same men before the autumn's fall / Shall bang old Vercingetorix out of Gaul.' Owen is quoting: 'The red-faced old centurion started up, / Cursed, battered on the table.'

[10] 'Letter to S.S. from Mametz Wood', in which the poet looks forward to travelling with SS after the war: 'Robert will learn the local *bat* / For billeting and things like that, / If Siegfried learns the piccolo / To charm the people as we go.'

[11] 'A Letter Home'. See Letter 551, n. 256.

[12] SS had this nickname in France on account of his bravery and exploits on the battlefield, which earned him the Military Cross.

[13] 'Golden Hair'. The first four lines of the sonnet read: 'High in her tower she sat in flowerful spring / And combed her, hair before her mirrored wall, / Sweet was she, slim and lissom, blithe and tall; — / Her hair shone gold as shone her golden ring.'

[14] 'Attar of Roses' (ll. 9–14): '—Her lips! red as the dawn of doubtful days, / And curved as are the sides of stately ships… / Oh! I must taste their sweet beyond all praise, / And crush her lips' sweet roses with my lips, / That they can neither murmur, laugh nor pout, / So I must kiss her lips, and draw the attar out.'

[15] The final thirty-nine words of this paragraph were omitted in *CL* and *SL*.

[16] 'From the Cardoc in June', verse (stanza) 3: 'Upon the hillside bracken sprouts are showing / In tender bright green stalks from out the grass; / Like craven croziers are the curled shoots growing / To bless me as I pass.'

[17] JS, in WO (pp. 242–5), convincingly argues that this was the first draft title of 'The Show' (CPF, p. 155).

[18] CPF, p. 182.

[19] DH identifies these words as a line from Robert Graves's 'The Caterpillar', in *Fairies and Fusiliers*.

[20] 'I am Merlin, / And I am dying, / I am Merlin / Who follow The Gleam.' Tennyson, 'Merlin and The Gleam', in *Demeter and Other Poems* (1889).

566. To Susan Owen

10 p.m. Monday [26 November 1917][21]   *Clarence Gardens, Scarborough*

Dearest my Mother,

I am writing in the uncertain privacy of my Office: to tell you that I did indeed forget to post a card written the hour of arrival in Scarborough. It went only one post before my Letter.

Concerning my re-entrance into the Battalion the thing that is most mentionable was the great unexpected consideration & respect shown me by all ranks. (I had risen from the dead.)

The Colonel is a terrible old misanthrope in the morning. (He has lost two sons) but the evening soothes him, and it is only then that I have dealings with him.

Captain Mather whose hints are my laws of life, is a good sort (i.e. kind and clever.) His father was a friend of Ruskin, and wrote a Ruskin Biography.[22] He has read Sassoon with great appreciation. Our Major is the substantial justification of his name: Major Frank.[23] He lives so courteous & pleasant to all that I knew he valued War Poetry before he told me so!

(This may seem a strange inference but it is worth thinking over.)

Have just been interrupted by two drummers who've been stavying[24] here with dish-washing working all day since 6, who need a note to pass the Barrack Sentry.

I was working all Sunday Evening with Mess Bills for 25 officers 'going out' in a few days.

The wind has been glorious for me as annoying for you. The sea was—not a thing for this notepaper to tell of. Much love to all at Alpenrose. I am well pleased with this job.

Dearest of my love. W.E.O.

Thanks for Boots.

[21] PN, p. 189.

[22] James Marshall Mather (1851–1916), *Life and Teachings of John Ruskin* (Warne, 1883).

[23] Major N. G. Frank, 6th Manchesters.

[24] *sic*.

567. To Susan Owen

Sunday [2 December 1917][25]　　　　　　　　　　　　　　　　[*Scarborough*]

Dearest Mother,

I wrote in the middle of the week. Did you get a complete letter? For I have discovered a page of writing to you among my papers. This afternoon I had a fire in my grate, which smokes horribly in the wind. Thus I finished an important poem this afternoon,[26] in the right atmosphere. I also drafted three others. I'm going to get up at dawn tomorrow to do a dawn piece which I've had in mind since those dismal hours at York, 3 to 7 a.m.! All dressed up, and nowhere to go.

I don't want to see York again. No use to me. Worse than Crewe. Here I have a certain amount of what might degenerate into worry, but it doesn't with me. I think my chief trouble is watching that hundreds of windows are shaded at 4 p.m. And no unnecessary lights burning. I think I have hereditary aptitudes for this. I housekeep on a scale that would fairly stagger you and Mary, don't you know.

Engaged two chamber-maids yesterday to polish furniture—or we shall have a big depreciation bill.

The men however do excellent work, and learn as quickly as a female forgets.

I took a joy-walk into Scarboro' yesterday, & discovered 3 genuine 'Hepplethwaite' Chairs. I think I must have 'em.

Did I tell you the Hotel stands on the edge of the North Cliff; just where we played cricket once?

The whole bay is white as milk, the wind being contrary to the breakers.

I was really <u>very</u> sorry not to be able to call at Alpenrose. But it was on your account, wasn't it?

I hope you'll see Dunsden & the Vicar.

Mary wrote the other day, enclosing my Edinburgh Mails. One of my Waiters here lives under the shadow of Holyrood. He's the best lad for work I've got— wounded in the leg. Our old Bar Corporal was at Bangower, & Blanche has written to him since! I wonder if you heard from H. today? I suppose he mustn't write to me yet. Give my messages to him.

　　　　　　　　　　　　　　　　　　　　　　　　Ever your boy Wilfred

Am writing on my knee.

---

[25] PN, p. 189.
[26] 'Wild with all Regrets'. See Letter 568.

568. To Siegfried Sassoon

6 December 1917   *Scarborough*

My friend,

I shall continue to poop off heavy stuff at you, till you get my range at Scarborough, and so silence me, for the time. This 'Wild with all Regrets'[27] was begun & ended two days ago, at one gasp. If simplicity, if imaginativeness, if sympathy, if resonance of vowels, make poetry I have not succeeded. But if you say 'Here is poetry,' it will be so for me. What do you think of my Vowel-rime stunt[28] in this, and 'Vision'? Do you consider the hop from <u>Flea</u> to Soul too abrupt?

Wouldn't our Theosophist[29] like the Thought Form of this piece? quite see the origin of Theosophy. It's the same as that of heaven, and Abraham's bosom, and of the baby that sucked Abraham's bosom, (supposing he lived long enough ago): desperate desire.

Your W.E.O.

[27] An early draft, dated December 5, 1917, of 'A Terre' (*CPF*, p. 178).
[28] Pararhyme. The assonant or 'falling', consonantal rhymes that effect a discordant, melancholy, and unsettling mood are a hallmark of Owen's mature poems.
[29] A fellow patient at Craiglockhart. '...I was fool enough to begin grumbling about the war....he merely replied: "Ah, Sherston, that is the Celestial Surgeon at work upon humanity"' (see Sassoon, *Sherston's Progress*, pp. 29–30).

569. To Susan Owen[30]

Friday Night [7 December 1917][31]   *[Scarborough]*

Dearest Mother,

I wanted Colin to come, hoping I should be in Billets. He could only have tea with me here. There are rooms vacant, but as the Hotel is quite taken over by the Gov't he couldn't sleep. I have made no friends even of the most temporary nature in the Town, but I could easily find him a lodgement, which I would offer him as a Christmas Present. I should be able to be with him either morning or afternoon for hours.

I think he could disport himself very well between times. I went to an Auction yesterday, & got an antique <u>side table</u>[32] wondrous cheap. It will arrive addressed to Father at Station. A beautiful old piece,—to be my Cottage sideboard. There were none but Dealers at this sale! They would double the price in their shop, I was told.

So glad to hear you feel weller. I'm all right. Best wishes to Uncle & Auntie.

Your W.E.O.

Tuesday. ! ! !
4 p.m.

My own Mother,

I wonder how you are disporting yourself at Alpenrose. Life here is a mixture of wind, sand, crumbs on carpets, telephones, signatures, clean sheets, shortage of meat, and too many money-sums. But I like it. For one thing I fell so suddenly into mental preoccupations that there was no dallying with regrets for leaving Home. I have not even written to Sassoon or anyone.

We are getting four maidservants and a page, as these boys are being over-worked at present. You would love to see me 'keeping an eye on the charwoman.'

Gen. Lovatt[33] called yesterday but didn't come in as I thought he would—to see that no fire was burning in my office, and generally look up the kitchen-taps.

I was flurrying round like any Mrs. Smith de Smith when 'Company' is expected.

I 'get out' for an hour or two daily, if only to promenade the 'arrested' subaltern, who is a *ci-devant* Sergeant Major, under arrest for laying hands on an A.P.M.,[34] a big fellow, and a gruff. On our first walk I kept on the landward side of the cliff. There is also a Major under arrest for striking a private. I have to keep looking them up.

The Hotel is a pleasanter place even than the Queen's at Southport, well furnished & commodious. My room has hideous furniture, but a comfortable bed—and fireplace. My personal servant had a bad shell shock in Gallipoli, while lying sun-stricken. He was about a year in hospital, but has all his wits about him now.

Concerning Leslie's book, I may say privately that it is a mere orgy of kissing, and does nobody any good. Were these poems founded on a single act or fact they might have been written to some poetic purpose or value. But that is not so, which is no doubt the more admirable from a <u>Pauline</u> point of view, but the more 'pitiable' in a <u>human</u> aspect. Nothing great was said of anything but a definite experience.[35]

I must now go and see that every blind is drawn, aye and double-drawn.

Always your own W.E.O.

[30] Two letters in one.
[31] PN, p. 189.
[32] HO inherited this, as well as the chest of drawers mentioned in Letter 670. These remain in the Owen family.
[33] Major General Lord Lovat (1871–1933).
[34] Assistant provost marshal.
[35] This paragraph was omitted in *CL* and *SL*.

570. To Susan Owen

13 December 1917   *Scarborough*

Dearest Mother,

It is the quarter of an hour after lunch. The coffee has given me satisfaction and everybody else. (I serve coffee after lunch as well as dinner.) So I sit in the middle of my five-windowed turret, and look down upon the sea. The sun is valiant in its old age. I draw the Venetian blinds, so that the shadow of the lattices on the table gives an illusion of great heat.

I thought Arnold Bennett's article of yesterday showed how much he wants Peace, but how little he knows of war.[36] I hope you read it. How do you find that book about the Fusiliers?[37]

Yesterday I was sent the Tynecastle School Magazine, very amusing. Mrs. Fullerton writes again this morning, reminding me how I promised to go up there for my first leave.

'You can imagine our welcome better than I can write' they say. Now, I find that Leave from Friday Night to Monday Night is granted every month! But Mrs. Fullerton is leaving the school for ever on the 21st. in order to be with her husband who will soon get sent out again.

There is much talk of Education for the 'A 4's' of the Battalion, that is the tender younglings. I have been 'approached' on the subject, but I shall not consent to lecture on Militarian subjects. The scheme either comes of a desperate feeling that the race is going to perdition intellectually or else it is a Jesuitical movement to catch 'em young, & prepare them for the Eucharist of their own blood.

Dearest love from W.E.O.

[36] 'That Inconclusive Peace' (*Daily News*, 13 December 1917).

[37] [Lt John] Bernard [Pye] Adams, *Nothing of Importance: A Record of Eight Months at the Front with a Welsh Battalion, October, 1915, to June, 1916* (Methuen, 1917). Adams did not live to see the book in print. He died of wounds, aged 26, in a field hospital on 27 February 1917 after leading an attack on Puisieux. He is buried in Couin New British Cemetery, Pas-de-Calais. His headstone reads, 'Kept by the Power of God'. SS gave Owen his own annotated copy, which lists 'in Sassoon's scrupulous hand on the back of the front fly-leaf the dead and wounded officers of the 1st Battalion Royal Welch Fusiliers' (*WO*, p. 233). As JS noted, 'One can imagine him savouring the understatement of that title' (*WO*, p. 233). It survives among Owen's books.

571. To Susan Owen

[*18 December 1917*]   *Scarborough*

My dearest Mother,

Glad to hear from Mary as well as you this morning. I hope she is not made to work too hard at that job, and wish she could get something in the Hospital less crockish.

If you hold to giving me a present this is what I most want:

Tides, Poems by John Drinkwater:

Sidgwick and Jackson. 2/6.[38]

Siegfried is going out next week, but may stay in Ireland on the way.

He feels like a condemned man, with just time to put things straight. One of his last deeds here is causing Robert Nichols (of the *Ardours & Endurances*) to write to me, and befriend me. I await Nichols's letter with much wonder.

Enclosed is an article[39] in which I am quoted pretty freely.

I feel immensely glad that Harold is at ease [*remainder missing*]

[38] Published 1917. Owen's copy survives among his books.
[39] This article has not survived.

574. To Susan Owen

20 December [1917]   *North British Station Hotel, Edinburgh*

Dearest Mother,

Train was an hour late at York. There had been an accident in front I believe. Thus I got in after 6 a.m. to Waverley—fortunately—for there was no bedroom vacant at all. But I had a big bath & big breakfast. Then went straight to Craiglockhart—mainly after my Chesterton Drawing Originals,[40] which had not yet been returned to me, & which it seems one Salmond has carried off: I saw Dr. Brock, whose first word was 'Antaeas!' which they want immediately for the next Mag! Shall have to spin it off again while up here. Crowds of the men I knew are still at the Hydro, and thought I had come back relapsed (N.B. I had very little sleep last night.)

Then I went off to Tynecastle. They were in the act of writing Christmas Letters to me! My address was on the Blackboard. And 'original' Christmas Cards were all over the room! I am going to see the Grays this afternoon & may stay with them tomorrow. Am feeling <u>very</u> fit, in spite of the wretched weather, & journey.

Hope your parcel comes all right –

And my table!   Always your lovingest W.E.O.

[40] A page of sketches by G. K. Chesterton appeared under the title 'Profiteers' in *The Hydra*, No. 1, New Series (November 1917).

575. To Susan Owen

Sunday [*23 December 1917*]   *Scarborough*

My own Mother,

Came back last night for Supper, leaving Ed. at quarter to two. A good journey, and as a show well worth the money in itself. The sun began to think of setting about two o'clock and so there was a three hours' winter sunset over the Northumberland moors. I liked what I saw of Berwick on Tweed.

———————————

Monday

I was interrupted here. Have now had your lovely parcel, & opened it but not broken into the scrumshies.

The Scotch boys gave me 100 Players Cigarettes. It was most touching, for I had given most of them nothing—beyond *Hiawatha*. We had a great time in Minnehaha's Wigwam on Thursday. Dined with the Grays and Mrs. Steinthal on Friday: stayed in digs of my own.

I can think of nothing at the moment but Robert Graves' letter,[41] which came by the same post as the parcel.

He says 'Don't make any mistake, Owen, you are a — fine poet already, & are going to be more so. I won't have the impertinence to criticize…

Puff out your chest a little, and be big for you've more right than most of us…

You must help S.S. & R.N. & R.G. to revolutionize English Poetry. So outlive this war.

Yours ever, *Robert Graves.*'

I have never yet written to him!

This aft. I am appointed to tea with Cousin May. This will give a Christmas feeling.

The weather is Septemberish.[42]

I little expected so large a parcel. I am upset in soul that no present will arrive to Mary or Father in time.

I left the tea-pot unpolished to emphasize its antiquity. So looking forward to see you pour out—early in Feby.

I shall gather round tomorrow with you in what Bob Cratchit calls a circle round the fire. This was in one of the many home made Christmas cards I got:

> The thoughts of love arc long long thoughts
> > But memories sweet are longer.
> The bonds of wealth are strong, strong bonds
> > But friendship's ties are stronger!

Pity it's not more banal than it is.

x W.E.O.

———

[41] This was included in full in *CL*, Appendix C.
[42] 'Mayish' struck out.

577. To Leslie Gunston

30 December 1917   *Scarborough*

My dear Leslie,

It is overlong since I wrote; but now, composed by my bedroom fire this Sunday afternoon, my thoughts impel themselves after you, & wish you were here to read a little Swinburne, whom I find particularly fine on Sundays.

Have you yet got Gosse's life of A.G.S.?[43]

I had a longish letter from Sassoon recently, saying he will get Robert Nichols to write to me, for he likes him much. Nichols' *Ardours & Endurances* you know, are in the 3rd or 4th Edition.

Graves also wrote to me, telling me to 'puff out my chest & look big', for I have as much right as most of Them.

Some poems of mine sent him by S.S. he is passing on to Nichols. They believe in me, these Georgians, and I suffer a temptation to be <u>satisfied</u> that they read me; and to remain a poet's poet![44]

S.S. who has your book, (for the letter which he acknowledges, was in it,) says <u>not a word</u> of the book. He may have unfortunately read the 'Nations' Debt'[45] first, and taken offence. Remember Poetry with him is become a mere vehicle of propaganda.

Already, by now, I believe he is in France.

I have had some good inspirations in Scarboro', but my need is to revise now, rather than keep piling up 'first drafts'. My duties, as you know, are in your Line, and I like 'em. Went to the most atrocious bad play ever witnessed, the other night: low melodrama shocking bad acting.

But there were a dozen girls who danced & sang by way of Interlude; & they being only 14 to 18 had adorable slender bare legs, nude as you could wish. What's more some of them came outside the Hotel next day. I waved and blew kisses from the window, but didn't speak to them. Anyhow it was better than overhearing conversation in a motor-car!

An old Bordeaux friend[46] of mine is now Interpreter in the American Y.M.C.A. near Bordeaux. Will write again soon.

Always your W.E.O.

---

[43] Sir Edmund Gosse (1849–1928), *The Life of Algernon Charles Swinburne* (Macmillan, 1917).

[44] See Letter 578.

[45] LG, 'The Nation's Debt', in *The Nymph and Other Poems* (A.H. Stockwell, 1917), ll. 1–5): 'Day by day now our debt grows deeper, / Day by day as we live the same; / Nor has death, grim and ruthless reaper / Stained our grass by our blood or with flame. / Why then and how is our land not weeping?'

[46] Pierre Berthaud.

578. To Susan Owen

31 December 1917   *Scarborough*

My own dear Mother,

Just a short note to thank you for the message enclosed with forwarded letters. I guess you saw the Cards, from Johnny & Bobby; characteristic cards: pictures of monkeys & the motto: 'Times change, & we with Time, but not in ways of Friendship.' So they are unchanged—from the old shallow waggery, and the old deep affection. I haven't written to them since my arrival in England.

The other letter was from my *cher ami* in Bordeaux who, unlike Raoul, persists in his expressions of fidelity. What I taught him of English has got him a post as Interpreter to the American Y.M.C.A. at Bordeaux. (*verb. sap.*) I think Bordeaux is first on my post-war Visiting List. Many & various, strange & multitudinous are the friends that befriend me in this world. Yet I never found one false, or that did not surpass me in some virtue.

Some are very young, and some are already old, but none are middling.

[*one line inked out*]

And there are no dogs among my friends.

No dogs, no sorcerers, nor the other abominations on that list. For I have been bitten by the dogs of the world; and I have seen through the sorceries and the scarlet garments.

And so I have come to the true measure of man.

I am not dissatisfied with my years. Everything has been done in bouts:

Bouts of awful labour at Shrewsbury & Bordeaux; bouts of amazing pleasure in the Pyrenees, and play at Craiglockhart; bouts of religion at Dunsden; bouts of horrible danger on the Somme; bouts of poetry always; of your affection always; of sympathy for the oppressed always.

I go out of this year a Poet, my dear Mother, as which I did not enter it. I am held peer by the Georgians; I am a poet's poet.

I am started. The tugs have left me; I feel the great swelling of the open sea taking my galleon.

Last year, at this time, (it is just midnight, and now is the intolerable instant of the Change) last year I lay awake in a windy tent in the middle of a vast, dreadful encampment. It seemed neither France nor England, but a kind of paddock where the beasts are kept a few days before the shambles. I heard the revelling of the Scotch troops, who are now dead, and who knew they would be dead. I thought of this present night, and whether I should indeed—whether we should indeed—whether you would indeed—but I thought neither long nor deeply, for I am a master of elision.

But chiefly thought of the very strange look on all faces in that camp; an incomprehensible look, which a man will never see in England, though wars should be in England; nor can it be seen in any battle. But only in Étaples.

It was not despair, or terror, it was more terrible than terror, for it was a blindfold look, and without expression, like a dead rabbit's.

It will never be painted, and no actor will ever seize it. And to describe it, I think I must go back and be with them.

We are sending seven officers straight out tomorrow.

I have not said what I am thinking this night, but next December I will surely do so.

I know what you are thinking, and you know me

Wilfred.

579. To Mary Owen

4 January 1918   *Scarborough*

My dear Mary,

Many, many thanks for the Parcel, and your charming little letter. I have seen the last of Cousin May, but her friend, an uncommonly plain lady, is going to continue her German lessons. It is very kind, & I shall make the best of my rare opportunities.

I hear *John Bull* has published an aspersion on the Officers of the 5th Manchester Regt. implying that their men get only ¼ hour for breakfast but the officers get more.[47] I met the C.O.'s train with a taxi this afternoon, and as we were riding together, he asked me what I would do about this lie of Bottomley's. I hoped he would prosecute.

My servant, a deplorable 'shock' case, is run down, & I am giving him a rest, and I think changing him for a secondary-school-educated youth, who has fought at Beaumont Hamel, and at Serre, and all those places, if they can be called places.

He was badly wounded, and his leg has been badly set. He still wears the shell-torn boots.

Lt. Whittaker has just arrived here, for a week's 'training' before going out. Most of our old Musketry Instructors at Oswestry etc. are now killed, he says. But we've got stacks of men, as Sassoon says.

Your cheery Brother

Please send Sassoon's *Daffodil Murderer*[48]—in Book<u>case</u>.

---

[47] 'A *Damnable order*. How long do the officers of the 5th Manchesters spend over their meals? Rather longer, we fancy, than the time granted to the men by a recent order—Tommy being allowed only a hr. for breakfast, and the same for dinner. Such haste is hardly conducive to digestion, even with rations on Lord Rhondda's scale' (*John Bull*, 5 January 1918).

[48] See Letter 548.

580. To Susan Owen

10.30 p.m. 5 January 1918   [*Scarborough*]

My dear dear Mother,

This has been a day of continuous work from 7 a.m. to 9 p.m. ! ! not excluding meals!

True I went out to tea to Miss Bennett,[49] but I worked at German Conversation all the time there and walking back—'home'.

We have dismissed the Mess Corporal, & I have all the sundry items as well. And winding up last year's accounts for the Auditors! O my!

On such days I always write to you—as you notice. Because on such days I have no time to settle down to my art. For it is an art, & will need the closest industry. Consider that I spend—what?—three hours a week at it, which means one fruitful half-hour, when I ought to be doing S I X hours a day by all precedents.

Leslie has been unfavourably reviewed by the *Times Literary Supplement*. Not attacked of course: one does not attack harmless civilians—They say he rimes with ease but has no originality or power.

I rime with wicked difficulty, but a power of five men, four women, three children, two horses, and one candle is in me.

I see I am hand-writing like a sick man. Indeed I am in pyjamas & my fleece, lying before my fire, airing my toes,—which have not yet forgotten Beaumont Hamel; and have turned septic in a mortifying manner (interpret this as you will) & cause my left ankle and knee to ache. The doctor applies iodine but he has not seen the 'breaking-out' up the leg. I am not lame enough to stop stair-climbing; but I think I shall rest tomorrow.

Much wondering how you are feeling.   Your own Wilfred x

[49] Miss Bennett was giving him German lessons.

581. To Leslie Gunston

8 January 1918   [*Scarborough*]

My dear Leslie,

I was glad to find you take up a strong attitude with regard to your poetry & mine.

You ask me if I saw the Reviews of S.S. I have read every word of them—in his huge book of Press Cuttings. The vast majority are entirely appreciative. As for Graves, have you seen *Chambers' Journal* lately, or the Sat. *Westminster?*[50] And remember the *Edinburgh Review:*[51] fame itself!

But these men are not out for fame.

They simply say what Everyman most needs. And everyman is glad.

Graves's technique is perfect. Did Poetry ever stand still? You can hark back if you like, and be deliberately archaic, but don't make yourself a lagoon, salved from the ebbing tide of the Victorian Age.

The *Times* is just in what it says. But you have only to go on with your quiet unassuming graceful style, and presently everybody else will so scream themselves hoarse that you will be the only happy voice remaining, then you will be indeed original, and a haven for many.

The more I think of your ease & rapidity in writing, the more I hope for an inimitable book next time. But not within five years.

We Georgians are all so old.

Tell me all the Reviews you get.

I am much in doubt whether to put forth any poems next Spring or not. Someday I'll lend you my *Georgian Poetry 1917*.[52] If you would like it soon I'll send it.

I don't forget I am in debt to you for 3/- isn't it?

I've been reading Wells' *What is coming*.[53]

Hazlitt's *Essays*,

and a glorious book of critical essays by A. K. Thompson, called *The Greek Tradition*.[54]

I read no fiction. Wells' *Wife of Sir Isaac Harman*[55] which I've just finished isn't fiction.

Ever your affectionate Wilfred

---

[50] *The Westminster Review.*

[51] *The Edinburgh Gazette* for October 1917 carried enthusiastic reviews by Edmund Gosse of Graves's *Over the Brazier* and SS's *The Old Huntsman*.

[52] SS, Graves, Nichols, and Monro were well represented. See Letter 585, n. 000.

[53] H. G. Wells, *What is Coming? A Forecast of Things after the War* (Cassell, 1916).

[54] J. A. K. Thomson, *The Greek Tradition: Essays in the Reconstruction of Ancient Thought* (Allen & Unwin, 1915).

[55] H. G. Wells, The *Wife of Sir Isaac Harman* (Macmillan, 1914).

582. To Susan Owen

17 January 1918   [*Scarborough*]

My own dear Mother,

Just had your lovely letter, together with an invitation to Robt. Graves's Wedding at St. James' Piccadilly, and afterwards at 11 Apple-Tree Yard,

St. James's Square.

on Jan. 23rd.

Suppose I got leave for this, would you be very sad? Nichols will no doubt be there, and a host of others. Graves is marrying Miss Nicholson, daughter of the Painter.[56]

I send you the Coal Poem.[57]— don't want it back. Yes, I got the Georgian Anthology while in London.

I suppose you saw how Subalterns are now getting 10/6 a day. I should soon be getting 11/6.

Foot's better.

Love to all.   Your W.E.O.

[56] Annie 'Nancy' Mary Pryde Nicholson (1899–1977), painter and fabric designer. She was the only daughter of the artists Sir William Newzam Prior Nicholson (1872–1949) and Mabel Pryde (1871–1918), and sister of Ben Nicholson (1894–1982), artist, and Christopher 'Kit' Nicholson (1904–48), architect and designer. Her brother John Anthony 'Tony' Nicholson (1897–1918) was a lieutenant in the Royal Field Artillery and died of wounds on 5 October 1918, aged 20.

[57] 'Miners' (*CP*, p. 135).

583. To Susan Owen

19 January 1918   *Scarborough*

My dear darling Mother,

That was a naughty tentative letter of mine. I meant to call at Home on the way. If I can get away on Tuesday Morning, I shall arrive Shrewsbury a few minutes to 5 p.m. There surely will be an early morning train to London, arriving noon or one p.m.

The wedding is at 2.30.

With your beautiful letter came a proof from the *Nation* of my 'Miners'. This is the first poem I have sent to the *Nation* myself, and it has evidently been accepted. It was scrawled out on the back of a note to the Editor; and no penny stamp or addressed envelope was enclosed for return! That's the way to do it.

'Miners' will probably appear next Saturday, but don't order a copy.

Will Colin be over on Tuesday Night?

Of course the Leave is not absolutely certain. It is a kind of duty both to myself and Graves to go to the Wedding. You know how hard it will be to start away on Wednesday Morning.

                                            Always your W.E.O.

584. To Susan Owen

Thursday, 24 January 1918   *Scarborough*

Just five minutes and half a sheet of paper left to tell you what a good, full, & profitable 24 hours I had in London.

Lunched with Ross. Wells was there, but at another table, whence he waved to me from afar. Had a few words after lunch, but we were in a hurry to drive off. The wedding was nothing extraordinary. Not a great crowd of people, but a very mixed one. Some were dressed in the dowdiest unfashion. Possibly these were celebrities in their way?

George Belcher[58] was the greatest surprise: togged up in 1870 costume, a very striking figure. Max Beerbohm[59] was also at the reception.

Graves was pretty worked up, but calm. The Bride, 18 years old, was pretty, but nowise handsome.

Heinemann was there. He is jibbing at Sassoon's new book, because of the 'violent' poems.

Dined at the Reform again with Roderick Meiklejohn[60] of the Liquor Control Board. (Lord Rhondda[61] was the nearest person to me at lunch!)

Then repaired to Half Moon St. with Meiklejohn, & passed the evening with Ross and two Critics.

At 2 a.m. found my way to Imperial Hotel, and started up this morning by the 10 a.m. from King's Cross.

Feel much refreshed.   Dearest love. W.E.O.

[58] George Frederick Arthur Belcher (1875–1947), cartoonist and painter, known for his work in *Tatler* and *Punch*.
[59] Sir Henry Maximilian 'Max' Beerbohm (1872–1956), caricaturist and writer, who contributed to numerous publications including *The Strand Magazine*, *The Yellow Book*, *The Sketch*, and *The Saturday Review*. His only novel, *Zuleika Dobson*, was published in 1911. He is regarded as one of the greatest caricaturists of his age.
[60] Sir Roderick Sinclair Meiklejohn (1876–1962), Private Secretary to Herbert Henry Asquith 1905–11, and at this time Deputy Controller of Supply Services in the Treasury. A poem in SS's *The Old Huntsman*, 'Liquor-Control', is dedicated to him.
[61] David Alfred Thomas, 1st Viscount Rhondda (1856–1918), politician and industrialist, was Food Controller at this time.

585. To Leslie Gunston

Saturday Night [*26 January 1918*]   [*Scarborough*]

Dear L.

Great thanks for your letter. I can't identify your 'A. & E.' without applying the method of superposition, coordinating the figures each to each, and so on.

Went up to Town for Robert Graves's Wedding last Tuesday, calling Home on the way. Arrived at Padd. on Wed. Mng. I hired a bath room, but had no time to get in the water as the page announced my taxi before I had finished shaving. So I arrived punctually at the Reform to lunch with Robert Ross.

Wells was there, but at a different table. But he waved to me from afar, and we had a few words on going out.

Lord Rhondda sat within reaching distance of me!

To you, Max Beerbohm and George Belcher will be the most interesting people at the Reception. Belcher appeared as a dandy of the 1870 period!—Very long Frock coat, very tall dull hat, Cravat, Choker Collar, Side whiskers, and a pole of a walking stick.

Max B. dressed fairly ordinarily, but when he looked at me, I felt my nose tip-tilting in an alarming manner; my legs warped; my chin became a mere pimple on my neck.

Heinemann was there; and Edward Marsh,[62] the Georgian Anthologist tho' I did not know him as such till afterwards. I was introduced as 'Mr. Owen, Poet' or even 'Owen, the poet'.

You may feel keen enough to buy this week's *Nation*. I have at last a poem in it, which I sent off on the same evening as writing ! !

Don't yet ask Matthews for *Keats* thanks very much, as Boots Ltd.[63] may lend it me. I subscribe for 3 months.

Always your W.E.O.

[62] Sir Edward Marsh (1872–1963). At this time Private Secretary to Winston Churchill, he also published *Georgian Poetry* with William Heinemann, anthologies of contemporary verse—five of which appeared between 1912 and 1921. Owen also met C. K. Scott Moncrieff (see Letter 619) at the wedding. In a letter of 1 February 1918, Robert Graves wrote, 'I hope you found Marsh and Scott Moncrieff worth talking to'.

[63] Boots the Chemist ran a subscription lending library 1898–1966.

587. To Susan Owen

8 February 1918   *Scarborough*

Dearest Mother,

I forget how much I borrowed for my travelling money last month; but I think it was less than this Cheque, which is fortunately on your Bank. For half an hour's work I think Two Guineas is good pay. I played with the poem afterwards a little, but the work was done in 30 minutes.

Leslie's 'musical ear' is offended by my rimes. Isn't that delicious?

I am sorry: there is nothing to tell you of my military destiny.

My foot showed improvement last week, but is now as bad as ever.

I have 'put up' my blue chevron for Foreign Service. You will no doubt see two or three chevrons on Officers in Shrews: each additional one means a year's service.

The 'Women' have not turned up, so things go on as before except that the dinner is slightly better cooked by two kitchen lads than by our late she-cooks who cost £10. a month: not including Beer.

Many thanks for all your letters. I heard from Harold yesterday and replied.

Still waiting for Colin's 'Story'.

Dearest Love, W.E.O.

589. To Leslie Gunston

Picture postcard addressed Y.M.C.A. Hazely Down Camp, Near Winchester.
The card bears the following verse, as amended by Owen:
A Little Health, A Little Wealth, A Little
House, and Freedom—and at The End,
I'd Like a Friend, And *Every* Cause to Need Him.

[*Postmark 12 February 1918*]   [*Postmark Scarborough*]

Quite as delighted to have your blunt criticism as your first postcard. I suppose I am doing in poetry what the advanced composers are doing in music. I am not satisfied with either. Still I am satisfied with the <u>Two</u> Guineas that half-hour's work brought me. Got the Cheque this m'ng!

Your W.E.O.

590. To Susan Owen

Wednesday [*13 February 1918*]⁶⁴   *Scarborough*

My own dear Mother,

How shall I cheer you up? This afternoon is all blanketed in sea-fog, but it is not at all desolate but quite a cosy kind of fog. All the same Scarborough is a moribund place. I would rather the back of behind Edinburgh than all the Front of Scarboro'.

Priestley⁶⁵ took me to a secret Old Shop where they sell to dealers more than to the public.

There I saw in a very frowsy condition something like the perfect chair; and, what's more, a filthy old Chest of Drawers of lovely proportions and precious oak.

I think I have found what I want at last.

It occurs to me that I should make a really workmanlike <u>Dealer in Antiques</u>. If I could get a shop in London and some experienced Hands I should be not uncontent. Colin might manage the business while I go foraging in Bagdad, Peru, Ceylon, Pompeii, or Market Drayton.

Tonight I am 'dining out' with Bainbrigge.[66] It is amusing to think of myself in the Masters' Rooms at Shrewsbury, as one who deigns not to enter the class-rooms, being above these things—as no doubt I shall be—after the war.

How is Mary keeping?

But I want you to write about yourself. I feel particularly fit today. Can it have been the Antique Shop?

Always your loving W.E.O.

[64] PN, p. 189.

[65] Lieutenant Henry Priestley, 7th Manchesters, was a manufacturer in Bradford before the war and enlisted in the Artists' Rifles in July 1915. President of the Mess Committee, he was known affectionately as 'Uncle Henry' (WOANB, pp. 381–3)

[66] Philip Gillespie Bainbrigge (1891–1918), was a master at Shrewsbury School 1913–17; his death is reported in Letter 666. 'A tall, delicate, weedy man with very thick glasses in his spectacles [....] He had a great sense of humour and enormous academic ability' (Nevil Shute, Slide Rule, 1954). For a discussion of Bainbrigge's erotic, homosexual poetry, his relationship with C.K. Scott Moncrieff, and the potential influences of these on WO's own poems and sexuality, see DH, WOANB, pp. 378–83 and GC, Wilfred Owen, pp. 256–62.

591. To Susan Owen

[13 February 1918][67]   Scarborough

My own Mother,

What happiness was in your card & letter for me. Your joke did me good, because I think it did you good.

For light reading there is nothing like Arnold Bennett. So I send you The Card.[68] It is notable among my books as the only novel I've read in which I did not in some manner identify myself with the hero.

It is because I loathe Machin that I consider A.B. a wonderful writer, for I read the book with avidity. And it was because I loathed Machin this book has done me so much good.

I consider Mrs. Machin as good a portrait as any novel contains.

It's hard to think of any books you would specially like from my hoard. Try the Life of Tennyson in the Bureau-Case: and, in conjunction, read some of The Idylls of the King.

Ross has got the majority of my war poems in his keeping, in order to study and ruminate them.

I am going to reconsider the Chair and Chest tomorrow.

I suppose I may get leave in a fortnight or so; but there is a new rumour of my going to a Command Depot; which is where most Light Duty Officers 'end up', doing physical drill, to fit them for serious warfare.

Our patrols shot a man last night, supposed to be a spy. I know nothing more.

Ever your own W.E.O.

[67] PN, p. 189.
[68] The Card: a Story of Adventures in the Five Towns (E.P. Dutton, 1911).

592. To Susan Owen

18 February 1918   *Scarborough*

My dear, dear Mother,

Yours was the letter among five others. I will send you Mrs. Gray's, for so you will learn much about her, and about myself!

You did not remark on the incidence that while you were writing to ask me whose 'Life' to read, I was writing to you the reply—Tennyson's.

I <u>have</u> a life of R.L.S. somewhere. I think on the Biography Shelf in the Bureau, by Graham Balfour.[69] <u>Not</u> a wonderfully good one.

I could make you like Scarborough. I could make you like anywhere I wished.

Last night I took an artist johnny—called Claus[70] (!) (exhibits & <u>sells</u> at the Carfax,[71] does Italian peasants in Italy, studio in London; reveres the name of Robert Ross, as one who with a word could raise him to eminence—). I took old Claus, (a fat old tub, with round spectacles, and a conical head)—took old Claus to <u>the</u> Scarborough, where there's not a house built since 1780, not a street much wider than Claus, and miles of it, mind you, miles of glorious eighteenth century. It was twilight and the Sunday evening bell.

Not a soul in the alleys.

Not a lamp lit. A dim moon—and the Past.

And we got excited. What excited us, who shall say? We jumped about, we bumped about, we sang praises, we cursed Manchester; we looked in at half open doors and blessed the people inside. We saw Shakespere in a lantern, and the whole of Italy in a Balcony. A tall chimney became a Greek Column; and in the inscriptions on the walls we read romances and philosophies.

It was a strange way of getting drunk. I wonder if the people in the officers' bar suspected that evening, how much more cheaply a man can get fuddled on fresh air and old winding passages?

I am sorry you have disturbing and daylight-lingering dreams. It <u>is</u> possible to avoid them: by proper thinking before sleep. I confess I <u>bring on</u> what few war dreams I now have, entirely by <u>willingly</u> considering war of an evening. I do so because I have my duty to perform towards War.

I will copy out the best bit of <u>Compression</u> I have accomplished—P.T.O.

You know with what feelings I think of you—well or unwell. They are such, when I hear you are at least bettering, as make me a better creature, and my dreams younger. So must you think of me, and Harold and Colin.

If I do not read hymns, and if Harold marks no Bible, or Colin sees no life-guide in his prayer-book, it is no bad sign. I have heard the cadences of harps not audible to Sankey, but which were strung by God; and played by mysteries to Him, and I was permitted to hear them.

There is a point where prayer is indistinguishable from blasphemy. There is also a point where blasphemy is indistinguishable from prayer. As in this first verse:

Last Words[72]

'O Jesus Christ!' one fellow sighed.
And kneeled, and bowed, tho' not in prayer, and died.
    And the Bullets sang—'In vain'
    Machine Guns chuckled 'Vain'
    Big Guns guffawed 'In vain'

'Father and Mother!' one boy said.
Then smiled—at nothing like a small child; being dead.
    And the Shrapnel Cloud
    Slowly gestured 'Vain!'
    The falling Splinters muttered 'Vain'.

'My Love!' another cried, 'My love, my bud!'
Then, gently lowered, his whole face kissed the mud.
    And the Flares gesticulated, 'Vain'
    The Shells hooted, 'In vain'
    And the Gas hissed, 'In vain'.

[69] Sir Graham Balfour (1858–1929), *Life of Robert Louis Stevenson* (Methuen & Co., 1901).

[70] DH suggested this could be Second Lieutenant W. M. Claus, 5th Manchesters, seconded to the 1 (Res.) Garrison, King's Own Yorkshire Light Infantry (see DH, *Wilfred Owen the Last Year*, p. 206.) and not, as *CL* states, Emile Claus (1849–1924), Belgian painter. However, Owen's description of Claus as 'a fat old tub' with a studio in London suggests HO and JB are more likely correct.

[71] In Bury Street, W1. Robert Ross was a Director of Carfax and Co. Ltd, picture dealers, 1900–8.

[72] Early draft of 'The Last Laugh' (*CPF*, p. 168).

593. To Susan Owen

Midnight, 21 February 1918   [*Scarborough*]

My own dear Mother,

My purple slippers & enchanter's fleece are on, and off is the brisk soldierly authority, which is such a hindrance to my writings to you.

All day I've been hoping you've had weather like to ours. The Elements left nothing to be desired except a mild fire at half past four.

Which I had.

In truth, I am very comforted in Scarboro'. 'For everything' that Solomon mentions, 'there is time' except the singing and dancing. I cut the Local Concerts and the Select Bachelor Dances. Yet I do dance, privately in my room, to the music of good news from you. I dance when the melody of a good line comes into my noddle; I dance also when I dash my bad foot against a stone.

I am looking forward to seeing some good Boxing on Sat. night.

Last week I went to an excellent play, a really charming Comedy *Quinney's*, by Vachell.[73] Am now reading a book by Vachell *The Hill*,[74] a tale of Harrow, and the hills on which I never lay, nor shall lie: heights of thought, heights of friendship, heights of riches, heights of jinks.

Lovely and melancholy reading it is for me.

Still, was there not Broxton Hill for my uplifting, whose bluebells it may be, more than Greek iambics, fitted me for my job.

Midnight, 22 February 1918

I got so thoughtful last night that I could not go on writing. I hope I did not Harrow you too much.

That 'Last Words' seems to have rather a harrowing effect on you. I have shown it to no one else as it is not chastened yet. It baffles my critical spirit.

What can I talk about tonight?

Priestley bought some wonderful large Ranunculi this morning; and they are so fine that nothing would do but he must buy a fine bowl to set them in. So we are winning at least the 'Warness' of War.

Things look stupefyingly catastrophic on the Eastern Front. Bainbrigge of Shrewsbury, (over some oysters we consumed in our little oyster-bar this afternoon) opined that the whole of civilization is extremely liable to collapse.

Let us therefore think of more enduring things, my lovely Mother. Such as the February flowers. These are they whose whiteness I have not yet suffered enough to buy. They are what I prayed to when Colin had Scarlet Fever. I could not buy them then for poverty. Now I cannot buy them for shame: For to my extraordinary thinking, it is a wicked traffic, this of grabbing up the Mediterranean Narcissi, and vending them to the rich. Still they are to be seen in the shop-windows of Grange Road West;[75] in Birkenhead; and in Scarborough, and I suppose in Bermondsey, Stockport, Dudley, and perhaps in the uttermost parts of Lybia about Berlin.

For that we must be thankful.

Their odour is disinfectant of souls, as Carbolic is of mortal breath. Narcissi and Carbolic: that is all Life. The Field Daffodils and the Field Dressing Station: these are the best ideas of Heaven and Hell for the senses.

You will notice that Christ is never represented with the Syrian Lilies in His hand. That is to be expected: for as one says 'There were many Christians before Christ; The astonishing thing is: there have been none since.'[76]

One Spring, Carbolic may have saved you and me. Every Spring the Narcissus is enough to save a man's soul, if it be worth saving.

Show now therefore the Narcissus to Colin at this time.

The immensity of our devotion to Childe Colin has yet to be achieved. A fever more scarlet is already inculcating in his veins; and you must take him apart to yourself, wash him with pure words of truth, feed him with the best, and that according to his desires. In the strangeness of his fever he will push you from him; and all your thought will not be able to quench his thirst. Deny him not the thing he craves, as I was denied; for I was denied, and the appeal which, if you watched, you must have seen in my eyes, you ignored. And because I knew you resisted, I stretched no hand to take the Doll that would have made my contentment.

And my nights were terrible to be borne.

For I was a child, and you laughed at my Toys, so that I loved them beyond measure; but never looked at them.

Yet no man is ashamed of his first doll.

With Harold it has been otherwise. He was always insensible to laughter.

Make easy, I say, the pillow of Colin's fever, for it will be soon; and let us draw aside and think together for him; and tremble before this thing of life and death.

I had meant this to be a consoling kind of letter, and if you read it rightly, it will prove so:—In spite of this Latest News: Leave only once in 3 months (8 days)!

Always your own loving Wilfred x

[73] Horace Annesley Vachell (1861–1955). *Quinney's* is the best-known play by this prolific novelist and playwright. It was first written as a novel (published in London by John Murray, 1914). The main character, Joseph Quinney, is an antiques dealer.

[74] *The Hill: a Romance of Friendship* (John Murray, 1905) is set partly during the Second Boer War (1899–1902), and both DH and GC note the influence of the novel on 'Spring Offensive'. GC argues that 'a badly written school story fed one of the greatest war poems, its clichés transformed into poetry' (GC, *Wilfred Owen*, p. 256).

[75] In Shrewsbury.

[76] Oscar Wilde, *De Profundis* (1905), p. 116.

596. To Susan Owen

Postcard

Sat. [*Postmark 11 March 1918*]   *Scarborough*

Just heard I've got to go to Northern <u>Command Depôt Ripon</u>—as a result of my last Medical Board. There I shall do physical drill and so on, till I am quite fit. Not a bad idea even if I be demobilized! Am glad it's not to Manchester I'm going. Shall be glad to explore this part of Yorkshire. I start on Tues. and the above is all my Address. Have tried to get home for this weekend, but Priestley is away, and they won't let me go. You might come & stay at Harrogate!

Am sending a big box of books & winter clothes home—to be left unopened. I did so want to see you getting well; and Colin before he left. Am writing to Colin tonight.

W.E.O.

597. To Susan Owen

Postcard

Tuesday [Postmark 12 March 1918]   *Officers Command Depot*
                                                       32 Lines, Ripon

An awful Camp—huts—dirty blankets—in fact WAR once more. Farewell
Books, Sonnets, Letters, friends, fires, oysters, antique-shops. Training again!
                                                       Your W.E.O.

Scroll arrived just in time to see Priestley open it. Thank you!

598. To Susan Owen

Postcard

Wednesday [13 March 1918]   *Ripon P.O.*

Off duty at 3 p.m.! Glorious weather. So strolled into the Town, & was just
going into Cathedral when I met Isaacson[77] the actor coming out. He is now very
much the Actor, having been discharged from Craiglockhart. Benson is giving
The Merry Wives of Windsor in the Garrison Theatre tonight. I am going round to be
introduced to B. & Lucy Benson. I feel much bucked after a tea with an old
Craiglockhartian!

[77] See Letter 536.

599. To Susan Owen

Friday [15 March 1918]   *Address to Officers Command Depot*
                                                       B. Coy., Ripon

Dearest my Mother,

    As you foretold, this place has made me completely ill. I am now in an Isolation
Hut, sweating under Army Blankets and the disappointment of not seeing the
Bensons. Don't know the name of my Complaint, but a staggering headache came
on yesterday, accompanied by pains in limbs, sore throat, fever etc. etc. It's not
influenza, and I am very much better today, (after a perfectly ghastly night.)
    But don't be bothered about me now. I am getting as suddenly better as I fell
suddenly ill. It was rather curious to have a bad sore throat for an hour or so, and
then—quite all right again.

I think the Disorder is traceable to my extreme disgust of the life here—and the badly served cold food. Will write tomorrow.

Am in for a good night.

Your W.E.O.

600. To Susan Owen

Sat. Morning [16 March 1918]   *[Ripon]*

This is a sorry Birthday Letter, my darling Mother, but I can assure you that this morning I already feel better than you—alas! Ate my breakfast egg, even without salt, and thirsted for the tea though without sugar. I am now able to be <u>amused</u> at the bad style of my attendance.

It is only the style that is bad: I was put into sheets stippled with somebody's blood, and blankets caked with mud, like a cow's flank.

The Doctor has just been in. He says this fever has no connection with previous fevers of mine, but is one which often attacks newcomers to this Camp.

I shall be going back to my hut tomorrow as I am not bad enough for hospital.

There are 14 officers in that hut and 13 too many. Most of them are privates & sergeants in masquerade (as were half the officers at Clarence Gdns.) I'd prefer to be among honest privates than these snobs.

It was something to have seen Isaacson and to be made welcome by the merry company of Shakesperians.

Just after I left Craiglockhart a great wave of Discharges swept in, and floated off Isaacson and crowds of others. I am left here 'bound in shallows & in miseries'.[78]

Please do let me have Mrs. Aslin's[79] address. I know nothing more of her than of her association—I will not risk the word friendship—with the Gunstons.

I will now think about Colin. If I were his age, with his obvious disqualifications for

1. steady business,
2. or a learned profession,
3. or pictorial or literary Art,

and <u>with</u>

1. great emotional faculties
2. the promise of great good looks in a year or two
3. high ideals

I should join the Benson Company. He has been given an excess of emotional faculty, and that excess he must turn to account in the form of bread & butter. But must I suppose he has only 3 months' liberty?

Then send him to school.

Or if pride forbids, call it an agricultural college.

Say, to Reading or the Shropshire College. You couldn't make a better investment.

Yes, this is my advice.

I will make another suggestion if this won't do.

Tell me how you all exactly 'are'.

Your lovingest Wilfred x

---

[78] *Julius Caesar,* IV, iii, l. 210.
[79] The name was omitted in *CL* and *SL*. Owen visited her.

605. To Mary Owen

Wed. [*27March 1918*][80]   *7 Borage Lane, Ripon*[81]

My dearest Mary,

So glad to have your cheery letter. You know, we scramble for letters, twice a day, almost as eagerly as when on Active Service Abroad. Many of the officers here have been wounded over and over again. People with crippled arms do <u>special</u> physical exercises. It is rather pitiful. The Senior M.O. is a Harley St. Heart Specialist. He put me in the 6th and Lowest Class of Fitness! But I shall be moved up any day. No leave longer than 48 hours is possible yet. Is it worth while? Every battalion, I understand, has sent two companies of A 4 (boys) on Draft Leave: in consequence of our <u>Straits</u>. (Don't see the joke, I didn't mean it.) It is specially cruel for me to hear of all <u>we</u> gained by St. Quentin having been lost. They are dying again at Beaumont Hamel, which already in 1916 was cobbled with skulls.[82]

Meanwhile I think less of leaving the Army: and more of getting fit.

My realest thanks to dear Mother for her packing of the Chinese Scrolls. Priestley (before he could have received the parcel) sent me some lovely Mediterranean Flowers. That's how we keep our war-weary spirits up!

I don't like the charwoman idea. I think I shall postpone my Leave till I hear you've a regular servant, what?

Your loving old Brother

---

[80] *PN*, p. 189.
[81] The cottage is now no. 24. Borrage is the correct spelling.
[82] The last German offensive of the war, the Second Battle of the Somme, was launched in March 1918 on a 50-mile front against the British 3rd and 4th Armies. British losses were heavy, and 100,000 men were taken prisoner. The tide turned on 1 May. See 'Insensibility' (*CPF*, p. 145), l. 5 of which runs, 'Sore on the alleys cobbled with their brothers'.

606. To Colin Owen

[*Circa 30 March 1918*]   *Ripon*

My dear Colin,

I send you a rather well-composed photograph of the village-city.

You'll see that it's quite pleasant, though not beautiful.

Note the grooved tiles of the roofs.

The five minutes walk from Camp to my Cottage is by a happy little stream—tributary of the Ure. There is boating of a kind on the Ure; but much better at Knaresborough on the Ouse itself, I think. How I look forward to your Invitation to a Pengwern[83] boat. Didn't know you were a member of the Club.

Evidently you need the bicycle more than I. Ripon is only a mile from my hut, and through Borage Lane (my lane) it is an interesting walk;—especially this morning when the buds all made a special spurt between dawn and noon, and all the Lesser Celandines opened out together.

I don't think there is the least probability of demobilization now. On the contrary, I am trying to get fit.

Our Physical Exercises are varied by tricks like doing the opposite of the order, or on the command Do This! you do what the instructor does, but on the command Do That! you don't move. It's really an old parlour game, but frightfully difficult done quickly. Last time we played this mental game I was the last man out, or rather I was never caught out. So I consider myself completely restituted now from Shell Shock.

Do tell me about your Farm, & farmers, and also what your arrangements are for joining the Royal Air Force.

Your dearly loving Wilfred

What have you read during March?

[83] The Shrewsbury rowing club.

607. To Susan Owen

Easter Sunday [*31 March 1918*]   *The Ante-Room, O.C.D., Ripon*

My Mother Dear,

I am writing crouched up in one of the good easy chairs with which we have stocked our Common Room Hut. We have also a good piano, which helps to drown the chinkling of silver on the Bridge Tables. I scarcely have spoken to any of this crowd of 'gentlemen' except to decline to make a Four at bridge.

I find myself growing more conventional in the matter of 'Proper Introductions' as I grow older. There are no less than five people made aware of my presence in Ripon, by friends who tell me I must go and see them

1) Mrs. Aslin.—done.[84]
2) A Major, friend of Bainbrigge of Shrewsbury—not done.
3) A friend and relation of Priestley's—not done.
4) A great friend of the Grays of Edinburgh—not done yet.
5) Two maiden ladies, benefactresses when he was in Ripon of the Scottie in Clarence Gardens (who faints and has undiscoverable parents). These old dears as I had been advised provide a mighty good tea to anything in khaki that strays into their house. They have also some inklings of breeding, and traces of Accent, having been in the service of the Marchioness of Ripon for 37 years. I shall go there again the next time there's a bad lunch in Camp.

Outside my cottage-window children play soldiers so piercingly that I've moved up into the attic, with only a skylight. It is a jolly Retreat. There I have tea and contemplate the inwardness of war, and behave in an owlish manner generally.

One poem have I written there; and thought another. I have also realized many defectuosities in older compositions.

The enormity of the present Battle numbs me. Because I perfectly foresaw these days, it was that I said it would have been better to make peace in 1916. Or even last Autumn. It certainly is 'impossible' now.

What did I say about America?

Why did I denounce them?

Fancy the old 13th C.C.S. being in German hands! Even Nesle,[85] a town hospital where I paused 3 days, is occupied. On Good Friday I believe the most frightful fighting was round about the Canal where I used to board the barges.

The Mystery Gun of St. Gobain Wood is about as romantic an episode as the whole war has provided. Paris, after all, has so many ugly buildings and unnecessary civilians…160 casualties in a second or two, and that in the heart of the enemy country, is pretty work.[86]

I wonder how many a _frau, fraulein, knabe and madchen_ Colin will kill in his time?

Johnny de la Touche leaves school this term, I hear, and goes to prepare for the Indian Army.

He must be a creature of killable age by now.

God so hated the world that He gave several millions of English-begotten sons, that whosoever believeth in them should not perish, but have a comfortable life.

I could face the world-facts better if I could be sure of at least your health and peacefulness at home. Don't let your fire burn low; don't leave off winter-clothing; don't eat pickles; and don't read newspapers. Thus you'll keep well.

I meant, when I said you must get a servant before I get leave, that it will be a severe discomfort to me,—not otherwise than as thus:—

That I will not eat from plates which you must needs wash. The moral discomfort, I say, will drive me to the Crown, aye the Britannia, aye the Oyster Bar, and finally the Cop Fried Fish Shop.

Now you know.

Your lovingest old Wilfred

[84] The name was omitted in *CL* and *SL*.
[85] See Letter 494.
[86] Paris was shelled by German long-range guns sited in St Gobain woods, some 75 miles away from the city, between March and August 1918. The deadliest incident occurred on Good Friday, 29 March, when one shell hit the church of St-Gervais-et-St-Protais during Mass, collapsing the roof and killing ninety-one people.

608. To Leslie Gunston

[*Circa 1 April 1918*]   *Ripon*

Opening sheets missing

are enjoying your pleasaunce of Alpenrose.

All the joy of this good weather is for me haunted by the vision of the lands about St. Quentin crawling with wounded. If the Line was as thinly held as when we held it, I don't wonder at the Breakage. Our Staff is execrable.

Was awakened yesterday by this sentence: long range guns firing on Paris.

Isn't it stupendous?

I must buck up and get fit!

'Yours to a cinder'* W.E.O.

*Borrowed this expression from a letter from *mon petit ami* in Scarboro!

609. To Susan Owen

[*April 1918*]   *The Ante-Room* [*Ripon*]

Mine own Mother,

Your portrait is certainly slightly camouflaged. I should tell the merchant to do less retouching, but you will never persuade him to let go a photograph purely <u>au naturel</u>, you know. I think the result will be <u>most</u> satisfactory, if you say you will not accept the present rendering. <u>Only</u>, don't they retouch the negative itself? I am loath to let this charming picture away—all the same. Hope he won't be long finishing off

This afternoon I was retouching a 'photographic representation' of an officer dying of wounds—[87]

Thus:

> Sit on the bed; I'm just a mass of shell:
> Don't touch me—can't shake hands now—never shall.

My arms have mutinied against me—brutes:
My fingers fidget like ten idle brats.
I tried to pop out soldierly—no use!
I'm dying of war like any old disease.
This bandage feels like pennies on my eyes.
My death won't cut much figure in your book.
A short life and a merry one, my buck!
We used to say we'd hate to live dead-old, —
But, now, not to live old seems—* (were you told
How long I've got?) etc.

I hear that of the 100 officers now in Clarence Gns. 53 are going out immediately, and practically the whole of the <u>men</u> (so called).

How curious that Warne[88] is there. Had I been there I might have got him a good job with me in the hotel, unless he be too very countrified?

Is he very 'superior'?

Immensely glad Colin is so content.

Numbers of officers have bunked away from here as far as London even— <u>without leave</u>. They have been discovered, poor chaps. There is to be a solemn assembly tomorrow.

A fair goodnight to all.

W.E.O. x

Piano, Flute & Violin are making most lovely music. I can't scarcely read, it's so fine. I am not ill pleased with Ripon generally.

*I can't find a word strong enough here.

[87] 'A Terre' (*CPF*, 178).
[88] Son of a Shrewsbury estate agent. His sister Mary was a friend of Mary Owen.

611. To Leslie Gunston

21 April 1918   *Ripon*

My dear Leslie,

I address to Alpenrose, though I believe you to be at Worple Road. Your job[89] seems to me the limit of good fortune. And what are the increments withal, excuse me?

Will this manner of war work in itself exempt you from encountering common foe, dam Hun, excuse me?*

See also p.54 *Sphere* for a good peep at Swinburne.[90] Dam disgusting, excuse me. How do you like the Prize Plaque Memorial?[91] Had I adjudicated I should have chosen this; yet, for my own name, I should prefer Sapper MacDougall's beautiful grief, among the realistic forests of wooden crosses. To me, the British

Lion in the Prize looks a thoroughly nasty animal; and the breasts of Britannia are somehow not the breasts of a chaste woman, excuse me.

Have you seen Arnold Bennett's *Pretty Lady*. Fortunately I just secured my copy before circulation was prohibited.[92] The book is one which the century needs, as much as the Victorians needed *Oliver Twist*. As an amusing narrative it is unsurpassed, in spite of its being a collection of pieced-together idylls. If you can't get it I will send you my copy. Or shall I bring it. I am due for a long week-end leave ! ! My 48 hours, (which I considerably overstayed) at home were an emergency affair. Since then Leave has been granted, as from the W.O., for 15% of the Camp weekly. I should like to spend some of it in Town: not of course Wimbledon. I have now risen to the 4th (of 6 Divisions) of Fitness. There is no doubt—from the elaborate soundings to which I'm subjected—that my heart is shock-affected.

Have you read Gilbert Frankau?[93] I have not. (See *Sphere*.)

In my Chaumbers under the roof of a cottage (7 Borage Lane, Ripon) I have written, I think, two poems: one an Ode which, considering my tuneless tendencies, may be called dam good, excuse me.[94]

It is a very parfit Bowre this Cottage of mine. I wish you could look in for a cup of tea and half a cigarette sometimes. No one here knows of my retreat. If I lived in London I should take two empty chambers somewhere in the Cardiac Region and furnish them with Camp kit.

Sorry you could not find the Word I wanted.

<u>Did you or did you not receive the letter[95] I once wrote from this Hut?</u>

It contained some wild statements, and I should like to be reassured that it's not lost.

Looking forward to a highly interesting account of your occupations.

Your affectionate W.E.O.

Harold has had some terrific adventures: but chiefly on land: & not connected with the war.

* See p. 46. *Sphere*, Ap. 20.[96]

---

[89] LG was engaged on architectural work at the Albert Dock, London.

[90] An account by G. B. Burgin, the novelist, of a depressing lunch with Swinburne at The Pines, Putney, at which the poet spoke once only to complain that the beer was flat.

[91] *The Sphere* carried a photograph of the prize-winning design for a Memorial Plaque for the Fallen by Ernest Carter Preston (1885–1965). Cast in bronze to be given to next-of-kin, the plaque became known as a 'Death Plaque' or 'Widow's Penny'.

[92] Published 1918. The book was not withdrawn and not prosecuted, possibly because of Bennett's connections, but there were objections from Roman Catholic clergy (the central figure is a prostitute who is a Catholic), which saw it banned from public libraries, while W. H. Smith's decided not to stock the work in their bookshops, as did Boots. (See George Simmers, 'The Pretty Lady' (2009), https://greatwarfiction.wordpress.com/2009/11/03/the-pretty-lady/).

[93] Gilbert Frankau (1884–1952), a writer whose war poems, in *The Judgement of Valhalla* (Chatto & Windus, 1918), received a favourable review in the same issue of *The Sphere*.

⁹⁴ The Ode was possibly 'Insensibility', but see *CPF*, p. 184, for an alternative; the other poem was the final version of 'A Terre' or 'The Send-Off', at this time called 'The Draft' (*CPF*, p. 172). See Letter 616.
⁹⁵ Possibly Letter 608, of which the opening sheets have been lost.
⁹⁶ 'Two Letters' by E. V. Lucas. A Japanese man enlisted in a British Columbia battalion in order to, in his words, 'encounter the common foe, dam Hun, excuse me'.

612. To Susan Owen

*Sunday Aft. [21 April 1918]*⁹⁷   O.C.D. [*Ripon*]

My dearest Mother,

Have had another lapse from letter writing, lasting a week or more.

The only news is that I am re-graded into Division 4. So it's a long way yet to the top: and a longer time before I shall go over it; again.

This date is somewhere near the Anniversary of my Shock.

I hear from Paris that Amiens is '*complètement évacué*'; and that the school-children of Paris are all being removed into the provinces.

Dr & Mme. Horteloup are both well. My old pupil and disciple Pierre of Bordeaux was not taken for Military Service when his *Classe* was called up; so he is still with the American Y.M.C.A.

This afternoon I am going over to the Officers' Y.M. to meet someone Mrs. A. wants me to meet.

We have a new padre, and his sermon this morning was as bad as they make 'em.

You will love to read (1) Thomas Hardy's *Under the Greenwood Tree* in my Novel Shelf. A most reposing book. Arnold Bennett's new book⁹⁸ has caused some stir, and has been withdrawn from circulation, but not before I secured my copy. It deals with nothing but truth, however; and is as much needed today as *Oliver Twist* was to the Victorians.

Possibly it was withdrawn owing to a slighting reference to the King.

I shall be very interested to know how you take to *The Greenwood Tree*.

Of Poetry there is no lack on the Poetry Shelf of the Bookcase.

I will write in a day or two: though to quote myself cynically 'Nothing happens.'⁹⁹ A certain gloom was, however, noticeable as I travelled from town to town. There was a hint of war.

Dearest Love to all. W.E.O.

⁹⁷ PN, p. 189.
⁹⁸ *The Pretty Lady*.
⁹⁹ The refrain in 'Exposure' (*CPF*, p. 185).

613. To Susan Owen

Saturday [28 April 1918]   *Crown Hotel, Boroughbridge*

Dearest Mother,

I walked over here to see the land, and how it lies around Ripon. Have been further than Boroughbridge to Aldborough where there are Roman Remains, and the finest tessellated pavement in Britain. It is in a cottage![100]

I am much too footsore to walk back, so I am now waiting for a train to take me to Harrogate.

The weather is superb, and I have spent an afternoon of great 'elation' in these fine old villages.

Many, many thanks for your last letter.

I thought of poor Stanley Webb when I was among the 'Remains'.[101]

If in 1913 I used to wish to live in the 4th Century, how much more now!

Your own, W.E.O.

[100] Near Boroughbridge. Three pavements, all now removed to the Aldborough Roman Site museum, represent the she-wolf suckling Romulus and Remus, a lion awaiting its prey, and the Muses.

[101] Stanley Webb was killed in France on 21 March 1918, aged 23. He is buried at Fouquescourt British Cemetery, Somme. The inscription on his headstone reads PRO CETERIS MORI CORONA ET JANUA VITAE.

615. To Susan Owen

Thursday [?2 May 1918]   *7 Borage Lane, Ripon*

My dearest Mother,

So Harold was not in this Zeebrugge Show.[102] What does he say about it? Its success will not be measured before a month or so. The secret was well kept, especially by Harold.

We had a Surgeon-General inspecting today, the same was responsible for the ghastly medical deficiencies & mismanagement on the Peninsula. In spite of the revelations of the Mesop: Commission, here he is still at large,—spoiling a fine afternoon for us.[103]

This morning we had a lecture from a captain from the War Office, designed to stimulate our fighting instincts.

Two 5th Manchester Officers are here; one 'went out' with me on my ship.

I am feeling very well.

I shall have to smoke less (as soon as my pre-Budget stock of cigarettes is exhausted.)

Leave is now possible from Friday to Tuesday, since our Commandant has been to the War Office about it. I could obtain it next week end, or the following. I should like to go to London with some MSS. What do you say?

If you are not very well I shall come home, go round to the Salop Orphanage, and try the power of my glamour on some of its inmates. Seriously <u>have you tried the Orphanage?</u>

Tell me how you really are.   Your lovingest Wilfred

[102] On 23 April a British naval force under Sir Roger Keyes (Vice-Admiral, Dover Patrol) destroyed the mole and temporarily blocked Zeebrugge harbour (one of the main U-boat bases) by sinking three concreted old cruisers at its mouth. HO was on the shortlist for this operation, but by the luck of the draw did not take part.

[103] Major General W. G. Birrell (1859–1918), Director of Medical Services in the Gallipoli campaign. He came under criticism in the *Final Report of the Dardanelles Commission: Part II, Conduct of Operations* (Cmd. 371, 1919).

616. To Susan Owen

Sat., 4 May [1918]   *Hut 23 [Ripon]*

Dearest my Mother,

Just a note for your Sunday. I discovered that one of my teeth wanted mending, so on Friday I stayed in my flea-bag till the Dr. came round to the Hut (to see 3 others who've now gone to hospital with influenza.)

I went to the Dentist in the afternoon.

The Army will do nothing.

It is interesting to note that by thinking of my tooth, I brought on slight toothache.

Have been to two of Hall Cain's[104] plays this week. How badly written they were! I can't stand Hall Cain. But then was he not my imagined rival in love, when he used to give presents of jewels, when I had not even nuts and apples to give.

I can recommend to you *Tides* by John Drinkwater: (on poetry shelf).

I have long 'waited' for a final stanza to 'the Draft'[105] (which begins.

I

'Down the deep, darkening lanes they sang their way
To the waiting train,
And filled its doors with faces grimly gay,
And heads & shoulders white with wreath & spray,
As men's are, slain.')

*   *   *   *

IV

Will they return, to beatings of great bells,
In wild train-loads?
—A few, a few, too few for drums and yells,
May walk back, silent, to their village wells,
Up half-known roads.

Today is pouring wet.

I hope to hear from Colin soon.

I can't get any Gillette Blades in Ripon. Will you please buy 1 dozen ready to send me at any moment? I forgot the 10/- note last letter! I know why I had no letter today! You are carrying out my Prescription and forbid yourself pen & paper as well as books!

Is there any improvement?

Your own W.E.O.[106]

[104] Sir Thomas Henry Hall Caine (1853–1931), novelist. His novels, including *The Bondman* (1899), *The Manxman* (1894), and *The Eternal City* (1901), were dramatized for the stage. He was heavily involved in the propaganda campaign during the First World War, writing numerous articles for *The Daily Telegraph* which were collected in *The Drama of 365 Days: Scenes in the Great War* (1915) and editing *King Albert's Book* (1914) to raise money for Belgium relief. The reference to 'my imagined rival in love, when he used to give presents of jewels, when I had not even nuts and apples to give' could have come from any number of Caine's novels.

[105] Subsequently 'The Send-Off'.

[106] On the following day he jotted down the following:

Projects: (5 May, 1918. Ripon)

1. To write blank-verse plays on old Welsh themes. Models: Tennyson, Yeats, 1920.

2. Collected Poems (1919)

3. Perseus

4. Idylls in Prose.

There is a British Museum fragment of a poem on Perseus. See also Letter 340.

618. To Susan Owen

Monday [13 May 1918]   [*Ripon*]

My dearest Mother,

Made a careful study of your letter, but for the life of me can't make any real conclusions how you are. Still, it is something to know names, and to have the complaints located.

I look forward to your holiday in Torquay as much as you do. You <u>must try for that Hotel</u>. Hotel would suit you better than boarding house: tho' I have no liking for either myself. I am lucky to get a room in London near Mr. Ross's flat. Leslie sends a card today saying he'll be at Alpenrose for Whitsun. Rather unlucky, but he may change his mind (!) There is also a danger that H. G. Wells etc. may be out of town. I particularly want to see him. But with the Landlady expecting me, as I divine from Mr. Ross's letter (I will enclose it) I won't try the impossible effort of changing the dates of my hard-earned Leave—precarious as the promise of it is.

Leslie informs me I've won a prize in the *Bookman*. (My first try.) I omitted to get a copy, so don't know what it is.[107]

If there's nothing much doing in London, on Sunday, I may drop in to you on Monday just for a little pow-wow and x.

W.E.O.

[107] WO won a consolation prize (a book) for 'Song of Songs', which was one of three winners in a Lyric competition in the May 1918 issue. See Letter 624.

619. To Susan Owen

Postcard

Frid. [*Postmark 17 May 1918*]   *Piccadilly*

Having a glorious time. Spent all aft. at War Office, Scott-Moncrieff[108] is trying to find me a job in England—lecturer to a Cadet Batt. Arrived last night. Report back on Sunday.   W.

[108] Charles Kenneth Scott Moncrieff (1889–1930), later to become the translator of Proust. A captain in the King's Own Scottish Borderers, with an MC, he had been invalided home and now had a staff job. See Jean Findlay, *Chasing Lost Time: the Life of CK Scott Moncrieff* (Farrar, Straus and Giroux, 2015). Findlay also explicitly addresses the alleged physical relationship between WO and Scott Moncrieff.

620. To Susan Owen

Monday [*20 May 1918*]   *Ripon*

My Mother,

You'll excuse a short letter yet awhile: it is hot; and I'm sleepy this afternoon. In 2 nights & days I have slept only 3 hours. I always have a week of freedom from the need of sleep somewhere about May; fortunately it has occurred during last week.

My 'reception' in London has been magnificent. The upshot is that I am to have my work typed at once, and send it to Heinemann, who is certain to send it to Ross to read for him!! This is very subtle. Ross first meant to take it himself but we thought this independent idea a great joke.

Judging from my own diffidence, <u>and</u> the state of the paper supply a book is not likely to appear before next Spring. I am rather proud—to have got so far on <u>one</u> published poem. Almost an unparalleled case, what! How far I have got, learn from this extract in the *New Witness* (Chesterton's weekly).[109] It is a criticism of an American Anthology of English Verse:[110] 'The book is curiously dull & undistinguished. Our younger fame seems not to have reached him: there is nothing by Robert Nichols, Robert Graves, Siegfried Sassoon, W. J. Turner, Wilfred Owen, Osbert Sitwell, or any of their contemporaries junior to Rupert Brooke...' Osbert Sitwell was 'phoned round to Half-Moon St. 'to meet me !'[111] I had a <u>whole flat</u> above Ross's for 7/6 with breakfast! And I had more invitations to lunch & dinner than I could manage!

More tomorrow. Shrewsbury as you saw was impossible.

[109] Cecil Chesterton (1879–1918) was editor of *The New Witness* until his death, when his brother G. K. Chesterton (1874–1936) took it over and renamed it *G.K.'s Weekly*.

[110] The book reviewed in *The New Witness* was W. Reginald Wheeler (ed.), *A Book of Verse of the Great War* (Yale University Press [1917]). The reviewer was Scott Moncrieff. *New Witness*, May 10, 1918, pp. 35–6.

[111] Sir Osbert Sitwell described the meeting in *Noble Essences or Courteous Revelations* (Macmillan & Co., Ltd., 1950) and the pages were included as Appendix D in *CL* (p. 597). Sitwell wrote of Owen's 'sturdy, medium build', his 'broad' face, 'width of eye and forehead', and eyes that were 'deep in colour and dark in their meaning'. He also tried to describe Owen's voice: 'what does his voice sound like across the years? A soft-modulation, even-toned, but with a warmth in it (I almost hear it now), a well-proportioned voice that signified a sense of justice and of compassion' (pp. 103–4).

621. To Susan Owen

Postcard

Tues. [*Postmark 21 May 1918*]   [*Postmark Ripon*]

I am much enjoying the hot weather: which, as weather, is pleasanter here than in London. All I can tell you about my worldly schemes (or rather the schemes of my friends) is: I have every chance of becoming Instructing Staff Officer to a Cadet Battalion.[112] I would <u>rather</u> work in the W.O. itself and that seems not impossible either. Really I would <u>like most</u> to go to Egypt or Italy, but that is not entertained by Scott-Moncrieff. Scott-Moncrieff, is a lamed captain, related to General[113] of that name, known as the 'Father of the War Office', who has just died.

I am now in Div. 2 awaiting <u>Board</u>, before W.O. friends can <u>do anything</u>.

[112] 'Graves's brother [turned up] yesterday, who wants to go and be a cadet at Oxford. We might send you to teach him.' Letter from Scott Moncrieff, headed War Office, 26 May 1918.

[113] Major General Sir George Kenneth Scott Moncrieff (1855–1924), Director of Fortifications and Works, War Office, 1911–18. Owen was anticipating his death.

622. To Susan Owen

Saturday [25 May 1918]   *Borage Lane* [*Ripon*]

Dearest Mother,

I've been 'busy' this evening with my terrific poem (at present) called 'The Deranged.'[114] This poem the Editor of the *Burlington Magazine*—(a 2/6 Arts Journal which takes no poetry)—old More Adey,[115] I say, solemnly prohibited me from sending to the *English Review,* on the grounds that 'the *English Review* should not be encouraged.' !!!!

Five years ago this would, as you suggest, have turned my head—but nowadays my head turns only in shame away from these first flickers of the limelight. For I am old already for a poet, and so little is yet achieved.

And I want no limelight, and celebrity is the last infirmity I desire.

Fame is the recognition of one's peers.

I have already more than their recognition: I have the silent and immortal friendship of Graves and Sassoon and those. Behold are they not already as many Keatses?

As I looked out into the untravelled world over the hedges of Dunsden Garden, I saw them in the dawn and made ready to go out and meet them.

And they were glad and rejoiced, though I am the gravest and least witty of that grave, witty company.

Today I climbed back over the hedges into Dunsden again and wandered round the parish for hours. (For this ordinary [*remainder missing*][116]

The King is said to be coming here next week—coming to see how his thin bullocks are fattening.

The W.A.A.C's[117] now wait on us. It is rather pleasant; a sort of communal home life without parents or children.

My train had just got out of London when the raid began. I suppose I ought to be glad, but a raid is much more thrilling than the daily thunderstorms up here. [*remainder missing*]

----

[114] This became 'Mental Cases' (*CPF*, p. 169).

[115] William More Adey (1858–1942), was a friend of Oscar Wilde and Robert Ross and joint editor of *The Burlington Magazine,* 1911–19. A description of him as an old man is given in SS's *Siegfried's Journey,* pp. 35–6.

[116] DH showed that *CL,* Letter 529, is the conclusion of Letter 622: 'Paper and handwriting match those of L. 622 and I take these fragments to be part of the "missing" page of that letter' (*The Library,* p. 283). The parts are joined here.

[117] Members of Women's Army Auxiliary Corps. The W.A.A.C. was founded in January 1917. Dr Mona Chalmers Watson was its first Chief Controller. Initially confined to auxiliary roles in Britain, they were allowed to serve in France under the command of Helen Gwynne-Vaughan. When Queen Mary became the Corps' patron in 1918, it was renamed Queen Mary's Army Auxiliary Corps (QMAAC).

624. To Susan Owen

[29 May 1918]   *Ripon P.O.*

Came into Town to find something for Mary & Father,[118] but the effort & responsibility are too great.

Will you yourself or Colin do the shopping?

Thanks for news this morning.

The heat is most enjoyable—am going bathing in river this afternoon. The *Bookman* affair about which you are so kindly importunate was a mere idle joke, an old lyric I condescended to send from Scarboro'.

It gained me only a book. The Bookman people are hopeless bad literary people.

You shall see 'Deranged'[119] some fine day when you feel strenuous enough.

Dearest love to Mary, and congratulations to dear Father.

What about a pipe for him?

So Colin is aware that such things as letters are written? Even perhaps he reads them sometimes? [*remainder missing*]

[118] Mary's birthday was the following day. Tom Owen's was 31 May.
[119] An early draft of 'Mental Cases'.

625. To Mary Owen

Wednesday Night. 11 p.m. to Midnight [29 May 1918]   *[Ripon]*

My dear Little Sister,

I am rather weary now, having Swum this afternoon, and—in consequence of the exercise—, having written a promising poem this evening. I can now write so much better than a year ago that for every poem I add to my list I subtract one from the beginning of it. You see I take myself solemnly now, and that is why, let me tell you, once for all, I refrain from indecent haste in publishing. So much for myself.

A pity and shame to myself that I was not able to choose you a present. To speak truth, it baffles me to know what you really are interested in; beyond Mother.

This is beautiful in itself, but I wish I knew there was some Sphere of human activity you played or worked at. Music—no bon! Painting—nah pooh! Literature—taboo! Horticulture, likewise, Medical work, ditto. Why not, then, specialise in Embroidery or some such craft,—design something remarkable, and produce something astonishing.

My dear I am as serious as I am rude. Chiefly for your own benefit I am saying this,—To give you some tie to Mother Earth. I feel that a light wind of grief, to say nothing of a storm, might blow you off your innocent feet.

Nor entirely for your benefit do I suggest these Interests. So many Activities that Matter are in the hands of non-good people.

Possibly I am quite wrong in asking you to hook on to something Material. You will wistfully wonder if I am a Pagan. It would be good if you would arise, and in a loud voice, <u>tell me so</u>. I am not, but such a discussion would get us to the bedrock of things. The bedrock of things should be—well, Who should it be?

My religion consists in a sort of beautiful and Christ-like Intervention between the disputing parties Paul of Tarsus and the ruined but skilful silversmiths of Ephesus. Very gently I should make some clever remark which should send the silversmiths contentedly back to their beautiful work, and give Paul a contract for as many tents as the army required for subjugating the Gauls, and exiling the soldiery.

My religion says it is better to design a church than sit and look at its design once a week.

Forgive the exuberance of this letter. It comes of my recent baptism in the pleasant waters of this River. It was an amusing afternoon. After toiling many miles to the bathing place I found it reserved for the Civilian Population on Wednesdays! However the civilian population were not dismayed to share the water with Officers. Anyone seeing these civilians (or rather in their father's old clothes, which they wore) would have kept well upstream of them. An Artist Cadet there, losing his head with joy, dived into 2 feet of water, and nearly lost it again. He cut it open, but as there was no brandy, he decided not to faint, and I got him safe into a cab.

This letter, writ with much rubbing of mine eyes, is my Birthday present, and <u>not</u> John Bradbury's little note.[120] God bless you as you are a blessing to us, and reward you from the treasury where your great heart is.

Wilfred

[120] John Swanwick Bradbury, 1st Baron (1872–1950), Joint Permanent Secretary to the Treasury 1913–19, whose name became a popular synonym for a treasury note.

627. To Susan Owen

Thursday [6 June 1918]   *5th Manchester Regt., Cavalry Barracks,*
Scarborough

Had a rather pleasant <u>arrival</u>. Priestley is still P.M.C.[121] & has two apartments in the Barracks, where he gave me a private tea—fine China tea,—in priceless porcelain.

Most of the officers here in March are 'gone' and a new crowd are here—junior to me fortunately.

The last of my old Mess Staff went yesterday. The W.A.A.C.'s do everything now.

I live in a tent with a cinder floor, a yard or two from the Main Entrance to Camp; so it is inundated with vile dust. Thus it is not necessary to try to grit my teeth: it is done without effort.

We get up at six, and work furiously till 6 p.m., after which we are too tired to move.

Priestley is powerless to give me a room in Barracks as all A officers must sleep under canvas.

I have informed the War Office of my Category & address. I cannot keep alive here long. Here one does not live at all. One eats, (badly) sleeps, (well) and works like a demented piece of clockwork.

We call the recruits Rookies because they are so thin.

The padre is going to find Warne as I don't know his Company.

My Company is B.

Drummer George of Dunsden <u>wept</u> when I said goodbye. (I had seen him 3 times!) This you must not tell <u>anybody</u>. Such things are not for this generation of vipers.

All thanks to dear Mary for her beautiful letters.

W.E.O. x

---

121 President of the Mess Committee.

629. To Susan Owen

Postcard

10 June 1918   *Scarborough*

Am wondering a little why no letter at all since I arrived here. Am earning my pay again with a vengeance. But a short bout of this work is not unpleasant. Have got a habitable tent now. Am going on Musketry for a few days, thanks to Whittaker, who is still here. What company is Warne? Letter from W.O. says I'll probably be sent to Artists. Tell Colin the R.A.F. are <u>asking</u> Infantry Officers to transfer to flying. Numbers of ones have gone for approval today.

Thanks: Letter received.

630. To Susan Owen

Saturday Morning [*15 June 1918*]   *Priestley's Rooms in Barracks*
[Scarborough]

Dearest Mother,

Have just been inoculated, so will write while able, and before I begin to roll about. Was working yesterday till 8 p.m. with 1 hr. for lunch, & ¼ hr. for tea.

Spent 2 solid hours seeing that the Rookies bathed themselves properly & washed their toes—especially the conscripts who came the same day from the Mills, awful specimens, almost green-pale, another Race altogether from the mahogany swashbucklers who have finished their training.

I found Warne, and interviewed him. He looks very well-treated, a little too strapping ponderous and bumpkinish a fellow for my much liking.

My week-end is wrecked. But it should not be many days before I am called to the W.O. and so to Berkhampstead for a month's preparatory course with the Inns of Court O.T.C.

It must not be thought I am unhappy here, meanwhile. I have now a waterproof tent with long grass & buttercups all round to act as dustscreens. Mine is the only single tent, thanks to Priestley, who also puts his apartments at my disposal when I have time to come here, which is this morning for the first time. I had magnificently resolved not to unpack my books or papers while in camp; when lo! an urgent request from the Sitwells in London for more of my poems for their 1918 Anthology[122] which is coming out immediately. This is on the strength of 'The Deranged', which S. Moncrieff showed them the other day. I know not what to do. For one thing I want to see the Sitwells' etc. works before I decide to co-appear in a book!

I suppose I must congratulate Colin.[123] Hope very much to see him at Hampstead.

I may have big expenses at the end of the month, but you must decide what Colin should have, & I'll do my fondest.

---

[122] *Wheels*, the annual miscellany of contemporary poetry founded and edited by Edith Sitwell with the assistance of her brother Osbert. In *Wheels*, 1919 (dedicated to Owen's memory), were included 'Strange Meeting', 'The Show', 'A Terre', 'The Sentry', 'Disabled', 'The Dead-Beat', and 'The Chances'.

[123] He had become a cadet in the RAF, and was undergoing initial training at Swiss Cottage, London. His birthday (24 July) was approaching.

631. To Susan Owen

Friday Evg. [*21 June 1918*]   [*Scarborough*]

Weary though I be, I must yet let you know before I sleep that I am well, & in humour with the life about me. The effects of inoculation wore off about Wednesday, & I do full duty. Today have been Revolver Shooting, & it may be a final proof of my normality (for Father's satisfaction)[124] that I shot better than most. We go on with this Course tomorrow.

I see my 'Hospital Barge' and another poem[125] appear in this week's *Nation*. I'll send you the Editor's cheque early in July, helping to launch Colin into Extravagance.

My Immortal Innocent has rather let himself down in my estimation by going to the Bing Boys[126] when he swore his first Theatre should be Shakespere.

The Regent Palace is no longer the Hotel it was when I used to stay years ago. My last visit was most unfavourable, and in the light of recommending it to a younger brother, alarming.

Was so pleased to get a letter from Father. Will write to him to Torquay—when will that be?

Will send a Card to Chubbie Cubbie. And to Colin. Have not seen again Warne, but have found under my care other Shropshire lads whose speech bewrayed them to me. These, and some Welsh chappies we have are indeed, look you, I am prout to say, the muscle, as well as the voice, look you, of the company.

The Lancashire Mill Hands are weeds, why, Weeds.

Nothing to report from War Office. Have been interrupted even at this hour, so Goodnight, my darling Mother.   x

[124] See Letter 634, closing lines.
[125] 'Futility' (*CPF*, p. 158). Published in *The Nation* on 15 June 1918.
[126] *The Bing Boys are Here*, which opened at the Alhambra Theatre in 1916, marked the first appearance in revue of George Robey (1869–1959). An enormous success, it was followed by *The Bing Boys on Broadway*.

632. To Susan Owen

Monday [24 June 1918]   *My Tent [Scarborough]*

STAND BACK FROM THE PAGE! and disinfect yourself.

Quite 1/3 of the Batt. and about 30 officers are smitten with the Spanish Flu.

The hospital overflowed on Friday, then the Gymnasium was filled, and now all the place seems carpeted with huddled blanketed forms. Only the very bad cases have beds. The boys are dropping on parade like flies in number. Priestley and the Adjutant are the two latest cases.

The thing is much too common for me to take part in. I have quite decided not to!

Scottie, whom I still see sometimes, went under today, & my servant yesterday.

Imagine the work that falls on the unaffected officers. Yesterday, I was Orderly Officer for the Battalion, & was not able to take off my frown for five minutes on end between Reveille & midnight. My temperature is normal, so don't be alarmed. I'm afraid my new servant,—a Herefordshire gardener's-boy, with the garden still lying in loamy beds about his ears—will 'drop' tomorrow.

There is no panic; most are already convalescent.

As no call has come from the W.O. has reached me, I shall likely be here another month—unless drafted out, which is not probable.

War Dreams have begun again; but that is because of the flapping of the canvas all night in the high winds; or else the hideous faces of the Advancing Revolver Targets I fired at last week. It is not because I am G.S. as I will prove to you another day.

Ever your W.E.O. x

633. To Susan Owen

Postcard

Sunday [Postmark 1 July 1918]   *[Postmark Scarborough]*

I wondered if Colin would be infected, and am now only hoping he won't carry it to you. I am quite immune—to everybody's amazement. Went a Cross Country Run last Wednesday, from which my calves are still suffering. Have seldom enjoyed any exercise so much.

Refereeed a Football Match yesterday !!

Had 2 long belated letters from Siegfried (in France). One letter had twice been sent from Craiglockhart to Dublin after some other Owen.

Siegfried sends a poem which I'll copy for you some day. Osbert Sitwell wrote to me yesterday, also sending a poem on the latest news 'M. Clemenceau is fully satisfied with the conditions at the front'.[127] O's father, Sir George is a magnate in Scarborough & his own estimation.

---

[127] Sitwell recalled in *Nobles Essences* (p. 105): 'I had sent him an epigram I had composed on Clemenceau, at the time French Premier. Whenever catastrophe threatened to overwhelm the Allied Cause, as it frequently did in 1917 and '18, and whatever the extent of human suffering involved, inevitably in the English papers some such reassuring sentence as this would appear: "On being informed of these happenings, Monsieur Clemenceau announced that he was fully satisfied"..."Ill Winds", as the epigram was called, remained unpublished.
It ran—
        "Up on the Cross, in ugly agony,
        The Son of Man hung dying—and the roar
        Of earthquakes rent the solemn sky
        Already thundering its wrath, and tore
    The dead from out their tombs...then Jesus died—
    But Monsieur Clemenceau is fully satisfied!"'

634. To Osbert Sitwell[128]

July[129] 1918   *[Scarborough]*

Dear Osbert Sitwell,

I rehearsed your very fine epigram upon our Mess President—rather a friend of mine. He did not immediately recognize Jesus. The rest of the Mess would not of course know the name of Monsieur Clemenceau. (To my mind this would be no indication of any man's ignorance of affairs.) May I send 'Ill Winds' to a French youth who might translate and circulate it where it would be appreciated?

Always hoping to find an hour in which to copy out and generally denebulize a few poems acceptable to you either as Editor or—may I not say—friend—I have delayed this letter so long. Tonight there is only time for a tedious brief speech with you before the mind wakes up for its only amusement these days—dreams.

For 14 hours yesterday I was at work—teaching Christ to lift his cross by numbers, and how to adjust his crown; and not to imagine he thirst till after the last halt; I attended his Supper to see that there were no complaints; and inspected his feet to see that they should be worthy of the nails. I see to it that he is dumb and stands to attention before his accusers. With a piece of silver I buy him every day, and with maps I make him familiar with the topography of Golgotha.

Last week I broke out of camp to order *Wheels, 1917.* Canning[130] refused to stock copies. I persisted so long that the Young Lady loudly declared she knew all along that I was 'Osbert himself'. This caused a consternation throughout the crowded shop; but I got the last laugh by—'No, Madam; the book is by a friend of mine, Miss Sitwell.'

Rigby's people would not order a single copy without deposit!

Is the 1918 vol. designed to go on the caterpillar wheels of Siegfried's Music Hall Tank?[131] If so I might help with the ammunition. Would you like some short War Poems, or what? Please give me a final date for submitting them to you.

I very much look forward to meeting you again, and if it be in Scarborough the pleasure will be that of all snatched joys. I am incarcerated more strictly than you imagine. Westborough[132] is now a weekly ambition. The Spa is beyond my hopes. This is the beginning of decadence. As is proved by my Father's message on hearing I was G.S.[133]: 'gratified to know you are normal again.'—Very sympathetically yours,

W. E. S. Owen

---

[128] The letter was first published in *Noble Essences.*

[129] At some time in July Owen listed the poems that would be included in his first collection. See *CPF*, p. 537. The proposed title was *Disabled and Other Poems,* in preference to two other possibilities, *With Lightning and with Music* and *English Elegies.* On the same sheet of paper he wrote down the names of those to receive copies. The list reads: 'S.S., R. Graves, Leslie, P. B. [Poetry Bookshop], Mrs. Gray, Mrs. Fullerton, Dr. Sampson, Dr. Brock, Miss Wyer (?), R. Meiklejohn, Dr. Rayner, Laurent Tailhade, A. Bennett, H. G. Wells, Johnny de la Touche, Bainbrigge, Lady Margaret Sackville, R. Nichols, W. B. Yeats, J. Drinkwater?'

[130] A Scarborough bookshop, no longer in existence.

[131] From SS's poem 'Blighters', in *The Old Huntsman*: 'I'd like to see a Tank come down the stalls, /…/And there'd be no more jokes in Music-Halls / To mock the riddled corpses round Bapaume.'

[132] The principal street in Scarborough.

[133] General Service.

636. To Susan Owen

Friday [12 *July* 1918][134]   [*Scarborough*]

Dearest of Mothers,

I started a letter on Tues. but didn't get far, so I'll abandon it altogether, & begin again. Since Tues. I have been Messing Officer to the Battalion in place of Stiebel who is away at Torquay for 10 days. This means that I am 'on my own', responsible to the Colonel & my conscience for the feeding of a thousand 'souls'. (I wish men's Souls were as hungry as these Bodies.)

My new job means no dimunition of work but it is more interesting. I have a dozen brawny W.A.A.C.s to do the cooking, two boy stokers, & 3 men Night Cooks.

The Rationing is a tremendous affair, but the reckoning & much of the ordering is done by 2 Corporals, skilled ledger-men both. The washing up is done by a little army of W.A.A.C.s in charge of a man-sergeant. When I scold, which is regularly every hour, you might recognize some of your own voice-tones such as you used when Phyllis was unusually 'trying'. I have never in my life had to appear so omniscient & omnipotent. Nor have I ever struggled so desperately or so vainly against dirt & disorder. I put on overalls & whitewashed the cookhouse this morning!

Time goes cruelly fast. The army seems to be a vast digestive apparatus, with hunger as eternal as the cookhouse fires.

To dip for a moment into more savoury things, let me remind you that because I am sacrificing my Thought and Time to the bellies of the multitude is no reason why no letters should be written to me. I've had a miserable Post all week. Leslie no doubt is influenced by the 1½ post, but it is a sad fact, that people want an i for i and a t for a t. (Except people such as Siegfried.) I've got his new book of things I looked over at Craiglockhart.

Priestley has obtained a fair price for my Chest of Drawers, & accordingly it will be sent on Monday next addressed to Father. I hope Father will get the Carriage Refunded. The drawers may be packed with books or other refuse in the form of valuable candlesticks.

I still wear one pip because nobody knows whether I am Lieut. or not.

Harold—where is he? Does he consider it fortunate to be sent to the Tropics—I think he should. I'd rather be sent to the North Pole—and going out into the blizzard like a gallant gentleman than go and get spattered with blood I am trying here to enrichen [*five words illegible*].

W.E.O.

[134] PN, p. 189.

638. To Susan Owen

Saturday [20 July 1918][135]   [*Scarborough*]

Dear, dear Mother,

Wonderful of you to write so bravely of your cares. I think of these things at night because I must not by day. The only comfort from my quarter is the Statement that I am well and all my anxiety here is what I share from you.

Your card came this morning.

Stiebel[136] came back tonight.

Priestley leaves tomorrow for hospital & wants me to take on his job permanently. I am not too keen. I am glad to Have Done with the W.A.A.C's. It is almost impossible to control them. They either weep or take flight when reprimanded. 2 of Priestley's deserted today. One of 'mine' cries' several times every day.

Their work it is true is terribly hard; but I was responsible for the men's food, and had to 'slave' them. Tell Mary I overheard one W.A.A.C. say after me 'I'd like to smack 'is brown face forrim.'

I wish I could get my Leave now to be with you. Would you like me to exaggerate matters (if indeed it is possible) and come. Colonel Mitchell is away and the acting C.O. is a Major with whom I am quite friendly & informal.

More tomorrow.

Your own W.E.O.

135 PN, p. 189.
136 Lieutenant J. S. Stiebel, 7th Manchesters.

641. To Susan Owen

[*Circa 30 July 1918*][137]   *Scarborough*

My own Mother,

I send you a precious letter, from the Greatest friend I have.

I was inoculated again on Sat. but it was Siegfried's condition and not my own that made me so wretched. This time surely he has done with war.[138]

The most encouraging thing is that he is writing already again.

Now must I throw my little candle on his torch, and go out again.

There are rumours of a large draft of officers shortly.

Sorry I only sent 10/- when the expenses were altogether about 14/-. Here is the residue for Mary.

Will try & get the books you mention, & also send you Siegfried's.

Dearest wishes to Mary,

Your lovingest W.E.O. x

137 'The Kind Ghosts' (*CPF*, p. 181) is dated 30 July 1918, and probably the poem referred to in Letter 642.
138 Returning from a dawn patrol on 13 July, SS was taken for a German and received a bullet wound in the head from one of his own NCOs. He was invalided home. See *Sherston's Progress*, pp. 264–7.

642. To Susan Owen

Thursday, 7.30 a.m. [*8 August 1918*]   *Scarborough*

Dearest Mother,

Am just about to start out for the day's work,—on the Butts today.

Have had another black week, alarms calling us out at 4 in the morning, & since Sat. continuous Rain, so that my tent floor was half under water for 2 days.

I shall be on Range Duty up to Friday Night, so my Leave will not start before Friday week, if then.

So sorry I've missed Colin, but if I go to London I'll see him there. Yes, with Colin and S.S. in London I really must pass 1 day there.

I send you S.S's last note. The first sentence refers to a poem[139] I wrote last week and sent him.

I can tell by many signs that Siegfried has been really unnerved this time.

All thanks for the news you've sent from time to time of yourself, Colin, & Mary. Harold sent the Refund this week. I hope he was quite well able. I don't understand your exclamations about the Boots.

Will pay that Dentist's Bill of course.

How are your eyes now?

Always your W.E.O. x

[139] Probably 'The Kind Ghosts'; see *CPF*, p. 181. SS's letter survives in the Owen Archive at Oxford.

643. To Susan Owen

Saturday [10 August 1918]   *Scarborough*

Dearest Mother,

Tomorrow I am for a medical inspection with 21 others, to be declared fit for draft. This means we may be sent on draft leave tomorrow, & I may reach you even before this letter! I know not. I am glad. That is I am much gladder to be going out again than afraid. I shall be better able to cry my outcry, playing my part.[140]

The secondary annoyances & discomforts of France behind the line can be no worse than this Battalion. On Friday we were called up at 3 a.m. and had the usual day's work. The Adjutant is ill, & Stiebel is ill. I did Stiebel's job on the Stunt, & am still doing it.

These are only mock alarms of course. But this morning at 8.20 we heard a boat torpedoed in the bay about a mile out, they say who saw it. I think only 10 lives were saved. I wish the Bosche would have the pluck to come right in & make a clean sweep of the Pleasure Boats, and the promenaders on the Spa, and all the stinking Leeds & Bradford War-profiteers now reading *John Bull* on Scarborough Sands.

Siegfried is being moved to Berwick on Tweed next week. Am trying to find which day. Imagine what wretched uncertainty I'm in tonight. All I feel sure of is my excellent little servant Jones, who'll pack my stuffs in quarter of an hour, night or day.

Let me thank Mary for her Boat Letter. Hope we'll all have a River Afternoon in spite of my wished-for torpedoes-nearer-home.

I like poor Doris better now I hear she understands *The Old Huntsman* Book.

My mind is a cobweb of lines radiating to Shrewsbury, London, Hastings,[141] Berwick, London, Shrewsbury, Berwick, Edinburgh, Portsmouth[142] - - -

Ever, W.E.O.

[140] 'You have cried your cry, you have played your part' (Letter 647, n. 143).
[141] Colin had been posted to Hastings.
[142] HO had been on a gunnery course at Portsmouth earlier in the year.

645. To Susan Owen

Monday Night [19 August 1918]   *My Tent, Scarborough*

I rushed off a note in time for this evening's post, which may seem very mingy. Work has not fallen hard on me yet; I have done nothing today because my trench feet are so bad I can't walk; & the Patrol last night was altogether enjoyable, and the Dawn this morning.

Still, I am quite wretched tonight, missing you so much. Oh so much!

Taking the world as it really is, not everybody of my years can boast, (or as many would say, confess) that their Mother is absolute in their affections.

But I believe it will always be so with me, always.

There is nothing in heaven or earth like you, and that is why I can't write a poem for you.

Next time I come, we must have a very long and very deep talk.

Meanwhile, eat, drink, and be merry. Here is for half a dozen bottles of red wine, which <u>must</u> be finished before I'll look at you again. I sometimes wonder if you are still haunted by the horror of wine 'taking hold' of me!! You are too absurd! That transgression at least will never bring a blush to my nose.

Eat, Drink, and Be Merry, for tomorrow we live, and the day after tomorrow <u>live</u>, <u>live</u>, <u>live</u>. Even in Scarborough I must live; though I feel dead to all these people.

I have done something towards my Contribution to *Wheels*, but the night watch has rather muddled me.

Strange how suddenly my toes went wrong! It is the old frostbite 'playing on' me again as Jones says. Because I said I was sad, little Jones is prattling to me now, & I am talking volubly while I write.

I am also thinking wildly and crying a little for only you to hear.

Wilfred x

646. To Susan Owen

Postcard

Sat. Mng. [Postmark 31 August 1918]   *[Postmark Folkestone]*

Am writing in a hairdresser's shop waiting for a shave. Found no room in
Hotels so got put up in an Officers' Club, thanks to S. Moncrieff's knowledge of
the region. Got up at 5.30 this mng. & caught train in good time. On the train I
was astonished to meet Major Fletcher, the P.M.C. you remember, who settled up
my accounts last Monday, not dreaming he himself would be pushed off on
Tuesday. But here he is, & I am very glad & shall try to keep with him; he used to
be 2nd in command of the 5th in France.

We go on board at 3 p.m. Will write from Boulogne.

Love and good cheer W.E.O. x

647. To Susan Owen

Sat., 31 August 1918   *E.F.C., Officers Rest House and Mess*

[*half page missing*] Arriving at Victoria I had to wheel my own baggage down
the platform & through the streets to the Hotel, which was full. But I got a bed (as
I [*half page missing*] My last hours in England were brightened by a bathe in the fair
green Channel, in company of the best piece of Nation left in England—a Harrow
boy, of superb intellect & refinement, intellect because he detests war more than
Germans, and refinement because of the way he spoke of my going away; and the
way he spoke of the Sun; and of the Sea, and the Air; and everything. In fact the
way he spoke.

And now I go among cattle to be a cattle-driver...

I am now fairly and reasonably tired & must go to my tent, without saying the
things which you will better understand unsaid.

O my heart,
Be still; You have cried your cry, you played your part.

Did I ever send you Siegfried's poem which he wrote on the boat:

For the last time I say War is not glorious;
Tho' lads march out superb & die victorious,
And crowned by peace, the sunlight on their graves;
  You say we crush the Beast; I say we fight
  Because men lost their landmarks in the night,
  And met in gloom to grapple, stab, & kill.
  Yelling the fetish names of Good & Ill
  Which have been shamed in history.

> O my heart,
> Be still; you have cried your cry, you have played your part![143]

Goodnight, goodnight.
You are at home; yet you <u>are</u> home;
Your love is my home, and I cannot feel abroad.

Wilfred x

---

[143] SS did not publish this. The closing lines, slightly modified, appear in 'To Leonide Massine in "Cleopatra"'(SS, *Collected Poems*). 'O mortal heart / Be still; you have drained the cup; you have played your part.'

648. To Siegfried Sassoon

Sat., 31 August 1918   *E.F.C., Officers Rest House and Mess*

Goodbye—
    dear Siegfried—
    I'm much nearer to you here than in Scarborough, and am by so much happier.
    I have been incoherent ever since I tried to say goodbye on the steps of Lancaster Gate.[144] But everything is clear now: & I'm in hasty retreat towards the Front. Battle is easier here; and therefore you will stay and endure old men & women to the End, and wage the bitterer war and more hopeless.
    When you write, please address to Mahim,

Monkmoor Rd.

Shrewsbury.

What more is there to say that you will not better understand unsaid.

Your W.E.O.

---

[144] SS was in the American Women's Hospital, Lancaster Gate, overlooking Hyde Park.

649. To Siegfried Sassoon

Sunday, 1 September 1918   *A Depot, A.P.O. S.17, B.E.F. France*

Dearest of all Friends,

    Here is an address which will serve for a few days.
    The sun is warm, the sky is clear, the waves are dancing fast & bright...But these are not Lines written in Dejection.[145] Serenity Shelley never dreamed of crowns me. Will it last when I shall have gone into Caverns & Abysmals such as he never reserved for his worst daemons?
    Yesterday I went down to Folkestone Beach and into the sea, thinking to go through those stanzas & emotions of Shelley's to the full. But I was too happy, or

the Sun was too supreme. Moreover there issued from the sea distraction, in the shape, Shape I say, but lay no stress on that, of a Harrow boy, of superb intellect & refinement; intellect because he hates war more than Germans; refinement because of the way he spoke of my Going, and of the Sun, and of the Sea there; and the way he spoke of Everything. In fact, the way he spoke—

And now I am among the herds again, a Herdsman; and a Shepherd of sheep that do not know my voice.

<u>Tell me how you are.</u>

With great & painful firmness I have not said you goodbye from England. If you had said In the heart or brain you might have stabbed me, but you said only in the leg;[146] so I was afraid.

Perhaps if I 'write' anything in dug-outs or talk in sleep a squad of riflemen will save you the trouble of buying a dagger.

Goodbye W.E.O.

[145] The opening lines of Shelley's 'Stanzas Written in Dejection, near Naples'.
[146] SS annotated this letter: 'I had told him I would stab him in the leg if he tried to return to the Front.'

650. To Susan Owen

Postcard

Aft. of Sunday, 1 September [1918] *Address: H Depot, A.P.O. S17,*
B.E.F., France

Have here caught up a number of our officers drafted out before me. This place is vastly more habitable than in 1917. Impossible to feel depressed. All Auguries are of good fortune. How blessedly different from last year!

All love. W.E.O.

651. To Susan Owen

2 September 1918 *[H. Depot, A.P.O. S17]*

My own sweet Mother,

The sun still shines, & everything is little more warlike than in Scarboro. Except that large numbers of wounded were being rushed down the road as I marched a party this morning.

I went to the sea-side by tram yesterday afternoon but there was nothing to do.

I am now in a Y.M.C.A. quite vacant of custom, which is the reason I came, and also to see the gentleman in charge, a man of letters whose name I know, but whose works are not much known, Mr. O'Riordan.[147] He has just come in—, an extraordinary hunch-backed little Irishman, of very pleasant manners.

I sent a card to you for Colin which you'll forward to Hastings.

Here is a list of things which sent at once should reach me here.

Paraffin, Toilet, Boots, small bottle.

1 pair pyjamas, flannelette.

1 lozenge-shaped identity disc;

Keys, 3 or 4 small, if found.

2 small towels now in wash.

No more now. Hoping to hear in 2 or 3 days.

Ever W x

---

[147] Conal Holmes O'Connell O'Riordan (1874–1948), an Irishman of letters who succeeded J. M. Synge as Director of the Abbey Theatre Dublin in 1909. He ran the YMCA Rest Hut at the Base Camp, Étaples, until the end of the war. He wrote under the pen name Norreys Connell. See Letter 652. DH quotes O'Riordan's recollections of Owen, published in *John O'London's Weekly* (6 June 1941) and in *Martial Medley* (1931): 'There could have been no cheerier companion than charming, young Wilfred Owen' (WOANB, 421). This is in contrast to the way that Roland Bate remembered Owen, who he felt had 'acquired a positive attitude of aloof superiority' (WOANB, p. 510, n. 5) since they were hut-mates at Romford.

652. To Susan Owen

Saturday [7 September 1918]   H. Depot, A.P.O. S17

My own Mother,

Still here, but may go up the Line any hour. Orders have come through that I rejoin the 2nd Battalion, so that will be my address.

> 2nd Batt.
> The Manchester Regt.
> B.E.F.
> France.

Was out all day yesterday, & came in too late for post.

It was a fine bold idea of yours to address a letter here, without waiting for my version of the address. I had that letter two days ago, and had great joy of it. Yours & Mary's came last night. Mary's must have a very long answer when I find one.

I have been seeing O'Riordan daily, 'O'Riordan', as G. K. Chesterton writes, 'whom all of us know and love as Norries Connell.'—'All of us' means the whole clan of English writers.

I sleep in a Dormitory, not a Tent, and discovered near by last night one of Erskine Macdonald's little Georgian Poets. He is, really, a big Scotchman,[148] of no genius, but useful as an audience.

The Staff here think they are doing me a favour by sending me back to my old Unit. It's certainly better than any other Lancs crowd, and there is no possibility of a Welsh Regt. from this Camp. If I can't transfer to anything better, I shall perhaps transfer to the 2nd to avoid the prospect of passing the rest of my days with the Scarborough mob.

My parcel will be sent on if I leave before it comes. Will write again tonight or tomorrow.

Ever W.E.O.

[148] Second Lieutenant Murray McClymont, 2nd/10th (Scottish) Kings Liverpool Regiment, who had three poems in *More Songs by the Fighting Men* (Erskine Macdonald, 1917). A copy of the book, which remains among Owen's library in the Bodleian, is annotated by Susan Owen: 'This came back with Wilfred's kit. Dec. 1918'. McClymont had inscribed it (7 September 1918): 'A little book and a little song, / The first all right and the last all wrong; / Which is but meet, let it be known, / Since mine's the song, and the book's for Owen!'

653. To Susan Owen

Saturday [7 September 1918]   [*H Depot, A.P.O. S17*]

My dearest Mother,

Just a memorandum that I start 'hence' tomorrow morning, with a body of troops as well as my luggage to pull after me. When I'll have delivered the troops to their destination, I make my way straight to my own battalion which, I repeat, is the 2nd.

O'Riordan will be at the station to see me off. I've just spent three hours in his hut, talking, not books, but life & people, as is the way between Authors. Especially authors who haven't read each other!

Thus my mind has been amused, & I must not allow this letter to <u>be</u>muse it.

If I see around me other officers whose faces bitterness is changing from their complacent English expressions, I laugh them to scorn.

You would not know me for the poet of sorrows.

Wilfred x

654. To Susan Owen

Monday, 9 September 1918   [*France*]

My own Mother,

I am at a Reception Depot, where I rest, having safely delivered my party of men, who behaved excellently. Our <u>Reception</u> here was not very warm, as we detrained in pitch darkness, & no one had the faintest idea where to go. Guides, however, turned up at last; & led on to billets in this now ruinous old town[149] which I've often spoken & written about.

It was frightfully nice of Haig to allow the French to be shelled out of it, & so leave us any amount of room & household goods. I have a good room in a large house, with a young officer,—quite bearable,—bound also for the 2nd. Man. There are no window panes, but the valuable hand-lace-curtains remain. I sleep on a table, for which a kind Kiltie has just found me a mattress. It's huge fun looting for furniture, & I sleep on my table in a serenity far different from, let us say, at Hastings.

I calculate I'll find several of your letters, & other's, waiting my arrival at the Battalion. In about a week (but I'll tell you again with details) I'd like a parcel with re-fill battery, cigarettes, & chocolate.

I enclose letter explaining the gloves, which I should like included in next parcel, please.

Send me such of Harold's and Colin's letters as you may.

Tell them, and them only, how peculiarly unreluctant I am to be back here with the Nation, & to have the Channel between me and all that the Gunstons[150] typify.

Your Wilfred x

---

[149] Amiens.
[150] The name was omitted in CL and SL.

[656.][151] To Susan Owen

Tues. 10 September 1918   *With The Australian Imperial Force*

[Letter Not to be hawked about.][152]

My own Mother,

I'm sitting in my Camel Hair Coat at my bed-table, by the light of 2 candles. Tomorrow, it seems, will be spent here like today—no duties, no cares, but no letters.

Plenty of French books, plenty of cigarettes, plenty of magnificent life about me, and—enough to eat. No wounded pass through here; as for the poor battered houses they make me merry at heart, for they were all in bad style. And since probably by now the soldiers whose these houses were or were to have been are Unreturning, no pity whatever for their destruction moves me.

I kick joyfully about the debris, and only feel a twinge of sadness when a little child's copy-book or frock or crumpled little hat is laid bare.

Near the Cathedral I picked up a delightful wee lace-surplice, my only souvenir so far.

Potts,[153] that is my comrade—in billets—, chose a Toby Jug, in very bad taste.

Potts is a science student at Manchester; only 20; book learned in certain 'Subjects', but not without ideas. Indeed we talked 3 good hours last night.

It is a pleasure to find someone worth disagreeing with, nowadays, and here-a-placed.

I think we are fond of each other, moreover, & will do each other much good.

The Australian Y.M. is a shack of a cottage, near a little place where I once had tea last year, & which Sassoon also knew.

It was strange to wander again by the Canal where the 'Hospital Barge' passed....

I had a strong poetical experience in a wrecked garden this afternoon, not an ordinary garden, but full of conservatories of tropical plants, aviaries, fish-ponds, palms & so on. I can't make a poem of it, because of Shelley's 'Sensitive Plant'[154] which you might turn up if you want the effect I enjoyed. I say enjoyed…

Here is a list for next parcel which you might send as soon as convenient after receiving this:

1 Pears Soap.

1 Euthymol Toothpaste.

1 Refill Battery.

2 Boxes Non Safety Matches.

2 pair Madoxes 2/6 socks.

The gloves.

20 Players Navy Cut or more if possible.

Horlicks Tablets.

No Chocolate, unless room is left.

? Handkerchiefs.

Goodnight; and may your peace be as divine as mine is tonight.

Your son, your son, your son…

[151] This letter was dated and printed out of sequence (PN, p. 189). It is here in chronological order.

[152] In Owen's own hand under the date.

[153] Second Lieutenant Frederick Potts, Manchester Regiment, was wounded on 1 October 1918. He became a chemistry teacher after the First World War and died in 1960.

[154] Written in 1820, 'The Sensitive Plant' describes an idyllic garden tended by a fair lady, on whose death it falls into neglect, becoming a wilderness. Its plants are finally ravaged by a cruel winter. 'That garden sweet, that lady fair, / And all sweet shapes and colours there, / In truth have never passed away; / 'Tis we, 'tis ours, are changed! not they.'

[655.][155] To Susan Owen

Thursday [12 September 1918]   Y.M.C.A.,
                                                          With The Australian Imperial Force

No move yet; and no news to better that news.

How many of your letters, I wonder are amassing in the Man. Regimental Postbags.

You might chance one card here to tell me you're well.

Because I <u>may</u> stay here indefinitely.

The weather is wet & cold, but my temper, it is proved, keeps independent of sunlight.

This afternoon I went forth in search of adventure, & took a joy ride in a tank.

I was accosted in the Australian Y.M. by an old Runner of mine who shared the miseries of the—Rly. Banks.[156] He has never had so frightful a time since.

Just as I was moving off at the Base, a private rushed out from the crowd & shook my hand. I just was able to recognize him as a drummer at Southport—he looks a middle-aged man now.

The augury was good, and I think the incident put my draft in a confident mood.

Potts is good solid companion, not without wit, & full of wisdom.

I hear the C.O. of the 2nd. is the Major or Colonel mentioned in all the papers the other day as wounded for the tenth time.[157]

I don't know where they are.

Literary Cuttings, and others from the news, would amuse me. At present I read Stevenson's Essays, & do not want any books.

Do not inform friends & relations that I pass my hours reading, sleeping, conversing, & gathering roses from bewildered gardens. But so it is, and I'm getting fat upon it.

I assure you the difference is noticeable when I come to shave my face, (about 11 in the morning).

I kiss your hand.

W.E.O.

[155] This letter was dated and printed out of sequence (PN, p. 189). It is here in chronological order.

[156] See Letter 605.

[157] Major J. N. Marshall, MC, Irish Guards, had joined 2nd Manchesters on 1 June 1918 as Second in Command. He had been wounded (for the tenth time) on 11 August. See Letters 658, 659 (in which Owen calls him 'the Major of the 12 wounds'), and 661.

657. To Susan Owen

Friday, 13 September [1918]   *Y. M. C.A.*
With The Australian Imperial Force

Dear, dear Mother,

News today that the Batt. is coming down here, instead of my going Hence. Excellent. I have been billeting troops today. Write to the 2nd. Man., <u>not</u> this Recep. Camp as I'll be joining about Sunday.

It is funny to think of your letters being brought down from the Front!

Do not, (as I afore-asked) undeceive the world which thinks I'm having a bad time, if it thinks at all. But take to yourself the fact that I've an amusing little holiday here; and know that nowhere in the universe, and at no time, can I experience anything again like—and—in 1917.

Ever your W.E.O. x

658. To Susan Owen

Sunday, 15 September 1918   *With the 2nd. Batt., The Manchester Regt.*[158]

My dear dear Mother,

I reported to the Adjutant at 9 this morning, & am now in <u>D Coy.</u>—which is part of my address. Your letter of Sept. 10 (unnumbered) (with the photograph), was on the table at lunch. After lunch, I went round to B.H.Q. for the rest, but found none, & could get nothing out of the post-corporal.

I hung about interrogating people till the Terrible Major, (he of the 10 wounds fame) asked me if he could help me! I departed. Mysteriously, at dinner, eight more letters were brought to me, including only one of yours, The No. 3. None from S.S. It is possible that his correspondence is specially censored—and intercepted.

All thanks for the parcels—in anxious anticipation!

Cigarettes are scarcer and scarcer. *Verb. Sap.* The poor Boys were smoking grass in envelopes in the line last week. I wish I could tell you what they have done in the making of last month's News.

Yesterday I had the honour (!) of preparing the Brigadier's Quarters: & supervising Guides for various units of the Brigade. I watched The Manchesters 'march in' and great cheer it was to see at least two lads instantly recognize me as they went by. They were, strangely enough, the very two I most hoped had survived. <u>Almost</u> they are the only survivors in the ranks....

Many of the N.C.O.'s I remember.

I like my Coy. Commander:[159] & the other four Coy. Officers are anything but blighters. Three, I believe are junior to me.

But Potts has been put in another Coy.

We billet together, nevertheless.

Of our billets (in a village close adjacent to where I was last week) I will write more next time—tomorrow, I hope.

By the writing you may judge I am not yet <u>very</u> comfortable.

W.E.O. x x

---

[158] The Germans were now in retreat, but were hitting back strongly as they withdrew. The 2nd Manchesters had been heavily engaged about Vermandovillers, Ablaincourt, and Cizancourt in the last days of August, and had been withdrawn to Berny, then to the Neuville area, on 6 September. Owen rejoined them at Corbie on 15 September.

[159] Captain Hugh Somerville, MC and Bar, commanding D Coy. See Letters 662a and 667.

659. To Susan Owen

Saturday [21 September 1918]   [*2nd Manchester Regt.*]

Just a tiny note as a sign of life, & to say that both your Parcels have reached me, one yesterday and one today! Tomorrow—Sunday —I will thank you in detail.

All news is told when I say I am still in the same billet, & no doubt shall be for long after you get this letter.

I have been appointed Bombing Officer to the Battalion. N.B. I know nothing specially about bombs. I told the Adjutant so, & he said something about making me Gas Officer; or 'some Battalion job'. I am flattered.

The Adjutant is a fine pleasant man.

My Captain is an Honours Student of Eng. Literature. Need I say more? (Yes, I need: he is <u>not</u> a producer).

The Colonel[160] is an agreeable non-ferocious gentleman. <u>But</u> the Major of the 12 wounds loves Soldiering & has passed his life wherever he could find any fighting. Need I say more?

Your W.E.O. x

---

[160] Lieutenant Colonel G. McM. Robertson, DSO, North Staffs., had become CO on 18 May 1918.

660. To Siegfried Sassoon

22 September 1918   *D Coy. 2nd Manchester Regt.*

My dear Siegfried,

Here are a few poems to tempt you to a letter. I begin to think your correspondence must be intercepted somewhere. So I will state merely

I have had no letter from you $\left\{ \begin{array}{l} \text{lately} \\ \text{for a long time,}^{161} \end{array} \right.$

and say nothing of my situation, tactical or personal.

You said it would be a good thing for my poetry if I went back.

That is my consolation for feeling a fool. This is what shells scream at me every time: Haven't you got the wits to keep out of this?

Did you see what the Minister of Labour[162] said in the *Mail* the other day? 'The first instincts of the men <u>after the cessation of</u> hostilities will be to return home.' And again—

'All classes <u>acknowledge</u> their indebtedness to the soldiers & sailors…'

About the same day, Clemenceau is reported by the *Times* as saying: '<u>All</u> are worthy…yet we should be untrue to ourselves if we forgot that the <u>greatest</u> glory will be to the splendid poilus, who, etc.'

I began a Postcript to these Confessions,[163] but hope you will already have lashed yourself, (lashed <u>yourself!</u>) into something…

O Siegfried, make them Stop![164]

W.E.O.

P.S. My Mother's address is <u>Mahim</u>
<u>Monkmoor Rd. Shrewsbury.</u>
I know you would try to see her, if _____ I failed to see her again.

---

[161] Owen is here mimicking the Field Service postcard.
[162] George Henry Roberts (1869–1928), Minister of Labour 1917–19.
[163] 'Smile, Smile, Smile' (*CPF*, p. 190).
[164] The last words of 'Attack' (SS's *Counter-Attack and Other Poems*) are: 'O Jesus, make it stop!'

661. To Susan Owen

Sat. 28 September 1918   *Same Address*

Dearest Mother,

Am still sitting on straw under our Tamboo,[165] for it is raining again. These few days have been dry & not really cold. You must not suppose I have been uncomfortable. Though I left the last vestige of civilization, in the Civil sense, behind at _____, there is here all but all that a man wants fundamentally; clean air, enough water to wash once a day; plain food and plentiful; letters from Home of good news, shelter from the rain & cold; an intellectual gentleman for Captain; 3 bright & merry boys for my corporals; & stout grizzled old soldiers in my platoon. My Sergeant is a tiny man. We get on very well together.

Major Marshall of the 10 wounds is the most arrant utterly soldierly soldier I ever came across. I have not 'come across' his path yet, & hope not to. Bold, robust, dashing, unscrupulous, cruel, jovial, immoral, vast-chested, handsome-headed, of free, coarse speech, I am not surprised he figures in a book. I don't know which book; must find out.

The Colonel is a mild, honourable gentleman, who lets us alone to do our work.

Two at least of the officers in D. Coy. are quite temporary gentlemen. They call me The Ghost, (which is a point in favour of their latent imaginations.)

So delighted with all your news of Harold.[166] Didn't I tell you it was 'A Good Thing.' You don't say where Colin is, after having left Hastings.

As I hope I said, I had his letter, but at present I'm borrowing note paper, of which a quire is not to be found in the Company.

The forthcoming news should be of intense interest to you.[167]

Here is my lunch; roast beef & baked potatoes! I'm hungry!

Ever your W.E.O. x

[165]   Bivouac or small trench dugout.

[166]   HO had reached Simonstown on the Western Cape of South Africa to join the light cruiser *Astraea* as sub-lieutenant. See JO III, ch. 12.

[167]   Later the same day the battalion moved (with its brigade, the 96th) to Vendelles, crossing the St Quentin Canal, and took up positions east of Magny-la-Fosse, near Bellenglise, on 29 September in preparation for a brigade attack on Joncourt to gain the Beaurevoir-Fonsomme Line round Chataignies Wood.

662. To Susan Owen

4th (or 5th) October 1918   *In the Field*

Strictly private

My darling Mother,

As you must have known both by my silence and from the newspapers which mention this Division—and perhaps by other means & senses—I have been in action for some days.[168]

I can find no word to qualify my experiences except the word SHEER. (Curiously enough I find the papers talk about sheer fighting!) It passed the limits of my Abhorrence. I lost all my earthly faculties, and fought like an angel.

If I started into detail of our engagement I should disturb the censor and my own Rest.

You will guess what has happened when I say I am now Commanding the Company, and in the line had a boy lance-corporal as my Sergeant-Major.

With this corporal who stuck to me and shadowed me like your prayers I captured a German Machine Gun and scores of prisoners.

I'll tell you exactly how another time. I only shot one man with my revolver (at about 30 yards!); The rest I took with a smile. The same thing happened with other parties all along the line we entered.

I have been recommended for the Military Cross;[169] and have recommended every single N.C.O. who was with me!

My nerves are in perfect order.

I came out in order to help these boys—directly by leading them as well as an officer can; indirectly, by watching their sufferings that I may speak of them as well as a pleader can. I have done the first.

Of whose blood lies yet crimson on my shoulder where his head was—and where so lately yours was—I must not now write.

It is all over for a long time. We are marching steadily <u>back</u>.

Moreover

The War is nearing an end.

Still,

Wilfred and more than Wilfred

[168] The brigade had attacked on 1 October and had gained its objectives. The Manchesters attacked with great gallantry, broke through the Beaurevoir-Fonsomme Line, and after stiff hand-to-hand fighting cleared 1,400 yards of the line, capturing 210 prisoners. Repeated counter-attacks were made during the following night. Five officers were killed, six wounded (including Potts); eighty-five other ranks were killed or wounded. On 3 October the battalion was relieved and pulled back to dugouts on the banks of the St Quentin Canal near Lehancourt; and on 5 October moved to Hancourt in the Vendelles area to rest. Owen writes during the march back to Hancourt.

[169] The citation in the London *Gazette* (supplement) of 30 July 1919 reads: 'For conspicuous gallantry and devotion to duty in the attack on the Fonsomme Line on 1st/2nd October 1918. On the Company Commander becoming a casualty, he assumed command and showed fine leadership and resisted a heavy counter-attack. He personally captured an enemy M[achine] G[un] from an isolated position and inflicted considerable losses on the enemy. Throughout he behaved most gallantly.' In CL, HO replaced the phrase 'inflicted considerable losses on the enemy' with 'took a number of prisoners'. A copy of the citation was kept by Tom Owen in his personal scrapbook.

[662a.] To Charles Scott-Moncrieff[170]

7 October 1918

My dear Scott-Moncrieff,

I received your note in a pill-box which I and my glorious little company had captured a few hours previously.

You may be able to inform yourself of the circumstances and Effects (in the Sassoonic sense) of our attack (2nd. Man. Regt.) of Oct. 1st.

I'm really glad to have been recommended, and hope a M.C. will come through—for the confidence it will give me in dealing with civilians.

I'm frightfully busy (as O.C.D.) and many glorious Cries of the blood still lying on my clothes will have to be stifled.

My Captain, wounded, was Somerville, M.C. of Edinburgh Univ. He thinks he knew you there. I find I never wrote a letter with so much difficulty as this. Perhaps I am tired after writing to so many relations of casualties. Or perhaps for other causes.

I am far enough out of the line to feel the acute discomfort of Billets (ram-shaks of corrugated iron). Do write soon, with all the news you can spare of Peace Possibilities.

Ever yours,
W.E.O.

[170] The letter was first published in the second edition (1978) of Dennis Welland's *Wilfred Owen: A Critical Study* (Chatto & Windus, 1958), and later appeared as Appendix A in the second edition (1998) of *SL*. It appears now in its original chronological place.

663. To Susan Owen

[6 October 1918][171]   [2nd Manchester Regt.]

It is 5 o'clock this Sunday Evening. You will be sitting at tea. I fear you are without news, and a little wondering…

You will understand I could not write—when you think of us for days all but surrounded by the enemy. All one day (after the battle) we could not move from a small trench, though hour by hour the wounded were groaning just outside. Three stretcher-bearers who got up were hit, one after one. I had to order no one to show himself after that, but remembering my own duty, and remembering also my forefathers the agile Welshmen of the Mountains I scrambled out myself & felt an exhilaration in baffling the Machine Guns by quick bounds from cover to cover. After the shells we had been through, and the gas, bullets were like the gentle rain from heaven.

My servant was wounded in the first hour of the attack. My new servant has just gone on leave this afternoon, carrying with him some books & binoculars[172] of mine, with instructions to call on you as he passes through Shrewsbury (to Manchester.) This Howarth is a 'scratch' servant not my choice; but I rather hope he'll call on you & tell you what he can.

So strange to read your letters again! And so good to hear you are at least try-ing to keep quite well. Glad you find your Help worth accommodating.

Must now write to hosts of parents of Missing, etc.

Your W.E.O. x

[171] PN, p. 190.
[172] A German pair of binoculars.

664. To Siegfried Sassoon

10 October 1918   [*2nd Manchester Regt.*]

Very dear Siegfried,

Your letter reached me at the exact moment it was most needed—when we had come far enough out of the line to feel the misery of billets; and I had been seized with writer's cramp after making out my casualty reports. (I'm O.C. D Coy).

The Batt. had a sheer time last week. I can find no better epithet: because I cannot say I suffered anything; having let my brain grow dull: That is to say my nerves are in perfect order.

It is a strange truth: that your *Counter-Attack* frightened me much more than the real one: though the boy by my side, shot through the head, lay on top of me, soaking my shoulder, for half an hour.

Catalogue? Photograph? Can you photograph the crimson-hot iron as it cools from the smelting? That is what Jones's blood looked like, and felt like. My senses are charred.

I shall feel again as soon as I dare, but now I must not. I don't take the cigarette out of my mouth when I write Deceased over their letters.

But one day I will write Deceased over many books.

I'm glad I've been recommended for M.C., & hope I get it, for the confidence it may give me at home. Full of confidence after having taken a few machine guns (with the help of one seraphic lance corporal,) I held a most glorious brief peace talk in a pill box. You would have been 'en pamoisons'.[173]

I found one of your poems in another L. Cpl's possession! The Theosophist[174] one it was: containing, let me tell you, the one line I resent.

In bitter safety I awake unfriended.

Please apologise—now.

Yes, there is something you can send me: 2 copies of *C. Attack*, one inscribed. One is for the Adjutant,—who begged a book of Erskine MacD's Soldier-Poets which I had with me—because I met one of these amalgamations at the Base. And liked him for his immediate subjugation to my principles and your mastery.

But he is now sending me V.A.D. love poems,[175] so he will remain a private in my section of poets.

Was so interested about Prewett.[176]

At the Base I met O'Riordan (of the Irish Theatre, & collaborator with Conrad.) A troll of a man; not unlike Robbie for unexpected shocks. It was easy, & as I reflect, inevitable to tell him everything about oneself.

I have nothing to tell you except that I'm rather glad my servant was happily wounded: & so away from me. He had lived in London, a Londoner.

While you are apparently given over to wrens,[177] I have found brave companionship in a poppy, behind whose stalk I took cover from five machine-guns and several howitzers.

I desire no more <u>exposed flanks</u> of any sort for a long time.

Of many who promised to send me literary magazines no one has succeeded, except the Ed. of *Today*[178] who sent me (by whose request?) Mais's[179] article & the picture, which I have at last managed to stick to the corrugated iron Wall of my Tamboo. For mercy's sake send me something to read which may help to neutralize my present stock of literature. I send you the choicest of specimens.[180]

Ever your W.E.O.

[173] 'in a swoon'.

[174] 'Sick Leave' (in SS's *Counter-Attack and Other Poems*).

[175] McClymont had written on 11 September: 'I have altered the sonnet as below. Sorry to trouble you, but I want your criticism.' The love poem followed. On the back of this letter, Owen drafted 'Smile, Smile, Smile' (*CPF*, p. 190).

[176] SS was now convalescing at Lennel, near Coldstream in Berwickshire, the home of Lady Clementine Waring. Among his fellow convalescents was a Canadian poet, Frank 'Toronto' Prewett, who published a volume of poems, *The Rural Scene* (1924), thereafter abandoning poetry for farming. See *Siegfried's Journey* and Joy Porter, *Trauma, Primitivism and the First World War: The Making of Frank Prewett* (Bloomsbury, 2021).

[177] 'I had described how, early one morning, a golden-crested wren had appeared in my bedroom and perched on my pillow, thereby affording me the innocent pleasure of releasing it at the open window. Reading his rejoinder to this almost maiden-auntlike piece of news, I probably told myself that war experience was mainly composed of acute contrasts, of which this—in conjunction with his—seemed a classic example' (SS, *Siegfried's Journey*, p. 73).

[178] Holbrook Jackson (1874–1948), author and bookman, editor of *T.P.'s Weekly* 1911–14 and of *To-day* 1917–23.

[179] The writer S. P. B. Mais (1885–1975), at this time a schoolmaster, was also literary critic on *The Evening News*.

[180] A Special Order of the Day by General Sir H. S. Rawlinson, BART., G.C.V.O., K.C.B., K.C.M.G., Commanding Fourth Army remains with the letter to SS. Owen quotes from this document in Letter 665.

665. To Susan Owen

10 October 1918   [*2nd Manchester Regt.*]

My own Mother,

I think all your dear letters have now reached me. By Oct. 3, your last, we had got out of the danger zone.

At five in the mng. I led the Company out, by the stars, through an air mysterious with faint gas. Such was our state that when dawn broke some of us were surprised, and for half an hour I had myself thought it was five in the evening! Since then I have been pretty busy with the Company, still in my charge, with 2 junior officers. At three this morning, a big number of lads from Scarborough turned up, several of them outgrown drummers, once my waiters in Clarence Gdns!

Nearly all have come to my Company, & <u>from</u> my company in Scarborough. Luck again! I'm in the horrible position of not having enough food for them, as they left their rations some ten miles away!

Some of them look pretty scared already, poor victims. Tonight I must stand before them & promulgate this General Order:

'Peace talk in any form is to cease in Fourth Army.

All ranks are warned against the disturbing influence of dangerous peace talk.' And so on.

It is amusing to think of anyone being upset by a friend's arm-amputation in hospital[181] ...

How would Father like—No, I will spare you.

Father would like to see mc on my Charger; or sitting at my Orderly Room Table, where I can inflict Field Punishment! In a few days a senior officer will no doubt turn up from Leave or somewhere.

Am looking out with hungry eyes for your parcel. None of my rich relations consider 20 cigarettes worth my life. They'll have a murderer's curse; if I should curse them. Meanwhile you have a martyr's blessing.

W.E.O.

[181] Tom Owen's superior, Mr Williams, Chief Superintendent of the West Region, London North-Eastern and Great Western Railways, had undergone the operation; and Tom Owen became Acting Chief Superintendent, a position he held until his retirement several years later. Williams refusing to retire, the much-increased pension Tom Owen would have received on his retirement in 1925 was not forthcoming. The family left Shrewsbury and settled in a house they named 'Wilmot' at 193 Peppard Road, Emmer Green, near Caversham. Tom Owen died in 1931.

666. To Susan Owen

11 October 1918   [2nd Manchester Regt.]

Not for circulation as a whole.

Dearest of Mothers,

No letter from you today, and no parcel. The great concerns which take my time have prevented me from properly thanking you for the many little blessings of your last parcel. The Munchie I ate over a period of several days & nights; and the fact that it was once eaten under a particularly nasty & accurate bombardment—(shells so close that they thoroughly put the wind up a Life Guardsman in the trench with me—so that he shook as the Guards shake on parade) these circumstances, I say, have not taken the good savour from Munchie-munchie.

The New Food[182] served me one night when we lay drenched to the bone, and the awful Cold had begun to paralyse my stomach. I don't like this Food.

On that night both officers & men lay in the mud utterly despondent; but a lance-corporal spread half his blanket (not supposed to be carried) over me, and the warmth came like the rising of the May-day sun. So I was saved from the nearest approach to the excruciation of my First Campaign. That time on the Somme in 1917 was so infinitely worse than this for cold, privation, and fatigue that nothing daunts me now.

The Sergeant, now acting my Coy. Sgt. Major, was a corporal with me in the first dug-out where the Sentry was blinded, you remember. He remembers it...

I still command D. Coy, and have now four junior officers.

It is delightful to have the Scarborough Drums to fill the Vacant Ranks. Censoring letters today I came across this: 'Do you know that little officer called Owen who was at Scarborough; he is commanding my Company, and he is a toff I can tell you. No na-poo. Compree?' Interpreted: 'a fine fellow, no nonsense about him!'

I record this because it is more pleasing than military medals with many bars.

———————————

Returning to the unpacking of my parcels: cigarettes: arrived just in time: sweets & (good) chocolate always welcome.

You see I live between the extremes of gross materialism—feeding savagely & sleeping doggishly—and of high spirituality—suffering & sacrificing.

Wilfred

Next day

Together with your last letter came one from S. Moncrieff, now in France supervising or piloting Beach Thomas[183] and Philip Gibbs.[184]

He hopes to motor over to see me some day. His letter told me the very sad news of Robert Ross;[185] and also of P. Bainbrigge of Shrewsbury School, my friend of Scarborough; killed.

I am glad you are finding courage to speak. In a previous letter you said you kept quiet. I was not proud of that. The 4th Army General has had to issue an Order:

'Peace Talk must cease in the Fourth Army.'

From another Letter to Scarboro'—Mr. Owen is my Coy. Commander, and his such a desent chap.

---

[182] New Food Committees had been set up on 8 October 1918 to fix compulsory percentages of potatoes in bread, meat in sausages, etc.

[183] Sir William Beach-Thomas (1868–1957), journalist and writer on the countryside. He was War Correspondent for the *Daily Mail* at this time.

[184] Sir Philip Gibbs (1877–1962), author and journalist, was War Correspondent for the *Daily Chronicle* and other papers throughout the war. His book, *The Soul of War* (1915), published by William Heinemann, is an unsparing view of the horrors of war.

[185] Robert Ross died on 5 October 1918, aged 49.

667. To Susan Owen

15 October [*1918*]   [*2nd Manchester Regt.*]

Dearest Mother,

No change of situation,, except that I now live in a tent, & a change of weather has made the place more miserable. On the night when the news was officially sent us of the German 'Acceptance' we spent a merry enough night; I even discovered I could sing. We still hope something may be concluded by the Mixed Commission before we go into the line again. By we, I mean every officer & man left, of the legions who have suffered and are dust.[186]

I am not depressed even by Bottomley's 'NO! NO! NO!'.[187]

It has had the effect of turning the whole army against its John Bull at last. My heart has been warmed by the curses I have heard levelled at the *Daily Mail*.

Robbie Ross's death is more affecting to me, almost, than many of the deaths that took place at my side. Thank you so much for the paragraph from the *Times*. It was marvellously true of him, and kind, considering the *Times* was never his friend.

A Senior Lieutenant has turned up from Leave so I am now only Second in command of D. Coy. He has returned from his first visit to London utterly disgusted with England's indifference to the real meaning of the war as we understand it.

The Parcel came all right; my only grouse is that it was too big. Suppose it had reached me nearer the line I should have had to dump most of it: as every ounce tells on the back after the tenth muddy mile and the fourth sleepless night.

Please note, once more, that I <u>don't</u> want old, shrunk, darned socks. No use at all. I must have new ones if my feet are to remain 'beautiful on the mountains' of victory. Nothing now lacks—but in, say, a week's time, you might send <u>only</u>

(1 <u>small</u> writing pad.
(1 small Toilet Paraffin.
(2 Munchies.

We have had cigarettes from Capt. Somerville's[188] parcels. His wound in the thigh has got him to Bristol now. Only Lt. Gregg[189] died of wounds. I had known him in Scarborough. He had been very fond of his wife, and proud of his little daughter.

I suppose the child will be told she should be proud of Daddie, now.

I <u>don't</u> like the new Coy. Officers.

I have sent one of my corporals away for a Commission: such was my august pleasure.

I would, if I could, send many of these officers away (to a secondary school) to train for corporals.

I await Colin's fate with great hope. Thank you for passing on news to Harold.

I am paralysed when I try to write to Leslie: so many of these boys are so <u>much less fit</u> than he.[190] Numbers have really bad chests from gas; but it is their own fault. They would <u>not</u> put on their masks, when I did. My health is perfect.

Later

Your letters of Oct. 10th & 11th & Mary's have just come.

Mary's hopes for Peace Next Summer are sanguine, not to say sanguinary. Next Summer! When Christmas is the Limit of our Extreme Patience! Time gets marvellously lengthened out between the first rustle of a shell coming down & the VRACH! It seems, when at night a plane over you shuts off its engines for a moment in order to drop a bomb, hours.

I have just been given this enclosed Cutting. The 4 p.m. was timed on my wrist-watch! I hope Pte. Howarth will have told you all he can. My letters are written under such disjointed circumstances that they must read disjointedly. Admire at least my soldierly braggadoccio to Father.

Ever Wilfred

[186] The closing lines of SS's 'Prelude: The Troops' in *Counter-Attack* run: 'The unreturning army that was youth: / The legions who have suffered and are dust.'

[187] 'I have no intention, as far as I have any power, of allowing the Gentlemen of Whitehall to come to an arrangement with the Kaiser. I don't want any more talk of not being out to destroy the German nation—that is just what I am out for….' Horatio Bottomley, 'I shall be there' (*John Bull*, 12 October 1918).

[188] Wounded in the Fonsomme Line battle, Owen taking over command.

[189] Lieutenant R. Gregg, 6th Manchesters, died of wounds on 1 October 1918, aged 38. DH notes how 'he has been confused even in his army files with Reginald Arthur Gregg (Letter 449), 5th Manchesters, who joined up as an Artist aged seventeen and survived the War' (*WOANB*, p. 516, n. 17).

[190] This sentence (of twenty-two words) was omitted in *CL* and *SL*.

668. To Susan Owen

Sat. 19 October 1918   [*2nd Manchester Regt.*]

My dearest Mother,

We left the Corrugated Iron & Red Tent Billet in a hurry early yesterday morning.[191] For future Reference I will call this the <u>False Floor Dug Out.</u> It goes down some 50 ft. but the Bosche has covered it in at a depth of 5 ft.—no doubt because he was having so many prisoners taken from the tunnels. I need not say these are not yet <u>The Trenches.</u>

We have the *Times* of Thursday, and the strange news makes us feel that the Rumble on the horizon may cease any hour.[192] I'm listening now, but it still goes on, a gigantic carpet-beating.

I wonder has my servant called on you, or has he sent the Binoculars.

In the hurry of our departure yesterday, I left behind my Boracic Powder & Perm. of Potash! Please include small quantities, with writing pad & Mixed Fruit & Nut! It is now six weeks since I saw a shop, or decent habitation.

Thank you indeed for the *Punch*. Parts were very good; though much was dastardly. Would you please send me the next *New Statesman?*—around a letter.

I'm afraid I leave many things in your letters unanswered.

All that I might say to Mary & Colin & Father (& you)—if I had a fair table to write on,—or even if there were not so many dead horses corrupting the wind—you must imagine for me.

Ever your own Wilfred

[191]　The battalion moved to Bohain and Bussigny, still rear areas, in the second half of October.
[192]　The news was the break-up of the Dual Monarchy. Hungary separated from Austria, and Austria was proclaimed a Federation of Germans, Austrians, Czechs, Ukrainians, and Yugoslavs.

669. To Susan Owen

20 October 1918　　　　　　　　　　　　　　　　　　[*2nd Manchester Regt.*]

Dearest Mother,

After a very heavy march on which I had the painful duty of collecting & goading along the stragglers, we have come upon the vestiges of civilization again: civilians, just liberated, still continue here. It is just like March 1917. We have a fairly good billet, but may move any hour. We have only been 'in' 4 hours. After a 7 hours march, (without food on the way), I fed, and revived, & questioned civilians,—instead of writing a longer letter than this is to be.

Please send Colin's address so that I can write direct to Hastings.

About a week ago, a letter of 2 Lt. Foulkes[193] was opened and examined by the Base Censor. If any of mine have received his attentions, tell me. So little of interest I may tell you and so ill I tell it, all letters are Private.

Did I tell you S. Moncrieff is now with B. Thomas[194]? Siegfried is thinking of Parliament (a Labour Seat!) A *Daily News* round your letter would be very welcome.

You write just seldom enough to avoid 3 letters coming together, & just often enough to keep me serene. I am conscious of your prayers. Please say more about your own restoration to health. Though I have read the opening chapters of *Little*

Dorrit (& carefully enough to remember them after marching umpteen miles) still I say Will is the best medicine.

Ever Wilfred

[193] Lieutenant John Foulkes, MC, Manchester Regiment, the only other D Coy officer to come out of the Fonsomme Line battle unscathed. He won his MC at the same time. For his recollections of Owen, see Edmund Blunden's memoir in *The Poems of Wilfred Owen* (Chatto & Windus, 1931).
[194] Beach Thomas. See Letter 665.

670. To Susan Owen

Tues. Mng., 22 October 1918   (*Same kitchen*) [*2nd Manchester Regt.*]

Dearest Mother,

Your last letter before going to Alpenrose, & the one from Alpenrose and the parcel reached me together yesterday. Two days ago I was thinking a great deal of your Restoration to health, and even managed to mention it, I believe! This is fine news of your visit to Dr. Armitage. Let nothing waver you from your treatment, however incommodious to other people (or yourself.) How happily I think of you always in bed. About the end of November you will start to move about your room. Your room must be arranged. All my Articles of Vertue which you like are to represent me there. My Jacobean Chest; (why not?) my carpets; my tall candlesticks; my pictures; my tables: have them all in.

About Christmas you will start the hardening processes. You will lengthen your walks and your paces. You will grow keen with the keenness of frost and cold, blue sunlight. So you will be ready, early in February, for my Leave. We will walk to Haughmond, and while you are resting on the top, I will run round the Wrekin and back, to warm my feet.

For even were Prussianism removed from London & Berlin and Peace happened before Christmas, I should not get home before January or February.

We move from here in a few hours, <u>not</u> for the front. Communication is frightfully difficult with the Base. It passes my wits how letters arrive so soon! Now the rain has begun, the roads are increasingly baffling: and though my letters cease for a week or more you <u>must not conclude I am in the fighting zone.</u> It is unlikely for a considerable time, time even for the British Government & its accomplices to save their Nations.

W.E.O. x

P.S. Thank you for everything in parcel, except socks which I had spared & exempted as unfit last August.

671. To Leslie Gunston

25 October 1918　　　　　　　　　　　　　　*2nd Manchester Regt., France.*

Dear Leslie

I rejoice with you over your success with the *Nation*.[195] Certainly that Roundel meant more to me than all the *Nymph* poems put together. Now you are recognized by Massingham, Sassoon will want to see your work: I'll tell him. He wrote to me on the 16th a letter which I got yesterday, telling how he was with dear Robbie Ross on the evening before our inestimable friend suddenly died.[196] Siegfried mentions that A. Bennett offered him a job under Beaverbrook, but that S.S. wrote to Beaver's Pte. Sec. saying he had no qualifications for War Propaganda <u>except that he had been wounded in the head</u>: that repartee deserves eternal fame.[197]

You must not imagine when you hear we are 'resting' that we lie in bed smoking. We work or are on duty <u>always</u>. And last night my dreams were troubled by fairly close shelling. I believe only civilians in the village were killed (Thank God). In this house where I stay five healthy girls died of fright when <u>our</u> guns shelled the place last fortnight. You & I have always been open with each other: and therefore I must say that I feel sorry that you are neither in the flesh with Us nor in the spirit against war. You know why I could find no word of greeting for Gordon (on the occasion of his marriage.) Concerning your fresh disappointment, I only hope the languid Italian will make a passable (to say the least) war time substitute.[198]

There are two French girls in my billet, daughters of the Mayor, who (I suppose because of my French) single me for their joyful gratitude for *La Déliverance*. Naturally I talk to them a good deal; so much so that the jealousy of other officers resulted in a Subalterns' Court Martial being held on me! The dramatic irony was too killing, considering certain other things, not possible to tell in a letter.

Until last night though I have been reading Swinburne, I had begun to forget what a kiss was. I shall be glad to hear more of the 'Zambardi', a finer name, for me, than Nina, which I detest.[199]

I have found in all these villages <u>no evidence of German atrocities</u>. The girls here were treated with perfect respect. All the material ruin has been wrought by our guns. Do you still shake your befoozled head over the *Daily Mail* & the *Times*?

　　　　　　　　　　　　　　　　　　　　　　　　　Love W.E.O.

P.S. I should be glad of <u>any literary literature</u>.

---

[195] LG's poem 'Les Morts' was published in *The Nation*.
[196] The evening is described in *Siegfried's Journey*, pp. 82–4.
[197] See *Siegfried's Journey*, p. 71.
[198] These last two sentences of the paragraph were deleted in *CL* and *SL*.
[199] This sentence was deleted in *CL* and *SL*.

672. To Susan Owen

29 October 1918   [*2nd Manchester Regt.*]

Dearest Mother,

Through so much marching I have not been able to write for a day or two. I don't want to send Field Cards in case you suppose they mean in the Line. In future, however, a F. Card will be no proof that I am actually there.

Last night I slept in a cottage, but in an hour or two we move on: <u>not</u> to fight.[200]

Your last letters were the two with the Permang: & the Boric. Many many thanks for sending this so quickly.

Yesterday evening I hear the post corporal fell into a river; I understand the letters are all right; but haven't got any yet.

Howarth came back a day or two ago, but I did not take him back to me. My present one is Pte. Roberts, whom I knew in Scarborough.

The civilians here are a wretched, dirty crawling community, afraid of <u>us</u>, some of them, and no wonder after the shelling we gave them 3 weeks go.

Did I tell you that five healthy girls died of fright in one night at the last village. The people in England and France who thwarted a peaceable retirement of the enemy from these areas are therefore now sacrificing aged French peasants and charming French children to our guns. Shells made by women in Birmingham are at this moment burying little children alive not very far from here.

———————————

It is rumoured that Austria has really surrendered.[201] The new soldiers cheer when they hear these rumours, but the old ones bite their pipes, and go on cleaning their rifles, unbelieving.

———————————

A little gleam of good news I discovered in your note which said <u>already</u> you felt rested by being in bed.

I wonder what your diet is?

For my next parcel, will Mary please get:

(1 small bottle Tatcho
(1 „ Oatine
(1 pair cork boot-socks, size 6.
(20 Players.
(Chocolate.

There is a pair of breeches too narrow in the knees left in a drawer. Would Father get the Tailor who made my last pair to enlarge the knees? & dispatch to me? I will send a cheque soon.

Thank Father very much for his last letter.

The cutting from the *News*, & especially Gardiner's article[202] was appreciated by us all.

Siegfried sent me a little book which he had in France. Offered a job in War Propaganda under Beaverbrook he wrote to B's private sec. saying he had no qualifications for such work, except that he had been wounded <u>in the head</u>.

So glad you liked Tolstoy.

All my dearest love, my darling Mother.

W.E.O.

---

[200] The battalion moved into the line at St Souplet on the evening of the same day, 29 October, taking over the line west of the Sambre–Oise Canal, north of Ors, on the following night, 30/31 October. An attack over and beyond the canal was to be mounted.

[201] An armistice was signed with the Italians on 3 November 1918.

[202] The article by A. G. Gardiner, the Editor, in the 19 October issue of *The Daily News*, entitled 'The Victory and its Uses', in which ways of making *final* peace terms were discussed.

673. To Susan Owen

Thurs. 31 October [1918] *6.15 p.m.*   [*2nd Manchester Regt.*]

Dearest Mother,

I will call the place from which I'm now writing 'The Smoky Cellar of the Forester's House'. I write on the first sheet of the writing pad which came in the parcel yesterday. Luckily the parcel was small, as it reached me just before we moved off to the line. Thus only the paraffin was unwelcome in my pack. My servant & I ate the chocolate in the cold middle of last night, crouched under a draughty Tamboo, roofed with planks. I husband the Malted Milk for tonight, & tomorrow night. The handkerchief & socks are most opportune, as the ground is marshy,[203] & I have a slight cold!

So thick is the smoke in this cellar that I can hardly see by a candle 12 ins. away, and so thick are the inmates that I can hardly write for pokes, nudges & jolts. On my left the Coy. Commander snores on a bench: other officers repose on wire beds behind me. At my right hand, Kellett, a delightful servant of A Coy. in <u>The Old Days</u> radiates joy & contentment from pink cheeks and baby eyes. He laughs with a signaller, to whose left ear is glued the Receiver; but whose eyes rolling with gaiety show that he is listening with his right ear to a merry corporal, who appears at this distance away (some three feet) nothing [but] a gleam of white teeth & a wheeze of jokes.

Splashing my hand, an old soldier with a walrus moustache peels & drops potatoes into the pot. By him, Keyes, my cook, chops wood; another feeds the smoke with the damp wood.

It is a great life. I am more oblivious than alas! yourself, dear Mother, of the ghastly glimmering of the guns outside, & the hollow crashing of the shells.

There is no danger down here, or if any, it will be well over before you read these lines.[204]

I hope you are as warm as I am; as serene in your room as I am here; and that you think of me never in bed as resignedly as I think of you always in bed. Of this I am certain you could not be visited by a band of friends half so fine as surround me here.

Ever Wilfred x

[203] The Ors Canal was some 70 feet wide bank to bank, except at the locks, with an average depth of 6–8 feet. All bridges had been demolished or prepared for demolition. Low ground on both sides of the canal had been inundated by the Germans; most of it was swamp. The Germans held the eastern bank.

[204] Strong patrolling continued till zero hour for the IX Corps attack, 5.45 a.m. on 4 November. 14 Brigade crossed; 96 Brigade, which included 2nd Manchesters, was not successful. The engineers got a bridge across, but the area was swept with shell and machine-gun fire. Two platoons made the crossing, but the bridge was then destroyed. The remainder of the battalion crossed at Ors, where 1st Dorsets had secured a crossing. Wilfred Owen was killed on the canal bank on 4 November. Lieutenant Colonel Marshall ('of the ten wounds') and one other officer, Second Lieutenant Kirk (posthumously awarded the VC) were killed, along with twenty-two other ranks; three officers and eighty-one other ranks were wounded; eighteen other ranks missing. A week later, the war was over.

APPENDIX A

*My Dear Old Wolf: An Undelivered Letter to Wilfred Owen
from His Brother Harold (Backwater Press, 1996)*

*Rodgarten Shaw
Ipsen
Oxfordshire*

LETTER TO W.O. FROM H.O.

*Haud facile emergent quorum virtutibus obstat
Res augusta domi*
They do not easily keep their heads above
water whose straitened circumstances at
home stand in the way of their talents

Juvenal III, 164–5

My Dear Old Wolf,

Forty-four years have disappeared—how little I have done with them—since I last wrote to you in 1918. You never read this letter. You were killed before it reached you. I have always been sorry about this—stop muttering, the letter I mean, of course, not you. It was one of my few good letters. I think it would have pleased you.

A strange impulse stirs me to write to you now. It is this book I have written for you which impels me to do this—mostly because if it is ever published, I would like, before it goes out for the world to read, to tell you a little about it in some way that will be more intimate than the book can be, so that you may know what I have done.

This is in no sense an apology—did we ever apologize to each other? It is not an explanation—did we ever explain? Above all this letter is not an excuse for an unease of conscience. Concerning anything I have said about you in this work I feel no guilt. Others will think I ought to and, doing this for me, will blame me for what I have done. I am prepared for this. Others will of course say this is not Wilfred Owen as we like to think of him, and accuse me of putting you in a bad light, even that we were jealous of each other. Of course we were, but not in the way they will mean. We'll let them, Wilfred—you and I can stand it (in 1962 nobody stands anything, they always take it) as we did in the old days.

Although individually we were so opposed, just the same, if collectively antagonized, we were jolly good at standing together.

I don't apologize, explain, or excuse. To you, none of these things are necessary. You do not need them. Others will, but they will not get them. What I want so much to talk to you about is my apprehension, not about what I have said, still less about what I have felt while I have been writing, but apprehension over my poverty of literary ability. This lack, as you will so swiftly see, does not always keep me from that yawning trap, the awful gap between the poignant emotion felt and lived in the mind and the frightening inadequacy of the same thinking when transported into words that are written down. Why won't the words come out on paper in the way we can feel them in the imagination? Is it that we do not actually use word forms to think and feel with? I don't know. I only know how futile they can be when written down.

When I am working through your manuscripts—some of them impossible to decipher—and see how you change word after word, line after line, crossing out, reimposing, arranging yet rearranging perhaps only for some small word, I see how much you yourself worked to lessen this maddening gap—not for the sake of the work itself, never that, but only that you might more surely know that between your mind and your written word the least possible gulf remained.

I too, in my halting way, have tried so hard—but unlike you have not succeeded.

I am tired now—no, not tired, but weary from writing this book—so in this letter to you I shall only write what I feel. I am not going to care what bad English creeps in (it's here already) and I shall jump about from one point to another just as I like. All right, all right, don't frown at me or tell me I have no choice, my English must always be bad—anyhow, what do you expect from me? To use your own youthful pungent prophecy, 'a dissolute bawdy sailor, roaring his way through the seaports.'

People will say I have made you appear hard with me and intolerant of me. Dammit, you were, you know. Why not? Wasn't it better for both of us and healthier all round? Of course it was. You will always be to me the Old Wolf that I have tried so hard to draw. For the rest, as I say, it is all there for those who can read. For the ones who can not—well, they did not bother us forty-four years ago. They won't now.

When I set out to write this book I swore to myself that I would not sentimentalize over you or the others. I would draw us all as I see us or not at all.

If I have, as I have, purposely avoided positive appreciation it is because to me, as it would be to you, any smearing on of sickly sentiment would not only be alien to both of us but intolerably nauseous as well. Whatever else I may have done or not done, at least I have spared you the indignity of over-sweet biographical distortion. I loved you as you were. I have never used this word to you before, have I....

If from time to time I have splashed acid over us all, this is clean and wholesome—and knowing you and us, I also know how much we prefer a little sting from acid rather than an overdose of sugar and syrup. My goodness, you weren't a bad hand at spraying the acid yourself; and looking back, I can't forget just how jolly good at this you really were.

I have worked hard on this book. Did I hear you say quite unbelievable? I refuse to work at all on this letter to you. All I will do is try to put down something I feel. Illiteracy won't matter. Has it ever, compared with feeling? Did I hear you mutter, you have no choice, no choice? All right, I haven't— but we must stop this snapping and muttering, or we shall be back where we were forty-four years ago—as we would have said then, we'd better shut up. But before I leave this I must tell you that you will find clumsy passages and—dare I breathe it—perhaps now and again, by accident, hackneyed phrases intrude, if not in actuality in a guise so thin that it will not deceive you. Don't, in your own classical manner, despise them—but try to remember, as I do, that these things for me, an untrained writer, are the only avenues through which I may travel to attempted achievement.

In many ways I feel rather pleased that the book shows so little trace of professional skill. How could it do otherwise—don't worry, I heard that last caustic remark of yours.

I am sorry about that last letter of mine you never got. In it I told you I had got, partly from experience, what I thought was a good idea for a short story. In my usual simple-minded way I also proposed that when you got back from France and I from the Cameroons I would write it in my bad English so that you could transcribe it into good English for me. I really thought this was a marvellous idea. Ah, you're at it again, I can hear you distinctly—hopeless task, quite hopeless. So it would have been, but if you ever get far enough into this wretched book you will find it tucked away somewhere towards the end. I have called it what I intended to call it then, 'Millie', but I have made no attempt to make a short story of it. I wanted you to do that for me. It was some time after this happened that I heard you had been killed.

It is strange that I can still write to you and feel you are not dead at all. If you don't tire of the book too quickly, you will find a bit more about this, also towards the end.

Yes, Father went to France to visit the little churchyard in Ors. I disappointed him bitterly by my absolute refusal to go with him. I dreaded the finality this might bring. I have always been glad that I did not do so—but my goodness, who is sentimentalizing now. I must stop this. Oh, how much news I have that I would dearly love to tell you, but of course I mustn't, or I shall be well on the way to another confounded book. Did I hear you say not another, Harold, please? But I will touch on one or two happenings, in tabulated form.

Father died in 1931, Mother in 1942. Mary owns a little house near Dunsden and goes to church there. Mr Wigan remained vicar of 'your' parish until he died in 1947. Colin is in Africa with a wife and young family—three fine sons.

In 1927 I married Phyllis de Pass. Phyllis has helped me so much by reading back to me from the typescript all that I have written in making this book. More important even than the necessity for this has been, for me, the great joy of listening to her beautiful voice, the lovely quality of which enriched, sometimes deceptively, the poverty of the writing.

You were edited by Siegfried Sassoon and the Sitwells and published in 1920. Prentice and Ian Parsons have been our family friends and literary advisers to us all in turn ever since. Did I hear you exclaim Chatto and Windus? Yes, I thought that would please you.

In 1931 a new edition was published, with a foreword by Edmund Blunden.

Your work has been broadcast many times.

England's fine poet Cecil Day Lewis reveres your work. This is a major tribute to you, which you in turn will revere. An accidental detail I must recount—it will give you so much pleasure. In his inaugural address at Oxford as Professor of Poetry he spoke at length of you and your poems. It was broadcast, and I heard it. So you see, Old Wolf, although you could not get to your coveted Oxford, your work has done this for you.

Osbert Sitwell, the first person to read my original version of this book—I have practically rewritten it since—wrote to me with so much kindness and appreciation that I had no choice but to continue it.

Patric Dickinson broadcast an understanding biographical study of you—this is really going to make you jump—and as an outcome of his stay here wrote a poem, not for you but for me.

The University of Texas has founded a Wilfred Owen Collection.

The more the years increase the more difficult I find it to remember that you were killed before any of these things even started to happen. You, the person most concerned, never in life knew that you were published.

Somebody else I want you to meet is Hope de Pass. Hope it was who out of the kindness of her heart acted as my honorary amanuensis and typist, and has done so much of the strenuous typing of this final version, following my difficult manuscript with splendid accuracy.

Your beloved France has produced many lovers and students of your work, embracing the universities and schools.

I must tell you of countless readers of your poems with whom I correspond. To mention them by name would be quite impossible.

As I say, all these names—which will give you so much delight—are merely tabulated here. They must be expounded elsewhere. Even Siegfried Sassoon, the Sitwells, and Blunden can appear only briefly, due to the accident of date, in the last chapter.

I could go on talking to you for years about all these things. But my goodness, that won't do, will it? What did I hear you say again? You talk too much? That wasn't what you said—I'm surprised—I thought it must have been that…Oh, you want to know what of me. My dear, there is altogether too much of me in the book already. And this I must say to you. With my moronic mind (your words) this is the only possible way I can do it, by painting you as a reflection of myself and others. (The reflection should be on to us from you, but I feel too weary to twist the words round and make it look right—but you will know what I mean.)

You see, Old Wolf—funny how this 'Old' term of affection crops us again in this letter after all these years—how much we used it in those Shrewsbury days as a form of endearment. Old Wolf, Old Mary—the Welsh coming out, I suppose. Wilfred dear, you didn't live long enough so that I could do it in any other way. You, I know, will see this immediately—others won't.

Let me divide your twenty-five years up for you. When I do so and take you out of the family you will see what happens. Seventeen very dull, plain, ordinary schools, two years acting curate—what did you say? No, no, of course I will not repeat what you just said—two years in Bordeaux, and the rest in war. This last you have already done yourself and I cannot add to it. What then is left for me without the family? Only prosaic tabulation. Anyhow, people just do want to know all about your background and family life. Your work they know so well, of you they know nothing. What little they glean is sometimes disastrously misleading.

If you had lived you could have done it so well, without bringing the others and me into it so much. I cannot. I did think of doing it for you, as if you were speaking and portraying all of us as we must have appeared to you but this project is too dangerous. I cannot speak for you. I can only speak for myself. Let's be honest with each other, we always were. Perhaps after all, hidden away in me, is something creative, and the egotism of the artist just insists upon inserting itself. I have found that to fix the truth I have had to bring myself in so much, and, without altering, yet alter, to really find the truth.

What are you muttering now? Oh yes, my painting. I can tell you all about that quickly. I have painted one or two good pictures, but not one single IMPORTANT one. I know now that I never shall, which is a difficult thought to live with. Without the Owen capacity to be able to smile over all those early hopes of ours which, except for you, have never come to anything much (in true Owen tradition even you were not permitted to know success) the thought would be impossible to live with. That, Old Dear, is how things have gone with me.

I wish I could write to you that I had my place among the painters as you have among the poets. You too would wish this. Not to be too serious, what a glorious opportunity I lose in not being able to say to you 'I told you so'. How much we should both enjoy the triumph.

I almost forgot to tell you that we have had another war since OUR War.

In a letter to me after a visit by you to Burlington House (I can't resist this)—it was, I think, when you were matriculating in London, you wrote to me: 'I wonder if I shall ever see a painting of yours hanging on those august walls. Unless you alter very much, I fear not.' Encouraging old beast, weren't you, and flamboyant too with your blasted august walls. If only you had not been killed you could have done just this, the Salon too. Yes, and the British Museum. An etching of mine is in the Print Room. All your published manuscripts, bought for the Nation, are there. It is rather nice, isn't it, that we are represented in the B.M. together. But as I was saying we would have gone round the exhibitions with each other, and perhaps, standing near to one of my paintings, we would have waited in hope that someone would pass remarks about it. What glorious fun we would have had— what heated arguments too. If only the war had ended seven days earlier...but this won't do at all.

One more thing. I was running through the typescript of the book when I came across this passage I have written about us: 'at times we hated each other'. Out of context it looks so startlingly impossible that I felt shocked and distressed, but reading it through again I saw that really is was quite all right, and I have left it. Between you and me it is meaningless. I like to think that at seventeen and thirteen we were able to feel strongly enough about each other to do this.

Something else I must talk to you about, your letters—I have found four hundred and twenty of them in my studio here. So far nobody else has seen them. Let your breath go, I heard you draw it in. Yes, I really have looked after you over this—not that this is much to have done for you, but I believe it will give you enormous relief. It has not been an easy thing to do. I have in turn been pleaded with, begged and bullied, one attempt at bribery, another I was suspicious of theft, to make me release them for publication. I have been accused, seriously, of malicious obstructionism.

Over this I have never wavered, so determined am I that not one word of them shall be published until my book is out.

For me to allow the publication of these letters without the explanation of background that this book will bring, and so explain them, would be not only grossly unfair to you but might even be disastrous. I see the relief in your warm brown smile. Thank you for that. But I think now, Old Dear, that when this book is published, if it ever is, the time will have come when I, not anybody else, should edit them, and then publish. They should come out a week or two after the book itself, in a separate volume, with only small comment, and with them some of the family—don't get panicky—photographs. My book is not suitable to put these last into, nor yet the letters either. You think I am right? My goodness, that didn't sound like you. For goodness sake don't change now....yes, yes, I heard you all right—DON'T let anyone else do this.

Perhaps your young water-colourist (your words) has progressed a little after all.

It is a terrible thing to say, perhaps even a wicked thing, but we of the lost generation who came back, in age so little more than boys, found ourselves not only lost indeed but with a restless unhappiness that would not let us return to ourselves. So if at times, especially in the early twenties, I became inclined to look towards you—so safely dead—with covet glances of envy, and to think with bitterness that after all you who did not come back were better off than we who did, do not think hardly of me but forgive me. I know you will.

You are I know impatiently wondering about the Latin tag I have quoted at the beginning of this letter. No, no, I am sorry to disappoint you. How I wish I need not....no, I have not become a Latin scholar. I chanced across the quotation in the *Daily Telegraph,* Peterborough. With the acquisitiveness of the artist I seized upon it as being extraordinarily apt for both of us. I felt I must use it. In nine words it so well explains our early difficulties. Too bad, isn't it, that I may not steal the wind from your sails with a claim to scholarship in Latin. All I can—but this will please you—is to tell you that I have, without permission, just lifted it.

In this book you will find feeling, you will not find erudition. Laugh away, it's so good to hear your Wolfish laughter. I'm enjoying it, so go on. Anyhow, I am laughing with you—yes, thank goodness, I am still able to do this.

All I can try to do is tell your story. In it you will find little mention of the poetry you made, only the manner of life you led while making it—and certainly no attempt at any critical study of your work. I am content, as I must be, to let others do this.

I have brought in this bit about erudition to try and raise your laughter. It has been worth it to hear it and I am glad.

Wilfred, here it is then. It is the best I can do. If in it things have gone wrong, then the wrong is in the telling. The wrong must never ever seem to lie in you or the others.

It is late now, and I am tired—so, my dear, if I may I will use your own sad words...

Let us sleep now.

H

APPENDIX B

Locations of Owen's Manuscripts

Within the family	No. of letters	Archival holding/Location
Susan Owen	554	Harry Ransom Humanities Research Center, University of Texas at Austin [HRHRC], https://norman.hrc.utexas.edu/fasearch/findingAid.cfm?eadid=00528
Mary Owen	41	HRHRC
Colin Owen	22	HRHRC
Harold Owen	9	HRHRC
Tom Owen	5	HRHRC

Outside the family	No. of letters	Archival holding/Location
Leslie Gunston	30	Bodleian Library, University of Oxford [Bodleian], https://archives.bodleian.ox.ac.uk/repositories/2/archival_objects/42314
Siegfried Sassoon[1]	7	Columbia University Rare Book and Manuscript Library, New York, https://findingaids.library.columbia.edu/ead/nnc-rb/ldpd_4079189
Alec Paton	3	Bodleian
Nelly Bulman	1	HRHRC
Charles Scott Moncrieff[2]	1	Dennis Welland Collection, John Rylands Library, University of Manchester, https://www.librarysearch.manchester.ac.uk/discovery/fulldisplay?docid=alma992976139314501631&context=L&vid=44MAN_INST:MU_NUI&lang=en&search_scope=MyInst_and_CI&adaptor=Local%20Search%20Engine&tab=Everything&query=any,contains,wilfred%20owen%20collected%20letters&offset=0&pcAvailability=false?
Osbert Sitwell	1	Reproduced in Osbert Sitwell, *Noble Essences: Or Courteous Revelations* (London: Macmillan & Co., 1950), p. 106

A selection of Owen's letters may be viewed via the First World War Poetry Digital Archive, http://ww1lit.nsms.ox.ac.uk/ww1lit/collections/owen

Letters 255, 370, 395, 476, 479, 480, 482, 491, 494, 498, 502, 503, 505, 506, 509, 510, 516, 531, 534, 535, 540, 541, 542, 545, 546, 548, 552, 564, 577, 589, 592, 622, 643, 662, 673.

---

[1] Sassoon wrote to Harold Owen on 23 September 1959 to say he had 'seven long letters written after he left Craiglockhart...As I have told you, those 2 destroyed seemed to me, at the time, to be a bit immature in expression, though satisfying to my Ego!'

[2] This letter came to light after the publication of the *CL* and was first published in *SL*.

SELECT BIBLIOGRAPHY

Editions

The Collected Poems of Wilfred Owen, ed. C. Day Lewis (Chatto & Windus, 1963).

Poems by Wilfred Owen, with an Introduction by Siegfried Sassoon (Chatto & Windus, 1920).

The Poems of Wilfred Owen, ed. Edmund Blunden (Chatto & Windus, 1931).

The Poems of Wilfred Owen, ed. Jon Stallworthy (Chatto & Windus, 1990).

Wilfred Owen: Collected Letters, ed. Harold Owen and John Bell (Oxford University Press, 1967).

Wilfred Owen: Selected Letters, ed. John Bell (Oxford University Press, 1985).

Wilfred Owen: The Complete Poems and Fragments, 2 vols, ed. Jon Stallworthy (Oxford University Press, 1984; new edn, Chatto & Windus, 2013).

Wilfred Owen: War Poems and Others, ed. Dominic Hibberd (Chatto & Windus, 1973).

Biographies

Guy Cuthbertson, *Wilfred Owen* (Yale University Press, 2014).

Dominic Hibberd, *Wilfred Owen: A New Biography* (Phoenix, 2003).

Dominic Hibberd, *Wilfred Owen: The Last Year* (Constable, 1992).

Harold Owen, *Journey from Obscurity: Memoirs of the Owen Family*, 3 vols (Oxford University Press, 1963–5).

Jane Potter, *Wilfred Owen: An Illustrated Life* (Bodleian Library Publishing, 2014).

Jon Stallworthy, *Wilfred Owen* (Oxford University Press, 1974; new ed., Pimlico, 2013).

Critical Studies

James Campbell, *Oscar Wilde, Wilfred Owen, and Male Desire: Begotten, Not Made* (Palgrave Macmillan, 2015).

Keith V. Comer, *Strange Meetings: Walt Whitman, Wilfred Owen, and Poetry of War* (Lund University Press/Chartwell-Bratt, 1996).

Santanu Das, *Touch and Intimacy in First World War Literature* (Cambridge University Press, 2005).

Dominic Hibberd, *Owen the Poet* (The Macmillan Press, 1986).

George Johnson, *Mourning and Mysticism in First World War Literature and Beyond: Grappling with Ghosts* (Palgrave Macmillan, 2015).

Douglas Kerr, *Wilfred Owen's Voices: Language and Community* (Clarendon Press, 1993).

Sally Minogue and Andrew Palmer, *The Remembered Dead: Poetry, Memory and the First World War* (Cambridge University Press, 2018).

BIOGRAPHICAL TABLE

1893 (18 March) Wilfred Edward Salter Owen born at Plas Wilmot, Oswestry, the son of Tom Owen, railway clerk, and his wife, Susan Shaw.

1897 The Owen family moves to Birkenhead.

1901 Wilfred Owen starts school at mid-term at the Birkenhead Institute.

1906–7 Tom Owen appointed Assistant Superintendent, GW and LNER, Western Region, and the family moves to Shrewsbury.

1910 The Owen family moves to Mahim, Monkmoor Road, Shrewsbury.

1911 (9 September) Owen takes the University of London matriculation exam. (28 September) He is interviewed by the Rev. Herbert Wigan, vicar of Dunsden, near Reading, and is offered an unpaid post as lay assistant and pupil in his evangelical church. (Early October) Hears he has matriculated at the University of London, but not with honours. (20 October) Arrives at Dunsden.

1913 (Early January) Owen determines to leave Dunsden and to break with evangelical religion. (16–19 May) He takes the Reading University scholarship examination, but in July hears he has failed to win it. (c.15 September) Leaves for Bordeaux to teach English at the Berlitz School of Languages.

1914 (25 July) Owen gives up his job at the Berlitz School. (31 July) Travels to Castel Lorenzo, Bagnères-de-Bigorre, Pyrenees, to act as tutor to Mme Léger, and meets the French poet Laurent Tailhade. (17 September) Returns to Bordeaux with the Légers, and starts to look for pupils as a freelance teacher of English. (4 December) He is offered a post as tutor to the two elder de la Touche boys, near Bordeaux.

1915 (October) Owen joins up in the Artists' Rifles, London, moves into lodgings, and meets Harold Monro at the Poetry Bookshop. (15 November) Goes to Hare Hall Camp, Gidea Park, Essex, as Cadet Owen, Artists' Rifles.

1916 (27 February–5 March) Owen on a ten-day army course lodges over the Poetry Bookshop, and shows his poems to Harold Monro. (5 March) Joins Officers' School, Gidea Park. (4 June) Commissioned in the Manchester Regiment. (18 June) Reports to the 5th (Reserve) Battalion, Manchester Regiment, at Milford Camp, near Witley, Surrey. (24 September) Owen and the 5th Manchesters move to Oswestry, under canvas. (29 December) He crosses to France and Base Camp, Étaples, with his regiment.

1917   (1–2 January) Owen joins 2nd Manchesters on the Somme near
            Beaumont Hamel, in a rest area. Assumes command of 3 Platoon,
            A Coy. (6 January) 2nd Manchesters on the move towards the front.
            (9–16 January) Owen holds a dugout in no man's land; his sentry is
            blinded; his platoon is exposed to severe frost. (4 February) Arrives
            at Abbeville for a course on transport duties. (March) Rejoins
            battalion near Fresnoy; suffers concussion following a fall at Le
            Quesnoy-en-Santerre; evacuated to Military Hospital at Nesle, and
            moved to 13th Casualty Clearing Station at Gailly. (4 April) Rejoins his
            battalion at Selency. (12 April) Goes into the line again at Savy Wood
            for twelve days. (2 May) He is evacuated to 13th Casualty Clearing
            Station with shell shock. (June) Sent to No. 1 General Hospital, Étretat,
            and then to Welsh Hospital, Netley, Hampshire. (26 June) Owen
            arrives at Craiglockhart War Hospital, Edinburgh. (July) Writes his first
            contribution to The Hydra; becomes editor. (c.17 August) He introduces
            himself to Siegfried Sassoon. (13 October) Owen is introduced to
            Robert Graves by Sassoon. (28 October) Owen appears before a
            Medical Board and is given three weeks' leave pending return to his
            unit. (9 November) Lunches and dines with Robert Ross at the Reform
            Club and meets Arnold Bennett and H. G. Wells. (24 November) Owen
            joins the 5th Manchesters at Scarborough for light duties; appointed
            'major-domo' of the Officers' Mess, Clarence Gardens Hotel.
            (4 December) Promoted Lieutenant.

1918   (26 January) Owen's poem 'Miners' is published in The Nation.
            (12 March) He is posted to Northern Command Depot, Ripon. (June)
            Graded fit for general service; rejoins 5th Manchesters at Scarborough;
            receives request from Edith and Osbert Sitwell for poems to include in
            Wheels 1918. (15 June) His poems 'Hospital Barge' and 'Futility' published
            in The Nation. (August) On embarkation leave; visits Sassoon, who has
            been wounded and invalided home, in hospital in London; spends
            evening with him and Osbert Sitwell; and reports again to Base Camp,
            Étaples. (9 September) Owen arrives at Reception Depot, Amiens, to
            await the arrival of 2nd Manchesters. (29 September–3 October) 2nd
            Manchesters launch a successful assault on the Beaurevoir–Fonsomme
            line. Owen is awarded the Military Cross. (30–31 October) Owen's
            battalion takes over the line west of the Sambre–Oise Canal, near Ors,
            in preparation for an attack across the canal at dawn on 4 November.
            (4 November) Owen is killed in the early morning on the canal bank at
            Ors. (11 November) News of his death reaches his family in
            Shrewsbury.

INDEX